The New Class Society

The New Class Society

Goodbye American Dream?

Fourth Edition

Earl Wysong, Robert Perrucci,
and David Wright

ROWMAN & LITTLEFIELD PUBLISHERS, INC.
Lanham • Boulder • New York • Toronto • Plymouth, UK

Published by Rowman & Littlefield Publishers, Inc.
A wholly owned subsidiary of The Rowman & Littlefield Publishing Group, Inc.
4501 Forbes Boulevard, Suite 200, Lanham, Maryland 20706
www.rowman.com

10 Thornbury Road, Plymouth PL6 7PP, United Kingdom

British Library Cataloguing in Publication Information Available

Library of Congress Cataloging-in-Publication Data

Perrucci, Robert.
  The new class society : goodbye American dream? / Earl Wysong, Robert Perrucci, and David Wright. — Fourth edition.
      pages cm
  Revised edition of: The new class society : goodbye American dream? / Robert Perrucci and Earl Wysong. 3rd ed.
  Includes bibliographical references and index.
  ISBN 978-1-4422-0527-7 (cloth : alk. paper) — ISBN 978-1-4422-0528-4 (pbk. : alk. paper) — ISBN 978-1-4422-0529-1 (electronic) 1. Social classes—United States. 2. United States—Social conditions—1980– I. Wysong, Earl, 1944– II. Title.
  HN90.S6P47 2014
  305.50973—dc23   2013012029

∞™ The paper used in this publication meets the minimum requirements of American National Standard for Information Sciences—Permanence of Paper for Printed Library Materials, ANSI/NISO Z39.48-1992.

Printed in the United States of America

Contents

List of Tables and Figures

FIGURES

TABLES

Acknowledgments

"Art is long . . . life is short, and success is very far [away]."

—Joseph Conrad (1897/2007)

Spinning social science straw into the gold of an artful narrative is an elusive endeavor. Paraphrasing Mark Twain on the power of language, we believe the difference between a class analysis that reflects an imaginative blend of art and science and one that lacks this quality is the difference between vivid lightning that illuminates the social world and the shallow glow of a cell phone screen that lights a single tweet. This project flashed into being in 1999 with the first edition. At that time, we were nearly alone in calling attention to the changing class structure, steadily widening inequalities, and declining opportunities—developments we saw as threatening the American dream. As we crafted our narrative for this edition, we aspired to recapture the lightning evident in that first edition. But it is up to you, our readers, to determine the extent to which the fourth edition approximates that lofty standard. We are mindful of the reality that printed works today compete with digital media products for readers' attention, time, and favor. To some, books may appear as quaint, dated, and "old school"; they are sometimes viewed as less glamorous, less entertaining, and less visually compelling than products of the digital universe. Recognizing those realities makes us doubly appreciative of readers who chose this book. We hope its content will convince you that the printed word remains a source of enduring value in today's digital world.

The publication of this new edition was facilitated by the efforts and contributions of many people. In its early stages the project benefited immensely from the support and vision of the late Alan McClare. As executive editor, Alan encouraged us to develop a fourth edition that would not just update our earlier work but also, in many respects, be a new book. He challenged us to imagine a new edition with more chapters than earlier versions, to develop a bold volume wherein our class analysis approach would be used to explore an expanded range of inequality issues and examine new economic, political, social, and cultural developments. Inspired by his vision and invigorated by our own enthusiasm for crafting a book that would link our new, class-focused research on recent important issues such as the new economy, the financial crisis, the political zeitgeist of the Obama era, social mobility, the culture industry, and many others, we developed an outline for a new edition. At that time, Alan was as excited by the promise of our new work as we were, but unfortunately he was unable to see it through to fruition. In recognition of his unwavering support for our work, we dedicate this edition to his memory

We appreciate the encouragement, support, and assistance of many individuals associated with Rowman and Littlefield who helped move the fourth edition from an outline of chapter titles to a completed manuscript. Sarah Stanton was a patient, supportive force over an extended period of time. As acquisitions editor, Sarah never wavered in her support for the book even as the project moved through numerous iterations, encountered unexpected headwinds, and took longer to complete than expected. Assistant editor Kathryn M. F. Knigge provided timely encouragement, support, and assistance as the manuscript moved to completion. Production editor Patricia Stevenson made numerous editorial contributions that added clarity and precision to the fourth edition; we are indebted to her for her detailed attention to the manuscript. The authors, however, are responsible for any and all errors or mistakes that may remain in the book.

To readers, supporters, and instructors who found earlier editions of the book to be thoughtful, informative, provocative, and useful, we offer a sincere and vigorous "thank you!" We are grateful for the observations and compliments many passed along to us. We are also appreciative of the comments we received from critical readers. The supportive and critical feedback helped improve our work. We look forward to learning of readers' reactions to this new edition.

We hope readers will find the book to be an artful and engaging rendering of class inequality issues. Written, we believe, with thunderclap clarity and imaginative imagery, its goal is to illuminate—in new and useful ways—the nature, power, and consequences of America's increasingly unequal class structure. To learn more, we invite you to turn the page.

Introduction

"Occupy Wall Street reminded the country of the deep economic divisions running through our society, but it appears the only way to keep the issue in the media discussion is to keep OWS—or some other form of large-scale protest—in the news."

—John Knefel, "Bored with Occupy—and Inequality," *Extra!* (May 2012): 7

This book is focused on what we and many others believe is the most important social issue in the United States today: the emergence and entrenchment, over the past four decades, of a new, increasingly unequal and ever more rigid social class system. We initially identified, described, and analyzed what we termed the *new class society* in the first edition of this book in 1999. Since then, much of our research has been devoted to enhancing our understanding of the many evolving facets of what we call America's "new class system." Through books, articles, and research papers we have sought to share our findings with interested readers.[1] Our latest exploration of, and most recent research on, the structures, processes, and consequences of our unequal class system are contained in this fourth edition of *The New Class Society*.

We have all been told that compared with other nations, our country is the richest and our economy is the most productive and efficient on earth. But what is less well known is the extent of inequalities in the rules, policies, and practices that direct the distribution of highly unequal shares of goods, services, income, and wealth to Americans. In short, when it comes to producing goods and services, America *is* indeed "Number One!" But when it comes to *fairly* distributing the goods, services, income, and wealth generated by our enormously productive and wealthy society, America is *not* "Number One."

The explanation for the disparity between our highly productive society and a more equitable distribution of its rewards lies, we believe, in the multifaceted

1

influence of the *new class system*. The main structural and dynamic features of this system, explored in the following chapters, include the following: (1) the central importance of large corporations and powerful policy-making government organizations to the creation and maintenance of an increasingly caste-like social class system; (2) the mobilization of enormous economic and political resources by wealthy elites, advocacy organizations representing their interests, and large corporations to facilitate, via corporate and governmental policies, an upward redistribution of income and wealth to the most affluent classes; (3) the intensification of social-class-based economic, political, and cultural inequalities via forty years of class-war policies directed by the wealthiest classes against the middle and working classes; (4) the increasing polarization of the United States into two distinct "have" and "have not" classes; (5) the perpetuation and legitimation of our unequal class system by several conventional social institutions, including federal and state governments, large corporations, the corporate media, and the culture industry. As we will see, these features, along with various economic, political, and social developments related to and spawned by them, have exerted, and continue to exert, profound effects on the lives and life chances of all Americans.

In sociology, the term *social classes*, as we note in chapter 1, refers to the organization of societies into stratified "layers" or "ranks" with each class (or rank) consisting of large numbers of people who possess similar levels of what are considered scarce and valuable resources in a given society. While the term *resources* can be thought of as taking many forms (e.g., power, education, occupation, opportunities, health), in advanced industrial societies the *quantity of money* people possess as wealth or receive as income is a critical "scarce and valuable" resource. Thus, the quantity of money people have is central to the general meaning of social class as a concept and to people's social class rankings in our society. Money, however, is not the only feature of social class, and it is not the only resource included in definitions of it. As we'll see in chapter 2, within sociology, social class has been defined differently by different scholars. And although *our* definition of social class does include money as a crucial resource, it includes other key resources as well (see chapter 2). But for our purposes in this introduction, the quantity of money people have, used here to represent the economic dimension of social class, provides a convenient and familiar way of referencing and measuring one crucial aspect of social class membership and related class inequalities.

In America's highly unequal class system, the concept of class inequalities includes the idea that not only do people in different social classes possess unequal levels of resources but these inequalities also lead to very unequal lives. In short, class inequalities, especially wealth and income differences, have powerful and enduring effects on people's opportunities and life experiences. The *quantity of money* people in different social classes have (in amounts such as large, modest, small, none) means people are substantially advantaged or disadvantaged in several ways (e.g., educational and occupational opportunities, access to health care, ability to influence government policies). The greater the quantity of money one has, the greater one's "life chances" for living a secure, long, happy, healthy, and rewarding life—and vice versa.[2] This does not mean that lots of money buys happiness. It means that having more money provides people with more opportunities, resources, and chances *to pursue and achieve* whatever they determine to be important goals in their lives. But we don't all have to be rich to enjoy an abundance of positive life chances. A large and growing body of research finds that societies with greater levels of equality produce higher levels of both mental and physical well-being among all people in all classes than more unequal societies. At the same time, people in more equal societies are less stressed, more trusting of others, and commit far fewer violent crimes than people in more unequal societies.[3] The evidence is clear: class inequalities matter for individuals and societies.[4] This reality underscores the importance of better understanding our unequal class system.

Chapter 2 describes the distinctive form of our new class system as essentially bipolar. It includes an affluent and secure *privileged class* and an increasingly impoverished and insecure *new working class*. Chapter 2 also identifies four important principles that define the new class system. These four principles are explored at length in chapters 3, 4, 5, and 6. As we will see, in this new class system, most people are members, or soon will be members, of the new working class—the class of people increasingly excluded from the likelihood of realizing or experiencing highly positive life chances. The once-upon-a-time traditionally large and secure American middle class is mostly absent in the new class system. Chapters 5 and 6 explore how and why the demise of the middle class has been hastened by a number of developments and inequality trends driven by corporate and government policies orchestrated by and for the wealthiest classes.

SEPARATE REALITIES: THE DREAM AND THE ICEBERG

"More than three-quarters of Americans . . . say that they believe in the American Dream."

—Michael Ford et al., *The Modern American Dream* (August 2011)

"That's why they call it the American dream; you have to be asleep to believe it."

—George Carlin, *Sacramento Bee* (December 2, 2005)

Some readers may wonder: Why do we need to explore the structures and dynamics of what we claim is an increasingly unequal new class system rife with structured class inequalities when, as many believe, we live in a society that routinely provides people with ample opportunities to achieve educational and economic success if they work hard and follow the rules? It's a good question. After all, as the first quote above indicates, a large majority of people in the United States today say they believe in the *American dream*—the belief, generally, that hard work leads to success. However, the second quote suggests we may need to be cautious. It implies that achieving the dream is not such a certain prospect. If that is not the case, then why not? Prudence suggests this question merits attention—especially if we suspect the certainty of the dream is "oversold."

From our perspective, the American dream of financial security and upward mobility stands in opposition to what we term the "iceberg" of the new class system. Thought of this way, the U.S. class structure, like an iceberg, consists of not only readily visible features and obvious inequalities but also a much larger mass of partially concealed, or even "hidden," components, including a wide array of structured class inequalities. As metaphors, these concepts call attention to and remind us of potent tensions that exist in our society between the cultural ideals and social realities associated with the U.S. class system. The dream represents a widely shared cultural ideal—what most Americans believe *should* be true about class-related opportunities and achievement in our society. The iceberg, however, represents the social reality of what *is* true regarding these qualities in our society—that they are battered and blunted by the iceberg-like reality of partially exposed, but largely hidden, patterned, enduring, and increasing class inequalities embedded in the new class system. These separate realities are threaded through the American social fabric as well as the lives and life chances of each of us. While the dream inspires optimism and hope for a brighter future, the iceberg, especially its hidden components and inequalities, grinds away at the dream, generating, as we will see, increasingly bleak life chances, opportunities, and experiences for most Americans.

The American Dream

"[Today] every element of the [American] dream is imperiled."

—Robert L. Borosage and Katrina Vanden Heuvel, *Nation* (October 10, 2011)

The foundation of the American dream, a term coined by historian James Truslow Adams during the Great Depression, rests on the belief that humble class origins are not destiny.[5] It includes the widely shared view that American society offers equal and nearly unlimited opportunities for upward mobility for those who embrace a strong work ethic, regardless of class origins.[6] Although the details of the American dream have varied somewhat over time, Americans—from the post-WWII period to the present—typically envision it as including financial security, home ownership, family, higher educational levels (leading to upward mobility), greater opportunities and rewards for the next generation (compared with the current generation), a successful career, freedom, happiness, and a comfortable retirement.[7]

In the 1920s and 1930s, the "modern American dream" (grounded in the growth of a secure middle class after World War II) was not yet part of the culture.[8] Today, of course, it is, but the ideals of the dream are increasingly at odds with the inequality patterns of the emerging new class system—which, in many respects, are similar to those evident in the 1920s and 1930s. As we note in chapter 1, the U.S. class structure during the Great Depression resembled a pyramid with limited mobility across class lines. Class membership in such a system was typically defined by family lineage— "The fruit doesn't fall far from the tree." Prior to the first three decades of the post–World War II period (1945–1975), this aphorism linking children, parents, and social class stood at the intersection of commonsense observations and social science research.[9] From wealthy elites to white trash, personal experiences, popular culture, and sociological data supported the view that social class tended to "run in families."

Following World War II, as chapter 1 points out, the pyramidal class structure of the 1930s began to change as real wages (adjusted for inflation) began trending upward for working-class Americans. At the same time, the postwar period witnessed improving opportunities for advancement from the working class into more prestigious occupations.[10] For members of the expanding blue- and white-collar middle-income groups of the 1950s and 1960s, these new patterns provided a reassuring vision of a comfortable and secure future for themselves and their children. Improved living standards combined with traditional beliefs in the open-ended economic and social opportunities in America contributed to an enthusiastic, shared embrace of the modern American dream as a cultural ideal among members of virtually all social classes.[11]

Somewhat paradoxically, the dream runs both parallel with and counter to the general pattern evident in the United States today whereby children tend to replicate the class rank of their parents (a topic explored in chapter 5). For privileged-class families, the dream offers a reassuring sense of continuity: the advantaged positions of parents can and will be passed on to, and extended by, their children. For working-class families, the dream represents a possible future of reward, fulfillment, and affluence, especially for their children. To some extent, the first thirty years of the post-WWII period provided middle-income workers and families with evidence that the dream was increasingly within reach. Thus, among the working and middle classes, the modern American dream resonated powerfully as a mythic cultural ideal and, at least for a time, as an attainable reality. Today, however, the opportunities once available to working-class Americans for realizing the dream are being shredded by powerful economic, political, and social forces that are part of the "iceberg" of the new class system—an iceberg of epic proportions and potency that spans the entire society and threatens to destroy the American dream.

The Three-Thousand-Mile Iceberg

> "The first lesson of sociology . . . [is] the importance of class consciousness."
>
> —Charles H. Anderson, *Toward a New Sociology* (1974)

Like a huge iceberg stretching coast to coast across the American social horizon, the new class system combines a dramatic profile of sharply defined and disturbing visible features with a submerged and hidden mass of potentially society-wrecking forces and consequences. While we appreciate Americans' interest in and attraction to the dream, we believe a close examination of the "iceberg" of the new class system and of the inequalities embodied in it is essential both to better understand it and to see how and why it threatens the ideals of the dream. We view the new class system as iceberg-like because although some of its class-relevant structures and processes are readily visible and obvious, meaning they are located "above the waterline of widespread public awareness," many other features are relatively invisible and less obvious, meaning they are submerged, or located "below the waterline of widespread public awareness." In our analysis, the former phrase (above the waterline) refers to widespread public awareness of many obvious forms and consequences of inequalities concerning the economic dimension of social class. By contrast, the latter phrase (below the waterline) refers to the relative lack of widespread public awareness concerning the details of crucial class-relevant organizational structures and dynamic processes that produce, legitimate, and perpetuate class inequalities.

Above-the-Waterline Inequalities: Media, Popular Culture, Protests

Widespread public awareness of above-the-waterline economic inequalities arises, we believe, from people's encounters with these issues via personal experiences (e.g., pay cuts, job losses, mortgage foreclosures), media reports, popular culture, and public protests. The term *media reports* refers to news and commentary about economic inequalities appearing in print and electronic mainstream corporate media outlets (large, for-profit firms), "alternative media" outlets (small, nonprofit organizations), and reports disseminated via Internet sources such as corporate and alternative media websites, social media (Facebook, Twitter), blogs, Web-based publications, and video websites (YouTube, Hulu). *Popular culture* refers to economic inequality references in the content of print, film, television, and Internet materials designed or intended to *entertain* large, general audiences or specific subgroups. The term *public protests* refers to organized, public demonstrations by groups opposed to a variety of economic inequalities.

In recent years, media reports and popular culture content, reflecting different ideological perspectives, have focused on several above-the-waterline forms or consequences of economic inequalities and thus have contributed to growing public awareness about them.[12] Examples of inequality topics that have become familiar to the public due to these sources include growing income and wealth inequalities, skyrocketing CEO pay, high unemployment rates, increasing poverty rates, high home mortgage foreclosure rates, mushrooming student loan debt, a shrinking "middle class," the growing divide between the "haves" and "have nots," federal tax policies favoring the rich over average Americans, taxpayer-funded "too big to fail" bailouts for Wall Street versus austerity policies for Main Street, "free trade" agreements that export American jobs, and corporate corruption of the democratic process through extensive, often secret funding of political campaigns and political advertising.[13] We believe that these topics and many others are interwoven, arise out of structures and processes inherent in the new class system, and deserve more attention. Thus, the connections between such topics and their links to features of the new class system are explored in chapters 3–9.

In addition to reporting on above-the-waterline inequality issues, the media have also covered public protests against various inequalities by groups on the political "right" and "left." On the "right," beginning in 2009 and continuing to the present, is the "Tea Party," which has sponsored protest rallies against inequalities like government-funded bank bailouts.[14] On the "left," beginning in early 2011 there have been mass protests against state-level legislative initiatives attacking workers' rights in Midwestern states, such as the large groups of workers and students that gathered in Madison, Wisconsin.[15] Also on the left is the Occupy movement, which began in New York City as "Occupy Wall Street" protests in late summer 2011 and spread to several other cities with protestors focusing on elite-driven public and corporate policies that favor the wealthy "1 percent" at the expense of everyone else—the "99 percent."[16]

The recent emergence of these inequality protest movements raises a number of questions about them: What are their messages? What do they want? Why are they emerging now? Why are different labels ("right" vs. "left") used by different media sources (corporate vs. alternative media) to describe the Tea Party and Occupy movements? Could they unite into a single movement for change? Answers to many of these questions are explored in chapter 14.

There is little doubt that the emergence of the Tea Party and Occupy movements are linked to growing economic inequalities spawned by the new class system. At the same time, there is also little doubt that these movements have contributed to widespread public interest in economic inequalities, substantial public support for policies to reduce such inequalities, and majorities supporting protests against inequalities. Evidence for such views is found in national surveys regarding Americans' opinions on these issues. For example, in a November 2011 *Wall Street Journal*/NBC News poll, 76 percent agreed that America's economic structure "favors a very small proportion of the rich over the rest of the country."[17] A *Washington Post*/ABC News poll in the same period found a 60 percent majority favored public policies "to reduce the gap between wealthy and less well-off Americans."[18] And a *Time* magazine poll taken in October 2011 found 73 percent of Americans favor "raising taxes on those with annual incomes of $1 million or more to help cut the federal deficit." This poll also found 56 percent of Americans favorably viewed "the protests on Wall Street and across the nation against policies demonstrators say favor the rich, the government's bank bailout, and the influence of money in our political system."[19]

Below-the-Waterline Inequalities: The Class Analysis Taboo

"That most unmentionable of topics . . . [is] class and how it determines the fate of millions of Americans."

—Susan J. Douglas, *In These Times* (January 2012): 15

Media reports, popular culture, and protest activities have helped focus public attention on several important inequalities found largely above the waterline. While these are welcome developments for those interested in gaining a more complete understanding of inequality in the United States, there is much more to the story of the new class system "than meets the eye" (above the waterline). In order to more fully understand and appreciate the scope, scale, and complexities of the new class system, and perhaps how to change it, we need to identify and explore a number of structural and dynamic features that are central to its nature—features largely hidden "beneath the waterline." Such features are the primary focus of chapters 6–14.

In earlier editions of this book we presented evidence documenting the reality that below-the-waterline features of the new class system, especially those involving class power issues, were largely *outside* of widespread public awareness. We demonstrated that this was the case, at least in part, because such features were largely excluded from attention or consideration by most major social institutions. This exclusion, we maintained, occurs because *social class analysis*, rigorous inquiry into below-the-waterline structures and processes undergirding class-based inequalities, has been a taboo topic in American society.[20] We view the taboo nature of social class analysis as a product of institutional biases that discourage and deflect public discussions of class issues—especially the topics of class power and conflicting class interests. These biases are grounded in privileged-class interests in encouraging public silence on, or even confusion about, class issues. Members of the wealthiest "1 percent" of the privileged class (what we call the "superclass" in chapter 2) have an especially strong interest in not having public attention called to their class-based advantages or to broader class inequalities. This is the case because a close examination of the origins of and basis for these inequalities, including the wealth, power, and privileges of the superclass, might call the entire class system into question.[21]

Superclass preferences for avoiding public discussions of class inequalities are paralleled by the interests of what we call "credentialed-class" members in maintaining their own positions of affluence and security (see chapter 2). Allied with and following the lead of their superclass sponsors, many credentialed-class members are rewarded for helping to keep class analysis out of the arena of public discourse. In their roles as government officials, organizational executives, media producers, and community leaders, credentialed class managers and professionals often pursue organizational policies and practices that have the effect of deflecting public attention away from class inequalities and class-based analyses of social issues and problems.[22]

Although the interests of the superclass and of the entire privileged class are major factors underlying the class taboo, we do not see a "class conspiracy" driving the neglect of class analysis in public discourse. Rather, we see the elite classes (the superclass and its credentialed-class allies) as bound by shared cultural assumptions, values, experiences, worldviews, and organizational memberships.[23] These shared qualities lead to strong, common commitments to maintaining the economic, political, and cultural status quo.[24] Such views lead most members of the elite classes, the rest of the privileged class, and the new working class to explain material and social success (or failure) on the basis of factors other than class-based resources.[25]

Today the class analysis taboo is still largely in place. Recent developments such as the Occupy movement have helped call public attention to *some* below-the-waterline inequality issues, such as how the economic power of the top 1 percent influences the political process. Even so, most below-the-waterline components of the new class system remain taboo. As in the past, this means they are *outside* the boundaries of mainstream political discourse, corporate media reports, most forms of popular culture, and thus outside of widespread public awareness.

Since the class taboo relegates most features of the new class system to below-the-waterline status, we believe this book, which is focused squarely on such topics, is essential reading for those interested in understanding the "hidden" aspects of our class system and how those features relate to inequalities that are part of it. If the material presented in the preceding "dream and iceberg" sections sounds a bit alarming, perhaps that's because it is—at least if you believe this is *not* the kind of society America *should* be in the twenty-first century. Would you like to know more? If so, we invite you to continue reading. We believe open-minded readers who join in our exploration of the many facets of the new class system will acquire a more complete understanding of, and an appreciation for, how and why this system emerged, how it is maintained and legitimated, and how crucially important its complex structures, dynamics, and consequences are to their own lives, families, communities, and the larger society. We hope this knowledge will facilitate critical discussions of the new class system, encourage readers to consider why and how this system may need to be changed, and empower readers to identify and engage in the kinds of actions and policies that need to be undertaken by concerned citizens interested in fundamentally transforming this system.

1

Class in America: The Way We Were

"My momma always said that life is like a box of chocolates. You never know what you're gonna get."

—*Forrest Gump* (1994)

The lead character of the popular film *Forrest Gump* demonstrates that despite limitations of intellect, his pure heart, guileless character, sincerity, hard work, and positive mental attitude enable him to prevail over life's hardships. Though the film was released many years ago, it has since become an American classic, largely because of the hero's endearing nature. Gump's disarming qualities defrost the cynicism of a heartless world and open the path to material success, social respect, and personal fulfillment. His achievements appear to affirm his momma's homily, reinforce belief in the American dream, and give testimony to the pervasive ideological belief that all men are created equal.

However, movie ideals often clash with social realities. Is life really as Gump said, like a box of chocolates—unpredictable and capricious in detail but essentially rewarding to the pure of heart? Consider the contrast between the fictional experiences of Forrest Gump and the real-life experiences of Jim Farley.

Jim Farley's fellow workers at Federal Mogul Corporation's roller bearing plant on the east side of Detroit called him Big Jim—not so much because of the size of his body, they said, as because of the size of his heart. They liked the soft-spoken yet tough manner in which he represented them as a union committeeman. And they liked his willingness to sit down over a shot and a beer at the nearby Office Lounge and listen to the problems they had with their jobs, their wives, or their bowling scores.

Jim Farley had come North from eastern Kentucky, because mechanization of the mines and slumping demand for coal made finding work there impossible. The idea of leaving behind the mountains where he had grown up for the punch-in, punch-out factory life in a big city like Detroit didn't appeal to him much—but neither did the thought of living on relief, like so many unemployed miners in his hollow and most others in Pike County. . . .

Federal Mogul announced that it would be phasing out its Detroit operations by early 1974 and moving bearing production to a new plant in Alabama. Farley, say those who knew him, became a different man almost overnight—tense, moody, withdrawn. A month after the announcement he suffered a heart attack. Physically, he recovered rapidly. Mentally, things got worse. His family and friends called it "nerves." . . .

With close to 20 years at Federal Mogul, the thought of starting all over again—in an unfamiliar job, with no seniority and little hope for a decent pension—was not pleasant. But Farley had little choice. Three times he found work, and three times he failed the physical because of his heart problem. The work itself posed no difficulty, but none of the companies wanted to risk high workers' compensation and health insurance premiums when there were plenty of young, strong workers looking for jobs.

As Farley's layoff date approached, he grew more and more apprehensive. He was 41 years old: what would happen if he couldn't find another job? His wife had gone to work at the Hall Lamp Company, so the family would have some income. But Farley's friends were being laid off, too, and most of them hadn't been able to find work yet either—a fact that worsened his outlook.

Farley was awake when Nancy left for work at 6:15 A.M. on January 29, but he decided to stay home. His nerves were so bad, he said, that he feared an accident at work. His sister-in-law Shirley stopped by late that morning and found him despondent. Shortly before noon he walked from the kitchen into his bedroom and closed the door. Shirley Farley recalls hearing a single click, the sound of a small-bore pistol. She rushed to the bedroom and pounded on the door. There was no response. Almost 20 years to the day after Jim Farley left the hills of eastern Kentucky, his dream of a secure life for his family was dead. And so was he.[1]

Most people would see Jim Farley's death as an unnecessary personal tragedy. Here was a man with severe psychological problems who simply could not cope with the stress of job loss. "Millions of people lose a job in this lifetime, but they don't commit suicide" might be the typical response. There is a strong tendency to see unemployment as individual failure and the inability to "bounce back" as further evidence of that failure.

But there is another way to look at Jim Farley's death, a way that recognizes the powerful impact that impersonal economic and social structures, and changes that affect those structures, have on people's lives. For some, these structures produce limited opportunities and hardship. For others, they open doors to bright futures and affluent lives. Farley's chances in life were powerfully shaped by being born into and working within the lower layers of the U.S. class structure, a structure that constrains opportunities for people like Farley. His life was like that of millions of others who barely finish high school and move through half a dozen jobs hoping to find one that will provide a decent wage and long-term security. And Farley did seem to find what he was looking for in a job at the Federal Mogul bearing plant—at least for a while.

It is important to note that Jim Farley's company, Federal Mogul, was closing its doors in Detroit in 1974 at about the time the "old economy" began changing. It was replaced by a "new economy," which we introduce in chapter 2 and explore in chapter 3. The new economy, as we will see in chapters 3 and 4, includes domestic and global dimensions that are inextricably intertwined. It emphasizes new labor-saving technologies, new rules about the relationship between employers and employees regarding job security, wages and benefits, and globalized production. This new economy has, as we'll see in chapters 3–6, led hundreds of companies to move thousands of U.S. plants to other countries, eliminating millions of U.S. workers' jobs.

The end of the old economy brought an end to the post-WWII class structure, which we briefly describe later in this chapter, and the new economy helped usher in a new class structure. This change, as we will see, is not a temporary aberration that will soon be put right but a fundamental shift in the distribution of economic and political power that helped reshape the U.S. class system. To understand the declining fortunes of millions of Jim Farleys and the corporate decisions of thousands of Federal Moguls, it is necessary to explore the links between the new economy and the new class system. As we will see, the structures and processes that are part of the new economy and the new class system have been and will remain enormously important in shaping corporate practices, government policies, and workers' lives.

When we ask, "What are the major characteristics that define a class structure?" it is important to recognize that a particular class structure is shaped by broad economic, political, and social conditions and events. A class structure can be influenced by long periods of economic growth, stagnation, or decline, as well as by tax laws that increase or decrease the incomes of wealthy persons and by tax rates that raise or lower corporate profits. The class structure Jim Farley was born into in the 1930s was different from the one he experienced as a twenty-five-year-old worker in the 1950s. During Jim Farley's working career in the 1950s and 1960s, the economy was growing and taxes on wealthy Americans and corporations were much higher than they would be in the new economy that emerged after his death. During this period, Jim Farley's income was growing, and the level of inequality between high- and low-income groups was much less than it would become. When Jim Farley died in 1974, the events that precipitated his death prefigured the emergence of what would be a new class structure very different from the one that preceded it. In the next two sections we briefly describe some major features of the U.S. class structure in the 1930–1945 and 1945–1975 time periods. The first period spans the years from the onset of the Great Depression to the end of World War II. The second period begins as World War II ends and continues to the dawn of the "new economy." These accounts help us see how class structures change over time and how that change is influenced by broader political and economic events.

THE U.S. CLASS STRUCTURE: 1930–1945

Prior to the Great Depression of the 1930s and despite the image many have of the "roaring twenties" as a period of great prosperity, the U.S. class structure was highly unequal. Most Americans were either mired in deep poverty or very poorly paid. They were part of a very large lower class that included a majority of all Americans. There was not much of a middle class as we understand this term today. The middle ranks of the class structure at this time ranged from those who had very modest incomes to those who, by the standards of that time, had relatively affluent incomes. But all of these middle ranks together accounted for less than a third of Americans. At the very top was a small class with levels of incomes and wealth that ranged from exceptionally affluent to robber-baron rich.[2]

In the 1930s, the decade preceding World War II, the United States experienced a long, deep, and widespread depression. During this Great Depression, industrial production and manufacturing output fell sharply, producing a sharp decline in individual incomes and corporate profits. The results were dramatic. There were major losses in tax revenues at all government levels. Unemployment reached 25 percent in 1933, and remained above 15 percent throughout the decade. Over ten thousand banks failed, wiping out the savings of millions of Americans. And although Americans in all social classes experienced at least some of the effects of the Great Depression, those at the bottom of the class structure were hardest hit.[3] The Great Depression did not reshape the U.S. class structure as much as it expanded the size of the lower class and made the boundaries between the classes more difficult to cross. It froze in place at the bottom for a decade or more a large majority of Americans—those with little in the way of stable incomes or long-term savings. Figure 1.1 provides an image of the U.S. class structure as it existed prior to the Great Depression and that became even more rigid by that steep economic downturn.

The pyramid-shaped class structure depicted in figure 1.1 helps call attention to several important features of a highly stratified class structure with a large lower class. First, its *shape* reminds us that the majority of people in such a structure are located at the bottom of the pyramid. This was the case in the 1930s when even more Americans found themselves at the bottom of the pyramid than in the 1920s. Those at the bottom always have the least amount of some scarce and valued resource (in this example, money). Second, it provides an idea of the *span* of the structure—namely, the size of the income gap between the top stratum and the bottom stratum. The ratio of average incomes for families in the top and bottom strata of the structure is very wide, perhaps 400:1 or more. (Figure 1.1 does not provide income estimates for each stratum.) Third, it provides an indication of the *permeability or rigidity* of the structure—that is, the opportunity for people to experience upward mobility. In figure 1.1 the three strata are separated by spaces, indicating that upward mobility is limited and that the newest generation born into each stratum will more than likely remain there in their lifetime.

The conditions of the Great Depression, and the pyramid-shaped class structure it reinforced, began to change when the United States entered World War II. Industrial production that was needed to supply the war machine revived the steel and rubber industries to produce what was needed in the way of planes, tanks, bombs, and guns. The textile industry expanded as it was pressured to keep up with the demand for

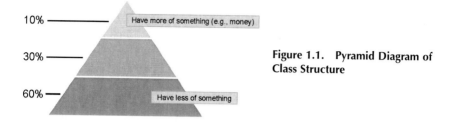

10% —————— Have more of something (e.g., money)

30% —————— **Figure 1.1. Pyramid Diagram of Class Structure**

60% —— Have less of something

military clothing needed by the hundreds of thousands of young men and women who entered the armed forces as volunteers or draftees. Women entered the labor force in record numbers to fill the gap created by military mobilization, thereby creating the iconic "Rosie the Riveter" symbol of women working in defense factories. By 1943, expansion of the military and industrial sectors reduced the unemployment rate to 3 percent, but the broader benefits of this military-based economy were restricted by the existence of wage and price controls, as well as gas and food rationing. The general population was still on a wartime footing, thereby limiting the benefits of full employment and an increase in consumer spending.

THE U.S. CLASS STRUCTURE: 1945–1975

When World War II ended, the United States was the dominant military and economic power in the world. U.S. industries that produced weapons of war for the armed forces, and for many U.S. allies, remained intact and unharmed by the war. In contrast, the industrial capacity of England, France, Italy, Germany, Japan, China, and the Soviet Union were totally or partially destroyed because the war was fought on their soil; their factories, rail systems, and infrastructure were destroyed by continual bombardment from air power and ground assaults. The war-torn nations lost not only the factories that could produce consumer goods needed by their people but also a generation of young men and women who would make up the workforce and do the work of rebuilding.

At the close of the war, there was concern that the United States would not be able to sustain the high level of employment that was stimulated by wartime mobilization, and that the country would slip back into the high level of unemployment and stagnation of the depression years. However, U.S. political and industrial leaders fashioned a new geopolitical system that would maintain American dominance. U.S. policy-makers created an ambitious foreign assistance program, known as the Marshall Plan, that extended billions of dollars in aid to European and Asian nations. The aid money was used by the war-ravaged nations to buy U.S. agricultural and industrial products. Meeting the demand for consumer and agricultural goods from other nations established the United States as the major exporter of goods and services and contributed to sustained economic growth. The United States continued its dominance of the world economy through its control of three-fourths of the world's investment capital and two-thirds of its industrial capacity. An added contributor to this growth was the phenomena of many returning veterans being readily reabsorbed into the labor force and hundreds of thousands of veterans using their "GI benefits" provided by Congress to enroll in colleges and universities throughout the nation. This new educated and skilled workforce was a further strength of America's renewed economy.

The postwar system described above served as the basis for U.S. growth and prosperity during the 1950s and 1960s. Industrial relations between labor and management during these decades took the form of what some authors have described as a "social contract." This means that management would provide workers with stable wage increases, pensions, health insurance, and paid vacations; in return, American workers, many of whom were members of large and powerful unions, provided high-productivity work performance, agreed-upon work rules, and minimal disruption of the workplace in the form of unauthorized strikes.[4]

The clearest evidence that the postwar economic expansion provided positive benefits for most Americans can be found in data on income growth across all income groups in the country. If we divide the entire population of income earners into five quintiles (each quintile includes 20 percent of the population), we can compare the relative income gains of each quintile during the period from 1947 to 1973. Income data for this period indicate that the four lowest income groups experienced gains in the shares of income they received while the top quintile experienced a slight decline in its income share.[5] The income gains of workers during the latter portion of the 1947–1973 period are illustrated by the sharp rise in median annual earnings of full-time, full-year workers. Median annual earnings rose from $37,940 in 1959 to $45,748 in 1973, a 22 percent increase (both amounts in 2011 dollars).[6]

The post–World War II economy of the 1950s and 1960s helped reconfigure the U.S. class structure from the pyramid shape shown in figure 1.1 to the diamond shape presented in figure 1.2. Using the same terms we used to describe the pyramid class structure, we can see that the diamond *shape* locates most Americans in the middle stratum. Regarding the *span* of the class structure, the income share data reported in the previous paragraph suggest that the degree of income inequality was lower at the end of the time period (1975) than at the beginning of the period (1945). Regarding *permeability or rigidity* of the class structure depicted in figure 1.2,

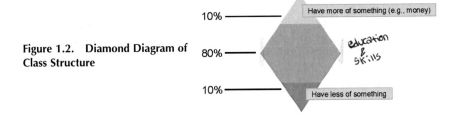

Figure 1.2. Diamond Diagram of Class Structure

the existence of a very large middle stratum (80 percent of Americans) indicates there was ample opportunity for people to move up or down into that large middle group. In sum, the image of class structure in figure 1.2 is that of a "middle-class society," which was the term most often used to describe the U.S. class structure in the 1950s and 1960s. How did scholars who studied the U.S. class structure account for the shift from a pyramid shape to a diamond shape?

MAPPING THE CLASS STRUCTURE: PAST TRADITIONS

During the 1960s, social scientists who were studying the changing class structure and defining what class means in America were well aware of the expanding opportunity and income growth taking place for over a decade. They often attributed the change from a pyramid-shape structure to a diamond-shape structure to the growing importance of educational credentials and occupational skills being acquired by the expanding labor force. Some analysts argued that as American workers expanded their skill levels they also became more productive, contributing to the expanding profits of their employing organizations. As the fruits of productivity and profits became shared more widely, the shape of the class structure became more and more of a middle-class society. Other analysts argued that the economic gains were temporary, and that regardless of expanded skills and education, workers were still workers and owners were still owners, and their interests would always be incompatible. However, despite their different views of the changing class structure, their theories of class were similar in that they believed that a person's location in the class structure was based on a person's occupation, although for very different reasons (which we examine below). We call these two approaches to class analysis the *production* model and the *functionalist* model.

The production model is a kind of single-factor approach in which people's positions in the production process (what they do in the workplace) occupies center stage. It views the shape of the class structure as organized on the basis of the relationship that people have to the means of production. People may be owners of productive resources—like factories, offices, malls, airlines, and rental properties—or nonowners—workers who own only their own labor power, which they must sell to the owner in order to earn wages. Owners make profits by buying a worker's capacity to work and applying it to the productive process and selling the products in the marketplace. A worker's capacity to work must be converted in actual work, thereby requiring the need for supervisors and managers who oversee production. The market value of the products that are produced by workers exceeds the value of the wages they are paid for producing them, thereby creating surplus value and the basis for exploitation of workers.

This approach is grounded in the work of Karl Marx, who focused on owner (bourgeoisie) and nonowner (proletariat) classes. But some contemporary sociologists (neo-Marxists) have refined and extended the original two-class model to reflect the reality that the production and corresponding occupational structures are much more complex today than they were in the 1880s.[7] Recent sociological variations of this approach move beyond the two-class model to produce a multilevel image of class structure with a relatively short list of levels or classes. However, unlike the image of classes shading into one another because of gradually shifting economic and lifestyle differences, Marxian production models view the class structure as more sharply divided by inequalities that reflect people's positions in the production process. In these models, classes are typically based on occupational categories such as owners, managers, small employers, semiautonomous employees, and hourly wage workers. In each instance, class position is based on a person's location in the production process—which also closely corresponds to the possession of income and wealth and to the occupational roles people perform. Owners (big and small) set policy and control the production process; managers assist owners and act as "order givers" who oversee the production process and often accumulate portions of productive wealth themselves; workers are "order takers" and typically do not share in the ownership of productive wealth (or at most own only very small portions); the poor are excluded from both ownership and most forms of desirable work. This model acknowledges the existence of conflicting class interests and examines the strategies used by owners and managers to pressure workers into accepting lower wages or less desirable working conditions.

The functionalist model was partly inspired by Max Weber's view that social stratification is a complex, multidimensional phenomenon and cannot be understood on the basis of a single factor, like a person's position in the production process. Unlike the Marxian production model, in which ownership and control (or the lack of it) are critical to producing the class structure (and defining class), Weber believed that inequality existed along two different dimensions of social life, which he called *class* and *status*.[8] According to Weber, class positions reside in the economic order and are based on a person's relationship to the market; there are propertied classes and nonpropertied classes. The propertied classes own land and the means of production and receive rent and profits in the marketplace. The nonpropertied class is made up of skilled and unskilled workers who sell their labor power at values determined by the supply and demand for labor.

Weber's view of class positions bears some resemblance to Marx's production model, but Weber did not stop with the analysis of class, because he argued that in addition to the economic order, there is a social order composed of status groups. Status groups are based on the prestige associated with one's style of life, including their values, beliefs, associations, and consumption behavior. Status groups exist independent of class groups, and it is possible for the same family to have a high class position and also be in a low status group.

The Weberian view of classes and status groups introduced the distinction between an "economic class" and a "cultural class." An economic class in both the production and functionalist models emphasized groupings of people with similar occupations, income, and educational levels. Although the production model might emphasize occupation-based power and income (owners versus workers), and the functionalist model might emphasize occupational prestige and education (socio-economic groups), both would view these groupings as economic classes that were similar in terms of similar occupation, income, and education. The idea of cultural classes was introduced by the Weberian concept of status groups, which focused on *lifestyles*, meaning the ways that people lived their lives, such as their choices of clothing, homes, leisure activities, or child rearing.[9] Taken together, such qualities produce what we can call a cultural class.

Many sociologists were attracted to Weber's multidimensional approach to inequality, and they gave greater attention to his views on status groups and prestige rankings of one's occupation and style of life. Application of the Weberian functionalist approach often produced a cakelike image of the class structure, with the layers (referred to as *strata*, not classes) organized according to variations in the levels of prestige. Prestige levels are viewed as reflecting a combination of several qualities individuals possess. These include the level of importance attached by cultural values to different occupational categories individuals occupy, educational levels they attain, and variations in their source of income. Although money does matter somewhat in some functionalist models, prestige (especially occupational prestige—not wealth per se) is the critical factor shaping the class structure and locating people within it. According to functionalist models, occupations requiring advanced formal education such as teaching and social work confer high levels of prestige on people who work at them, even though their income levels may be lower than some factory or business occupations requiring less education.

As noted, functionalist models encourage a layer-cake view of the class structure. In contrast to production-model views of sharp class divisions based on production positions and economic wealth, functionalist models envision a multilayer class structure with shaded degrees of prestige and income dividing the social classes. Thus, functionalist models are somewhat similar to the public image of class structure. But functionalist models often omit references to class and instead use the term *socioeconomic strata* (SES) as a way of describing the layered rankings of people possessing similar levels of occupational prestige and education. The ranks that make up the SES structure are typically arranged by functionalist models into descriptive categories that are further subdivided. For example, the highest rank is often divided into upper-upper and lower-upper SES groupings with the same upper- and lower-prefix designations also applied to the middle and lower ranks. Approached in this way, class structure takes on a kind of shaded, layer-cake image with classes more akin to statistical categories than groupings of real people.[10]

While the competing production and functionalist models of the class structure provided reasonably good accounts for the pyramid structure that existed during the depression and the diamond structure that emerged with the economic expansion after World War II, both models failed to anticipate the historic changes in the U.S. economy that began to take form in the mid-1970s and would become known as the "new economy."[11] The conditions that led to Jim Farley's death in 1974 included his employer's decision to move its plant from Detroit to Alabama, probably because of lower wage markets and a nonunion environment. Federal Mogul executives could make this move because the law says corporations have "property rights" over their factories and may close them and move them elsewhere with little or no consideration of the workers or the community. Workers' jobs are not considered to be protected by property rights, and communities have no legal means to prevent a company from leaving.

The economic conditions that led to Jim Farley's death in 1974 began to spread across the land as millions of workers in once-secure, high-wage jobs in America's basic industries were told that they were no longer needed. During the next four decades, thousands of manufacturing plants in auto, steel, rubber, textiles, glass, and consumer electronics industries either went out of business, moved to lower-wage locations in the United States, or moved production overseas to low-wage countries. As the flight of manufacturing jobs to foreign shores proceeded, corporate America's appetite for ever-higher profits began to focus on its white-collar labor force. Giant corporations like AT&T, GE, GM, and IBM began to implement "downsizing" or "restructuring" policies to reduce the number of white-collar workers they employed. This often occurred through the use of new technologies and the reorganization of white-collar work, which not only reduced the number of white-collar workers but also increased the workload of and demands on those who remained employed. The appearance of the *new economy* in the mid-1970s set the stage for four decades of economic changes that would help transform the U.S. class structure—the topic for chapter 2.

2

The New American Class Structure

"If calling America a middle-class nation means anything, it means that we are a society in which most people live more or less the same kind of life. In 1970 we were that kind of society. Today we are not, and we become less like one each passing year."

—Paul Krugman, "The Spiral of Inequality,"
Mother Jones (November–December 1996)

Early warning signs of a slowdown and redirection of the American economy started to appear in the mid-1970s as many of the war-torn economies in Europe and Asia resumed production of goods for export and became competitors with the United States. The U.S. merchandise trade balance of exports and imports recorded a double-digit deficit in 1977 ($29.2 billion), which had never happened before.[1] It marked the beginning of America's switch from a creditor to a debtor nation. At the same time, many of America's largest corporations experienced declining profit rates compared to the 1960s.[2] Corporate executives, government leaders, and the mainstream media held discussions concerning global competition and declining profits, searching for answers about what could be done.[3] Many of the "answers" considered by these elites focused on a need for policies that would: (a) reduce the power of organized labor in order to reduce labor costs, (b) reduce excessive government regulations on U.S. business to reduce the cost of doing business, and (c) reverse what was claimed to be a declining work ethic among American workers in order for the United States to compete with more diligent workers in other nations in the global economy.[4]

Rather than responding to the increased competition in autos, steel, textiles, and electronic product markets by investing in more efficient technology or new product innovation, corporate leaders, with the assistance of both political parties, embarked

21

on a forty-year program of increased foreign investment, mergers and joint ventures with foreign corporations, and outsourcing and offshoring domestic production by closing plants and downsizing the domestic workforce. By 1981, the United States "was importing 26 percent of its cars, 25 percent of its steel, 60 percent of its televisions, tape recorders, radios, and phonographs, 43 percent of its calculators, 27 percent of its metal-forming machine tools, and 53 percent of its numerically-controlled machine tools."[5] By 2010, imports from developing nations reached $872 billion, up from $30 billion in 1980, and up from $3.6 billion in 1970.[6]

Forty years of plant closings, shifting investment abroad, downsizing, and outsourcing by America's largest and most well-known corporations resulted in the drastic erosion of high-wage jobs that were the backbone of "middle-class" America. ⌈At the same time that the middle class was disappearing, a large new group of highly paid business owners, corporate executives, managers, and professionals were riding the crest of a new wave that would produce a large and dominant privileged class with high incomes, great wealth, and political power.⌋

MAPPING THE NEW CLASS STRUCTURE

The production and functionalist models discussed in chapter 1 are inadquate frameworks for understanding the changing class structure. Both models emphasized the importance of occupation as a key factor in determining class location—although for different reasons. As we noted in chapter 1, the production model emphasizes how the location of an occupation in the system of production determines one's class; those who own and control the means of production are in one class and those who sell their labor for wages are in a different class. The functionalist model emphasizes how the prestige of an occupation confers rewards and determines one's socioeconomic position. Although both models have made useful contributions in analyzing class inequalities in the past, their exclusive focus on the occupationally linked factors of production and prestige is inadequate to the tasks of both describing and understanding the emerging realities and complex dimensions of the "new American class system." Millions of workers who were in highly skilled occupations and who would have been comfortable in the middle-class society of the 1960s and 1970s are now displaced from jobs shipped to foreign workers, and those jobs are not coming back. The production and functionalist theories could not explain these new facts. In their place, we propose what we call the *distributional model.*

To more fully understand the origins, nature, and dynamics of the new class system, in this book we develop and apply a new model of class analysis. Our model retains the focus on occupations that is central to production models, and incorporates consideration of organizations and the distributional processes they control, such as wages, benefits, and taxes. Organizations employing workers provide wages and salaries, and they may provide health care and pension programs. Government organizations set trade policies, establish individual and corporate tax rates, and define employer-worker rights and responsibilities. Educational organizations like universities confer specialized skill credentials for graduates to use in the labor market. We argue that a combination of location in the occupational structure (production model) and organizational membership (distributional model) can be used to identify class membership, describe our map of the stratification system, and consider the consequences of class inequalities. We refer to our approach as the distributional model of class analysis, and it includes at least four major features that distinguish it from previous models of class analysis.

The first distinctive feature of our model is that the emerging new class system is organizationally based. This means that the class structure is increasingly organized around and through large, organizational structures and processes that control the distribution of several forms of valuable economic and social resources. We maintain that large organizations—through various levels and groups of "gatekeepers" within them—direct, channel, and legitimate the distribution of these resources to individuals and groups. Occupations are still important in our approach, not simply because of their role in production but because of the organizations in which their work is conducted. Lawyers are not important as lawyers; they are important because of the firms in which and for which they do their work. This means that a corporate lawyer with a very high salary could be a member of the privileged class, while a small-town lawyer who handles divorces, wills, and criminal cases could be a member of the working class. In the production and functionalist models the two lawyers would be in the same class because they have the same occupation and education level.

The first feature is directly linked to the second important feature of our approach. We define classes as collectivities of individuals and families with comparable amounts of four forms of economic and social resources, or forms of capital: investment, consumption, skill, and social capital (discussed below). People possess variations in these forms of capital in large measure owing to the nature and extent of the links they have to upper-level authority positions in the organizations in which they are employed. Thus, we view the class structure as being largely shaped by the distribution of organizationally controlled forms of capital that, held in greater or lesser amounts, determine the class locations of individuals and groups.

A third major feature of our approach concerns the idea that large organizations are centrally involved in legitimating the distributional processes as well as the class inequalities that arise from them. As we will see in later chapters, this means that large organizations are key sources for generating beliefs and explanations that justify the distribution of the four forms of capital to various individuals and groups, and describe the distribution as fair and legitimate. The fourth and final major feature of our approach rests on our assertion that the U.S. class structure is increasingly polarized by class inequalities into two broad class divisions. This leads us to argue that the new class system more closely approximates a double-diamond image of class structure than the cakelike, stacked-layer images evoked by earlier models of class analysis.

Our distributional model takes into account the reality that large organizations dominate the economic, political, and cultural landscapes today and, through complex distributional structures and processes, shape the nature and details of the new American class system. In this system, social classes consist of collections of real people (not statistical categories) who hold similar levels of, and have similar access to, the four forms of generative capital. These forms of capital are distributed to class members through organizationally based structures and processes that, as we will see, are dominated by privileged groups who themselves possess high levels of all four forms of capital.

GENERATIVE CAPITAL AND CLASS STRUCTURE

Our image of a double-diamond class structure is based on the way that the four forms of capital are distributed and the availability of these resources over time. In American society today, capital is the main resource used in exchange for what we need and want, and it is found in four forms: consumption capital, investment capital, skill capital, and social capital. We call these resources generative capital because they can produce more of the same resource when invested, or they can contribute to the production of another resource (e.g., social capital can produce investment capital).

Consumption Capital

Consumption capital is usually thought of as income—what we get in our wages, salary, social security, unemployment, disability, or welfare checks. The lucky people have enough of it to buy food and clothing, pay the rent or mortgage, and pay off their debts. The really lucky people have a little money left over. But for many people, there is plenty of month left over when the money runs out. In 2010, 46.6 million Americans lived below the Census Bureau's "official" poverty line, but 49 million lived below its "Supplemental Poverty Measure."[7] (In 2010 the federal government's "poverty line" income level was $22,050 for a family of four.)

Figure 2.1 illustrates the distribution of income among families in the United States in 2011. Slightly more than 26 percent of families had incomes above $100,000 per year. At the other extreme, 17.5 percent of families had annual incomes below $25,000. About one-fourth (23.5 percent) had annual incomes from $25,000 to $49,999, and about a third (32.4 percent) had annual incomes between $50,000 and $99,999. Comparing income data for 1969, 1979, 1989, 2000 (data not shown here), and 2011 reveals two trends in the distribution of family incomes over the last forty years. First, there has been an increase in the proportion of families in the top income level ($100,000 or above). Second, there has been a decrease in the proportion of families with middle-level incomes ($25,000 to $49,999). In 1969, about 4 percent of families had incomes of $100,000 or more. This percentage increased to 8 percent in 1989, 18 percent in 2000, and 26.6 percent in 2011. In this same period, middle-level incomes ($25,000–$49,999) declined from 41 percent of

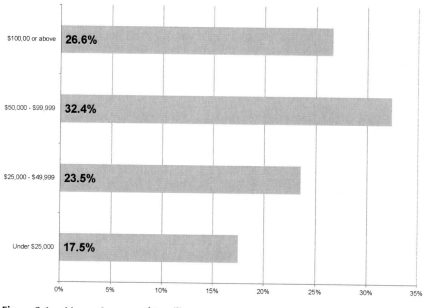

Figure 2.1.   Money Income of Families, 2011
Source: U.S. Census Bureau, Current Population Survey, "2012 Annual Social and Economic Supplement"

families in 1969 to 33 percent in 1979. In 1989 it fell to 30 percent, then to 27.5 percent in 2000, and to 23.5 percent in 2011.[8]

Consumption capital is closely linked to position in the system of production, or occupation. Some jobs pay a lot more than others, but there is also large variation in the incomes of people with the same occupation. Salaries of lawyers, professors, and engineers may vary from upper six figures at the high end to incomes barely above the national average for wage and salaried workers. (In 2011, the median annual income for full-time, full-year employed wage and salaried workers was $42,000, in 2011 dollars. See chapter 5, table 5.1.) Thus, position in the system of production is important, but it does not tell us the full story when considering the question of income. Attempts to map the class structure by using only occupational categories or occupational prestige rankings will invariably combine persons who are getting vastly different returns on their educational assets. The salaries of lawyers, professors, and engineers are due partly to their occupation but also partly (and importantly) to the characteristics of the specific organizations where they work (in addition to other resources discussed later).

Investment Capital

Investment capital is what people use to create more capital. If you have a surplus of consumption capital (the money left over when the month ends), you can save it and earn interest each month. You can buy a house, pay off the mortgage over twenty to twenty-five years, and wait for the rising market value of homes to build equity, which you can recover if and when you sell the house. Or you can create an Individual Retirement Account (IRA) and invest in stocks or bonds to earn dividends and capital gains. You can buy an old house, a "fixer-upper," renovate it, divide it into apartments, and collect rent. If your annual rent receipts exceed the combined cost of mortgage payments, property taxes, insurance, and maintenance costs, you will earn a profit.

Most Americans have very little investment capital. Home ownership is a major source for the accumulation of family wealth for many Americans. In 2009, 67.4 percent of households were occupied by homeowners.[9] Almost 90 percent of people in the top 25 percent income group own homes, versus just under 50 percent in the bottom 25 percent income group.[10] Many families depended on the rising market value of their homes as their source of retirement income. A very rosy scenario says that if you bought a house for $50,000 and sold it twenty-five years later for $150,000, that would be the main source of your retirement income. When the housing market bubble exploded in 2008, many Americans who expected that the values of their homes would continue to rise found themselves with homes that were worth less than their mortgages.

What about retirement accounts? As we point out in chapter 5, in 2009 fewer than half of all private-sector workers were covered by any type of employer-provided pension plan. It is possible to save for retirement without such a plan, but few Americans do. In 2010 only 41.1 percent of all U.S. households owned some type of IRA, and the median value of all IRAs was only $36,000.[11] If you owned a median-value IRA and it doubled to $72,000 at your retirement, you *might* be able to buy an annuity that would provide a $400 monthly income. Of course, if that was your only income, you would still need $500 more per month to bring you up to the poverty level for a one-person household. As we note in chapter 5, many employers once provided workers with defined-benefit pension plans, but not today. This leaves most Americans with only Social Security benefits for income when they stop working.

There are many ways to use investment capital to produce wealth, which provides power and independence and is a major source of well-being for families. Wealth is determined by the total current value of financial assets (bank accounts, stocks, bonds, life insurance, pensions) plus durable assets such as houses and cars, minus all liabilities such as mortgages and consumer debt. Thus, we can describe a family's wealth in terms of total net worth (financial assets, plus durable assets, minus liabilities) or total financial wealth (total financial assets held). The distinction is important because financial assets can generate income (interest, dividends), but durable assets like homes or cars are "lived in" or used for "driving around."

The level of wealth inequality in the United States is much greater than the level of income inequality. Much less is known about wealth than about income distribution in the United States, but wealth is a more significant indicator of economic inequality because of the role it plays in transmitting affluence and privilege across generations. Some sociologists have described wealth inequality as "the buried fault line of the American social system."[12] Figure 2.2 presents the shares of total net worth and total financial wealth in 1983, 1992, 2001, and 2010 for the top 1 percent, the next 19 percent, and the bottom 80 percent of U.S. households. It is clear that there is enormous disparity in the amount of wealth held by the richest 20 percent of the population compared with the bottom 80 percent. In 2010 the "privileged class" (the top 1 percent plus the next 19 percent) held 89 percent of total net worth and 96 percent of total financial wealth—both figures representing increases over the years since 1983. Wealth provides security, well-being, independence, and power to a privileged minority in American society, who can use that wealth to advance their privileged-class interests. Members at the higher levels of the privileged class have accumulated wealth from positions that are at the intersection of their occupations and the organizations in which their occupations are located.[13]

Those with significant wealth are likely to hold top occupational positions in elite, resource-rich organizations. Examples include senior executives in the Fortune 500 firms, physician-executives in large health care firms, senior corporate lawyers, congressional leaders, senior White House staff, cabinet officials, professors at

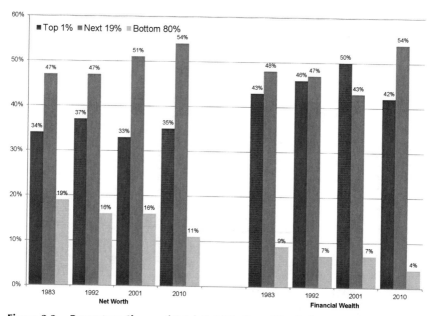

Figure 2.2. Percentage Shares of Total Net Worth and Total Financial Wealth, 1983–2010

Source: Edwin N. Wolff, "Changes in Household Wealth in the 1980s and 1990s in the U.S.," Working Paper No. 407, Levy Economics Institute and New York University, May 2004; Wolff, *The Asset Price Meltdown and the Wealth of the Middle Class* (New York: New York University Press, 2012); Lawrence Mishel, Josh Bivens, Elise Gould, and Heidi Shierholz, *The State of Working America*, 12th ed. (Ithaca, NY: IRL Press, 2012)

elite universities, top corporate media pundits, producers, reporters, and assorted cultural elites. They span a wide variety of political, religious, and social labels (e.g., Democrats, Republicans, conservatives, liberals, Christians, Jews, pro-choice, anti-abortion), but they share a common bond: professional employment in large organizations. As a result, they have high incomes, job security, and wealth. And they help shape the rules of the game in order to preserve and extend their wealth, power, and privileges.

Skill Capital

Skill capital is the specialized knowledge that people accumulate through their work experience, training, or education. Skilled electricians learn their craft through apprenticeship programs and years of on-the-job experience. Skilled doctors learn their craft in medical schools, but their skills are developed further through work experience. Skill capital is exchanged in a labor market, just as investment capital is used in connection with a financial market. Both electricians and doctors try to get the highest return for their skill in the form of wages or fees, and they do this through collective associations like labor unions (United Auto Workers, United Electrical Workers) or medical societies (American Medical Association).

The most important source of skill capital in today's society is located in the elite universities that provide the credentials for the elite classes within the larger privileged class. (The elite classes include the superclass and the credentialed class.) For example, the path into corporate law with seven-figure salaries is provided by about two dozen elite law schools where the children of the elite classes enroll. Similar patterns exist for medical school graduates, research scientists, and those holding professional degrees in management and business. The market value of the credentialed skills minted by elite universities is provided by large corporate employers and professional associations that enable and ensure high incomes, wealth, and security.

Social Capital

Social capital is the network of social ties that people have to family, friends, and acquaintances. These ties can provide emotional support, financial assistance, and information about jobs. Social capital is used by immigrants in deciding which communities they will settle in when they come to the United States. These same immigrants use social capital to get settled and to find jobs. Social ties are also used by doctors, lawyers, and other professionals to facilitate their affiliations with more or less prestigious organizations where they will practice their work.

The basis of social ties can be found in school ties and in kinship, religious, and political affiliations. For example, graduates of elite universities often become the new recruits at national law firms, major corporations, foundations, and government agencies.[14] But social capital is used for more than just getting high-paid secure jobs.

It is also used to solidify class interests by making sure that people marry within their corporate or professional class.

Although everyone has at least a minimal level of social capital, it should be clear that access to different forms of social capital (like consumption, investment, and skill capital) is distributed very unequally. Having a family member able to loan you $100 or a friend who works in a retail store and can tell you about a job opening is not the same as being a member of a fraternity or sorority at an elite university. Social capital refers to current memberships people hold in social networks that are linked to varying levels of organizational power, prestige, and opportunities. A person's position in these social networks provides access to information and opportunities that can be converted into important financial and social benefits.

Many scholars concerned with class analysis have discussed social capital in conjunction with cultural capital, and sometimes the two terms are used interchangeably. While *social capital* refers to network ties, *cultural capital* refers to cultural knowledge (art, music, dining etiquette) that can be an important resource in establishing ties with elite groups.[15] We view these terms as related, but we also see them as having distinct meanings. In our view individuals and families are likely to acquire high levels of social capital through their participation in class-based social networks, and in the process they also are likely to increase their level of cultural capital (i.e., detailed knowledge of elite class cultural elements) acquired or held by network participants

GENERATIVE CAPITAL AND POWER

"In the 2012 [election] cycle . . . more than half (57.1%) of individual Super PAC money came from just 47 people giving at least $1 million [totaling $131.6 million]."

—Adam Lioz and Blair Bowie, "Million-Dollar Megaphones," Dēmos: Ideas and Action to Promote the Common Good (August 2, 2012)

The distribution of these scarce and valued resources—consumption capital, investment capital, skill capital, and social capital—is the basis for class inequality among individuals and families in the United States. This inequality is revealed when resources are converted into economic power, political power, and social power. *Economic power* is based on the resource of money (consumption capital and investment capital), and it can be used to provide food, clothing, shelter, and even luxuries. People who have more economic power can buy more things and better things and thereby make their lives more comfortable and enjoyable. Money also has the special quality of being transferable to others and can also be used to transmit advantage.

Consumption capital can be used to procure social capital. For example, families with money can use it to help secure the futures of their children by purchasing special experiences through travel, tennis lessons, scuba diving, dance, and creative arts, expecting that such experiences will foster or strengthen social relationships with others having similar experiences. It is also done by buying entry into prestigious educational institutions that provide their students with lifelong advantages. Families who buy elite educational degrees for their children use their consumption capital to develop both social capital and skill capital. Graduates of elite universities have special advantages in terms of converting their credentialed skill capital into better jobs. And they establish social contacts that can be used later to solidify or enhance their social positions.

Three out of four families in the United States have very little economic power. Even so-called middle-class families on the "brink of comfort" find themselves in a constant struggle to make ends meet.[16] The problem facing three of every four families in the United States is not only that their consumption capital is limited but also that it is unstable and unpredictable.[17] The predictability of resources allows people to plan and save in order to provide for the future. Most American workers have very unstable incomes, even if they are sometimes earning what seems like a high income. Some skilled, unionized workers sometimes earn $10,000 a month because of overtime opportunities. But this monthly income rarely continues throughout the year. It can be lost when economic declines lead to layoffs or when plants are moved to low-wage locations elsewhere in the United States or in other countries—which is exactly what happened to millions of well-paid blue-collar workers over the past four decades.

Political power is the result of collective actions to shape or determine decisions that enhance people's opportunities. The tenants of a housing project can combine their time to collect signatures on a petition calling on the housing director to provide better services. Corporations in a particular sector of the economy can combine their money (economic power) to hire lobbyists who will seek to influence members of Congress to support or oppose legislation that will affect those corporations. Individuals and organizations with more economic power have a different set of opportunities for exercising political power than groups without economic power.

The clearest examples of how collective economic power can be converted into political power can be found in the lobbying activities of large corporations and wealthy Americans. As we point out in chapter 9, lobbying by coalitions of large corporations, trade associations, and CEO-headed groups has produced enormous economic benefits for large firms across several economic sectors. At the same time, these and other elite class-organized coalitions have also effectively lobbied for and won, over the past thirty years, tax cuts that have benefited all members of the privileged class, but especially the top income groups in this class.

Groups with little economic power usually try to exercise political power through mass mobilization of persons with grievances. Bringing together hundreds or thousands of persons for a march on city hall conveys a visible sense of a perceived problem and an implied threat of disruption. The capacity to disrupt may be the only organized weapon available to those without economic resources. Such actions usually get the attention of political leaders, although they do not always produce the results desired by aggrieved groups.

Social power involves access to public services and the interpersonal networks that can be used to solve many of the day-to-day problems that confront most families. Public services like police, fire protection, and public transportation can provide people with the security to use public space for living, leisure, and getting to and from work, stores, and day-care facilities. Interpersonal networks consist of the informal groups and formal associations that are available in a community for persons with certain interests and concerns. The availability of community groups concerned about the presence of toxic waste dumps, the spread of crime, and the quality of the schools in their community provides opportunities for people to learn about many things in addition to toxic waste, police protection, and education. Such groups often provide links to how to find information about jobs, how to approach a local banker for a loan, or how to obtain information about financial aid for college students.

There is considerable evidence from social research that Americans with greater economic resources, and those holding upper managerial positions in organizations, are more likely to actively participate in a variety of community affairs.[18] As a result, members of the privileged class tend to dominate community-level educational, business, and service organizations. This means that, as with the other forms of power, the members of this class have access to and exercise greater levels of social power than do nonelite members at the community level and at state and national levels as well.

THE DOUBLE-DIAMOND CLASS STRUCTURE

"In [2012] . . . 76% of the public agrees with this statement [that] . . . 'today it's really true that the rich just get richer while the poor get poorer.'"

—Pew Research Center, *Trends in American Values: 1987–2102* (June 4, 2012)

The four forms of capital described above—consumption, investment, skill, and social—are scarce resources now held in varying amounts by people within two broad classes that form the basis of a new class structure that we describe as a double-diamond shape. We term the two large groupings in this structure the *privileged class* and the *new working class*. Within these two major classes we also identify five class segments that are clusters of people who share similar occupational characteristics and organizational affiliations that link them to similar levels of the four forms of capital. The double-diamond structure is depicted in figure 2.3. The *shape* of this new structure includes a small top diamond representing the privileged class (20 percent of the population) and a much larger bottom diamond representing the new working class (80 percent of the population). The figure does not provide specific information on the *span* of this new structure (the income gap between the top and bottom strata), but the "Capital capacity" column on the right suggests a wide and

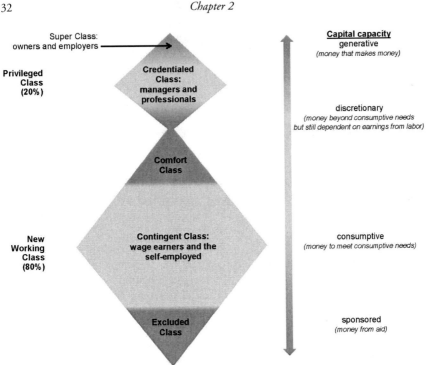

Figure 2.3.   Double-Diamond Diagram of Class Structure and Class Segments

growing income gap between the top and bottom strata. Details on the structure's span are provided in the next two sections. The *permeability* of the structure is limited, as indicated by the narrow passageway between the two large classes. This means there are very <u>few opportunities for upward mobility</u> in this structure.

Table 2.1 provides brief descriptions of the five class segments in terms of the occupational characteristics, organizational affiliations, and consumption capital levels people in each segment hold in common. One of the upper and one of the lower class segments are subdivided into two broad "segment categories" that reflect important occupational, organizational, and consumption capital subdivisions within those two segments. As the table indicates, the credentialed-class segment is subdivided into the "managers" and "professionals" categories and the contingent-class segment is subdivided into the "wage earners" and "self-employed" categories. Table 2.1 also provides estimates of the percentage of the population associated with each class segment or category. Examples of the occupational activities, organizational affiliations, and income levels of those who are located in the two large classes, the class segments, and the segment categories are provided in the next two sections.

Table 2.1. Class Structure in America

Class Position	Class Characteristics	Percentage of Population
Super Class segment:	Owners, employers and senior executives. Income from investments, business ownership and senior management in large firms; incomes from upper seven to nine figure levels; exceptional consumption and investment capital.	1-2%
Credentialed Class segment:		
Managers	CEOs and mid- and upper-level managers of mid-size corporations and public organizations. Incomes from top seven-figure range among CEOs and upper-level managers in six figures.	9-11%
Professionals	Possess credentialed skill in form of college and professional degrees. Use of social capital and organizational ties to advance interests. Incomes from $200K to upper-six figures.	12-14%
Comfort Class segment:	Nurses, teachers, civil servants, very-small business owners, and skilled/unionized workers such as machinists or electricians. Incomes in the $40-$80K range but little investment capital.	14-16%
Contingent Class segment:		
Wage earners	Work for wages in clerical and sales jobs, personal services, and transportation as truck drivers, clerks and machine operators. Members of this group are often college graduates. Incomes at $40K and lower.	44-46%
Self-employed	Usually self-employed with no employees, or family workers. Very modest incomes with high potential for failure.	3-4%
Excluded Class segment:	In and out of the labor force in a variety of unskilled, temporary and low-wage jobs.	10-15%

Privileged Class (20%) applies to Super Class through Professionals. *New Working Class (80%)* applies to Comfort Class through Excluded Class.

The Privileged Class

The activity of some people in the system of production is focused on their role as owners of investment capital. Such a person may be referred to colloquially as the "boss" or, in more respectful circles, as the CEO, but in the language of class analysis they are all owner-employers. The owner may actually be the sole proprietor of the XYZ Corporation and be involved in the day-to-day decisions of running that corporation. But ownership may also consist of possessing a large number of shares of stock in one or several corporations in which many other persons may also own stock. However, the ownership of stock is socially and economically meaningful only when (1) the value of shares owned is sufficient to constitute "making a living" or (2) the percentage of shares of stock owned relative to all shares is large enough to permit the owner of said shares to have some say in how the company is run. Members of this superclass segment, along with those in the credentialed class, control most of the wealth in America. The point here is to distinguish wealthy owners of investment capital from the millions of Americans who own only a few shares of stock in companies, or in mutual funds, or whose pension funds are invested in the stock market. The typical American stock owner does not make a living from that ownership and has nothing to say about the activities of the companies they "own."

A second activity in the system of production is that of manager, the person who makes the day-to-day decisions involved in running a corporation, a firm, a division of a corporation, or a section within a company. Increasingly, managers have educational credentials and degrees in business, management, economics, or finance. Managers make decisions about how to use the millions of dollars of investment capital made available to them by the owners of investment capital. The upper levels of the managerial group include the top management of the largest manufacturing, financial, and commercial firms in the United States. As we discuss in chapter 6, corporate executives and managers receive substantial salaries and bonuses, along with additional opportunities to accumulate wealth in the form of company stock. Those in some managerial positions would be hard pressed *not* to accumulate substantial wealth. For example, the top twenty-five hedge fund managers received average incomes of $556,000,000 in 2011.[19]

The lower levels of the managerial group carry out the important function of supervising the work done by millions of workers who produce goods and services in the economy. The success of this group, and their level of rewards, is often determined by their ability to get workers to be more productive, which means to produce more at a lower cost.

Professionals carry out a third activity in the economic system. This group's power is based on the possession of credentialed knowledge and professional skills. Some may work as "independent professionals," providing service for a fee, such as declining numbers of medical doctors, dentists, and lawyers. But most professionals work for corporations, providing their specialized knowledge to enhance the profit-making activities of their firm or of firms that buy their services. The professional group is made up of university graduates with professional degrees in medicine, law, business, engineering, pharmacy, and a variety of newer fields such as computer sciences that serve the corporate sector. The possession of credentialed knowledge unifies an otherwise diverse group of occupations, which includes, for example, physicians who may earn $500,000 a year as well as MBA graduates from elite universities who may earn $250,000 a year or more in large corporate or government agencies.

The potential to accumulate wealth is very great among certain segments of professionals. Physicians, for example, are the most highly paid professional group. The average net income in 2012 for male physicians in all specialties was $242,000; female physicians averaged $173,000 mainly because they are concentrated in lower-paying specialties such as family medicine. There are large differences between the incomes of lower-paid general practitioners such as family medicine physicians (at the low end), who averaged $158,000 in 2012, and specialty physicians (at the high end) such as radiologists, who averaged $315,000, and cardiologists ($314,000).[20] After six years of practice, these income differences become even larger, with, for example, family medicine physicians averaging $199,850 and radiologists averaging $469,800.[21]

Similar opportunities to earn high incomes and accumulate wealth exist among lawyers, where partners at the nation's two hundred largest law firms averaged over $800,000 in 2009, but "some top . . . partners at firms in New York, Los Angeles, Washington and Chicago earn $10 million or more a year compared with $640,000 for the average partner at a U.S. firm."[22] On the other hand, the mean starting salary for lawyers was only $78,653 in 2011, 15 percent lower than in 2009 ($93,454).[23] Among all lawyers, the median annual wage was $113,310 in 2011, but incomes vary by firm size: "Eight-year veterans at firms with no more than 25 employees had a median wage of $111,250. Lawyers with the same amount of experience at firms with . . . 701 or more attorneys had a median wage of $225,000."[24]

Professors at elite universities in fields like law, medicine, business, and biomedical or electrical engineering have opportunities to start businesses or serve as consultants for industry in ways that can significantly enhance their incomes. For example, professors at prestigious law schools have many opportunities to amass wealth via part-time law practices or consulting contracts.[25] Modest activities, like serving as an outside director for a bank or a mid-size corporation, can be very financially rewarding for elite university faculty and administrators.

Why would the president of a university, or its board of trustees, allow professors to engage in such lucrative "outside activities"? Maybe it's because the president, whose annual salary is $400,000, holds four director positions that provide him or her more than $100,000 a year in additional income. Maybe it's also because some two dozen college presidents receive in excess of $1 million in annual compensation, and may serve as well-compensated directors of major companies. Consider the president of Brown University, an elite school, who served on the board of directors for Goldman Sachs for ten years. In 2009, she received $323,539 for her work on Goldman's board, and has accumulated $4.3 million in Goldman Sachs stock.[26]

Not everyone with a credentialed skill, however, is in the professional credentialed class. We exclude from this class most college-educated workers such as teachers, social workers, and nurses who, despite their professional training and dedication, earn incomes far below those in the top professional groups. We distinguish between elite and marginalized professional groups, with only the former being in the privileged class and the latter largely located in the "comfort class" segment, the top portion of the new working class.

The New Working Class

This class includes the large majority of Americans who work as employees; they sell their capacity to work to an employer in return for wages. Most members of this class carry out their daily work activities under the supervision of "managers" who may be members of the privileged class. At the top of this class in terms of credentialed skills, organizational affiliations, and income are the many college-educated workers who work in occupations that are excluded from the credentialed class of professionals and are located, as we noted above, in the "comfort class" segment of the new working class.

Examples of workers in the comfort class segment include university professors at nonelite schools and attorneys working for legal services agencies, franchise law firms, and public defender agencies. Faculty at nonelite schools are included because most earn only modest salaries and many do not hold tenure-track positions. The attorneys we include here are not linked to large resource-rich law firms at top salaries. As a result, they, like most workers generally, have limited job security, modest incomes, and little investment capital. Other examples of workers in this segment include teachers, social workers, and nurses who appear to be professionals by training but in fact are members of occupations often labeled "semiprofessions," implying that they fall short of being full professionals. This is partly due to the fact that most "semiprofessionals" are not linked to large resource-rich organizations at highly paid positions such as those held by workers in the top 20 percent of all paid employees in such organizations. In addition to the groups noted above, this segment also includes small business owners and skilled, often unionized craft workers such as machinists and electricians.

The "contingent class" segment makes up the largest share of the new working class (47–50 percent including the self-employed). Workers in the "wage earners" category hold jobs that can be terminated with virtually no notice. An exception would be the 6.9 percent of private-sector workers who belong to labor unions, but even union members are vulnerable to having their jobs eliminated by new technology, restructuring and downsizing, or the movement of production to overseas firms. This segment also includes the many thousands of "self-employed" persons and family businesses based on little more than "sweat equity." Many of these people turn to self-employment as a protection against limited opportunities in the general labor market. But many are attracted to the idea of owning their own business, an idea that has a special place in the American value system: it means freedom from the insecurity and subservience of being an employee. But for wage workers, the opportunities for starting a business are severely limited by the absence of capital. Aspirations may be directed at a family business in a neighborhood where one has lived, such as a dry-cleaning store, a beauty shop, or a convenience store.

The "excluded-class" segment, the lowest-income but still sizable portion of the population (10–15 percent), has very weak links to the labor market. It includes the "working poor," such as those who work full time for low wages at or slightly above the federal minimum wage of $7.25 per hour.[27] Such low wages produce annual incomes for the working poor in the $15,000–$20,000 range. This segment also includes low-income workers with transient work patterns. This means they work for wages for short periods of time followed by long stretches of unemployment, when they rely on unemployment compensation, food stamps (Supplemental Nutrition Assistance Program, or SNAP), welfare, or disability benefits.[28] The excluded segment also includes very-low-income retirees who attempt to supplement their retirement incomes with low-skill, low-wage, part-time, temporary work such as part-time service work.

In short, figure 2.3 provides an overall picture of the shape of the double-diamond class structure, and table 2.1 summarizes information regarding the five major segments of that structure. It is important to keep in mind that a person's location in the double-diamond class structure is related to his or her occupation but not determined by it (as is the case in the production and functionalist models of class structure, discussed in chapter 1). As we pointed out, it is not occupation but access to generative capital—stable, secure resources over time—that determines class position. These resources are provided by the organizations within which specific occupations are located and where work-related responsibilities are carried out.

ORGANIZATIONS AND INEQUALITY: CLASS, GENDER, RACE

"It is important to remember that gender is intertwined with . . . race and class.
. . . The categories all work together to construct the complexity of a person's life."

—Kerry Ferris and Jill Stein, *The Real World* (2012), 257

While our primary concern is with examining the nature and consequences of the new class structure in the United States, we also recognize that inequality has many faces. It is our view that a wide array of class as well as gender and race-based forms of inequalities exist in American society and that they are grounded in and linked to large organizations, especially corporations, and the resources that they control.

In order to understand the structures and processes that undergird the origins and reproduction of class as well as gender- and racial/ethnic-based forms of inequality, we focus first on organizations. To clarify and illustrate how organizationally based factors underlie and are critical to all three forms of inequality, we begin by considering this question: What factors facilitate or impede people's access to affiliations with stable, resource-rich organizations at the levels and types of links (e.g., occupation) that yield high levels of all (or most) forms of generative capital associated with privileged class membership? The short answer is that organizational policies and practices shape the processes by which people become affiliated with organizations at various levels. Organizational policies and practices that shape and guide the affiliation process (especially employment decisions) are routinely claimed by policymaking and policy-executing organizational representatives to operate according to principles of meritocracy. However, substantial evidence documents that such policies actually function as class-, gender-, and racially biased gatekeeping mechanisms.[29]

We view organizational policies and practices governing affiliation processes as being composed of two "inequality scripts," one formal, the other informal. At the formal level, these scripts identify organizational roles (e.g., career positions) and specify the formal credentials necessary to access the roles (e.g., educational level, experience). The informal level represents the covert dimension of affiliation decisions made by organizational gatekeepers. At this level, informal qualifications including class background, gender, and racial/ethnic membership enter into affiliation decisions. Upper-level positions, or positions on career ladders that lead to the top, are typically filled via informal inequality scripts that selectively advantage the children,

friends, and associates of current members of the privileged class. High-level positions are compensated by high incomes, are linked to long career ladders within
the organization, and typically require elite educational credentials. Persons from
privileged-class backgrounds are most likely to successfully negotiate the organizational affiliation process and "fit" into these organizational roles that demand and
yield high levels of generative capital.

Abundant evidence exists to show that women and blacks especially have been
negatively affected by organizationally based inequality scripts in at least three
ways. First, working-class women and blacks have historically been more likely than
working-class white males to be employed in smaller and less capitalized organizations, resulting in lower wages, fewer benefits, and greater job insecurity.[30] Second,
even when working-class women and blacks win jobs with resource-rich organizations, they are often employed in gender- and racially segregated positions. There is
substantial evidence of such segregation within the American workplace. Women
comprise 92 percent of nurses but only 32 percent of doctors; 85 percent of legal
assistants but only 32 percent of lawyers; 97 percent of secretaries; 97 percent of
preschool teachers; 90 percent of maids; and 71 percent of food servers.[31] The top
occupations for black and Hispanic men are truck driver, janitor, security guard,
construction laborer, farm worker, cook, and gardener. The most segregated occupations by gender and race also have the lowest incomes.[32]

Third, when women or people of color achieve privileged-class positions, the
promotion process often includes an invisible "glass ceiling" and/or tokenism. These
features are evident in studies documenting the disproportionate representation of
white males versus women and blacks in organizational positions at privileged-class
levels.[33] Women in management positions are often viewed as having dual commitments to work and family, and thus as less suitable for fast-track careers.[34] African
Americans who have benefited from affirmative action policies to attain upper-man-
agement positions in corporations are often placed in racialized positions involved
with black consumer markets or dealing with politically based community issues.[35]

The gender- and race-based inequalities and grievances experienced in everyday
life make it more difficult for working-class men, women, and people of color to
recognize their common class interests as members of the working class. Most fail
to recognize that such inequalities are grounded in and linked much more closely to
the organizationally based inequality scripts that create and perpetuate class divisions
than to informal, micro-level social scripts. Even though we view class-, gender-, and
race-based inequalities as organizationally based and driven, we also view class inequalities as qualitatively different from gender and racial grievances. This is the case
because we believe class inequalities transcend gender and racially based grievances
and have the potential to unite all members of the new working class in efforts to
promote changes that would reduce all three forms of inequality.

Gender and racial inequalities are real and far from unimportant as features and
experiences. Indeed, we return to these issues in our final chapter and consider how
they help reinforce our unequal class structure. But now, since it is our view that a

focus on social class is central to understanding the overarching inequality structures and trends affecting all Americans in our society today, we return to the issue of class structure. In the final section of this chapter we identify four key features of the new class system.

THE NEW AMERICAN CLASS STRUCTURE DEFINED

"The ladders of upward mobility are being dismantled. America, the land of opportunity is giving way to ever deepening polarization between rich and poor."

—Paul Craig Roberts, "The New Face of Class Warfare,"
CounterPunch (July 13, 2006)

Earlier in this chapter, figure 2.3 presented our basic view of the new American class structure as a two-class, double-diamond system. This image identifies the two major classes, but it does not identify or explain the structures and processes that gave rise to this two-class system. It also does not tell us how the class structure operates, what consequences it produces, how it has been perpetuated and legitimated (made acceptable to most people), or what might happen to it in the future. We begin our consideration of these topics by first identifying four important principles that define the new American class structure and influence how it affects people. In chapters 3, 4, and 5 we examine each of these four principles in more detail. Then, beginning with chapter 6 and continuing through chapter 14, we consider additional topics that relate to the major structures and processes that are central to the new class system.

#1: The New American Class Structure Is Anchored in the "New Economy"

Dramatic workplace-related changes began to unfold in the mid-1970s that would reshape the lives of blue-collar and white-collar workers; these changes have often been described as part of the "new economy." One of the central features of this new economy was the focus of a 1982 book by Barry Bluestone and Bennett Harrison titled *The Deindustrialization of America*. These authors defined *deindustrialization* as the "widespread systematic disinvestment in the nation's basic productive capacity."[36] This term refers to corporate policies that have led to the decline of core manufacturing activities in traditional areas of strength in the U.S. economy like autos, steel, textiles, and consumer electronics. Executives in large firms in the manufacturing sector began making decisions to redirect their resources in ways that would produce higher corporate profits, often leading to plant closings in the United States and investments in other countries. One result of these decisions was the loss of millions of high-wage jobs in the manufacturing sector.

Deindustrialization was soon followed by a variety of forms of corporate restructuring such as "downsizing." The focus of downsizing was on reducing costs by reducing the number of employees, typically white-collar workers employed as middle managers, data entry employees, and customer call center workers. These jobs were eliminated by advances in computer-based work activities that required fewer workers and enabled the transfer of many jobs to lower-wage workers in other countries.

The combined effect of decades of deindustrialization and other corporate restructuring practices like downsizing had a profound impact on the once stable and secure jobs held by unionized blue-collar workers and white-collar supervisors in the manufacturing sector. The decline of the "middle-class" jobs these workers held was facilitated by the expansion of computer-based technologies, government trade policies, and the emergence of an international labor force. In chapters 3 and 4 we discuss the "new economy's" domestic and global dimensions and consider how both have been involved in reshaping the U.S. class structure.

#2: A Disappearing Middle Class

The functionalist view of class structure, as noted earlier, presents a "layer-cake" image of class differences. This image encourages the view that there is a "center" or a large "middle class" that stands between the upper and lower classes. The different groups in the middle may think of themselves as being "better off" than those below them, and they may see opportunities to move up the "ladder" by improving education, job skills, or income.

The functionalist view of the class structure as including a large middle class is also the view held by most Americans. As we will see in chapter 5, despite the new economy, plant closings, and the financial crisis, most Americans still consider themselves to be middle class. However, we think the evidence suggests otherwise. Our chapter 5 title, "How the Middle Class Died," provides a sense of our view on the fate of the middle class. As we will see in that chapter, much evidence indicates that the middle class has largely vanished. In our view, there can be no middle class unless Americans have stable jobs and secure financial resources that grow over time. An approximation of those conditions may have existed a generation ago, but not today. We explore the issue of the disappearing middle class in more detail in chapter 5.

#3: Class Structure Is Polarized and Rigid

One of the most significant aspects of class structures is their persistence over time. The inequality that a person experiences today provides the conditions that determine the future. Most discussions of class structure ignore its persistence and view it, and one's place in it, as temporary and ever changing. The belief in equality of opportunity known as the American dream states that regardless of where a person starts out in life, it is possible to move up through hard work and education. At the same time, Americans tend to see "social class" as a constantly changing part of American society, as indicated by shifting income statistics, emerging new job categories, and the ways that new technologies are changing people's lifestyles. In short, the popular image of class differences is that they are temporary and constantly changing. But in fact, nothing could be further from the truth when it comes to the U.S. new class system.

The "rules of the game" that shape the class structure also help reproduce it. Let's consider a few of those "rules" and how they work. First, our legal system gives corporations the right to close plants and move them overseas, but it <u>does not give workers a right to their jobs</u>. Second, people in the elite classes have almost <u>unrestricted opportunities to accumulate wealth</u> (i.e., extensive consumption and investment capital). As we will see in chapters 6 and 9, the accumulation process is based on tax laws that favor the rich, a variety of loopholes to avoid taxes, and an investment climate that enables the rich to get richer. In figure 2.2 we saw that the share of net worth and financial wealth held by the top 20 percent of the population is staggering. This extraordinary disparity in wealth not only provides evidence of a polarized two-class structure but also provides the basis for persistence of that structure. Because inheritance and estate laws make it possible to do so, wealth is transmitted across generations, and privilege is thereby transmitted to each succeeding generation.

Third, the so-called <u>equality of opportunity in America is supposedly provided in large part by its system of public education.</u> Yet everyone who has looked at the quality of education children receive at the primary and secondary levels knows that it is linked to the class position of parents. As we will see in chapter 11, schools that largely serve poor students and their low-income families have the poorest physical facilities, libraries, laboratories, academic programs, and teachers. Some children who survive this class-based public education are able to think about some sort of postsecondary education. But here again, the game is rigged against them. Going to college is tied to the ability to pay the costs of tuition, room, and board. Even at low-cost junior or commuter colleges, the expenses exceed what many working-class families can afford. On the other hand, even if college attendance were not tied to ability to pay, it is not likely that many youngsters from low-income families would think of college as a realistic goal, given the low quality of their educational experience in primary and secondary grades.

These "rules of the game," combined with the new economy as well as with other structures and processes reshaping the class structure, have helped generate three effects related to class polarization and rigidity. First, compared with the recent past, the class structure today is more sharply divided into two broad, polarized classes; the middle class is largely missing. Second, the likelihood of being located in either the privileged class or new working class today is largely determined by the class rank of one's parents—"the fruit doesn't fall far from the tree." Third, the likelihood of upward mobility for persons from low- and middle-income social backgrounds is small and declining. In chapter 5 we will examine recent evidence that relates to these three effects, including results from our intergenerational mobility research project.

#4: Classes Have Conflicting Interests

In the functionalist, layer-cake theory of class structure, each class is viewed as having more or less of some valued resource such as education, occupational skill, or income. Members of each class may aspire to become members of classes above them, and they may harbor negative opinions and prejudices of those in classes below them. But classes, in this theory, are not fundamentally opposed to one another. Of course, there is often discussion of why members of certain classes might support or oppose particular political candidates because of their social or economic policies. But these alliances or oppositional views are seen as linked to shifting issues and are not tied to class interests.

Our view is more closely aligned with the central ideas of Marxist class analysis, which stresses the role of exploitation and dominance in class relations. We see the privileged class and the new working class today as having fundamentally different and opposed objective interests. This means that when one class improves its situation, the other class loses. The advantages of the privileged class, expressed in its consumption capital, investment capital, skill capital, and social capital, are enjoyed at the expense of the working class. Any action to make the resources of the working class more stable—by improving job security or increasing wages and pensions, for example—would result in some loss of capital or advantage for the privileged class. Given the existence of oppositional interests, it is expected that members of the privileged class will work to advance their interests. This principle of conflicting class interests as well as the related issue of "class war" are explored at length in chapter 6.

These four principles—(1) the new class structure is anchored in the new economy, (2) the middle class is disappearing, (3) class structure is polarized and rigid, and (4) classes have conflicting interests—provide a basis for understanding key features of the American class structure today. Most Americans have a good understanding of inequality but very little understanding of the class structure that creates and perpetuates inequality because *social class analysis* is a taboo topic not open for discussion in the United States. Although public officials and the corporate media sometimes mention poverty, homelessness, or income inequality, the average American is rarely presented with a sustained discussion of America's *social class structure*. Thus, we are almost never asked to consider how and why this structure came about, how it operates, how it is legitimated, its many consequences and the inequalities it generates, or the prospects for changing it. We propose to defy the taboo and use a class-analysis approach to explore the topics noted above as well as many others in the chapters ahead.

3

The New Economy
and the New Class Structure

"NAFTA and CAFTA have given us the shafta."

—Jennifer Granholm, former governor of Michigan (2006)

In the summer of 2011 we were interviewing a cross-section of Americans about their views of the economic recession. One of our respondents, a seventy-year-old retiree, reflected on the country's economic and social problems and said, "I think we are headed to a third-world type of situation." Is it possible that the United States could be sliding toward becoming a third-world nation? What happened to the world's "most powerful nation, the sole superpower"? What happened to the "shining city on the hill," the standard and beacon for all those nations and peoples of the world trying to emulate and acquire the prosperity and democracy enjoyed by Americans?

A few months after our seventy-year-old retiree uttered his dire prediction, the corporate media were presenting daily reports of the thousands of people occupying public spaces in over one hundred cities as part of the Occupy Wall Street movement. While the Occupy movement differs significantly from the Tea Party movement, which began in 2009, both were energized by the same deep sense of dissatisfaction many Americans have with "business as usual." This means they are upset with how the federal government ignores average people's needs while slavishly shoveling trillions of taxpayer bailout dollars to the Wall Street firms, bankers, and hedge fund managers whose actions led to the 2008 financial crisis and the recession that followed.

The foundation for these movements grows out of many years of public dissatisfaction with America's major institutions. In 2004, a Gallup poll reported 61 percent of Americans were concerned they might lose their job because their employer might move jobs to a foreign country. In 2007, 78 percent said the economy was "getting worse," and when polled again in a *New York Times/CBS* poll in 2008, only 21 percent of Americans said that the overall economy was in good shape.[1] By 2010, seven of ten Americans believed that the country was heading in the wrong direction. In 2012, barely one in ten said they had "a great deal" or "quite a lot" of confidence in Congress, and only 37 percent said the same about the presidency.[2]

Likely sources of America's growing pessimism about U.S. institutions and anxiety about job losses include growing public awareness of high U.S. unemployment and underemployment rates and the failure of public and private policies to remedy the situation. Such public angst is also likely magnified by coverage in alternative media outlets, such as Internet blogs and social justice websites, or corporate leaders' repeated announcements of job cuts. From Internet sources more so than from corporate media, Americans may learn, for example, that IBM executives plan to move high-technology jobs in computer programming and software design to foreign workers in India and China. Such stories make Americans even more aware of *outsourcing*, which, in the case of IBM and many other firms, means shifting more and more U.S. jobs to low-wage nations.

Another reason for the public's growing disenchantment with corporate America and the federal government is personal experience. People have years of "facts on the ground" all around them that tell a story of national decline, a story that seeps into everyday consciousness and tells people something is wrong. What are these facts on the ground? Older Americans may recall that after World War II, manufacturing as a share of total U.S. jobs was at a peak of 40 percent; it slipped to 27 percent in 1981, then fell to 8.1 percent in 2010.[3] The result has been a loss of 8 million U.S. manufacturing jobs between 1979 and 2012.[4] Even younger Americans may know that the United States lost 2.4 million manufacturing jobs just between 2005 and 2012.[5]

If Americans are not aware of national trends, they might be aware of recent job cuts by the three major U.S. auto firms. After all, the U.S. auto industry once employed hundreds of thousands of American workers, and it still sells millions of cars in the United States. But between 2007 and 2011, job cuts by the "Big Three" auto firms sent economic shock waves through thousands of families and communities as even more "middle-class" auto jobs disappeared. "GM is down to 50,000 workers [in 2011], from 78,000 in 2007. Ford is at 40,000, down from 54,000. Chrysler employs 22,000 hourly, down from 40,000."[6]

These job losses were just the latest in a long series of blows to the U.S. auto industry and its unionized work force. Automakers in the United States have been steadily losing market share to foreign auto producers, especially the Japanese companies like Toyota, Honda, and Nissan, since they built auto plants in the United States during the 1980s. U.S. presidents and Congresses during this period did little to protect U.S. auto manufacturers and unionized U.S. autoworkers from foreign competition.[7] Under the banner of "free trade" and "globalization," foreign automakers were first allowed unrestricted access to the U.S. auto market with their exports and then were encouraged to establish plants in the United States, where they would build cars with nonunion workers.

If all of these blows weren't enough, the 2008 financial crisis and the recession that followed had devastating effects on American families. Millions saw the values of their homes decline and their retirement savings shrink or disappear. Unemployment soared and peaked at 10 percent in October 2009, with 14.8 million people out of work.[8] *Underemployment,* a broader measure of U.S. joblessness, was even worse. This term refers to the unemployed plus those who have stopped looking for work and those who are working part-time but desire full-time jobs. In 2010, the U.S. underemployment rate was 16.7 percent, consisting of 25.2 million Americans.[9] An even broader measure of how the recession affected Americans, one used by the Pew Research Center in 2010, found that one-half of all adults in the labor force experienced some work-related hardship, including unemployment, reduction in work hours, or involuntary movement to part-time work.[10]

In this chapter we summarize developments that over the last forty years have, in our view, led to the transformation of the U.S. economy and helped reshape America's class structure. We call this transformation the "new economy." It has emerged as the result of a number of factors, including a constellation of practices followed by major corporations and Wall Street financial firms plus tax and trade policies enacted by the U.S. Congress with support from both political parties and signed into law by Republican and Democratic presidents. The new economy began to emerge in the 1970s, but it has become more pronounced in the past three decades. In the next section we focus on five features of the new economy: neoliberalism, financialization, new technologies, global production and transnational power, and dual labor markets. These features are not the result of natural changes nor the "invisible hand" of market forces; rather, they are the result of calculated corporate and government actions shaped by the interests of the superclass that occupies the top rung of the double-diamond class structure.

THE NEW ECONOMY

> "In the late 1920s . . . the U.S. economy was regarded as a 'New Economy.' . . . We all know how that vision ended in October of 1929."
>
> —Abby Scher, *Dollars and Sense* (July–August 2012): 12

The five features of the new economy include abstract ideas about how an economy works best, as well as corporate and government practices and policies built around such ideas. The effects of theory-inspired policies and practices are found in new forms of economic activities, technologies, global production, and labor markets. We begin with an overview of a major theoretical perspective that has helped energize and justify the new economy.

Neoliberalism

Neoliberalism as an economic and political philosophy has roots in Adam Smith's classic work, *Wealth of Nations.* But its contemporary version is derived from the work of Friedrich August von Hayek, an early twentieth-century Nobel Prize–winning Austrian economist.[11] While the history of this idea is interesting, our focus here is on its contemporary expression in the economic policies and practices of the federal government and large corporations. Neoliberalism today refers to government and corporate policies at the national and global levels that are based on "[free trade], financial liberalization, privatization, deregulation, openness to direct foreign investment . . . fiscal discipline, lower taxes, and smaller government."[12] Neoliberalism views unfettered capitalism as the only system capable of providing the most efficient economic production possible as well as prosperity for all. In the short run, proponents of neoliberalism acknowledge that "free market capitalism" may lead to some problems and dislocations (e.g., job losses, problematic working conditions for some), but in the long run this system is viewed as assuring both freedom and prosperity for all.[13]

One way to understand neoliberalism is to contrast two different economic systems: a social economy and a market economy. In a social economy the production of goods and services takes place with reference to the larger society. That is, a social economy is *embedded* in society. This means in part that the prices of goods and the value of labor is overseen by government to ensure that the positive effects for society as a whole outweigh any negative effects. For example, a company that wishes to produce its products in a new way (with new technology) or in a new place (in another country) would be asked to consider the effects that such decisions would have on the needs of people and the community. Author Severyn Bruyn has argued persuasively for the development and application of a social economy as a broader and more inclusive system, stressing the full array of institutional linkages between economy and society.[14]

In contrast with a social economy, a market economy is viewed as operating apart from the larger society. It views individuals and corporations as rational actors that seek to maximize their economic gains. Market economy advocates claim that for the economy to be most effective, it must be free from interference with the economic principles (or "laws") that are thought to set the value of goods, services, and wages. Neoliberalism views unfettered free markets as key elements of a market economy. As noted above, it requires unrestricted free trade involving goods and services. It views the private sector as far more efficient than the public sector, and it includes the idea that most social exchanges can be converted into monetary values.

In many respects neoliberalism has become the dominant economic idea system in the United States. It is powerfully influential among top government and corporate leaders at the national and international levels, and its influence extends down to state and local leaders as well. The power of neoliberalism is evident today in many government policies that reflect its influence. Such policies include laws that privatize public assets and that strictly limit government spending (austerity). Privatization is based on the view that the private sector can manage a variety of public assets more efficiently than can government. This is the case partly because private firms do not have to answer to voters or unions when they manage public assets. Austerity policies are based on the idea that limiting spending makes government more efficient and causes people to be more self-reliant by reducing their "dependency" on government "handouts."

While there are many illustrations of privatization policies being proposed or enacted in the United States today, one of the largest nationwide examples centers on "education reform." This large-scale privatization scheme involves efforts to "reform" public education by transforming it into a privately operated enterprise. These efforts are being led by the private education industry with the aid and support of several large foundations, policy-planning groups like the American Legislative Exchange Council (discussed in chapter 9), and many government officials. The story behind the drive to privatize our nation's public school system is too long and complex to be told here. Even so, it is important to know that when the corporate media report on education reforms, failing public schools, and the growth of charter schools, they report on the most visible features of a massive iceberg of school privatization interests, initiatives, and policies. The debate over education reform is never framed as a privatization scheme aimed at remaking schools into profit centers for large corporations, but that is precisely what is occurring.

Efforts to privatize public education were greatly enhanced by the "No Child Left Behind Act," which President Bush signed into law on January 8, 2002. The effects of this act, combined with initiatives funded by the Bill & Melinda Gates, Walton, Broad, and Michael & Susan Dell foundations, have promoted what author Naomi Klein has called "the shock doctrine" or a form of "disaster capitalism," "destroying the public education system in order to open it up for privatization."[15] The reality is that "financial circles now increasingly refer to public education in the United States as an unexploited market opportunity."[16] (The drive to privatize public education is also part of an effort by the elite classes to erode the resources and political clout of public-sector unions.[17])

Austerity policies are evident in the calls by many "conservative" members of Congress for reduced government expenditures on a variety of so-called "safety net" social programs like Medicare, Medicaid, and Social Security. There are also calls for reduced government spending on housing and mass transit programs. The argument of neoliberalism is that such programs often involve extensive waste and inefficiencies, and the benefits are difficult to document. Moreover, the neoliberal view is that the potential benefits of such programs would be better realized if they were in the hands of the private sector, which would run them on a for-profit basis.

Financialization

Financialization "can be defined as the long-run shift in the center of gravity of the capitalist economy from production to finance."[18] This means that large financial firms, the financial "products" they create and market, and the profits they generate increasingly dominate the U.S. economy. It also means that large financial firms and the financial transactions they generate and oversee have become, or soon will become, more important to the U.S. economy than the production of all material goods and all other types of services.

The rise of financialization can be illustrated with some facts about the U.S. economy. When we look at financial profits as a percentage of total U.S. corporate profits over time, we see a substantial increase over the past fifty years. In 1960 U.S. financial firms' profits accounted for 17 percent of total domestic U.S. corporate profits. This share increased to 20 percent in 1987, then peaked at 44 percent in 2005 before falling to 27 percent in 2007 (on the brink of the financial crisis). It rebounded to 31 percent in 2009 and rose to 33 percent in 2011.[19] In contrast, the financial profits of U.S. manufacturing firms as a share of total profits have fallen over the past thirty years. In 1980, U.S. domestic manufacturing firms' profits accounted for 47 percent of total domestic U.S. corporate profits. This share fell to 38 percent in 1990, 24 percent in 2000, 20 percent in 2007, and 18 percent in 2011.[20]

When we look at the richest Americans today and the sources of their wealth, we see the influence of financialization. Each year *Forbes* magazine publishes a list of the four hundred richest Americans. In 2012, "the source of wealth for nearly a quarter (96) of the Forbes list is 'investments.' That's twice as many as technology, the second greatest source of wealth for members of the Forbes 400. Nearly one third of the Forbes 400 (123, or 30.75 percent) made their fortune in real estate and investments. . . . The source of wealth for more than half (208) of the Forbes 400 list comes from four fields: investments, technology, real estate, and energy."[21]

If we combine the information in the previous two paragraphs, we begin to see what financialization means for our economy and for the wealthiest Americans. But what about the rest of us? One recent study links financialization and U.S. income inequality over a thirty-year period. The authors describe the connection by noting that "the result [of investment in the financial sector] was an incremental exclusion of the general workforce from revenue generating and compensation setting processes. . . . Our analysis shows that increased dependence on financial income, in the long run, decreased labor's share of income, increased top executives' share of compensation, and increased earnings dispersion among workers."[22]

Federal laws and regulatory policies (or the lack thereof) helped facilitate the growth of financialization. Between 1970 and 2006, Wall Street partnerships, taking advantage of incorporation laws that reduce business owners' personal liability risks, transformed themselves into public corporations, thereby reducing personal financial risks for shareholder-executives in those firms. This shift led to a "bonus culture in which employees felt free to take huge risks with other people's money in order to generate revenue and big bonuses."[23] Another factor, discussed in chapter 9, was congressional enactment of the Financial Services Modernization Act (also known as the Gramm-Leach-Bliley bill). This act, passed in 1999 with the full support of the Clinton administration, repealed the 1933 Glass-Steagall Act, which had prevented banks from engaging in speculative ventures by separating investment and commercial banking activities.[24]

Financial-sector growth was also encouraged by a U.S. Securities and Exchange Commission rule change, in 2004, which allowed investment banks to increase their debt-to-capital ratio from 12:1 to 33:1 in 2008.[25] This meant that banks could issue loans valued at thirty-three times their total assets. Meanwhile, both Congress and federal regulatory agencies chose not to engage in any meaningful efforts to control the activities of private investment groups such as "hedge funds" and private-equity groups.[26] These unregulated entities provide wealthy investors with investment opportunities not available to small public investors. An additional growth incentive was the decline in federal taxes on capital gains as the rate fell from 28 percent in the 1990s to 15 percent in 2003, where it has remained for the past decade (see chapter 9).

As profits and investment shifted from manufacturing to finance, so did the incomes of Wall Street executives and stock traders employed in the financial sector, contributing to increasing levels of income and wealth inequality in the United States. When manufacturing profits fell, so did the number of manufacturing jobs. As that happened, middle-income jobs disappeared, the wages of most workers turned stagnant, and the double-diamond class structure began to take shape.

New Technologies: Production, Communication, Transportation

The introduction of new technology into existing systems of production is nothing new. It has been going on since the beginning of the industrial revolution. New labor-saving technology has always displaced workers, but it has also created new industries and a need for new workers. Workers displaced by new technology would soon find jobs in emerging industries or in plants or offices created by new technology. The same thing has been happening in the U.S. economy over the last forty years, but with one big difference—the new workplaces and new jobs were created not in the United States but in other countries. Let's look at the new technology and how it has been used.

The first new technology feature involves computer-based production systems. One of the early forms introduced into traditional manufacturing operations was called CAD-CAM, or computer-assisted design and computer-assisted manufacturing. It represented the dawn of the "smart machine" age and was introduced in manufacturing, banking and financial services, customer services, and midlevel managerial jobs. The early impact occurred in manufacturing. It increased productivity while reducing the need for many existing workers or new workers.[27] Computers also created new ways of organizing work and controlling workers, such as the use of computer-guided control of the work pace and continuous machine-based measurement of productivity. This reduced the need for midlevel supervisors whose job was to oversee machine operators by monitoring their quality and productivity. The use of human supervisors is less essential when smart machines can inform operators when they're falling behind their established work rate or their machines are producing output below some established quota.

The second new technology feature involves computer-based telecommunications, which enables almost instantaneous coordination and feedback with people and facilities scattered around the globe. The combination of computer-based production and telecommunications makes it possible for the home office of a corporation to coordinate widely dispersed production and inventory control activities without direct face-to-face contact and coordination.

The third new technology feature involves the development of transportation systems that make the large-scale movement of raw materials and finished products possible on a global scale. Most products are transported by a combination of land- and sea-borne cargo-transport vehicles. The use of standardized cargo containers and transport cranes coordinated by computerized tracking and control programs transformed once-colorful seaports from anchors, ropelines, and stevedores to mammoth factory-like intermodal facilities. These huge city-sized operations utilize elevated rail cranes that skim, on mobile steel skeletons, above transport vehicles and staging fields where standardized shipping containers are temporarily stored.[28]

The transport process begins after cargo containers, resting on semitruck or rail platforms, are filled with products at the point of production (often third-world factories). They are then transported via truck or rail to massive intermodal ports, where elevated cranes move them first to staging fields and then to huge containerized ships. When the ships reach their destination ports, the containers are offloaded by reversing the loading procedures. The containers then travel by rail or semitrucks to their final consumer market destinations, most often in first-world nations. For some products, the transport process involves utilizing large commercial aircraft, but the land- and sea-based system described above is more commonly used than airfreight. During the transport process, the containers are monitored and controlled by computerized tracking and control systems that are in constant communication with corporate inventory managers. This brings us to the fourth feature of the new economy.

Global Production and Transnational Power

The combination of new technologies described above made it possible to produce a "global car," a vehicle that had many of its components produced in separate countries (e.g., engine, drive train, electronics) and then shipped to a designated location for final assembly. All the pieces would "fit" because they were computer-designed to precise specifications and quality standards. This same combination of new technologies could also be used to produce a global washing machine or a global refrigerator, and so on. But producing even complex products via this kind of globally *dispersed* production system is typically less profitable than what could be called an *offshored* and *outsourced* production system. In this system complex products such as automobiles, television monitors, computers, and smartphones are produced in low-wage nations by factories that sometimes utilize components from other low-wage nations (a variation of dispersed production), but the finished products are intended for sale in the United States or in some other advanced industrial nation. However, the factories in low-wage nations that produce the finished products are typically not directly owned by U.S. corporations but by "independent vendor" firms that have contracts to produce products bearing the corporate brand names and logos of iconic U.S. companies such as Apple and Nike.[29]

The globalization of production was and is justified by neoliberalism doctrines that favor corporate-mediated international trade and openness to direct foreign investment. The resources of transnational (or multinational) firms were put in the service of national and international elites to help shape policies to facilitate two-way trade. In the United States, trade policies were enacted that encouraged the flight of manufacturing to other countries with lower wages and more favorable environmental regulations. For example, the North American Free Trade Agreement (NAFTA) was enacted in 1993 with the promise that it would create more U.S. jobs, but the effect has been the opposite.[30] Other free trade agreements with other countries allowed for the creation of export processing zones, whereby plants built in these zones received favorable tax agreements in return for producing goods that were only for export.[31]

Multinational corporations that chose to invest overseas had additional incentives to do so because of numerous ways to delay, defer, and avoid taxes. Employees of U.S. multinational corporations also receive tax breaks that serve as additional incentives to establish or expand overseas operations. Jeffrey R. Immelt, CEO of General Electric, was appointed by President Obama as chair of the President's Council on Jobs and Competitiveness, which is the ultimate irony given that fewer than half of GE workers are based in the United States and that Immelt presided over GE plant closings and the shedding of 34,000 GE jobs in the United States. If that wasn't enough, in 2009 GE not only paid no federal income taxes on $10.8 billion in earnings but also "realized a $1.1 billion tax benefit."[32]

U.S.-based transnational or multinational corporations like GE, IBM, Nike, and Microsoft have their corporate headquarters in the United States but conduct their business operations on a global scale. The huge size of these firms provides their executives with substantial economic resources that undergird the firms' economic and political power. As we discuss in chapter 8, the political power of transnational and domestic corporations in the United States derives in part from extensive campaign contributions ("investments") made by such firms and their executives to candidates from both parties for federal offices, including the presidency. Such contributions are legal and at the very least afford large donors "access" to federal office holders and agency appointees.[33]

The power of U.S. multinational firms is further expanded by the existence of a transnational corporate community. Multinational firms, through interlocking board members and financial relationships, have the potential to act in concert and to exert their influence on the nation-states in which they operate and on international regulatory bodies. Such developments suggest that senior multinational executives may represent the core of an emerging global power elite.[34] A study of interlocking directorates among the Fortune Global 500 in 1983 and 1998 found "a significant increase in both the total number of interlocks and an even greater growth in transnational ties."[35] A different approach to understanding the rise of a transnational capitalist class looks beyond the interlocks that may link multinational industrial corporations and international banks. Leslie Sklar explores how a shared ideology may unify the common interests of a transnational corporate and capitalist class.[36]

Dual Labor Markets

The easiest way to understand the idea of dual labor markets is to ask the average American to describe the characteristics of a "good job" and a "lousy job." Their answer is likely to be that a good job is secure, pays well, provides many benefits, has opportunities for advancement, and offers improvements in each area over time. In contrast, a lousy job is likely to be viewed as one that pays the minimum wage, has no benefits (or very few), is insecure, and leads nowhere (it's dead-end work). That is the everyday-language description of what sociologists call a dual labor market. It simply means that American jobs are divided into the primary labor market (good jobs) and the secondary labor market (lousy jobs). In the language of dual labor market theory there is also an intermediate labor market, meaning jobs with a mixture of good and lousy traits.

Dual labor market theory provides a view of how jobs are allocated that is different from the functionalist model of class structure described in chapter 1. In the functionalist model, good jobs go to people who have more human capital like education, skills, and work experience than other people. The functionalist model also takes the view that those who hold good jobs have worked harder to get more education or more valuable skills and thus deserve their more rewarding jobs. In short, the reason why people get good jobs or lousy jobs is because of differences in their individual characteristics. In dual labor market theory, the presence and extent of good jobs versus lousy jobs are determined largely by the structure of the economy, including the power of labor unions in the workplace; these *structural* factors are reflected in the labor markets.[37]

From the standpoint of dual labor market theory, the largest and most profitable companies have more resources to allocate to employees than small, low-profit-margin firms. If large numbers of workers are organized into powerful unions, they are more likely to get large, high-profit firms to provide workers with higher wages and better benefits than if workers are not unionized. As unionized workers win higher wages, a high-wage "norm" may spread to nonunion workers in high-profit firms or in resource-rich nonprofit organizations.[38] In this model, having a good job has little to do with the individual qualifications or experiences of workers.

Today, large firms with high profits do not always create good jobs for large numbers of their workers (think Wal-Mart), but firms with such attributes have the resources to create more good jobs than would be the case for small, low-profit firms. A key factor affecting workers' ability to obtain high wages and substantial benefits from large, high-profit firms is the power of organized labor in society. This power is directly related to the percentage of workers covered by collective bargaining agreements.[39] Workers today are less likely than in the past to be organized into powerful unions that can force employers to negotiate with and to meet at least halfway some of the wage, benefit, and working condition issues raised by their workers.

A concrete example of how the intersection of organizational resources and the power of unionized workers impact labor market location and job quality involves the work experiences of the three authors of this book. We are all university faculty members with tenure at the rank of full professor. According to dual labor market theory, our jobs would be located in the primary labor market because our positions provide job security, comfortable salaries, extensive benefits, and substantial job autonomy. While we are relatively advantaged in the labor market, fewer and fewer college faculty have opportunities that would allow them to replicate our experiences and positions. As recently as ten years ago, more than half of the instructional faculty at four-year universities were tenure track professors, but by 2010 "nearly 64 percent of the instructional faculty . . . [were not] eligible for tenure. . . . About 70 percent of the instructional faculty at all colleges is off the tenure track."[40] Most nontenure-track faculty do not have job security; they typically earn much less than tenure-track faculty, and they may not be covered by pension or health insurance plans; in short, they are in the secondary labor market.

Why has the proportion of nontenured faculty increased over the last several years, even in resource-rich universities? The answer appears to be less a matter of resources than the declining power of U.S. labor unions. Recent research indicates that strong unions "contribute to a moral economy that institutionalizes norms for fair pay, even for nonunion workers."[41] Thus, we (the authors) are likely the beneficiaries of wage and benefit "norms" that spread, in the past, via the moral economy from heavily unionized workplaces to universities. It is no coincidence that as unions have declined, so have the wages, benefits, and working conditions of university faculty.

The primary and secondary labor markets have long existed in the United States, but in the last forty years the dual labor market for workers has become increasingly polarized. One reason for this polarization is the new economy wherein employers have become more hostile toward labor unions over the last four decades.[42] As a result, there has been a sharp decline in the share of U.S. workers who are union members. Total union membership fell from 24 percent in 1973 to an eighty-year low of 11.3 percent in 2012, with only 6.6 percent of private-sector workers now in unions.[43] This decline has contributed significantly to the growth of jobs in the secondary labor market as more and more employers are not bound by either union contracts or "moral economy norms" when it comes to workers' job security, wages, and benefits. The decline in union membership and in the moral economy norms facilitated by strong unions has also led to the growth of nonstandard work arrangements, including part-time, temporary, and contract workers.[44]

Dual Labor Markets and the Double-Diamond Class Structure

The dual labor market is in part reflected in the double-diamond class structure described in chapter 2. The top diamond includes secure, highly paid professional and managerial positions located in resource-rich organizations. People in those positions have high levels of the four forms of "generative capital" identified in chapter 2 (consumption, investment, skill, social capital). The bottom half of the double-diamond includes *some* workers with jobs that have at least *some* qualities associated with primary labor market employment. Such workers are largely located in the "comfort class" segment as illustrated by examples shown in table 2.1 in chapter 2. But most workers in the bottom diamond are part of the "contingent class" segment.

Dual labor market theory envisions not only the two general labor market types (primary and secondary) but also two employee categories within firms (or entire industries) described as "core" and "peripheral" jobs. The former are thought of by senior executives as essential to a firm's operations and are relatively well compensated to encourage worker identification with the firm and to minimize employee turnover. The latter are viewed by management as less important to a firm's operations than core jobs. As a result, peripheral workers are paid less, receive few benefits, are often intermittently laid off, and have little or no job security.[45] They may be hired directly by firms as "temps" or hired through agencies as contract workers.

In the new economy most large firms (and entire industries) increasingly employ workers in two-tier arrangements much like the core and peripheral divisions described above even though employers may use different terms to identify the categories used in their workforce. This employment arrangement is reflected in the jobs held by members of the new working class in the bottom diamond of our double-diamond class model. In the next two sections we illustrate how the two-tier employment categories apply to selected subdivisions of the new working class.

Core Workers

As noted above, the workers at the top of this lower diamond are part of what we call the "comfort class" segment. Most workers in this segment are considered core employees by their employers. This is the case because they are viewed by management in their firms as possessing the skills, knowledge, and experience essential to the primary mission of the organization. In the case of private employers, they are viewed as essential to activities that generate revenue and profits. In the case of nonprofit employers (like schools and some hospitals), they carry out the functions that are the center of the organization's reason for existence. Because of their value to employers, core workers are reasonably well compensated and enjoy a measure of job security.

But being in the core is not the same as being a member of a specific occupational group. A firm may employ scientists or engineers with advanced degrees, but only some of them might be considered core employees. Skilled blue-collar workers may also be in the core. The decision regarding which jobs and workers are included in the core is made by senior executives in private firms or by elected officials that oversee some nonprofit organizations like schools. One advantage of core membership apart from employment benefits is that core workers' credentials, skills, and experience can be "traded" in the external labor market for a core job in another firm, especially if one's employer experiences revenue losses leading to job cuts. Finally, core workers have protected positions because of other employees like them who are considered noncore.

Peripheral Workers

Peripheral jobs are major threads in the social fabric of what we call the "contingent class" and "excluded class" segments of the new working class. The term *contingent* suggests the kind of employment arrangements many workers have in this class segment. The jobs held by many workers in this segment are dependent (or contingent) upon marketplace demand for various kinds of products and services produced by employers. But this demand is often subject to fluctuations over time, making it somewhat unpredictable. Thus, employers are only interested in hiring workers on a temporary or contract basis. Employers want a "flexible workforce" that can be quickly expanded or contracted; they are not interested in providing workers with long-term, stable employment.

Workers who make up the "wage earners" category of the contingent-class segment may be directly employed by a given company or organization and hold standard, full-time jobs. But even if they do hold such jobs, they are less likely to be employed in core positions than workers located in the comfort-class segment. Many other workers in the "wage earner" category work in peripheral jobs. This usually means they are employed in one of many types of "nonstandard employment" categories such as part-time, direct hire temporary, temp agency, regular self-employed, independent contractor, on-call, or contract employees. In 2006, 30.6 percent of all U.S. workers were employed as "nonstandard workers."[46] Since the 2008 financial crisis and recession, the proportion of the labor force employed as nonstandard workers has increased.[47]

A good example of jobs performed by nonstandard, temporary workers is found in the so-called auto transplants—the Japanese auto firms like Toyota, Honda, and Nissan that have located assembly plants in states like Kentucky, Indiana, and Tennessee. Such firms employ between two thousand and three thousand American workers in their plants, and they have made explicit no-layoff commitments to workers in return for high productivity and also in the hope that it would discourage unionization. However, in a typical plant employing two thousand production workers, the no-layoff commitment was made to twelve hundred hires at start-up time; the other eight hundred hires were classified as temporary. Thus, when there is a need to cut production because of weak sales or extensive inventory, the layoffs occur among the temporary workers rather than among core workers. Sometimes these temporary workers are not even directly employed by the firm but are hired through temporary help agencies like Manpower. These temporary workers are actually contingent workers who are hired when needed and fired when not needed. Often there is no path from temp to permanent, core employee status, but because so many workers are desperate for a job, many may work as auto transplant temps for several years.

As noted above, almost one-third of Americans are employed as "nonstandard workers."

The occupations held by such workers are highly varied; examples include secretaries, engineers, computer specialists, lawyers, managers, and accountants. They may be hired to complete a specific task or project, or simply as a low-cost option that gives the company great flexibility. Often, they are paid by the temp agency and do not have access to a company's benefit package of retirement or insurance programs. Many of the professionals and specialists who work for large firms via temp agencies are often the same persons who were "downsized" out of their jobs by these same companies. The following experience of a downsized worker is an ironic example of how the contingent-class segment of peripheral workers is created:

> John Kelley, 48, had worked for Pacific Telesis for 23 years when the company fired him in a downsizing last December. Two weeks later, a company that contracts out engineers to PacTel offered him a freelance job.
> "Who would I work for?" Kelley asked.
> "Edna Rogers," answered the caller.
> Kelley burst out laughing. Rogers was the supervisor that had just fired him. "That was my job," he explained. "You're trying to replace me with myself."[48]

The two-tier employment arrangements described above illustrate the range of work and employment relationships experienced by workers in the bottom diamond of our double-diamond class structure. Most workers in the bottom diamond have no chance to move into the top diamond, but the American dream encourages them to believe that they can. Only core workers have even the slightest chance to make it into the privileged class. This is the case because core workers often have the credentials, skills, or social capital necessary for long-term job security or to start a successful business. As a result, they may have enough excess consumption capital (savings) to invest that they might realize substantial profits. Evidence relevant to the prospects of workers' *children* moving up across class lines (as adults) is presented in chapter 5, where we discuss the findings of our intergenerational social mobility research project.

THE NEW ECONOMY: ACUTE AND CHRONIC CRISES

"The financial crisis and the subsequent slow recovery have caused some to question whether the United States . . . might not now be facing a prolonged period of stagnation."

—Ben Bernanke, chairman of the Federal Reserve Board (August 2011)

Our overview of the new economy has provided a descriptive account of its main features and suggested how it serves as a foundation for the new class system. But the new economy is not just a static structure consisting of five distinct parts; it is also a dynamic force that generates recurrent and ongoing economic crises in acute and chronic forms. To some extent these forms are iceberg-like. The acute crises are highly visible, like dramatic spires of ice rising above a submerged foundation. The chronic crisis is somewhat like the submerged mass of an iceberg floating beneath the surface. Though largely hidden, it is nonetheless a powerful, dangerous, grinding force capable of great destruction.

The acute form is evident in the recurring economic recessions and increasingly "jobless recoveries" experienced by the United States since the 1970s. As the economy became increasingly dependent on financialization for economic growth, the result was a series of economic bubbles and busts. This pattern was illustrated by the high-tech stock market bubble and crash in the early 2000s. And it was especially obvious in 2008 and after as the financial crisis rocked the U.S. economy and created economic hardships and problems that many Americans are still facing today. The chronic form, as we will see, is less obviously evident than the acute form. Its core feature is economic entropy: a downward stagnation spiral. It involves the slow, gradual, but cumulative erosion of good jobs and educational opportunities following acute crises.

The 2008 Meltdown: Acute and Recurring Crises

The 2008 financial crisis and its aftermath are the most recent reminders of the acute, recurring economic crises generated by the new economy. Some analysts suggest such events are the "new normal" and will occur periodically as long as the new economy is allowed to continue in its current form. The story regarding how and why the 2008 financial crisis occurred has been the subject of numerous scholarly and popular books and articles (and even movies).[49] Our purpose here is not to explore that story (there isn't time or space here to do so) but to point out that a number of researchers believe credible evidence supports the view that 2008 was not an aberration and that our new economy will inevitably generate periodic acute economic crises.[50] The reasons for this tendency are linked to the trend toward economic entropy mentioned earlier. Economic stagnation leads large corporations to search for higher profits especially through financialization "products" and schemes that lead to economic bubbles and collapses followed by ever-weaker economic recoveries.

The new economy is essentially a "death star." It is designed to create high profits for the wealthy few, and it does. But in the process of doing what it does best, it radiates financial death rays that destroy not only workers' wages but also the entire middle class and the underlying labor market structures that created, supported, and sustained it. It has no choice. It must fulfill its nature, deploying ever more esoteric financial products (like derivatives, which Warren Buffett called "financial weapons of mass destruction"[51]) in an unending quest for ever higher profits and at the same time incinerating all forms of economic employment capable of sustaining an American middle class. Additional details concerning the emergence of this death star via class war and political lobbying are discussed in chapters 6–9. We invite you to join us there.

America since the 1970s: The Hidden Chronic Crisis

In addition to the acute crises, the new economy has also produced an ongoing, but somewhat hidden, iceberg-like chronic economic crisis over the last forty years. The "cause" of this chronic condition is the same as the new economy's basic problem: the rate of economic growth has slowed since the 1970s, leading to economic stagnation. Why has growth slowed? The answer lies in systemic contradictions built into the new economy: "A central cause of this stagnation tendency is the high, and today rapidly increasing, price markups of monopolistic corporations, giving rise to growing problems of surplus capital absorbtion."[52] What this means in ordinary language is that giant corporations are able to set prices without any meaningful competition. And it means the profits these firms generate are less likely to be reinvested in the United States in either goods-producing or service-sector businesses because of slack demand due to workers' wages stagnating relative to prices. In short, fewer workers have jobs that pay enough to support a long-term, robust expansion of U.S. businesses. In the search for higher returns, corporate profits are increasingly channeled into either high-risk, *potentially* high-profit financial ventures (like the financial "products" that fueled the housing bubble) or investments in other nations as investors bet on higher returns there than in the United States. One result of this self-reinforcing stagnation loop is that workers' share of national income has dropped to its lowest level ever while corporate profits (in 2011) accounted "for the largest share of gross domestic product since 1950."[53]

A major feature of this crisis has been the forty-year decline in U.S. jobs that pay a "living wage." If we define "good jobs" as those that pay a minimum of $18.50 per hour and provide health insurance and retirement plans, we find about 24 percent of U.S. workers held jobs with those qualities in 2010, compared to 27 percent in 1979. But during that period, output per worker rose from $69,903 in 1979 to $103,659 (in 2011 dollars).[54] As we noted earlier, millions of high-wage jobs in the auto, steel, and durable goods sectors disappeared over the last forty years. And as each recession occurred, the good jobs lost were, for the most part, not replaced. As one source puts it, "What are often called 'jobless recoveries' (the weak job growth following the last three recessions) should actually be called 'growthless and jobless recoveries.'"[55]

The massive loss of good jobs has changed the employment landscape for millions of Americans and erased the upward social mobility chances for most workers and their children. Many Americans are not fully aware of the scope or consequences of this chronic crisis because it has unfolded over many years. And during some periods there was *some* new job growth; the problem was the growth was often in service-sector jobs that provided low wages and limited benefits. During this forty-year period the class structure has been reshaped from the diamond form, "middle-class" structure into the polarized double-diamond form described in chapter 2.

The chronic and acute crises produced by the new economy are reflections of underlying processes that have facilitated an enormous transfer of wealth from those in the bottom diamond of the class structure to those in the top diamond. But the elite classes (the superclass and the credentialed class) have benefited far more than the other segments in the top diamond of the privileged class. And the superclass (the wealthiest 1 percent) has benefited the most. This group experienced not only a dramatic increase in wealth over the past forty years but also, and more important, a dramatic increase in the economic and political power it holds at both the national and global levels. As we will see in chapters 6–10, the increase in both the wealth and power of the superclass is inextricably linked to its ownership and control of large, powerful national and multinational corporations.

CONCLUSION

In the remaining chapters we explore in more detail the structures and processes that drive and support the new economy and the double-diamond new class structure. We also document the consequences of this new class system for Americans in both the top and bottom diamonds. An amusing but revealing anecdote involving famed consumer advocate Ralph Nader helps set the stage for our exploration of the global economy in the next chapter. Nader tells of being asked, in 2011, to look over an L.L. Bean catalog to see what he might want for a Christmas gift. Nader reports he looked through the eighty-eight-page catalog and discovered 97 percent of the items were listed as "imported" by L.L. Bean.[56] This vignette is an ironic example of how decades of "free trade" laws that were promised by government and corporate leaders to be "win-win" agreements actually impacted our economy: more choices for U.S. consumers but not more jobs for U.S. workers. In the next chapter we shift our attention from the new economy to the larger global economy. Our objective is to explore how the growth of the global economy transformed jobs and production, intensified class inequalities, and benefited multinational corporations, the elite classes, and the larger privileged class.

4

The Global Economy and Class Inequalities

"At the same time as U.S.-based corporations have been shifting America's production base to low-wage, high repression states like China and Mexico, America has undergone such a startling polarization that its income distribution pattern resembles that of a 'banana republic.'"

—Roger Bybee, "A Three-Point Plan to Save Democrats,"
In These Times (January 2011)

In many ways the global economy is like a sports arena where the United States is both a participant and a "subject." The *participant* term is easy to understand. Our government and U.S. companies are "players" in this arena. But the latter term reminds us that the U.S. government as well as U.S. firms, workers, and consumers are *affected* by the structures, processes, and other nations that are part of the global arena. U.S. participation in the global economy occurs via trade and investment policies of the federal government and U.S. multinational firms. For average Americans, most of these policies are iceberg-like in that they are not evident or obvious unless they generate effects that are experienced at the level of everyday life. When the global economy produces changes that directly affect American communities, workers, and their families in dramatically negative ways, then its iceberg-like qualities and power are revealed.

Thirty years ago we came face to face with the negative effects of the global economy during the course of our research on factory closings in Indiana in the 1980s. The workers affected by plant closings in the communities we studied were somewhat like the caged canaries coal miners carried into the mines to detect hidden dangers. These workers were among the first to experience what would be many waves of plant closings that would cost millions of blue-collar workers their jobs. The lives of the workers we studied were changed by their experiences, almost always in negative ways. But for the corporate executives who made the calls to close American plants, the decisions weren't personal. It was just part of doing business in the global economy.

On December 1, 1982, an RCA television cabinet-making factory in Monticello, Indiana, closed its doors and shut down production. Monticello, a town of 5,000 people in White County (population 23,000), had been the home of RCA since 1946. The closing displaced 850 workers who were members of Local 3154 of the United Brotherhood of Carpenters and Joiners. Officials at RCA cited the high manufacturing costs and foreign competition as key factors leading to the closing.

Reactions of displaced workers from RCA were varied, with most expressing either a general sense of despair or a feeling of confidence that they would survive. One worker was hopeful, stating, "Losing one's job is a serious jolt to your attitude of security, preservation, and well-being. However, I feel strongly that we must look forward to hope and faith in our country and its people. Deep inside I want to believe that tough times won't last, but tough people do. This will mean a lot of sacrifice, determination, and change in those people affected by losing one's job." Less hopeful views are revealed in the following remarks gleaned from personal interviews with RCA workers:

> We are down to rock bottom and will probably have to sell the house to live or exist until I find a job here or somewhere else. I have been everywhere looking in Cass, White, and Carroll counties. We have had no help except when the electric company was going to shut off the utilities in March and the Trustee [County Welfare] paid that $141. My sister-in-law helps us sometimes with money she's saved back or with food she canned last summer. The factories have the young. I've been to all the factories.[1]

Whether the personal response to the closing was faith, fear, or anger, the common objective experience of the displaced workers was that they had been "dumped" from the "middle class." These displaced factory workers viewed themselves as middle class because of their wages and their lifestyles (home ownership, cars, vacations). Most had worked at RCA for two decades or more. They had good wages, health care benefits, and a decent pension plan. They owned their homes (with mortgages), cars, recreational vehicles, boats, and all the household appliances associated with middle-class membership. All the trappings of the American dream were threatened as seemingly stable jobs and secure incomes disappeared. In the space of a few months these workers and their families joined the growing new working class—the 80 percent of Americans without stable resources for living.

The RCA factory that closed in Monticello, Indiana, was, as noted above, one of many plants closed as waves of such closures swept across the nation beginning three decades ago. According to a study commissioned by the U.S. Congress, between the late 1970s and mid-1980s more than 11 million workers lost jobs because of plant shutdowns, relocation of facilities to other nations, or layoffs. Most displaced workers had been in manufacturing. Subsequent displaced-worker surveys commissioned by the Bureau of Labor Statistics estimated that between 1986 and 1991 another 12 million workers were displaced, but most of those were predominantly located in the service sector (about 7.9 million).[2] The data show that when displaced workers then and today find new jobs, they often receive wages that are significantly lower than what those workers had previously earned and many are part-time and lack health insurance and other benefits.[3]

This chapter describes and illustrates how the elite classes (superclass and credentialed class) have contributed to and benefited from the growth of the global economy and how this growth benefited many others on the lower rungs of the privileged class. It also calls attention to how most of the benefits produced by the expanding global economy have come at the expense of the working class. As we'll see, corporate profits and stockholders' dividends increased over the last several years as large segments of the U.S. manufacturing base were shifted to plants in low-wage nations. Increases in profits and dividends were further reinforced by wage freezes or cuts for most remaining workers in U.S. manufacturing plants and by increases in the speed of the production process. Low wages for foreign workers plus wage cuts and speed-ups for domestic workers lead to the production of more goods and services at lower costs. What firm couldn't generate higher profits in this global production scheme?

How are the increased profits distributed? Not to workers. Their share has fallen. Corporate profits are distributed mostly to executives, managers, and professionals in the form of higher salaries, bonuses, and other benefits. As we saw in chapter 3, this arrangement is justified in part by the neoliberalism argument that free markets in the global economy benefit the "risk takers" and "job creators" who richly deserve their handsome rewards. Neoliberalism also claims that in the long run, everyone benefits from the free-market global economy. And as we'll see in chapters 10–13, the elite classes employ a wide array of techniques and processes both to justify the unequal distribution of rewards produced by the global economy and to distract workers from these inequalities. Of course, if justification or distraction fail, the superclass holds the ultimate trump card: an armed state. It controls the means of violence (military, national guard, police, and the investigative and security apparatus) that can be used to suppress any rowdy or serious large-scale dissent.

CREATING THE GLOBAL ECONOMY: THE PATH TO CORPORATE PROFITS

"We have entered the era of Empire, a 'supranational' center consisting of networks of transnational corporations and advanced capitalist nations led by the one remaining superpower, the United States."

—Michael Hardt and Antonio Negri, *Empire* (2000)

The existence of a global economy is not new. Immanual Wallerstein and others maintain that "world economic systems" have existed in various forms since the fifteenth century.[4] What makes today's global economy different from earlier versions is the scale and variety of international commerce and the central significance of large transnational (or multinational) corporations in organizing and controlling global commerce. During earlier periods, nation-states, sometimes in conjunction with firms that worked hand-in-glove with the interests and policies of national governments, were the primary actors organizing global trade. In contrast, the contemporary period has witnessed the emergence of stateless and homeless multinational corporations. These entities lack allegiances to any specific national government and they make no long-term commitments to specific geographic locations, communities, or people. Some of these homeless qualities were evident in some firms prior to World War II, but it was not until well after 1945 that truly stateless transnational firms began to emerge. By the early twenty-first century such firms were relatively commonplace around the world.

When World War II ended in 1945, all but one of the industrial nations involved had experienced widespread destruction of their industrial system and the infrastructure necessary for a healthy economy to provide sufficient food, shelter, and clothing for its people. Although all nations that participated in the war suffered terrible human losses, the United States alone emerged with its economic system stronger than it was at the start of the war. As we pointed out in chapter 1, for decades following the war, the United States dominated the world economy through its control of three-fourths of the world's invested capital and two-thirds of its industrial capacity. At the close of the war, there was concern in the United States that the high levels of production, profits, and employment stimulated by war mobilization could not be sustained. The specter of a return to the stagnation and unemployment experienced only a decade earlier during the Great Depression led to the search for a new economic and political system that would maintain the economic, military, and political dominance of the United States.[5]

This system was the basis for U.S. growth and prosperity during the 1950s, the 1960s, and the early 1970s. By the mid-1970s, steady improvements in the war-torn economies of Western Europe and Asia had produced important shifts in the balance of economic power among industrialized nations. The U.S. gross national product was now less than twice that of the Soviet Union (in 1950 it was more than three times), less than four times that of Germany (down from nine times in 1950), and less than three times that of Japan (twelve times in 1950). With many nations joining the United States in the production of the world's goods, the U.S. rate of growth slowed. As England, France, Germany, and Japan produced goods for domestic consumption, there was less need to import agricultural and industrial products from the United States.

Declining Profits and "Explanations": 1960s–1970s

Profits of U.S. corporations steadily declined from the late 1950s through the 1970s. In 1959 the average after-tax profit rate of U.S. firms was 8 percent. The rate fell to 7.8 percent in 1969, 6.1 percent in 1973, and 5.1 percent in 1979.[6] The

U.S. elite classes were very concerned about declining profit rates. It affected their accumulation of wealth from stocks, bonds, dividends, and other investments. It also affected corporate, managerial, and professional salaries indirectly, through the high rate of inflation that eroded the purchasing power of consumption capital (i.e., salaries) and the real value of investment capital (i.e., value of stocks, bonds, etc.). To account for declining profits, business leaders and the corporate media listed the usual suspects.

The leading "explanation" was that U.S. products could not compete in the global economy because of the power of organized labor. This power was reflected in the high labor costs that made products less competitive and in cost-of-living adjustments that increased wages at the rate of inflation (which was sometimes at double digits). Union control of work rules also made it difficult for management to adopt new innovations to increase productivity and reduce dependence on labor. Next on the list was the American worker, who was claimed to have embraced a declining work ethic, resulting in products of lower quality and higher cost. U.S. workers were portrayed as too content and secure and thus unwilling to compete with the ambitious workers of the rapidly developing economies. The third suspect was the wide array of new federal regulations on businesses enacted to protect workers and the environment. Corporate executives complained about increased business costs that came from meeting the workplace standards of the Occupational Safety and Health Administration (OSHA) or the air and water pollution standards of the Environmental Protection Agency (EPA).[7]

The explanations business leaders put forth for declining profits (selfish unions, lazy workers, government regulations) were said to make American products less competitive in the global economy. They provided the rationale for an attack on unions and on workers' wages and helped to justify massive plant closings and capital flight to low-wage areas. They also served to put the government on the defensive for its failure to be sensitive to the "excessive" costs that federal regulations impose on business.

What was rarely discussed in the business pages of the *New York Times* or the *Wall Street Journal* was the failure of corporate executives in major U.S. firms to respond to increasing competition in areas once dominated by U.S. companies including autos, steel, textiles, and electronics. In the early 1960s, imports of foreign products played a small part in the American economy, but by 1980 things had changed. In the early 1960s, imports accounted for less than 10 percent of the U.S. market, but by 1980 more than 70 percent of all the goods produced in the United States were actively competing with foreign-made goods.[8]

American corporations failed to follow the well-established management approach to the loss of market share, competitive advantage, and profits. Instead of pursuing long-term solutions, like investing in more efficient technology, new plants, research and development, and new markets, corporate executives chose to follow short-term strategies that would make the bottom line of short-term profits the primary goal. This focus led to increasing corporate investments in other nations, company mergers, plant closings, downsizing, and outsourcing.

CREATING THE NEW WORKING CLASS

"We do not stay in America to optimize employment; we stay to improve our productivity."

—Intel executive, *New York Times* (May 11, 2004)

When a large multinational firm closes its U.S. facilities and invests in other firms abroad or opens new facilities abroad, the major losers are the production workers who have been displaced and the communities with lower tax revenues and increased costs stemming from expanded efforts to attract new businesses. But this does not mean that the firms are losers, for they are growing and expanding operations elsewhere. This growth creates the need for new employees in finance, management, computer operations, and information systems. The total picture is one of shrinking production plants and expanding corporate headquarters, shrinking blue-collar employee rolls and expansion of high-wage professional-managerial positions.

The layoffs in Monticello in 1982 followed even earlier layoffs in other communities and industries in the mid- to late 1970s. Such events were part of several processes still in motion today that have reshaped the American class structure from a diamond-shaped "middle-class" society into the double-diamond structure described in chapter 2. In response to declining corporate profits, the first step corporations took involved a superclass-led attack on high-wage unionized workers, eliminating their jobs in the auto industries, steel mills, rubber plants, and textile mills. The reshaping continued through the late 1980s to the mid-1990s, when the strategy was expanded to include not only plant closings and relocations but "restructuring and downsizing" strategies as well, often directed at eliminating white-collar jobs.

Having been extraordinarily successful in closing U.S. plants, shifting investment and production abroad, and cutting both labor and labor costs (both the number of production workers and their wage-benefit packages), major corporations now turned their attention to saving money by cutting midlevel white-collar employees. In the 1990s, there were no longer headlines about "plant closings," "capital flight," or "deindustrialization." The new strategy was "downsizing," "rightsizing," "reengineering," or how to get the same amount of work done with fewer middle managers and clerical workers.

Downsizing

Job losses in the 1990–2000 decade appeared to hit hardest those who were better educated (some college or more) and better paid ($40,000 or more). Job losses affecting production workers in the 1980s was "explained" by the pressures of global competition and opportunities to produce in areas with lower-wage workers. The "explanation" for the 1990s downsizing of white-collar workers was either new technology or redesign of the organization. Some middle managers and supervisors were replaced by new computer systems that track the work of clerical workers. These same computer systems eliminate the need for many middle managers responsible for collecting, processing, and analyzing data used by upper-level decision makers.

The rush to downsize in some of America's largest and most prestigious corporations became so widespread in the 1990s that a new occupation was needed to handle the casualties. The "outplacement professional" was created to put the best corporate face on a decision to downsize—that is, to terminate large numbers of employees—as many as ten thousand. The job of these new public relations types is to get the general public to accept downsizing as the normal way of life for corporations that have to survive in the competitive global economy. Their job is also to assist the downsized middle managers to manage their anger and to get on with their lives.

The *Human Resources Development Handbook* of the American Management Association provides the operating philosophy for the outplacement professional: "Unnecessary personnel must be separated from the company if the organization is to continue as a viable business entity. To do otherwise in today's globally competitive world would be totally unjustified and might well be a threat to the company's future survival."[9] In a case of art imitating life, a 2009 Hollywood movie (*Up in the Air*) presented the story of a professional "terminator" (played by George Clooney) who travels around the country firing middle managers whom companies want to eliminate. The professional terminator is hired so that the company executives do not have to experience the discomfort and stress of firing their long-time associates. In real life, companies have used outside professionals to perform the job Clooney played in the movie.

Downsizing is often viewed by corporate executives as a rational response to the demands of competition and thereby a way to better serve their investors and ultimately their own employees. Alan Downs, in his book *Corporate Executions*, challenges four prevailing myths that justify the publicly announced layoffs of millions of workers.[10] First, downsizing firms do not necessarily wind up with a smaller workforce. Often, downsizing is followed by the hiring of new workers. Second, Downs questions the belief that downsized workers are often the least productive because their expertise is obsolete. According to his findings, increased productivity does not necessarily follow downsizing. Third, jobs lost to downsizing are not replaced with higher-skill, better-paying jobs. Fourth, the claim that companies become more profitable after downsizing, and that workers thereby benefit, is only half true—many companies that downsize do report higher corporate profits and, as discussed earlier, often achieve higher valuations of their corporate stock. But there is no evidence that these profits are being passed along to employees in the form of higher wages and benefits. After challenging these four myths, Downs concludes that the "ugly truth" of downsizing is that it is an expression of corporate self-interest to lower wages and increase profits.

The impact of corporate plant closing and downsizing decisions on the new working class was hidden from public view in part by the steady growth of new jobs in the latter part of the 1990s, and by the relatively low rate of unemployment. In his second term in office, President Clinton made frequent references to the high rate of job creation during his administration (without mentioning they were primarily low-wage service jobs) and the relatively low unemployment rate. Of course, the official rate of unemployment can conceal larger truths about the nation's economic health—as we noted in our chapter 3 discussion of the difference between the unemployment and underemployment rates.

Another way of looking at the unemployment rate is to contrast rates across different income groups. The Center for Labor Market Studies at Northeastern University divides the population of Americans into deciles based on annual household income. In 2009, the top decile of households earning $150,000 or more had an unemployment rate of 3.3 percent. The next decile of households earning between $100,000 and $149,999 had an unemployment rate of 4 percent. The lowest-earning decile of households earning $12,499 or less had an unemployment rate of 30.8 percent, and for the next lowest earners ($12,500 to $20,000) the rate was 19.1 percent. The difference in unemployment rate between the top and bottom deciles is dramatic. If we add the percentage of those in each decile who are underemployed (working part-time but looking for full-time, and those who have stopped looking but would take a job if available), the rate for the top decile was 1.6 percent, and for the lowest decile 20.6 percent. More than one-half of Americans in the lowest income decile are either unemployed or underemployed.[11]

Outsourcing

In the 2000–2010 decade the corporate strategy of global "outsourcing" became a common tactic for eliminating American jobs. Outsourcing today involves using the capabilities of the Internet and new telecommunications technology to hire workers in other countries to perform jobs formerly held by American workers. For example, workers in India or China may be hired by a U.S. computer company to work in their customer service department. So when a customer in Kansas or Indiana calls the computer company for help in solving a user problem, they may be talking to a service representative in Calcutta or Beijing. More highly educated engineers or computer specialists may also be hired to work in software development while remaining in their home country being paid a small fraction of what would be paid to an American professional.[12]

The elite classes work hard explaining and justifying to the new working class the harsh realities of the changing global economy. "Lifetime employment," we are told, is out (it was never in, anyway). The goal, workers are told, is to attain "lifetime employability." Workers are told they can acquire this quality by accumulating skills and being dedicated employees. Even Japan's once highly touted commitment to lifetime employment (in some firms) has unraveled, as reported more than a decade ago in a feature article in the *New York Times*.[13] It should not surprise us that a corporate media outlet like the *Times*, whose upper-level employees belong to the elite classes, should join in disseminating the myth of the global economy as the "invisible hand" behind the downsizing of America. The casualties of plant closings and downsizings are encouraged to see their plight as part of the "natural laws" of economics.

This enormous transformation of the U.S. economy over the last forty years has been described by government leaders and the corporate media as the inevitable and therefore normal workings of the new global economy. Some, like former president Ronald Reagan, have applauded the changes as representing historic opportunities to revitalize the U.S. economy. In a 1985 report to Congress, he stated, "The progression of an economy such as America's from agriculture to manufacturing to services is a natural change. The move from an industrial society toward a postindustrial service economy has been one of the greatest changes to affect the developed world since the Industrial Revolution."[14]

A contrasting view posits that the transformation of the U.S. economy is not the result of natural economic laws or the "invisible hand" of global economic markets but, rather, the result of calculated actions by multinational corporations to expand their profits and power. When corporations decide to close plants and move them overseas where they can find cheap labor and fewer government regulations, they do so to enhance profits and not simply as a response to the demands of global competition. As we will see, in many cases, U.S. multinational firms are themselves the global competition putting pressure on U.S. workers to work harder, faster, and for lower wages and fewer benefits. Only rarely do corporate media pundits or mainstream economic analysts acknowledge that the "invisible hand" is actually controlled by multinational firms that increase profits by shipping high-wage jobs to low-wage nations, downsizing firms, and outsourcing jobs.

THE GLOBAL ECONOMY: TRADE DEFICITS AND JOBS

"The [U.S.] goods-producing industries . . . have lost jobs over the last half-century and so it has been in the service sector that employment growth has occurred."

—Fred Magdoff, *Monthly Review* (June 2011): 35

Discussions by mainstream media pundits and corporate leaders on how the global economy is a positive force for businesses and workers ("win-win") often focus on three developments. (You may notice they overlap with some features of the new economy we presented in chapter 3.) The first development concerns the remarkable extent of change in the global economy as indicated by the appearance of many new producers of quality goods in parts of the world that are viewed as less developed. Advances in computer-based production systems have allowed many nations in Southeast Asia and Latin America to produce high-quality goods that compete effectively with those produced by more advanced industrial economies in Western Europe and North America.

The second development concerns the creation of computer-linked telecommunications systems that permit rapid economic transactions around the globe and the coordination of economic activities in locations separated by thousands of miles. Advances in computer-based production and telecommunications make it possible for large firms, especially multinationals, to decentralize production and locate facilities around the globe. The third development concerns the emergence of a large, diverse international labor force with a rainbow of skills. This large pool of workers makes it possible for corporations to employ competent, dependable workers in jobs ranging from production technicians to engineers to medical professionals anywhere in the world. The existence of this labor force gives corporations great flexibility when negotiating with their domestic workforce over wages and benefits.

These three developments are claimed by corporate leaders to benefit companies, consumers, and workers around the world. There is no doubt these developments have changed how products are produced, and they have resulted in expanded imports and exports and an enlarged role for trade in the world economy. But in order to ramp up production in less developed nations, the large investments needed for plants and infrastructure typically must come from outside sources. The leading sources of capital investment for production facilities in less developed nations have been large multinational firms headquartered in the advanced industrial nations. It is estimated that two-thirds of international financial transactions have taken place within and between Europe, the United States, and Japan.[15]

The U.S. Trade Deficit and Global Competition?

The effects of these investments on the U.S. trade deficit might appear to be problematic from the standpoint of U.S. national interests. For example, throughout the 1980s, the United States became a debtor nation in terms of the balance between what we exported to the rest of the world and what we imported from other countries. The gap between what we buy from other countries and what we sell to them is called the trade deficit, and it has been growing for thirty years. In the 2005–2010 period, the U.S. trade deficit indicated imports of goods and services exceeded exports by an average of about $610 billion per year. These deficits were far larger than in the 1990s ($90 billion average) or early 2000s ($490 billion average).[16] But what do these figures tell us? On the surface, they appear to be the result of the routine operation of the global economy. The figures indicate that in 2010 we had merchandise trade deficits of $60 billion with Japan, $273 billion with China, $66.5 billion with Mexico, $34 billion with Germany, and $28.5 billion with Canada.[17] It appears companies in those nations are doing a better job of producing goods than those in the United States and thus we import products rather than producing them ourselves. But is this the correct conclusion? The answer lies in how you count imports and exports.

Trade deficit figures are based on balance of payment statistics, which tally the dollar value of U.S. exports to other countries and the dollar value of foreign exports to the United States; if the dollar value of Chinese exports to the United States exceeds the dollar value of U.S. exports to China, the United States has a trade deficit with China. This would appear to mean that Chinese companies are producing the goods being exported to the United States. But that is not necessarily the case. According to the procedures followed in calculating trade deficits, "The U.S. balance of payments statistics are intended to capture the total amount of transactions between U.S. *residents* and *residents* of the rest of the world."[18] If *resident* simply identifies the geographical location of the source of an import, then some portion of the $273 billion U.S. trade deficit with China could be from U.S.-owned firms that are producing goods in China and exporting them to the United States.[19] Those U.S. firms are residents of China, and their exports are counted as Chinese exports to the United States. For example, Nike Corporation has seven hundred plants scattered around Southeast Asia and elsewhere, and the products those plants export to the United States contribute to our trade deficit even though a U.S. company "produced" the exports.

Thus, the global economy that is *out there* "forcing" U.S. firms to keep wages low so we can be more competitive might actually be made up of U.S. firms that have located production plants in countries other than in the United States. Such actions may be of great benefit to the U.S. multinational firms that produce goods around the world and export them to the U.S. market. Such actions may also benefit U.S. consumers, who pay less for goods produced in low-wage areas. But what about U.S. workers in a manufacturing plant whose wages have not increased in forty years because of the need to compete with "foreign companies"? What about workers who may never get jobs in manufacturing because U.S. firms have been opening plants in other countries rather than in the United States? Could it be that U.S. multinationals are creating the "global competition"?

Good-bye Manufacturing Jobs, Hello Service Work

American multinational corporations' foreign investments have changed the emphasis in the U.S. economy from manufacturing to service. This shift has changed the occupational structure by eliminating high-wage manufacturing jobs and many middle-management jobs and creating a two-tiered system of service jobs. The top tier consists of high-skilled, high-paid workers in the business and professional services sector, while the bottom tier consists of low-skilled, low-paid workers in the health care and food service sectors. Between 1979 and 2012, employment in the manufacturing sector declined by 52 percent (from 24.7 million to 11.8 million workers).[20] But during about the same period (1983–2010), employment in management occupations increased by 39 percent (from 10.7 million to 15 million).[21] For the 2010–2020 period, U.S. Bureau of Labor Statistics employment projections call for a continued decline in manufacturing jobs but sharp increases in upper-level business and professional service jobs. However, the occupations that will experience the largest numeric growth in jobs over the next decade will be, as we discuss in chapter 5, low-skill, low-wage service jobs. For example, five of the ten occupations the BLS projects as adding the largest numbers of new U.S. jobs in 2010–2020

(2.7 million) require *less than a high school diploma* and will pay "very low" annual incomes (under $21,590).[22]

There have been big winners and big losers in this social and economic transformation. The losers have been the three out of four Americans who work for wages—wages that have been declining since 1973; these American workers constitute the new working class. There is growing evidence that globalization not only eliminated jobs in the United States but also depressed the wages of workers in both rich and poor countries.[23] The biggest winners have been the elite classes, but the larger privileged class has also benefited as job opportunities and incomes for those in the bottom portion of this class have also expanded. Corporate executives, managers, scientists, engineers, doctors, corporate lawyers, accountants, computer programmers, financial consultants, health care professionals, and media professionals have all registered substantial gains in income and wealth in the last forty years. The changes that produced the "big losers" and "big winners" have been facilitated by the legislative actions of the federal government and elected officials of both political parties, whose incomes, pensions, health care, and associated "perks" have also grown handsomely in the past two decades.

THE ADVANTAGES OF HOMELESSNESS: STATELESS MULTINATIONAL FIRMS

"A majority of U.S. corporations in the top one hundred multinationals experienced, between 2000 and 2008, substantial (and in some cases huge) increases in the share of assets, sales, and employment of their foreign affiliates."

—John Bellamy Foster and Robert W. McChesney,
Monthly Review (June 2011): 5

The movement by U.S. multinational firms of production facilities from the United States to foreign countries in the 1980s and 1990s was not simply the result of a search for another home where they could once again be productive and competitive. It appeared as if RCA closed its plant in Monticello, Indiana, because it was old and required too much renovation to make the investment worthwhile. Perhaps some people believe that RCA executives were saddened by having to leave the thirty-five-year-old plant in Indiana to search for another home where the company could stay for the next thirty-five years or longer. If anyone did believe that, they were wrong. U.S. plants were not closed by multinational firms just so they could find permanent homes elsewhere. The closures reflected the business logic of a new breed of corporations: homeless and stateless multinational firms—mentioned earlier in this chapter.

The rash of plant closings in the 1970s and 1980s seemed to begin as responses by corporate executives to the economic challenges of declining profits and increased global competition. As such, they appeared to be rational management decisions to protect stockholder investments and the future of individual firms. Although things may have started in this way, it soon became apparent that what was being created was the *spatially decentered firm*. A company with this form has numerous advantages that yield increased profits. It can produce the same finished product at several different sites at once or it can produce a finished product using components manufactured in a half-dozen different plants around the globe for assembly at a location separate from the component production sites. Although spatially decentered, these new transnational firms are centralized in decision making, allowing them to coordinate decisions regarding matters such as production, marketing, international investments, and the distribution of profits. These new firms with global production, distribution, and marketing systems were made possible, as we noted earlier, by advances in computer-assisted design, manufacturing, and telecommunications that enabled management at corporate headquarters to coordinate research, development, design, manufacturing, and marketing decisions at sites around the world.

In 2012 the five largest U.S. multinational firms (by annual revenues) as identified by *Fortune* magazine were: (1) ExxonMobil ($453 billion), (2) Wal-Mart ($447 billion), (3) Chevron ($245 billion), (4) Conoco Phillips ($237 billion), and (5) General Motors ($150 billion).[24] It is interesting to note that three of these five largest firms are oil companies, but regardless of the industries these firms represent, all five are deeply engaged in the global economy with various kinds of business operations in nations on almost every continent. These firms and many others like them (from Apple to McDonald's to Nike to Xerox) did not become giant multinationals by accident. As they grew over time, their superclass executives, with the assistance of their credentialed-class colleagues along with many privileged-class professional and technical workers, took advantage of global investment and production opportunities, including the use of low-wage workers in developing nations, economies of scale, and the U.S. tax code.

Stateless multinational firms like ExxonMobil, Wal-Mart, and General Motors are able to move their production facilities quickly when they spot competitive advantages such as lower wages, cheaper raw materials, preferential monetary exchange rates, more sympathetic governments, and greater market proximity. Since these advantages can only be realized by global operations, they encourage U.S.-based multinational firms to increase capital investments in other nations, mostly low-wage countries. Doing so expands the options of multinationals in terms of where to locate their production operations, and it makes them less vulnerable to pressures from workers for higher wages and benefits. And because these firms are so large, they enjoy the advantages associated with economies of scale—meaning, for example, they pay lower prices for production materials because they purchase them in very large quantities and they pay lower rates on business loans because they borrow and repay very large sums.

The tax advantages multinational firms enjoy regarding profits earned on foreign investments are partly a product of U.S. and foreign tax codes. What this means is that profits generated by multinational firms' foreign investments are typically taxed at much lower rates in most nations where those profits are earned than in the United

States. For example, "China's rate is just 15 percent; Ireland's is 12.5 percent."[25] (But this doesn't mean all U.S. corporations pay the official federal tax rate of 35 percent on domestic profits—see the next paragraph.) Because taxes on corporate profits are lower in other nations than in the U.S. and because U.S. laws provide tax benefits for U.S. firms that invest in other nations, many U.S. multinationals have dramatically increased their foreign investments. For example, in 2000 only 7 percent of Ford's $283.4 billion in total assets were invested in company operations outside the United States, but in 2008, 46 percent of Ford's total assets ("downsized" to $223 billion) were invested outside the country.[26] One result of the increase in foreign investments by U.S. multinationals over the past decades has been that increasing shares of U.S. corporate revenues are generated overseas and are not subject to U.S. taxes (unless they are returned to this country). Partly because of these developments, the corporate share of federal revenues has declined while the share paid by taxes on individuals has gone up. As we point out in chapter 9, in 1953 federal income taxes paid by U.S. corporations accounted for 30 percent of all federal revenues, but this share fell to 12 percent in 2013.

Another reason why the share of federal revenues paid by taxes on corporate income has fallen over the past several years is that the effective tax rate corporations pay on U.S. profits has fallen. This change is largely due to the insertion, by various congressional actions over the years at the urging of corporate lobbyists, of numerous "loopholes" in the U.S. tax code. In fact, the tax code has become so "corporate friendly" that many firms now pay taxes on corporate profits at extraordinarily low rates or, in many cases, pay no taxes at all. A study of 250 of the nation's largest corporations reported that in 1998, twenty-four firms received tax rebates totaling $1.3 billion, despite reporting U.S. profits before taxes of $12 billion. A total of forty-one corporations paid less than zero federal income tax in at least one year from 1996 to 1998, despite reporting a total of $25.8 billion in pretax profits.[27] A 2008 Government Accounting Office study of corporate income taxes found that between 1998 and 2005 over half (55 percent) of large U.S. firms paid no taxes for at least one of the years in that period. "In 2005 alone, 25 percent of those companies paid no corporate income taxes, even though corporate profits had more than doubled from 2001–2005."[28] More recently, a 2011 study by the fair tax advocacy group Citizens for Tax Justice reported that 280 of the biggest publicly traded American corporations paid taxes at an average rate of 18.5 percent on their profits, which is far below the official federal corporate tax rate of 35 percent.[29]

As noted above, as long as the foreign profits earned by U.S.-based multinational firms are not brought back into the United States, they are exempt from federal taxes on corporate profits. As one might suspect, this feature of the U.S. tax code provides executives in U.S. multinationals with strong incentives to not return foreign profits to the United States. From a business perspective, it makes more sense to reinvest those low-taxed profits abroad rather than return them to the United States, where they will be taxed by the federal government. The end result is that a growing pool of corporate profits is removed as a potential revenue source from the federal government. For example, in the year prior to the Bush administration initiative described below, Hewlett-Packard had $14 billion in untaxed foreign profits; for pharmaceutical giants Merck and Johnson & Johnson the amounts were $15 billion and $12.3 billion, respectively. Recognizing the growing size of the pool of untaxed foreign profits, in early 2005 the Bush administration proposed a one-time tax break for companies to bring their foreign profits home. The proposal would have taxed foreign profits at a rate of 5.25 percent instead of the standard corporate tax rate of 35 percent.[30]

Another federal tax advantage benefits employees of U.S. multinational firms who work overseas. For example, an executive employed overseas by a U.S. multinational firm typically receives additional compensation for home-leave air fare, medical benefits, housing subsidies, and tuition for school-age children. If an executive lived in Hong Kong, he or she would receive (estimated amounts in parentheses) an employer-paid housing allowance ($70,000), school tuition ($40,000), and home-leave airfare ($20,000). These company-paid benefits received by overseas employees are either exempt from U.S. taxes or taxed at very low rates. Federal tax laws in the mid-2000s excluded from taxation the first $80,000 earned as income overseas. The next dollar earned beyond $80,000 was taxed as the first dollar earned. So an executive who worked overseas and earned $200,000 a year in the mid-2000s received additional benefits of $130,000 (housing allowance, tuition, home-leave airfare) and had a total income of $330,000, but paid U.S. income taxes on only $120,000.[31] This "sweet deal" for multinational firms and their senior executives further incentivizes them to continue to invest abroad. If the president and Congress were really concerned about protecting American workers' jobs, they could curb the use of offshore contractors by limiting the tax deductions multinationals get to cover the payroll costs of jobs performed by employees in other countries.

CONCLUSION

"The overriding imperative of government policy is to do whatever it takes, using all available tools—fiscal, monetary, political, even military—to keep stock prices from falling."

—David Graeber, *Nation* (September 24, 2012): 22

Opposition to the superclass-defined global economy agenda is fragmented and operates with very limited resources. Some U.S. union leaders and others critical of "free trade" agreements and the foreign labor and investment practices of multinational firms find it difficult to have their voices heard by large numbers of Americans. They are overwhelmed by the resources of corporate America. As we will see in chapters 7–10, groups such as the Business Roundtable, the National Association of Manufacturers, and the U.S. Chamber of Commerce, plus the corporate media and the elite universities have enormous power in the public arena. These and other superclass-dominated institutions set the agenda for and control public discussions about international trade agreements, labor policies, and corporate investment practices. Dissenters may be allowed to speak in measured tones, but not to many people and not for too long before the "powers that be" mobilize an array of resources to neutralize or discredit their views. After you complete chapters 6–14, you may better understand how and why those who disagree with or attack superclass interests are marginalized, co-opted, or otherwise silenced.

The first four chapters of this book have begun the process of identifying and exploring the basic structures and processes that shape and energize the new U.S. class system. These chapters also begin the process of documenting the largest-ever transfer of wealth from working-class Americans to those in the elite classes. Our focus in the first four chapters on the history of the U.S. class structure, the nature and shape of the new class system, the new economy, and the global economy provides an important foundation for more fully understanding the connections that link the wide range of issues and materials covered in the remaining chapters.

The core theme of the book is the same throughout all chapters: the U.S. class structure is the center of the social universe. It generates a force field as powerful in the social world as gravity in the physical plane. And like gravity, it is largely invisible. It is also iceberg-like in that we can easily see some of its obviously visible features, yet at the same time a major portion of its structures and processes that powerfully shape our lives are concealed unless we look closely beneath the surface of conventional social awareness. So now we turn from the global economy to a related issue in chapter 5, "how the middle class died." As you read chapter 5, keep in mind that much as Dickens's ghosts of Christmas Past, Present, and Future stalked and haunted Scrooge, so, too, do the new economy, the global economy, and multinational firms stalk and haunt the American middle class. But unlike the happy ending presaged by Dickens's ghosts in *A Christmas Carol*, today's ghostly trinity has contributed mightily to an *unhappy ending* (thus far)—the demise of the middle class and the evisceration of the American dream.

5

How the Middle Class Died

"America was once the great middle-class society. Now we are divided between rich and poor, with the greatest degree of inequality among high-income democracies."

—Jeffery D. Sachs, "Why America Must Revive Its Middle Class,"
Time (October 10, 2011)

Are you middle class? Many readers, we suspect, are likely to answer yes. In national surveys, most Americans say they are middle class.[1] Many Americans also say they believe the middle class—like the American dream—is in trouble, and in recent years, numerous scholars and journalists have documented a wide range of problems facing this class.[2] The "problems facing the middle class" issue became the focus of national public policy when President Obama signed an executive memorandum in early 2009 establishing the "White House Task Force on Middle-Class Working Families."[3] A major goal of the task force was "to achieve a secure future for middle-class working families."[4] Since then, the Obama administration claims, in a task force *Annual Report*, to have implemented major policy initiatives providing real support for the middle class.[5] But based on our review of the "evidence" presented in the *Report*, we conclude that task force–initiated policies have been more symbolic than substantive in terms of supporting the middle class. We find the Obama administration has *not* implemented significant public policies that would provide substantial, secure, long-term forms of material assistance to middle-income Americans. Indeed, despite the efforts of the task force as well as the Obama administration's more general economic policies, the middle class today is viewed by many as still hurting and still in trouble as the United States experiences what is widely regarded as a tentative and fragile "economic recovery."[6]

In our view, the situation facing middle-income Americans is more dire than "problems and troubles." From our perspective, *there is no secure middle class* in

America today. Our double-diamond model of the U.S. class system (chapter 2) does not include a middle class because, in our view, middle-range incomes today do not constitute middle-class membership. We believe a relatively secure American middle class *did* exist in the recent past but that it has since disappeared—along with the economic and social context that gave rise to and briefly supported it.[7] However, we do not believe the recent past represents a "golden age" of secure middle-class membership for most Americans. Some union and nonunion segments of the labor force did achieve modest middle-class lifestyles, but many other Americans did not—especially the poor, single women, and minorities. In the post-WWII period, the U.S. labor movement lacked the political muscle in Congress to enact legislation that would create a secure, middle-class "social wage" for all citizens. Instead, the large industrial unions negotiated labor contracts that essentially created "private welfare states" within large industrial firms that supported middle-class lifestyles for their members—for a few decades.[8] Middle-class wage and benefit packages won by large industrial unions served as workplace templates creating pressures on nonunionized employers that led many to provide similar wage and benefit packages to their workers—at least for a while.[9]

Although our views on the existence of the middle class differ from those held by most Americans (as expressed in national surveys), we believe this disagreement underscores the importance of exploring how the middle class is defined, what has become of it over the past several years, and what has become of the class structure generally. Thus, in this chapter our focus is fourfold. First, we consider the meaning of the middle class, including how it can be defined and measured. Second, we examine changes in measures of middle-class components over time and consider how such changes have adversely affected this class. Third, we consider the extent to which structural opportunities for employment in middle class–compensated occupations and for upward mobility have changed over time. Fourth, we document the trends of increasing class polarization (a growing two-class system) and class rigidity using various types of data such as income distribution measures and recent intergenerational mobility patterns. The research findings presented in this chapter illustrate and support the second and third principles of the new class system noted in chapter 2: a disappearing middle class, and a class structure that is polarized and rigid.

Many of the findings presented in this chapter center on what we call *inequality trends*. These are measures of economic and social conditions that, when tracked over the past thirty-five to forty years, trend in directions indicative of growing class inequalities. We view these inequality trends as embedded in and magnified by the *new economy*. But it is important to recognize that the new economy is not by itself the causal factor responsible for creating and driving these trends. Rather, to the extent that these trends have underlying causes, they are located in the conditions of conflicting class interests and class war—topics considered in the next chapter.[10] Major inequality trends explored in this chapter focus on incomes (of individuals and families), productivity, job stability, health insurance, pension benefits, occupational and educational opportunities, income concentration, and intergenerational mobility. We believe our exploration of these topics will help readers better understand our view of "how the middle class died."

WHAT IS THE MIDDLE CLASS?

"Middle class is a social construct that reflects occupational status, education and income among other factors."

—Gregory Acs, *Downward Mobility from the Middle Class* (September 2011)

To explore how inequality trends have adversely affected the middle class, we need a definition of this class that allows us to identify its basic characteristics. Unfortunately, there is no single, widely agreed upon definition of the U.S. middle class. This situation was acknowledged by a U.S. Commerce Department report, "Middle Class in America." The report stated, "No single accepted definition of middle class appears in the academic or popular literature, but numerous definitions have been suggested."[11] Our review of a large body of middle-class literature confirmed this observation. Among the "numerous definitions" alluded to by the U.S. Commerce report, we found many by social scientists who have offered a variety of models as the basis for conceptualizing, analyzing, and defining the middle class as well as social classes generally. Outside of social science, we also found many journalistic, popular media, governmental, and public opinion–based middle-class definitions—such as the one quoted above.[12]

Despite the absence of a "single accepted definition," a variety of "operational definitions" have been developed for the purpose of conducting research on the middle class (such definitions specify how this class will be measured in empirical studies). In our review of the substantial and wide-ranging middle-class literature, we found that different approaches used to study the middle class utilized different operational definitions. Among the various orientations found in such studies, two approaches used by scholars, researchers, journalists, and others appear well suited to our goals of developing a useful operational definition of the middle class and exploring the impact of inequality trends on this class over time. These are (1) the "income approach" and (2) the "resource approach." Related to these two is a third orientation we call the "opportunities approach." It has been used in some studies to explore, for example, how changes in the occupational and income distribution structures over time impact the middle class and the chances members of this class have for upward social mobility.[13]

The first approach refers to a distinct income range with upper and lower dollar amounts, which is used as the basis for identifying individuals and/or families located within the middle class. The second approach refers to material resources people possess, apart from income, which are viewed as important hallmarks of middle-class membership. Examples include job security, employer-provided health insurance, and secure pension benefits. The third approach refers to the extent to which opportunities for employment in middle class–compensated occupations and upward social mobility exist within a society. It conceptualizes such opportunities as constituting an important *structural dimension* of the class system.

Unlike the first two approaches, the opportunities approach does not identify individual-level characteristics that workers or families must possess to be considered middle class. Rather, it identifies *structural features* that must be present in the larger society in order for a middle class to exist and for people to have opportunities to move into it and, perhaps, to move up from it into more affluent classes. Structural features that undergird opportunities for middle-class membership and upward mobility include, for example, large numbers of middle class–compensated occupations in the private and public sectors and widely available and affordable higher education programs. Such structural features are crucial to the existence of a large middle class and opportunities for upward mobility; if they are not present, then this class cannot exist because opportunities to join it or advance beyond it will not exist.

income approach: money focused
resouce approach: material goods
that aren't $
opportunities approach: structure of society

Middle Class: An Operational Definition

Using variations of the first two approaches noted above, our operational definition of the middle class consists of two basic components: (1) incomes and (2) resources. Measures of these two components allow us to begin exploring how "middle-class" *workers* and *families* (as operationally defined in this chapter) have been adversely affected by inequality trends over the past several years.[14] Our operational definition of the *opportunities dimension* of the middle class identifies structural features in society we view as essential for the existence of a large middle class and the chances members of this class have for upward social mobility into higher classes.

The following section specifies how we measure the two basic components and how we define opportunities for middle-class membership and for upward mobility. It also identifies "expectations" associated with the two basic components and the opportunities dimension. These expectations are based on traditional American values and cultural ideals regarding the meaning of middle-class membership. Examples of these values and ideals, which are also central to the American dream, were mentioned in the U.S. Commerce Department report that noted, "Fairly standard middle class values and aspirations . . . include economic stability, a better life for one's children, and a current lifestyle that allows for a few creature comforts. . . . One characteristic that stands out in the literature on the middle class is that middle class families emphasize their expectations about the future; this means they work hard, plan ahead, and expect to save in order to attain those plans."[15] This means members of the middle class expect their plans and efforts will "pay off" by leading to greater economic security and a better life in the future for themselves and their children.

American Dream?

In short, they expect their efforts will allow them and their children to realize the American dream.

Components, Opportunities, and Expectations

For the income component we define annual *middle-class incomes* as $30,000 to $100,000 for *individual workers or families*.[16] For the resource component we define as middle class those *workers* (and their families) who are provided, *by their employers*, three major resources: (1) secure job tenure, (2) comprehensive, low-cost health insurance plans, (3) and substantial and secure "defined-benefit" pension plans.[17] Regarding the *opportunities dimension*, we define opportunities for widespread membership in the middle class and realistic chances for upward social mobility as conditions that exist when three structural features are present in society. These are (1) large numbers of readily available entry-level jobs that provide "middle-class" incomes and resources to workers; (2) a large and readily available pool of openings in college-degree-required occupations, professions, and careers at "middle-class" or higher income and resource levels for new college graduates; and (3) a large and readily available pool of openings located in classes above the "middle" for workers from middle-class family backgrounds (or even lower) who obtain the credentials necessary to move up into higher class ranks.[18]

Three expectations based on traditional American values are associated with the income component of our operational definition. Over time, it is expected that middle-class incomes will (1) increase at rates that exceed inflation, (2) increase as worker productivity increases, and (3) increase at rates that substantially exceed inflation for workers who complete higher levels of education (beyond a high school diploma). The resources component of our definition includes one expectation linked to the idea that middle-class membership has historically implied a class location grounded in stability and security. Thus, it is expected that middle-class workers and families will, over time, experience improvements or increases in the three types of resources identified by our operational definition.

Three expectations are associated with the opportunities dimension. These parallel the structural features of this dimension and reflect traditional values and ideals embodied in the American dream. First, it is expected that substantial numbers of entry-level job openings providing middle-class levels of income and resources (i.e., benefits) will be readily available over extended periods of time to individuals seeking employment. Second, it is expected that substantial opportunities will be readily available for new college graduates to move directly from college into occupations and professional careers that require college degrees. Third, it is expected that substantial opportunities will be readily available within the U.S. class structure for large numbers of workers from middle-class family backgrounds (and from lower-class backgrounds as well) who obtain the credentials necessary (educational and work experience) to move up into higher classes and that such upward mobility will be a frequent occurrence in the class structure.

INEQUALITY TRENDS: MIDDLE CLASS
INCOMES, RESOURCES, OPPORTUNITIES

"The trends are clear. . . . The next generation is likely to see a vanishing middle class."

—Eric Michael Moberg, *Class War* (2012)

Income Trends

We begin our review of inequality trends with three figures and a table that focus on changes in earnings over time for individual workers that fall within the range of our middle-class income definition ($30,000–$100,000). While the figures provide information for long periods of time, trends evident over the last thirty-five to forty years (1970s–2011) are our primary focus. The figures and table report *real income* for all years in 2011 inflation-adjusted dollars.[19] Figures 5.1–5.3 and table 5.1 document three largely *negative* income trends experienced by most "middle class by income" American workers in the 1973–2011 period. These are as follows: (1) *reductions* in average hourly and weekly earnings for production and nonsupervisory workers (figure 5.1), (2) *declining* median annual earnings for full-time, full-year workers (figure 5.2), and (3) *reductions* in median annual earnings for the vast majority of all full-time, full-year *middle-class-income* workers—those located in four of the five income quintiles (figure 5.3 and table 5.1).

Figure 5.1 illustrates that average hourly earnings (real earnings in 2011 dollars) *declined* -7.4 percent for production and nonsupervisory workers from $20.97 in 1973 to $19.42 in 2011. Also, average weekly earnings declined -12.4 percent from $744 in 1974 to $652 in 2011. In contrast, real hourly and weekly earnings trended steadily *upward* throughout the 1947–1973 period, each rising more than 60 percent. Multiplying the average hourly earnings reported in figure 5.1 for 1973 ($20.97) and 2011 ($19.42) by 2,000 hours (considered a full year of work) generates *estimates* of average annual incomes of $41,940 for 1973 and $38,840 for 2011. These amounts place workers in both years within the boundaries of our operational definition for middle-class incomes, but clearly *the wage trend is not in the direction predicted by our first expectation* linked to the income component (middle-class incomes will increase at rates that exceed inflation). One limitation of figure 5.1 is that it does not tell us if the workers receiving the average hourly or weekly earnings held jobs that employed them full-time, all year long. Thus, we don't know if workers actually received annual incomes in the amounts we estimated above. To get a better sense of how the incomes of full-time, full-year "middle-class-by-income" workers have changed over the past thirty-five to forty years, we turn our attention to figures 5.2 and 5.3 and table 5.1.

Figure 5.2 displays the median annual earnings for *all* full-time, full-year employed U.S. workers for the 1960–2011 period (real earnings in 2011 dollars). (This group is *smaller* than the one used to calculate average earnings in figure 5.1.) Figure

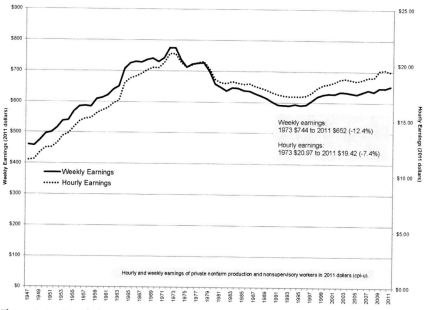

Figure 5.1.   Trends in Average Hourly and Weekly Earnings, 1947–2011
Source: U.S. Department of Labor, Current Employment Statistics (CES)

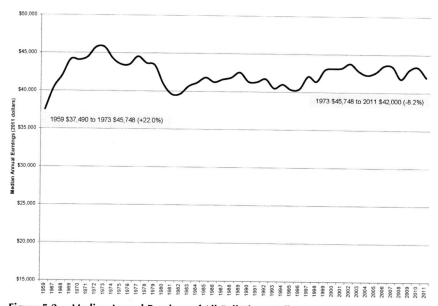

Figure 5.2.   Median Annual Earnings of All Full-Time, Full-Year Employed, 1959–2011
Source: U.S. Census Bureau, Current Population Surveys, "1960 to 2012 Annual Social and Economic Supplement"

5.2 shows us that the earnings of full-time, full-year workers declined by -8.2 percent in the 1973–2011 period. Real earnings fell from $45,748 in 1973 to $42,000 in 2011. In contrast, median real earnings for this group trended steadily *upward* throughout the 1959–1973 period, rising by 22 percent over those fourteen years (from $37,490 in 1959 to $45,748 in 1973).

Figure 5.3 displays the median annual real earnings of all full-time, full-year workers by quintiles for the 1959–2011 period and specifically compares 1973 and 2011 earnings within each quintile. Table 5.1 provides a side-by-side listing of median annual real earnings for each quintile in 1973 and 2011 (in 2011 dollars) and the percentage change for each quintile over the 1973–2011 period.

The information presented in figure 5.3 and table 5.1 reveals two important facts about middle-class earnings. First, in 2011 about 60 percent of all full-time, full-year workers had incomes that placed them within the range ($30,000–$100,000) of our middle-class-income definition (all workers in Q3 and Q4 plus about half of the workers in Q2 and Q5).[20] Second, of the approximately 60 percent of full-time, full-year workers with "middle-class" incomes, about 83 percent experienced losses in real earnings over the 1973–2011 period while the other 17 percent experienced only a modest increase. Regarding the second fact, we can see in figure 5.3 and table 5.1 that for the 1973–2011 period, the real earnings of workers in the second (Q2), third (Q3), and fourth (Q4) quintiles fell by -10.6, -6.1, and -0.5 percent, respectively. Since half of the workers in Q2 were above the $30,000 median, they fall within our middle-class income range, as do all of the workers in Q3 and Q4. These three groups make up 50 percent of all workers and 83 percent of all middle-class-by-income workers. They all had *income losses* over the 1973–2011 period.

The other 17 percent of "middle-class" workers consists of those workers in Q5 with earnings below the $102,400 median for this quintile (half of the quintile = 10 percent of all full-year, full-time workers). These workers *appear* to have experienced an increase of +12.3 percent in their earnings over the 1973–2011 period. However, the "middle-class" workers located in the lower half of Q5 were likely to have experienced only a modest increase in earnings for this period. This was the case because

**Table 5.1.	Median Annual Earnings by Quintiles for Full-Time, Full-Year Employed**

Quintiles	Year and Wage/Salary (2011 dollars)		Percentage change 1973-2011
	1973	2011	
All Full-time Full-year Employed:	$45,748	$42,000	-8.2%
Quintile 5 (top 20%)	$91,191	$102,400	12.3%
Quintile 4	$60,794	$60,500	-0.5%
Quintile 3	$45,798	$43,000	-6.1%
Quintile 2	$33,558	$30,000	-10.6%
Quintile 1 (bottom 20%)	$20,265	$18,000	-11.2%

Source: U.S. Census Bureau, Current Population Surveys, "1974 and 2012 Annual Social and Economic Supplement"

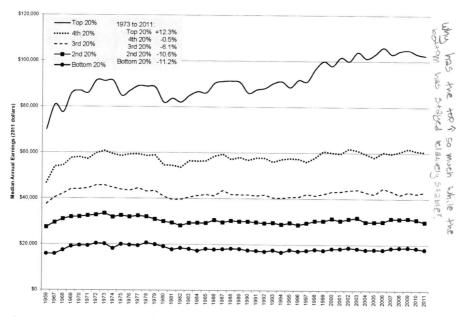

Figure 5.3. **Median Annual Earnings of All Full-Time, Full-Year Employed by Quintile, 1959–2011**
Source: U.S. Census Bureau, Current Population Surveys, "1960 to 2012 Annual Social and Economic Supplement"

most of the gains in earnings for Q5 workers went to the highest-income workers in this quintile. Other sources reveal that the highest-earning 5 percent of all workers experienced a 36 percent increase in real wages in the 1973–2009 period and that the top 1 percent received an increase in real income over 200 percent.[21] The 12.3 percent increase in earnings for Q5 (figure 5.3, table 5.1) is the *average* for all Q5 workers. As such, it *masks* both the dramatic earnings increase experienced by the *highest-paid* Q5 workers and likely the modest increase in earnings experienced by workers in the bottom half of Q5.

The relationship between changes in worker productivity, real wages, and family income is examined over the course of several decades in figures 5.4 and 5.5.

Figure 5.4 illustrates that during the 1973–2010 period, the *productivity* of U.S. nonagricultural workers *increased by about 100 percent* (from about 140 in 1973 to about 280 in 2010), while workers' real hourly wages actually *declined by about -9 percent* (from about 138 in 1973 to about 120 in 2010). In contrast, both productivity and real wages grew together throughout the 1960–1973 period.

Figure 5.5 continues the figure 5.4 comparison of productivity growth and income but switches the focus from individual workers' real wages to *real median family income*. The information presented in figure 5.5 illustrates that while worker productivity increased by 58.8 percent in 1973–2000, real median family income

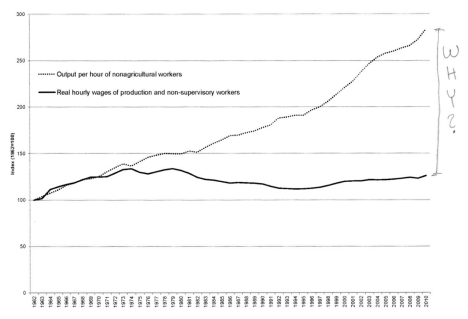

Figure 5.4.   Changes in Productivity and Hourly Wages, 1962–2010
Source: Economic Report to the President, 2012

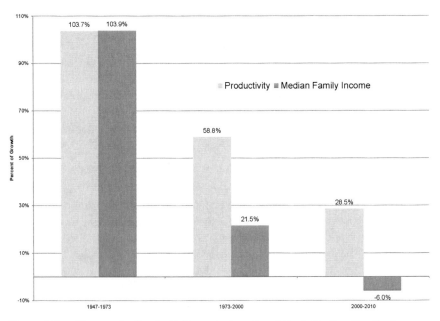

Figure 5.5.   Changes in Productivity and Growth of Real Median Family Income, 1947–2010
Source: Economic Report to the President, 2012

rose only 21.5 percent for this period. Over the last ten years of data shown in the figure (2000–2010), we see *productivity increased by 28.5 percent*, but *real median family income fell by -6.0 percent*. In contrast, both productivity and real median family income *grew* by 103.7 and 103.9 percent, respectively, in the 1947–1973 period.

The relationship between full-time, full-year workers' educational levels and their median real hourly and annual earnings for the 1973–2011 period is examined in figures 5.6 and 5.7.

Figure 5.6 displays annualized median hourly earnings for full-time, full-year workers in five different educational levels for 1973 and 2011 (in 2011 dollars). Figure 5.7 displays *changes over time* from 1959 to 2011 in median annual real earnings for workers within the same five educational levels used in figure 5.6, but our primary interest is in the 1973–2011 period. If we multiply the median hourly earnings displayed for each educational level in figure 5.6 by 2,000 hours (a full year of work, used earlier with figure 5.1), the resulting amounts are close to the median annual earnings for each educational level displayed in figure 5.7 for 1973 and 2011. For example, multiplying the hourly earnings of workers with less than a high school diploma in 1973 ($17.73) by 2,000 produces an annual income of $35,460—about the same as shown in figure 5.7. (See the bottom trend line and the "dot" on the line above 1973.)

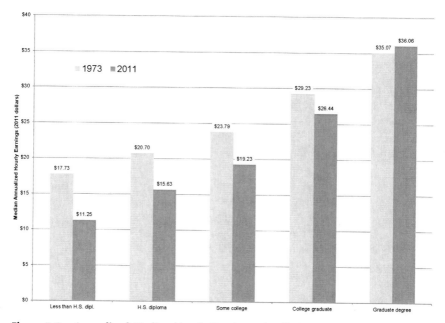

Figure 5.6. Annualized Median Hourly Earnings of Full-Time, Full-Year Employed by Education, 1973 and 2011
Source: U.S. Census Bureau, Current Population Surveys, "1974 and 2012 Annual Social and Economic Supplement"

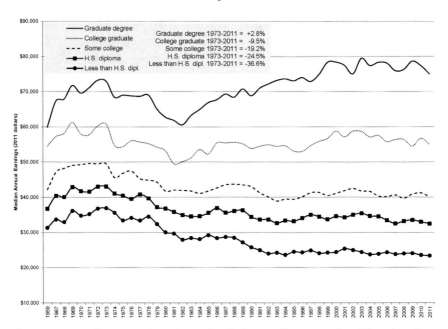

Figure 5.7. Median Annual Earnings of Full-Time, Full-Year Employed by Education, 1959–2011
Source: U.S. Census Bureau, Current Population Surveys, "1960 to 2012 Annual Social and Economic Supplement"

Figure 5.7 shows us that in 1973, the median annual earnings of individual workers in each of the five educational levels were within the boundaries of our middle-class-income definition. However, figure 5.7 also reveals a *downward trend* in median annual real earnings in the 1973–2011 period for workers in four of the five educational levels. Of these four, the less than high school diploma group experienced the largest decline in earnings—a stunning -36.6 percent drop! As a result, the annual earnings of workers at this level in 2011 (about $22,000) were *below* the minimum needed to be included in the middle class—$30,000 by our definition. Figure 5.7 shows us that the incomes of workers in the other three groups suffered, but not as badly as the bottom group: high school diploma, -24.5 percent; some college, -19.2 percent; college graduate, -9.5 percent. Only graduate-level workers experienced an increase in real earnings in 1973–2011, up 2.8 percent, but this was only a raise of 0.07 of 1 percent for each of the thirty-eight years.

While figure 5.6 shows that each educational level increment in 1973 and 2011 is associated with higher median hourly earnings, figure 5.7 graphically illustrates that the median annual earnings *trend* for each of the four lowest educational levels was *negative* in the 1973–2011 period. The earnings trend was positive only for the graduate-level degree group. By contrast, the earnings trend was *positive* for workers in *all five* educational levels in the *1960–1973 period*—as shown by the left side of figure 5.7.

Income Expectations Revisited

The three expectations associated with the income component of our middle-class definition were not supported by the income inequality trends we presented. First, our findings revealed that middle-class incomes *did not* increase at rates that exceeded inflation for most workers in this class during the 1973–2011 period—findings contrary to the first expectation. Second, our findings revealed that, for the most part, not only did middle-class incomes *not* increase as productivity increased but the reverse was also found to be the case for the 1973–2011 period—findings contrary to the second expectation. While figure 5.5 did show an increase in both median family income (+21.5 percent) and productivity (+58.8 percent) for the 1973–2000 period, the income increase was less than half the productivity increase. Moreover, based on our analysis of family income growth in this period, we believe it was due mainly to either more family members going to work or an increase in the number of hours worked by already employed family members. It does not appear that wages were increased to reward productivity growth. Third, our findings revealed that workers' incomes did not increase at rates that substantially exceeded inflation for middle-class workers with higher levels of education—findings contrary to the third expectation.

Resources Trends

The following sections illustrate that inequality trends affecting job stability, health insurance, and pensions have significantly diminished these middle-class resources over the past thirty-five to forty years

Job Stability: Reductions in Years on the Job and in Shares of Workers with Long-Term Jobs

Job stability as measured by "mean tenure"—the average number of years on the job—declined in all age categories from 1973 to 2006. The decline was six months for workers aged twenty-five to thirty-four, ten months for workers aged thirty-five to forty-four, and one year for workers aged forty-five to fifty-four. Educational levels were related to declining job tenure, but no group was spared the trend of growing instability. Workers aged forty-five to fifty-four with a high school diploma or less experienced a decline in job tenure of nineteen months from 1973 to 2006, whereas those with a college degree experienced a decline of seven months.[22] More recently, "median years of job tenure"—the point at which half of all workers had more tenure and half had less tenure—rose slightly from 4.0 in 2006 to 4.4 in 2010. Such a change *appears to suggest* job stability has improved in recent years, but that is *not* the case. Instead, this slight gain in median job tenure "reflects, in part, relatively large job losses among less-senior workers in the most recent recession."[23]

Job stability as measured by changes in the percentage of workers holding long-term jobs for more than ten years declined for all workers in the 1973–2006 period. In the more recent 1996–2010 period this pattern of decline continued for workers aged twenty-five to fifty-nine.[24] In 1973, 29.9 percent of workers between the ages of thirty-five and forty-four had worked at their current job for more than ten years, but in 2006 that share had fallen to 24.6 percent. This same pattern held true for workers in the same age group with educational levels typically tied to middle-class membership. In 1973, 28.6 percent of workers (thirty-five to forty-four) with "some college" and 29.2 percent of college graduates had worked at their current job for ten years or more, but in 2006 those shares had fallen to 24.9 percent (some college) and 24.6 percent (college graduates).[25] More recently, the 2006–2010 period witnessed a slight increase in the percentage of workers over age sixty holding long-term jobs.[26] This change, however, like the slight improvement in median job tenure, was due *not* to improving job stability but to large job losses among less-senior workers in the current recession—as noted above.

Among workers employed for even longer time periods, those with twenty years or more at their current job, we find the same pattern as with ten-year workers—smaller shares of workers employed today than in the recent past. In 1973, 21.9 percent of all workers between the ages of forty-five and fifty-four had worked at their current job for more than twenty years, but in 2006 that share had fallen to 17.4 percent. Workers in this age group with education levels typically associated with middle-class membership had the same experience. In 1973, 19.9 percent of workers (forty-five to fifty-four) with "some college" and 20.2 percent of college graduates had worked at their current job for twenty years or more, but in 2006 those shares had fallen to 18.2 percent (some college) and 19.0 percent (college graduates).[27] For older workers close to retirement, we find the same pattern. In 1983, 33 percent of private-sector pre-retirees aged fifty-five to sixty-four had worked twenty years or more with their current employer, but in 2010 that share declined to 25 percent.[28]

Health Insurance: Reductions in Coverage, Increases in Costs

The share of private-sector workers covered by employer-provided health care plans declined to 51 percent in 2010 from 69 percent in 1979 (where employers pay anywhere from partial to full premiums).[29] Among the entire under-sixty-five population covered by employer-sponsored health insurance, there have been substantial declines in all gender and racial categories. This trend was especially pronounced over the last ten years. Over the 2000–2010 period, employer-sponsored health insurance coverage for under-sixty-five males fell from 69.1 percent to 58.2 percent and from 69.3 to 59.1 percent for females. During the same period, employer-sponsored coverage for under-sixty-five whites fell from 76.2 to 66.9 percent, coverage for blacks declined from 57.5 to 45.3 percent, and coverage for Hispanics fell from 47.3 to 39.2 percent.[30]

Parallel with the trend of declining coverage were increases in costs workers paid for health insurance and increases in the percentages of workers required by employers to help fund their health care plans. Large increases in workers' health care costs in the 1975–2010 period are evident in part by the steep rise in the average per-month premiums *paid by workers* for *family* health insurance plans (in 2010 dollars): $18 per month in 1975, $72 in 1988, $122 in 1996, $129 in 1999, $226 in 2005, and $383 in 2010.[31] For many professional white-collar occupations, average monthly health care premiums paid out-of-pocket for family coverage ranged between $377 and $420 in 2010.[32] Nationally, workers' contributions to premiums for employer-sponsored family health insurance plans increased 168 percent from 1999 to 2011. This increase was far above overall inflation for this period (38 percent) and increases in workers' earnings.[33] In 2010 dollars, workers' annual contributions to premiums for family health insurance coverage totaled $1,543 in 1999; in 2011 this amount increased to $4,129.[34] The proportion of full-time private-sector workers required to make contributions for *single medical coverage* increased from 26 percent in 1980 to 69 percent in 1997 to 80 percent in 2010. For *family medical coverage*, the percentage of workers required to make contributions rose from 46 percent in 1980 to 80 percent in 1997 to 89 percent in 2010. For most white-collar workers, the proportion was 91 percent in 2010.[35]

In addition to higher costs to workers for employer-sponsored health insurance, there have also been large increases in workers' "out-of-pocket" expenditures for health care needs. Ever-larger amounts of workers' earnings are being spent to cover ever-higher health insurance co-payments and deductibles as well as to pay for health care services and prescription medications once covered by more comprehensive employer-sponsored health insurance plans. These "cost-shifting" changes are illustrative of significant reductions in the *quality* of health insurance coverage. The effect of declining quality of coverage on workers is evident in part by the increasing numbers of families spending more than 10 percent of their disposable income on health insurance premiums as well as on medical costs not covered by their insurance plans. In 2009 about 28 percent of U.S. families had health care costs in excess of 10 percent of their disposable income compared to 19.2 percent in 2003 and 15.8 percent in 1996.[36] The reduction in health insurance quality is also a likely source of the difficulties many families report they have in paying their medical bills. A 2011 survey conducted by the Centers for Disease Control and Prevention (CDC) found 20 percent of U.S. families were having trouble paying their medical bills and half of those said they were totally unable to pay any of their medical bills.[37]

Although the 2010 Patient Protection and Affordable Care Act will presumably increase the percentage of insured Americans as the 2014 insurance exchange provisions take effect, the act also includes a 40 percent excise tax starting in 2018 on the most comprehensive health care insurance plans (those with total annual premiums over $27,500). The effect of this tax on what Republicans in the 2010

Congress called "Cadillac coverage" (to demonize comprehensive plans covering unionized workers) will be "to effectively reinforce a new lower standard of acceptable coverage."[38] In other words, the extent of coverage provided by the few current comprehensive employer-sponsored plans remaining (union and nonunion) will be diminished after 2014—another blow to middle-class resource security.

Pensions: Reductions in Coverage, Increases in Costs, Reductions in Benefits

The proportion of private-sector workers covered by *all types* of employer pension plans declined to 42.8 percent in 2010 compared to 50.6 percent in 1979.[39] Not only has the trend of pension coverage declined generally, but since 1979 "the erosion . . . was widespread, occurring among both high school and college graduates at every wage level. In fact, the groups with the highest coverage have tended to lose the most ground in recent years."[40] Vice President Joe Biden recently highlighted the dearth of pension coverage today when he pointed out that "[in 2007] just 60 percent of working heads of families were eligible to participate in any type of job-related pension or retirement plan. . . . Even among those who *were* eligible, more than 15 percent did not participate in the plan, leaving roughly . . . 78 million working Americans with no employer based retirement plan."[41]

Adding to the problem of coverage has been the declining quality of pension plans, which tend to fall into two categories. First, *defined-benefit* plans "are generally considered the best plans from a workers' perspective because they guarantee a worker a fixed payment in retirement based on pre-retirement wages and years of service regardless of stock market performance."[42] Second, *defined-contribution* plans are funded by employer contributions to workers' individual retirement accounts (typically 401[k] plans—to which workers often can also contribute).[43] Under these plans, a worker's retirement income depends upon the investment options provided by employers and a worker's investment decisions over time. Because of these conditions associated with defined-contribution plans, workers are often presented with substantial limitations and uncertainties that can make retirement income problematic and unpredictable.[44]

The proportion of full-time private-sector workers in medium and large firms (one hundred workers or more) covered by defined-benefit plans fell from 84 percent in 1980 to 50 percent in 1997. For workers in small firms, such coverage declined from 20 percent in 1990 to 15 percent in 1996.[45] In 1995 the proportion of workers covered by defined-contribution plans exceeded the proportion covered by defined-benefit plans. Since then, the percentage of workers covered by defined-benefit plans has continued to decline while the percentage covered by defined-contribution plans has continued to rise.[46] In 2010 only 19 percent of U.S. private-sector employees were participating in defined-benefit plans (offered by 10 percent of employers) while 41 percent were participating in defined-contribution plans (offered by 44 percent of employers).[47] Given the important differences between the two types of pension plans, it is clear that "the shift from traditional defined-benefit plans to defined-contribution plans represents an erosion of pension quality."[48]

Reductions in the availability and quality of pension plans make it certain that substantial numbers of retirees—including many in the middle class—will lack "adequate retirement income." "A common test of retirement income adequacy is the ability in retirement to replace at least half of current income, based on expected pensions, Social Security benefits, and returns on personal savings."[49] Based on this standard, the percentage of workers aged forty-seven to sixty-four with *expected* retirement incomes of less than 50 percent of current income *rose at every education level* in the 1989–2004 period.[50] For example, among workers aged forty-seven to sixty-four with less than a high school diploma, the proportion rose from 39.2 percent in 1989 to 46.6 percent in 2004; among college graduates, the proportion rose from 20.8 percent in 1989 to 21.2 percent in 2004.[51]

Since 2004, the proportion of workers with expected retirement incomes of less than half of their pre-retirement earnings has continued to rise.[52] We estimate that *over half of all current workers*, including those in the middle class, will receive annual retirement incomes (from pensions, Social Security, and savings) that are *less*, and in many cases *much less*, than 50 percent of their pre-retirement earnings. For example, consider "middle-class" private-sector workers who retired in 2009 earning the then median annual income of $40,000 for full-time, full-year workers. If those newly retired workers received the 2009 median retirement income ($19,697—pension income plus Social Security), this amount would equal 49.2 percent of their pre-retirement earnings.[53] Since *more than half of all workers earn less* than the full-time, full-year median income, when these workers retire, they will receive *less than half* of the median annual pension income—in whatever year they retire. Illustrating this point are the very low incomes received by 60 percent of all retirees—those in the three lowest retiree income quintiles. In 2009 the total annual income for retirees in the lowest retiree income quintile was $10,685 *and below* while the income ranges for the second and third retiree income quintiles were $10,686 to $14,487 and $14,488 to $19,478. In contrast, the next-to-the-highest (fourth) quintile range was $19,479 to $29,666; the highest quintile included retirees with total retirement incomes of $29,667 and up.[54]

An additional threat to workers' retirement income security comes from employers abandoning their pension obligations. Since the enactment of the Employee Retirement Income Security Act (ERISA) of 1974, increasing numbers of employers have shifted their responsibility for defined-benefit plans to the Pension Benefit Guaranty Corporation (PBGC—created in 1974 by Congress in part to protect defined-benefit pensioners if their company failed). Pensioners who have had their plans taken over by the PBGC receive far less—typically about 50 percent less—than they were promised in benefits.[55] In 2011, the average monthly pension benefit paid by PBGC was $573 (about $6,900 per year).[56] However, even these reduced payments may be at risk, since in 2011 the PBGC had a deficit of $26 billion and it is likely to grow as more firms turn their pension plan obligations over to this federal agency.[57]

Resources Expectation Revisited

The expectation associated with the resources component of our middle-class definition was not supported by the resources inequality trends data we presented. While the expectation was that over time middle-class workers and families would experience improvements or increases in the three major resources associated with membership in this class, the reverse actually occurred. The evidence we presented illustrates that the last thirty-five to forty years have witnessed a continuous and substantial erosion of these resources. As we documented, not only are middle-class jobs more insecure today than in the past, but ever-larger shares of increasingly limited middle-class incomes must now be devoted to health care and retirement needs than was the case in the past. But as middle-class incomes have stagnated, workers and families in this class are increasingly unable to adequately fund these needs.

In the not-too-distant past, many middle-class workers and families could reasonably expect that substantial levels of all three resources would be available to significantly reinforce their financial security and class rank. That is obviously not the case today. In fact, resource losses and declining incomes led the authors of a 2007 study to estimate "that 69 percent of middle-class families lack the basics they need to ensure financial security" and are at risk of slipping out of the middle class.[58] The sharp declines we documented in the levels of resources available to middle-class families combined with falling or stagnant incomes *before and after* the 2008 financial crisis suggest that even higher levels of middle-class insecurity prevail now than when the 2007 study was published. The extent of resource and income losses, we believe, calls into question the existence of a "secure middle class" in America.

Opportunity Trends

Middle-Class Membership Prospects

What about opportunities for middle-class membership? Will substantial numbers of entry-level job openings providing middle-class levels of income and resources be readily available over extended periods of time to individuals seeking employment—per our first opportunities expectation? A useful baseline for considering this issue is the Center for Economic and Policy Research's estimate that a "good job" today is one that pays "at least $18.50 per hour, has employer-provided health insurance, and some kind of retirement plan."[59] Jobs of this sort provide income and benefit levels that are middle class by our definition. Figure 5.1 in this chapter illustrates that such "good jobs" were common in 1973 when average real hourly earnings exceeded $20 an hour and many jobs had health insurance and pension benefits. But current and future middle-class job opportunities are increasingly uncommon. An economist at the Economic Policy Institute estimates that only about a third of all U.S. jobs projected to be created in the next few years would meet the "good job" criteria.[60] In fact, the average pay of recently created jobs suggests this projection may be overly optimistic. For example, the U.S. Bureau of Labor Statistics (BLS) reported that 41.4 percent of the new jobs created in the first half of 2011 paid an average wage of less than $15 per hour (less than $30,000 annually) and 68.2 percent paid less than $20 per hour.[61]

Over the next several years the U.S. labor market is expected to reflect the impact of growing *job polarization*, a term that refers to "the increasing concentration of employment in the highest- and lowest-wage occupations as job opportunities in middle-skill occupations disappear."[62] This means that as in the recent past, the U.S. economy will continue to create many more low-wage jobs than good jobs with "middle-class" compensation levels. Evidence for this trend comes from the BLS, which projects that 69.2 percent of all job openings due to growth and replacement needs in the 2010–2020 period will require only a high school diploma or less and that the largest number of job openings will be located in low-paid service-sector occupations.[63] For example, seven of the top ten occupations the BLS projects in 2010–2020 as having the largest numeric growth in jobs require either *less than a high school diploma* (five of the seven) or *only a high school diploma* (two of the seven) and provide annual incomes described by the BLS in 2008 as "very low" (under $21,590) or "low" ($21,590–$32,380). These seven occupations include retail salespersons, home health aides, personal care aides, office clerks (general), combined food preparation/servers (including fast food), customer service representatives, and laborers and freight, stock, and material movers.[64]

Middle-Class College Graduates and Career Prospects: Surplus of College Graduates

What about college graduates? Will substantial opportunities be readily available for new college graduates to move directly into occupations and careers that require college degrees—per our second opportunities expectation? It appears many in the middle class believe this *should* be the case. Traditional middle-class expectations regarding education and work typically view college graduation as leading to professional careers, higher incomes, and comfortable lifestyles.[65] These expectations were recently echoed by the White House Task Force *Annual Report*: "Postsecondary education . . . [offers] one of the most reliable routes to a good career."[66] The reasons for such expectations are likely due to the positive life experiences of many in the middle class. For example, a recent national survey found that a larger percentage of college graduates in the middle class (60 percent) saw themselves as likely to have a better life in five years compared to the percentage of adults who held such a view in all other education categories (some college, 55 percent; high school graduate or less, 47 percent). The survey also found that among Americans who defined themselves as middle class, college graduates had the highest median family income ($75,198) of all educational categories of adults who located themselves in this class.[67]

Despite middle-class expectations, projected trends in the U.S. occupational structure suggest that substantial numbers of professional job openings *will not* be available for current and future college graduates. In fact, at least one-third or more of all job seekers with bachelor's degrees will be unlikely to find jobs requiring that credential in the next decade (table 5.2). As we noted above, the BLS projects that seven of the top ten occupations with the largest projected numeric job growth in 2010–2020 require either less than a high school diploma or only a high school diploma. The job with the largest projected growth, registered nurses (711,900 jobs), requires only a two-year associate degree. The occupation with the tenth-largest projected job growth, postsecondary teachers (305,700 jobs), is the only job in the top ten that requires a doctoral or professional degree.[68] Of the *top twenty* occupations with the largest projected numeric job growth in 2010–2020, *only one* requires a bachelor's degree alone—elementary school teachers. Collectively, the top twenty occupations will add a total of 7.41 million new jobs over the ten-year period, but of this number, just 248,800 (3.3 percent) will require only a bachelor's degree.[69]

Of course many occupations will require a bachelor's degree over the next ten years, but the number of available jobs for college graduates will be less than many in the middle class may expect. The BLS projects a total of 8,562,000 job openings due to growth and replacement needs for college graduates with bachelor's degrees in 2010–2020.[70] During this decade, however, U.S. colleges and universities will produce about 1.6 million bachelor degree graduates each year (over 16,000,000 for the entire ten years).[71] This disparity will produce a substantial surplus of college graduates each year. Table 5.2 displays two annual "surplus" projections based on two different postgraduate educational assumptions.

As table 5.2 indicates, there would be an annual surplus of 744,000 more graduates than available job openings through 2020 if we *unrealistically* assume that *none* of the annual 1.6 million bachelor's degree graduates enter full-time graduate/professional programs each year. The surplus would, however, be reduced to 594,000 if we *more realistically* assume that 150,000 bachelor degree graduates will enter full-time

Table 5.2. College-Level Job Openings versus College Graduate Job Seekers, 2010–2020

Annual Number of Job Openings for U.S. College Graduates, Bachelor's Degree: 2010-2020	Annual Number of U.S. College Graduates, Bachelor's Degree: 2010-2020	Annual "Surplus" of College Graduates Each Year: 2010-2020
856,000	1,600,000	744,000 [1]
		594,000 [2]

[1] Assumes *none* of the bachelor degree grads enter graduate/professional programs each year.

[2] Assumes *200,000* bachelor degree grads *will* enter graduate/professional programs each year.

Source: Lockard and Wolf, "Occupational Employment Projections to 2020," 206; U.S. Census Bureau, *Statistical Abstract of the United States: 2012,* 190

graduate/professional programs (e.g., PhD, MD, JD) each year.[72] Even under the second assumption scenario, it is clear that over the next decade large numbers of bachelor's degree graduates each year will have sharply limited opportunities to move directly into professional careers. In 2011, for example, 53 percent of U.S. college graduates under age twenty-five were either unemployed or underemployed.[73]

Middle-Class Upward Mobility Prospects: Recent Intergenerational Mobility Trends

What about upward mobility? Will substantial opportunities be readily available for workers from middle-class backgrounds (or below) to move into higher-class ranks and will such upward mobility be a frequent occurrence—per our third opportunities expectation? Recent studies report that the likelihood of upward intergenerational mobility in the United States *declined* in recent decades compared to the past for adults from poor or modest family backgrounds.[74] Most studies use annual income as a basis for comparing the economic status of parents and their adult children and most focus on father-son comparisons. While income is a convenient and useful measure of economic rank, it does not measure other attributes thought to be important indicators of class membership, such as various levels of education and occupational prestige—as suggested by sociologist Max Weber.[75] Also, while father-son comparisons are useful, such studies obviously ignore daughters and thus track only half of all intergenerational mobility outcomes.[76]

To more fully explore the upward mobility experiences of *all* adult children (not just sons) from middle-class (and other) backgrounds and move beyond the limitations of income as a one-dimensional indicator of class rank, we conducted our own study. We included sons and daughters and utilized a multidimensional measure of class, inspired by Weber, known as "socioeconomic status" (SES). This indicator combines measures of income, education, and occupational prestige into SES scores that range from low to high values. The data for our study were drawn from the National Longitudinal Surveys (NLS)—1979 to 2006 series. We created a standardized SES variable and used it to calculate the SES rankings of our sample consisting of 2,352 father–adult son pairs and 2,085 father–adult daughter pairs. We divided the SES values into four ranks (quartiles): Highest = SES Q1, Second = SES Q2, Third = SES Q3, Fourth = SES Q4. We then compared the SES ranks of the adult sons and daughters in 2006 (median age, both genders, 2006 = 43) with their fathers' SES ranks in 1979 (median age, 1979 = 43).[77]

We identified the SES Q2 rank in our study as "middle class" and used it as the basis for assessing the extent of upward intergenerational mobility for children from this class. This rank was chosen because the income, educational, and occupational levels of our subjects (fathers, sons, daughters) located in the SES Q2 rank closely approximate the levels of these components held by middle-class adults—as operationally defined in studies using one or more of these factors to identify membership in this class. The results of our analysis are shown in table 5.3 for both sons and daughters. The percentages shown in the last four lines on each side of the table

Table 5.3. Socioeconomic Mobility by Quartile

		Son's SES in 2006					Daughter's SES in 2006				
		highest			lowest		highest			lowest	
Father's SES in 1979		SES Q1	SES Q2	SES Q3	SES Q4	(totals)	SES Q1	SES Q2	SES Q3	SES Q4	(totals)
highest	SES Q1	**304**	175	92	45	616	**235**	143	79	34	491
	SES Q2	170	**153**	121	150	594	128	**149**	148	92	517
	SES Q3	93	151	**177**	192	613	82	127	**173**	167	549
lowest	SES Q4	49	98	135	**247**	529	48	113	184	**183**	528
	(totals)	616	577	525	634	2,352	493	532	584	476	2,085
% upward mobility (lower left quadrant)		29.6%					32.7% *				
% downward mobility (upper right quadrant)		33.0%					31.8% *				
% no mobility (diagonal)		37.5%					35.5% *				
% downward or no mobility		**70.4%**					**67.3%** *				

* p <0.05 difference between sons and daughters

(sons—left, daughters—right) depict the proportions of *all* sons (2,352) and *all* daughters (2,085) in our sample who experienced one of three mobility outcomes: upward, downward, no mobility; the fourth line shows downward plus no mobility combined. These topics are discussed in more detail later in this chapter in the "Class Rigidity" section.

To clarify the intergenerational mobility experiences of *sons* whose fathers were located in what we view as the *middle class* (SES Q2), we need to look at the *left side* of the table. Here we see that a total of 594 sons had fathers located in SES Q2 (1979). The SES ranks and mobility experiences of these 594 sons in 2006 were distributed as follows: 170 were in SES Q1 (28.6 percent, *upward mobility*, one rank), 153 were in SES Q2 (25.8 percent, *no mobility*), 121 were in SES Q3 (20.4 percent, *downward mobility*, one rank), and 150 were in SES Q4 (25.3 percent, *downward mobility*, two ranks). The mobility experiences of *daughters* from middle-class fathers (SES Q2) are shown on the *right side* of the table. Here we see that a total of 517 daughters had fathers located in SES Q2 (in 1979). To track the distribution of SES ranks and mobility experiences of these 517 daughters in 2006, the same procedures used for sons were followed.

Comparing daughters with sons, we find that 24.8 percent of daughters (128 out of 517) and 28.6 percent of sons (170 out of 594) from SES Q2 middle-class fathers moved *upward* into a higher class rank; at the same time, 46.4 percent of daughters (148 + 92 = 240 out of 517) and 45.6 percent of sons moved *downward* from the middle class into lower class ranks; finally, 28.8 percent of daughters (149) and 25.8 percent of sons (153) with SES Q2 fathers experienced *no mobility*—as adults they held the same SES Q2 rank as their fathers. We can see that the mobility patterns of *middle-class* sons and daughters are both somewhat different and similar at the same time. That is, sons are slightly more upwardly mobile than daughters, but both sons and daughters are about equally downwardly mobile.

Our findings regarding the likelihood of *upward* intergenerational mobility among adult children from middle-class backgrounds are generally consistent with those reported for father-son comparisons in income mobility studies such as those mentioned earlier. That is, we found that *the sons as well as the daughters* of middle-class fathers were *less likely* to experience *upward* mobility than in the past.

Opportunity Expectations Revisited

Based on the evidence we reviewed relating to our first opportunity expectation, it is clear that substantial numbers of entry-level middle-class jobs are *not* currently available and are not likely to be available in the future. In fact, as the evidence indicates, recent years have witnessed substantial *reductions* in the availability of the kinds of jobs that once provided middle-class employment. It is clear that the ongoing decline in middle-class employment openings and compensation levels has seriously compromised opportunities for workers to join—or remain in—the middle class.

With regards to our second opportunity expectation, the divergent employment and educational trends we documented indicate that large numbers of bachelor degree graduates will *not* have opportunities to move directly from college into professional careers. Over the 2010–2020 period, the mismatch between the large number of bachelor degree graduates and the limited number of job openings ensures that opportunities for new bachelor-level graduates will be substantially constrained.

The evidence related to our third opportunity expectation is also grim. The mobility patterns evident in table 5.3 indicate substantial opportunities are *not* readily available for large numbers of workers from middle-class backgrounds to move up in the class structure; they also tell us that upward mobility, among sons or daughters, was hardly a "frequent experience" among those who came from middle-class backgrounds. Moreover, when the evidence related to all three opportunity expectations is considered together, it supports conclusions that are the *reverse* of each expectation regarding opportunities for middle-class membership, employment of college graduates, and upward mobility.

CLASS POLARIZATION AND CLASS RIGIDITY

Class polarization refers to the growing division of the United States into two main, polarized classes, the privileged class and the new working class. One important result of this process has been the gradual elimination of a secure middle class as a meaningful component of the class system. *Class rigidity* refers to the hardening of the class structure with family background becoming the primary determinant of class rank for life. It is marked by an increasing impermeability of the boundary dividing the two major social classes resulting in very little upward mobility from the new working class into the privileged class, and very little downward mobility from the top to bottom class ranks. And as meaningful social mobility disappears, privilege at the top and privation at the bottom—with very little in between—become frozen in place and perpetuated in perpetuity. The concepts of class polarization and rigidity are related and represent ongoing processes associated with a number of increasingly obvious middle-class-destroying inequality trends—as explored in this chapter. And as noted earlier, they are related to the conditions of conflicting class interests and class war—topics explored in the next chapter.

Class Polarization: The Shrinking Middle Class

Increasing class polarization in the United States over the past thirty-five to forty years is linked to the three inequality trends described earlier and is especially evident by three related income trends. The first involves the shrinking middle class—measured by reductions in the percentage of American *families* and *households* with annual incomes that fall within a broad "middle-class range." If for *families* we define this range to be between $25,000 and $100,000, we find the proportion of American families in this category *declined* from 71.9 percent in 1969 to 58.3 percent in 2006 (using 2006 dollars for both years).[78] If for *households* we define this range to be plus or minus 50 percent of median *household* income, we find the percentage of American *households* (not families) with incomes in this range *fell* from 50.3 percent in 1970 to 42.2 percent in 2010 (using 2010 dollars for both years).[79] In 2010 the median U.S. household income was $49,445; thus, the "middle-class" income range, plus or minus 50 percent of the median, was $24,723 to $74,167.[80] Both definitions highlight income trends indicative of a shrinking "middle class"—as a percentage of the U.S. population.

Class Polarization: Income Concentration

The second trend related to increasing class polarization concerns income concentration. It includes changes in the shares of national income received by U.S. families at different income levels—including those in the "middle class"—and the increasing concentration of national income in the hands of the wealthy. Figure 5.8 illustrates changes in family income shares within five family income quintiles over time. The solid bars shown in figure 5.8 depict the percentage shares of all national income distributed to families within each quintile in 1973 and 2010. For example, families with the lowest incomes (the bottom quintile, annual incomes up to $20,000) received 4.3 percent of all national income in 1973, but only 3.3 percent in 2010. The long rectangular box at the top of figure 5.8 reports the percentage change in the family income share for each quintile group in 2010 compared to 1973. It also reports the 2010 family income ranges for each quintile (in 2010 dollars).

The references in the box at the top of figure 5.8 to the percentage change in family income shares shows us that during the 1973–2010 period, families in the four lowest quintiles experienced losses in their shares of national income. If we define "middle-class" families here as including *only* those in the third ($38,044–$61,735) and fourth ($61,736–$100,065) quintiles, we see that their shares of national income *declined* by -14.1 and -4.8 percent, respectively. But families in the bottom and second quintiles fared even worse, experiencing income share *losses* of -23.9 and -20 percent, respectively. Meanwhile, families in the top 20 percent (annual incomes of $100,066 and up) saw their income share *rise* from 43.5 percent of all national income in 1973 to 50.2 percent in 2010—a 15.5 percent increase.

It is clear from figure 5.8 that growing income concentration at the top occurred throughout the 1973–2010 period. The figure shows that while a highly unequal

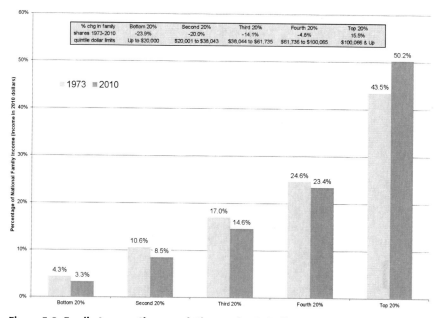

Figure 5.8. Family Income Shares and Changes by Quintiles, 1973 and 2010
Source: U.S. Census Bureau, Current Population Surveys, "1974 and 2012 Annual Social and Economic Supplement"

distribution of family income shares existed in 1973, income inequality was even greater in 2010. The *upward redistribution* of income evident in figure 5.8 makes it clear that as middle-class families (and lower-income families) lost income shares over time, the most affluent family quintile gained income shares—a "zero-sum" outcome. As a result of this increasing concentration of national income in the hands of a relatively small number of affluent families over the past thirty-seven years, *class polarization* between "the rich and the rest" became even more pronounced.

While figure 5.8 documents an upward shift in income shares over the past thirty-seven years, more specialized data reveal that the general trend of increasing income concentration at the top is also found *within* the most affluent quintile. Research on income distribution within the top quintile indicates the highest-income families in this group experienced the largest income gains over the 1973–2010 period and collected most of the income received within this quintile. For example, families in the *top 10 percent* income group collected 95 percent of the income received by all families in the top quintile in 2010. Just the *top 1 percent* income family group (average annual income, $1,371,000) saw its share of national income grow from 13 percent in 1974 to 20 percent in 2010.[81] Thus, even though all families in the top quintile experienced rising incomes over the past thirty-five to forty years, income growth among the highest-earning families in this group far outstripped that of the merely affluent. This development illustrates that the general trend of growing income concentration extends to families within the most affluent quintile.

Class Polarization: The Growing Underclass

The third income trend related to increasing class polarization calls attention to the growth of what we call here the American "underclass." We use this term to refer to that portion of the U.S. population defined by the federal government as poor and "near poor." (In our model the "underclass" would include the "contingent" and "excluded" class segments.) The U.S. Census Bureau recently reported that, using a new Supplemental Poverty Measure (SPM), 146.4 million Americans representing *48 percent* of the total U.S. population in 2010 either fell below the poverty line (49.1 million) or fell into a low-income category (97.3 million—those earning 100 percent to 199 percent of the poverty level).[82] The 146.4 million figure represents an increase of 4 million over 2009, the earliest year for which numbers are available using the Census Bureau's new measures. Since the Great Recession began in late 2007, the share of low-income working families rose three straight years to 31.2 percent in 2010—the highest in nearly a decade. In contrast, in 2002 low-income families made up 27 percent of all American families. Over the last thirty-one years, the inflation-adjusted average annual earnings of low-income families (the bottom 20 percent of all families) have fallen from $16,788 in 1979 to less than $15,000 in 2010.[83]

Class Rigidity

The reality of increasing class rigidity in the United States is illustrated by our intergenerational mobility study results (table 5.3) and by comparisons of our research with the findings of similar studies from the 1970s. Perhaps the most striking findings from our research related to class rigidity are the large percentages of *all* sons and daughters with SES ranks that were below or equal to their fathers' SES ranks and the small percentages who moved from the bottom to the top. As table 5.3 shows us, *70.4 percent of all sons* and *67.3 percent of all daughters* in our sample *either were downwardly mobile or experienced no mobility*. These large percentages mean that less than a third of all sons and daughters experienced upward mobility of any sort. And among sons and daughters who did move up, most rose only a short distance; very few made it to the top. For example, 25.5 percent of sons and 34.8 percent of daughters with fathers in the lowest (Q4) SES rank (135/529 sons and 184/528 daughters) moved up one level to the SES Q3 rank. But only 9.3 percent of sons and 9.1 percent of daughters with fathers in the lowest (Q4) SES rank moved up three levels to the top (Q1) SES rank.

When we compare the mobility experiences of the sons in our sample with those in Featherman and Hauser's 1978 father-son study of occupational intergenerational mobility (using 1973 data), we find three important differences indicative of increasing class rigidity. First, compared with the 1978 findings, our study reveals much less upward mobility, far more downward mobility, and a higher proportion of sons replicating their fathers' SES rankings. In the 1978 study, 49 percent of the sons were upwardly mobile, 32 percent were nonmobile (stationary), and 19 percent were downwardly mobile.[84] In contrast, only 29.6 percent of all sons in our study were upwardly mobile, 37.5 percent were nonmobile, and 33 percent were downwardly mobile. The latter two results indicate that *70.4 percent* of all sons in our study (rounded value) versus *51 percent* of the sons in the 1978 study were either downwardly mobile or nonmobile.

Second, compared with the 1978 findings, our study found a much larger share of positions in the "top class" rank (SES Q1 in our study) held by sons with fathers who held top or next-to-top class ranks. Featherman and Hauser's study found 46 percent of positions in the top occupational rank were held by sons with fathers in the top or next-to-top occupational ranks.[85] In contrast, our study found 77 percent of the positions in the top SES quartile (Q1) were held by sons with fathers in the top two SES quartiles (Q1 and Q2). This finding indicates that top SES/class positions today are far more likely to be occupied by sons with fathers who held top or near-top positions than was the case in the 1970s.

Third, compared with the 1978 findings, our study found much less mobility from the lowest ranks into the highest ranks. In the 1978 study, 16.4 percent of sons with fathers in the lowest occupational rank and 22.9 percent of sons with fathers in the second lowest occupational rank rose to the top occupational rank.[86] In contrast, our study found only 9.3 percent of sons with fathers in the lowest quartile (SES Q4) and 15.2 percent of sons with fathers in the second lowest quartile (SES Q3) rose to the top SES quartile. These differences indicate that sons from the bottom ranks in our study found it much harder to rise to the top than was the case for sons from the bottom ranks in the 1970s.

It is our view that the three income trends—a shrinking middle class, growing income concentration in the hands of the affluent, and an expanding underclass—along with our findings on intergenerational mobility, bring into focus and vividly illustrate the twin realities of class polarization and class rigidity in the United States today. As the data suggest, these two important and interrelated phenomena have emerged over the past four decades as central features of our class structure and shared social experiences.

HOW THE MIDDLE CLASS DIED: DEATH BY A THOUSAND CUTS

We believe the evidence presented in this chapter illustrates "how the middle class died." This phrase refers to our view that the "disappearing middle class" has ceased to exist as a meaningful component of the class structure. This is the case, we maintain, because the incomes and material resources that formed the foundation of middle-class membership have declined so significantly over the last thirty-five to forty years for so many Americans that the *secure middle class* has largely vanished. As we discovered in this chapter, the inequality trends and other evidence we presented reveal a gradual but inexorable decline in the material well-being of the American middle class—since about 1973. When we track the downward-pointing inequality trends and related data, we do not find them marked by dramatic or sharp turning points; rather, we find what appears to be a long, slow, gradual slide—always downward. It is a slide akin to the process of inflicting legions of small knife wounds on an organism—individually each slice seems to be of little consequence, but collectively they kill as the life blood oozes through a thousand cuts. This is how the middle class died. And while many people still believe they are in the middle class, we think most are not. In our class model, remnants of the post-WWII groups that attained modestly secure middle-class lifestyles are now found in the "comfort-class segment" of the new working class. This segment contains those individuals and families who have been able—thus far—to avoid at least many of the thousand cuts that killed the once-upon-a-time relatively large, modestly secure American middle class.

It is useful to recall, as we noted at the beginning of this chapter, that the thirty years after World War II was not a "golden age" of secure middle-class membership for most Americans. While *some* Americans did attain a modest middle-class lifestyle, many did not. However, prior to 1973 many U.S. workers *did* experience increasing real incomes and expanding workplace benefits. The result for some workers was membership in a growing middle class and for others, the promise of joining that class in the not-too-distant future. The middle class then was somewhat like the American dream—part reality and part aspiration. But middle-class membership, like the American dream, seemed closer in 1973 than today. Of course, many students and workers today still believe the steep upward mobility version of the American dream will soon be theirs. Indeed, these Americans are probably more inclined to view themselves as members of the "pre-rich class" than the middle class! Those convinced that they will soon be rich are less likely to be concerned with the death (or life) of the middle class. Since in their view they're just "passing through" the lower rungs of the class system, they are likely to view the study of class inequalities as irrelevant and tiresome. We would, of course, disagree, but what do we know?

Some may ask: If the middle class has died, what about the millions of Americans with middle incomes? Statistically, we can, of course, always calculate the middle of the U.S. income distribution and identify as "middle class" those located in that range.[87] But, as we suggested earlier, it is our view that middle incomes today do not constitute middle-class membership. The pre-1973 reality of rising incomes and expanding workplace benefits experienced by many American workers provided important measures of economic security and social stability that are hallmarks of middle-class membership and expectations. As those qualities have faded, being located in the middle of the income distribution confers neither security nor stability. Middle income simply points to a statistical location; it does not represent middle-class membership. In our view, the "disappearing middle class"—the second principle of the new class system—has, for all practical purposes, virtually disappeared! At the same time, class polarization and rigidity—comprising the third principle of the new class system—have grown and intensified.

It is important to recognize that while this chapter describes and illustrates *how* the middle class died and *how* the unpleasant phenomena of class polarization and rigidity can be illustrated, it does not explain *why* these developments have occurred. Exploring answers to the "why question" as it relates to these topics as well as other class inequalities is a primary concern of chapter 6, which focuses on the fourth principle of the new class system: classes have conflicting interests.

6

Conflicting Class Interests and Class War

"The Right in America stands for the interests of the employers and the investing class. . . . The Left stands for the interests of those who have to work for a living. . . . The haves and the have-nots have different and opposing interests.

—Robert Fitch, "How Obama Got His Start," *CounterPunch* (January 2012)

The idea that "classes have conflicting interests"—the fourth principle of the new class system—and the idea that such conflicts may find expression as "class war" are associated with Marxist analyses of inequality under capitalism. But because Marxist-based inquiries have long been condemned by opinion leaders in the elite classes, they are routinely marginalized, discredited, and dismissed by conventional social institutions such as the corporate media, both major political parties, and higher education. As a result, the merits of Marxist-inspired ideas as a basis for understanding and explaining the dynamics of the American economic, political, and class structures are seldom explored. But the "economic tsunami" (i.e., the 2008 financial crisis and Great Recession that brought worlds of economic pain and hardship to millions of workers) helped change this situation. The dramatic changes this tsunami produced in the lives of many Americans and the questions it raised about our institutional structures helped alter conventional worldviews held by many and fostered interest in alternative views and explanations.

Despite the interest many Americans now have in alternative ways of understanding recent economic changes, as illustrated by public support in 2011 for the Occupy movement, elite leaders suggest that they're not necessary. Privileged-class pundits and elected officials tell us, "We're all in this together," and that "shared sacrifices" are necessary to solve our current economic problems. We view such pronouncements as self-serving attempts to neutralize public outrage about and opposition to growing economic inequalities, austerity budgets, the corrupting influence of corporate money in politics, tax policies favoring the rich, Wall Street bailouts, corporate greed, and arrogant billionaires—issues that remain of great concern to Americans.[1]

Understanding and addressing the important and legitimate grievances of workers requires, we believe, a class analysis approach that begins with attention to conflicting class interests. Taking this approach, we view superclass corporate owners, their credentialed-class allies, and many other privileged-class members as having economic, political, and cultural interests that are directly opposed to those of the working class. We also view the elite classes (i.e., the superclass and its credentialed-class allies) as controlling and deploying far more economic resources in support of their interests than the working class. And, as we will see, these resources fund a wide range of activities in the economic, political, and cultural arenas aimed at preserving and extending the dominance of the elite classes' interests over those of the working class.

Taking our class analysis approach a step further, in this and other chapters we maintain that over the past four decades the superclass and its allies have pursued their shared interests by actively engaging in a comprehensive anti-working-class campaign we call *class war*. The true nature of this war has little to do with conservatives' claims that proposals to increase taxes on the rich represent "class warfare."[2] Rather, the purpose of this superclass-funded, one-sided, top-down war has been (and is) to reinforce and expand the supremacy of the economic, political, and cultural interests of the elite classes vis-à-vis the working class. But unlike conventional wars wherein powerful opposing armies engage in violent combat with each side attempting to impose its will on the other by force, class war, as waged by the elite classes on the working class, only *occasionally* involves the use of physical violence or armed conflict.[3]

The U.S. class war is conducted on many fronts via strategies that may be difficult to discern but by tactics that often involve obvious assaults on workers' interests. For example, the superclass *strategy* of creating an organizational base to plan, coordinate, and advance its interests (e.g., conservative think tanks and potent lobbying groups like the Business Roundtable) may not be readily apparent as a class war component. In contrast, numerous superclass-initiated *tactics* that directly harm workers' interests but advance those of the elite classes are readily apparent as class war attacks. Such tactics frequently involve actions and policies carried out openly, and examples abound in the corporate, government, and cultural arenas. In business they include outsourcing, downsizing, union-busting, wage and benefit cuts, and plant closings; in government they include tax cuts for the rich, austerity budgets, anti-labor laws, and international "free trade" agreements; in the cultural arena they include corporate media-disseminated attacks by conservative organizations, pundits, and other superclass allies on "big government" and trade unions as the primary sources of our major economic and social problems. These attacks often focus on so-called "dependency-producing" programs like Social Security or Medicare and "inefficient" public institutions like schools; they also describe unions as roadblocks to efficiency and progress. The conservative cultural critique claims that only the private sector

they say these things because they've never needed these programs

can correct problems created by government, that greater privatization of public programs and institutions will enhance our nation's well-being, and that unions foster entitlement attitudes.

The waging of class war by the elite classes is facilitated by giant corporations and the enormous profits they produce—both of which are largely controlled by the superclass. This control ensures that large shares of corporate-generated profits will be distributed as income and wealth to the superclass along with much smaller shares to its credentialed class allies and many other members of the privileged class. A portion of the concentrated wealth and income this distributional order produces has been and is used by the elite classes to create and sustain a variety of organizations (e.g., conservative think tanks and the Business Roundtable), activities (e.g., elite class lobbying, campaign funding), and idea systems (e.g., neoliberalism, "free markets") that are sharp points of the class war spears used to advance their interests.

CORPORATIONS AND CONFLICTING CLASS INTERESTS

"Millionaires and billionaires . . . have been waging class warfare mercilessly over the last four decades, and they've been taking no prisoners."

—Matthew Rothschild, *Progressive* (November 2011): 7

Large corporations and the wealth and income they generate are at the heart of conflicting class interests, class war, and *class power*—the ability of a class to protect and advance its interests based on the resources it possesses or controls. Since corporations exist to produce profits, the economic interests of the elite classes that benefit from their distribution—including superclass corporate owners, senior executives, and major stockholders—are served by the practice of profit maximization. As we saw in chapters 3, 4, and 5, in today's "new economy" the profits of large firms are often maximized via corporate policies and practices that not only reduce workers' wages and benefits but also erode or eliminate workers' rights to bargain collectively with employers. When corporate profits increase, the elite classes' economic interests are, of course, served. But increased profits also serve their political interests as well. This is the case because rising profits allow the superclass and its allies to expand their political power by increasing expenditures for lobbying activities and political campaigns. These "investments" game the governing process, producing laws and regulations that protect and advance their shared interests. And as the elite classes' political power increases, working-class political power is diminished.

The economic resources controlled by major U.S. corporations are staggering. Although the entire for-profit U.S. "corporate population" today numbers about 6 million firms with total annual business receipts over $30 trillion, a small number of huge companies dominate the U.S. economy as well as all major sectors of American business.[4] The five hundred largest firms by revenues (the Fortune 500) make up less than .001 percent (one-thousandth of 1 percent) of all U.S. corporations.

Even so, in 2011 the revenues of these five hundred firms totaled $11.8 trillion and their profits totaled $825 billion.[5] Those amounts represented about 40 percent of all U.S. corporate revenues ($30 trillion) and profits ($1.94 trillion) in 2011.[6] Such enormous revenues and profits illustrate that "size matters" in the business world. However, large firms are significant not simply because of their overall size but also because small numbers of very large corporations have such enormous resources that they dominate the marketplace in several business sectors.

Concentrated corporate dominance is highly visible in the financial and insurance sectors, which, as we saw in the chapter 3 section on "financialization," have become increasingly important in the new economy. In the financial sector, the United States has over six thousand commercial banks insured by the Federal Deposit Insurance Corporation (FDIC). Even so, the ten largest banks (by revenues) held 84 percent ($10.2 trillion) of the total assets ($12.1 trillion) of all FDIC-insured commercial banks in 2011.[7] By comparison, in 1990 the ten largest U.S. financial firms held only 10 percent of the total assets held by all U.S. financial companies.[8] In the insurance sector, the ten largest U.S. life and health insurance companies (by assets) held $2.98 trillion in assets in 2011. This amount represents 52 percent of the total assets ($5.78 trillion) held by all 946 U.S. life and health insurance firms.[9] It is important to note that large U.S. firms not only dominate virtually all sectors of the American economy today but also play increasingly dominant roles in the global economy, since many large U.S. firms are multinational companies with subsidiaries scattered around the globe.[10]

Large Corporations: Patterns of Ownership, Wealth, and Income

Large U.S. corporations are primarily owned and controlled by members of the superclass, many of whom serve as senior executives in such firms along with a trusted and upwardly mobile cadre of credentialed-class members sponsored by superclass mentors. Although not all superclass members choose to hold leadership positions in the economic, political, or cultural arenas, all members of this class are, by definition, wealthy. As we noted earlier, the superclass includes the top wealth-owning and income-receiving groups in the United States—including the 425 U.S. billionaires, out of 1,226 billionaires in the world in 2012.[11] Those superclass members who are actively involved in corporate governance, along with a select group of trusted credentialed-class members, hold virtually all of the seats on the boards of directors of the largest U.S. firms, which in 2012 included approximately 5,350 director positions in S&P 500 firms.[12] Many of these corporations are "interlocked" by superclass members who simultaneously serve as directors on the boards of multiple firms—often across different industries.[13]

Superclass corporate leadership and interlocks are facilitated by stock ownership. Ownership of all common stocks not held in retirement accounts in 2010 was highly concentrated at the top. The wealthiest 1 percent of U.S. households, the superclass core, owned 47.4 percent of all such stocks. Below the top 1 percent, concentrated stock ownership and high levels of participation in senior corporate governance roles are also common among the next wealthiest 4 percent, which owned 32.5 percent of stocks. The stock ownership and governance characteristics of the top two groups are present to some extent but are much less common among the next 5 percent, which owned 10.1 percent of stocks. Below the top three groups, concentrated stock ownership and participation in senior corporate governance fade very quickly, as the next 10 percent owned just 6.4 percent but the bottom 80 percent owned only 3.5 percent.[14] Declining concentrated stock ownership below the top 1 percent indicates that a substantial wealth divide separates the top group from the groups below it. It also suggests that the next 4 percent (the wealthiest credentialed-class group), like the 1 percent above it, stands significantly above and apart from the next 15 percent—the upper, middle, and lower ranks of the modestly to barely wealthy privileged class.

Where income is concerned, the superclass is located in the top 1 percent group, as is the case with wealth. In 2011 the average cash income of this group (about 1.2 million households) was $1,371,000 (in 2011 dollars).[15] At the top of the 1 percent group (the top 1/100th of one percent) the *average* income was $23,846,950 in 2010.[16] But even this figure was dwarfed by the *average* income of $556,000,000 for the top twenty-five hedge fund managers in 2011 (down from $882.8 million in 2010).[17] Below the superclass are the top-earning members of the credentialed class, making up the next 9 percent income group with *average* incomes of $200,500 in 2011.[18] The lower-earning privileged-class members make up the bottom 10 percent of the highest income quintile; the 11.8 million households in this group had *average* incomes of $105,000 in 2011.[19]

Various forms of data concerning the *sources* of personal income illustrate that the higher the income, the lower the percentage derived from salaries and wages and the greater the percentage derived from wealth—most often in the form of dividends, interest, and other forms of corporate-based compensation—and vice versa. For example, 80 percent of American households (the bottom four income quintiles) receive about 70 percent of their income from wages and salaries; only 7 percent comes from business income and all types of investment capital (over 22 percent comes from other sources, mainly Social Security and unemployment compensation). In contrast, for the top 1 percent of households (by income) business income and investment capital income sources account for 53 percent of all income this group receives; only about 35 percent (or less) of income in this group is derived from wages and salaries.[20] Illustrating the latter point, executive compensation studies reveal that salaries plus bonuses represent a small portion of CEOs' total incomes. For example, a *USA Today* survey of 138 large U.S. firms reported CEO median income to be $9.6 million in 2011. Of this amount, CEO median *cash income* totaled $3.1 million ($1.1 million salary plus $2.1 million cash bonus). The remainder of median CEO income was paid in the form of stock and stock options.[21] Thus, for the CEOs in the *USA Today* survey, salary and bonus income made up only 33 percent of *total* CEO compensation in 2011. But among the highest-paid CEOs, salary and bonus income often represent only single-digit percentages of their total compensation.

The incomes of many credentialed-class managers and white-collar professionals who assist superclass elites in waging class war, legitimating inequalities, and
managing corporations are well below those of superclass members, but they are
still substantial. In Washington, the salary for members of Congress has often been
viewed as the "income floor" of the upper-middle class.[22] In 2012 that floor was
$174,000.[23] This figure represents an approximate baseline salary minimum for
midlevel privileged-class managers and professionals—especially those in private-
sector firms. However, salaries for senior corporate executives such as chief financial
officers (CFOs) in midsized and larger firms are well above congressional salaries. For
example, CFOs located in six hundred "middle market" companies received average
incomes of $927,743 in 2010.[24] The incomes of CFOs in larger firms are much
higher—typically seven or eight figures. In smaller firms (five thousand to twenty
thousand employees), the low end of the 2011 CFO income range ($98,589) fell
below the 2012 congressional salary, but the high end ($458,691) was well above it.[25]

From newly rich corporate officers to the oldest American family fortunes, sky-
box-levels of wealth and income are linked to the ongoing production of corporate
profits. Elite class corporate officers understand this connection. Thus, superclass
members actively involved in corporate governance, along with a select group of
upwardly mobile credentialed-class members groomed by superclass sponsors, work
diligently to ensure the continued financial health, power, and growth of the corporate enterprise. At the highest wealth levels, the corporate basis of immense personal
wealth is illustrated by current or former CEOs with large fortunes linked to specific
firms as well as by family members who inherited large fortunes due to their ties to
the founders of large firms. Examples in the former category include, in 2012, Bill
Gates's $66 billion Microsoft fortune, Warren Buffett's $46 billion Berkshire-Hatha-
way empire, Philip H. Knight's $13.1 billion Nike holdings, and Mark Zuckerberg's
$9.4 billion Facebook fortune. Examples in the latter category include Christy
Walton's $27.9 billion Wal-Mart–based fortune and those of five other Walton heirs
($115.5 billion in combined wealth for all six Wal-Mart heirs), as well as Laurene
Powell Jobs's (Steve Jobs's widow) $11 billion Apple fortune.[26] Large corporations
are clearly the engines that generate the wealth and income of the superclass and its
credentialed-class allies.

How Superclass Corporate Control Serves Privileged-Class Interests

As a result of superclass ownership and control of large firms, the economic, political, and cultural interests of this group, their credentialed-class allies, and many other
members of the privileged class are served in three ways. First, much of the value of
the goods and services produced by workers is distributed through corporate-based
channels and practices to superclass corporate owners, their credentialed-class allies,
and many other privileged-class members. The heart of this process is simple and
increasingly transparent in today's new economy. It begins with corporations paying
workers far less in wages and benefits than the market value of what they produce.

The difference between wages paid and the market value of what workers produce is retained by corporations as profits. *why can't workers earn the market value of what they are producing?*

Senior company executives today typically embrace corporate policies that produce ever higher profits even if they reduce workers' wages and benefits. Such policies are quite apparent in the current highly uneven and largely jobless "economic recovery" (so long to the Great Recession?). Corporate profits, as noted earlier, soared to an all-time record $1.94 trillion in 2011, while workers' wages and benefits declined—clearly illustrating the connection between low wages and high profits. Executives in the corporate community are quite aware of the empirical nature of this connection. For example, JPMorgan Chase chief investment officer Michael Cembalest, in an analysis sent to his bank's top investors, concluded that "reductions in wages and benefits explain the majority of the net improvement in [recent profit] margins."[27] In a separate study, Northeastern University's Center for Labor Market Studies reported, "Corporate profits from 2009's second quarter through 2011's first . . . have increased 39.6 percent. Over that same span, median weekly earnings of full-time U.S. workers have dropped 1.0 percent."[28] As a result of these policies, profits per worker among Fortune 500 companies in 2011 "hit a record of $32,000, 50% above the level in the early 2000s."[29]

While inequalities between corporate profits, executive compensation, and worker pay can be documented in virtually all firms in every economic sector, the U.S. auto industry provides an instructive case study. Following years of financial losses, General Motors (GM) and Chrysler entered bankruptcy and were "bailed out" by loans from the federal government in early 2009. (Ford managed to avoid bankruptcy.) Despite these setbacks, sales and profits at all three U.S. auto firms rose dramatically in the 2010–2011 period. The combined net revenues of GM, Ford, and Chrysler increased from $13 billion in 2010 to $18.2 billion in 2011.[30] And as profits rose, CEO pay at GM and Ford jumped sharply. (Chrysler CEO income changes are less clear.[31]) Table 6.1 shows that total compensation for the CEO at government-bailed-out GM went from only $181,308 in 2009 (the bailout year) to $7.7 million in 2011. Compensation for the CEO at "no-bailout-necessary" Ford Motors rose from $17.9 million in 2009 to $29.5 million in 2011.

Despite providing the labor power that made the recent surge in U.S. automakers' profits *and* CEO pay levels possible, hourly autoworkers did not share in these gains. Wages have been frozen since 2007 for "first-tier" U.S. hourly autoworkers—high-seniority workers who receive the highest levels of union-negotiated wages and benefits. And they will remain frozen through 2015 due to labor contracts negotiated by the United Auto Workers (UAW) union in 2011. Even worse, hourly autoworkers hired after 2007 receive only 50 percent of "first-tier" workers' wages.[32] As a result of these policies, wages for "first-tier" workers will remain at about $28 per hour (roughly $45,000 per year after taxes) through at least 2015, but wages for "second-tier" workers (as well as "contract" and "temporary" auto workers) will be stuck at about $15 per hour (roughly $24,000 per year after taxes). Moreover, the number of "first-tier" autoworkers will shrink as they retire, leave, or die and as plant managers

Table 6.1. Total Compensation for GM and Ford CEOs, 2009–2011

Auto Company CEOs	Total Compensation per Year (nominal dollars)		
	2009	2010	2011
General Motors CEO	$181,308	$2,257,419	$7,702,743
Ford Motors CEO	$17,916,654	$26,250,515	$29,497,572

Source: Ford and GM Corporate Reports, 2009, 2010, 2011

hire low-wage workers to replace them—despite UAW assurances that this will not happen.[33] In fact, the trend of wage cuts in the auto industry is being replicated today across a wide range of U.S. manufacturing companies.[34]

The seeming paradox of rising profits and executive pay levels along with stagnating and/or declining wages for rank-and-file workers so evident in the auto industry has become the "new normal" in much of corporate America. While workers create profits, they have no control over their distribution—or redistribution. Instead, superclass control of large corporations via stock ownership, corporate board seats, and senior executive positions ensures that what we call the "profit redistribution process" will proceed according to corporate compensation, stock option, and dividend policies established by the superclass with the assistance of their credentialed-class allies. The end point of the "profit redistribution process" occurs when corporate profits, derived from workers' productivity and undercompensation, are "redistributed" *from* workers whose labors produce profits *to* superclass corporate owners, CEOs, credentialed-class senior managers, and privileged-class stockholders in the form of salaries, bonuses, stock options, and dividends. Thus, superclass control of large corporations is essential to the economic interests of this class, its allies, and the privileged class generally.

The second way superclass ownership and control of large corporations serves its interests and those of the privileged class generally involves deploying high levels of personal and corporate economic resources to influence public policy–making—a topic explored further in a later section in this chapter ("The Political Dimension of the Class War") and in chapters 7–9. The corporate-derived income and wealth of the superclass are used to penetrate and powerfully influence government via massive campaign finance expenditures and intensive lobbying efforts. As we will see in the chapters 7–9, these activities have permitted the superclass, along with its credentialed-class allies, to implement legislation and public policies that have, over the past forty years, institutionalized its economic and political interests—at the expense of the working class. Examples (explored in the coming chapters) include the following: (1) steep cuts in federal income tax rates, (2) reduced government regulation of businesses, (3) more international "free trade" agreements, (4) the erosion of federal and state labor laws originally enacted to protect workers' rights to unionize and bargain collectively, and (5) cuts in social programs such as government subsidized housing, food stamps, and medical care. The end result of these and similar policies is an economic and political order that not only favors elite class interests over working-class interests but also makes such disparities appear "normal" or even "natural."

The third way superclass ownership and control of large corporations serves its interests and those of the privileged class generally involves utilizing personal and corporate resources in ways that influence the *content* of U.S. culture. As we discuss in "The Cultural Dimension of the Class War" section later in this chapter and in chapter 9, the superclass and its credentialed-class allies directly control and/or powerfully influence numerous for-profit and nonprofit organizations engaged in the production and dissemination of many different and widely shared "cultural products" that are important components of American culture. Examples range from large corporate media firms to superclass-funded conservative "think tanks" such as the American Enterprise Institute, the Heritage Foundation, and many others. These think tanks produce and disseminate to corporate media outlets, pundits, members of Congress, and other "opinion leaders" large numbers of books, policy papers, and press releases designed to mobilize public and governmental support for so-called "conservative" viewpoints and policy preferences. Large media firms in turn produce, for example, television news programs that often report on or cite think tank–provided materials.[35] In this way, among many others, public opinion (one aspect of culture) is shaped by news reporting that reflects and projects elite class ideas and values.[36]

ʃWe are not suggesting that the elite classes are engaged in a calculated conspiracy to shape the culture in ways that benefit their interests. A conspiracy is not necessary. All that is necessary is superclass ownership and/or control of media firms and other organizations involved in the production of "cultural products." The managers of such firms and organizations are not only aware of the ideas and views of the ownership class, they most likely share them. Thus, the many subtle and not-so-subtle links between, for example, the views of superclass media owners and those of media managers ensure that the cultural content produced by such firms will generally fall within a range of ideas, views, and values acceptable to the ownership class. Thus, superclass ownership of large firms helps ensure that the ideas of the elites become those of the masses.ʅ

CLASS WAR IN AMERICA

"The war by the Right to restore the 'natural' order of our economy and society as it existed in the 1920s has achieved many victories. Inequality is at the highest levels since the 1920s, government regulation of industry and finance is hopelessly weak, and the union movement is battered. Indeed, this war may be entering a decisive phase."

—James Crotty, *In These Times* (February 2012): 22

Nowhere is the reality of conflicting class interests more apparent than in the ongoing class war that has been instrumental in driving the transformation of the American class system in the period from the 1970s to the present. The inequality trends we discussed in chapter 5 are the direct result of activities and policies initiated and implemented by superclass-dominated organizations over the past forty years—large corporations, federal and state governments, and many nonprofit organizations. Collectively these developments represent, in our view, total class war. Although various approaches have been offered as explanations for the current configuration of the U.S. class system, none approaches the explanatory power of a class war analysis. While the details of the forty-year class war story are complex, the main actors, events, and policies underlying it are stunningly simple. Grounded in conflicting class interests, the class war is sponsored and directed by the superclass, implemented and managed by its credentialed-class allies, and funded by corporate-generated profits.

The story behind the class war and the highly unequal new class system it produced begins in the 1950s and early 1960s. At that time, the U.S. elite classes were split on the issue of launching a class war to aggressively attack gains made by workers under President Roosevelt's New Deal programs "because profits were so high."[37] But this split was soon reversed by economic, political, and social developments in the 1960s and early 1970s. During this period, several progressive political and social movements supported by civil rights groups, organized labor, consumer and environmental organizations, and other reform-minded persons led to an expansion of New Deal–based national policies that effectively increased a wide range of opportunities for—as well as the economic, occupational, and physical well-being of—working-class Americans. These policies included some of President Johnson's Great Society programs such as federal civil rights laws, Medicare, Medicaid, the War on Poverty, and new federal regulatory acts in six major areas: consumer product safety, discrimination in employment, traffic safety, consumer finance, job safety, and the environment.[38] Among these were groundbreaking measures such as the 1969 Coal Mine Health and Safety Act, the 1969 National Environmental Policy Act, and the 1970 Occupational Safety and Health Act. For the working class, the net effect of this body of progressive legislation was a welcome expansion of the U.S. welfare state–social wage.

Members of the superclass viewed the expansion of pro-working-class policies with fear and loathing. As one progressive author observed, "The expansion of the welfare state in the 1960s and 1970s created panic among the U.S. capitalist class."[39] This reaction was undoubtedly magnified by the parallel trend of *declining* corporate profits during this same period and by the shock, in 1973, of the first major oil price increase.[40] The superclass response to these events was to close ranks in support of a concerted, large-scale mobilization for total class war: "The leadership of the capitalist class tended to reject political moderation and, through their inner circle connections, came to share a belief in the need for a right-wing offensive."[41] At the heart of this effort was the conscious creation of political, economic, and cultural strategies for the purpose of waging class war on a scale unprecedented in American history. The general goals of this war were and are to increase corporate profits, the wealth and income of the elite classes, and the political and cultural power held by these classes. The following sections briefly describe the political, economic, and cultural dimensions of this war as if they are distinct and separate features, but in fact they are intertwined and inseparable.

The Political Dimension of the Class War

In the political arena, superclass leaders and their credentialed-class allies wage class war via a variety of organizations and activities that promote their political and economic interests. The primary political interests of the elite classes are to maintain and expand the extensive political power these classes hold and exercise in the political and public policy arena. These interests are pursued by intervening in (or some say manipulating) the "democratic" election and governing processes. The point of intervening is to elect candidates who will enact legislation and produce regulatory policies that support elite-class economic interests. At the same time, efforts are made by and on behalf of the elite classes to legitimize the extent to which their economic resources and political power influence both elections and the content, enactment, and enforcement of public policies and regulations. As we will see, such efforts often involve disguising the nature and extent of elite-class interventions in the election and governing processes. Of course, elite-class leaders are not concerned with influencing *all* types of public policies or regulations. They are primarily concerned only with those that affect their central economic interests of maximizing corporate profits and accumulating ever-higher levels of personal income and wealth. Thus, the elite classes' interest in acquiring, expanding, and wielding political power must be understood for what it is—an important *means* of realizing and reinforcing the economic interests of elites, and often those of the entire privileged class.

To achieve their political and economic objectives, elite-class leaders began mobilizing for class war in the political and public policy arena some forty years ago. The immediate goal of this war in the early 1970s was to blunt growing public support for higher taxes on the rich and large corporations.[42] By 1980, the larger, long-term goal of the war as envisioned and endorsed by superclass leaders involved creating "a modern version of the 1920s economy situated in a global economic system."[43] Class war assaults mounted in the political arena in support of this goal, attacks that continue to this day, center on four specific objectives: first, contest and roll back the New Deal, Great Society, and working-class gains dating from the 1930s to the early 1970s; second, reduce tax rates on wealthy individuals and corporations; third, significantly reduce government spending; fourth, substantially limit the power of federal regulatory agencies.[44]

The early phase of this war began with a dramatic expansion of the organizational and resource base undergirding the elite classes' political lobbying and policy-influencing capacity. Such developments were precisely what Lewis F. Powell Jr. envisioned in a 1971 memorandum to the U.S. Chamber of Commerce two months before his nomination to the U.S. Supreme Court by President Nixon. Powell's memo was the result of a request by his friend Eugene Sydnor, a powerful member of the chamber who believed the American business system was threatened and needed a plan outlining what the chamber could do to help save it. Powell shared Sydnor's concerns and, as a former American Bar Association president and member of top corporate boards, he was well connected and respected within the business community.[45]

In his memo, Powell warned that the free enterprise system was under attack by anti-business forces. He called on the business community to take "direct political action" in support of its shared interests and added that "political power . . . must be used aggressively and with determination."[46] He reminded the business community that success depended not on the actions of individual business leaders or single corporations. Instead, he made the case for developing a unified, class-wide approach in support of shared elite class interests. Powell wrote, "Strength lies in organization, in careful long-range planning and implementation, in consistency of action over an indefinite period of years, in the scale of financing available only through joint effort, and in the political power available only through united action and national organizations."[47] One researcher summarized Powell's message on the need for collective political mobilization and action by the corporate community: "To truly succeed in resetting the terms of American politics, corporations needed to systematize their approach, creating new institutions and giving those institutions sustained support."[48]

The list of heavyweight superclass-supported political lobbying developments that emerged following Powell's memo begins with the Business Roundtable. Organized in 1972 by John Harper, head of Alcoa Aluminum, and Fred Borch, the CEO of General Electric, it included two hundred CEOs from the largest banks and corporations, and it remains one of the most formidable corporate lobbying and policy-setting organization today.[49] In that same year, to further beef up elite-class political pressure on Congress, the National Association of Manufacturers (NAM) moved to Washington, DC. Also, the number of corporations represented by registered lobbyists grew dramatically, from 175 in 1971 to 650 in 1979, and membership in the U.S. Chamber of Commerce more than doubled, from thirty-six thousand in 1967 to eighty thousand in 1974.[50] By 2010, Washington lobbying organizations numbered over two thousand and employed over twelve thousand registered federal lobbyists.[51] "These lobbyists were employed . . . by more than 14,700 companies, unions, trade associations, universities, and other organizations."[52] Of course, most lobbyists and the firms that hire them represent superclass interests. Total lobbying expenditures by all Washington lobbying organizations in 2011 ($3.32 billion) were nearly double the amount of money contributed directly to the campaigns of all congressional candidates in the 2010 elections ($1.86 billion).[53] And, of course, much of the congressional campaign money comes from the same elite-class groups and superclass-controlled organizations that hire Washington lobbyists.

Superclass Funding of Political Campaigns

Powell's memo did not specifically address the issue of increasing corporate support for the political campaigns of candidates sympathetic to the interests of business. Even so, increasing superclass support for the political campaigns of candidates who favor corporate and elite classes' interests *and* legitimizing this support are important aspects of the political dimension of class war. As we will see in chapter 8, the rising costs of political campaigns have led to ever greater dependence, especially at the national level, by Republican and Democratic candidates on two types of funding provided by elite class sources. First, candidates rely on large *direct* campaign contributions—those regulated by federal election laws and Federal Election Commission (FEC) rules. Second, candidates also increasingly rely on substantial *indirect* support for their campaigns—support that takes forms not regulated by FEC rules.

Since the 2010 U.S. Supreme Court's *Citizen United* decision, indirect forms of election campaign funding have grown in importance. The two major vehicles for such funding are super PACs and nonprofit 501(c) "social welfare" groups. Both organizations can legally raise and spend unlimited amounts of money to support candidates running for office.[54] These organizations and the court ruling that begat them have led to the "end of the world as we know it" with regard to election campaign funding. But the effects of these new developments have been entirely predictable. As we will see in chapter 8, compared with the past, they enable the superclass and the corporations they control to exert even greater influence over elections and the legislative process, resulting in the enactment of an ever-expanding range of public policies that support their economic and political interests. They serve as reminders that the political dimension of the class war takes many forms.

The Economic Dimension of the Class War

In the economic arena, superclass leaders wage class war via many of the same organizations that promote their political interests. The general objective of the class war in the economic arena was and is to enact government policies and implement corporate practices that increase both corporate profits and elites' personal wealth and income levels. To achieve this objective, superclass leaders, following the general strategies outlined in Powell's 1971 memo, initiated and continue to support ongoing class war campaigns in five areas central to their economic interests: (1) expand managerial autonomy, (2) restrict workers' rights, (3) reduce workers' wages and benefits, (4) implement international "free trade" agreements, and (5) reduce taxes on large corporations and wealthy individuals.

Campaigns in the first and second areas often involve utilizing superclass organizations and resources in support of lobbying, legal actions, and the reshaping of federal regulatory agencies (when necessary) to expand a wide range of "managerial rights" held by corporate executives. As these rights are expanded, they help ensure the legality of an array of corporate policies—even those implemented to undermine union power (e.g., outsourcing, plant closings, and relocations) in order to reduce labor costs and increase profits. Outsourcing, a practice described in chapter 4, provides an instructive example of how superclass cohesion, managerial rights, and reductions in union power are linked. The term refers to the corporate practice of shifting the production of goods or services from relatively high-wage workers (often unionized) to low-wage, nonunion workers, often in poor nations. The use of outsourcing is often justified by corporate executives in economic terms as necessary to profit growth, but in the class war it is a tactic used to reduce or eliminate union power in a firm or industry.

While many reports on outsourcing have appeared in the media, the *history* of how this corporate practice came to be legally enshrined as a managerial right, thereby making it a legitimate tactic corporations may freely use to undermine unions, is likely unknown to most Americans. It is a history that begins in the 1960s. As Domhoff has pointed out, "Outsourcing first seemed to be a feasible option for reducing union power as far back as 1961, but it took a decade for corporations to make use of it in the face of liberal-labor opposition."[55] In 1961 the National Labor Relations Board ruled that outsourcing did not violate union contracts, but this decision was overturned in 1962 due to the appointment of more liberal board members by President Kennedy. As a result, the corporate community began mobilizing against what many business executives saw as an attack on "management prerogatives," and this effort included firms that had, up to that point, maintained positive relations with unions.[56] Summing up the links between management rights, outsourcing, and attacks on unions, Domhoff observed:

> Top executives from these companies claimed they were willing to bargain with unions over wages, hours, and working conditions, but not over an issue that involved their rights as managers, including their right to weaken unions. Their successful battle, won through court cases and influence on appointments to the National Labor Relations Board, culminated in 1971 with a series of rulings against the need for collective bargaining over management decisions. These decisions opened the way for greater outsourcing, plant relocations, and plant closings.[57]

Following the outsourcing victory, many other notable superclass achievements have been won in the second area of the economic class war—attacks on workers' rights and unions. They stretch from President Reagan's 1981 firing of striking air-traffic controllers to recent state laws reducing or eliminating workers' bargaining rights. High-profile examples include the 2011 passage in Wisconsin of Governor Scott Walker's plan to eliminate most collective bargaining rights for public-sector employees and the approval of "right-to-work" laws in Indiana and Michigan in 2012 (the first such laws to be passed in a decade).[58] Moreover, Governor Walker's victory in the June 5, 2012, recall election that sought his removal from office "is encouraging Republicans in other states to push ahead with their efforts to curtail unions' power."[59] These and many other anti-workers' rights and anti-union developments have been led at the state level by the American Legislative Exchange Council (ALEC). Discussed in chapter 9, ALEC is another key organizational component of the class war that emerged in the early 1970s.

The success of the superclass-initiated war on workers' rights and unions is evident by the forty-year decline in U.S. unionization rates. The share of U.S. workers belonging to trade unions fell from 24 percent in 1973 to 11.3 percent in 2012—the lowest level in eighty years.[60] Among private-sector U.S. workers, only 6.6 percent belonged to unions in 2012, but 36 percent of public-sector (government) workers belonged to unions.[61] However, new state laws attacking public-sector unions are shrinking union membership in that sector. In Wisconsin, for example, "since the new Wisconsin law took effect, the state's second-largest union, the American Federation of State, County and Municipal Employees, has lost nearly half of its members in the state. . . . Wisconsin membership in AFSCME dropped from 63,577 [in 2011] to 34,942 [in 2012]."[62]

The third aspect of the economic class war (reductions in worker compensation) is evident by numerous cases of wage cuts and freezes in both the public and private sectors. A high-profile example of this development was cited earlier in this chapter in our discussion of autoworkers' wages. As we noted, "first-tier" autoworkers' wages have been frozen since 2007 and will remain frozen through 2015; at the same time, "second-tier" autoworkers hired after 2007 (an increasing share of workers in this industry) receive only half the first-tier pay rate.

In the fourth area of the economic class war, the elite classes successfully secured passage and implementation of a number of international "free trade" agreements by the federal government—despite public opinion polls showing a majority of Americans opposed to such trade deals.[63] As we noted in chapter 4, these agreements have been supported by presidents from both political parties beginning with Clinton's support for the 1993 North American Free Trade Agreement (NAFTA). Presidents Bush and Obama followed Clinton's lead by supporting similar trade deals. More recently, president Obama secured congressional passage of and signed "free trade" agreements (negotiated under the Bush administration) with South Korea, Colombia, and Panama. These agreements, as we discuss in chapter 9, will increase corporate profits, expand the U.S. trade deficit, and result in the loss of thousands of American jobs.[64]

In the fifth area of the economic class war, over the past thirty years the elite classes advocated and won large reductions in federal taxes on wealthy individuals and large corporations. In chapter 9 we discuss several major federal tax "reforms," meaning reductions in federal income taxes on the rich and on corporations, enacted over the 1981–2012 period. As we will see in more detail in chapter 9, the success of the economic class war in reducing taxes on the rich is evident by the sharp decline in federal income tax rates on this group.

As an illustrative snapshot of how far taxes on the wealthy have fallen, let's consider some "tax facts." The federal tax rate on incomes over $808,680 (in 2010 dollars) fell from 70 percent in 1975 to 50 percent in 1985, to 39.6 percent in 1995, and to 35 percent in 2011.[65] While this 50 percent drop in tax rates was substantial, the decline since 1955 in *effective* federal tax rates for the highest-income Americans was even greater. Internal Revenue Service (IRS) data show that in 1955 the top 398 U.S. taxpayers had average incomes of $13.2 million (in 2009 dollars). After exploiting every tax loophole available, these taxpayers paid 51.2 percent of their 1955 incomes in federal income taxes (an average of $6.76 million each). In sharp contrast, in 2009 the top four hundred U.S. taxpayers had average incomes of $202.4 million (illustrating the growing concentration of income at the top). After taking advantage of the generous tax cuts and loopholes provided by federal "tax reforms," especially those passed since 1980, in 2009 the top four hundred paid just 19.9 percent of their incomes in federal income taxes (an average of $40.3 million each).[66]

The Cultural Dimension of the Class War

In the cultural arena, superclass leaders wage class war via a number of for-profit and nonprofit organizations to *promote* an array of ideas that legitimate the numerous inequalities generated by the economic and political dimensions of the class war. At the same time, class war in this arena is waged *against* ideas that would reinforce or promote the economic and political interests of the working class. The purpose of the cultural dimension of the class war is to shape the content of culture in ways that promote widespread public acceptance of the ideas, values, and worldview of the elite classes—a universally accepted superclass "cultural narrative."

All types of "cultural products" are the focus of class war in this area. Obvious examples include news, information, commentary, and entertainment disseminated by large media firms via electronic and print formats. Print products include, for example, newspapers, magazines, books, and even textbooks. Electronic products include, for example, television programming (e.g., news, commentary, entertainment), movies, websites, blogs, and video games. Less obvious examples of cultural products are those produced by nonprofit, superclass-funded organizations such as conservative think tanks like the American Enterprise Institute, the Heritage Foundation, and many others. These organizations produce and disseminate to corporate media outlets, pundits, members of Congress, and other "opinion leaders" large numbers of books, policy papers, and press releases designed to mobilize public and governmental support for so-called conservative ideas, views, and policy preferences. The materials they distribute typically provide the ideological rationale (e.g., "free markets," "neoliberalism") and "empirical evidence" (selectively chosen "facts") justifying policies that would "reform" (often via "privatization" schemes) government programs and institutions anathema to superclass values, interests, and policy preferences (e.g., Social Security, Medicare, Medicaid, public schools).

It is our view that much of the content woven into many of the cultural products noted above is both *class-biased* and *socially potent*. By class-biased we mean that the content tends to reflect and reinforce the values and interests of the elite classes. This means, in part, that most of the content of widely shared cultural products is framed and communicated in ways that tend to ignore, conceal, marginalize, contest, disguise, or misrepresent class inequalities and the ways such inequalities favor the interests of the elite classes; such content also typically fails to identify or legitimate the class-based interests and grievances of workers.

By socially potent we mean that the widely disseminated body of elite-class-biased cultural content powerfully, but indirectly, influences the economic, political, and social perspectives, attitudes, and opinions held by large numbers of working- and privileged-class members in ways that favor the interests of the elite classes. We view this content as influencing consciousness through the power of "cultural hegemony"—what we envision as a largely invisible but potent force field at the center of the cultural arena emanating from elite-class-based resources and elite-class-biased ideas. This hegemonic force field shapes the components and contours of culture in directions and forms that largely serve the elite classes' interests.[67]

As we illustrate in chapters 12 and 13, the potency of elite-class-biased content infused into cultural products is significant. It influences peoples' information-processing abilities, including how they understand and interpret economic, political, and social events or developments. It helps shape their preferences on public issues, public policy priorities, and even their entertainment and popular culture choices. Thus, what people imagine to be *their own* ideas, opinions, and preferences in many areas are in fact derived from the consumption of cultural products infused with class-biased content that reflects and serves the interests of the elite classes, not those of the working class. We view elite-class disseminated cultural products as helping to prevent the development, among workers, of *class consciousness* that reflects their own interests.[68]

An example from the 1980s illustrates how "cultural products," in this case policy documents produced by superclass-funded conservative think tanks, can influence national political discourse and help shape public policies. In 1980, the Heritage Foundation published a 1,100-page paperback volume titled *Mandate for Change*. It provided a "conservative blueprint" for eliminating virtually all of the progressive social and tax policies enacted in the twentieth century; it also included a "fact-based" narrative supporting and justifying its policy reversal proposals. Despite the transparent ideological nature of this document, the ideas and policy suggestions it contained were endorsed by elite national opinion leaders and the Reagan administration. As one example of the cultural dimension of class war, this document provided potent ammunition in support of ideas and policies favored by elite-class leaders. A progressive pundit commenting years later on the policy significance of this publication observed, "The Reagan White House . . . put into play nearly two-thirds of the recommendations this blueprint . . . advanced. By 1989, the New Deal would never be deader. Taxes on the rich would never be lower."[69] (Actually, taxes on the rich dropped even more in the 1990s–2000s, and even more New Deal programs were cut.)

THE ICEBERG OF INEQUALITY:
CLASS WAR, MAINTENANCE, AND LEGITIMATION

"To maintain their power and privilege, elites have learned to . . . exploit nonelites without their realizing they are being exploited."

—Harold R. Kerbo, *Social Stratification and Inequality* (2012), 408

As we have suggested, many aspects of the class war are visible and obvious—like the ice peak soaring above the submerged mass of a large iceberg. But beneath the waterline are less obvious features of the class war. These include the structures and processes used to conduct the war, to disguise some of the most obvious class war tactics and assaults, and to maintain and legitimate the highly unequal new class system. Of course, elite classes in stratified societies have always devoted a portion of their considerable resources to subduing dissent, reinforcing inequalities, and legitimating the class system, thereby ensuring their continued possession of disproportionate levels of wealth, power, and privilege. However, the problems of maintaining and legitimating the increasingly unequal new class system have been rendered more complex by the class war, which has intensified class inequalities, and by the tension between those inequalities and the relentless, media-driven promotion of the American dream as a cultural ideal. Thus, current class war strategies associated with its conduct and with the maintenance and legitimation of growing class inequalities combine sophisticated extensions of approaches used in the past with emerging, innovative forms of control and distraction.

The Class-Power-Network Model

Our perspective on how the class war is conducted and disguised as well as how the unequal new class system is maintained and legitimated is based on an organizational model of class interests and power. It views large firms as repositories of superclass resources and also as dominant sources of power in virtually all sectors of society. According to this approach, elite class leaders use corporate-based resources to create, fund, and control extensive, overlapping organizational networks within the economic, political, and cultural social arenas. These networks consist of organizations linked by various connections such as interlocked board members, shared public policy interests, and common goals—including the maintenance and legitimation of concentrated wealth and power held by the elite classes.

In the economic arena, network examples include superclass-controlled trade associations and peak corporate groups—such as the Business Roundtable. Superclass-funded think tanks, lobbying organizations, super PACs, and 501(c) groups are examples of organizational networks within the political arena. In the cultural arena, network examples include the corporate media, superclass-funded think tanks, superclass-controlled organizations such as foundations and civic and cultural entities, and the boards of trustees at elite universities. We view these interlocked organizational networks as directed by elite class leaders who use them to design and implement class war strategies and tactics that reinforce the shared economic, political, and cultural interests of their class. These include attacking unions; legitimating corporate autonomy, power, profit maximization, and class inequalities; and maintaining the organizational structure of the new class system so as to perpetuate the advantaged positions, interests, and privileges of the elite classes. However, we also maintain that the organizations within these networks typically present public facades that disguise or deemphasize their elite class biases and the ways they function as surrogate actors in support of elite class interests.

Although our class-power model views elite class leaders as participating in conscious and deliberate activities such as class war strategies and tactics to protect and advance their shared class interests, it is not based on a conspiracy theory of power. We do not view superclass leaders as a group that secretly conspires to promote its interests and maintain class inequalities. Rather, following G. William Domhoff, we view the coordinated, interest-supporting activities of the "power elite," consisting of superclass leaders and their credentialed-class allies, as grounded in a complex structural system populated by a relatively homogeneous group that is similar in many important respects.[70] Superclass leaders tend to have similar elite educational backgrounds, to be officers of large, interlocked firms, and to be members of a small number of elite social and cultural organizations. The elite, class-based, family, business, and social experiences of this group lead to shared common values, worldviews, and commitments to maintaining the status quo.[71] From where superclass leaders stand, life is good and the system works. The shared culture of the elite classes leads not to conspiracy but rather to an authentic boosterism for the corporate model and the "magic of the market." There's no need for a conspiracy when the most common question among superclass leaders is this: "Why change what works? (for us!)"

Dominant Class-Power Networks

Figure 6.1 illustrates the main features of our class-power-network model. At the top, the model views the dominant class power base as grounded in the power elite—the organizationally active superclass leaders and their credentialed-class allies (see chapter 7). This group is centrally involved in directing and coordinating the three overlapping corporate-based dominant power networks. Class war strategies as well as those associated with the maintenance and legitimation of all forms of class inequalities extend downward through four basic social institutions: the national economy, the state, media and culture, and the educational system. Chapters 7–14 in part explore how the class war and the maintenance and legitimation strategies identified by the model are linked to organizational policies and practices directed by elite class leaders. And they illustrate how these strategies and related policies serve elite class interests and those of many members of the privileged class—especially by helping to expand, perpetuate, and legitimate structured inequalities within the new class society.

By focusing on the top half of the model, we can begin to see how the abstract notion of superclass dominance is channeled through real organizations that collectively merge into powerful networks. From the top down, the dominant power networks pursue elite class interests through corporate-based activities penetrating the four routine institutional structures of society. As we will see, the corporate practices and public policies that emerge from these structural linkages weave class war strategies as well as those of legitimation, co-optation, distraction, and coercion into a dense organizational web that sustains the new class system's inequalities.

Members of both the working and privileged classes are targeted by the dominant power networks depicted by the model. Specific public policies, programs, business practices, and cultural ideas that extend, maintain, and legitimate elite class interests, the corporate empire, and class inequalities are routinely and repeatedly directed at working-class members and privileged-class consumers through the four basic social institutions shown in the model.

For members of the working class, the cumulative effects of lives lived under super-class-dominated social institutions encourage acceptance of class hierarchies, extensive corporate power, and the inequalities associated with these arrangements. The working class is constantly reminded by ideas and experiences infused into the cultural fabric that private businesses are "good" but public enterprises are "bad" (or at best they are inefficient).[72] Such reminders come, for example, from oligopolistic corporations that control the economy (e.g., finance, insurance, media), corporate-funded bashing of big government (e.g., by "conservative" politicians, the Fox News Channel, media pundits like Rush Limbaugh), and corporate-media celebrations of the free enterprise system (e.g., CNBC programs like *Mad Money* and the *Kudlow Report*).

In short, working-class behaviors and attitudes are shaped in ways that promote public acceptance (ideological legitimation) of class inequalities. Such outcomes ensure that the distribution of capital resources in the new class society remains relatively unchallenged and unchanged: A small number of highly rewarded positions are reserved for members of the elite classes within the privileged-class top diamond while virtually everyone located in the new-working-class bottom diamond is restricted to a narrow range of low-reward positions. — How did this happen?

Alternative Class-Power Networks

Of course, the top portion of figure 6.1 is only part of the story. At the bottom of the figure we find an alternative class-power base grounded in several organizations and groups. The labor movement along with other progressive groups such as many women's rights, civil rights, environmental, gay rights, "net roots," media-reform organizations, and some religious groups form the heart of three overlapping alternative power networks. These alternative networks challenge, with varying degrees of vigor and with limited resources, class war strategies and tactics, inequality–extending and -maintaining policies, and the legitimation messages all of which flow via dominant power networks into the economy, the state, media, culture and the schools.

The alternative-network dimension of our model underscores the point that we do not equate superclass dominance in the economic, political, and cultural arenas with total control. On one hand, class war is waged and class inequalities are expanded, maintained, and legitimated by the actions, policies, and ideas orchestrated by superclass-sponsored and credentialed-class-managed organizations within the dominant power networks. But on the other hand, all of these activities and ideas are subject to challenges by alternative-power-network actors in the economic, political, and cultural arenas, with labor unions serving as the core organizational force.

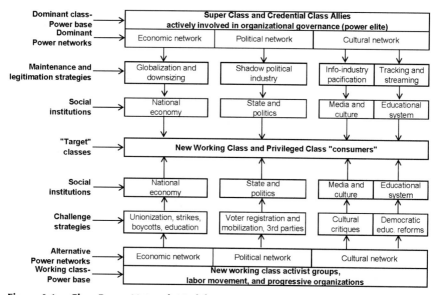

Figure 6.1.   Class-Power Network Model

Our inclusion of trade unions as a key feature of the alternative power networks does not mean we view unions as speaking with a single voice for workers or that we view all unions as consistent progressive advocates for workers' common class interests. We recognize that the labor movement includes diverse and sometimes contradictory trends and actions. Even so, among organizational alternatives to corporate power, trade unions possess the greatest concentration of human and economic resources and represent the most significant alternative organizational force countering elite class corporate dominance—which helps explain why they are frequent targets of the superclass-led class war. But this recognition does not diminish the importance of other organizations and groups in the alternative power networks—some of which are linked to leaders and funding sources with privileged-class backgrounds. Such groups, often in conjunction with unions, frequently challenge class war initiatives and activities that seek to expand, maintain, and legitimate class inequalities through the dominant power networks.

The Clash of Conflicting Class Interests

We believe the interests of the working class, in contrast with those of the elite classes, trend in the direction of reducing class-based economic, political, and cultural inequalities. This means, first, that workers have economic interests in receiving a much larger share of the value of the goods and services they produce in the form of

higher wages as well as more extensive and secure benefits. Such outcomes would occur at the expense of superclass owners of productive property and their credentialed-
class allies by reducing profit margins. Second, workers have political interests in
contesting superclass-privileged class control of government in order to use law and
public policies on behalf of the working class as instruments for reducing economic
and political class inequalities. For example, workers' opportunities and economic
security would be enhanced by an expansion of the social wage including increased
public-sector spending on education, a national health care system, and a substantial
expansion of environmental protection policies. Third, at the cultural level, workers
have interests in producing and disseminating cultural products and components
(via, for example, nonprofit media outlets, the Internet, and public schools) that
would explore and expose the wide range of class-based inequalities favoring elite
class interests and legitimate the class-based interests and grievances of workers.

Our view of the existence of conflicting class interests does not mean we see all
segments of the elite classes and the working class as equally aware of or equally well
organized to work toward the active realization of their interests. On the contrary,
as chapters 7–9 illustrate, we see members of the elite classes, especially those in the
superclass, as much more conscious of their collective class interests, more cohesive
in pursuing them, and in possession of much greater and more unified organizational
resources than the working class. The net result is that compared with the working
class, the elite classes at the peak of the privileged class, led by the superclass, are
much more aware of, and able to effectively pursue and realize, their common class
interests.

Inequality and Inequity

The efforts of alternative power network groups to promote economic, political,
and social policy changes that would reduce class-, gender-, and racial/ethnic-based
inequalities call attention to the distinction between inequality and inequity. *Inequality* refers to the objective reality (factually verifiable) that various distinct and
identifiable groups (e.g., class, gender, racial/ethnic groups) receive unequal shares
of various forms of scarce and valued resources distributed within the society. For
example, much of the evidence presented thus far concerning differences in the distribution of consumption and investment capital illustrates that the highly unequal
economic and political outcomes people experience in the United States are often
based on their membership in class, gender, and racial/ethnic-based groups.

Inequity refers to a subjective judgment that the unequal access to scarce and
valued resources experienced by groups distinguished by class, gender, and/or racial/
ethnic membership is unfair and unjust. This concept interprets the organizationally
based policies and practices used as the bases for unequally distributing scarce and
valued resources as fundamentally flawed in the sense that they arbitrarily privilege
some groups over others and thereby violate basic standards of fairness in the dis-

tributional process. Thus, people who observe class and other group-based forms of inequality through the lens of inequity view organizational policies and practices that produce highly unequal resource outcomes for such groups as requiring substantial revision and change.[73] From an inequity perspective, class, gender, and racial inequalities in areas such as the distribution of income, wealth, health care, economic security, and educational and occupational opportunities are not viewed simply as reflections of merit-based distributional processes; rather, they tend to be viewed as evidence of fundamental biases and flaws embedded in a variety of distributional processes that perpetuate unfair economic, political, and cultural advantages of existing privileged-class groups at the expense of nonprivileged-class groups.

Almost by definition, a worldview of class (and other) inequalities based on an inequity interpretation necessitates and legitimates changes in the economic, political, and cultural arenas aimed at substantially narrowing the current range of inequalities. This is the orientation and approach taken by most individuals and groups that are part of the alternative power networks. While most participants in these networks are unlikely to envision total equality as a realistic goal, the pursuit of *equity*—the distribution of scarce and valued resources in a fair and just manner—does appear to be a widely shared objective among the members of these networks.

Of course, it is possible to argue that substantial inequalities are legitimate and justified. For example, contemporary justifications of class inequalities are often grounded in Herbert Spencer's late-nineteenth-century ideology of social Darwinism. Spencer celebrated the supposed superiority of the wealthy, viewed the poor as inferior and deserving of their fate, and justified class inequalities on the basis of a pseudoscience of "survival of the fittest."[74] Echoes of Spencer's views still resonate strongly in the United States today—especially among the elite classes.[75] For example, research indicates that individuals with higher-class backgrounds are more likely than those with lower-class backgrounds to view people with higher-level occupations and educations as deserving greater incomes than people with lower-level occupations and educations.[76]

THE ICEBERG, THE DREAM, AND THE DETAILS

"Titanic came around the curve, into the Great Iceberg. Fare thee, Titanic, Fare thee well."

—Leadbelly (H. Ledbetter), "Fare Thee Well, Titanic" (1912)

As the *Titanic* sinking a century ago reminds us, icebergs can be treacherous—especially the huge frozen mass below the waterline. Our exploration of the hidden portion of the class iceberg is also fraught with danger, though not of the physical sort. Because of the taboo nature of class analysis, people are less likely to venture below the waterline of conventional social analysis. Down there, visibility is limited and images are murky. Dangers of miscommunication and misunderstanding abound. And those in "respectable quarters" claim it is unproductive or even un-American to make the trip: Better to stick with the dream than explore the iceberg. Even so, we'll take our chances. We think the potential rewards are worth the risks, and we invite you to join us.

In the following chapters we continue our tour of territory that for most Americans is familiar and yet, in many ways, unknown. Our class-power-network model serves as the basic map for exploring several hidden features of the new class system. As we will see, the dominant power networks are not abstract, ivory-tower inventions but real organizational webs of power we all encounter daily. By tracking the strategies and activities of superclass-dominated organizations, the model helps us understand how this class dominates organizations, public policies, programs, ideas, and social behavior in the economic, political, and cultural arenas.

Like a magnifying glass, the model serves as a lens bringing into focus the ways the dominant power networks are used to wage class war and to maintain and legitimate the many inequalities of the new class system. Using this lens, we will explore how the web of power spun by the dominant power networks impacts the election and governing processes and public views on superclass-favored policies and regulations and how it influences the production and distribution of values and beliefs related to personal fulfillment, the mass consumption of goods and services, and the uses of work and leisure time. And we will use it to explore how and why the cultural dimension of the dominant power networks is especially useful in legitimating class inequalities. As we will see in chapters 10–13, the cultural network is important in this regard because it includes potent organizations (e.g., the corporate news media, commercial websites, schools, corporate entertainment media) that disseminate ideas, information, and images that not only help legitimate numerous inequalities embedded in the new class system but also often serve as vehicles for distracting public attention away from the class war and related class inequalities.

The class-power-network model will also help us see and better understand another important dimension of the class iceberg—the "underdogs" of class conflict. The alternative-power-networks portion of the model provides us with a map for understanding how dominant-power-network strategies, policies, programs, and ideas favoring elite class interests are contested and challenged in specific terms by real organizations and real people. These challenges are grounded in an agenda based on fair play, an end to arbitrary class inequalities, and greater opportunities for all Americans to actually achieve the American dream—rather than to continue the present course where the dream is betrayed and crushed by the massive iceberg of class inequalities.

For those who may be interested in joining the cause of justice in the class war, it might be useful to consider how you would answer this question: "Is your hate pure?" It is a question the late radical journalist Alexander Cockburn "would ask a new *Nation* intern, one eyebrow raised, in merriment or inquisition the intern was unsure. It was a startling question, but then this was—still is—a startling time. For what the ancients called avarice and inequity Alex's hate was pure, and across the years no writer had a deadlier sting against the cruelties and dangerous illusions, the corruptions of empire."[77] When Alex died in 2012, the working class lost one of its most articulate and passionate advocates. Now more than ever, the cause, his cause, needs new recruits who will answer his question: Yes!

7

The Invisible Class Empire

> "The way our ruling class keeps out of sight is one of the greatest stunts in the political history of any country."
>
> —Gore Vidal, *Progressive* (September 1986)

Americans have an enduring interest in how powerful and invisible forces impact people's lives and the world around us. It is often manifested by a fascination with mysterious paranormal and supernatural story lines—such as those in the *Paranormal Activity* and *Twilight* film series as well as television dramas including *Fringe, Supernatural*, and *The Vampire Diaries*. A common script device in this genre uses cryptic remarks as clues to elusive truths that, if understood, can unlock mysteries embedded in the unfolding drama. Viewers are led to believe these clues will help them figure out what's going on, but mysterious events—often linked to paranormal phenomena or shadowy and sinister human interventions—keep "the truth" just out of reach.

Like the viewers of such tales, we also believe it's possible to unravel elusive truths about what's *really* going on. But unlike fans of the paranormal, our focus is on the reality of economic and political inequalities rather than fictional events in shadowy settings. More specifically, our concern in this chapter is with superclass political power and evidence that reveals "the truth" about this highly charged issue. As Vidal's quote suggests, ruling-class political dominance is a long-standing, but typically unacknowledged and unexplored, feature of American society. Occasionally, it has been candidly recognized—sometimes by writers of elite-class origins such as Vidal as well as by players at the top of the political game. President Woodrow Wilson once observed that "the masters of the government of the United States are the combined capitalists and manufacturers of the U.S."[1] However, such public candor is rare and may entail negative personal and professional consequences. Vidal, for example,

maintained that his public musings on ruling-class political power earned him un-
dying elite enmity as a class traitor and that, as a result, both he and his work were
marginalized and demonized by the elite-class-controlled media.[2]

Superclass elites have long recognized that publicly acknowledged, front-page
robber-baron plutocracy is inconsistent with American cultural ideals of democracy
and political equality—and dangerous to their interests. Up-front publicity revealing
the nature and extent of superclass political dominance would magnify the tensions
between democratic ideals and concentrated class-power realities by calling into
question the institutional legitimacy of American politics and public policy. For
these reasons, superclass leaders prefer to keep the existence of and details about the
extent of their class-based power out of sight.

THE INVISIBLE EMPIRE AND THE GOLDEN TRIANGLE

> "It is the interaction of class and organizational imperatives at the top of all Ameri-
> can organizations, including government institutions, that leads to [upper] class
> domination in the United States."
>
> —G. William Domhoff, *Who Rules America?* (2010), 219

We believe the superclass preference is for Americans to know less, not more, about
"the truth that is out there" concerning the invisible class empire that dominates our
national political system. The term *invisible class empire* refers to the hidden structures and processes through which leaders of the "elite classes" (i.e., the superclass
and its credentialed-class allies) penetrate and dominate the American political system. And it refers to the processes used to disguise this reality as well as the concealed
political, economic, and cultural dimensions of elite-class power.

It is an empire in the sense that the leadership of the elite classes has crafted a
far-flung and widely dispersed collection of resources, organizations, and processes
into a coherent political force that ensures the perpetuation of not only elite class interests but also the interests of large segments of the privileged class. It is invisible in
the sense that the class-based dimensions of the resources and control processes that
undergird the empire are largely excluded from American public attention. In the
political arena, the silence of incumbents, wannabes, and pundits on elite class power
promotes public inattention. In the cultural arena, public inattention grows out of
an almost total mass-media blackout of reporting on the empire combined with a
nearly total neglect of the subject by the U.S. educational system—at all levels.

As we noted in chapter 6, superclass leaders and their credentialed-class allies
who guide and direct this empire are sometimes referred to as the "power elite."[3] At
the top, this group consists of superclass leaders active in organizational governance
(e.g., corporations, government). It shades downward to include a second tier of
semi-autonomous, credentialed-class executives and managers. This junior partner
portion of the power elite includes upwardly mobile corporate officers, national

political leaders and office holders, federal lobbyists, and other specialists drawn largely from the credentialed class. These groups directly assist superclass power elite leaders or indirectly serve their interests. All of these groups together, with superclass leadership at the center, form a kind of directorate that charts and oversees general economic and political policies as well as routine institutional practices necessary to maintain the class empire.

This chapter begins the process of peeling back the cloak of invisibility that shields the empire by exposing the organizational foundations of what we call the golden triangle of class power. As figure 7.1 illustrates, superclass resources, grounded in the investment capital that members of this class personally hold or control as corporate officers, serve as the basis for financing and controlling two major "industries." The shadow political industry (explored here and in chapters 8 and 9) and the information industry (explored in chapter 10) both drive and conceal superclass power. The convergence of these twin structures leads to *superclass political dominance.* This term refers to the ways the routine operation of the two industries promotes superclass domination over public policy issues that involve the core economic and political interests of this class. It also reflects the reality that superclass ownership of the media and its control over many nonprofit organizations that influence culture (e.g., elite universities) provides this class with substantial cultural influence (e.g., to shape public opinion and popular culture content), which has important political and class power implications and consequences.

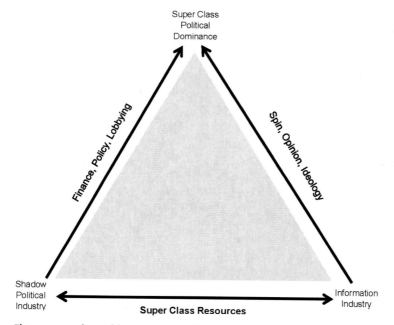

Figure 7.1. The Golden Triangle of Class Power

Control everything keeping them there?

How could they fall out of the loop when they are the...

The shadow political industry extends upward as the left flank of the triangle. It consists of several real-life organizations that provide the political muscle underlying the class empire. This industry parallels, or shadows, all branches of the federal government, federal elections, and federal public policy–making processes. Largely created, funded, and dominated by the superclass, this industry's core consists of four interrelated, organizationally based communities: (1) the federal lobbying community—Washington, DC–area lobbying groups largely funded by superclass-based resources to influence policy-making in Congress and federal agencies; (2) the political finance community—superclass and corporate donors fund the election campaigns of candidates for federal offices (president and congress) via contributions to candidates and to "independent" groups for "outside spending" on election activities; (3) the policy-planning community—superclass-funded think tanks, research institutes, policy discussion groups, and foundations develop short- and long-term policies supporting elite class interests; (4) the classwide lobbying community—"peak" corporate groups (e.g., the Business Roundtable, corporate coalitions, and corporate-professional alliances) conduct lobbying campaigns to advance the shared economic and political interests of the elite classes. The goal of this industry is to intervene in the political arena in ways that protect and advance superclass economic and political interests. Its primary "product" is dominance of politics and government—meaning the election and governing processes. This chapter explores the first community; chapter 8 explores the second community; chapter 9 explores the third and fourth communities.

The information industry anchors the right flank of the triangle. Grounded in the largest mass media corporations, this industry serves superclass members' political and economic interests in two ways. First, much of the news and commentary disseminated by firms at the heart of this industry help legitimate or conceal the nature and extent of superclass power. Second, large portions of the megaprofits generated through the operations of large media firms are channeled back to superclass owners, with smaller profit shares flowing to credentialed-class, second-tier media executives and managers.[4] This industry operates via three interrelated control processes generating the information, ideas, images, and commentary (economic, political, social) that reinforce superclass interests. Explored in detail in chapter 10, these are (1) the mainstream ideology process, (2) the opinion-shaping process, and (3) the spin-control process.

The structures and processes of both industries converge at the top of the triangle into *superclass political dominance*. This term, as noted earlier, refers to the domination of superclass interests over class-relevant political and economic public-policy outcomes as well as their potent influence in shaping cultural content. As we will see, public-policy and cultural-content outcomes often reflect and reinforce superclass dominance by legitimating or disguising (or both) the nature, extent, and consequences of superclass power generally. In the political and economic arenas, superclass leaders, along with their credentialed-class allies, are viewed as directing and controlling most major class-relevant national public policy outcomes. Examples of superclass-dominated policy outcomes, especially those resulting from classwide lobbying (e.g., federal tax rates on the wealthy), are discussed in chapter 9. The concept of superclass political dominance also includes the idea that elite class leaders influence cultural content in ways that reinforce superclass interests. This influence occurs through the information industry, which disseminates news and commentary friendly to superclass interests. And it occurs through the "culture industry," which shapes the content of popular culture, including entertainment "products," in ways that often reinforce superclass interests. Elite class leaders' influence of cultural content via the information and culture industries is explored in chapters 10 and 13.

The triangle model develops selected features of the more general class-power-network model introduced in chapter 6, but it does not attempt to address all dimensions or features of superclass power. Even so, it provides a powerful tool for conceptualizing the core of superclass economic, political, and cultural power in the United States. By locating superclass power and dominance in organizationally based resources, structures, and processes driven by class interests and unified by a class-based ideology, the model avoids conspiracy-based theories as the basis for understanding superclass cohesion and power.

The model also calls attention to the reality that many superclass leaders often know and interact with one another because they occupy interlocked top positions in large organizations; in addition, they control high levels of investment capital, participate in overlapping corporate, political, and social arenas, and come from similar class backgrounds. These circumstances, combined with high levels of investment, consumption, social, and skill capital held by superclass members and their credentialed-class allies, serve as the foundation for a widely shared worldview, or political-economy ideology. This idea system blends assumptions grounded in elite-class interests concerning how the political and economic systems should be organized and function together. In general, it tends to view the political and economic status quo as reasonable, legitimate, and just.[5] The model views the common bonds of economic resources, interests, social identity, and ideology as foundations upon which elite-class leaders create, maintain, and justify the linked structures and processes that drive the triangle.

Acting on the basis of a shared worldview and through routine organizational structures and processes, elite-class leaders orchestrate political strategies and media policies that preserve and expand their wealth, power, and privilege. The model views those at the top as holding a strong, shared sense that the "system" works and as pursuing concerted, but nonconspiratorial, strategies and tactics that preserve it.[6]

THE SHADOW POLITICAL INDUSTRY

"I think the current system is rigged, frankly, in favor of the wealthy."

—Newt Gingrich, televised interview (*Too Much* [June 18, 2012]: 1)

Although the shadow political industry is not a totally new development, in the new class system this flank of the triangle has expanded to unprecedented levels of size, complexity, and sophistication. Compared with the recent past, this industry has also become a much more widely shared, class-collaborative project linking super-class leaders with growing numbers of credentialed-class allies and with lower-tier

privileged-class professionals who work, either directly or indirectly, on behalf of superclass interests. These professionals possess specialized lobbying, political finance,
policy-planning, legal, research, and communication skills plus informal political
contacts that are critical to the maintenance of superclass interests and power.

Nonstop media coverage of the 2012 U.S. presidential campaign produced mo-
ments of rare candor regarding the power of the superclass when some political leaders
made unexpected comments, such as Gingrich's quote at the start of this section, which
seemed to confirm what many suspected: the wealthy largely control U.S. politics, elections, and government. The extent of political power held by the wealthy has also been
partially revealed by media reports on two issues: (1) influence peddling in Congress
by wealthy special-interest groups and their well-paid lobbyists—especially those representing Wall Street; (2) the U.S. Supreme Court *Citizens United* decision (explored
in chapter 8) permitting unlimited spending by the rich and corporations to influence
elections.[7] Such reports have helped call public attention to some superficial features of
the first two shadow industry communities. Even so, the corporate media continues its
long-standing practice of *not* reporting on the policy-planning and classwide lobbying
communities. They remain largely unnamed and unknown to most Americans.

Despite a lack of detailed reporting on the shadow political industry, recent polls
suggest many Americans are aware of and concerned about features of this industry
that are known to them—especially those that adversely impact democratic elections
and government. For example, *nearly two-thirds* of Americans polled say the *Citizens
United* decision negatively affects elections.[8] Another survey found *over two-thirds* of
Americans think that lobbyists, major corporations, banks, and financial institutions
have too much power.[9] A third poll found *fewer than one-third* of Americans believe the
federal government is honest and addresses people's needs.[10] Given these views, it is not
surprising that an earlier *New York Times* poll found 77 percent of Americans believed
that lobbyists bribing members of Congress "is the way things work in congress."[11] Such
results indicate the public is aware of *some* of the most visible features of the wealth-
corporate-government linkages found in the iceberg-like shadow political industry. But
we think Americans need to know much more about this industry—including (1) the
class-based organizational structures and processes that undergird its various components
and (2) the way it adversely impacts our democratic traditions and institutions, including open debates on public issues, fair elections, and representative government.

FEDERAL LOBBYING:
ELITE-CLASS INFLUENCE IN WASHINGTON

"Corporations spend far more money on lobbying than their officers give to political candidates."

—G. William Domhoff, *Who Rules America?*, 6th ed. (2010), 176

Class collaboration in the shadow industry is particularly evident in the large numbers of credentialed-class professionals who work for the numerous organizations

that are part of this industry—including those employed by several lobbying firms located in the Washington, DC, area. Most of these firms represent superclass-controlled organizations and actively lobby both the Congress and federal agencies on behalf of their interests. To accommodate superclass-connected clients, Washington lobbying firms employ a small army of professional lobbyists and spend billions of dollars annually. This "army" is deployed along two fronts. The first front involves special interests. Much lobbying by and on behalf of superclass-controlled corporations and industries seeks legislative or regulatory favors (e.g., tax breaks, reductions in regulations) that will advance their short-term interests. This kind of special interest lobbying often produces narrow economic advantages for a specific firm or industry and for a small group of superclass owners and investors. The second front involves classwide interests. What we call classwide lobbying is aimed at producing federal policies that advance the economic and political interests of virtually all elite class members but harm working-class interests. From our perspective, classwide lobbying is far more significant than special interest lobbying because it has been a crucial factor in creating, maintaining, and hardening our highly unequal new class system; yet, despite its importance to the class structure, it receives no coverage by the mainstream media and is seldom studied by academic researchers.

Members of the federal lobbying community participate in both lobbying types described above. We will take a closer look at both types in chapter 9, but before we get to that chapter, here we explore the class-based and class-biased nature of the federal lobbying community. Attorneys figure prominently in this community because as a group they often possess the knowledge, skills, and political contacts essential to effectively influence congressional and agency policy-making processes. While not all DC-area attorneys are lobbyists, some DC lawyers own well-known lobbying firms, many others either work directly for lobbying firms or perform contract work for such firms, and some are *former* lobbyists who have taken jobs *in* Congress.[12] In recent years there has been a substantial increase in the number of DC attorneys, which has paralleled the growth of the Washington lobbying community. For example, in 2012, more than 80,000 attorneys were members of the District of Columbia Bar, compared with 73,000 in 2001 (up from 10,925 in 1972).[13] Based on data reported per the federal Lobbying Disclosure Act (LDA) of 1995, the number of unique, registered lobbyists who have actively lobbied in Washington grew from 10,408 in 1998 to 12,655 in 2011.[14] Although this group is relatively large, the LDA definition of a lobbyist is very narrow and does not cover many professionals involved in lobbying activities such as "'strategic advisors' and consultants who devise lobbying strategies."[15] Using more expansive definitions of lobbyists than set forth by the LDA and also recognizing that some lobbyists fail to register, the total Washington-area lobbying community is estimated by some analysts to include at least eighty thousand and maybe more than one hundred thousand lobbyists.[16]

Focusing only on the conservative LDA reporting requirements, we can see that lobbying is a big business within the shadow political industry. According to LDA reports, total lobbying expenditures reached $3.32 billion in 2011, up from $1.44 billion in 1998. As a result of continued increases in the numbers of lobbyists and lobby spending, in 2011 there were twenty-four active lobbyists and $6.1 million in annual lobbying expenditures *for each member of Congress*—compared to nineteen active lobbyists and $2.6 million in annual lobbying expenditures per each congressional member in 1998.[17] To more fully comprehend the *scale* of congressional lobbying expenditures, it is useful to recall, as noted in chapter 6, that the *reported* expenditures of all Washington lobbying firms in 2011 ($3.32 billion) were nearly double the amount of money contributed *directly* to all congressional candidates in the 2010 elections ($1.86 billion).

Lobbyists are likely to have favorable access to members of Congress and federal agencies not only because of the resources they command but also because of personal connections many have with current members of Congress and federal agency heads. Illustrative of these links are the approximately four hundred current and former members of Congress who "have appeared as paid lobbyists or foreign agents in the past decade."[18] Examples include former Senate majority leaders Robert Dole and Trent Lott, former House majority leaders Richard Armey and Richard Gephardt, and former House speakers Newt Gingrich and Dennis Hastert.[19] Of the members of Congress who left office since 1998, 43 percent had registered to lobby by the mid-2000s.[20] In addition to members of Congress, nearly 5,400 current and former congressional staff members have gone through the "lobbying 'revolving door' in the past decade"—meaning they left congressional staff positions to go to work as lobbyists. Of this large group, "more than 2,900 filed lobbying paperwork in 2011, indicating they are currently lobbying."[21] At the same time, some lobbyists are leaving their jobs to work in Congress and federal agencies. For example, "605 former lobbyists have gone to work for members of congress in the past decade."[22] What explains this "reverse lobbying revolving door"? While the reasons vary, one experienced insider suggested that "lobbyists return to Congress not for the salary, but because it can help polish their résumés. . . . It's an opportunity to embellish their backgrounds and thus become more valuable [when they return to lobbying]."[23]

One seldom mentioned issue in discussions of lobbying is the potentially corrupting influence of secret, post-government-service-job offers made to members of Congress or federal regulators by lobbyists representing lobbying firms, large corporations, or other resource-rich organizations interested in legislative or regulatory favors. Such offers are, of course, illegal, but if tendered secretly, they are both unknown and unknowable. As *Republic Report* asks and answers:

> If you're a corporation or lobbyist, what's the best way to "buy" a member of Congress? Secretly promise them a million dollars or more in pay if they come to work for you after they leave office. Once a public official makes a deal to go to work for a lobbying firm or corporation after leaving office, he or she becomes loyal to the future employer. And since those deals are done in secret, legislators are largely free to pass laws, special tax cuts, or earmarks that benefit their future employer with little or no accountability to the public. . . . The everyday bribery of the revolving door may be the most pernicious form of corruption today.[24]

Most members of the federal lobbying community are employed (directly or indirectly) by large corporate clients or trade associations representing corporate interests because these groups have the most money to spend.[25] This is especially evident when we consider that, as noted in chapter 6, the Fortune 500 firms accounted for 40 percent of *all* U.S. corporate revenues and profits in 2011. The links tying DC-area lobbyists, and many other credentialed-class professionals, to superclass-controlled corporate clients form a dense, reciprocal web, weaving together superclass and corporate interests, credentialed-class professional skills, and political contacts. These links are cemented by steep-green salaries for lobbyists that range from $300,000 for veteran Capitol Hill staffers to millions of dollars for "well regarded top officials" like former members of Congress.[26] How many millions? A recent study of twelve former members of Congress found when they became lobbyists, their salaries increased an average of 1,452 percent over their congressional pay. This means the salary of a former-member-of-Congress-turned-lobbyist would increase from $174,000 (2012 congressional pay) to an average of $2.5 million as a lobbyist.[27] These salaries reflect the fact that nearly all *highly paid* lobbyists are employed by superclass-controlled corporations and/or resource-rich organizations that are funded (directly or indirectly) by the superclass, such as corporate-based trade associations, research groups, and lobbying firms. Collectively, these organizations, which make up 72 percent of the Washington lobby community, are the major employers of highly paid professional lobbyists.[28]

The web of superclass corporate influence in the lobbying community is also illustrated by the reality that some Washington lobbying firms are subsidiaries of huge public relations and advertising corporations that are themselves owned by even larger multinational corporations. For example, in the early 2000s the lobbying firm BKSH & Associates was part of Burson-Marsteller (the largest U.S. public relations firm), which was part of Young & Rubicam (a huge U.S. advertising company), and all three were owned by "the WPP Group plc, the world's most comprehensive communications services group."[29] In October 2009, WPP (based in Dublin, Ireland) announced BKSH and another WPP-owned lobbying firm, Timmons & Company, would "merge to form Prime Policy Group . . . a single leading bi-partisan firm that will offer a team-oriented approach to strategic thinking and execution, built on a distinguished record of delivering results for clients—in Washington and around the globe."[30] Today, "WPP is the world's largest communications services group, with [2011] billings of $71.7 billion and revenues of $16.1 billion. WPP companies provide communications services to clients worldwide including 344 of the *Fortune* Global 500; 63 of the NASDAQ 100 and 33 of the Fortune e-50. . . . WPP employs over 158,000 people . . . in 2,500 offices in 107 countries."[31]

Superclass Dominance of Shadow Industry Professionals

The group that generally supervises and controls the shadow industry and drives the market for credentialed-class professionals' lobbying, political finance, and policy-planning services consists largely of the top twenty thousand senior corporate officers and directors located in the one thousand largest U.S. financial, service, and industrial firms.[32] These top corporate officers form the heart of the institutional power elite, and their firms represent the core of the superclass organizational power base. This group exercises control over enormous levels of investment capital and tends to intersect or overlap with the wealthiest 1 percent of all Americans.[33] The members of this group also either possess or are hardwired into the highest levels of social capital and command extremely high levels of consumption capital. And many members of this group occupy their positions due to inherited wealth from family fortunes.

Studies of what we term *superclass leaders* indicate that about 30 percent come from very wealthy families. The largest group (about 59 percent) comes from families in the top 20 percent income group (the privileged class by our definition), about 3 percent comes from families located in the bottom 80 percent income group (the new working class), and the remaining 8 percent could not be classified.[34] Some superclass leaders, such as Steve Case (former CEO, AOL-Time Warner), Bill Gates (Microsoft), and Mark Zuckerberg (Facebook), are "newly rich" as a result of entrepreneurial ventures. While often described in the media as having "middle-class" origins, many superclass entrepreneurs such as Case, Gates, and Zuckerberg actually come from wealthy or very affluent family backgrounds and attended elite secondary schools and universities (e.g., Phillips Exeter Academy and Harvard).[35]

Other current superclass leaders have in fact "moved up" in major corporate hierarchies to elite positions, but in almost every case such rising executives are from credentialed-class family origins.[36] This route typically involves assistance from superclass "sponsors." Such individuals act as gatekeepers in identifying and grooming a few rising executives and political operatives from non-superclass backgrounds for membership in the power elite—typically, first as junior members and later as full partners. Nonelites who are sponsored in this fashion are usually selected and assisted on the basis of their acquisition of critical social and cultural capital (e.g., elite educational credentials) and relevant personal qualities such as allegiance to superclass ideology, organizational effectiveness, talent, and charm.[37] Indeed, Barack Obama's career reflects such a pattern. His path from the elite Punahou School in Honolulu to Columbia and Harvard, then to the Illinois State Senate, the U.S. Senate, and finally the U.S. presidency was facilitated at crucial points by superclass sponsorship—especially during his political campaigns.[38] While there is no doubt that Obama's personal qualities—his intellect, ambition, and charisma—have been important to his successes, without superclass sponsorship he would not have become the Democratic presidential nominee in 2008, nor would he have been elected president.[39]

Despite commanding huge resources, great power, and high status, the superclass is still a relatively small group. Its leadership base is too small to attend to the detailed activities necessary to translate general superclass policy preferences into specific public policy outcomes favoring its interests and perpetuating its political dominance. Superclass leaders need junior partners to help ensure that their interests are protected and served in the political and economic arenas. Thus, through their presence on policy-making boards of corporate, cultural, civic, and other organizations, the most organizationally active superclass leaders (the senior power elite) recruit, cultivate, utilize, and generously reward the expertise and assistance of a wide range of professionals who serve superclass interests in the shadow industry. These are the individuals who direct the industry's daily activities. As a group, they are typically able, ambitious, well-educated professionals who often move from shadow industry positions to high-level government posts to senior corporate positions. A recent example is Peter Orszag. At one point in his career he was a senior fellow at the Brookings Institution (perhaps *the* major "centrist" policy-planning think tank), where he helped develop pro-corporate economic, trade, and health policy initiatives. He later served as President Obama's director of the Office of Management and Budget from 2008 to 2010. After leaving the Obama administration, Orszag became vice chairman of Global Banking at Citigroup—one of the largest U.S. banks.[40] Professionals like Orszag located in the various superclass-funded lobbying, political finance, and policy-planning organizations form the core of the shadow industry, but they also often "move on and *up*."[41]

Largely faceless and unknown to the American public, the shadow industry's professional cadre, along with the staff members they supervise, have an increasingly routine presence in the political life of our society. Their careers are closely linked to the success of the superclass project of controlling U.S. politics and the state. One example is the Hamilton Project—what author William Grieder has called a sophisticated "deep lobby" group. It was organized in early 2006 by Robert Rubin, executive co-chair of Citigroup and former Treasury Secretary in the Clinton administration; it was directed by Peter Orszag while he was at Brookings. The project consists of economists and financiers supposedly "developing ameliorative measures to aid the threatened [U.S.] workforce."[42] The project helped develop trade and economic policies for the Obama administration such as the NAFTA-style "free trade" agreements Congress passed in 2011 with Korea, Colombia, and Panama—agreements that will result in more U.S. job losses.[43] But given the elite-class origins of the project's founders and supporters, the content of these agreements is not surprising.[44] The project is unlikely to advocate trade policies that would challenge the basic features of the existing global trading system that favors superclass interests. The Hamilton Project participants, and many other credentialed-class professionals like them in similar organizations, are the shock troops for and key political allies of the class empire. They are active participants in the federal lobbying, political finance, policy-planning, and classwide lobbying organizations that are central to superclass power and dominance in the United States.

8

Political Finance:
It's Money That Matters

"Our democracy has become a plutocracy. The rich rule."

—Sam Pizzigati, "This Week," *Too Much* (August 6, 2012): 1

The story of superclass domination of politics and the state through the shadow political industry continues with the financing of political campaigns. Money has always been an important factor in politics, but it has taken on even greater importance as a result of three recent developments. First has been the increasing reliance by candidates' official campaigns and by "independent" groups on highly paid specialized staff (e.g., high-tech professionals, public relations specialists) and expensive multimedia advertising utilizing many outlets and platforms (e.g., television, print, websites, e-mail, social media). Second was the U.S. Supreme Court's ruling in the *Citizens United v. Federal Election Commission* case (discussed later), which permitted unlimited "outside spending" by independent groups to influence elections as long as it is not coordinated with candidates' campaigns.[1] Third has been the expansion, especially in recent years, of "parallel" or "two-dimensional" campaigns. In the first dimension, political donors make direct contributions, regulated by federal laws, to candidates' official campaign committees, which spend the money on allowable campaign expenses. In the second dimension, enlarged by the *Citizens United* ruling, individuals, corporations, unions, and others may make unlimited contributions to independent groups that fund election-influencing activities outside of candidates' official campaigns (hence, "outside spending"). Since contributions to groups in the second dimension are now unlimited, this dimension's spending is growing rapidly—pushing up campaign costs. Increased spending in this dimension increases spending in the first dimension as candidates targeted for defeat by independent groups try to blunt the effects of outside spending attacks by increasing their official campaign spending.

Sharply rising campaign costs have magnified the reliance by candidates and independent groups on contributions from superclass and corporate donors. As this reliance grows, so does the influence of these donors and their interests on the supposedly democratic election and governing processes. Superclass campaign donors are not disinterested citizens motivated by altruistic civic obligations. Their motives and priorities are different from those of average citizens. They make large campaign contributions as investments on which they expect a return—including policies that will expand their investment and consumption capital. Regarding motives, one survey of wealthy donors "revealed that 76 percent said 'influencing policy/government' was a 'very important' reason why they gave money."[2] Regarding policy priorities, a more recent survey of wealthy respondents in the top 1 percent of U.S. wealthholders found they were far more likely than average-earning Americans to identify the federal deficit as America's "most important problem."[3] Moreover, they preferred to address deficits by spending cuts targeting entitlement programs, including Social Security and Medicare, rather than by raising taxes on the wealthy (or anyone else). In short, their views are "significantly different from the views of most members of the general public."[4]

FEDERAL CAMPAIGN FINANCE LAW: PAST AND PRESENT

"Campaign finance law underlies all other substantive laws."

—Paul S. Ryan, *Mother Jones* (July–August 2012): 25

Federal efforts to regulate campaign finance are based on the view that concentrated wealth held by individuals, corporations, and other special interests should not be permitted to flow unchecked into the democratic election process because it would corrupt that process. A Federal Election Commission (FEC) summary of campaign finance reform from 1905 to the 1960s notes that

> President Theodore Roosevelt recognized the need for campaign finance reform and called for legislation to ban corporate contributions for political purposes. In response, Congress enacted several statutes between 1907 and 1966, which, taken together, sought to: [1] Limit the disproportionate influence of wealthy individuals and special-interest groups on the outcome of federal elections; [2] Regulate spending in campaigns for federal office; and [3] Deter abuses by mandating public disclosure of campaign finances.[5]

The 1970s witnessed the enactment of new federal campaign finance statutes beginning with the 1971 Federal Election Campaign Act (FECA), which consolidated earlier reforms.[6] The FECA established more stringent financial disclosure requirements for federal candidates, political parties, and political action committees (PACs) but failed to create a central oversight and enforcement agency. Serious campaign finance abuses in the 1972 presidential campaign resulted in amendments to FECA in 1974 that set limits on campaign contributions made directly to candidates by individuals, political parties, and PACs; they also created the U.S. Federal Election Commission and charged it with supervising the disclosure of contributions and with administering the presidential election public funding program.[7] Conservatives challenged the constitutionality of the amendments in *Buckley v. Valeo.* The U.S. Supreme Court's ruling in this case "upheld the law's contribution limits, presidential public financing program, and disclosure provisions. But it struck down the limits on spending, including so-called independent expenditures—money spent by individuals or groups 'totally independent' of campaigns. . . . *Buckley* not only wiped out chunks of the 1974 law—it has shaped most major campaign finance court decisions ever since."[8]

Since 1974, the only major amendment to the FECA was the 2002 Bipartisan Campaign Reform Act (BCRA). "The BCRA banned national political parties from raising or spending nonfederal funds (often called 'soft money'), restricted so-called issue ads, increased the contribution limits and indexed certain limits for inflation."[9] Conservatives challenged the constitutionality of BCRA (*McConnell v. FEC*), but a U.S. Supreme Court ruling in late 2003 "upheld nearly the entire law."[10] The ruling appeared to be a victory for modest campaign finance reform, but in retrospect it turned out to be the high-water mark of reformers.

Federal laws and FEC rules currently permit individuals, PACs, political parties, and political committees to make direct contributions in limited amounts to candidates in federal elections and to political parties (e.g., individuals may give only $2,500 to each candidate or candidate committee per election). Corporations and unions are not permitted to make direct contributions to candidates, but they can establish PACs, which may raise money and make direct, but limited, contributions to federal candidates and political committees.[11] Candidates, parties, and PACs are required to file reports with the FEC identifying contribution sources, amounts, and spending.[12] The FEC refers to regulated contributions as "hard money" or "federal funds."

The FEC designations of *unregulated* "soft money" or "non-federal funds" refer to funds that are "raised outside the limits and prohibitions of federal campaign finance law for activity affecting federal elections."[13] When the FEC was created, it was not anticipated how important these funds would become in election financing. But by the mid-1990s, elite-class political operatives devised tactics allowing them to legally raise and spend large amounts of unregulated soft money to influence federal elections.[14] As an example, the Democratic National Committee raised more than $122 million in soft money to support President Clinton's reelection.[15] The reliance of candidates' supporters on unregulated funds grew in the 2000s despite the BCRA's ban on soft money contributions to political party committees for use in federal elections. The ban actually facilitated the growth of other forms of unregulated spending as wealthy donors increased their contributions to organizations not encumbered by BCRA or other FEC contribution limits—especially "527 committees" (the number

527 refers to an Internal Revenue Code section granting tax-exempt status to political committees[16]). Contributions to 527 committees went from $114 million in the pre-BCRA 2000 elections to $534 million in the post-BCRA 2004 elections—a nearly fivefold increase.[17] But the massive growth of unregulated spending on election campaigns due to the *Citizens United* ruling has since dwarfed these earlier 527 spending totals—as we will see later in this chapter.

Information today about the financing of federal elections comes largely from FEC records compiled in accordance with laws and rules published in the *Federal Register*.[18] This includes information about hard money contributions to and spending by candidates for federal offices (as well as political parties) *and* about the sources of *some* soft money contributions made to independent groups for outside spending. Additional information on funds contributed to and used by tax-exempt nonprofit organizations for outside spending comes from Internal Revenue Service (IRS) records as mandated by the Internal Revenue Code (IRC).[19] But despite FEC and IRS rules, large amounts of unregulated money—hundreds of millions of dollars—are raised and spent today to influence federal elections by groups operating outside all reporting requirements.

Citizens United: The Case and the Consequences

The U.S. Supreme Court agreed in 2009 to hear on appeal from the U.S. District Court for the District of Columbia, the *Citizens United v. Federal Election Commission* case. It involved an effort by Citizens United, a small conservative nonprofit organization, to broadcast a rabidly anti–Hillary Clinton film it had produced (*Hillary: The Movie*) "on on-demand TV during the [2008] Democratic primaries. . . . The FEC told Citizens United it couldn't air or advertise the film during primary season because it amounted to a 90-minute campaign ad that didn't identify who'd paid for it." Citizens United attorney James Bopp (from Terre Haute, Indiana) told the DC Court the movie wasn't much different from what viewers see on *60 Minutes*, and "its creators deserved first amendment protections."[20] The DC Court rejected Bopp's logic and upheld the FEC ban. The U.S. Supreme Court, however, reversed the DC Court. Building on the 1976 *Buckley v. Valeo* decision, the Court, in January 2010, "ruled 5–4 . . . that corporations and labor unions are entitled to the same free speech rights as people and can spend directly from their general treasuries on unlimited independent expenditures [in election campaigns]."[21]

In mid-2010 a DC federal appeals court, relying on the *Citizens United* verdict, issued a ruling in the *SpeechNow.org v. FEC* case that struck down limits on contributions to independent expenditure organizations.[22] Elite-class political operatives quickly developed two new organizations to raise and spend the unlimited amounts of unregulated campaign finance money now permitted: super PACs and 501(c) groups. These two types of organization are now the dominant sources of outside spending on activities intended to influence federal elections. And while similar groups such as 527 committees still exist, they lack advantages associated with the new groups and now account for only a very small share of outside spending.[23]

The FEC defines a super PAC as an "Independent Expenditure-Only Political Committee."[24] It provides such groups with a "form letter" or template to be completed by a super PAC's treasurer and returned to the FEC. This letter, which registers the super PAC with the FEC, states that it may "raise funds in unlimited amounts" but requires it to "not use those funds to make contributions, whether direct, in-kind, or via coordinated communications, to federal candidates or committees."[25] Super PACs must also report to the FEC their donors' identities and the amounts contributed.[26] But details about donor's identities can easily be concealed through the use of "shell corporations."[27] Distinct from super PACs are 501(c) groups—named for the IRC sections granting tax-exempt status to nonprofit "social welfare" organizations.[28] These groups can raise unlimited amounts of money from *anonymous* sources and use it to influence elections by, for example, donating unlimited amounts of money to super PACs or by funding their own election-related messages on television and elsewhere.[29] Like super PACs, 501(c) groups cannot make direct contributions to candidates or coordinate their support for specific candidates with the candidates' official campaign organizations.[30]

Despite the *Citizens United* ruling, federal campaign finance laws and FEC rules regarding *regulated* election funds remain intact. This situation was underscored by an FEC statement aimed at clarifying the effect of *Citizens United* on FEC regulations; it said, "The ruling did not affect the ban on corporate or union contributions or the reporting requirements for independent expenditures and electioneering communications."[31] Since the amount of money contributed to candidates' campaigns in the form of regulated funds appears to substantially exceed outside spending on elections, FEC regulations do provide some measure of transparency to federal election financing. However, if outside spending continues to increase with each new election, one consequence of the *Citizens United* ruling will be a reduction in the significance of FEC regulations because hard money will play a diminishing role in funding elections. On the other hand, some observers expect the U.S. Supreme Court will, in a future case, lift all limits on direct contributions to candidates. If this occurs, all hard money/soft money distinctions will vanish.

THE RISING COSTS OF ELECTION CAMPAIGNS

"The rate of increase in campaign spending . . . is now at an all-time high."

—Robert W. McChesney and John Nichols, *Monthly Review* (April 2012): 1

In 2012, with the *Citizens United* ruling fully in place, we estimate about $1.6 billion was required to mount a *winning* presidential campaign. This amount includes spending by Obama's campaign committee, independent groups that report expenditures to the FEC (e.g., super PACs), party committees, and outside groups *not required* to report expenditures to the FEC (e.g., 501[c] groups and 527 committees). By official estimates, all *reported* spending by and on behalf of both major candidates totaled $1.12 billion for Obama and $1.3 billion for Romney.[32] These figures place the total cost of the 2012 presidential election at $2.42 billion. However, we estimate at least another $700 million was spent on the election by outside groups *not required* to report their expenditures to the FEC.[33] If we add this amount to the $2.42 billion official estimate, the total cost of the 2012 presidential race would be $3.12 billion. Whatever the final cost, it is clear that the 2012 presidential election was the most costly in U.S. history. But we may never know with certainty how much more expensive it was than past elections. This is because "dark money," a reference to funds spent by 501(c) groups *not required* to reveal donors' identities or amounts donated and spent, accounted for a substantial share of outside spending.[34]

Four years earlier (before *Citizens United*), the total cost of the 2008 presidential campaign was estimated at $2.9 billion—including all money spent by *all* candidates in the primary and general elections.[35] The two major party candidates spent a combined total of $1.1 billion. (Senator Obama's campaign raised $745.7 million, while Senator McCain's raised $351.5 million.) The FEC also reported that "individuals, parties and other groups spent $168.8 million independently advocating the election or defeat of Presidential candidates [in 2008]."[36] In sharp contrast with the costs of the 2012 and 2008 elections was the relatively modest amount raised by former President Bush for his 2004 reelection: $423 million (in 2010 dollars).[37]

Congressional Campaigns

As with presidential contests, the costs of congressional elections have also soared over the past decade during both presidential and midterm elections. In the most recent presidential election (2012), we estimate *total spending on all congressional races* by all candidates, political parties, and independent groups amounted to about $4 billion.[38] By comparison, total spending on the congressional races during the previous presidential election (2008) amounted to $3.2 billion (in 2012 dollars).[39] In the most recent *midterm* congressional elections (2010), spending by all candidates, political parties, and independent groups totaled $3.65 billion.[40] That amount was substantially higher than the total inflation-adjusted costs of the 2006 and 2002 midterm elections, which were $3.1 billion and $2.7 billion, respectively (in 2010 dollars).[41] The *Citizens United* ruling added to total congressional election costs by sharply increasing the amount of outside spending by independent groups advocating for or against congressional candidates. For example, the total *reported* outside spending by all groups in the first post–*Citizens United* midterm congressional elections (2010) amounted to $484 million compared with $341 million in 2006 (in 2010 dollars).[42]

As total election costs have risen, so have the amounts of money needed to fund *winning* congressional campaigns. In 2012, the cost of *winning* a congressional election (excluding outside spending) averaged over $9.7 million for a Senate seat and $1.5 million for a House seat.[43] By comparison, the average cost of a winning election in 2002 amounted to $4.8 million for a Senate seat and $1.2 million for a House seat (in 2012 dollars).[44] These increases have been driven by the three developments noted earlier and also by the winner-take-all nature of the American political system. Politicians clearly understand the sentiment expressed in Vince Lombardi's well-known sports aphorism: "Winning isn't everything. It's the only thing." To increase their chances of winning elections, candidates typically try to raise and spend more campaign dollars than their opponents. While candidates who spend the most money are not guaranteed election victories, they win far more often than they lose. On average, 92 percent of congressional candidates who spent the most money on their campaigns (from donations to their official campaign committees) won over the past six election cycles.[45] In *close* congressional elections (a victory margin of 10 percent or less), the proportion of top-spending winners averaged only 63 percent in the past six election cycles.[46] But only 14 percent of all congressional races in those cycles were close.[47]

In the post–*Citizens United* era, outside spending in some congressional elections can equal or exceed the amount of money spent by a candidate's official campaign. This means substantial outside spending support can increase a candidate's odds of outspending his/her opponents (in total spending) and thereby increase his/her chances of winning—especially in close elections. The importance of such spending was "confirmed by a simple statistic from the 2010 races: of fifty-three competitive House districts where [Karl] Rove and his compatriots backed Republicans with 'independent' expenditures that easily exceeded similar expenditures made on behalf of Democrats, often by more than $1 million per district, according to Public Citizen, Republicans won fifty-one."[48] Knowing that outside spending can be crucial to winning, future congressional candidates must consider how to cultivate or neutralize such spending.

As the dollar figures rise higher for each new election cycle, it is important to recall that campaign expenditures are not one-time costs. As campaigns become increasingly permanent and seemingly never ending, each new election cycle requires more money. To cover the spending needed to conduct average-priced *winning* campaigns in the *next election cycle*, representatives and senators need to raise, for their official campaign committees, *at least* $13,500 and $28,500, respectively, *every week* of their current terms in office. And now they also need to cultivate close relationships with leaders of independent groups willing to fund outside spending in support of their reelection campaigns. Being a serious candidate today requires cordial ties to wealthy contributors willing to donate serious sums of money to one's official campaign and to independent groups for outside spending in support of one's candidacy.

THE POLITICAL FINANCE COMMUNITY: SUPERCLASS DONORS ARE CRITICAL

"Billions of dollars [are] raised and spent [in U.S. elections] by secretive outside groups and Super PACs with most of that money coming from a small group of giant corporations and super-rich individuals."

—Robert Weissman, president, Public Citizen (July 25, 2012)

So where does the cash come from for federal candidates' campaign committees and for outside spending by independent groups? The answer is the same in both cases:

the political finance community—composed primarily of the superclass, second-tier elite class members, and large corporations. While labor unions and the small group of nonelite-class Americans who make small contributions to selected candidates are also part of this community, their importance is clearly secondary in financing election campaigns. As we will see, the vast majority of political contributions made *directly* to candidates for federal offices comes from individuals located in the elite classes and from traditional PACs—which are largely funded by wealthy individuals, large corporations, and trade associations. And we will see that nearly all contributions made to independent groups for outside spending also come overwhelmingly from wealthy individuals and large corporations controlled by the superclass.[49] In all instances we will see that superclass donors are especially important sources of all types of political contributions.[50]

In the last two presidential elections, contributions *from individuals* to candidates' official campaign committees accounted for a majority of all direct donations made to these committees. For example, in 2012 contributions from individuals accounted for over 75 percent of both Obama's and Romney's campaign receipts.[51] By comparison, in 2008 contributions from individuals accounted for 85 percent of Obama's campaign receipts but only 55 percent of McCain's; the remaining 45 percent came from other sources, including federal funds and transfers from other authorized funding committees.[52]

In the last three congressional elections, an average of 65 percent of Senate and 55 percent of House candidates' total receipts (respectively) came from contributions individuals made directly to candidates' campaign committees.[53] Contributions from PACs represented the second largest source of direct contributions to congressional candidates' campaigns, making up an average of 14 percent of Senate and 30 percent of House candidates' total receipts.[54] In the 2010 and 2012 congressional elections, the total receipts of all candidates from contributions by individuals and PACs plus loans were about four times larger than all reported outside spending. For example, in the 2010 elections all congressional candidates raised a combined total of $1.86 billion in direct contributions and loans.[55] By comparison, reported outside spending in support of congressional candidates in that election totaled $484 million.[56]

Individual Contributors—Top of the Class

As we've seen, contributions from individuals represent the single largest source of campaign funds raised and spent by federal candidates—a pattern evident in all federal elections for which FEC records exist. (Even self-funded campaigns rely on contributions from the *individual* wealthy candidate to his or her campaign.) And while many people make small donations ($200 or less) to candidates, a majority of individual contributions to federal candidates comes from donors contributing over $200. We know this is the case because the FEC requires federal candidates and political parties to publicly disclose the names of donors who contribute $200 or more to support their election activities. (Candidates and parties are not required to identify the names of donors who contribute $200 or less.)

Most of the money contributed by individuals to federal candidates' campaigns is in amounts over $200, and the evidence indicates these donors are *not* average-income Americans. Only about *one-third of 1 percent* (0.30) of American adults contributed $200 or more to political candidates, parties, or PACs in the 2012 elections.[57] In the 2010 elections the over $200 contributor group was about the same size (0.35).[58] The reality that a tiny "donor class" largely funds federal elections is not new; it has long been the norm.

The 2010 midterm congressional elections usefully illustrate this norm because it is the most recent federal election since the *Citizens United* ruling not complicated by a presidential race. In the 2010 elections, contributions over $200 from individuals in the tiny donor class (0.35 of all American adults) to federal candidates or PACs totaled $1.3 billion—an amount representing 90 percent of all individual contributions that year.[59] An even smaller group of "fewer than one out of 2,000 citizens (0.04) contributed amounts of $2,300 or more accounting for two-thirds of total funds in 2010."[60] But the smallest group of all, just 26,783 individuals (less than 1 in 10,000 Americans), contributed more than $10,000 each to federal political campaigns. This "1 percent of the 1 percent" contributed $774 million—an amount representing 24.3 percent of all contributions from individuals to federal candidates, parties, PACs, *and* independent expenditure groups in 2010.[61]

In terms of our class model, political contributions of over $200 to federal candidates, parties, PACs, and independent expenditure groups come largely from individuals and families in the top one-half of the privileged class, but those in the superclass contribute the most. To illustrate, among *all* political donors in the early 2000s, "one out of five makes $500,000 a year and another three out of five make over $100,000."[62] In the mid-2000s, over 80 percent of donors who contributed over $200 to political campaigns or parties had annual incomes of $100,000 or more.[63] By comparison, only 4 percent of *individuals* in that time period had annual incomes of $100,000 or more.[64] But even $100,000 is well below the annual incomes of the 146,715 Americans who, in amounts of $2,400 or more, gave a total of $1.1 billion to federal candidates, parties, and PACs in the 2010 election cycle.[65] A similar-sized group of 134,451 high-income donors contributed over $1 billion in amounts of $2,500 or more in the first eighteen months of the 2011–2012 election cycle.[66] The income levels of donors who make political contributions of thousands of dollars or more are well known to businesses specializing in campaign fund-raising. One example is NextMark, a marketing firm that sells mailing lists of wealthy contributors to political fund-raising groups. While it offers several lists for sale, an illustrative example is one it describes as the "Major Republican Political Donor" file. It includes "fiercely loyal Republicans who have donated a minimum of $5,000 to . . . Republican [candidates]." The NextMark website says the current *median* household income for members in this file is $218,337.[67] Income levels of large campaign donors have also been studied in statewide elections. One study found nearly 60 percent of donors who gave $500 or more to gubernatorial and state legislative candidates in Connecticut had incomes of $250,000 or more and 25 percent had incomes over $500,000.[68]

Corporate PACs: Another Class Act

At the start of 2012, a total of 4,657 traditional PACs were registered with the FEC, which classifies them into six categories or types.[69] We view about 3,500 of these PACs, those that fall into three of the six FEC categories, as very closely linked to superclass and corporate funding sources and interests.[70] Based on our review of PAC funding sources, corporate PACs (1,652), corporate-dominated trade-member-ship-health PACs (985), and corporate domination of what we estimate to be *at least one-half* of nonconnected (800/1,601) PACs are of special importance to reinforcing superclass political dominance—for four reasons.[71]

First, these PACs collect, control, and disburse a majority of all PAC money. Second, they are almost exclusively administered by committees of upper-level corporate managers from large corporations who share a common worldview reflecting superclass interests. Third, corporate and corporate-dominated PACs consistently reflect classwide business unity growing out of shared interests and the effects of FEC limits on PAC donations. (PACs may contribute only $5,000 to each candidate or candidate committee per election.) Fourth, corporate and corporate-dominated PAC dollars closely parallel the contribution patterns and political preferences of most superclass donors. While it is true that *some* superclass donors contribute to candidates who appear to favor policies that would constrain the interests of large corporations, most superclass donors, most corporate PACs, and most corporate-dominated PACs support conservative, pro-business candidates. Regarding the fourth point, the author of one PAC study observed, "On this point, at least, the behavior of individual capitalists and of corporate PACs are more alike than different."[72] These four factors lead to contribution patterns whereby most corporate and corporate-dominated PAC contributions flow to politicians who endorse policies that protect and extend the wealth and power of large corporations and the superclass elites who control them.

Contributions from traditional PACs have not been significant sources of funding for recent presidential campaigns. To illustrate, PAC contributions accounted for less than 1 percent of total receipts reported by Obama and his Republican opponents in the 2008 and 2012 presidential elections.[73] In contrast to the minor role PACs play in presidential campaigns, PAC funds, as noted earlier, *are* important to congressional candidates because they represent the second largest source of direct contributions to their campaigns. For example, in the 2010 elections 3,613 traditional PACs (of all types) donated $431 million directly to all congressional candidates.[74] Of that amount, $330 million (representing 77 percent of all PAC contributions) came from 1,470 corporate PACs plus about 1,400 other PACs representing corporate interests.[75]

Even though PAC contributions accounted for an average of only 30 and 14 percent, respectively, of total campaign receipts among *all* House and Senate candidates in the last three congressional elections, PAC money was (and is) much more important to the campaigns of incumbents (who win over 90 percent of elections). For example, PAC contributions over the last three elections accounted for an average of 43 and 22 percent, respectively, of total campaign receipts among incumbent House and Senate candidates.[76] Focusing on just the 2010 elections, we find that PACs contributed an average of $2 million to each Senate incumbent and $702,000 to each House incumbent.[77] Since corporate-linked PACs account for 77 percent of all PAC contributions, this means donations from such PACs averaged $1.5 million and $540,000, respectively, to each Senate and House incumbent.

In 2012, about 4,000 corporate and corporate-dominated PACs were actively engaged in raising money for federal candidates, political parties, and other committees.[78] Control of these PACs rests in the hands of PAC committees almost exclusively composed of corporate managers and officers in the elite classes.[79] These committees bring together superclass members and upwardly mobile credentialed-class corporate professionals.[80] The two groups are closely linked through their shared involvement with and concern for shaping corporate policies that favor superclass and corporate interests and through a shared political worldview. The political unity, consensus, and cohesion typically found among corporate PAC managers is based on "a set of underlying material relations—loans from the same banks, sales and purchases from each other, interlocking boards of directors, common interests in accumulating capital and avoiding government regulations that might restrict their power."[81] These material and social relations reinforce PAC managers' interpretations of, and decisions and actions on, both politics and business—in favor of superclass interests. Thus, the millions of dollars that corporate PACs raise, control, and disburse tend to be directed by PAC committees to those candidates most favorable to shared, superclass-based business interests.

Although corporate PAC contributions are sometimes disbursed in ways that appear to reflect efforts by competing firms or economic sectors to promote their narrow interests at the expense of other firms or sectors, such patterns are not the norm. More often, corporate PAC contributions tend to be mutually supportive. Convergent patterns of corporate PAC giving indicate classwide business unity on a wide range of regulatory and labor policy issues, rather than hardball competition. Superclass unity is especially evident in cases of policies affecting corporate control over labor markets—including issues such as working conditions and unionization campaigns.[82]

Studies of corporate PAC contributions consistently document the pattern of classwide business unity rather than competition or conflict in the political arena as the dominant reality. Although a few examples of competing business PACs can be found, "opposed to this [behavior] are literally dozens of examples of companies that 'hate each other,' are 'suing each other all of the time,' and are each other's major competitors but that nonetheless work well together in Washington. They cooperate in promoting the same policies, sponsoring joint fundraisers [for candidates], and in general behaving as a unified bloc." One study of corporate PAC donations found business to be unified in three out of four political races, giving, on average, nine times more money to one candidate than to the other. Moreover, "PAC officers may disagree with their counterparts at other corporations, but the unstated rules forbid public disputes, and only reluctantly will one business directly oppose another."[83] The superclass leadership of the corporate community recognizes that only by acting together can business PACs use their combined resources to exert substantial sustained power over the campaign-funding dimension of the political process.

Outside Spending by Independent Groups: The Superclass Rules

The sources and amounts of contributions to independent expenditure groups known as super PACs for outside spending to influence federal elections are a matter of public record. These organizations are required to report all of their donors monthly or quarterly to the FEC and all of their spending in real time; thus, FEC records show us who contributes to these organizations and how much. As a result of these requirements, we know that contributions from individuals make up most of the funds raised by super PACs and that for-profit businesses account for the second-largest share of funds raised by these groups. In contrast, 501(c) groups, as noted earlier, operate in secret. They are not required to disclose donors' identities or the amounts donated, and they can easily evade reporting how much they spend. As a result, we know less about the funding sources and spending patterns of these groups than is the case for super PACs.

FEC records reveal that in the first two quarters of the 2012 elections, super PACs reported raising $312 million, with $230 million of that amount (74 percent) contributed by individuals. Of this $230 million, 94 percent came from contributions of at least $10,000 from just 1,082 individuals. But 57 percent came from just 47 people—each giving *at least* $1 million. "These same 47 people were responsible for 42.1 percent of *all the money Super PACs raised for the cycle* [italics added] (counting contributions from individuals and organizations)."[84] In the same time period, 515 for-profit businesses contributed $34.2 million to super PACs, accounting for 11 percent of their fund-raising.[85]

Where 501(c) groups are concerned, we don't have access to the details that would allow us to document the full extent to which wealthy individuals and large corporations contribute the money used by these organizations to fund their election activities—for the reasons noted above, Even so, the evidence we do have suggests "that a huge percentage of the money raised and spent by these groups is coming from a tiny number of wealthy individuals and institutions."[86]

We know that 501(c) groups spend large sums on activities intended to influence federal elections—which means they must also be raising lots of money. The scale of spending by these groups is truly impressive, especially when we consider that "dark money groups . . . [planned] to spend up to $900 million through the 2012 cycle."[87]

Research on dark money expenditures by 501(c) groups underscores the extensive resources of these groups. One study found that in the 2010 elections "501(c) groups outspent Super PACs by a ratio of three-to-two."[88] A more recent study found that over 50 percent of outside spending on television ads for the 2012 presidential election was paid for by "'dark money' groups that do not disclose their donors."[89] In this study, the top *four* 501(c)(4) spenders bought $43.3 million in TV ads for the presidential race (through July 1, 2012), but reported only $418,920 in spending to the FEC. A similar study found that just *two* 501(c)(4) groups spent $59.9 million on TV ads for the 2012 presidential election (through August 8, 2012)—$4.2 million more than all super PACs combined.[90] One group, Crossroads GPS, was organized by former Bush strategist Karl Rove, and the other, Americans for Prosperity, is associated with the billionaire Koch brothers.[91]

The political contribution patterns of wealthy individuals indicate they constitute a major source of donations to 501(c) groups. We know, for example, that 17 wealthy individuals made political contributions of $500,000 or more in the 2010 elections and that the total amount contributed by this group amounted to $27.7 million. Of that total, 92.4 percent was given to independent expenditure groups.[92] We also know that 47 wealthy donors contributed at least $1,000,000 to super PACs in the 2012 election cycle and that *at least some* of these donors were also contributors to 501(c) groups.[93]

Despite reporting gaps, two types of information suggest corporate contributions represent a second major source of funding for 501(c) groups. First, FEC records reveal that the proportion of all funds received by all super PACs from for-profit companies fell from 17 percent in 2011 to 11 percent in 2012.[94] A likely reason for this decline is that corporations are redirecting their political contributions from super PACs to 501(c) groups. Corporate officers increasingly appear to prefer anonymous avenues for their political contributions to avoid any negative exposure risks that may come from public disclosure of their donations. Second, substantial corporate contributions to 501(c) groups have been disclosed by accident: "A few accidental disclosures in recent months—for example Aetna's inadvertent reporting of $7 million given to the U.S. Chamber of Commerce and a 501(c)(4) corporation—have given credence to the uspicion that secret contributions are the new favorite avenue for businesses to influence elections."[95]

WHAT ABOUT THE INTERNET?

"Without the Internet, Barack Obama would still be the junior Senator from Illinois."

—Colin Delan, *Learning from Obama* (2009)

What about the Internet as an alternative source for democratizing the funding of political campaigns? Are small contributions made via the Internet by average-income donors to tech-savvy candidates' websites likely to supplant or significantly alter superclass donors' dominance of campaign funding for federal candidates? The short answer is no—based on some overlooked realities of Obama's Internet fund-raising record, the *increasing* importance of superclass mega-donors and dark money to federal election campaigns in the post–*Citizens United* era, and the views of consultants who specialize in using the Internet to fund political campaigns.

Obama's 2008 presidential campaign raised more money via Internet contributions from individuals (over $500 million) than any previous political candidate. And his campaign *reportedly* raised much of that money from over three million small donors who contributed less than $200 each. While these successes seem impressive, they are *not* indicative of a shift away from the dominant role played by elite-class donors in funding federal election campaigns for two reasons. First, the significance of the funds raised via the Internet *from small donors* to Obama's campaign was less important than many believe. A study by the Campaign Finance Institute found the amount raised from donors whose *total contributions aggregated $200 or less* accounted for only 26 percent of the total funds Obama raised from individuals—about the same as for George W. Bush in 2004. Second, the same study found that almost half of the money donated to Obama came from people who gave $1,000 or more.[96] As one "e-politics" author put it, in the case of Obama's donors, "'online' doesn't necessarily mean 'small.'"[97]

The *major* sources of *direct* contributions to Obama's 2008 and 2012 campaigns as well as to the independent groups that supported him with outside spending on election-related ads were wealthy individuals, PACs, large corporations, and, to a lesser extent, labor unions.[98] Admittedly, contributions from individuals made via the Internet *were* crucial in funding Obama's campaigns (totaling 76 percent of all individual donations in 2008). However, the large contributions (those that *totaled more* than $200, often up to $1,000 and more) donated both by the Internet and by traditional fund-raising events were far more important in funding the campaign than the small ones.[99] Most of the funding for both of Obama's presidential campaigns came from wealthy donors—the traditional funding source for Democratic *and* Republican presidential candidates.

In the post–*Citizens United* era, small numbers of "mega-donors," who can legally contribute unlimited amounts of dark money to fund outside spending, have become increasingly important to financing elections (as we have shown). Candidates' websites and Internet solicitations are *not* relevant to securing dark money donations from mega-donors for outside spending. (It is illegal for candidates to solicit dark money.) The mega-donors who contribute and/or raise dark money prefer to avoid public scrutiny; they sponsor and participate in exclusive, secretive fund-raising events closed to the public and press.[100] Absent of major legislative reforms, the importance of mega-donors and dark money to election campaigns will continue to grow, dwarfing by far small campaign contributions made to candidates via the Internet.

Consultants who advise candidates on how to raise political donations online point out that the Internet *can* be a significant source of campaign funds if it is "properly used." But enthusiasm among consultants about the Internet's potential as a *major* campaign revenue source is tempered by a realistic appraisal of what the Internet is likely to provide in terms of campaign donations. As one consultant puts it, "In some ways the Internet has totally revolutionized the way campaigns fund-raise. But the net will never replace fund-raising calls, events, and direct mail as the way in which the majority of campaigns raise most of their money."[101] Consultants recognize that the people most likely to contribute to political campaigns via the Internet or more traditional methods are primarily elite-class members—as Obama's 2008 and 2012 campaigns illustrate. Internet-based solicitations *can and do* expedite contributions from elite-class members to their favored candidates, but Internet fund-raising *does not* significantly alter the reality that most campaign funds, regardless of how they are raised, still come largely from elite-class donors.

WHAT ABOUT THE DEMOCRATS?

"Traditional Democratic solutions [to social problems] as well as the ideology behind [them] . . . are totally unacceptable to the people who increasingly fund Democratic campaigns."

—Thomas Frank, *Pity the Billionaire* (2012), 172

As noted earlier, superclass donors and the corporations they control are not the only players in the political finance community. But as we've seen, compared with organized labor and nonelite-class donors, they are the largest sources, by far, of contributions to candidates, political parties, and outside spending groups. And while superclass donors generally favor Republican candidates and conservative outside spending groups, many also support Democratic candidates and their outside spending groups. Today, the Democratic Party leadership, most Democratic candidates for federal offices, and supportive outside spending groups depend primarily on contributions from superclass and corporate donors. The history of this situation, summarized below, parallels the superclass-sponsored and directed class war described in chapter 6 and reflects, in part, the increasing concentration of wealth and income in the hands of the superclass.

Since the late 1970s, the traditional superclass dominance of the Republican Party has been complemented by its "colonization" of the Democratic Party. This process was facilitated by the takeover of the Democratic Party leadership by the corporate-linked Democratic Leadership Council (DLC). Founded in the mid-1980s, the DLC was directly and indirectly linked (via the New Democrat Network—NDN) with dozens of corporate contributors from the Fortune 500 such as Bank One, Dow, DuPont, Merrill Lynch, Microsoft, Morgan Stanley, and Raytheon.[102] By the mid-1990s one researcher summarized the effects of the increasing penetration of the Democratic Party by superclass interests through its political funding practices in these terms: "Fifteen years ago when the Democrats became more adept in attracting corporate money, a *Wall Street Journal* article stated that 'Business already owns one party and now has a lease, with an option to buy, on the other.' The disregard for labor by centrist Democrats has less to do with ideology, analysis, or changing demographics. It's simply a reflection of Democrat dependence on corporate money."[103]

More recently, President Obama, who epitomizes the new breed of "nonideological," but supposedly technocratically competent, "new Democrats," reflected on some characteristics of the superclass and the effects of his—and by extension all new Democrats like him—dependence on superclass campaign funding in his book, *Audacity of Hope*:

> Increasingly I found myself spending time with people of means—law firm partners and investment bankers, hedge fund managers and venture capitalists. As a rule, they were smart, interesting people, knowledgeable about public policy. . . . They believed in the free market and an educational meritocracy. . . . They had no patience with protectionism, found unions troublesome, and were not particularly sympathetic to those whose lives were upended by the movements of global capital. . . . I know that as a consequence of my fund-raising I became more like the wealthy donors I met.[104]

Obama's musings about the effects of his fund-raising experiences on his own views are consistent with and reflective of the experiences and views of many contemporary Democrats. Today's new Democrats typically do not identify with or embrace an explicit, working-class-populist-progressive ideology or embrace the anti–big business, anti-wealthy rhetoric that energized the party and many of its candidates in the rapidly receding past. Nor do they embrace or advocate policies that would explicitly advance the interests of average workers against those of the entrenched elite classes.[105] Instead they tend to seek the safe political "center" and prefer to view themselves and to be viewed by others as nonideological, pragmatic problem-solvers.[106]

Illustrative of this approach is the Hamilton Project's mission statement, which says, in part, "The Project puts forward innovative proposals from leading economic thinkers—based on credible evidence and experience, not ideology or doctrine—to introduce new and effective policy options into the national debate."[107] Funded by and indebted to the superclass, albeit a somewhat moderate subgroup within that class, the Hamilton Project endorses what *seems* to be a nonideological problem-solving approach without ever recognizing that *all* political-economic policy options are inherently ideological. New Democrats, funded by the same sources as the Hamilton Project, are cut from the same bolt of "nonideological, technocratic" cloth. They pride themselves on being reasonable and willing to compromise with their political opponents in the interests of national "progress and unity"—even if such compromises would betray the working-class interests they often claim to support.

The technocratic ideas, style, and policy proposals of today's new Democrats are off-putting to many—including Tea Party–types on the right and many in the working class who have historically supported the Democratic Party. This is the case because new Democrats often come across as opportunistic elites motivated *not* by closely held and clearly defined principles, but by an elitist sense that *they* know what's in people's best interests. They know because they rely on experts and facts, not ideology. As technocrats, they claim good policy choices are driven by irrefutable "empirical evidence." They fail to recognize that any evidence used as the basis for public policies is inherently ideological and subject to manipulation. Interestingly, almost none of the "evidence-based" public policy proposals put forth by new Democrats would discomfort their superclass sponsors or intrude upon superclass interests or preferences.

Given the ideas and policy preferences of today's new Democrats, it is not surprising that progressive third-party candidates view Obama, and Democrats generally, as hopelessly compromised by their reliance on superclass and corporate funding. As Jill Stein, the 2012 Green Party presidential candidate, said, "There are marginal differences between [Obama] and Romney, but to pull the lever for either corporate-sponsored candidate is to give them a mandate for four more years of the same."[108] Commenting on what he views as the capture of the Democratic Party by corporate elites, Rocky Anderson, former Democratic mayor of Salt Lake City and the 2012 presidential candidate of the new Justice Party, said, "It is a gutless, unprincipled party, bought and paid for by the same interests that buy and pay for the Republican party."[109]

CONNECTING THE DOTS

The central importance of elite-class individuals, especially those in the superclass, and large corporations to the financing of political campaigns for federal offices ensures that superclass and corporate interests dominate the election process. After elections, due to how campaigns are funded and the influence of similarly funded federal lobbying, those interests not only go unchallenged but also are actively privileged above working-class interests by most elected officials in the governing process. Consider the following "dots":

- Presidential campaign contributions. Elite classes: 76 percent; working class: 24 percent. Elite-class donors (>$200) contributed over three times more than working-class donors (<$200) to presidential candidates in the past two elections (2008 and 2012).[110]
- Congressional campaign contributions. Elite classes: 79 percent; working class: 21 percent. Elite-class donors (>$200) contributed nearly four times more than working-class donors (<$200) to House and Senate candidates in the past three elections.[111]
- Contributions from corporate-dominated PACs: 19. Contributions from labor PACs: 1. Corporate-dominated PACs contributed 19 times more ($325 million) than labor PACs ($64.1 million) to House and Senate candidates in 2010.[112]

- Elite classes and corporate funding of super PACs: 92 percent. Union funding of super PACs: 4.6 percent. In 2012, about 92 percent of all funds raised by all super PACs came from elite-class donors (74 percent), corporations (11 percent), and other elite-class or corporate-linked groups (6–7 percent) compared with 4.6 percent from unions.[113]
- Elite classes and corporate funding of 501(c) groups for "secret outside spending." The precise extent of such funding is unknown because these groups are not required to identify their donors. We estimate such funding at over 90 percent.[114]

If we connect the "dots" denoting the extent of contributions from the elite classes (especially the superclass) and corporations for federal candidates, PACs, super PACs, and 501(c)s, a distinct pattern emerges in the electoral arena. We see a massive aggregation of superclass and corporate money that acts as a powerful political force field dominating both major parties, federal candidates' campaign funding, and outside spending. As a result, all key components of the entire election process revolve—like planets—around the giant "green sun" of superclass money.

The bipartisan nature of superclass contributions helps ensure that only candidates with such support can readily access the resources necessary to mount expensive, credible campaigns for federal offices. And it helps ensure that most candidates *in both parties* will be sympathetic to and supportive of superclass and corporate interests. As a result, no matter what the party affiliation of winning candidates may be, most winners will be deeply indebted to superclass and corporate donors for most of the resources that made their victories possible. Once in office, Republican winners are likely to be more aggressively supportive of policies favoring superclass and corporate interests than Democratic winners because they usually benefit from higher levels of campaign support from these sources. We recognize that some Democrats win elections due in part to support from organized labor.[115] Some of these winners even oppose superclass-friendly policies, but such individuals make up a small minority of elected federal officeholders. Under the current system, they provide, at best, only token opposition to the many policy initiatives put forward by their superclass-supported colleagues who favor superclass and corporate interests.

We believe the evidence supporting our contention that the mountain of superclass cash distributed in each election cycle helps ensure that this class retains an iron grip over U.S. politics is more than circumstantial. As we have shown, the political finance dimension of the shadow political industry rests on a dense web of financial connections woven by the superclass and organizations it controls. As a result, the cash donated and controlled by the superclass represents the dominant financial resource that underwrites the entire political process.

9

Policy Planning
and Classwide Lobbying

"The policy-planning process begins in corporate boardrooms. . . . It ends in government, where policies are enacted and implemented."

—G. William Domhoff, *Who Rules America?*, 6th ed. (2010), 87–88

Are austerity policies necessary to reduce the federal deficit, promote personal responsibility, and grow the economy? Is big government the source of many national problems today? Are the wages and benefits of unionized public employees bankrupting state and local governments? Do we need to slash programs for the 47 percent of Americans who pay no federal income taxes? Should taxes on wealthy "job creators" be lowered even more? Are vampire-like "greedy geezers" draining the financial lifeblood of younger generations—pushing Social Security and Medicare toward bankruptcy? Does the threat of terrorism require curtailing personal privacy rights and freedoms? The short answer to these questions is yes—at least according to many organizations that are part of the superclass-funded national policy-planning network.[1]

THE POLICY-PLANNING NETWORK

The policy-planning network consists of several superclass-dominated organizations, including think tanks, research institutes, policy discussion groups, and foundations.[2] Grounded in superclass resources and institutions, this network is dedicated to setting the national policy agenda, establishing policy priorities, and shaping public policy outcomes. It is based on a superclass worldview, shared by credentialed-class professionals who manage and implement routine network functions, that sees the existing economic and political reward, opportunity, and power structures as the most legitimate and the preferred national organizational arrangement (especially compared with more egalitarian alternatives).[3] The network functions through a variety of organizations and processes that collectively promote superclass interests by promoting policies to sustain the economic and political status quo—or slight variations thereof.

The links between this network and superclass political dominance are tied to the reality that "policy planning in the United States takes place largely outside of government, in private policy-planning organizations funded by private corporations and foundations."[4] This means that the organizations in the superclass-funded policy-planning network generate most of the research, ideas, and policy discussions that dominate and shape the national policy agenda, priorities, debates, and most legislative or regulatory "solutions." The multifaceted input from this network to the federal and state governments is clearly tilted in favor of policies that support and extend existing class-based wealth, income, and power inequalities and thereby reinforce superclass economic and political interests. We recognize that despite the shared economic and political interests of the superclass, some divisions exist within this class segment. Even so, more often than not, there is a superclass consensus in favor of policies that support "economic growth, a stable business cycle, incentives for investment, economy and efficiency in government, a stable two-party system, and maintaining popular support for political institutions."[5]

Network Members: Naming Names

Think tanks and research institutes are nonprofit organizations "supported by foundation grants, corporate donations, and government contracts."[6] They provide settings where experts from academic disciplines and former public officeholders research and discuss a wide range of domestic and international issues and explore policy alternatives to deal with them.[7] Although the classification of specific organizations as think tanks or research institutes is contested terrain in the social sciences, researchers generally agree that the policy-planning network core consists of a short list of five superclass-connected and politically influential "centrist" organizations. The Business Roundtable and two center-right think tanks, the Brookings Institution and the RAND Corporation, are key players in the formation of U.S. domestic policies; the Council on Foreign Relations (CFR) and the Trilateral Commission play similar, central roles in the establishment of American foreign policies.[8] In addition to the five core players, four other major center-right organizations play important roles in the network: the Business Council, the U.S. Chamber of Commerce, the Conference Board, and the National Association of Manufacturers (NAM).[9]

The five organizations listed above are linked to numerous other organizations involved in the policy-planning process. One that has been and is actively engaged in class war activities at the state level is the American Legislative Exchange Council (ALEC). Mentioned in chapters 3 and 6, ALEC was "founded in 1973 by Paul Weyrich and other conservative activists. . . . ALEC is a critical arm of the right-wing network of policy shops that, with infusions of corporate cash has evolved to shape American politics."[10] "ALEC is a 501(c)(3) not-for-profit organization that in recent years has reported about $6.5 million in annual revenue. ALEC's members include corporations, trade associations, think tanks, and nearly a third of the nation's state legislators (virtually all Republican)."[11] ALEC develops "model legislation" for legislators to introduce in states across the nation that reflect its "long term goals: downsizing government, removing regulations on corporations and making it harder to hold the economically and politically powerful to account."[12] The organization's recent priorities "included bills to privatize education, break unions, deregulate major industries, pass voter ID laws and more."[13] Its website claims, "Each year close to 1,000 bills, based in part on ALEC Model Legislation, are introduced in the states. Of these, an average of 20 percent become law."[14]

We can see evidence of ALEC's class war activities in several areas. State-level efforts to privatize public education, aided by national-level policies such the 2002 No Child Left Behind Act (discussed in chapter 3) and President Obama's "Race to the Top" initiative, have been led by ALEC.[15] The war on workers' rights and unions is another area where ALEC has been active and effective, as illustrated by the passage of "right-to-work" laws in Indiana and Michigan and attacks on public-sector unions (discussed in chapter 6).[16] In late 2012 early 2013 ALEC took steps to extend its work to the federal level. "This fall [2012], at the behest of the Heritage Foundation—[now] headed by former Sen. Jim DeMint (R-SC)—ALEC began meeting with . . . a caucus of 165 Republican members of Congress who have dedicated themselves to 'advancing a conservative social and economic agenda' in the U.S. House of Representatives."[17]

One form of evidence indicative of some superclass segmentation regarding members' support for the policy-planning network and the policies it develops is the existence of several second-tier think tanks that exercise varying levels of influence in the policy-planning process. Most embrace highly or ultraconservative perspectives, but a few reflect modestly liberal points of view. The general objectives of the right-wing think tanks include promoting an intensely neoliberal policy agenda and encouraging lawmakers and the public to embrace highly conservative views on major policy issues; such views include unquestioned allegiance to free markets, the merits of privatization, and the need to end government regulations on business.

Most closely paralleled with the main organizations at the center of the policy-planning network are two large, highly conservative think tanks that promote policy preferences held by the most conservative superclass segment. The American Enterprise Institute (AEI) is the most influential right-wing think tank linked to the policy-planning network as measured by the extent to which its board members also serve on the boards of the main network organizations and the boards of large corporations. The AEI's close ties to the network are not surprising given that it was "formed in 1943 as an adjunct to the U.S. Chamber of Commerce."[18] The Heritage Foundation, founded in 1974, is well known but has been rather limited in terms of board member interlocks with the main network organizations and large U.S. firms.

This is partly due to the fact that it is funded by "a few highly conservative men of inherited wealth."[19] But this situation may be changing as it becomes more involved with ALEC (see above). Other well-known, highly conservative think tanks that vie for attention in the policy-planning network include the Cato Institute, the Hudson Institute, the Hoover Institution, and the Manhattan Institute.[20]

While right-wing think tanks are not at the core of the policy-planning network, their expanding budgets have increased their policy-planning visibility (if not their influence). A study by the National Committee for Responsive Philanthropy (NCRP) estimated spending by the top twenty right-wing think tanks exceeded $1 billion in the 1990–2000 period.[21] Our analysis of these organizations' 2001–2006 budgets found their spending again surpassed $1 billion—in just five years.[22] More recently, spending by the *two* largest and most influential right-wing think tanks, the AEI and Heritage Foundation, totaled over $500 million in 2007–2011.[23]

In an effort to counter the policy influence of right-wing think tanks and advocacy groups, a small group of wealthy liberals established the Democracy Alliance in 2004. This "new partnership" affiliated with the Democratic Party was created in part to increase funding for progressive think tanks (e.g., Economic Policy Institute, Center on Budget and Policy Priorities). As one journalist put it, "The goal of the Alliance, according to organizers, is to foster the growth of liberal . . . institutions to take on prominent think tanks on the right."[24] Membership is by invitation only, and founding alliance partners agreed to "give $200,000 or more a year for at least five years to Alliance-endorsed groups."[25] "By 2008, [Alliance] members had contributed at least $100 million to liberal causes, according to the Capital Research Center."[26] Alliance spending, however, is difficult to determine because its members and organizational recipients are prohibited from "speaking publicly about its operations."[27]

The Democracy Alliance is an interesting organization, but whether it will be able to effectively counterbalance the relatively potent influence of right-wing think tanks in the policy-planning process remains to be seen. In any event, the Alliance, the groups it supports, and the highly conservative think tanks illustrate that the superclass is not totally unified on policy issues. Despite this evidence indicating modest superclass segmentation on some policy issues, most superclass members strongly support the core network organizations. However, even among this superclass majority more appear to be sympathetic to and supportive of highly conservative think tanks and the policies they promote than those who endorse or support liberal think tanks and policies.[28]

Policy discussion groups are often affiliated with think tanks and research institutes, but these groups have somewhat different goals and function in ways that are distinct from think tanks. They serve as important meeting grounds where superclass corporate elites and their professional allies from various venues come together. The purpose of these informal weekly or monthly meetings is partly to share ideas but also to allow superclass leaders opportunities to identify, recruit, and groom talented individuals from the professional ranks for top leadership positions within government and other key organizations in the policy-planning network. The meetings also help to legitimate the organizations and their activities by portraying both in altruistic terms and by emphasizing the nonprofit, and "independent," status of the organizations. The key organizations that serve as policy discussion groups (or facilitate such activities) often overlap with think tanks and include the National Association of Manufacturers, the U.S. Chamber of Commerce, the Conference Board, the CFR, the American Assembly, and the Brookings Institution.[29]

Foundations and Board Interlocks

As we saw earlier, federal lobbying and campaign funding are two central features of superclass influence where public policy–making and the election process are concerned. The same principle of superclass dominance also applies to policy planning, but instead of wealthy lobbyists and political donors, superclass-dominated foundations serve as the major financial engines providing much of the funding for the core policy-planning network organizations.[30] These tax-exempt, nonprofit organizations are often the creations of corporate entrepreneurs and wealthy families who founded them in part to reduce their own taxes as well as to use them as vehicles for encouraging policies favorable to their class interests.[31]

The resources controlled by foundations are staggering. The Foundation Center identified a total of 76,545 grant-making foundations in the United States in 2009. In 2012, the top one hundred U.S. grant-making foundations (by asset size) held combined assets of $243.8 billion, which accounted for 41 percent of all assets held by all U.S. grant-making foundations ($590.2 billion). The top one hundred U.S. grant-making foundations (by total giving—nearly identical to the top one hundred by asset size) awarded grants in 2010 that totaled more than $19.6 billion annually; this amount accounted for 43 percent of all foundation annual giving in 2010 (about $46 billion). In 2012, the top fifteen U.S. grant-making foundations (by asset size) held over $126.7 billion in combined assets, which accounted for 21.5 percent of all assets held by all U.S. grant-making foundations. The top five foundations are all linked to large, well-known corporate firms and fortunes. In 2012 they included the Bill & Melinda Gates Foundation (Microsoft, no. 1, $37.4 billion), the Ford Foundation (Ford Motor Co., no. 2, $10.5 billion), the J. Paul Getty Trust (Getty Oil, no. 3, $10.5 billion), the Robert Wood Johnson Foundation (Johnson & Johnson, no. 4, $9.2 billion), and the W. K. Kellogg Foundation (Kellogg Corp., no. 5, $8.5 billion).[32]

Foundations are managed by boards of directors or trustees composed primarily of superclass and closely allied credentialed-class members. One study found over 34 percent of the directors or trustees of the fifty largest U.S. foundations were members of exclusive upper-class social clubs. The boards of these top fifty foundations included a total of 402 director positions that were filled mainly by men (85 percent) who attended Ivy League or other prestigious universities. Moreover, many Rockefellers, Mellons, Lillys, Danforths, and members of other wealthy families (such as the Waltons of Wal-Mart fame) sit on the boards of directors of their family foundations and also often serve on corporate boards of several other firms.[33]

For example, recent Rockefeller foundation trustees include David Rockefeller Jr.; Richard D. Parsons, chairman of Citigroup, Inc.; Ann Fudge, former CEO of Young & Rubicam; James F. Orr III, CEO of LandingPoint Capital; and Ngozi Okonjo-Iweala, managing director of the World Bank.[34]

Foundation budgets come mainly from dividends received through their ownership of large blocks of corporate stock. The largest foundations spend their annual budgets on a variety of activities, but a consistent, long-standing funding priority has been to provide substantial support to the core policy-planning network organizations. One example is the Brookings Institution, a core network think tank with, in 2010, a staff of four hundred, expenditures of $89 million, $271 million in endowment net assets, and $410 million in total assets.[35] It received a total of $61 million in grants and contracts in 2011 plus $31 million in contributions from all sources, including over $9 million from eleven large foundations.[36] Over the years Brookings has benefited from both foundation and corporate funding, attracting in 2010, for example, sixty-two foundation donors (gifts over $25,000) and sixty-five corporate donors (gifts over $25,000). Six large foundations contributed over $1,000,000 to Brookings in 2010, including the Ford, Gates, and Rockefeller foundations.[37] The Council on Foreign Relations is another example of a core network organization supported by the largest foundations. Over the years it has received substantial funding from the Ford, Lilly, Mellon, and Rockefeller foundations.[38]

Highly conservative policy-planning think tanks have also benefited from foundation support, but it has come mainly from smaller foundations established by highly conservative individuals or families to promote their views (e.g., the Lynde and Harry Bradley, Sarah Scaife, and John M. Olin foundations). The NCRP report cited earlier estimated over a third of the $1 billion spent by the top twenty conservative think tanks in the 1990–2000 period was from conservative foundations. Contributions from large corporations and wealthy individuals accounted for most of the rest of conservative think tank spending in that decade.[39] This support continues; recent annual reports of right-wing think tanks identify smaller, highly conservative foundations and wealthy individuals with highly conservative views as major sources of funding for their organizations.[40]

The influence of superclass-controlled foundation funding on policy planning is reinforced by superclass members serving as directors or trustees on boards of core policy-planning network organizations. These individuals often simultaneously serve as senior executives or directors at major U.S. firms. An obvious example is the Business Roundtable; it has annual expenditures of $22 million and two hundred CEOs as members—from the largest U.S. corporations such as Goldman Sachs, General Motors, and ExxonMobil.[41] In our research, we found all seventeen members of the Roundtable Executive Committee in 2012 also served as CEOs at Fortune 500 firms.[42] The Brookings Institution is another example. Of the forty-eight members on the Brookings board of trustees in 2010, thirty-five also held positions as senior corporate officers or board members at Fortune 500 firms including Alcoa, Nike, PepsiCo, and State Farm.[43] The Council on Foreign Relations is a third example. A recent study found nineteen of the forty members on the CFR board of directors "were on one or more corporate boards linking the council to twenty-nine companies across the country."[44] An earlier study also found that more than two-thirds of the directors of the CFR, the Business Roundtable, and Brookings graduated from just twelve prestigious universities.[45]

CLASSWIDE LOBBYING: INVESTING IN PRIVILEGE

"[Lobbyists] are the emissaries of this nation's wealthy and immortal—corporate citizens. . . . They are impervious to term limits, impeachment, or sane regulations."

—Beau Hodai, *In These Times* (2011)

As we noted in chapter 7, in American politics, lobbying has two faces: special -interest competition and classwide practices. The former is familiar and widely reported, but the latter, consistent with the taboo on class power analysis, is virtually never the topic of media reports or public discussion. Mainstream media reports on lobbying typically emphasize that although lobbying is a big business, it is also a highly competitive enterprise involving intense rivalries among powerful organizations contending with one another to promote their own narrow agendas and interests. High-profile media coverage of the clash between powerful groups lobbying for and against the Protect Intellectual Property Act (PIPA, in the U.S. Senate) and the Stop Online Piracy Act (SOPA, in the U.S. House) in early 2012 illustrate this story line. Both bills were "aimed at foreign websites that infringe on copyrighted material . . . [or that sell] counterfeit consumer goods and medication."[46] Both bills allowed copyright or patent holders to obtain "court orders requiring payment providers, advertisers, and search engines to stop doing business with an infringing site."[47] Opponents objected on several grounds, including lack of protection against false accusations, expensive monitoring of users' behavior (on user-generated content websites), privacy concerns, and fears that Web firms would incur revenue losses and expenses due to court orders stopping business with *alleged* infringing sites—allegations that later might be proven false but in the meantime could cost Web firms millions of dollars.[48]

Lobbying for and against the bills made for colorful headlines like "Hollywood and Silicon Valley Are at War in Washington."[49] Some major supporters of the bills had Hollywood ties such as with the Motion Picture Association of America (MPAA) and large media firms such as ABC, CBS, Comcast-NBC Universal, ESPN, SONY, and Viacom.[50] A few strong opponents had links with Silicon Valley companies, but many major Internet and high-tech firms such as Amazon.com, Craigslist, eBay, Google, Microsoft, Twitter, Wikipedia, and Yahoo! opposed the bills.[51] Since supporters and opponents included large corporations and trade associations that spend millions of dollars lobbying congress, the PIPA-SOPA battle was reported in the media as a clash of special interest titans. The conflict was resolved, at least temporarily, when, due to widespread opposition, the Senate vote on PIPA was cancelled in late January 2012.[52]

While the PIPA vote cancellation is unlikely to end lobbying for antipiracy measures in congress, the PIPA-SOPA battle illustrates how lobbying in Washington is typically portrayed. Mainstream media accounts of special-interest lobbying leave readers and viewers with the impression that although it is not necessarily fair to poorly funded groups, the high-stakes, special-interest competition among "heavy hitters" leads to a rough balance of power. In fact, such stories often imply that competition among the "big boys" combined with the spotlight of media attention act as a kind of checks-and-balances system limiting the most egregious excesses of undue government influence among well-heeled lobby groups. While we agree that special-interest competitive lobbying is an important feature of our political system, we view it as less important than the political-influence dealing and policy-shaping power of lobbying's other face.

Classwide lobbying is very different from special-interest lobbying. The former is supported by an array of superclass-dominated organizations acting in concert to promote legislative and regulatory policies supportive of the classwide interests of superclass members. Also, this form of lobbying nearly always pits highly unified corporate-based coalitions against coalitions of organized labor, consumer, and citizen's groups in policy contests. The next five sections describe and illustrate classwide lobbying. First, we provide a brief overview of the classwide lobbying community. Second, we discuss how classwide coalitions produced policy outcomes favoring superclass interests at the federal level in four areas: deregulation of financial services, bankruptcy law, class action lawsuits, and free trade. Third, we briefly review the failure of the superclass-led effort to "reform" Social Security in 2005 and consider the extent to which the Obama administration's views are consistent with those of the superclass on this issue. In the final two sections we explore how superclass-supported federal tax and spending policies benefit the superclass, its allies, and corporations at the expense of the working class. We could have chosen many examples to illustrate the nature, extent, and consequences of classwide lobbying, but we believe our choices exemplify how superclass unity and political dominance are reflected in classwide lobbying campaigns and policies. Our choices also provide illustrations of how groups within the alternative power networks have challenged superclass-supported classwide lobbying and how, at least in one case, they prevailed (for now).

The Classwide Lobby Community

The classwide lobby community comprises a core of peak business groups, which are mainly nonprofit trade associations consisting of several individual corporate members with shared views and policy objectives. Depending on the issues, peak groups can and do participate in both classwide and special-interest lobbying, and some also serve as members of the policy-planning network. Peak groups tend to be organized around groups of top corporate leaders from large firms (e.g., CEOs) and specific industries (e.g., financial services, oil, electronics) as well as general, shared business interests (e.g., commerce and trade). Historically, peak groups have formed the organizational core of classwide lobbying efforts. On several issues that have reached congressional legislative or regulatory reform policy contests, a small number of peak groups have consistently been at the center of lobbying activities representing the interests of the business community as a whole as well as the class interests of wealthy elites.

Among the most influential classwide lobbying groups are the CEO-dominated organizations, including the Business Roundtable, the Business Council, and the Conference Board.[53] Industrywide peak groups that frequently play leadership roles in promoting, coordinating, and supporting classwide lobbying campaigns include the American Bankers Association (ABA), the American Chemistry Council (ACC), the American Council of Life Insurance, the American Mining Congress (AMC), the American Petroleum Institute (API), the Health Insurance Association of America (HIAA), the National Association of Manufacturers (NAM), the Pharmaceutical Research and Manufacturers Association (PhRMA), and many others. More general shared business-superclass interests are represented by peak groups such as the U.S. Chamber of Commerce and the National Federation of Independent Business (NFIB).[54]

Classwide Coalitions and Policy Outcomes

Industrywide and CEO-headed peak groups have historically taken the lead in creating ad hoc coalitions to promote classwide business unity and to spearhead lobbying campaigns aimed at influencing legislative outcomes on policies where shared superclass and broad corporate interests are at stake. Four federal policy contests spanning the Clinton, Bush II, and Obama administrations illustrate the potency of classwide lobbying efforts.[55] First, the Financial Services Modernization Act (FSMA) was approved by Congress in 1999 after years of superclass-led lobbying for similar bills dating back to the Reagan administration. The FSMA was enacted with support from the Business Roundtable, the Financial Services Roundtable, the U.S. Chamber of Commerce, a "$300 million financial services industry lobbying campaign, unprecedented campaign contributions, [and mainstream] media cheerleading."[56] It gutted the 1933 Glass-Steagall Act, which prohibited conservatively managed, tightly regulated commercial banks from also serving as high-risk investment banks and insurance companies. After signing the FSMA, President Clinton, unaware of how ironic his remarks would sound a decade later, gushed, "What we are doing is modernizing the financial services industry, tearing down those antiquated laws and granting banks significant new authority."[57] The scope of the FSMA was expanded in 2000 when the same classwide lobby that secured its passage won enactment of the Commodity Futures Modernization Act (CFMA). A key feature of this act banned federal regulations on over-the-counter financial derivatives (speculative products that "involve buying and packaging financial risk and selling it based on a system of grades").[58] The FSMA and CFMA achieved for the financial industry, and the super-class generally, long-sought-after deregulatory objectives. But they also led directly to the 2008 financial crisis, the too-big-to-fail bank bailouts, the Great Recession, and the "endless crisis" today in the United States and global economies.[59]

Second, the Bankruptcy Abuse Prevention and Consumer Protection Act of 2005 was pushed through Congress by a corporate coalition led by the finance, insurance, and real estate industries. This same group also accounted for "more than $306 million in individual and political action contributions during the 2004 election cycle" to federal candidates (59 percent went to Republican candidates).[60] Similar bills introduced in every Congress since 1998 had failed, but this time the combination of classwide lobbying, large campaign contributions, and the political composition of Congress led to a superclass victory over labor and consumer groups. Signed by President Bush on April 20, 2005, the law makes it difficult for middle-income families "to use Chapter 7 of the bankruptcy code, which provides an immediate fresh start." Instead, most debtors now must enter chapter 13 bankruptcy, "which requires a court-supervised payment plan that can last up to five years." Interestingly, the law includes a "millionaire's loophole" that permits wealthy individuals to set up "asset protection trusts" (not available to average-income families) to shield substantial assets from creditors.[61]

Third, the Class Action Fairness Act of 2005 was enacted following a six-year corporate campaign led by the Business Roundtable, the U.S. Chamber of Commerce, and one hundred major corporations and trade associations that together spent millions of dollars on campaign contributions, lobbying, and advertising expenses.[62] Signed by President Bush on February 18, 2006, the law requires that most large class action lawsuits, often involving consumer and worker grievances against large firms, be shifted to federal courts, which are considered to be "less friendly to plaintiffs."[63] This law was a major victory for the superclass, but it was only one of "a series of measures aimed at curbing lawsuits" sought by the superclass. Other "tort reform" efforts that superclass-sponsored corporate lobby coalitions hope to pass in the future "take aim at medical malpractice judgments and asbestos exposure claims."[64]

Fourth, in late 2011 Congress approved and President Obama signed free trade agreements (negotiated earlier by the Bush administration) with South Korea, Colombia, and Panama. Most significant was the U.S.-Korean pact because the Korean economy is the fourteenth largest in the world and because Korea is the seventh-largest trading partner of the United States.[65] The sixteen-month lobbying campaign that led to the approval of all three agreements was orchestrated by several superclass-controlled classwide organizations. At the point of the lobbying spear was the U.S.-Korea Free Trade Agreement Business Coalition, a group organized by the U.S. Chamber of Commerce and led by the top lobbyists for several large U.S. firms, including Boeing, Pfizer, Goldman Sachs, and Citigroup. This group was reinforced by the lobbying efforts of the Business Roundtable, NAM, the Financial Services Roundtable, Big Pharma, the American Farm Bureau, and the Retail Leadership Association, "along with a slew of individual mega-corporations."[66] The supporters claimed, parroting statements from the Brookings Institution, that the trade deals would bolster the U.S. economy and in the case of Korea would "create new American jobs and opportunities for economic growth by immediately removing barriers to goods and services in Korea."[67] This claim was repeated and supported by the U.S. corporate media, Secretary of State Hillary Clinton, and the Obama administration.[68]

Opponents of the trade agreements, mainly the AFL-CIO and other U.S. unions, citing a study by the Economic Policy Institute, argued that the Korean deal would increase the U.S. trade deficit with Korea "by about $16.7 billion and displace 159,000 American jobs in its first seven years."[69] Opponents also pointed to an NBC/*Wall Street Journal* poll that "found that only 18 percent of Americans think free-trade agreements create jobs, compared to 69 percent who said they cost jobs. Only 17 percent said such agreements had helped the U.S., while 53 percent said they had hurt."[70] But the opponents' arguments were dismissed as "President Barack Obama worked with most congressional Republicans and a handful of Democrats to shove [the trade deals] through Congress . . . even [though] the government's own studies show [they] will increase the U.S. trade deficit."[71] Obama's support for the deals was viewed by some as an effort "to win back the support of the wealthy Wall Street Democrats who contributed so richly [to his campaign] in 2008."[72] Whatever his motives, it was clear that Obama, "who won several swing states [in 2008] by pledging to overhaul our flawed trade policies . . . [did] a complete flip-flop [when he signed the bills into law]."[73] In the first 2012 presidential debate, President Obama claimed the free trade deals with Korea, Panama, and Colombia expanded U.S. exports. But by then "the data [on the trade deals were] in, and they show the president's assertion—made a year after Congress approved the deals—is wrong." U.S. automotive exports to Korea declined by 7 percent since the deal passed, while Korean auto imports increased by 25 percent. "The combined U.S. trade deficit with Korea and Colombia increased 29 percent above the 2011 levels for the same months. . . . The Panama deal went into effect only days before the election."[74] Perhaps even worse, in 2012 we learned the Obama administration was "hammering out the biggest, farthest-reaching, and most secretive 'free trade' deal ever, the Trans-Pacific Partnership (TPP)."[75] Based on secret, leaked documents, the TPP would establish NAFTA-like trade rules with several Pacific Rim nations and would "extend the incentives for U.S. firms to offshore investment and jobs to lower-wage countries."[76]

Challenging Classwide Lobbying and Superclass Dominance

In the mid-2000s, a classwide lobbying campaign to "reform" Social Security organized and funded by superclass sponsors was defeated by a labor-led alternative power network coalition. In early 2005 President Bush put forward a Social Security "reform plan." It called for shifting Social Security from an old age and disability pension federal program funded by individual and employer contributions into a system that would divert a significant share of contributions into private individual investment accounts administered by for-profit financial firms.[77] Despite being the centerpiece of Bush's second-term agenda, by the end of 2005 his plan to privatize Social Security was dead. The plan failed in spite of over $200 million in spending by corporate-backed groups on public relations and lobbying campaigns supporting Bush's initiative.[78] So what went wrong? Why did the superclass privatization scheme fail to drive a stake through the heart of Social Security? The short answer is that the superclass-controlled dominant power networks are not all-powerful. In this instance, the alternative power networks, energized by organized labor, were able to mobilize enough resources and allies to defeat this superclass initiative. The main features of this classwide lobbying campaign and resistance to it are summarized in the third edition of this book; interested readers are invited to visit to that source for more details.

The failure of the 2005 classwide lobbying campaign to privatize Social Security illustrates that superclass political dominance does not equal absolute control over all class-relevant policy contests.[79] Even so, this was not a stake-through-the-heart loss for the superclass. While losing this battle was a setback, the superclass war against workers continues on many issues, including Social Security "reform," collective bargaining rights, free trade, and tax policies. President Obama conveyed his willingness to side with superclass interests when he appointed Erskine Bowles and Alan Simpson, two outspoken foes of Social Security, to cochair his "bipartisan" National Commission on Fiscal Responsibility and Reform.[80]

In late 2010 the commission issued a report that economist Joseph Stiglitz described as "not a deficit-reduction package, but a downsizing government package."[81] It included recommendations for raising the retirement age, cutting Social Security benefits for future retirees, and establishing personal savings plans to "supplement" Social Security (akin to Bush's scheme).[82] While Obama did not embrace the report, in mid-2011 he *did* offer to cut entitlement programs (e.g., axing billions from Medicare and cutting Social Security cost-of-living increases) as part of a "grand bargain" with House Speaker John Boehner to reduce the federal deficit, if Republicans agreed to modest tax hikes on the rich.[83] Republicans refused and the bargain collapsed. But by his commission appointments and his expressed willingness to cut entitlement programs, Obama signaled which side he favored in the long march by the superclass to "reform" Social Security.

The historical record reveals that when superclass economic and political interests are at stake in classwide struggles, the organizations representing this class are persistent, resourceful, and often victorious—even after sustaining initial defeats.[84] The historical record also makes it clear that superclass policy losses almost never equal capitulation—especially where classwide superclass and corporate interests are at stake. Given the power elite's long-term perspective and persistence, it seems certain that the failure of Bush's Social Security privatization scheme was only a temporary setback for superclass interests. The policy-making process is still in motion on this issue, especially given Obama's apparent interest in "compromise," and the jury of history is still out. Superclass policy preferences on core economic issues such as federal entitlement programs, labor law, taxes, and trade are akin to the qualities of characters in classic science fiction films such as *Dawn of the Dead* and *The Terminator*. Like undead zombies, superclass-promoted policies are continually reanimated, and like futuristic cyborgs, *they never stop!*

Classwide Lobbying: Federal Taxation and Spending Policies

The jury is not out on the issue of superclass dominance over federal tax and spending policies. These are, however, two areas where classwide and special-interest lobbying sometimes intersect and overlap—thereby obscuring the nature of superclass-led, classwide campaigns. Journalists tend to focus on special-interest lobbying and point out that political contributions by the wealthy often lead to tax breaks or federal subsidies for specific firms or industries. Although such policy outcomes are often both obvious and outrageous, they are of secondary importance to classwide lobbying. The cumulative effects of classwide campaigns dating from the 1960s aimed at shaping federal (as well as state and local) tax and spending policies to further advantage superclass interests are evident in current federal, state, and local laws. Classwide tax-cut campaigns described in the following five sections illustrate how unified superclass efforts under the Reagan, Clinton, and Bush II presidencies produced major changes in federal tax laws benefiting the wealthy and corporations. The sixth section considers the relationship between superclass preferences and the Obama administration's tax policies.

Classwide Campaigns and Tax Reform: 1981

Ronald Reagan's early political career was made possible by substantial financial support from western-state superclass members.[85] He was elected president in 1980 due in large part to massive support from most of the superclass members. They knew Reagan shared their economic and political views and would be an effective advocate for policies supporting their interests. As president, he did not disappoint his superclass sponsors. A central objective of his administration was to "restore the economic incentives of the Roaring Twenties."[86] As a practical matter, this meant first and foremost reducing taxes on the rich and the corporations they controlled.

Early in Reagan's presidency, a classwide coalition of business organizations including the Business Roundtable, NAM, and the U.S. Chamber of Commerce supported his administration in securing congressional approval for the Economic Recovery Tax Act of 1981—the first of Reagan's tax cuts for the wealthy.[87] The act lowered the top federal income tax rate on high incomes from 70 percent to 50 percent in 1982 and created new charitable deduction rules, which further reduced taxes for the wealthy.[88] Other provisions, such as business depreciation changes and investment tax credits, cut corporate taxes and raised profits.[89] And as corporate incomes increased, superclass investors prospered.

Classwide Campaigns and Tax Reform: 1986

Reagan's tax cutting efforts continued throughout his two terms, but the Tax Reform Act of 1986 was the most comprehensive tax reduction law enacted during his presidency. The record of the 1985 House hearings on the bill fills nine volumes (over nine thousand pages); the vast majority of the nearly one thousand witnesses represented corporate interests. Although many corporate representatives sought specialized benefits for individual firms or industries, some of the most potent corporate players advocated preserving and extending tax breaks that reinforced the classwide interests of wealthy corporate owners and officers. This message was evident in testimony from witnesses representing the Business Roundtable, NAM, the U.S. Chamber of Commerce, NFIB, and many others.[90] One of the most obvious classwide benefits of the 1986 act for the superclass and top-earning privileged class members was a reduction in the federal tax rate on high incomes from 50 percent (set by the 1981 act) to 38.5 percent.[91]

Classwide Campaigns and Tax Reform: 1997

During the Clinton administration, the "same old gang" lobbied for additional reductions in federal corporate taxes, capital gains taxes, and inheritance taxes. The tax cuts mandated by the Budget Reconciliation Act of 1997 (BRA), which President Clinton signed, primarily benefited members of the superclass and large corporations. As the tax bill was being considered, members of Congress listened closely, as in 1981 and 1986, to lobbyists from NAM, the U.S. Chamber of Commerce, and NFIB, who coordinated their efforts to win business tax cuts—ostensibly to improve fairness, investment, and productivity (and not just to juice profits).[92] This lobbying effort was reinforced by classwide coalitions seeking cuts in the capital gains and estate taxes.[93]

The pro-BRA classwide campaigns paid big dividends to the superclass and its privileged-class allies. The BRA cut capital gains taxes from 28 to 20 percent. The minimum corporate tax was eliminated, and the federal estate tax exemption was raised from $600,000 to $1 million ($1.3 million for family farms and businesses).[94] The act distributed three-fourths of individual tax cuts to people with $100,000+ incomes. Over one-third of all tax cuts went to the wealthiest 1 percent, who ended up with more tax relief than the bottom 80 percent. Also, "changes in the Alternative Minimum Tax (AMT) . . . lowered the tax burden for corporations by $18.3 billion over 10 years."[95] The richest 5 percent of American families got 83 percent of the benefits from cuts in the capital gains tax, elimination of the minimum corporate tax, and the near doubling of the estate-tax exemption. Families in the top 20 percent income group won annual tax breaks of about $1,000, but the top 1 percent received tax breaks averaging $16,157 per year; families in the middle 20 percent income group received a tax break of only $153 per year; families in the lowest and second-lowest income groups saw either no tax cuts or slight tax increases.[96]

Classwide Campaigns and Tax Reform: 2001

Introduced on February 8, the Economic Growth and Tax Relief Reconciliation Act of 2001 was swiftly passed by Congress and signed by President Bush on June 7.[97] Marketed to the public and Congress on the grounds of fairness and as a recession-fighting measure, the act cost the U.S. Treasury an estimated $1.35 trillion in lost revenue over the 2001–2010 period.[98] As advertised, it was "the largest income tax rollback in two decades."[99]

Nearly 71 percent of the act's tax cuts went to those in the top 20 percent income group.[100] But many reductions benefited only the richest 1 percent. For example, the act increased the estate tax exemption (for married couples) to $4 million in 2006 (with even higher exemptions through 2009)—meaning only one in two hundred estates would owe any federal estate taxes.[101] By contrast, the law left tax rates unchanged for Americans with incomes of less than $27,050 (singles) or $45,200 (married couples).[102] Benefits for the wealthy were phased in over time. For example, the average annual tax cut for an individual in the top 1 percent income group was $2,991 in 2001, but it rose to $42,075 in 2007 and to $69,042 in 2010.[103] In short, "after 2001, the richest 20 percent [got] 84.1 percent of the overall benefits and the top 1 percent alone [got] more than half of the overall benefits."[104]

So how did this lopsided tax law loaded with benefits for the highest income groups and laden with many negatives for working-class Americans pass so quickly?[105] Polls showed little public support for the plan. Moreover, a coalition of organizations representing middle-income workers' interests, known as Fair Taxes for All, actively opposed it.[106] The reason Bush's bill moved so expeditiously through Congress was because of classwide lobbying by powerful organizations representing the material, political, and ideological interests of the superclass and its credentialed-classs allies. A group called the Tax Relief Coalition was organized in February 2001 to coordinate the classwide lobbying campaign; its founding members included the U.S. Chamber of Commerce, NAM, the National Association of Wholesalers-Distributors, and NFIB. Another 250 business and taxpayer groups were invited to join the coalition and were asked to pay $5,000 each in dues, mainly for advertising "in Capitol Hill publications."[107]

The coalition members set aside individual organizational interests for specialized forms of tax cuts in favor of a unified, classwide approach in support of Bush's plan. Jerry Jasinowski, president of NAM, pointed out that "loading up the bill with too many [special] provisions could doom it." He emphasized the need for business unity and said, "We need to be very judicious and forego trying to add a lot of things to this bill because it will just be seen as a corporate Christmas tree."[108] The coalition's objective was simply to get the Bush plan through Congress. Other corporate trade groups that were considering lobbying efforts to add specialized tax cuts to the bill, which might have complicated congressional support for it, were waved off by the Coalition.[109] Based on the end results and the final form of the law, it is clear the coalition was the major political force behind the successful classwide campaign for the 2001 act.

Classwide Campaigns and Tax Reform: 2002–2006

As was the case with the 2001 tax reductions, superclass interests prevailed as more federal tax cuts were enacted in 2002–2006. Four major tax laws were passed during this period that cut taxes for individuals and corporations. In each case, the tax cuts rewarded the classwide lobbying efforts and campaign finance contributions of the superclass.[110] The two tax cuts for individuals were the Jobs and Growth Tax Relief and Reconciliation Act of 2003 (JGTRRA) and the Tax Increase Prevention and Reconciliation Act of 2005 (TIPRA).[111] The JGTRRA was "the third largest [tax cut] in U.S. history" and mainly benefited wealthy taxpayers.[112] It cut the top tax rate to 15 percent on both capital gains (from 20 percent) and stock dividends (from 35 percent) and "accelerated the 2001 rate cut for top income brackets."[113] In addition, 71 percent of its economic benefits went to individuals with annual incomes over $200,000 and nearly 43 percent of the capital gains and dividend cuts went to those with incomes over $1 million.[114] The TIPRA extended the capital gains and stock dividend tax cuts enacted by the JGTRRA through 2010.[115]

The two corporate tax cut laws were the Job Creation and Worker Assistance Act of 2002 (JCWAA) and the 2004 American Jobs Creation Act (AJCA); both clearly favored superclass interests. Although the 2002 law provided workers with additional unemployment insurance benefits totaling $14 billion, U.S. corporations were the biggest winners, receiving $114 billion in tax cuts.[116] The 2004 AJCA was a follow-on to the 2002 JCWAA. It was supported by 428 major U.S. corporations and trade associations (including the Business Roundtable, NAM, and the U.S. Chamber of Commerce).[117] The AJCA provided "$137 billion in new tax breaks for corporate America."[118] The classwide nature of this corporate tax cut (like the 2002 act) was evident in that "almost every industry in America received special favors."[119]

Obama's Tax Policies and Superclass Interests: 2009–2013

No *new* major federal tax cuts reflecting superclass preferences were enacted during Obama's first term as President. But perhaps that's partly because this class benefited so enormously from the trillions of dollars it received from various federal bailouts and Federal Reserve programs. While middle- and lower-income groups received short-term, modest tax cuts via the 2009 stimulus package (the Recovery Act) and the temporary 2 percent payroll tax reduction that ended January 1, 2013, these initiatives were irrelevant to the superclass.[120] More important to superclass interests was the two-year extension of the 2001 Bush tax cuts Congress passed with Obama's support in late 2010. Mainly benefiting the rich, this measure was widely supported by superclass-led groups such as the Business Roundtable and the U.S. Chamber of Commerce.[121]

Following Obama's reelection, the so-called fiscal cliff, ignored during the campaign, quickly became the dominant political issue. The term, attributed to Federal Reserve Chairman Ben Bernanke, referred to the expiration, on January 1, 2013, of the 2001 Bush tax cuts and the imposition of several federal spending cuts agreed to by Congress and the president in 2011 as part of a "compromise" that raised the national debt ceiling.[122] The metaphor was seized on by both parties and the corporate media to give Americans the impression that dire economic consequences would occur if the president and Congress did nothing before 2012 ended.

The tax portion of the fiscal cliff was resolved by a last-minute compromise between the Obama administration and congressional Republicans. The deal, the American Taxpayer Relief Act of 2012, made permanent nearly all of the Bush tax cuts.[123] It did include a token tax increase on the rich, raising the federal income tax rate from 35 to 39.6 percent for households with incomes over $450,000 (less than 1 percent of households). And dividend and capital gains taxes for the over $450,000 crowd went from 15 to 20 percent.[124] By comparison, "in Denmark the rich pay 57 percent of what they earn in taxes."[125] And as we saw in chapter 6, wealthy Americans once paid a similar rate—51.2 percent in federal income taxes in 1955. The Obama tax deal means the rich will continue to pay far less than their fair share of the federal tax burden.

The issues of spending cuts and reducing the federal deficit were put off for another day, but when they return, "Social Security and Medicare benefits could end up back on the chopping block."[126] We know that Obama's first-term tax and spending policies firmly supported Wall Street, not Main Street—despite his pose as a populist defender of the middle class in the 2012 campaign. It is certain that high-priority superclass preferences will find their way into Obama's fiscal policies—despite what *candidate* Obama *appeared* to promise. We have already seen how the president sided with superclass leaders calling for Social Security "reform." And we know that despite what Obama campaign managers say about the importance of small donors to his 2012 campaign, his reelection was largely funded by superclass and credentialed-class donors. These wealthy elites may not agree with all the details that will be included in yet-to-be-agreed-upon federal spending cuts and deficit reduction deals, but their shared preferences are certain to be reflected in them. It is important to remember that "if the past tells us anything, it tells us that positions favored by President Obama's supporters in the corporate community will be taken into account when it comes time to make . . . [tax, spending, and labor policy] decisions."[127]

50 Years of Federal Tax Cuts: Two Measures of Benefits for the Wealthy

During World War II, federal income tax rates on top earners reached their highest point in U.S. history; the top rate remained at 91 percent until tax cuts in the 1960s reduced it to 70 percent. As we have seen, classwide lobbying campaigns in the 1981–2006 period led to even more dramatic cuts in federal income tax rates for the wealthiest Americans. Figure 9.1 graphically illustrates the sharp decline in federal tax rates on top-earning taxpayers over the last fifty-plus years.

Figure 9.1 shows us that Americans with the highest incomes faced a tax rate of 91 percent in 1955, but top earners didn't actually pay this rate. The four hundred top earners in 1955 *did*, however, pay an average of 51 percent of their incomes in

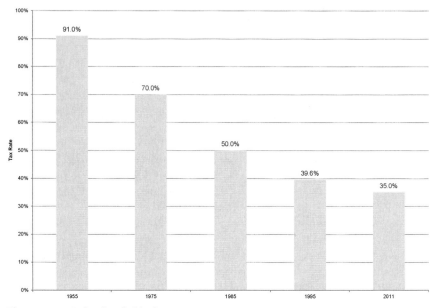

Figure 9.1.   Federal Individual Income Tax Rates on Top Earners, 1955–2011
Source: Senate Committee on Finance, "Federal Tax Treatment of Individuals," Prepared by the Staff of the Joint Committee on Taxation, September 12, 2011, JCX-43-11, p. 10; Tax Foundation, "Federal Individual Income Tax Rates History," Nominal Dollars, Income Years 1913–2011

federal taxes (as noted above).[128] In contrast, top-earning Americans today not only face a much lower top rate but also pay far less than this rate. For example, the 2012 Republican presidential candidate Mitt Romney, according to his 2010 tax return, earned $21.6 million that year and paid $3 million in taxes. Thus, his tax rate was only 13.9 percent—far below the 35 percent federal income rate for top earners that year.[129]

Figure 9.2 compares the average share of income *actually paid* by high-income Americans in 1961 and in 2011. The percentage shares paid can be thought of as representing the *average tax rates* paid by many in the credentialed class (the two lower-income groups) and by the superclass.

As figure 9.2 indicates, members of all three subgroups paid a substantially smaller share of their incomes in 2011 than in 1966, but the share paid by those earning over $1 million fell the most. These results illustrate that while fifty years of tax cuts have greatly benefited credentialed-class top earners, the superclass benefited the most. Figure 9.2 also reveals that the *average* share of income paid in taxes by those in the top group in 2011 (23.1 percent) is much more than the rate paid by Romney (13.9 percent), but far less than the maximum top rate (35 percent—see figure 9.1). Romney and tip-top earners like him pay less than the *average* share for those in the top income category in figure 9.2 for two reasons. First, most of the income received by the very highest earners is from capital gains, which was taxed at 15 percent, not

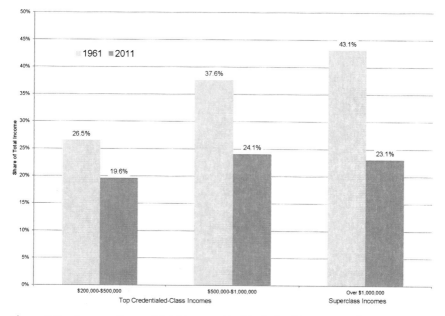

Figure 9.2. Average Share of Total Income Paid in Federal Income Tax by Income Categories, 1961 and 2011 (2011 dollars)
Source: Chuck Collins, Alison Goldberg, Scott Klinger, and Sam Pizzigati, "Unnecessary Austerity, Unnecessary Shutdown," Insitute for Policy Studies, April 2011

35 percent, in 2011.[130] Second, the very highest earners have access to tax loopholes not available to the "merely rich." (As noted above, federal income and capital gains taxes rose slightly in 2013 for households with incomes over $450,000.)

Taxploitation and Spendsploitation

We view superclass-dominated federal tax and spending policies as examples of *taxploitation* and *spendsploitation*—two types of exploitation by which the wealthy take advantage of workers. Unfair and selfish practices in both areas compound the more general levels of wealth and income inequality. Our review of federal tax cut laws reveals that the working class had little influence in shaping these laws. The history of federal spending policies that benefit the rich illustrates a similar pattern. In both areas the working class is increasingly exploited by policies governing how taxes are collected (on individuals and corporations) and by policies dictating how government spends tax revenues. Tax and spending policies in the United States do not redistribute wealth or income in any progressive sense but rather extend their maldistribution and concentration. Federal (and state and local) policies guiding how tax dollars are collected and distributed have resulted in the collection of an increasing share of tax revenues from workers and expenditures of these revenues in ways that disproportionately benefit the privileged class—especially the superclass and creden-tialed class. The federal government's bailout of Wall Street banks using trillions of taxpayer dollars is one of the most obvious examples of such policies. In this section we illustrate both forms of exploitation with figures depicting "American pies."

Taxploitation: Wealth and Tax Pies

The basic idea of the "wealth pie," shown in figure 9.3, was introduced in our chapter 2 discussion of wealth inequalities in the United States. It shows that in 2010 the richest 20 percent of Americans owned about 96 percent of the "financial wealth" of the country (e.g., stocks, bonds, financial securities). What the figure *doesn't show* is that the richest 10 percent held 85 percent of all U.S. investment assets and that *the top 1 percent alone* held 42 percent. The other 80 percent of Americans held the remaining 4 percent of U.S. financial wealth.[131] This means millions of workers (80 percent of the U.S. labor force) work every day producing wealth that goes largely to others, while they receive a few "crumbs" from the pie.

This extraordinary extent of wealth inequality is primarily the result of federal laws that have, over the last few decades, dramatically reduced taxes on the elite classes and large corporations. Laws favoring the rich and corporations have accel-erated the accumulation of ever-larger shares of wealth by the superclass and, to a lesser extent, the credentialed class. This inequality could, of course, be reduced if the wealthy were required to pay higher taxes on their incomes and assets and if they were prevented from transferring their wealth to their children and if corporations paid higher taxes. But as we have seen, that is not the way U.S. tax laws have been written.

The "tax pie" shown in figure 9.4 illustrates the share of total federal revenue paid by individuals and corporations. In fiscal year 2013 the share of total federal revenues paid by taxes on the incomes of U.S. corporations was 12 percent. This figure is down sharply from the 30 percent share corporations paid in 1953. By contrast, in

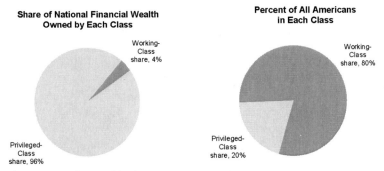

Figure 9.3.   The Wealth Pie, 2010
Source: Wolff, *The Asset Price Meltdown and the Wealth of the Middle Class* (2012)

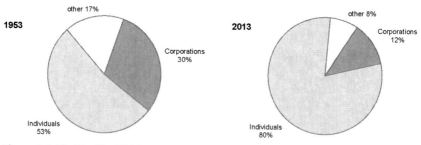

Share of Total Federal Revenue Paid by Individuals and Corporations

Figure 9.4. The Tax Pie, 2013
Source: Office of Management and Budget, 2013
Note: The "other" includes taxes (such as excise) that are typically paid by individuals. Thus, the individual share shown in the diagram is lower than the actual shares paid by individuals.

FY 2013 the taxes paid by individuals (income taxes plus payroll taxes) made up 80 percent of federal tax revenues. This figure is up sharply from the 53 percent share paid by individuals in 1953.[132]

While the tax pie reminds us that individuals, compared with corporations, now pay a much larger share of federal tax revenues than in the past, it is important to recognize that this trend negatively impacts workers more than the wealthy. This is the case because paying taxes is far more problematic for workers than for the wealthy. Most workers have little discretionary income *before* taxes and *even less after taxes*; by contrast, the wealthy have extremely high levels of discretionary income before *and* after taxes. And as we have seen, the U.S. tax code is filled with ways for rich individuals and corporations to reduce their taxes (often to less than zero), but workers don't have these advantages. Instead, when taxes on the rich and corporations are cut, it is working-class Americans who must make up for the lost taxes.[133]

Our review of major federal tax cuts makes it clear that the U.S. tax code is written by the superclass, for the superclass. Today, as in the past, the superclass justifies its advantaged status with the widely shared ideological aphorism, "When the rich do well, everyone does well." Why would this be the case? Because, as the rest of the story goes, wealthy "job creators" invest their money, which in turn creates more jobs and more wealth shared by all Americans. This "trickle-down" fairy tale, akin to the former divine right of kings myth, was invented by the superclass, seconded by the credentialed class, widely believed by the working class, and turned into law by Congress. As we have shown, Congress is receptive to this tale because the superclass provides them with huge campaign contributions and lobby-bestowed benefits in exchange for their votes that cut taxes on the rich. This "receptivity" is also enhanced by the fact that most members of Congress are either already millionaires themselves or well on the road to the 1 percent kingdom.[134] Meanwhile, the reality the fairy tale disguises becomes more evident every year as thousands of wealthy Americans and corporations not only pay ever-lower taxes but also often receive large tax refunds or credits paid for by taxes on individual workers.[135]

It should be noted that many conservative pundits and politicians, including Mitt Romney, complained in 2012 that nearly half of all Americans pay no federal income taxes.[136] These critics ignore the fact that all wage earners have payroll taxes withheld from their paychecks to fund the Medicare and Social Security programs. And they ignore the reality that workers and retirees pay many other kinds of federal, state, and local taxes, such as gasoline, excise, sales, and property taxes.[137] Finally, they ignore the basic reason why so many American *workers* pay no federal income taxes—they receive such low wages that their annual earnings are below the minimum taxable income levels established by the U.S. tax code.

Spendsploitation: The Redistribution Pie

Figure 9.5 presents a "redistribution pie." It provides a vivid illustration of how the many super-rich, merely rich, and nearly rich members of Congress chose to allocate some of the $3.8 trillion in the 2013 federal budget ($2.9 trillion in taxes plus $900 million borrowed). This pie illustrates the relative size of two federal "spending slices." One we call "wealthfare" spending (the defense budget). The other we call "welfare" spending (the budget for the Temporary Assistance to Needy Families [TANF] program). We refer to defense spending as "wealthfare" because large shares of the defense budget juice military contractors' profits and ensure the employment of hundreds of thousands of high-paid scientists, engineers, and civilian employees who work in government, industry, and university research and administration units throughout the "national security state."[138] We refer to federal spending for TANF as "welfare" because it is a cash assistance program available only to low- or no-income families; it provides very meager benefits to individual recipients and only for a limited period of time. TANF is funded by general tax revenues, but unlike defense spending, it produces few profit-making opportunities for large corporations and is generally outside the interests and experiences of the privileged class. It is a stigmatized program—in a word, it is "welfare."

There is a sharp contrast in how these two forms of spending are viewed by policymakers and the public in the United States today; one is widely applauded (defense) and the other (welfare) is widely condemned. Unlike the sharp political attacks on

Figure 9.5. The Redistribution Pie, 2013
Source: Office of Management and Budget, 2013
Note: Temporary Assistance to Needy Families (TANF) is the current federal program providing cash assistance to poor families. In 1997 it replaced the previous Aid to Families with Dependent Children (AFDC) federal program.

TANF (welfare) $17

Defense (wealthfare) $673

welfare spending, there is almost no national debate over defense-spending-generated "wealthfare" for the superclass (or most other forms of superclass wealthfare). This is the case because the wealthfare recipient group (large corporations and wealthy individuals) has strong lobbies in Washington and its members control the major media and educational institutions. The poor, of course, have no powerful lobbyists in their corner. As Bob Dole (Republican candidate for president in 1996) once said, "Poor people don't have a PAC." All they do is irritate the rich by their presence— and sometimes serve as a convenient scapegoat to blame for the fading fortunes of the working class. Poor people do not vote and they have no political clout, so their programs are cut. Meanwhile, defense spending grows—justified today not by the "red menace" but by global terrorism and vague threats to national security and world peace posed by "rogue states" (such as Iran and North Korea).

While some portion of defense spending can be defended as legitimate on the grounds of protecting U.S. national security, *how much* spending is necessary to fulfill this function is a politically loaded question and open to debate. What is not open to debate is that U.S. defense spending is huge. The *Budget of the U.S. Government: Fiscal Year 2013* estimates total outlays for the Department of Defense to be $673 billion (compared with $527 billion in 2007).[139] But total defense spending is much higher than the budget estimate. This is the case because each year Congress passes supplemental defense spending bills. Also, the defense budget doesn't include spending for a variety of military-related expenses such as veterans' benefits or interest on the national debt for loans that paid for past military spending. Taking these considerations into account, the War Resisters League estimates U.S. military spending to be $1.36 trillion in 2013 (out of $3.8 trillion in total federal spending).[140] Whatever the actual amount, we know that much defense spending benefits the wealthy and powerful; therefore, we rarely see such spending attacked by politicians or pundits. And we certainly do not hear politicians or pundits complain that defense spending produces "dependency" among those who benefit from it.

In contrast to widespread support for "wealthfare" defense spending are the energetic attacks, especially from conservative politicians and pundits, on what is claimed to be massive "welfare" spending and the widespread "dependency" it supposedly produces. Examples range from Reagan's derogatory "welfare queens" comments in 1976, to Romney's 2012 remarks implying the 47 percent of Americans who pay no income taxes are lazy, to CNBC pundit Lawrence Kudlow's recent claim that "growing government dependency is ruining America's traditional work ethic."[141] Missing in these attacks are some basic facts about how welfare programs really work and the amounts of money actually spent on them.

The main welfare program available to poor American families today is TANF. It was created when President Clinton signed the "welfare reform" bill known as the Personal Responsibility and Work Opportunity Act in 1996. This stingy and punitive law ended the long-standing federal Aid to Families with Dependent Children (AFDC) program and replaced it with TANF. Among other things, the 1996 law ended federal guarantees of cash assistance to poor families, set time limits on how long families can receive TANF assistance (sixty months), mandated cuts in food stamps and Supplemental Security Income (SSI), and placed financial penalties on states that do not force substantial portions of their adult TANF recipients into narrowly defined work programs.[142] Like the AFDC program it replaced, the TANF program accounts for less than 1 percent of the total federal budget. In 2013, federal spending for the TANF program amounted to $17 billion, less than 1 percent of the total federal budget.[143] The reality of welfare spending is very different from the claims made by politicians and pundits who attack it. Compared with the military budget, welfare spending is a pimple on an elephant's rear. But for superclass warriors who thrive on stirring public resentment against the poor, facts are irrelevant. Apologists for the rich tell us: *welfare* spending: bad!, but *wealthfare* spending (on defense): good!

It is clear that classwide lobbying helps juice federal spending in ways that ensure the superclass and its credentialed-class allies get large shares of the American pie. But it's also true, as Ringo Starr once sang, "You know it don't come easy." Keeping the federal cash spigot open requires that the superclass funnel millions of dollars to prime the congressional pump. Classwide political campaign financing and lobbying practices are expensive. But for the superclass and its credentialed-class allies, the tax and spending payoffs are huge.

SUPERCLASS INTERESTS, POLITICAL POWER, AND LEGITIMACY

"The upper class . . . is a dominant class . . . because the cumulative effect of its various distributive powers leads to a situation where its policies are generally accepted by most Americans."

—G. William Domhoff, *Who Rules America?*, 5th ed. (2006)

The superclass has always had critical interests in controlling politics and government. These political interests are logical extensions of its economic interests. Superclass control over great wealth has historically provided this group with a critical resource for influencing the selection and election of political candidates, the electoral process, and policy formation, implementation, and enforcement. As we have seen, superclass funding of political campaigns leads to powerful influence over elected officials and helps ensure superclass dominance over the formation and implementation of laws and public policies as well as major appointments to the state bureaucratic apparatus. Under this system, the state becomes a vehicle for legitimating existing class-power relationships and the production and distribution of wealth. Laws governing incorporation, corporate rights, taxes, and the regulation of labor markets ensure the dominance and legitimacy of large corporate enterprises in the economy. The stamp of state legitimacy combined with ancillary laws and regulations affords corporations control over workers' terms of employment and control over the production and distribution of wealth. Completing the circle of power, corporate-generated wealth provides superclass members with the economic resources they need to access and dominate the political process and the state. And, lest we forget, it is an *armed state*. The ultimate trump card of the power elite if legitimacy is insufficient to maintain superclass dominance is the armed might the state can deploy as needed: lethal force that can be legally wielded by armed police, the military, and now drones—against "enemies of the state."

Although economic wealth and the shadow political industry provide the super-class with the structural foundation facilitating its domination of politics and government, this arrangement is inconsistent with American democratic ideals. Superclass domination of the political and economic arenas is contradicted by widely shared democratic values and equal opportunity ideals. Left unaddressed, these contradictions could lead working-class members to call into question the legitimacy of the U.S. political and economic systems. However, superclass-owned organizations that make up the information industry have developed control processes that help obscure—and thereby reduce—the tensions generated by the clash between economic and political realities and cultural ideals. These control processes help minimize the prospects of a "crisis of legitimacy" for superclass-controlled economic and political institutions. Chapter 10 explores the role of the information industry in maintaining the legitimacy of superclass power.

10

The Information Industry

"Old and new [communication technologies] . . . serve a corporate minority that is inherently contradictory to the values of democracy."

—Patrick Morrison, "Media Monopoly Revisited," *Extra!* (2011)

"All the news that's fit to print." This quote published daily as part of the *New York Times* masthead suggests the ideal of news reporting in the U.S. media: diverse, impartial, balanced, and complete. But this ideal is far from reality. As we will see, there is substantial evidence that subtle and insidious forms of censorship are pervasive throughout virtually all electronic and print news media outlets owned and operated by large corporations in the United States (i.e., the corporate or mainstream media). Media censorship in the United States doesn't involve overt, heavy-handed, formal rules of reporting or the killing of new stories by government censors. "Instead, it comes stealthily under the heading of Missed Opportunities. . . . [It is] a subtle system of information suppression in the name of corporate profit and self interest."[1]

For nearly four decades Project Censored, a nonprofit media watch group, has been identifying and researching "important censored . . . news stories that the corporate media has failed to cover."[2] "Censorship, as defined by the Project, includes anything that interferes with the free flow of information in a society that purports to have a free press."[3] The project makes it clear that censorship in the United States today grows largely out of the routine structures and operations of the mega-merged corporations that own and control the major U.S. news media outlets. To illustrate this view, each year the project publishes the "Top 25 Censored Stories," which span and link both domestic and international issues. To accentuate connections between the censored stories, in 2012 the project said, "This year, we divide our top stories into categories and analyze them in what we call Censored News Clusters." These seven clusters are "topical categories . . . [that help] draw attention to the nature of censorship in the U.S. press."[4]

Project Censored's work helps call attention to two important information industry features concerning superclass-corporate power and the news media. First, contrary to what conservatives imagine to be the case, corporate media reports critical of superclass-controlled corporate power or of corporate and government policies that favor superclass interests over those of workers are extremely rare.[5] Second, media reports that *do* focus on class-power issues appear mainly in noncommercial sources—as the project's "censored stories" illustrate. Only sources relatively free from the influence of superclass and corporate power have the autonomy necessary to produce critical, investigative reports on issues such as superclass domination of elections and government; corporations defrauding or abusing workers, consumers, and communities; and corporate-government collusion against the public or workers' interests. Many of Project Censored's stories, especially prior to widespread use of the Internet as an information source, were first published by nonprofit alternative news magazines such as *CounterPunch*, *In These Times*, the *Progressive*, and *Mother Jones*. More recently, increasing numbers of the project's stories have come from Web-based sources, including nonprofit, independent media outlets, social justice and human rights groups, academic researchers, and independent news blogs.[6]

This chapter explores how organizationally based structures and processes produce what Project Censored describes as "information suppression." It focuses on the links between class interests, mega-media firms, and powerful media-driven processes that shape public views on economic, political, social, and cultural issues. We consider how the corporate media shape, censor, manage, and disseminate news, including information, ideas, and images, in ways that promote the interests of the superclass, their credentialed-class allies, and, to some extent, the entire privileged class, while ignoring or marginalizing working-class interests. As we will see, information industry executives prefer media content that will maximize profits and promote superclass interests. Their message is "Keep it light, keep it bright, and keep it moving."

get people to click on it

THE MAINSTREAM CORPORATE MEDIA

"Corporate media is the information control wing of the global power structure. The corporate media . . . censors news stories that challenge the propaganda of empire."

—Peter Phillips, *Censored 2012*, 29

The information industry consists of giant interlocked electronic and print-media corporations that are largely owned by superclass members and managed by a small number of superclass leaders in conjunction with credentialed-class junior partners.[7] The media outlets owned by the large firms at the core of the information industry constitute the mainstream corporate media. Together, they disseminate information, ideas, and images about, and interpretations of, national and global economic, political, and cultural news and issues to local, regional, national, and international audiences. The information industry can also be viewed as part of an even larger enterprise that some critics have termed "big media," the "culture industry," or the "national entertainment state."[8] Such labels suggest that in addition to generating news and commentary largely consonant with superclass interests, the large firms in this industry also serve as major conduits for disseminating most forms of popular culture, entertainment, corporate public relations propaganda, product ads, promotional campaigns, and paid political advertising.

The content of the news and information delivered by the electronic and print-media arms of the information industry is not neutral in terms of viewpoints conveyed or class interests served. But the content is also not "liberal" in the sense of being critical of mainstream economic and political institutions, policies, or cultural traditions—despite the claims of many conservative media pundits. Studies of media content do reveal consistent biases—but of a pro-business, pro-superclass sort. News story lines and accompanying images typically begin with pro-business sources, such as superclass-funded think tanks.[9] And the corporate media most often "favor style and substance that [are] consonant with their corporate [economic] interests."[10] In fact, "major advertisers have insisted that [messages consistent with their products and interests] . . . be expressed not in the ads, but in the ostensibly 'independent' news reporting . . . of newspapers, magazines, radio, and television."[11] The information industry consistently delivers news and information that effectively reinforce superclass and corporate interests—at the expense of working-class interests in an informed citizenry and participatory democracy.

Polls suggest deep public skepticism exists concerning news media credibility.[12] Even so, the information industry dominates national attention regarding news about current issues, with most Americans getting most of their news from a small number of large corporations that own large media outlets. A recent national survey found 66 percent of Americans report getting most of their news about national and international issues from television (down from 82 percent in 2002). The Internet was second at 41 percent (up from 14 percent in 2002); newspapers were third at 31 percent (down from 42 percent in 2002); radio was fourth at 16 percent (down from 21 percent in 2002).[13] While the Internet is increasingly reported to be a primary news source by many Americans, much Internet *news content* is developed and delivered to consumers online via websites owned and operated by the same five U.S. commercial television networks that deliver nationally televised news programs to broadcast or cable viewers each day (ABC, CBS, CNN, FOX, NBC). The televised *and* online news operations of these networks are owned by five huge parent firms. As a result of current media use and news production patterns, the companies that own these five large U.S. television networks are the primary sources of news for a large majority of Americans today—via the content of their TV news broadcasts and news websites.

Today, the core of the information industry and the corporate media consists of five giant corporations. Three large conglomerates—CBS Corporation (CBS),

Comcast (CC), and Walt Disney (WD)—own national television network news operations broadcast via *publicly licensed* frequencies managed by the Federal Communications Commission (FCC); they also own online news websites. The other two firms—the News Corporation (NC) and Time Warner (TW)—own national *cable-distributed* network news operations and online news websites. All five are U.S.-based firms. (NC, headed by CEO Rupert Murdoch, relocated its corporate headquarters from Australia to Delaware in 2004.[14]) In addition to owning U.S. TV network news operations, these five firms own or control several other media companies, including cable television networks, film studios, radio stations, newspapers, magazines, book publishing firms, and websites.[15] The five corporate profiles that follow include (1) 2011 total revenues, (2) 2011 total media revenues (all media types), (3) each firm's television network news unit, and (4) a *partial* listing of other media companies owned or jointly operated by each parent firm through various subsidiaries.[16]

- *CBS Corporation.* CBS's 2011 total corporate revenues were $14.2 billion; total media revenues were $11.8 billion. CBS operates five business segments: entertainment, cable networks, publishing, local broadcasting, and outdoor. CBS owns CBS News and the CBS Television Network. Its broadcast holdings include 29 television stations and 130 radio stations (CBS Radio). CBS owns three cable networks: Showtime Networks, CBS Sports Network (college athletics), and the Smithsonian Networks; it also jointly operates the CW broadcast network with Warner Bros., Entertainment. Through CBS Television Studios, CBS Studios International, and CBS Television Distribution, CBS produces, acquires, and/or distributes TV programming (examples of first-run syndicated series include *Wheel of Fortune*, *Jeopardy!*, *Entertainment Tonight*, and *The Dr. Phil Show*). Other CBS media holdings include publishing (Simon & Schuster, Pocket Books, Scribner, Free Press), numerous websites (e.g., CBS.com, CBSNews.com, CBSMarketWatch.com, CBSSportsLine.com, and CSTV.com), and outdoor adverting (CBS Outdoor).
- *Comcast.* CC's 2011 total corporate revenues were $55.8 billion; total media revenues were $53.8 billion. CC operates five business segments: cable communications, cable networks, broadcast television, filmed entertainment, and theme parks. CC owns *NBC Nightly News* due to its purchase of 51 percent of NBC Universal from General Electric in January 2011. (GE retains a 49 percent stake in the company renamed by CC as NBC Universal Media, LLC.) CC, through its NBC holdings, owns ten NBC television stations and provides programming for two hundred affiliated stations in the United States. CC also operates fifteen national cable networks (e.g., Bravo, CNBC, the Golf Channel, MSNBC, USA Network, Oxygen), thirteen regional sports and news networks, and more than sixty international channels. In addition, CC produces and distributes theater movies through Universal Pictures and Focus Features; it distributes DVD products for home viewing. Finally, CC owns Universal theme

parks in Orlando, Florida, and Hollywood, California. (CC's theme park revenues were $2 billion in 2011.)

- *The Walt Disney Company.* WD's 2011 total corporate revenues were $40.9 billion; total media revenues were $26 billion. WD operates five business segments: media networks, parks and resorts, studio entertainment, consumer products, and interactive media. WD owns *ABC World News,* the ABC Television Network, and eight television stations, and it has 238 affiliated U.S. TV stations. WD owns four major cable networks (ESPN, Disney Channels Worldwide, ABC Family, SOAPnet) and holds a 42 percent share of the A&E/Lifetime network (seven channels including A&E, HISTORY, The Biography Channel). WD owns the Radio Disney radio network broadcast by thirty-four terrestrial radio stations (thirty-one owned by WD) and by satellite in North and South America. WD releases theater films through Walt Disney Pictures, Pixar, Marvel, and Touchstone Pictures and through DVDs for home entertainment. Disney Publishing produces children's books, magazines, e-books, and, through ESPN, *ESPN Magazine.* Through Marvel Publishing, WD publishes comic books such as *Captain America, Spiderman,* and *X-Men.* The Disney Music Group includes Walt Disney Records, Buena Vista Records, Hollywood Records, and Lyric Street Records. WD's second largest business segment consists of several theme parks and resorts in the United States, Europe, and Asia (2011 revenues, $11.8 billion).
- *The News Corporation.* NC's 2011 total corporate revenues were $33.4 billion; total media revenues were $32.3 billion. NC operates six business segments: cable network programming, filmed entertainment, television, direct broadcast satellite television, publishing, and other. In the United States, NC owns *Fox News* broadcast via one of its cable networks, the FOX Broadcasting Company. Other NC-owned cable networks include MyNetwork TV, FX Networks, Regional Sports Networks, the National Geographic Channels, SPEED, the Big Ten Network, and twenty-seven television stations; NC also has 171 affiliated U.S. TV stations. NC's satellite TV includes STAR and Sky channels. In the United States, NC releases theater films through studios such as Twentieth Century Fox, Fox Searchlight Pictures, and Shine; it also rereleases films and TV products via DVDs and on-demand deals with Netflix and Amazon.com. NC's U.S. publishing segment includes magazines (e.g., *TV Guide*), newspapers (e.g., *Wall Street Journal, New York Post*), and books (e.g., HarperCollins). Finally, NC owns Amplify, education technology businesses that produce K–12 digital products and services for instruction and assessment.
- *Time Warner.* TW's 2011 total corporate revenues were $28.9 billion; total media revenues were $28.9 billion. TW operates three business segments: networks, filmed entertainment, and publishing. TW owns Cable News Network (CNN) through Turner Broadcasting. TW operates domestic and international cable television networks, premium pay channels, and digital media properties. TW's U.S. entertainment cable networks include TBS, TNT, Cartoon

Network, truTV, Turner Classic Movies, and Boomerang. TW's news networks include CNN and HLN; it operates premium, multipay channels on HBO and Cinemax. TW operates the CW broadcast network through a joint venture with CBS. Warner Bros. Television Group (a TW subsidiary) develops and releases television programming for TW's networks and for third parties. TW's film holdings include Warner Bros. Pictures and New Line Cinema, which release several feature films each year; TW, through Warner Bros., also rereleases films and television products via DVDs and video-on-demand (VOD) services. TW owns Time, Inc., which publishes over ninety magazines (twenty-one in the United States and over seventy in other countries) including *Time*, *Sports Illustrated*, *People*, *Money*, and *Fortune*. TW also owns smaller media properties such as DC Comics, the publisher of *Mad Magazine*.

The pattern of concentrated corporate ownership found in television news is also found in newspaper publishing. Of the estimated 1,350 daily U.S. newspapers, most are owned by large media conglomerates.[17] And like network television news operations, newspapers also provide news content to consumers via their corporate websites. The pattern of concentrated corporate ownership in newspapers is revealed by the fact that virtually all U.S. cities now have only one daily newspaper and most of those are controlled by huge companies that own dozens of papers.[18] To illustrate, Gannett, the largest newspaper chain, owned eighty dailies in 2011 with a total weekday circulation of 4.8 million.[19] The company reported 2011 revenues of $5.2 billion and ranked 465 on the Fortune 500 list.[20] As media concentration increases, more and more newspapers are now owned by large parent firms that also own television and online news businesses. The News Corporation illustrates this trend. As we've seen, NC owns the *Wall Street Journal* and the *New York Post* as well as television properties such the Fox News Channel and news websites.[21]

Corporate interlocks linking the boards of directors of the largest media firms to nonmedia companies illustrate how the web of superclass owners and employers cuts across the top levels of corporate America. In the 1990s, the six largest electronic media firms at that time (Time Warner, Disney, Viacom, NC, CBS, GE) had eighty-one directors on their boards. This group held "104 additional directorships on the boards of *Fortune* 1000 corporations."[22] The top eleven electronic and print media firms in the 1990s had "thirty-six *direct* [corporate] links, meaning two people who served on different media firm boards of directors and also served on the same board for another *Fortune* 1000 corporation."[23] The pattern of numerous director interlocks linking large-media and nonmedia firms continues. The corporate boards of the five giant media firms listed above plus the five largest newspaper corporations (in 2004— New York Times Co., Washington Post Co., Tribune Co. [*Chicago Tribune/L.A. Times*], Gannett [*USA Today*], and Knight-Ridder) included 118 directors who "sit on 288 different U.S. and international corporate boards."[24] The substantial number of media-nonmedia board interlocks underscores the reality that "the media in the United States effectively represent the interests of corporate America."[25]

The complex and extensive web of media and nonmedia corporate interlocks illustrates how the parent firms of the major U.S. TV news networks, and most of the other large media firms outside of the current five corporate giants, are integrated into a tightly woven superclass-based corporate structure. Through interlocks and joint ventures, the media segment of this corporate structure is largely owned or controlled by the same twenty thousand officers and directors of the one thousand largest firms that also supervise and control the shadow political industry.[26] This means that mainstream electronic and print media firms embrace business practices, personnel policies, and reporting styles that reflect and support superclass and corporate interests.[27]

Many of the fortunes of the wealthiest Americans are directly tied to media or media-related firms. In 2011, about 17 percent of the richest four hundred Americans on the *Forbes* list held fortunes based in media, entertainment, Internet services, or software. But among the top fifty wealthholders on the list, 30 percent derived their fortunes from these businesses.[28] This outcome, however, should not be surprising, since "the truth about the news industry has always been that rich businessmen (and a few rich women) own it."[29] And although news media ownership today more often takes a corporate rather than patriarchal form, the top news media CEOs are structurally bound to policies that advance superclass interests.[30] Today, the combined influence of superclass-based ownership and credentialed-class management practices where the news media are concerned have produced a kind of "corporate ministry of information." As one media critic put it, "It is normal for all large businesses to make serious efforts to influence the news, to avoid embarrassing publicity, and to maximize sympathetic public opinion and government policies. Now they own most of the news media that they wish to influence."[31]

Corporate interlocks that tie media firms' news operations with superclass interests of political control and profits lead to interesting contradictions. As a cultural ideal, news is supposedly delivered by "objective" media sources free from biases. In practice, as we have glimpsed and as we will see in more detail later, this is never the case. The stakes are too high. For superclass members and their credentialed-class allies to maintain their positions of wealth, power, and privilege, the working class must be persuaded that the economic and political status quo and the institutions that comprise and sustain them are legitimate. This means the news media must provide those who are not members of the privileged class with ideas, information, and interpretations that support a superclass worldview while ignoring or discrediting alternative views. Thus, news and editorial content trend heavily in the direction of reports and interpretations of events that legitimate the status quo, thereby protecting the interests of superclass members at the top of the class structure.

Of course, the existence of dominant, pro-superclass media reporting trends does not mean oppositional trends, views, or interpretations are totally absent from the media. They do exist, mainly as fragmented and minority positions, but our focus here is on superclass dominance of the mainstream corporate media. The following sections explore three major control processes that operate through the information industry. The mainstream ideology, opinion-shaping, and spin-control processes function in ways that not only promote superclass domination of economic and political thinking in the United States but also help conceal the operation and effects of both the shadow political and information industries.

THE MAINSTREAM IDEOLOGY PROCESS

"The ideology process consists of the numerous methods through which members of the power elite attempt to shape the beliefs, attitudes and opinions of the underlying population."

—G. William Domhoff, *The Powers That Be* (1979)

The mainstream ideology process is the most general of the three control practices operating as part of the information industry. But before we discuss this process, the term *ideology* needs a bit of clarification. This concept may seem like a remote, abstract reference. In fact, ideology is quite simple. It refers to idea systems that organize our thinking on various subjects. If we think sex is pleasurable or disgusting, or that sports are fun or boring, it is because of a complex set of ideas we have learned and accepted that surround those topics and color our experiences with them. Our sex and sports ideologies (i.e., "idea systems") include assumptions and conclusions about these subjects as well as selected "facts" (gleaned from personal experiences or conveyed to us by credible sources) that "prove" our views are right and those held by others are wrong.

In the economic and political arenas, ideologies exist that have the same basic features as our sex and sports idea systems. Political-economy ideologies consist of assumptions about how power and wealth are (or should be) organized and distributed along with selected "facts" that "prove" that the views people hold on these topics are "correct." Political-economy ideologies are most often referred to as ranging from "left" to "center" (or middle of the road) to "right." These labels can take on many meanings, but leftist ideologies are basically grounded in the view that democratic government can and should serve as an agent promoting political, economic, and social justice for all citizens. By contrast, ideologies on the right today tend to portray "big government" as an enemy "of the people." However, rightist views typically endorse government subsidies to businesses and favor powerful, government-funded and -controlled police, military, and security agencies. Right-wing views also tend to see nothing wrong with powerful *private* concentrations of wealth and power—as held by the superclass and large corporations.

Whether we know it or not, most Americans have little experience with leftist ideologies but lots of experience with centrist and rightist ideologies. This situation reflects the ongoing socialization of the working class to economic and political ideas and views that promote and reinforce superclass economic and political interests. Such training occurs through several social institutions, including schools and the corporate media, with the latter serving, in part, as a major conduit for the ideology process.

The *mainstream ideology process* refers to the powerful, indirect influence that the superclass has, especially through the corporate media, upon the political-economy ideological views held by most Americans—including those in the new working class. It refers to the numerous ways that superclass-supported pro-corporate, free market, individual-choice, "government is bad" (or at best inefficient) ideas get woven into and subtly dominate the content of corporate media-disseminated news and commentary. As a result of this process, public debates and discussions on political and economic issues and policies tend to reflect superclass ideological views, preferences, and interests.

Credible evidence exists to support our view that the superclass shares a rather uniform political-economy ideology that in turn dominates public thought via the mainstream ideology process. We also believe that the operation of the process whereby superclass ideological views dominate news and information content delivered to working-class members via the corporate-media-based information industry can be illustrated by an examination of three key topics. These are (1) the corporate media-management structure, (2) the influence of corporate interests and advertising on media content, and (3) the deep structural ideological foundation of the media.

Superclass Political-Economy Ideology

The mainstream ideology process is grounded in superclass leaders' ownership of and control over the corporate media and their shared economic and political ideas, which comprise a dominant "ideological umbrella" spanning a short, neoliberal-centrist-conservative spectrum.[32] Of course, it would be an oversimplification to argue that all superclass members share the same political-economy ideology. But the apparent consensus among superclass leaders favoring domestic austerity policies in the United States, Europe, and elsewhere in the world, as well as corporate-mediated international trade, suggests widespread superclass support for national and international "neoliberal" economic and political policies. As we noted in chapter 3, such policies are based on "[free trade], privatization, deregulation, openness to direct foreign investment . . . fiscal discipline, lower taxes, and smaller government."[33] Differences in superclass leaders' ideological views appear to be matters of nuance, emphasis, and degree across the dominant ideological umbrella rather than fundamental differences in values and policy directions.[34] Thus, the core values underlying the superclass neoliberal ideological spectrum emphasize free enterprise, competition, equal opportunity, individualism, and minimal government involvement in business activities.[35] These values and principles reinforce what is claimed by superclass leaders to be a superior (compared to the alternatives) and preferred (for all citizens) political and economic status quo.

With the information industry owned and controlled by the same core of superclass leaders who direct the shadow political industry, it is hardly surprising that the political-economy ideological preferences of this group cover a short spectrum. Research on this topic reveals that corporate media CEOs are typically economic conservatives interested in profits and markets and that they use the media to promote corporate values consistent with their interests.[36] As one researcher put it, "Media moguls—from Rupert Murdoch . . . to [network news] executives—may not exactly be 'movement' conservatives. But neither are they 'liberals.'"[37]

A study of CEOs who headed parent firms controlling the major TV networks characterized their political views as conservative. Moreover, three of the four at the time of the study—Jack Welch (GE/NBC), Michael Jordan (CBS), and Rupert Murdoch (News Corporation/Fox)—were described as taking actions aimed at influencing news and commentary content in their media divisions in support of conservative political causes or neoliberal-conservative corporate economic policies (e.g., aggressive downsizing and opposition to government regulation). Michael Eisner (Disney/ABC), characterized as a Democratic Party centrist, was described as holding views that were not much different from those of the first three.[38]

The Corporate Media-Management Structure

Although conservative superclass corporate leaders control enormous media resources, as a group they are too few in number to supervise the details necessary for the translation of their shared ideological views into routine media policies and content. Dependable corporate media managers who hold compatible views are recruited by superclass-dominated corporate boards to handle those tasks. These upper-tier, credentialed-class professionals operate under a supervision and reward structure that ensures pro-corporation content standards are met—along with high profits and bonuses for superclass owners and upper-level media management.[39] The CEOs that oversee large firms with large media divisions are handsomely compensated. In 2011, the average total compensation (salary, bonuses, and stock options) received by the CEOs at the five firms profiled earlier was approximately $27.5 million.[40] Looking only at newspapers, the CEOs at the three largest publicly held newspaper companies (by total weekday circulation) averaged $5 million in total compensation for 2011—despite declines in ad revenues and profit margins.[41]

Top media executives make sure superclass ideological views are extended downward in the corporate hierarchy. They richly reward their immediate subordinates and a small number of top media professionals who prepare and deliver on-air "news" content including network TV news anchors, producers, reporters, writers, and commentators. These top professionals are highly compensated for performing three important tasks: (1) structuring news content that will, for the most part, reflect superclass views, (2) attracting the largest possible audience (with the right demographics, usually young, affluent adults), and (3) not offending corporate advertisers. The third issue is not inconsequential, because most media profits come from advertising revenues. U.S. corporations spent an estimated $182 billion on advertising in 2012. Approximately $99 billion of that amount was spent on television, newspaper, and radio ads; another $30 billion was spent for all types of online and digital advertising.[42] Total expenditures on corporate advertising (about 30 percent of all marketing expenditures) *plus* all spending on all other marketing forms in the United States are estimated to be 5.5 percent of GPD or about $1 trillion.[43]

Corporate Interests, Advertising, and Media Content

Because the news divisions of media firms serve as major profit generators, media managers, producers, and reporters are under increasing pressure to generate media content that conforms to pro-corporate views. For members of this group, the result is a collection of news media policies, practices, traditions, and personal experiences that favor "soft news" (i.e., bland, noninvestigative news reporting and toothless commentary). This style of news frequently lapses into corporate cheerleading ensuring that media ad revenues are not interrupted by negative news stories or controversial, critical commentary concerning high-spending corporate advertising clients.[44]

Soft news reporting practices are shaped sometimes by covert links between corporate interlocks and media reporting practices and sometimes by direct corporate pressure on the media. Both types of influence result in corporate censorship of the news—in one form or another. The influence of covert links, such as how internal corporate pressures shape news reporting, is described by a reporter for *Extra!* (a media-watch magazine): "Most people who work for large corporations understand without being told that there are things you should and should not do."[45] As an example, consider the initial failure in 2011 by NBC Nightly News to report that its minority-ownership parent company (General Electric owns 49 percent of NBC) paid no federal taxes in 2010 on $14 billion in profits. After questions were raised in the print media about NBC's noncoverage of this topic, NBC News finally covered the story on March 31, 2011, "in a report that mainly provided an opportunity for GE CEO Jeffrey Immelt to rebut criticism." In the report, NBC correspondent Lisa Myers said, "Today Immelt defended GE, saying taxes were unusually low in the past two years because of losses during the financial crisis. . . . Immelt says that everyone should pay their fair share of taxes, including GE, and that the corporate tax code needs to be reformed to make it more competitive and eliminate loopholes."[46] In a sarcastic commentary on Myers's report, *Extra!* observed, "Yes, NBC allowed its boss to argue that the fact GE pays no taxes is a reason to lower its tax rate."[47]

Direct corporate pressure to change or kill news stories is also placed on media firms, but obviously the most successful efforts are those the public never hears about. One case illustrating how such pressure can kill a story became public in the late 1990s. It involved an investigative news series prepared by reporters Jane Akre and Steve Wilson and Fox TV station WTVT in Tampa, Florida. Akre and Wilson's series focused on Posilac, a drug based on the genetically engineered recombinant bovine growth hormone (rBGH) sold by the Monsanto Corporation. The series raised questions about how the drug was tested for safety, possible negative health effects of the drug on cows, and possible health hazards people might face by consuming milk from cows injected with the drug (which increases milk production by up to 30 percent).[48]

As a result of pressure by Monsanto against Fox News, the investigative series was never broadcast. In a February 21, 1997, letter to Fox News CEO Roger Ailes, an attorney representing Monsanto warned "enormous damage can be done by the reckless presentation of unsupported speculation as fact." The letter prompted a series of internal discussions and reviews at WTVT concerning the series. The reporters stood by their story, but the station management decided not to run it. As the station manager told the reporters, "We paid three billion dollars for these television stations. We'll tell you what the news is."[49] Over the next few years the case took a number of strange twists and turns, including legal proceedings by and against the reporters.[50] This case and others, such as the 1998 "mad cow" lawsuit against Oprah Winfrey, illustrate that corporate efforts to directly influence (or silence) news media content are real and powerful.[51]

Although direct corporate actions aimed at altering news media content do sometimes occur, such cases appear to be less significant in shaping news reports than routine business-media links. A more common route of corporate influence over news media content occurs through the informal clout businesses have as a result of their massive expenditures for media advertising. Some sense of the extent of this clout is evident in surveys of reporters and media executives: "In survey after survey, journalists report that they feel outside—or inside—pressure to avoid, slant or promote certain stories that might affect . . . powerful interests."[52] As an example, a 2008 survey by the Project for Excellence in Journalism of print and television reporters found "that large majorities of print and television reporters believe that financial pressures on their news organizations have increased; about a quarter say owners and advertisers exert either a great deal or a fair amount of influence in their newsrooms. Nearly half of Internet-based reporters (who, in the PEJ study, are mostly employed by those same print and TV outlets) see such influence."[53]

Deep Structure

Deliberate corporate efforts aimed at influencing media content to ensure a favorable advertising climate are paralleled by a deeper and more pervasive penetration of media organizations by superclass and corporate ideological views and values. *Deep structure* refers to the institutionalization of superclass-favored political-economy views and values in the training and reward structures of, and working conditions experienced by, most mainstream media professionals. In part, this concept is similar to what media critic Ben Bagdikian has termed "internalized bias"—the unstated and taken-for-granted understanding that journalists working for corporate media develop concerning what constitutes "acceptable" (to corporate interests) reporting topics, practices, and news content.[54]

Deep structure acts as a kind of hidden context. It is the vehicle through which the values and beliefs of the superclass are woven into the organizational hierarchies, management policies, content decisions, and daily reporting practices of the corporate news media. And these are the firms that generate most of the electronic and printed news and commentary in the United States. Like a transparent fishbowl shaping and bounding the water world of fish, deep structure imposes constraints and patterns on media policies and practices that are nearly invisible—unless its configurations are consciously perceived.

The deep structure of superclass ideological influence in the electronic media is reflected in many ways, but it is especially evident in how resources are granted or withheld in programming decisions. Corporate media managers routinely select, showcase, and lavishly support conservative, "free market" corporate cheerleaders. Current examples include Lawrence Kudlow (CNBC), Wolf Blitzer (CNN), Bill O'Reilly (Fox News Channel), and Rush Limbaugh (Clear Channel–Premier Radio Networks). Examples on Public Broadcasting Service (PBS) television include Tom Hudson and Susie Gharib (co-hosts of *Nightly Business Report*, purchased in 2011 by the private investment firm Atalaya Capital Management) and Charlie Rose (*The Charlie Rose Show*, sponsored by undisclosed corporations).[55] By contrast, the same media managers closely scrutinize and often quickly ax the few corporate critics or progressive commentators that typically find short-lived corporate media exposure.

Examples of popular progressive reporters and commentators fired, forced to quit, or with shows cancelled because of their views are infrequent, in part because the deep structure filtering process prevents people with such views from accessing high-profile corporate media positions. Also, when such events do occur, media managers routinely deny such firings or cancellations are related to the views of those who lost their jobs.[56] Four high-profile examples of progressive television program hosts who lost their shows and their jobs apparently because of their "liberal" political views are Michael Moore (2000, Bravo), Phil Donahue (2003, MSNBC), Keith Olbermann (2011, MSNBC), and Cenk Uygur (2011, MSNBC). The last two hosts were terminated shortly after Comcast's purchase of NBC, but even prior to that event, both had experienced conflicts with MSNBC managers concerned with the "liberal" content of their shows.[57] MSNBC executives would likely disagree with the conclusion that hosts who express "liberal" views are not welcome on the network. As evidence they might point to several alleged liberals who currently host MSNBC TV political talk shows such as Chris Hayes, Rachel Maddow, Lawrence O'Donnell, Ed Schultz, and Al Sharpton.

The hosts of television and radio shows critical of corporate power clearly have problems remaining on the air. This situation illustrates that the combination of corporate sponsorship and informal censorship leads to a very narrow range of neoliberal-centrist-conservative, pro-business news, information, and commentary disseminated by corporate and "public" media outlets.[58] This reality is in sharp contrast to the frequently repeated charge (most often by conservative pundits) that a "liberal bias" exists in mainstream media news reporting.[59]

Mainstream Ideology Results

The results of an information industry dominated by superclass ownership, political-economy views, pro-corporate managers, and co-opted journalistic professionals are threefold. First, the superclass-approved "pluralistic" model of political power is promoted at several levels and in a variety of forms through the major media firms that make up the information industry. Second, political-economy views that differ from superclass views—and the groups that promote them—are ignored, marginalized, or demonized by the information industry. Third, the working class is encouraged to embrace superclass views and to accept the superclass-dominated economic and political order as the most desirable and legitimate institutional arrangement.

Pluralism Promoted

The extensive promotion of a "pluralism model" of politics and government by the information industry is evident by the ideas and imagery used by nearly all corporate media where political reporting is concerned. This model rests on an interest-group interpretation of politics in America. A wide range of interest groups is claimed to exist, but the model argues that no one group is dominant in the political process. Such a view of American politics is constantly reinforced by corporate media reports and commentary and effectively neutralizes or excludes alternative perspectives that focus on the class-based nature of U.S. politics and political power.[60]

Corporate news media reports on the huge sums spent by billionaires and corporations on political campaigns reflect, at an implicit level, pluralist interpretations. Reporters typically point out that a wide array of wealthy individual and corporate campaign donors exist, but go on to explain that this situation actually promotes democracy. Such a reporting focus reinforces the view that American politics consists of competing, interest-based "veto groups" that check and balance one another's power. From this viewpoint, politics and public policies are seen as a kaleidoscopic swirl of pluralistic confusion with a multitude of wealthy individuals, corporations, super PACs, and so forth competing for political influence in a kind of rotating king-of-the-hill game of governance. The various campaign funding sources and vehicles are presented in media reports as agents of fragmented interest groups more often competing than cooperating with one another for narrow gains in the political process. This comforting view reinforces the notion that the U.S. political system ensures that no single interest group can corrupt or dominate the democratic process.

The problem with "pluralist-based" reporting on large campaign contributions as sources of political influence is that viewers and readers are encouraged to focus on *divided interest-group* power, rather than *unified superclass* power; such a focus, in effect, calls attention to the trees while ignoring the forest. Pluralist-based reporting leads viewers and readers to the conclusion that no single group dominates the political process—and thereby disguises the true nature of superclass political power and the operation of the shadow political industry.

Marginalization of Alternatives

In addition to promoting pluralist-based reporting, the mainstream ideology process also encourages media marginalization and demonization of economic and political views or groups disfavored by the superclass. For example, corporate media reports on unions are rarely framed in favorable or positive terms.[61] Union campaign contributions or super PACs are routinely subjected to media attacks as efforts by "union bosses" to manipulate and control the political process. In fact, virtually all organizations, ideas, and public policies or programs promoting working-class interests are often subject to negative corporate media reporting.[62] The negation of alternative worldviews is a necessary part of superclass efforts to control the terms of economic and political discourse in the United States. The reality of conflicting class interests means that the experiences, policy priorities, and legislative preferences of the working class are not the same as those of the superclass (or their credentialed-class allies). The consequences for the superclass of allowing the working class to translate its shared interests and experiences into legitimate political discussion, debate, and coherent policy alternatives without the benefit of "ideological coaching" from the information industry would be to risk the growth of class consciousness and class politics. The mainstream ideology process is part of superclass efforts to prevent these prospects from becoming reality.

Embracing Superclass Values?

Superclass ideology legitimates centrist-conservative politics, predatory corporate business practices, and the existing class system, including the wide array of advantages and privileges it provides for the superclass and its credentialed-class allies combined with extensive inequalities for the working class. As a result of our exposure to the mainstream ideology process, most of us tend to take the way the world is organized politically and economically—including the whole catalog of extensive class inequities—for granted. We assume that it is sort of natural and that there is not much we can do about it, so we tend to accept it, perhaps with some grousing and complaining, and go on. In fact, what this attitude reflects is our familiarity with only one ideological perspective: the superclass view. This is the case because it is the one that is subtly and powerfully woven into much of what we see, hear, and read in corporate-media-provided news and commentary via the mainstream ideology process.

Unfortunately for superclass leaders, their political-economy ideological foundations are problematic because the public principles they espouse are often at odds with the routine business practices pursued by the large firms they control. For example, superclass leaders claim to favor the ideals of free enterprise, competition, and equal opportunity. But in practice, large firms, owned by the superclass, clearly prefer to dominate markets and maximize profits through monopolistic or oligopolistic practices that exclude competitive free enterprise or equal opportunity. Also, although corporate executives pay lip service to individualism, they clearly prefer a labor force tightly regimented by unchallenged corporate rule and a consuming public manipulated and dominated by mass advertising. Finally, whereas large firms oppose government regulation of business as well as government policies that would expand the "social wage" (i.e., economic programs that would increase the income and economic security of working-class Americans), they typically support the existence and expansion of government programs that channel tax dollars into business revenues and profits. Reducing the tensions between publicly promoted superclass ideological values and contradictory corporate practices is a major concern of the information industry—often pursued via the opinion-shaping and spin-control processes.

THE OPINION-SHAPING PROCESS

"I promise you, *CBS News* and *ABC News* and *NBC News* are not influenced by the corporations that may own those companies."

—Charlie Rose, *Charlie Rose Show*, 2003 (in *Extra!* [November 2010]: 14)

The mainstream ideology process morphs seamlessly into the opinion-shaping process. The two processes overlap in many ways, but the key difference is that whereas the former promotes general neoliberal-centrist-conservative ideological values and principles, the latter involves their detailed infusion into the specifics of news programming, content, and commentary. The opinion-shaping process is most evident through the information industry's consistently favorable treatment, through reports, images, and interpretations of superclass-dominated ideas, organizations, and policies. Two widespread media practices help create and reinforce public opinion favorable to superclass interests: deck stacking and selective reporting.

Deck Stacking

Deck stacking refers to the overwhelming preponderance of pro-superclass and pro-corporate media managers, producers, editors, commentators, reporters, correspondents, anchors, and hosts within the information industry. One way for superclass media owners and their credentialed-class top-level media managers to achieve this result is through staffing and pay practices that distance upper-tier media professionals from average workers' experiences and pay levels and link them more closely to the interests (and views) of elite owners and managers. At the highest reaches of the media hierarchy are elite professionals earning millions. For the most part, the values and beliefs of this elite group reflect the pervasive, covert power of deep structure.

Elite media professionals can be counted on to "stack the news deck" with reports and commentary consistent with the interests of their superclass owner-employer bosses. Examples of such elites with multimillion-dollar annual incomes include all of the network TV news anchors and hosts of "public affairs" programs. In 2012 the three publicly broadcast network TV anchors included Brian Williams ($13 million, NBC), Diane Sawyer ($12 million, ABC), and Scott Pelley ($4 million, CBS). Major Sunday network TV public affairs shows, which supposedly inform viewers on public policy issues, all feature highly paid male hosts with superclass-friendly views: David Gregory (NBC's *Meet the Press*, $5 million), Bob Schieffer (CBS's *Face the Nation*, $6 million), George Stephanopoulos (ABC's *This Week*, $6 million), and Chris Wallace (*Fox News Sunday*, $1 million).[63] A recent slice of Gregory's off-camera social world provides instructive insights into the informal ties linking top news media personnel and the superclass. Wealthy real estate developers sponsored Gregory's 2012 bid to join the Chevy Chase Club, "a country club that has served wealthy Washingtonians since 1892." The club's initiation fee and annual dues are reported to be $80,000 and $6,000, respectively. This information, as the media-watch magazine *Extra!* notes, provides "something to keep in mind next time you hear Gregory talking about the need for 'shared sacrifices'—meaning cutting Social Security."[64]

Other elite media pundits, commentators, and "infotainment" personalities with multimillion-dollar incomes and superclass value orientations include (in 2012) Anderson Cooper ($11 million, CNN), Bill O'Reilly ($15 million, Fox), Matt Lauer ($21.5 million, NBC), and Oprah Winfrey ($165 million, syndicated; in 2012 Oprah was listed by *Forbes* as having a net worth of $2.7 billion). On radio, Rush Limbaugh's contract reportedly pays him $38 million per year (Premier Radio Network). Even the hosts of TV's premier news parody shows are well paid: Jon Stewart ($16 million, *The Daily Show*) and Stephen Colbert ($6 million, *The Colbert Report*).[65] The latter two shows are broadcast on Comedy Central, a cable TV channel owned by Viacom.

The uniform staffing of information industry managers, reporters, and pundits leads to an ideological filtering and opinion-shaping system generating news content and commentary that parallels and reflects but virtually never challenges superclass views. This situation begins with built-in structural biases grounded in corporate ownership of the media, leading to owners' hiring and rewarding of managers and editors who reflect pro-superclass and pro-corporate values and views. Acting as gatekeepers, media managers and editors hire and reward reporters who share their views—or who are willing to self-censor their work to conform with the ideological boundaries imposed by the corporate structure and enforced by editorial oversight.

Deck stacking extends across all media formats and is especially evident in the lop-sided spectrum of viewpoints presented by network television news programming, nearly all cable TV news programming, and the news websites owned by the largest media firms. This same pattern applies to "public" television news programming and nearly all nationally distributed, for-profit television, radio, print, and Internet-based pundits and commentators. In television news, an instructive example of deck stacking can be found in the views of the hosts of public affairs programs. The national commercial and public television public affairs programs with the largest audiences all feature centrist or conservative hosts (e.g., CBS's *Face the Nation*, NBC's *Meet the Press*, ABC's *This Week*, *Fox News Sunday*, and PBS's *Washington Week*).[66]

With the "host deck" stacked, centrist-conservative points of view are presented far more often than "liberal" or "progressive" perspectives on these programs; this same pattern extends to the programs' guests and panelists—as documented by three studies. The first study analyzed nearly seven thousand guests who appeared on the Sunday morning network TV public affairs programs broadcast by ABC, CBS, and NBC over eight years (1997–2005). This study concluded these programs "are dominated by conservative voices from newsmakers to commentators."[67] The second study analyzed nearly one thousand guests who appeared on the same three programs as the first study, plus those who appeared on *Fox News Sunday* from June 2011 through February 2012. This study "found a distinct conservative skew in both the one-on-one interview segments and roundtable discussions."[68] The third study focused on twenty-nine reporters-panelists who made a total of sixty-four appearances on the weekly PBS program *Washington Week* over four months (June–August) in 2010. This study concluded that "what the reporters offer on the show is mostly a forgettable mush of conventional wisdom. . . . Only one guest . . . did not represent a corporate media outlet. . . . *Washington Week* provides exactly the type of apolitical discussion . . . deep-pocketed corporate interests want to see on public television."[69]

The media watch group Fairness and Accuracy in Reporting (FAIR), which sponsored the latter two studies, says that the conservative biases in TV news programming are predictable. "As FAIR has argued, it's likely that the politically connected corporations who sponsor these shows prefer a center/right spectrum of debate that mostly leaves out strong progressive voices who might raise a critique of corporate power."[70] This assessment relates to an earlier observation FAIR made many years ago: "True advocates for the left—people who actually push for progressive social change and identify with left-of-center activists—are almost invisible on TV."[71] Both of these statements accurately describe news media biases—then and now.

Selective Reporting

Selective reporting refers to unstated but routine corporate news media reporting policies and practices that produce a preponderance of flattering news coverage of superclass-favored topics (i.e., views, issues, organizations, activities, policies, people). And it refers to reporting that ignores, downplays, or discredits the merits or significance of all topics that threaten superclass interests. Selective reporting is especially evident in media coverage of business and labor issues.

Business Good, Unions Bad

Selective reporting begins with much greater chunks of news media time and space devoted to covering business issues compared to labor and union issues. One study of TV news found that "union representatives made up less than 0.2 percent of sources on the [three network] evening news shows, making company representatives 35 times more likely to be heard." The study also found workers are almost never interviewed or portrayed as "experts."[72] Although ABC World News made the "American Worker" its March 4, 2011, "Person of the Week," a FAIR report found "U.S. workers are not the person of most weeks at ABC. . . . Labor representatives account for less than 0.2 percent of sources on the network newscasts."[73] In addition to the business community receiving far more network TV news coverage than workers or unions, it receives even more extensive media coverage via cable TV programming (e.g., CNBC, Bloomberg News), corporate media-linked websites (e.g., CNBC.com, CBSMarketWatch.com), and national business publications (e.g., *Wall Street Journal, Forbes, Fortune*); these widely watched and read sources have no parallels among labor union–produced media outlets.

Media portrayals of business interests, corporate actions, and company executives in positive terms, plus profiles glamorizing corporations-as-heroes, are prominent, routine features of selective reporting. Such presentations stand in sharp contrast to complaints by some corporate officials that the media often treat businesses harshly. The evidence overwhelmingly supports the conclusion that "the standard media—mainstream newspapers, magazines, and broadcasters—have always been reliable promoters of the corporate ethic."[74] This conclusion is further illustrated and supported by *Extra!*'s "Fear & Favor Review," which, every year, documents the flattering, preferential, and indulgent treatment and coverage afforded to corporations and wealthy elites by corporate media firms via their various media outlets.[75]

There is a sharp contrast between how the mainstream news media report on corporations versus unions. Unions are frequently treated harshly by corporate news media reports, which often describe them as outdated, confrontational, out of touch with global economic realities, selfish, and corruption riddled. Several studies have documented the reality that corporate news media coverage of unions, their leaders, and their activities is overwhelmingly hostile and negative.[76]

The Chicago Teachers Union (CTU) strike in September 2012 was a high-profile example of negative corporate news media reporting on unions. National and local television and print coverage suggested "teachers were primarily concerned with matters of obvious self-interest—how much they make, how they can keep their jobs, how to avoid accountability."[77] Largely ignored by the media were teachers' concerns with keeping public schools "necessary community institutions" and their opposition to privatization and standardized testing as part of a corporate agenda to close public schools, create profit-making opportunities with charter schools, ignore the needs of low-income students, and destroy teachers' unions.[78] Instead, the media favored "a storyline that suggested teachers were simply protecting their turf." Reflecting the negative tone of media reporting was a *USA Today* editorial condemning the strike that began with the headline "Chicago's Striking Teachers Flunk the Sympathy Test."[79] But despite negative corporate media reporting on the union and the strike, parents and students overwhelmingly supported the teachers' actions, their union, and the contract won by the CTU.[80]

The corporate news media's negative "framing" of the CTU, the strike, and the teachers who supported it was consistent with earlier negative media reports on both teachers' and public-sector unions.[81] In those instances, it is interesting that extensive negative media reporting occurred *despite* polls revealing widespread public support for teachers' and public-sector workers' unions and their pay and benefit levels.[82] Media critic Ben Bagdikian's observations regarding corporate power and media reporting on unions echo the findings of most research in this area: "The result of the overwhelming power of relatively narrow corporate ideologies has been the creation of widely established political and economic illusions in the United States. . . . [One is] that labor-union-induced wages are a damaging drag on national productivity and thus on the economy. [It is] false but [it has] been perpetuated by corporate-controlled media for decades."[83] (The lessons here? Unions are bad! Silence criticism!)

(handwritten margin note: How do unions threaten corporations?)

Think Tanks (Again!)

Selective reporting on a wide range of topics is reinforced through extensive media reliance on information from superclass-funded "official sources" such as think tanks. Studies of media references to think tanks according to their ideological orientations have consistently found an overwhelming reliance on conservative and centrist organizations. A recent study found 15,967 citations by U.S.-based major newspapers and U.S. radio and TV transcript databases to think tank sources. There were 5,300 references (33 percent) to conservative or right-leaning think tanks such as the Heritage Foundation and 7,512 references (47 percent) to centrist organizations such as the Brookings Institution. By contrast, the study found only 3,155 references (20 percent) to progressive think tanks such as the Economic Policy Institute (602 references).[84]

Given extensive superclass funding of and media firms' links to conservative-centrist think tanks, the study results are not surprising. Illustrating such links is the Heritage Foundation, the conservative think tank most widely cited by the U.S. media in 2011 (1,540 citations). Of its total 2010 operating revenues ($81.7 million), over 87 percent ($71.3 million) was contributed by ultra-conservative individuals, foundations, and corporations.[85] Among the organization's largest 2010 supporters were Richard M. Scaife, the Allegheny Foundation ($1 million each), the Sarah Scaife Foundation ($500,000), the Adolph Coors Foundation ($100,000), and Exxon-Mobil ($50,000). Heritage's board of trustees includes, for example, Steve Forbes (*Forbes* magazine) and Richard M. Scaife.[86] Heritage officers and fellows are well paid to promote conservative views. CEO Edwin J. Feulner Jr. received $1,025,922 in total compensation in 2010; in that same year most of the organization's eleven vice presidents received incomes in the $200,000 range; the five highest-paid Heritage fellows received average incomes of $234,000 each.[87]

THE SPIN-CONTROL PROCESS

"We face a Truth Emergency in the United States, largely as a result of dominant, top-down, managed news agencies of information control."

—Mickey Huff, *Censored 2012*, 289

The *spin-control process* refers to a wide array of deceptive and propaganda-driven media practices. It involves media owners, managers, reporters, pundits, and advertising-public relations firms using the information industry as a platform for disseminating news, commentary, images, and advertising slanted in favor of superclass and corporate interests. The objectives of spin control include marketing and legitimizing superclass-favored public policies (especially national economic, military, educational, and social policies), political candidates and public officials, and corporate products, services, and images. Spin control involves a symbiotic linkage between the information industry and the public relations (PR) industry, a multibillion-dollar corporate enterprise based on the twin goals of manipulation and deception.[88] Using the information industry as a platform, the public relations industry provides a wide array of services—mainly to superclass, corporate, and political clients—ranging from conventional press releases to commercial and political advertising campaigns to "the hiring of spies, the suppression of free speech, and even the manufacture of 'grass roots' movements."[89] "Surveys show that PR accounts for anywhere from 40 to 70 percent of what appears as news."[90]

The spin-control process operates at two levels. The first involves interpretation: it consists of information-industry-channeled news reporting and commentary that is "shaded"—through corporate media professionals' choices of value-laden terms, images, references, context, and illustrations—in directions that reflect positively on superclass-favored ideas, policies, organizations, and interests and negatively on topics disfavored by elites. The second level involves propaganda, deception, and calculated manipulation. It consists of all forms of advertising and public relations strategies and tactics aimed at manipulating target populations' opinions, attitudes, tastes, and behaviors (those of the privileged and working classes) on behalf of goals most often established by superclass-controlled corporate and political clients.

Spin control is a complex process with many facets extending beyond the scope of this book. The purpose of this section is simply to highlight, through illustrative examples, how each spin-control level furthers superclass interests, often in ways that conceal the nature and extent of these interests and of superclass power as well.

Spin Control: Interpretation

As noted earlier in this chapter, tensions between superclass ideological assertions that the U.S. economic and political systems are the best in the world and routine corporate practices producing a variety of negative economic and political consequences for the working class are problematic for elites. Efforts to reduce or rec-oncile these tensions are a routine focus of the spin-control process. Most corporate media reporters and pundits (supported by superclass leaders and most top elected and appointed government officials) typically address these tensions with news and commentary that "spin" U.S. economic and social problems through interpretations that deflect attention from the class-based structured inequalities that underlie many such problems.

In the world of spin control, problematic societal conditions, such as America's chronic economic malaise and high unemployment, are typically interpreted as highly complex, difficult to fully comprehend, and challenging to resolve. These qualities are claimed to stem in part from the complicated causal factors that are typically represented in the corporate media as causing such problems. Of course, the "causes" of problematic societal conditions are never identified as class power inequalities. Instead, they are more often interpreted as stemming from multiple sources such as individual-level qualities (e.g., low levels of intelligence, psychological problems, or dysfunctional cultural qualities), subcultural pathologies, governmental meddling, and temporary, unavoidable, but good-for-everyone-in-the-long-term consequences of large-scale "natural laws." These latter forces often include the wonderful and mys-terious "free market" or the equally magical "global economy." Two important effects of spin control regarding societal problems are (1) the public is distracted from the problematic effects of superclass domination of the media and indeed of most other institutions in the society; and (2) "solutions" to societal problems that would in-volve substantial redistributions of resources from the superclass (and corporations) to the working class are rarely articulated, considered, or implemented.

Spin Control and Austerity Policies

Corporate media reporting on government budget deficits, the rising federal debt, and the "need" for austerity policies to contain government spending illustrate the interpretation form of spin control in the United States today. In recent years the corporate news media have frequently called attention to the triple realities of trillion-dollar federal budget deficits, a rapidly rising national debt (up from $8.4 trillion in 2006 to $17 trillion in 2013), and continuing large shortfalls of tax rev-enues (versus expenditures) for many state and local governments.[91] These accounts often include the views of conservative pundits who favor austerity policies as the only realistic way to deal with the deficit and debt issues. Such policies involve deep cuts in government spending for programs that benefit the working class, such as Social Security, Medicare, and Medicaid, but leave in place previous tax cuts benefit-ing millionaires, billionaires, and corporations.[92]

Findings of recent studies concerning how the corporate news media cover defi-cits, debt, and austerity policies indicate that the interpretation level of spin control is a key feature of reports and commentary on these issues. A 2010 study found that "mainstream media discussions of budget deficits and state debt . . . [tend to] make sensational and deeply conservative assertions about the costs of already threadbare social safety nets in the United States. [And] they rely almost exclusively on the assumptions, arguments, and data of 'free market' think tanks and economists, failing to incorporate the views of left or liberal economists who dispute [conservative claims]."[93] A 2011 study regarding how the U.S. news media report on the causes of the federal deficit found that "media coverage of the policy change that contributed most to the deficit, the Bush tax cuts, 'was tenuous at best.'" Instead, this study found, "TV journalists have frequently given the impression that Social Security and Medicare are responsible for the deficit . . . [when in fact] Social Security and Medicare contribute nothing to the deficit."[94] A 2012 study looked at U.S. media support for the austerity policies of conservative British Prime Minister David Cameron and American pundits' arguments that the U.S. government should emulate those policies. The study found that after two years, the British austerity policies led not to economic recovery in the United Kingdom but to another recession. And it found that the U.S. news media and pundits have not acknowledged either the failure of Britain's austerity policies or that they were wrong to suggest the United States should emulate those policies.[95]

In late 2012 and early 2013 the range of U.S. political debate on austerity policies and deficits was, as reported by the corporate news media, limited to center-right views. The dominant interpretative narrative embedded in corporate media coverage of these issues endorsed austerity policies (i.e., sharply reduced government spending on social programs) as the only "realistic" means by which the financial health of government and the economy could be restored.[96]

As we pointed out in chapter 9, in late 2012 President Obama side-stepped the so-called fiscal cliff peril via a "compromise" bill that increased taxes on households earning more than $450,000 and put off the issues of spending cuts and deficit-debt reduction for another day. In early 2013 Obama publicly opposed cuts in "entitlement programs" (e.g., Social Security, Medicare, Medicaid), but as one progressive observer noted, "In [the] past round of budget bargaining, Obama proposed alarming cuts to key safety net programs that will be considered in upcoming negotiations."[97] Obama's willingness to cut these programs in the past as part of a "grand bargain" means that "Social Security and Medicare benefits could end up back on the chopping block."[98] Meanwhile, the Campaign to Fix the Debt, led by more than ninety CEOs of major U.S. corporations, "has set its sights on so-called entitlements—to the delight of the mainstream media. Jonathan Alter, of *Bloomberg View* . . . wrote 'Democrats must learn to live with—and vote for—changes in entitlements.'"[99] Thus, the corporate media spin entitlement cuts as a necessary form of "shared sacrifice"—despite opposition by a majority of Americans to austerity policies that would cut government spending on social programs.[100]

Spin Control: Propaganda

The public relations industry is the major force driving explicit, calculated spin control through the use of propaganda of all sorts, advertising, and newer techniques such as the production and placement of difficult-to-spot "fake news" in conventional news outlets and contrived "astroturf movements" (represented as authentic "grassroots movements") to support any given client's interests.[101] The industry is led by large firms, such as Burson-Marsteller, which, as noted in chapter 7, is owned by the WPP Group, a huge, transnational communications and lobbying conglomerate. In 2012 the U.S. PR industry employed about 210,000 PR professionals (53,000 PR managers and 157,000 PR specialists), which was more than twice the 85,000 U.S. news analysts, reporters, and correspondents employed that year.[102] As we noted earlier, the impact of PR on news content in the mainstream media is staggering in that it "accounts for anywhere from 40 to 70 percent of what appears as news."[103] While propaganda-based spin control takes many forms, we focus here on one form used to promote and conceal superclass and corporate interests and power: corporate image advertising.

Corporate Image Advertising

Billions of dollars are spent annually on all methods, including advertising, to promote free market ideology and the image of corporations as "heroes."[104] Ads attesting to the altruism and benevolent good works of corporations such as Apple, DuPont, ExxonMobil, Ford, General Motors, Google, Microsoft, Toyota, Wal-Mart, and many others are routinely aired on network and cable television, published in the print media, and woven into the fabric of the Internet via Facebook, Twitter, and corporate media websites: "On so-called 'public TV,' a dozen big corporate polluters—including BASF, Goodyear and Mobil—polish their images by underwriting nature shows."[105] The head of a large advertising agency described the purpose of corporate advertising as follows: "It presents the corporation as hero, a responsible citizen, a force for good, presenting information on the work the company is doing in community relations, assisting the less fortunate, minimizing pollution, controlling drugs, ameliorating poverty."[106]

The point of corporate advertising is to create favorable public opinion regarding corporate ideas, motives, and actions. This helps maintain the legitimacy of corporations—and by extension helps protect not only their business interests but also the economic and political interests and power of superclass corporate owners.

THE INFORMATION INDUSTRY: CONCLUSIONS

"Those who are concerned about growing inequality in this country . . . are the silenced majority, silenced by the corporate media."

—Amy Goodman, *In These Times* (December 2012): 35

The mainstream ideology, opinion-shaping, and spin-control processes are driven not by a superclass conspiracy but rather by superclass media ownership and a shared ideology that views the economic and political status quo as the best possible world, in accordance with common classwide interests and routine business practices. These factors weave the threads of superclass preferences and ideological biases into the fabric of virtually all news reporting, commentary, and advertising generated by the information industry. This industry consistently tilts reporting and commentary on events, institutions, personalities, and policies relevant to superclass interests in directions consistent with those interests. Of course, the three processes operating through the information industry may not always lead to a uniform, superclass-blessed "corporate ministry of information party line" on all issues and topics. But they clearly produce a lopsided presentation of ideologically infused news and commentary that trends in the direction of superclass interests on most issues, most of the time. Empirical support for this conclusion is provided by a study on inequality and the media that found that "higher inequality is associated with lower media freedom [and] this effect is stronger in democratic regimes."[107] The study also suggests that "in democracies where wealth tilts toward the top, the wealthy have a vested interest in 'capturing' the media and limiting the range of policy options that media grant time and attention."[108]

Acceptance *and* Resistance?

National surveys suggest many in the working class agree with some views supportive of superclass interests, but such surveys also indicate significant shares of the working-class oppose some views and policies favored by the superclass. Illustrative of widely shared views supportive of superclass interests are results for two items in a 2012 survey. First, 72 percent of Americans agreed that "the strength of this country today is based on the success of American business." Second, majorities in all income categories agreed that "Wall Street makes an important contribution to the American economy" (similar to 2009 findings). Agreement ranged from 52 percent among those with incomes of less than $30,000 to 70 percent among those with incomes of $100,000 or more. Thus, *despite* the 2011 advent of the Occupy Wall Street movement, most members of the working class still hold *positive views* of Wall Street.[109]

Illustrative of views held by many in the working class that are divergent from or opposed to views and policies supportive of superclass (and credentialed-class) interests are findings from attitude surveys on "free trade," large corporations, banks, the national news media, and socialism. A majority of Americans (55 percent) "say that free trade agreements lead to job losses in the United States compared with just 8 percent who say these agreements create jobs" (24 percent said they make no difference, 13 percent had no response). More than half of survey respondents with family incomes less than $75,000 said their personal financial situation had been hurt by free trade agreements compared with only 30 percent of those with family incomes of $100,000 or more.[110] Large majorities of Americans (67 percent) say that major corporations and banks have too much power.[111] Also, 57 percent of Americans say large corporations are having a negative effect "on the way things are going in this country today." This "negative effect" view was held by 68 percent of respondents toward banks and by 61 percent toward the national news media. Only small minorities had positive views of large corporations, banks, and the news media (28, 22, and 26 percent, respectively).[112] Finally, nearly one-third (31 percent) of Americans viewed socialism positively (60 percent viewed it negatively). More than four of ten (43 percent) with family incomes below $30,000 viewed socialism positively compared with only 22 percent among those with family incomes of $75,000 or more. A near majority (49 percent) of the eighteen to twenty-nine age group viewed socialism positively. And within two groups, socialism was viewed positively by clear majorities: liberal democrats (59 percent) and black Americans (55 percent).[113]

The results of polls such as those cited above illustrate that despite the pro-superclass biases inherent in the operation of the information industry, working-class members are not totally passive vessels filled with superclass-generated information and propaganda. Instead, these and other poll results provide evidence of resistance among nonelites to the massive dissemination through the information industry of news and commentary that overwhelmingly supports superclass interests. It is apparent that increasing awareness of class-based inequalities among the nonprivileged is fostering a growing awareness of and concerns about the nature and extent of superclass interests, motives, and power in the economic and political arenas.

A further effect of the control processes operating via the information industry relates to the extent of political awareness and engagement among the working class in politics, voting, and governance. Superclass dominance of news media content restricts the expression of alternative perspectives and often leads to confusion or cynicism among working-class members regarding the extent to which the shadow political industry is grounded in superclass resources and how it serves the interests of this class. It also reinforces circumscribed, sterile politics and fatalistic or de facto support among many workers for superclass-favored economic and social policies. With only center-right positions and policies endorsed as legitimate by most government leaders and media pundits, only stunted political debate is possible on key economic and social issues. Corporate news media coverage of tightly constrained political debates on economic and social policy options "leaves most citizens without a coherent view of politics . . . [and] a population unable to select alternative patterns of power sustains the status quo."[114] To the extent that large sections of the working class become confused, disgusted, or disillusioned with the political process, they may then withdraw from it. One result of the disengagement of workers from the political process is that many will no longer take an active part in that process. This outcome, termed "depoliticalization" by media scholar Robert McChesney, favors superclass interests because it removes large numbers of voters who might vote for candidates opposed to superclass-favored policies (should such candidates appear on ballots).[115] The disengagement of potential anti-superclass voters helps ensure the election of pro-superclass candidates and reinforces the legitimacy of government-enacted public policies that favor superclass interests.

The Stealth Industries

Despite the information industry's size, power, and success in promoting super-class interests, most features of it, including details concerning superclass funding and control of its operations, are seldom reported by the corporate media.[116] The dearth of media attention to superclass control of both this industry and the shadow political industry reveals their stealthy qualities: They're there, but they do not register on corporate media "radar screens" or generate much public attention. Why not? We believe the answer has three parts.

First, these industries are cloaked in the same powerful political force field that drives the class taboo on public discussions of superclass power: the corporate media avoids reporting on class power issues because it, along with most government and political leaders, is dominated and funded by the superclass. As a result, there are virtually no serious corporate media inquiries into the organizational foundations of class inequities.[117] Second, the information and shadow industries consist of numerous legitimate organizations with extensive resources and payrolls. Their links to major corporations, the corporate media, and the federal, state, and local governments make them a routine part of society—a nonstory, by media standards. Third, when either industry does become the focus of media reports or books, the "pluralist-special-interest group" model typically organizes and drives these accounts.[118] Viewers and readers are left with the impression that both industries consist of a diverse collection of competing organizations and sectors. No mention is made of the existence or importance of the superclass to funding, organizing, and coordinating the activities of these industries.

These factors help ensure that for each industry, the superclass-based political control structures and processes as well as the class consequences of their actions are largely shielded from media reporting and public attention. The result is the "stunt" Gore Vidal described in the quote at the start of chapter 7: superclass political dominance vanishes behind the unreported, widespread business-as-usual routines and legitimacy accorded to most features of the information and shadow political industries. In effect, the organizational foundations of the class empire and the results of its activities are hidden—in plain sight.

11

Educating for Privilege: Dreaming, Streaming, and Creaming

"The educational system is an integral element of the reproduction of the prevailing class structure of society."

—Samuel Bowles and Herbert Gintis, *Schooling in Capitalist America* (1976)

Nick Caradona and Arnie Seebol were an unlikely pair to become good friends in high school. They were from different parts of the city and from widely different ethnic and religious traditions—one Italian and a nominal Catholic, the other from a Jewish family with practicing parents and recalcitrant kids. Nick's and Arnie's paths would never have crossed if they had not both passed a citywide exam to get into an "elite" science-oriented high school. Most of the kids in the high school were college bound, but the idea of college had never occurred to Nick or Arnie, or to their parents for that matter.

Nick's and Arnie's parents had a tough time making ends meet, because of their unstable low-income jobs. Only one of the four parents claimed a high school diploma. Nick's parents were separated. When Nick was five years old, his father went to Washington, DC, to look for work; he drove a cab in DC for the rest of his working years, but he never returned to his family. Nick's mother worked as a domestic until he was twelve years old and then took a job as a clerk in a laundry. Arnie's father drove a truck for the *New York Daily News*, and his mother did "home work" for shops in the garment district. Nick and Arnie were both urged by their junior high teachers to take the exam for admission to the select high school and, after being admitted, they both enrolled.

At first, the bond between Nick and Arnie was based on the extremity of their shared differences, focusing on the "dirty secrets" of their elders and their ethnic cultures—namely, the disparaging terms and put-downs they had heard used against members of the in-group and the out-group. Arnie taught Nick the fine points of distinction between a *putz* and a *schmuck*. Nick also learned to smack himself in the head and exclaim "*goyisha kopf*" whenever he did something stupid. Arnie told him that Jews would use this routine whenever they did something foolish, exclaiming with the phrase that they were acting like Gentiles. It reminded Nick of his grandfather's frequent practice of referring to someone as an American in broken English ("You must be 'Merican"), pronounced in such a way that it sounded very much like "merde de cane," which Italians would understand literally as "shit of the dog." It was an unschooled double entendre, which Nick taught Arnie to use against other kids in school.

Arnie and Nick soon discovered other bonds. They both liked baseball (Nick a Yankees fan, Arnie a Dodgers fan), and both had a flair for "hustling," as they were always short of money. They took bets in school from other students, who would choose three baseball players whom they expected would get a total of six hits in that day's ball games. The odds on each bet were three to one. Thus a kid would bet a nickel that his three favorite players would get a total of six hits that day. If the three players scored the six hits, the bettor won fifteen cents; if not, Nick and Arnie won the nickel. The odds were always with the "bookmaker" as long as there were a sufficient number of bettors. Many kids had favorite ball players who rarely got more than one hit a game, but they bet on them nonetheless. Nick and Arnie would also "pitch pennies" and play cards during the lunch hour. Their high school was huge (five thousand students), so there was always plenty of "action" for Nick and Arnie.

Late in their senior year, Nick started to have problems, academically and otherwise. He went "on the hook" too many times and faked letters of excuse from his mother. In the midst of these problems, he quit high school a month before the end of term, failing to take any final exams. He went to work as a "runner" for a bookmaker and was soon "promoted" to a "writer" in a betting room where men assembled to talk about horse racing and to make bets on races at a number of tracks in New York, New Jersey, and the New England area. Off-track betting was illegal, but it was carried out openly with the paid-for cooperation of local police. Arnie graduated on schedule and went to work for his uncle in his dry cleaning store. Arnie would learn all about the business, and he hoped one day to own his own store or several stores.

The preceding vignette calls attention to how the intersection of students' social class backgrounds and educational opportunities for upward mobility can sometimes be both serendipitous and problematic. Nick and Arnie were kids who showed some talent in elementary school. Their teachers had a "dream" that they were worthy of moving into an educational tracking system that gave talented kids a chance to "make it" in the opportunity contest—meaning a chance to go to college. But Nick and Arnie themselves did not have the dream, and they never gave any thought to the track that could lead to a college education and beyond. It was partly because the cost of college-going was beyond the means of Nick and Arnie's parents. But it also required Nick and Arnie to forgo the income they would earn from working and the claim to adult status that comes with the end of schooling. Many of Nick and

Arnie's classmates were middle class and college bound from years of anticipatory socialization. They were "hot-house" kids who had been cultivated for years in an environment of controlled feeding and sunlight. They did not yearn for the freedom of adult status, for their sense of self was fused with the wishes held for them by their parent cultivators.

Nick and Arnie were working-class kids from low-income, working-class families, and their parents were working too hard to be involved in the school activities of their children. The opportunity provided by their admission to an elite high school does not exist in a vacuum. In Nick and Arnie's case, it existed within the working-class culture that was their everyday reality. Thus, if all the poor kids in East St. Louis were suddenly enrolled in a school with good teachers, facilities, and programs, it would be great for the kids, but only so much can be expected to follow from an enriched educational experience. The kids will still be poor, as will their parents and friends. Their educational system and experience is contained within a context, a class structure that shapes events that extend far beyond the classroom. The American dream of equality of opportunity is contradicted daily in primary and secondary schools throughout the country. A substantial body of research indicates that when students come to the "starting line" in first grade, they do not come as equals. They are advantaged and disadvantaged by their class situation, their race or ethnicity, and their gender; all of this shapes school experiences and educational outcomes.[1]

THE AMERICAN EDUCATIONAL SYSTEM

"A fundamental premise of the so-called 'American Dream' is that the postponement of personal gratification, especially in the pursuit of educational goals, will result in social rewards attached to a prestigious occupational position. . . . In the end, the American Dream is a barrier in public education."

—Adalberto Aguirre Jr. and David V. Baker, *Structured Inequality in the United States* (2000)

In effect, if not by design, the American education system functions primarily to transmit advantage and disadvantage across generations. This assertion flies in the face of a powerful and dominant ideology that permeates all levels of society—namely, that education is the great equalizer.[2] Education is what brought Abe Lincoln from a log cabin to the highest office in the land. Education is what gave millions of poor but aspiring immigrants in the United States the chance to be whatever they were willing to work for. This is the ideology of the American dream. The dream is so powerful that parents will compete vigorously to control local schools, so that their programs, teachers, and curriculum will serve the interests of their children. Middle-class parents, in particular, work very hard to see that their child gets the teachers with the reputation for being the best math, or science, or literature teacher. In order to improve their child's chances of getting into an elite college, they are also very supportive of efforts to add advanced placement courses from a local college into the curriculum. In the dream, education is the passport to a future that exceeds (if you are poor) or matches (if you are privileged) the economic situation of your parents.

For the dream to become a reality, schools have to be organized to meet the aspirations of the dreamers. In schools in which all the kids are from professional families, only one kind of education is needed—a college preparatory program. But when the kids in school come from diverse economic backgrounds, a system must be devised to provide not only the best education to the college-bound children from professional families and to some of the poor kids—who, based on probabilities alone, would be able to compete with the college bound—but also a quality educational experience for those who are not heading to college. The idea behind this system is that the educational experience should be designed to meet the "needs of the child."[3] The system is called *tracking*.

Tracking seems to be a very progressive idea, permitting teachers "to tailor instruction to the ability level of their students. A good fit between a student's ability and the level of instruction is believed to maximize the effectiveness and efficiency of the instructional process."[4] Does it not make sense to identify students who are headed to college, white-collar employment, or mechanical trades and provide them with the particular knowledge and skills that will be most useful—vocational and shop courses for the young men and women going to work in factories, keyboarding and word processing for those who would be clerks and secretaries in corporate bureaucracies, and literature, languages, mathematics, and the sciences for those headed toward colleges and universities? The problem with this theory of tracking is that students' vocations need to be identified fairly early in their young lives to make use of this system. Of course, this is no easy task, but the ideology of the American dream states that with the help of "objective" testing, student's strengths can be identified and tracked to make the best use of their abilities. Unfortunately, even though well intentioned, tracking can lead to a "dumbing down" curriculum and lowered expectations for those students who don't appear to be college material.

Tracking may have made some sense in the 1950s and 1960s, when the non–college bound could get good blue-collar jobs in the auto, steel, and rubber industries, and schools were responsible for providing basic numeracy and literacy for skilled and semiskilled workers. It may also have been useful when schools were heterogeneous in terms of the economic backgrounds of their students. If a school had the children of professionals, white-collar clerks, and unskilled workers, tracking was useful to meet the needs of the students who were college-bound or heading into the labor market. But today, many schools are much more homogeneous in terms of students' backgrounds and educational plans. Children from the corporate and managerial classes are generally either in private schools or in suburban schools limited to members of their social class. Virtually all of these students are college bound;

so what would be the point of tracking? At the other end of the class-structure spectrum we have poor rural schools or inner-city schools filled with children from the bottom one-third to one-half of the economic system. The closest thing you might have to tracking in these schools is the effort of dedicated teachers to reach out and identify those with the greatest potential and to groom them for college, hoping that they might have a chance to attend.

Resource-rich homogeneous schools, which today largely serve the children of the affluent and privileged class, are involved in *streaming*, not tracking. *Tracking* is a competitive metaphor, implying a contest among entrants in a race where all the "runners" have an equal chance to win. *Streaming* is a noncompetitive metaphor, implying that participants are "carried along" to their destination without any substantial competition with their peers. If you go to the right private schools or the better suburban schools, college attendance is an assumed outcome for everyone.

An excellent example of the streaming metaphor at the graduate level of education is found in the dean of the Harvard Law School's remarks greeting a new class of students at an orientation session:

> The fact is that you are not competing with each other. Your life at the school and your life as a lawyer will be happier and more satisfying if you recognize that your goal is to become the best possible lawyer so that you can serve your clients and society with maximum skills. Although you will experience frustrations from time to time, I think that rather than the *Paper Chase* you will see the school as much closer to the image involved in a letter we received some years ago from a Japanese lawyer who had just been admitted: "Dear Sir: I have just seen the movie *Love Story* with Ryan O'Neal and Ali McGraw and I am looking forward to a very romantic time at the Harvard Law School."[5]

Compare this "laid-back" welcoming speech by the Harvard dean with the prototype competitive welcome offered by a dean or chancellor to undergraduate students at less "prestigious" universities: "Look at the person on your right and the person on your left. At the end of the first year, only one of you will still be in the program." Those in the privileged classes attempt to create an elementary and high school educational structure that is characterized by streaming, so that their children are "guaranteed" good grades, high test scores, an enriched curriculum, extracurricular activities, and advising that will get them admitted to the country's elite schools. Privileged-class parents also frequently supplement the school's programs by providing their children with special prep classes for college admission tests. Such classes may cost close to $1,000, but, as parents know, "It isn't a matter of just getting into college, but of making it into UC-Berkeley or UCLA or MIT."[6]

Children from privileged-class backgrounds have parents with the time, energy, and money to shape experiences outside of school that provide the social and cultural capital needed for continued academic success. One study compared the summer experiences of fourth-grade students from professional families and from lower- to working-class backgrounds. Consider the following descriptions of summer activities from two students from professional families:

Top 10 Things I Did This Summer: (1) I went to Italy; (2) I read a lot; (3) I went bike riding and did much better at it; (4) I had play dates; (5) There was a book club meeting at my house; (6) I got a new piano teacher, and my piano playing really got better; (7) I went on-line more often and improved my typing; (8) I made candy dots and gingerbread cookies; (9) I was involved in a C. U. [California University] research project; (10) I got my school supplies early, and I am looking forward to getting back to school.

We had sleep-away camp for two weeks—that was so great. Then Vacation Bible School for a week. Then I think we had a free week. This week they had Boy Scout Camp and swimming lessons—next week just swimming lessons. Then, after that grandparents come, they have Science Adventure Camp for a week. Then we all go to Hawaii for two weeks.[7]

In discussing these how-I-spent-my-summer stories, the authors note, "None of the working-class or poor children in our study had summers that were this full of organized and varied activities." And more importantly, they report finding little evidence that these social class differences in summer experiences stemmed from parents' values and preferences. The differences could be traced to time, energy, and money. In short, parents from privileged backgrounds have the resources to shape the in-class and out-of-class experiences of their children, and they do so while supporting the myth of the dream, and extolling the virtues of equality of opportunity as the hallmark of American society.

THE POWER OF THE DREAM

"Schools are less about education than a kind of behavior modification, preparing the vast majority of students for a life . . . in which most will end up employed in essentially unskilled, dead-end jobs. . . . Even those set aside for college graduates require precious little formal education."

—John Bellamy Foster, *Monthly Review* (2011): 8

The myth of the American dream is a powerful force in American life, and it is based on two distinct beliefs: First, that everyone can aspire to levels of success that exceed their starting points in life, because where a person starts life is an accident that can be remedied; and second, that there is equality of opportunity to reach one's goals, and that the game has a set of rules that are fair and capable of producing the desired success goals.

The dream can be a source of inspiration for the young and a source of hope for parents who push their children to better themselves. But it also serves to legitimate the great inequality in society in wealth, power, and privilege by fostering the belief that those who receive high rewards are deserving because they have contributed more in terms of effort and hard work. This is the "myth of meritocracy" that neglects the reality that those born into privilege enjoy the benefits of privilege, which can hardly be called merit.[8] Thus, the dream is a comfort to the privileged but mostly an illusion for the nonprivileged.

Our intergenerational mobility research project (discussed in chapter 5) found that as adults, most children either replicated their fathers' SES rank or moved down in the class structure. As we saw, children from privileged class backgrounds very often replicated that rank as adults. For them the dream was fulfilled. But children whose fathers were at or near the bottom of the SES ladder rarely rose to the top as adults. However, a few *did rise* to the top, thereby "proving" the dream is *possible*. The rare examples of upward mobility reinforce the power of the dream for non-privileged children. What they and their parents see is that the *possibility* of rising exists, but what they don't see is that the odds are overwhelmingly stacked against such outcomes. Those in the bottom ranks (parents and children) are encouraged (by the media, schools, cultural lore, myths, and traditions) to believe that through education and hard work, the dream can become a reality for anyone, even if they were born into poverty (see figure 11.1).

The dream is so pervasive in our culture, so embedded in our family rituals and significant celebrations, that we often follow its logic without examination. It is a kind of cultural reflex leading us to continually search for evidence of the dream in action, and to urge it on others as a guide for living. Consider the following obituary, which the writer, with little or no evidence, chooses to frame within the myth of the dream. The headline reads, "B. Gerald Cantor, Philanthropist and Owner of Rodin Collection, Is Dead at 79." This headline, in half-inch type, is accompanied by an almost full-page story reporting the achievements of the deceased. The story begins,

> B. Gerald Cantor, who started out as a boy selling hot dogs at Yankee Stadium, became a wealthy financier and philanthropist, amassed the world's most comprehensive collection of Rodin sculpture in private hands, and gave much of it away to dozens of cultural institutions, died on Wednesday in Los Angeles after a long illness. . . .
>
> Mr. Cantor, who was raised in modest circumstances in the Bronx, and his wife Iris, who grew up three blocks from the Brooklyn Museum, came to be widely known in New York for their generosity to the Metropolitan Museum of Art, the Brooklyn Museum, and to medical institutions in the city. . . .
>
> Before he was 15, Bernie Cantor became a vendor at Yankee Stadium. "I only worked during Sunday double headers," he recalled, because "you could sell more things" in the delay between the two games. . . .
>
> He graduated from DeWitt Clinton High School and went on to study law and finance at New York University from 1935 to 1937. He originally planned to become a lawyer, but he changed his mind when he spotted a lawyer friend who had had to take a job working with a pickax on a construction project of the Works Project Administration.[9]

This fifty-five-paragraph story about a well-known philanthropist manages to create, for the casual reader, the clear impression in its opening sentence, and in the first few paragraphs, that we are dealing with yet another personification of the "rags to riches" American dream.[10] Poor boy works hard—selling hot dogs, no less, at

Yankee Stadium (a double dose of the dream being played out in the playground of dreams)—achieves phenomenal success, and gives all his money back to the "people" (actually to museums, hospitals, and at least a half-dozen universities).

But before we can make sense of Cantor's life, we need to know what it meant to be raised in "modest circumstances" when he was a child. We also need to know how these modest circumstances carried him to New York University during the depths of the Great Depression. The point of these questions is neither to ignore Cantor's achievements nor to diminish his generosity. The point is to call attention to one of the many ways by which the culture industry (discussed in chapter 13) reinforces the powerful myth of the American dream. Even this straightforward story of one person's life and achievements was "torqued" to feed into the myth. The story not only pumps up the dream but also legitimates the wealth of multimillionaires by first saying they "did it themselves, with hard work and dedication," and by then dwelling on how many millions they "gave back."

Factors of Success?

It is precisely because of such obituaries, *Forrest Gump*–genre films, and other rags-to-riches cultural products that most Americans appear to accept the myth of the American dream. Figure 11.1 reports the results of a national survey that asked

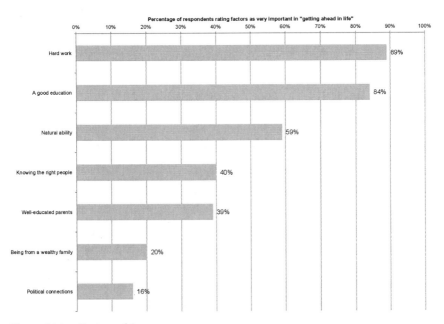

Figure 11.1.   Factors of Success
Source: James A. Davis and Tom W. Smith, *General Social Surveys, 1972–1998* (Storrs, CT: The Roper Center for Public Opinion Research, 1989)

Americans to rate the importance of various factors in "getting ahead in life." Almost nine out of ten Americans report that a good education and hard work are the keys to "getting ahead," whereas only six out of ten say the same about natural ability. In contrast, only two out of ten surveyed say that being from a wealthy family and having political connections are very important. The other factors involving social capital (knowing the right people or having well-educated parents) are considered very important by four out of ten Americans.

Americans put their faith in education and hard work as the keys to success. In answering the survey questions, respondents did not have to make a choice between a wealthy family and a good education. They could have chosen both as being very important. The power of the American dream is that it not only defines the paths to success (education and hard work) but also defines what is not related. The dream cannot tolerate a simultaneous belief in the value of education, which makes great sense in a credentialing society, and the advantage that comes from wealth. The myth creates facts that do not exist (you can be whatever you want to be) and denies facts that do exist (the chances for a poor child to rise to the privileged class are very slim).

The power of the dream among minorities is revealed by findings of a recent study of low-income African American high school students. Students were asked to provide a personal perspective on the importance of their race, class, or gender in limiting or enhancing opportunities for upward mobility ("What can prevent students from doing well in school?" "What is the best way of getting ahead in American society?"). Almost all students accept the "dominant narrative" of how one makes it in America: "When they were asked the best way of getting ahead in American society, without hesitation they discussed the importance of hard work, individual effort, and education."[11] However, they also provided alternative narratives of how race, class, or gender can limit an individual's efforts to improve his or her life chances.

The dream is manufactured in the popular culture, but the main vehicle for achieving it, as claimed by leaders in business, education, and government, is the school system. Equality of opportunity for all, regardless of birth, is the dominant American ideology. Education is said to be the great equalizer, providing the requisite skills, knowledge, attitudes, and values. But the dream was not always located in the school system. The Horatio Alger success stories popular in the early 1900s described the poor boys who "made it" because of their virtues of thrift, honesty, and hard work.[12] The path to success ran not through the classroom, but through the workplace, where the street-urchin-turned-stockboy caught the attention of the boss due to his virtues. The Horatio Alger secular success myth was consistent with the social realities of that time. Then, preparation for success in work often involved acquiring skills and training in the workplace. Even the so-called knowledge-based professions of law, medicine, and the ministry were open to entry through apprenticeship forms of preparation.

Increasing Educational Attainment

At the beginning of the twentieth century, about 72 percent of the U.S. population, aged five to seventeen years, was attending public elementary and secondary schools. In 1960 the figure was 82 percent; in the mid-1990s it reached 92 percent; and in 2000 it was 95 percent—nearly all elementary-age children are now in school. More telling is that in 1900, only 6.4 percent of seventeen- to eighteen-year-olds graduated from high school; that figure had risen to 68 percent by 1960. In 1995 it rose to 71 percent and then to 75.5 percent in 2009.[13] In 2010, among Americans aged twenty-five or older, 87.1 percent had attained a high school diploma or more.[14] At the top of the educational process, in 1900 about 29,000 Americans received college degrees (associate's, bachelor's, master's, doctor's, and first professional degree); this figure climbed to 477,000 in 1960, to 2.3 million in 2000, and to 3.2 million in 2009. (In 2009, 1.6 million received bachelor's degrees.)[15]

This virtual explosion in America's enrollment at different levels in the educational system probably does not owe simply to the love of learning. Increasingly in the twentieth century, and especially after World War II, good jobs have been linked to educational credentials. First, it was the high school diploma, then the bachelor's degree, and finally the specialized professional degree. Some analysts believe that the strong connection between education and jobs is the result of major technological advances that have changed the skill requirements of jobs. As the proportion of jobs requiring high levels of skill have increased, there has been increased reliance on the formal educational system to provide the required knowledge and skills. However, it is also possible that the increase in educational requirements for jobs is a way that privileged groups protect their access to those jobs that provide the greatest rewards.[16]

As more people enrolled in elementary schools, the high school diploma became the credential for many jobs that were formerly held by people with an eighth-grade education. Then, as enrollments in high school increased, the bachelor's degree became a requirement for many jobs formerly held by people with a high school diploma. And so it goes. With the expansion of higher education and 1.6 million graduates per year from four-year programs, the new credential becomes the answer to the question: What *school* awarded *you* your bachelor's degree? The elite classes (the superclass and their credentialed-class allies) that control the major corporations and universities keep raising the educational bar whenever too many members of the nonprivileged class gain too much access to formerly rare degree credentials.

Once schools became established as the place where people's futures were determined, their programs, activities, and curricula took on a larger significance. Schools became the models of a "small society" where the things that were learned formally and informally were relevant for the larger society. Schooling is carried out on a very rigid schedule, starting and ending at a predetermined time. Weekends are free, and there is an established schedule of vacations. Tardiness and absences must be explained, and if they are excessive, they will be punished. The school has established authority figures who must be followed without question. The Pledge of Allegiance and acceptance of God and country all serve to reaffirm the legitimacy of the established order. The daily activities and classes are built around respect for rules, self-discipline, grades, and performance according to externally imposed standards.

Within this "small society" framework, there is variation among schools, usually reflecting the class composition of its students. Schools for the privileged typically provide students with more opportunities for creativity, autonomy, and self-directed activities, whereas schools for the nonprivileged are more concerned with discipline, obedience, and job-related skills. Pressure for these different emphases often comes from parents. Parents who know their children are going to college emphasize enrichment in the arts, music, and cultural activities; those who know their children are headed for jobs emphasize the need for job-related activities.

Education Effects: Political Participation, Attitudes, Ideology

In addition to the social and technical skills learned at school, students are also prepared for their futures as citizens of a political and economic system. Does schooling have a "liberating" effect on students, calling upon them to question the political-economic order and to play an active role in promoting change or reform? Or does schooling lead students to accept things as they are, believing that they are living in the best of all possible worlds? A number of studies of the schooling experience indicate that schooling has a conservative effect on students and that there are important class differences in this experience.[17]

Earlier research findings on the effects of education on political participation indicate that students from different socioeconomic levels are socialized in schools to play very different roles in the political system, and this is done in a way that legitimates existing forms of economic and political inequality. Children from working-class and lower-middle-class communities are being prepared to continue the low levels of political participation exhibited by their elders. Moreover, they are prepared for a passive role in the political process because they have been taught that the institutions of government work for the benefit of all citizens.[18] Students from the privileged upper-middle-class community are clearly being prepared to participate in and influence the political agenda. The privileged are made aware of the role of power, influence, and conflict in public affairs, whereas the nonprivileged are encouraged to work together in harmony.[19]

Other research on the political effects of schooling indicates that students' early socialization leads them to develop positive and trusting orientations toward the symbols and institutions of political authority.[20] Moreover, schools transmit the idea that government is the main center of power in society, thereby neglecting the role of large corporations and the conflict that exists among competing political and economic interests.[21] This shaping of students' attitudes toward the economic and political order tends to bring them into conformity with the dominant ideology that serves the interests of the privileged class.

The longer students are in school the greater is their exposure to the dominant ideology. In a study of elementary and secondary students from urban schools in the southwestern United States, two-thirds of third-graders supported government intervention in the economy through assistance for those out of work and for the poor. The same level of support was found among sixth-graders, but less than one-third of the ninth- and twelfth-graders supported an active role for government. Student attitudes toward private ownership of major industries became increasingly positive across the four grade levels, with 16 percent of third-graders being positive compared to 63 percent of twelfth-graders. Finally, attitudes toward trade unionism became increasingly negative as they progressed across grade levels. Third-graders were least negative toward unionism (17 percent) and twelfth-graders were most negative (59 percent).[22]

There may be naiveté and uncertainty in students' attitudes (especially third-graders), but it is clear from this research that the ideology that benefits the privileged gains greater strength in the minds of students as they move from third to sixth to ninth to twelfth grade. Students do not necessarily start school supporting the ideas of private property, government restraint, or anti-unionism, but that is clearly where most of them wind up at high school graduation. Schools function to affirm the legitimacy of the dominant political and economic order and perpetuate the myth of equality of opportunity. In so doing, they serve the interests of the privileged class.

TRACKING AND STREAMING

"The school creates legitimacy and imparts the dominant ideology in a variety of ways."

—Martin N. Marger, *Social Inequality* (2011), 236

One of the main concerns of the privileged class is to protect their advantage and to transmit it to their children. In a society where educational credentials are used by the privileged to justify their rewards, it is critical that the rules of the game are designed to give advantage to the children of the privileged class. Of course, others can also play by these rules if they choose, but it may be comparable to poker players who try to draw to an inside straight—a risky bet.

Tracking and streaming are two ways in which the rules of the game are used to give advantage to children of the privileged class. In order to understand how these strategies work, it is important to remind ourselves how pre-college U.S. public education is financed. In general, states use state-level taxes "to provide about 48 percent of the budget for elementary and secondary schools. Local districts contribute around 44 percent, drawn mostly from local property taxes. . . . The federal government [provides about] 8 percent of state education budgets."[23] The amount of money raised through property taxes depends on the tax rate applied to the assessed value of homes and businesses. Communities with more expensive homes and a strong business community can generate more tax revenue for educational purposes than those without these features. We should note that the property tax–school funding link in the United States is changing. Some states, like Indiana, have shifted school funding from property tax–based formulas to statewide taxing and funding systems.[24] But even in Indiana and other states that are changing how schools are funded, property taxes remain an important revenue source for funding some features of public education such as buildings and equipment.[25]

In funding public schools, families in more affluent districts may pay higher property taxes in total dollars than families in poorer districts, but they often pay a lower tax rate than families in poorer districts. This is the case because the aggregate value of their homes and businesses is larger than in poor districts. Thus, a lower tax rate in affluent districts generates more total dollars than a higher rate in a poor district. An additional advantage enjoyed by affluent home owners is the fact that property taxes and mortgage interest are deductible from their federal income taxes, thereby giving the privileged classes a larger indirect subsidy for the education of their children than that received in poorer communities.

Evidence from research on the effects of school expenditures indicates that higher per-pupil expenditures for instruction are associated with higher levels of student achievement.[26] Higher student achievement comes from smaller class size and a higher ratio of teachers to students. The more money a school can spend on instruction, the more teachers they can hire and the more money they have to pay experienced teachers. The presence of more teachers and better-paid teachers also improves the social environment of the school, as lighter workloads both improve teacher morale and enable teachers to get to know students better. Thus, spending more money for more and better-qualified teachers improves student achievement, but such spending is often not an option in poorer school districts.

In heterogeneous school districts, where children of the privileged and nonprivileged may be in the same school, there is a single pool of money to fund that school. That money is used to get the best teachers, the most up-to-date instructional technology, the best laboratory equipment, films, computers, and other educational resources. In order to give an advantage to privileged-class children, it is necessary for the school to develop programs that allocate the best teachers, the most computers, and the best resources to programs that are most likely to be taken by the privileged class. The money is not given to the children of the privileged class, but to programs in which they are more likely to enroll. Thus, tracking is invented—a system that allocates resources to programs that are tied to distinct outcomes—a college preparation or a vocational preparation. Tracking is a form of inequality within schools.

In some heterogeneous school districts children of the privileged and nonprivileged may not be in the same school but in different schools in the same school district. In theory, each school in the district should receive the same per-pupil expenditure because the tax money was obtained to support all the schools in that district. Most past research on school funding has compared per-pupil expenditures across school districts, and to no one's surprise the school districts with affluent families had the highest per-pupil expenditures and the poorer districts had lower expenditures. But in one study, several enterprising researchers obtained data on spending among schools *within* the same school district.[27] They studied spending and student achievement across eighty-nine elementary schools in the same district. Instead of each school having the same per-pupil expenditure for their district, "total per-student spending among elementary schools within the district ranged from $3,045 to $8,165."[28] They also found that inequality in spending appears to reflect the class composition of schools—schools with the highest proportion of poor students were allocated fewer local tax dollars to spend on instruction and operations that promote a learning environment. Finally, students in schools that received more tax dollars to spend on instruction and operations exhibit higher levels of academic achievement, as measured by performance on state proficiency tests in reading, writing, math, science, and citizenship.

The presence of inequalities in per-pupil spending across schools within the same district is quite different from the well-known spending inequalities that exist between affluent and poor school districts. Spending inequalities within the same school district point to the existence of the powerful and hidden effects of class power on how economic resources are distributed to schools. Why two schools in the *same* school district should receive significantly different levels of per-pupil funding can only be understood by examining how school officials, local political leaders, and more affluent parents shape the school budget process in a class-biased manner.

Public School Streaming

In homogeneous school districts, where almost all the children are from the privileged classes or almost all are from lower classes, there is no need for tracking. In the rich schools, almost all children are headed for college. Rich school districts have more money to spend on educational programs than poor districts in part because they are located in areas with higher property values. Higher assessed property values produce more tax revenues for those school districts because this is how a large share of public schools' budgets is funded in most states.

Even if more states move away from using property taxes as the primary source of school revenue, affluent school districts are likely to continue to find ways to fund the schooling of their children at higher levels than poor districts. We know that schools with more money hire more qualified teachers, purchase better equipment, provide more extracurricular activities, offer better guidance and counseling, and provide a better all-around education than is the case in poor school districts. In poor schools, perhaps only one or two out of ten children may go to college. In rare cases where the proportion of students from a poor school district who go on to attend college exceeds one in ten, it is usually because of special circumstances. For example, a local state college or a community college may be located nearby, enabling poor students to work or live at home while attending school. The availability of such resources to students from poor school districts is obviously advantageous to some of those students. But even if such resources are available, students from poor districts find it difficult to compete in college because the quality of earlier education they received was often lacking in all areas of their schooling experience.

Rich school versus poor school comparisons remind us that streaming is a form of inequality that is most evident in comparisons of student experiences and opportunities between these two types of schools. Streaming students through elementary and high school to privileged-class educational and career destinations occurs in rich schools, but not in poor schools. This is the case because rich schools provide students with school-based experiences, opportunities, and other forms of support not typically available in poor schools.

Public School Tracking

Tracking, despite its official noble intentions, is a process that segregates students by ability groupings, curriculum choices, race, and socioeconomic status. It is a process that separates winners from losers in the contest for good jobs and high income, and it has been used in primary and secondary education to provide different and unequal education for those believed to be college bound and those believed to be heading directly to the labor market. In the early 1970s, about 85 percent of public schools used a system of tracking.[29] In the mid-1990s, two-thirds of high schools were moderately tracked and 60 percent of elementary schools practiced some form of whole-class ability grouping.[30] In the mid-2000s, the percentages of public high schools and elementary schools using some form of tracking were about the same as in the mid-1990s.[31]

Some tracking programs provide maximum separation, as students remain in the same track for all their courses, and some provide minimum separation with all students taking at least some courses together. Placing students in tracks based upon beliefs about their abilities can produce a powerful self-fulfilling prophecy effect. Track placement is directly and indirectly related to the class and racial background of students. The direct effects are a result of the expectations that teachers and administrators have of children from higher-class backgrounds.[32] The indirect effect occurs because less privileged children may express less interest in college, receive less parental and peer encouragement to attend college, and lack necessary achievement scores to be selected for placement in the college track.[33] There is substantial agreement among analysts of tracking, based on strong research evidence, that tracking has negative consequences for low-income and non-white students.

Inequalities in School Spending and Student Experiences

Inequalities between schools are revealed most sharply in the differences between school districts in the amount of money they spend to educate their students. Per-pupil expenditures are the best single indicator used to compare schools on the quality of their teachers, programs, and facilities. The national per-pupil average expenditure was $10,905 in 2009. Some states spent more, as illustrated by

Vermont ($18,913), New Jersey ($15,983), and Wyoming ($15,742). Other states spent much less, as illustrated by Nevada ($7,777), Mississippi ($7,814), and Utah ($8,141).[34] Within states, comparisons between rich and poor school districts (based on land values and family income) provide the most revealing evidence of class-based inequality. Urban school districts in larger cities spend far less money than suburban districts. Per-pupil expenditures in 2011 in the Chicago area ranged from a high of $11,864 in a suburban school district to $9,860 in the inner city.[35] Earlier studies of schools in New Jersey and New York revealed that per-pupil expenditures were between $4,000 to $7,000 higher in suburban schools as compared to per-pupil expenditures in inner-city schools.[36]

Per-pupil spending disparities are also found in comparisons of urban and rural schools. For example, earlier studies found spending in New York urban school districts was about $4,300 higher per pupil than in nonurban districts.[37] Rural areas, which are often predominantly white, spend far less money on schooling than either the urban or suburban school districts.[38] Wealthy suburban schools that spend nearly twice as much per pupil as poor, inner-city districts can readily afford better teachers, better facilities, smaller classes, and a variety of educational enrichment activities and programs. Such advantages will never find their way into inner-city schools as long as much school funding is based on property taxes.[39]

Both tracking and streaming are linked to and reflect class inequalities. One of the most important consequences of both practices is their effect on college enrollment. Large numbers of students in wealthy school districts are "streamed through" their elementary and high school years and are well prepared academically, socially, and emotionally to succeed in college. However, in school districts that have heterogeneous student populations and that track students, only those in the college-prep track have access to the resources needed to prepare for college.

Students who are in vocational tracks or in high schools composed primarily of students from low-income families are at a great disadvantage. Their educational aspirations are reduced because they receive little encouragement from peers and parents in their social milieu. Even students with high academic achievement and potential are less likely to think about college as a goal.[40] This occurs because students who are the children of doctors, lawyers, and other professionals are likely to receive sustained social encouragement from parents, friends, and teachers to view college attendance as a "natural destination" in their educational careers. Ample research evidence indicates that even students with high academic achievement and high measured intelligence are not likely to enter college if they are from lower economic groups. For example, several studies have found that students from low-income backgrounds who score high on academic achievement tests are far less likely attend college than students from affluent backgrounds who scored low on such tests.[41]

Inequalities: College, Incomes, Opportunities

The advantages of a college degree, apart from the life experiences and social and cultural capital gained by four years of study, include better chances for employment in higher-prestige jobs and higher incomes. In 1979, a male college graduate received almost 50 percent more income than a high school graduate.[42] "[But] in 2010 college graduates' lifetime earnings were nearly twice (97% more than) those of high school graduates."[43] The advantage in earnings for college graduates is also clearly evident in annual income comparisons by education completed. As we saw in chapter 5, in 2011 the median annual earnings of full-time, full-year workers who were high school graduates was about $32,000. In contrast, the median annual earnings of college graduates with a bachelor's degree was about $55,000 in 2011 (see figure 5.7). Over a lifetime, a college graduate will now earn about $1 million more than a high school graduate. In short, access to high-prestige and high-income positions is more closely tied to educational credentials today than was the case several decades ago.

Evidence from the past forty years indicating how education is linked to better jobs and higher earnings has led many government and business leaders to propose more and better education as the solution to many of society's problems. Workers displaced by new technology or plant closings are told that they must improve their skills to find work in the "new economy" (explored in chapter 3). Young men and women from the poorest families are encouraged to get a high school diploma and to think about going to college, even if only a community college.

Government leaders often give inspirational speeches encouraging young people to attend college, and they sometimes talk about increasing financial aid to students, but government assistance falls far short of college costs. In 2010–2011, the average annual cost of attending a four-year U.S. university totaled $16,712 at public schools and $44,619 at private schools (tuition, fees, room and board).[44] Pell grants, the major source of federal assistance to financially disadvantaged students, provided a maximum grant of $5,550 per year to students in 2011, but the average Pell grant award was only $3,800 that year.[45] For students with low incomes or who are from low-income families, the gap between the cost of attending college and the limited financial assistance they receive is largely covered by loans. As a result of money borrowed by poor students and others, including many from more affluent families, student debt has grown rapidly over the past several years. In 2011, "among the two-thirds of Bachelor's students who graduate with debt, the average size of their loan is just under $28,000 (not including interest)."[46]

It is difficult to argue against the claim that a college education improves a person's career and income prospects. Even after taking into account the gloomy statistics cited in chapter 5 regarding the stagnation of college graduates' earnings over the last forty years, college graduates are far better off economically than those who do not complete college. Having a college degree has certainly proven beneficial for members of the privileged class who have converted their credentialed skills into high-paying positions in business, finance, and the professions. Perhaps that's one reason why a large percentage of privileged-class parents send their children to college. Data from the U.S. Department of Education indicate that about 70 percent of high school graduates from wealthy families attend college, compared to only 21 percent from low-income families. Extensive data collected over many years indicate that a person's social class position is the best predictor of college attendance and graduation.[47]

Many Americans have gotten the message about the importance of advanced educational credentials to career success in the new economy. The privileged class sends the vast majority of its children to college, and today a substantial share of middle-income families make the financial sacrifices necessary to send a large share of their children to college as well. The problem for the latter group is that not all college credentials are created equal. Students in this group often find out too late that a college degree is no guarantee of full-time work, pay raises, or employment in jobs requiring a degree. For example, in 2011–2012 "the unemployment rate for young college graduates (ages 21 to 24) averaged 9.4%." And, as we saw in chapter 5, median earnings of college graduates fell 9.5 percent over the 1973–2011 period (figure 5.7). A large share of that decline occurred in just the last decade as "average wages for full-time workers fell by 5.4% . . . between 2000 and 2011." Finally, about 40 percent of college graduates under twenty-five are now working at jobs "that [do] not require a college degree."[48]

As the next section explains, the less than pleasant post-college scenarios described above are more likely to be experienced by those who graduated from nonelite colleges, especially those with majors that are not much in demand in today's new economy or that do not lead to admission into professional programs (e.g., law, medicine, pharmacy, business, engineering). Unhappy outcomes are much less likely for students from privileged-class backgrounds who graduate from elite colleges and universities. And they are less likely for graduates, even from nonelite schools, who wisely chose specialty majors much in demand in the new economy (e.g., software engineering, accounting, actuarial sciences, architecture).

PRINCETON VS. PODUNK: GETTING "CREAMED"?

> "It is often asserted that new technologies will equalize learning opportunities for the rich and poor. It is devoutly to be wished for, but I doubt it will happen."
>
> —Neil Postman, *Nation* (October 9, 1995)

Up to this point, we have demonstrated the strong influence schooling has on the reproduction of class inequality. Contrary to the beliefs contained in the American dream, education is not the means for providing equality of opportunity to all Americans regardless of their social position at birth. Schooling serves to reproduce inequality through the power of the myth of the American dream and through the effects of tracking and streaming as the way to deny equal access to the means for upward mobility. We now continue our analysis of schooling by examining the question of who goes to college and where they go.

As noted earlier in this chapter, rates of college attendance have increased dramatically in the past seventy years. In 1940, 216,000 degrees were awarded by U.S. col-

How has the dream changed over time? Manifest Destiny? coming to America? owning land?

leges and universities. Forty years later, 1980 saw nearly 1 million bachelor's degrees award by accredited institutions. In 2010, U.S. colleges and universities awarded 833,000 associate's degrees, 1.6 million bachelor's degrees, 611,000 master's degrees, and 140,000 doctorates (e.g., PhD, MD, EdD, DDS, JD).[49] This great expansion in college enrollment has introduced greater diversity in the college environment as compared with 1940, especially with regards to women, who now earn a majority of all associate's, bachelor's, and master's degrees awarded each year in the United States. Even so, college populations are still largely white. Excluding degrees earned by non-resident aliens, in 2009 white men and women accounted for 72 percent of all U.S. college degrees. Among minorities, 11 percent of all degrees were earned by blacks, 9 percent by Hispanics, and 7 percent by Asians.[50] In terms of class backgrounds, the 21 million students enrolled in U.S. colleges today are largely from middle-income and higher-income families—evident from the data cited earlier regarding family income and college attendance. Even so, a significant number of college students are from working-class and low-income family backgrounds. Perhaps what we have today is a modified version of the American dream, where some members of the nonprivileged classes are actually able to gain access to a measure of equality of opportunity. Perhaps.

The main argument of this section is that although the expansion of college enrollments has resulted in larger numbers of nonprivileged youth attending colleges and universities today as compared to the past, there has, at the same time, been movement toward a more rigidly class-based system of inequality within the framework of higher education. This more subtle and less visible form of inequality is reflected in the schools that privileged and nonprivileged students attend and in the areas in which they choose to specialize. Students from homes with modest finances may be more likely to select two-year or four-year programs with immediate employment opportunities rather than to aim for advanced or professional degree programs. In addition to class-based choices of academic majors, there is some evidence that female and nonwhite students also make career choices that result in lower incomes.[51]

The consequences of class-, race-, and gender-based systems of inequality within higher education are as serious in terms of wasted human resources as the class- or race-based systems of tracking and streaming in high school that determine who goes to college. Let us begin with the 4,495 institutions of higher education (in 2009) that are available to serve the needs of America's aspiring youth. About 38 percent (1,721) of those institutions are two-year colleges that students attend typically because they either lack the academic credentials to be admitted to a four-year institution or lack the money to pay for tuition, room, and board, or they are already employed and trying to improve their credentials and career opportunities.

Outside of the two-year schools, we find 2,774 four-year schools (62 percent of all higher education institutions) that are highly differentiated.[52] About two hundred of these institutions are the larger and more prestigious research universities that award almost all the professional and advanced degrees in the United States. These institutions graduate the doctors, lawyers, engineers, scientists, economists, and managers that populate the privileged class. These two hundred "top" universities can be further subdivided into the Ivy League (Brown, Columbia, Cornell, Dartmouth, Harvard, Pennsylvania, Princeton, and Yale), top twenty private universities (e.g., Chicago, Stanford, Columbia, Duke), top twenty state universities (e.g., California-Berkeley, North Carolina, Pennsylvania, UCLA, Texas), the so-called Big Ten (Illinois, Indiana, Iowa, Michigan, Michigan State, Minnesota, Nebraska Northwestern, Ohio State, Penn State, Purdue, and Wisconsin), and other state universities. And then there are the thirty or so small "elite" liberal arts colleges that provide high-quality education, strong social ties (the basis of social capital), and very high tuition (e.g., Amherst, Bates, Bowdoin, Clark, Colby, Franklin and Marshall, Hamilton, Haverford, Hobart, Oberlin, Reed, William Smith, Swarthmore, and Tufts).

The point of this little exercise (aside from the fact that some will complain we have misclassified many schools) is to illustrate that higher education is highly differentiated, with a small number of schools that are very selective about their admissions and consistently rated by many sources as among what those in the privileged class view as the fifty or so "elite" colleges and universities. The differences between the elite and nonelite schools grow larger each day as already-rich colleges get richer through fund-raising programs aimed at their wealthy alumni.[53] The number of elite schools in the United States that confer great advantages on their graduates probably stands at about fifty, or less than 1 percent of all the colleges and universities in the country. The competition to get into elite schools is brutal, and students with wealthy parents are better prepared for the competition.[54] It is no accident that students at elite schools, like Harvard, are often from families with annual incomes well above $250,000. If you are admitted to one of these elite schools, after graduation the odds are dramatically increased that you will also be admitted to one of the elite graduate or professional schools if you apply. And when schooling is completed, the graduates of elite schools will enter high-level positions in the major institutions of American society that are led by the superclass and managed by the privileged class. Students admitted to the "elite 1 percent" are getting "creamed," which is the positive meaning of this term used at the beginning of this section. Those who rise to the top in this system will enjoy the "good life" with all of its material and psychological benefits.

Many students who are enrolled in the 1,721 two-year colleges, and in most of the 2,724 *nonelite* four-year schools (2,774 minus 50 elite schools), are getting creamed in the negative meaning of the term—that is, they are getting "clobbered." Most of these students are caught between a rock and a hard place. They choose to go to college because it is their only hope of getting a "good job." The absence of such jobs for people with only a high school diploma drives most into college. Their parents cannot afford to pay the costs of even nonelite colleges, so many students work and take out loans in the hope that all the debt and sacrifice will pay off in the end. They forego income for four years and incur debt, yet when they graduate, all they may find is a job paying $10–15 an hour, or $20,000–$30,000 per year.

The median starting salary for 2009 college graduates varied widely, from liberal arts majors ($36,715) to chemical engineering majors ($65,142). In between these groups were nursing ($39,920), K–12 teachers ($34,707), business ($45,887), and computer science ($56,128).[55] Clearly, graduates with technical-professional degrees receive higher starting salaries, but as many as 40 percent of graduates reported that the job they held did not require a college degree (only 17 percent of engineering graduates said this, but about 50 percent of graduates in humanities and social sciences said a college degree was not required for their current job).[56] To be sure, at the 2,724 *nonelite* schools there is a small minority of graduates who do well career-wise. They are usually graduates in one of the specialty programs noted earlier who have the skill capital and credentials to command better incomes, but they are not likely to join the privileged class.

Two-Tiered System of Schooling for Privilege

What we envision as a two-tiered system of schooling for privilege is depicted in figure 11.2. The top panel of the figure focuses on the streaming process described earlier in the section on tracking and streaming. The children of the wealthiest members of the privileged class enter the stream in the elite prep schools that prepare students primarily for Harvard, Princeton, and Yale. The remaining children of the privileged class are educated in the resource-rich suburban high schools that are homogeneous in terms of the economic class backgrounds of their students and that are well funded, often by property taxes. Students located in the top panel, members of the privileged class, compete among themselves for admission to a small number (about fifty) of elite universities and liberal arts colleges. These schools are elite because they are well endowed by financial contributions from wealthy alumni, their admissions procedures are highly selective (i.e., they get many more applications than they admit), and degrees from these schools are given preferential "social placement treatment" by employers and elite graduate school programs.[57] Some graduates from these elite schools enter the elite schools of law, medicine, business, and engineering, and most of the rest go into entry-level positions in America's major corporations.

The lower panel of figure 11.2 indicates where most students are located. In 2012–2013, some 3.2 million students graduated from U.S. high schools; of that number, about three hundred thousand graduated from all types of private high schools (including religious-based schools).[58] But of all graduates of private high schools, only a tiny fraction come from elite prep schools such as Groton, Phillips Andover, and Cate.[59] Enrollments in the fifty elite colleges and universities make up a small fraction of the millions enrolled in higher education; thus, the overwhelming proportion of nonprivileged students are enrolled in the 2,724 *nonelite* colleges and universities and the 1,721 community colleges. A very small percentage of nonprivileged high school graduates "escape" the lower panel paths and are granted admission to elite schools, usually owing to their academic record and standardized test scores.[60] A study of Harvard's admission process indicates that the school does attempt to admit a small number of "working-class" students and "students of color"

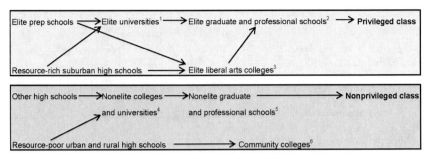

Figure 11.2.   Two-Tiered System of Schooling for Privilege
Notes
Elite universities: approximately twenty, including Harvard, Yale, Princeton, Chicago, Stanford, North-
    western, California–Berkeley, Michigan, Wisconsin, UCLA, North Carolina, Columbia, Duke, Penn-
    sylvania
Elite graduate and professional schools: approximately fifteen, including Harvard, California–Berkeley,
    Yale, Chicago, Wisconsin–Madison, Michigan, Columbia, Stanford, Princeton, Cornell, Illinois–
    Urbana, Pennsylvania
Elite liberal arts colleges: approximately thirty, including Amherst, Bates, Bowdoin, Brown, Bryn Mawr,
    Reed, Strathmore, Tufts, Colgate, Smith, Wellesley, Williams, Oberlin, Hamilton, Franklin and Marshall,
    Wesleyan of Connecticut, Barnard, Brandeis, Mount Holyoke, Haverford, Hobart, Skidmore, Union
Nonelite colleges and universities: approximately 2,700
Nonelite graduate and professional schools: approximately two hundred
Community colleges: approximately 1,700

who have demonstrated academic merit based on their high school grades, college
admissions tests, and other criteria.[61] This possibility of "moving up" describes the
small amount of creaming from the bottom tier of figure 11.2 into the schooling
streams of the privileged class.

One interesting feature of this two-tiered system of schooling for privilege is that
the way it works has not changed very much in the past forty years. Graduates of
the elite colleges and universities obtain higher rates of admission to professional
programs in elite schools and/or better jobs (i.e., prestige, opportunities, and income) than graduates of the nonelite schools, and this is true independent of merit.
The prestige of the degree-granting institution has an effect on postcollege jobs and
incomes over and above the ability of their individual graduates.

In the 1950s, research compared the incomes of graduates from Ivy League
schools, prestigious "technical" schools (e.g., Cal Tech, Carnegie, MIT), elite private
colleges, the Big Ten, other Midwestern colleges, and other eastern colleges. The
findings indicated that the median incomes of male graduates are directly related
to the prestige ranking of the schools, and this pattern was found across different
fields of study; earning power rises with each increase in prestige of the school and
independent of grades.[62]

The patterned advantages enjoyed by graduates of elite schools sixty years ago
are still in place today. Students from privileged-class backgrounds are more likely
to enroll in the most prestigious schools, and they choose programs of study that
have the greatest potential for high income.[63] In fact, the effects of privilege on who

goes to what college may be greater today than they were sixty years ago. Sons and daughters of the privileged class go to better high schools (if not private schools) and are provided with an educational experience that is geared to satisfy entrance requirements at the most selective elite colleges. And privileged-class families have the money to help their children prepare for college entrance exams.

The effects of class background on college-going are enduring, as evidenced by the fact that students from families with parents having high levels of education are more likely to obtain advanced education beyond the baccalaureate degree. Among students who obtained a baccalaureate degree, those who entered professional programs (MD, JD) and doctoral programs were more likely to come from families with higher levels of parental education.[64]

The final barrier for even the brightest working-class high school graduate is the cost of attending an elite college. As we pointed out earlier, in 2010–2011 the average annual cost of attending a four-year U.S. university totaled $16,712 at public schools and $44,619 at private schools (tuition, fees, room and board). How can "middle-class" U.S. families earning the median family income of $62,301 (2010 in 2011 dollars) afford to send their children to college, especially to private schools?[65] Even privileged-class families earning the median income of $161,252 (2010) for those located in the top one-third of the income distribution may find it difficult to pay for their children to attend private colleges or universities.[66] Because the parents of nonprivileged students have limited incomes and because federal assistance in the form of Pell grants for low-income students is capped at $5,550 (as noted earlier), these students go to lower-cost state colleges, borrow money, and work to cover their expenses. Choosing a major is often driven by practical considerations, such as the need to get a job immediately after graduation. This can lead students to choose vocationally oriented programs such as education, nursing, and technology degrees, which assure jobs after the baccalaureate degree but provide very limited opportunities for achieving high incomes or for accumulating significant amounts of wealth.

The College-Route Version of the American Dream

The American dream puts great emphasis on a college education as the one true path to upward mobility (along with hard work, of course). Traveling down the "yellow brick road" paved with academic tracks, good grades, and high college admission test scores should result in a college degree and entrance into the Emerald City. However, one of the important real-world details missing from the college-route version of the American dream is that most degrees from "generic" colleges and universities are *not* tickets to the privileged class. Elite school credentials are, as we have shown, a necessary component for admission to membership in the privileged class (absent, of course, a substantial trust-fund income from family wealth—per the Waltons).

Another real-world detail missing from the college-route version of the dream concerns the ways that a working-class background can disadvantage college aspirants. The dream appears to assume that poor but talented adolescents are adequately prepared for college because they are motivated, upwardly mobile achievers. It further appears to assume that such students have the "right stuff" in terms of social qualities such as the values, aspirations, and cultural capital needed to succeed in college. In short, the dream appears to assume that poor but talented black and white students who make it to college are there because of *socialized choices* to attend. This view assumes the choice to attend college follows a temporal sequence whereby the values and aspirations for college come first, and mobility opportunities follow.

For some college-bound working-class students, the dream's assumptions and the socialized choice model are relatively applicable. Some possess college-relevant values, aspirations, and cultural capital because of socialization experiences provided by parents who value education, like-minded college-oriented peers, and teachers who have worked hard to help them prepare for college. But even well-prepared working-class high school graduates, usually the first members of their families to attend college, often find their pre-college preparation failed to provide them with a realistic awareness of the nonacademic obstacles college presents, such as financial, social, and emotional pressures. Many well-prepared and determined working-class students will eventually adapt to college life, but often only after going through a number of personal struggles, disappointments, and frustrations.

A number of working-class students are likely to find college even more of a challenge than their relatively well-prepared working-class peers. This is the case because some low-income students may wind up in college not because of *socialized choices*, but because of *situational choices* that are unplanned and lacking in preparation for college life. Let us consider this possibility and the difficulties of college-life-working-class students' experience by returning to the story of Nick Caradona, whom we met at the beginning of this chapter.

Nick Caradona: College Students Then and Now

When we left Nick, he had dropped out of high school and was working as a runner and writer for a "bookmaker." He did this work for several years and aspired to start his own "handbook" as soon as he accumulated enough money and found a good spot (the right neighborhood/ethnic niche). Unfortunately, the Korean War intervened and Nick was drafted into the marines. After two years of service he returned to his old neighborhood with two goals—to buy a car with money he had accumulated in the military and to take advantage of all his GI benefits while avoiding going to work. After he bought a car, the next thing he did was go to the Veterans Administration (VA) and sign up for the 20/20 club—collect $20 a week for twenty weeks while allegedly looking for a job ($20 then was equal to $125 today). Nick collected $20 for twenty weeks and returned to the VA to see what was next. The clerk advised that since he didn't graduate from high school he should consider getting his high school diploma in a night school program. While enrolled, he would get $90 a month. So Nick went to night school, took an English course and a history course, and received a high school diploma. He then went back to the VA with the "What's next?" question.

This time the VA clerk said, "Why not go to college?" The idea had never crossed Nick's mind. The clerk told Nick that his weak academic record would prevent him from getting into a "good" college and suggested that he apply for admission to one of the state teacher's colleges. The most attractive part of this idea to Nick was that he would continue to get $90 per month while going to school. A "no-brainer" for Nick!

Nick enrolled in the teacher's college and found it to be a very alien environment. He checked into a motel for his very first night at the college, in preparation for the next day's orientation for freshmen. That night he took some records with him to the student union in search of a record player. On the way, he bought a bottle of wine to drink while he was listening to his favorite records (he was into sax players, and he had selections from Benny Carter, Vido Musso, and Coleman Hawkins, among others). Nick set up his records and wine and settled into an easy chair to sip and listen. It didn't take long before he was told, politely, that he would have to leave because alcohol was not permitted on campus. Nick was astounded. You could drink at age eighteen in the state, but you couldn't drink on campus.

Remaining at college was a struggle for Nick, not academically but socially. But for a fortuitous event, Nick would probably not have lasted beyond the first semester. During his first month at school he ran into a neighborhood buddy he hadn't seen since before the war. Tony Lembo was a neighborhood kid who had played softball with Nick when they were about fifteen. Tony's father had a hot-dog pushcart that he set up every day near the subway. Tony had been in the army in Korea, and he was using his benefits to become a phys-ed teacher. Tony and Nick decided to room together, and soon they met several other ex-GIs and formed a drinking and card-playing circle that sustained them while facing the ambiance of academe.

Nick was pursuing the college-route version of the American dream, but not exactly according to the conventional script linked to it. Nick never quite became a part of the college scene but sustained and protected himself by hanging out with other working-class guys who found themselves in the same place facing similar problems of adjustment. In some ways, Nick's experiences many years ago were much different than those of working-class students who aspire to college today. First, when Nick was growing up, the diamond-shaped class structure was emerging in post-WWII America—as we saw in chapter 1. Second, the educational and labor market opportunities associated with that diamond-shaped class structure were much more open than is the case in today's double-diamond class system. Third, the college admission process then contained far fewer academic and bureaucratic hurdles and paying for college was far less problematic. Tuition was inexpensive partly because at that time most of the costs of running state colleges and universities were paid for by tax revenues collected by state governments.

While many features of the American class and educational systems were different when Nick was growing up, some aspects of his college experiences were similar to those facing many working-class students who are the first in their families to attend college today. First, Nick's "fish-out-of-water" experience of not fitting in to the college social scene is likely to resonate with many working-class college students today, whether they are white, black, Hispanic, Asian, or "other." We know, for example, that people of color who attend predominantly white colleges face significant hurdles in trying to become a part of academic life.[67] Second, just as Nick withdrew into a circle of working-class friends as a way of coping with college life, many working-class students today seek out those with similar backgrounds for social comfort. (But with fewer working-class students on college campuses today, companions may be harder to find than in Nick's day.) Third, just as Nick was encouraged to choose a second-tier "teacher's college" (due to weak preparation), many working-class students today are likely to have similar experiences, but maybe for different reasons. Today, few working-class high school grads who are relatively well prepared academically aspire to attend elite colleges. The costs of such schools put them out of reach. But even the cheapest four-year college isn't cheap. The financial pressures on working-class students to get through college quickly may lead good students to bypass four-year schools in favor of cheaper, two-year community colleges so they can finish in less time, with less debt, and quickly get to work—taking pressure off of them and their families.

A FUTURE OF CONTINUING INEQUALITIES?

The main argument of this chapter has been that the American educational system operates in ways that reproduce the existing structures of inequality in the larger society, especially those grounded in class and racial distinctions. It achieves this end, first of all, by promoting an ideology that proclaims schooling to be the great equalizer and the main avenue for upward mobility. Second, inequality is perpetuated through a multitiered system of education made up of elite schools, average schools, and weak schools in terms of academic quality. The different quality of these schools is directly linked to class and racial categories of their students. The quality of the educational experience in primary and secondary schools helps to determine a student's chances for attending college.

We see little evidence of major changes in primary, secondary, or higher education that promise to expand equality of opportunity in schooling for young women and men. Public schools at the primary and secondary level are likely to continue to be funded by inequality-perpetuating methods (such as property taxes). The results will be continuing sharp divisions between resource-rich and resource-poor schools in terms of the quality of the educational experiences they provide.[68] Access to higher education will become more restricted as tuition costs rise faster than the incomes of most families. The gap between the small number of elite schools and the nonelite colleges will become magnified, limiting access to elite schools and conferring ever-greater advantage for their graduates.

The inequalities in primary and secondary schools linked to students' social class membership and/or their racial/ethnic identities are likely to be reinforced and extended in the years ahead. Projections of demographic trends suggest that primary and secondary schools will have increasing proportions of students of color in highly segregated settings. This may result in increased demands from parents for improvements in the quality of education provided for their children. Privileged-class parents may respond by moving their children from public to private educational settings. Working-class parents may also be attracted to opportunities to move their children out of failing schools into new, so-called charter schools or other alternatives that appear to offer some benefits to students as public school budgets decline.

Concern about the quality of public education and the call for reforms such as standardized testing, vouchers, and charter schools have been most forcefully and persistently expressed by elite class leaders in the business community. While parents' and teachers' groups have long-standing interests in democratic educational reforms that would assist the cause of learning, they have often opposed the kinds of "reforms" favored by corporate America. As we pointed out in chapter 3, much of the interest in "reforming" public education is driven by corporate interests in privatizing schools in order to turn them into profit-making enterprises.

The story regarding how and why educational reform has become the sharp point of the superclass spear aimed at reshaping schools into profit centers is too long and complex to be explored here. Suffice it to say here that in the guise of promoting greater educational quality and more freedom of choice through vouchers, charter schools, and other programs, the superclass and its allies are seeking to divert attention from their core agenda priorities, which are to crush public-sector teachers' unions and increase corporate profits.[69]

Based on the realities of the new class system, the new economy and the superclass-corporate educational "reform" agenda, educational inequalities in the United States will not only continue, in all likelihood they will also intensify. Students from families in the bottom of the double-diamond class structure will find it increasingly difficult to attend and complete college and find full-time jobs with long career ladders. It is likely to become increasingly apparent that large numbers of college graduates will find work only in low-paid service-sector jobs. Such a trend will highlight the growing reality that there is a significant mismatch between the kinds of careers that most colleges prepare most students to enter and the kinds of jobs available to most nonprivileged-class college graduates in the occupational structure associated with today's new economy.

12

The Pacification of Everyday Life

"The strongest is never strong enough to be master, unless he transforms his
strength into right, and obedience into duty."

— Jean-Jacques Rousseau, *The Social Contract* (1782)

Pacification refers to the transformation of potentially disruptive social situations
or restive populations into serenity: passive, peaceful, and calm. In the context of
conflicting class interests, pacification also implies the manipulation and control
of subordinate classes by dominant classes (but not necessarily in a conspiratorial
sense). By linking pacification with everyday life, the title of this chapter is meant to
call attention to how the class-related consciousness of average people going about
their day-to-day routines is shaped and muted. Pacification, when "successful,"
leads most nonelites to accept class inequalities and the institutional arrangements
that produce them as "legitimate"—meaning they are largely accepted as "normal,"
perhaps "natural," and maybe even "fair" in an odd kind of way. Thus, what we call
pacification has much in common with what sociologists who study inequality refer
to as the "legitimation process"—the process by which willing acceptance of class
inequalities occurs among most people in unequal, class-divided societies.[1]

In this chapter and the next we consider how the power and advantages of the
superclass, the credentialed class, and large segments of the entire privileged class
are exercised, reinforced, and legitimated at the level of everyday life. Because pacification is a multifaceted process, a full exploration of it would fill a separate book.
Our purpose here is to bring this complex process down to earth by exploring how
selected economic, political, and cultural topics are linked to the pacification of
everyday life. Our topics include economic development in small towns, the war
on drugs, the Patriot Act, and the culture industry. These phenomena link national
trends with local activities and illustrate how superclass-dominated organizations

promote class-based economic and ideological hegemony, social control, and the legitimation of class inequalities among nonelites. They show us how superclass power and ideas are embedded in taken-for-granted institutional practices and technologies that drive the pacification process.

GROW OR DIE: THE ELITE
CLASS THREAT TO SMALL-TOWN AMERICA

"The departure of a major corporation can have a devastating impact on a local growth coalition. . . . The net result is often a 'race to the bottom' as [rival] cities offer tax breaks, less environmental regulation, and other benefits to corporations in order to tempt them to relocate."

—G. William Domhoff, *Who Rules America?*, 6th ed. (2010), 50

As we have seen, the superclass has been very successful in capturing the largest shares of income and wealth. We have also seen that this outcome is not easy or cheap. It requires the constant care and feeding of the shadow political and information industries by the superclass. Moreover, shaping and delivering politics and policies favorable to superclass interests does not stop at the national level. It continues in states, cities, and towns throughout the United States. In this section, we consider linkages between the location of Japanese automobile assembly plants in Midwestern communities in the 1980s and the pacification process. Although our study of this topic may appear dated, its findings remain relevant today. It illustrates how the elite classes (i.e., the superclass and its credentialed-class allies) create local crises, demand sacrifices from citizens, legitimate these sacrifices, and benefit from "solutions" to the problems they created. While the transplants of the 1980s are "history," the class-based dynamics that drove those projects and public acceptance of them in many small towns live on in today's "new economy."

The past few decades have shown us how fragile the economic foundations are of small American communities. Many small towns have only one large firm with perhaps a thousand workers, a few midsize companies, and dozens of small retail and service businesses. Large firms, especially those with manufacturing plants, have been and remain central to many small-town economies. When a large employer announces plans to shut down, it is a crushing blow for a small town's economy. The loss of a thousand jobs paying an average of $30,000 takes millions of consumer dollars out of the community. Moreover, lost payroll taxes and plant property taxes significantly reduce the city's revenue. Also lost are contributions to local charities and churches by the plant's employees plus the volunteer work performed by workers and their families in community organizations. Due to the importance of such plants in small towns, when plant closings are announced, they tend to generate predictable, patterned scenarios.

The announcement of a plant closure in a small town is often accompanied by a corporate statement that "spins" the decision in these terms: the plant is old, and, based on a cost-benefit analysis, it would cost too much to upgrade it. At that point, the mayor probably asks company executives what it would take to make them reconsider. If a union represents the workers, its leaders may agree to discuss wage and benefit concessions. The local business community would probably ask the mayor and the city and county councils to spend more money on community development activities. To make matters worse, other businesses may remind the city and county of their costs. They may say tax waivers are needed for *their* survival. While the city had likely given tax abatements before, doing so now would mean even less money for schools, fire and police protection, city services, and a new professional community development office.

Some of what is described in this story about a hypothetical small town sounds a bit like extortion, blackmail, and bribery—although these activities are not called by those terms in political and business circles. And it is not just a hypothetical story. This story line reflects the basic outline of what has happened—and is still happening—in hundreds of small communities across the United States over the past forty years. These towns are essentially told: grow or die!

In the 1980s, six towns with populations ranging from 6,500 to 85,000 shared the experience of becoming the site of a large Japanese automobile assembly plant: Marysville, Ohio (Honda); Smyrna, Tennessee (Nissan); Lafayette, Indiana (Subaru-Isuzu); Normal, Illinois (Mitsubishi); Flat Rock, Michigan (Mazda); and Georgetown, Kentucky (Toyota). Each city and state was the "winner" in a multistate competition to attract foreign investment. The story behind how these winners embraced transplant-driven growth to avoid "fading to black" reveals how the elite classes create crises, benefit from solutions to the problems they created, and pacify nonelites.

Rust Belt states like Michigan, Illinois, and Ohio were hard hit by plant closings involving major corporations and as a result were drawn into "regional wars" of competition for new businesses.[2] So how do communities attract new firms to replace the jobs lost by plant closings? The short answer is by providing attractive incentives. State "incentive packages" for large industrial firms typically include a list of freebies that often begins with land and usually includes site preparation (roads, water, sewer lines), worker training, and property tax waivers—with the total incentive package value reaching $100 million or more. In 1985, for example, Kentucky gave Toyota $12.5 million for land, $20 million for construction preparation, $47 million for roads, $65 million for worker training, and $5.2 million to meet the educational needs of Japanese managers' children. But these features were just part of the deal. With bond interest payments added, the total incentive package cost Kentucky taxpayers $350 million.[3] Why? Why is our society like this?

While the purpose of incentives is to attract companies and new jobs, their costs place an increasingly high price tag on economic growth. In the 1980s the incentive packages amounted to $50,000 for each job in the Japanese transplants. The following decades witnessed a sharp rise in the total value of incentive packages. For example, in 1991 all fifty states gave $16 billion to businesses to locate or relocate plants and other corporate operations in their borders. In the early 2000s, this amount rose to $26.4 billion annually.[4] By the early 2010s, state-local governments were offering companies "almost $50 billion in location incentives and over $70 billion in total subsidies annually."[5] Per-job incentive costs also rose sharply. For example, incentives that led BMW to open a plant in Spartanburg, South Carolina, cost $79,000 per job (1994); the incentives that brought a Mercedes plant to Vance, Alabama, cost $167,000 per job (1997).[6]

The Elite Classes Come Calling: Pacification in the Heartland

Returning to the 1980s, we find Michigan, Tennessee, Ohio, Illinois, Kentucky, and Indiana collectively chipped in more than 1 billion "incentive package" dollars to land the Japanese auto assembly plants. For the two thousand or so workers hired in the new plants, the incentive money was seen as well spent. And it was certainly seen as a good idea by the business community that benefits from growth—especially the banks, lawyers, and realtors who would facilitate the new growth-related business transactions. But most residents in the communities (and states) where the plants were located (probably 90 percent) would not reap the benefits. Instead, they had to pay higher taxes to cover the incentive packages. They also "won" increased traffic congestion, higher housing costs (for rental units and new homes), and more municipal spending to cover school costs for children of parents who got jobs created by the "growth boom." Obviously there are economic benefits associated with growth, but benefits for whom? Also important is that nobody asked people in the towns if they thought it was a "good deal" to spend $50,000 of taxpayers' money for each new transplant job. The deals were made between the executives of incoming corporations and state and local members of the elite classes (government, business, and professional leaders); then the deals were "sold" to the people in the affected communities.

The transplant stories were told (and sold) locally by the electronic and print media. Local newspapers were especially important because they have reputations of journalistic objectivity and civic responsibility. Although local newspapers are known to have political biases (i.e., to be conservative or liberal, favoring Republicans or Democrats), they are also often seen as having broad community interests in mind when reporting on issues such as community-financed schools, libraries, roads, and recreational facilities. But we must recall that newspapers are, first and foremost, businesses. They are expected to make profits for their stockholders, just like any other business. And the sale of advertising is the engine that drives newspaper profits. Thus, newspapers in the transplant cities had a vested (but typically hidden and un-acknowledged) interest in growth, which was shared by bankers, realtors, attorneys, construction firms, and the chamber of commerce. So when newspapers in the cities competing for transplants told the story about incentives and transplant benefits for communities, it was a story spun by card-carrying members of the superclass and its credentialed-class allies.

Local Spin: All the News That's Fit to Print?

We examined newspaper stories written in conjunction with the process of locating Japanese transplant firms in three Midwestern communities by three different hometown newspapers. Our purpose was to see how local newspapers dealt with the complex task of assessing the potential costs and benefits of competing for and having a new, large manufacturing firm come to their community. Each of these projects had the potential of producing opposition from a variety of community groups such as environmentalists, organized labor, and concerned taxpayers. Given the potential for public controversy and community conflict, we were interested in how the local newspapers presented the story and shaped community thinking on this issue.

The three newspapers and time periods analyzed were the *Lafayette Journal and Courier* (Indiana, December 1986–September 1987), the *Murfreesboro Daily News Journal* (Tennessee, September 1980–September 1981), and the *Lexington Herald Leader* (Kentucky, December 1985–December 1986). In all, 490 transplant stories were published by the three newspapers in the time periods we examined. These stories were analyzed to answer the question: Who speaks on the transplants? We ask this question because newspaper reporters and editors make choices about which people and organizational representatives will be asked to express their opinions about the transplants, incentive money, and what it will mean for the community.

In the 490 stories, 1,769 persons were named and their views on the transplants presented. Our analysis of all persons cited in the stories found 36 percent were from business and industry (corporate executives, attorneys, chambers of commerce), 50 percent were elected officials (mayors, state representatives, congressional representatives) or officials in state or local government agencies, and only 13 percent were outside of the business-political sectors, such as labor leaders, educators, and social welfare services. Thus, almost 90 percent of the opinions expressed in the transplant stories came from persons who could be expected to be pro-business or pro-growth or to have pro-transplant interests. In effect, representatives from the privileged class did most of the talking in the newspaper stories. This outcome hardly reflects an effort by the local newspapers to provide balanced information and analysis to their readers.

When we examined the space devoted to the 490 stories, we found they accounted for a total of 19,331 square inches in the three newspapers. Our analysis of the *content* of the reports filling that space found 83 percent was devoted to positive accounts of the transplant projects. In contrast, only 17 percent of the space was devoted to stories that were "negative" or "critical" of some aspect of the transplants. In short, the overall *tone* of newspaper coverage of the transplants was unequivocally positive and supportive of awarding taxpayer-funded financial incentives to private corporations. Rather than being objective providers of balanced information and opinion, the newspapers acted as cheerleaders for the transplants and economic growth. Their coverage and biased story lines on the transplants were consistent with the profit-oriented, class interests of the newspaper owners, publishers, and editors—members of the elite classes.

The overwhelming representation of pro-growth views in local newspapers illustrates the dominance of state and local privileged-class members' views in media reports on economic issues with class-based implications and consequences for local communities. In the case of the transplants, the actions of local privileged-class members had the effect of reinforcing and reproducing at the local level the interests of national-level superclass corporate and political elites. The transplant cases illustrate how many communities are caught in a corporate squeeze that starts with multinational firms closing local plants and shipping jobs overseas. Faced with fiscal crises brought on by unemployment and declining tax revenues produced by plant closings, these communities are then forced to compete with other towns and states facing the same squeeze for the "privilege" of handing out millions of dollars in taxpayer money as "incentives" to lure other large corporations to bring new jobs to their towns.

The New Catch-22: Private Profits, Public Costs

The all-too-familiar scenario of plant closings followed by competition for the transplants illustrates how a new kind of "catch-22" is built into the double-diamond class structure.[7] The essence of the catch is this: profits are private, costs are public, and both are largely underwritten by the working class. Because the profits from doing business are private, they flow largely intact back to members of the elite classes—with few dollars skimmed off by ever lower corporate and capital gains tax rates. But the *social costs* of plant closings, such as higher unemployment, higher welfare costs, more family violence, increased crime, and higher rates of mental and physical illness, as well as the tax-funded costs of financial incentives to attract new businesses, are public. And both kinds of costs are primarily paid for by the working class. The routine business practices of corporations owned by the superclass create social problems while generating private profits, but the working class pays, in one form or another, most of the costs associated with the corporate system. Most obviously this includes higher taxes for the working class, but it also includes absorbing most of the human costs associated with corporate-generated social problems: the pain of unemployment, the confusion of disrupted lives, and the frustration of diminished community services. The double diamond leads to a double deal: a winning hand for the elite classes and many other privileged class members, a raw deal for the working class.

This new catch-22 provides useful insights into the contradiction between class benefits and class burdens where corporate practices and public policies are concerned. But as we have seen, newspaper accounts of the auto transplants did not acknowledge the existence of such a catch. The win-win vocabulary that dominated much of the local reporting on the transplants helped obscure the existence of conflicting class interests and coaxed local populations into accepting the deals as being in the best interests of all parties concerned. In a sense, the newspapers were an important part of a community-wide, street-level pacification project aimed at winning the "hearts and minds" of the working class in favor of the transplant projects. No conspiracy was necessary. The routine operation of elite class-dominated institutions, as the newspaper coverage illustrates, was sufficient to ensure local pacification. This outcome was evidenced by the absence of significant or sustained local opposition to the transplants in the chosen communities.

Grow or Die: Conclusion

While our study dealt with auto transplants, the insights these cases offer into the class-based dynamics of plant closings as well as the deployment of economic incentives by state and local governments to attract new firms are relevant today to a variety of businesses. Many companies in nearly all economic sectors have shown a willingness to close plants that are inconsistent with their interests and goals and to locate new operations or relocate existing facilities in states and communities that offer them substantial, government-funded incentives. A useful way of viewing plant closings and incentives offered by states and communities to attract new businesses (like the auto transplants) can be found in the work of Naomi Klein and what she calls "The Shock Doctrine."[8] This doctrine, as we noted in chapter 3, is associated with "disaster capitalism"—a business model where disruptive events, like natural disasters or economic crises, create opportunities for corporations and superclass-friendly government officials to implement major economic and public policy changes. Disasters, she says, help convince the public a crisis is real and serious. This is essential because it is average taxpayers who will pay for solutions—usually in the form of increased taxes. Many of Klein's examples illustrating how "disaster capitalism" works are drawn from international events in Poland, Russia, and Chile, and from the aftermath of Hurricane Katrina in New Orleans. But her concept can also be effectively applied to corporate-induced community "shocks" (e.g., plant closings) and corporate-encouraged competition between states and local governments using taxpayer-funded incentives to lure new businesses. As in the past, taxpayers are first frightened by the disaster of a plant closing. They are then told, via the media, that economic incentives and the increased taxes to pay for them are necessary to attract new businesses, but that everyone will benefit from this policy. Finally, they are encouraged to feel relieved (pacified) when a new firm comes to town, collects the incentives, and opens for business.

THE DRUG WAR AND PACIFICATION

"Domestically, the "drug war" has always been used as a pretext for social control. . . . Essentially the drug war is a war on the poor and dangerous classes, here and elsewhere. How many governments are going to give up on that?"

—Ken Silverstein and Alexander Cockburn, *CounterPunch* (1998)

Efforts by federal, state, and local elected officials to control the sale and use of illicit drugs in the United States have involved the implementation of several harshly punitive anti-drug laws over the past thirty years. These efforts, collectively constituting the "war on drugs," have frequently involved the use of symbolic politics by U.S. political leaders. *Symbolic politics* describes the political strategy of choosing and using "safe" political issues and public policies on the part of elected leaders to advance their interests and those of their elite class supporters. This approach is safe in that it involves a focus on programs that appear to address social problems—but in ways that do not threaten elite class interests and also have wide appeal among the working class. Symbolic politics are associated with at least three levels of symbolic action. First, to promote their own political interests, elected leaders "construct threats" to public well-being. This means these leaders, with the help of superclass sponsors and media attention, select social conditions perceived by many citizens as undesirable and transform them, by policy pronouncements and the mobilization of political resources, into high-priority public "threats" requiring policy interventions. Second, elected leaders propose programmatic interventions that they claim will ameliorate the problematic conditions associated with the "constructed threats" and that will also reassure voters that public office holders and institutions are responding appropriately to the dangers such threats pose. Third, elected leaders may invoke a "scapegoating strategy" whereby the "constructed threats" are explicitly or implicitly linked to unpopular or stigmatized groups, which encourages public perceptions of these groups as the source of the threats or problems.[9]

While the U.S. political landscape today includes many examples of symbolic politics (e.g., terrorism, predatory pedophiles, immigration, abortion), we view the so-called war on drugs as a classic illustration of this concept. Growing out of a high-profile, politically constructed "threat" (the "drug plague"), the drug war now includes numerous multifaceted government policies and programs with national and local class-related implications and consequences. Illicit drug use can be readily portrayed as a threat to public well-being at the national, state, and community levels. Most government leaders at all levels have, over time, embraced this symbolic politics approach to the problem of illicit drugs and have incorporated it in their political campaigns and their work as elected officials. Elevated public concerns about illicit drugs (due largely to symbolic politics) have encouraged government officials at all levels to "solve" the drug problem by implementing pervasive anti-drug laws, policies, programs, and law enforcement practices. These developments and their consequences constitute the heart of the drug war—a war that has become a powerful, unadvertised force in our society. Several features of the symbolic politics–driven drug war now shape everyday legal, economic, political, and cultural routines in ways that reinforce elite class interests, help legitimate class inequalities, and thus contribute to the pacification of everyday life. Examples of drug war features that contribute to these outcomes include harshly punitive drug control laws, multiyear mandatory prison sentences for drug offenses, seizures by law enforcement agencies of drug traffickers' assets, lifetime disenfranchisement for convicted drug offenders, and drug testing of students (by schools) and workers (by employers).

Some citizens may view the drug war features listed above positively and see them as necessary to "win" the war on drugs. Those who hold such views are unlikely to see how these features reinforce elite class interests, help legitimate class inequalities, or contribute to the pacification of everyday life. Such a "disconnect" is, in some ways, to be expected, given the low levels of class consciousness present in the U.S. population and the lack of exposure most Americans have had to class analysis and class power concepts. In order to see the connections we suggest exist, it is useful to think of the drug war in terms of our iceberg metaphor. Some drug war features appear "above the waterline" of conventional social analysis and are readily apparent, but other important features of the war, like class interests and pacification, are hidden "beneath the waterline"—below our culturally conditioned level of social awareness. Seeing and understanding these features requires us to utilize the "sonar equipment" called class analysis.

The National Drug Control Strategy and Its Effects

National public and political interest in the "drug problem" surged in 1986 after President Reagan's televised "War on Drugs" address to the nation and the subsequent passage of the Anti-Drug Abuse Act of 1986. Once set in motion, the drug war has remained a popular focus of political and media attention.[10] Over time, the war's scope was expanded by additional federal laws that facilitated its development into a powerful, complex, and multifaceted force. A major federal initiative that helped expand the drug war was the Anti-Drug Abuse Act of 1988. It led to the creation of a "national drug control strategy" aimed at systematically controlling both the supply of and demand for illicit drugs in the United States. This basic strategy has guided the drug war since 1988 over the course of Republican and Democratic presidential administrations up to the present.[11] While the drug war strategy calls for reducing both drug supply and demand, its primary focus has been upon supply reduction. This is evident by past and current patterns of federal drug control spending. Today, as in the past, far more federal dollars are spent to reduce the supply of drugs than to reduce the demand for drugs. Of the total 2013 National Drug Control Budget ($25.6 billion), 59 percent ($15.1 billion) was spent on supply reduction efforts (drug control by federal law enforcement agencies), but only 41 percent ($10.5 billion) was spent on demand reduction ($1.4 billion for prevention and $9.1 billion for treatment).[12]

Even though supply reduction spending accounts for most federal drug control spending, the amount budgeted for this function substantially understates total spending on illicit drug control by law enforcement agencies in the United States for at least two reasons. First, the federal supply reduction budget amount does not include federal dollars spent to pay the incarceration costs of federal inmates convicted of federal drug offenses. Second, federal supply reduction spending does not include the large amounts spent by state and local law enforcement agencies for this function. The latter point is important because drug control spending at the state and local levels is even more focused than federal spending on supply reduction via law enforcement.

An important effect of the major emphasis placed on the supply reduction dimension by the drug war strategy is that the criminal justice system has become the primary vehicle responsible for reducing the supply of illicit drugs in the United States. The various components of the criminal justice system are charged with enforcing the large body of federal, state, and local drug control laws enacted over the past thirty years and maintaining the courts and penal institutions essential to the law enforcement process. This means law enforcement agencies, officers, courts, judges, jails, and prisons are at the center of a multilevel, societal-wide effort to reduce the supply of drugs by arresting, convicting, and incarcerating drug users, dealers, and traffickers. Despite these efforts, many people, including former president Jimmy Carter, maintain the war on drugs has failed to reduce either the supply of or demand for drugs.[13] Almost everyone, however, agrees the drug war has succeeded in dramatically increasing the U.S. prison population, as the number of inmates incarcerated for drug offenses soared over the past thirty years. To illustrate, during the 1980–2010 period, the total number of inmates incarcerated in U.S. federal and state prisons and local jails rose from 502,000 in 1980 to 2.3 million in 2010.[14] Increased numbers of offenders incarcerated for drug offenses account for a large proportion of this increase. In 1980, only 13 percent of all U.S. federal and state prisoners were incarcerated for drug offenses, but in 2010, 51.1 percent of federal inmates and 17.8 percent of state inmates were imprisoned for drug offenses.[15]

The vast majority of all U.S. prison inmates, including those incarcerated for drug offenses, come from poverty-level or working-class backgrounds.[16] And while national studies show most illicit drug users are white, the 2010 inmate population of federal and state prisons by race and ethnicity was 32.2 percent white, 38 percent black, and 22.3 percent Hispanic (7.5 percent—"other").[17] By comparison, 2010 census data show the general U.S. population was 64.9 percent white, 12.1 percent black, and 15.8 percent Hispanic (7.2 percent—"other").[18]

Class Interests, Inequalities, and Pacification

The drug war reinforces elite class interests, helps legitimate class inequalities, and contributes to the pacification of everyday life in several specific ways. First, the drug war facilitates the "demonization of drugs" and promotes social unity against the common enemies of drug sellers and users. Second, both the supply and demand reduction dimensions of the drug war strategy encourage the adoption of individual-level explanations for and solutions to the social problems associated with illicit drugs. Third, the drug war encourages an uncritical acceptance of, and deference to, elite class-controlled authority and power structures including, at the community level, the police and local institutions associated with drug control efforts such as drug-testing in schools and workplaces. Fourth, the drug war helps legitimate a punitive law enforcement, anti-drug control model as well as the harsh legal sanctions central to drug control efforts. Fifth, the drug war, by sharply expanding the prison population, reinforces elite class dominance over and social control of the working and excluded classes.

The first of the five points above is a reminder that symbolic politics typically begins with the creation, by public officials and the corporate media, of a frightening "threat" to public well-being. In the case of the drug war, illicit drugs, users, and sellers are claimed to be mortal threats to everyone in society. The dire nature of the threat requires, we are told by elected officials, unity against those who sell or use illicit drugs. Social unity against a common foe tends to erase the significance of class distinctions and helps shift public attention away from class inequalities. Such conditions virtually eliminate the likelihood that discussions of the class structure or class inequalities will occur or be viewed as relevant by a population focused on the drug war. We are not suggesting the drug war is part of some kind of conspiracy by the elite classes to distract the working class from class inequalities. But to the extent that constructed threats like the drug war shift public attention away from our highly unequal class system, they make class inequalities less of a public focus or concern.

The second point suggests the U.S. drug war strategy encourages the view that the sale and use of illicit drugs are due to people making free-willed choices. While this view may be true in part, it omits any recognition of the ways that class inequalities shape peoples' life experiences, educational options, and career choices. For example, chapter 11 illustrated for us how class-stratified, unequal educational and career opportunity *structures* operate in our society. As we noted then, a large body of research finds children from elite-class family backgrounds usually become, as adults, well-educated, affluent professionals located in resource-rich organizations. In contrast, the drug research literature reveals that children from such backgrounds very rarely, as adults, become problem drug users or drug dealers.[19]

To the extent that an individual-level explanation is widely shared regarding the causes of America's illicit drug problems, most people would not see any need to alter the existing distribution of class-based and biased opportunities and resources. If the causes of the drug plague are viewed as located *within* people and *not* in structured class inequalities, then such inequalities do not need to be considered in drug problem discussions. Thus, symbolic politics-based policies aimed at "solving" the drug problem that are based on an individual, free-will causation model do not threaten the interests of the elite classes. Such policies never suggest that "solutions" to the drug problem require some redistribution of the wealth, power, and privileges concentrated in the elite classes. Therefore, drug war policies that focus on the need to alter individual choices regarding illicit drugs and that harshly punish those who "freely choose" to sell or use drugs protect the interests of the elite classes.

The third point serves as a reminder that the drug war is a potent, widely respected legal, economic, political, and cultural force in our society. This is the case because it is embedded in and operates through powerful, conventional social institutions. Examples include the federal, state, and local levels of the criminal justice system, large nonprofit organizations (e.g., the Brookings Institution, the Drug Abuse Resistance Education [DARE] "company"), and local schools. These institutions, largely controlled by the superclass, are managed and staffed at the upper levels by the credentialed class. Elements of this impressive array of institutions and resources marshaled to make war on drugs extend down to local communities across the United States. Working-class citizens, parents, and children are exposed every day to the operation of various institutions associated with the drug war. One example would be the participation of students and parents in local police-coordinated DARE programs conducted in local schools.[20] This familiarity promotes recognition of as well as appreciation and respect for the power and resources used by these institutions to advance the widely shared goal of a "drug-free America." As a result, at the local level the public is likely to uncritically accept the drug war because it is, in part, waged by and through local institutions citizens know and respect. Such attitudes make it highly unlikely that many local citizens will develop a critique of the drug war that considers how it advances and protects the shared economic, political, and cultural interests of the elite classes.

The fourth point reminds us that the drug war, with its two-track strategy, helps legitimate policies involving the use of law enforcement and harsh penalties to control drug sales and use. This is the case because the demand reduction track, which includes government-funded drug prevention and treatment programs, provides ideological cover and justification for harsh supply reduction policies. Since the drug war budget includes some funding for drug prevention and treatment programs, government officials can claim these efforts provide people with resources that enable them to avoid drugs by choosing abstinence or, if prevention fails, to enter treatment programs rather than continue illicit drug use. The existence of demand reduction programs allows officials to say to drug users and dealers, "If you choose to ignore our drug prevention program messages and drug treatment options (as well as our drug control laws) and persist in using or selling illicit drugs, the criminal justice system will discover your deviance and harshly punish your free-will choices to use or sell drugs. Such punishments are justified because you turned your back on our prevention and treatment efforts and *chose* to be a deviant druggie."

The fifth point reminds us of the quote at the start of the "drug war and pacification" section. The drug war can be viewed as a mechanism for intimidating and controlling the working class and the poor. It reminds people daily, at the national and local levels, of the extensive power the state (an armed state) holds over peoples' lives and lifestyle choices in areas chosen for control by the government lawmaking and enforcing apparatus controlled by the elite classes. Why would the elite classes care about controlling illicit drug sales or use? Perhaps it is in part because the elite classes have historically had an economic interest in controlling those features of workers' lives thought relevant to a disciplined labor force.[21] To the extent that elites view illicit drug use as interfering with disciplined production in the workplace, drugs need to be outlawed and employees tested for drug use.

In the neoliberal era, low-paid prison labor is a source of substantial profits for many firms, including those companies that own and operate private, for-profit prisons. These developments mean that some superclass investors have financial interests in policies (such as drug control and "three strike" laws) that generate "a large and increasing incarceration rate."[22] The very real *threat* of imprisonment for drug use can be viewed as a source of discipline keeping large segments of the working class "in line" (off drugs) and willing to work at low-wage jobs outside of prisons. At the same time, high rates of incarceration provide an extremely low-paid prison labor force that enriches those firms (and executives and stockholders) that employ prisoners as workers and/or that own private prisons.[23]

POLITICS AND PACIFICATION: THE USA PATRIOT ACT

"Never let a serious crisis go to waste. What I mean by that is it's an opportunity to do things you couldn't do before."

—Rahm Emanuel, former White House chief of staff (November 2008), quoted in the *Wall Street Journal* (January 28, 2009)

The Constitution of the United States includes guiding principles as well as limitations that are binding on all federal government officials. The Fourth Amendment to the Constitution states, "The right of the people to be secure in their persons, houses, papers, and effects, against unreasonable searches and seizures, shall not be violated, and no Warrants shall issue, but upon probable cause, supported by Oath or affirmation, and particularly describing the place to be searched, and the persons or things to be seized." One of the consequences of the September 11, 2001, terrorist attacks on the World Trade Center and the Pentagon was the expansion of federal laws concerning domestic security issues. Within days of the 9/11 attacks, many new legislative proposals that dealt with such issues were introduced in both houses of Congress. Members of Congress and the American people were in shock over the terrorist attacks, and the pressure for quick action was understandable. The crisis produced by the attacks created opportunities for federal government leaders to enact legislation that would not have been possible without it. It was as if President Bush's administration and congressional leaders, in the immediate aftermath of 9/11, were following Rahm Emanuel's advice—except they were doing so seven years before he offered it. Emanuel's comments dealt with the 2008 financial crisis and referred to plans being developed by President-elect Obama to address it when his administration took office in early 2009.[24] While the post-9/11 crisis was very different from the 2008 crisis, both created opportunities for new legislative initiatives. A key difference was that one of the most significant legislative responses to 9/11, the USA Patriot Act, focused on curtailing personal rights and freedoms in the name of fighting terrorism, whereas major federal responses to the 2008 financial crisis expanded the federal government's role in the economy. The act's sweeping changes (described below) appear to infringe upon, if not abridge, traditional citizenship rights that are guaranteed by the U.S. Constitution—as illustrated by the Fourth Amendment.

In the immediate post-9/11 period, many new "anti-terrorism" legislative initiatives were introduced in the House and Senate, but they were fragmented and disconnected. However, a small group of Democrats and Republicans (Pat Leahy, Orrin Hatch, and Arlen Specter) and then Attorney General John Ashcroft developed a comprehensive bill that eventually became the USA Patriot Act. The first version was introduced in the U.S. House of Representatives on October 2 and days later in the U.S. Senate. The bill quickly passed the House without a vote (the rules were suspended) and the Senate with one "no" vote. It was signed by President Bush on October 26, 2001.[25] This rapid sequence of events occurred because the 9/11 attacks resulted in the suspension of the usual process followed by Congress when considering proposed legislation. That process typically includes hearings where individuals and groups with interests in legislative proposals have opportunities to speak in favor or in opposition to the legislation and to offer suggested amendments. Such hearings, which might have set the stage for amendments to the legislation, were never held. Indeed, in the rush to pass the Patriot Act, many members of Congress who voted for it had not even read the bill, and most members of the public were unaware of its existence before it passed. It was only after the act passed that the corporate media began to report on its content and implications.

The Patriot Act permits the Department of Justice and the newly formed Department of Homeland Security to conduct unwarranted searches of dwellings and possessions and to engage in surveillance of personal records (e.g., library visits; financial, medical, and telephone records; personal computer files). Many of these surveillance procedures may be undertaken without any need by the government to specify the kind of information that is being sought from personal records or emails or whether the subject is suspected of any particular crime.[26] The act also made major changes related to foreign intelligence surveillance, extending the use of wiretaps, electronic bugging, and government access to business records of U.S. citizens.

Although the Patriot Act was intended to prevent terrorists from conducting new attacks on the United States, it can be applied to a wide range of so-called suspicious activities, such as those involving political activism. Thus, it can have a chilling effect on a wide range of free speech and free assembly rights guaranteed by the Constitution. The freedoms guaranteed by the Constitution and the rights of citizens to be protected against government intrusion on those freedoms are of great importance to average Americans. The powerful and the wealthy can buy legal protection if they feel government is treating them unfairly or violating their rights. But those without power or money depend upon the constitutional guarantees to protect their rights. Awareness of the potential ways that the Patriot Act can be applied and fear regarding how the consequences of its application might harm them personally may cause some Americans to engage in self-censorship in the expression of their opinions or to avoid engaging in legal forms of social activism. Such effects constitute, in our view, an extreme form of pacification. This is the case because the Patriot Act can be used to inhibit the expression of what are supposed to be constitutionally guaranteed forms of free speech. And since it can be used this way, the act encourages citizens to remain politically passive and even fearful because they know government agencies that are supposed to protect their political rights may, instead, be used to suppress those rights and punish those who dare to assert them.[27] While the act was thought to be urgently needed at the time, little attention was given to its important collateral effects—including the fact that it significantly expanded the power of the state over individuals and limited traditional personal freedoms that are supposedly guaranteed by the U.S. Constitution.

The act did include a "sunset clause" requiring periodic reauthorization by the Congress and approval by the president. Since its passage, the act was reauthorized twice. In 2005 and 2011 it was reauthorized with large congressional majorities voting yes. President Bush signed the first reauthorization on March 8, 2006, and President Obama signed the second reauthorization on February 26, 2011, and a four-year renewal on May 26, 2011.[28] To their credit, before, during, and after the reauthorization votes, some members of Congress, concerned public interest groups, and civil liberties organizations expressed concerns regarding the effect of the act on protected rights, especially those guaranteed by the Fourth Amendment to the Constitution.[29] In an apparent response to such concerns expressed by some after the passage of the original act, the U.S. Department of Justice set up a website to "dispel myths" about and defend the act—the website remains to this day.[30] While concerned Americans continue to work for changes in the act, it remains politically popular, as indicated by the large majorities in the House and Senate that voted in favor of both reauthorizations.[31] The political popularity of the act reminds us that once state power has been expanded, most federal officials, in both political parties, tend to support and justify its continued existence. The Patriot Act, like the drug war, is likely to remain as an instrument of pacification as long as the elite classes view it as useful to their interests and as long as nonelites remain passively silent about it.

13

The Culture Industry and Pacification

"An omnipresent commercial culture that emphasizes consumption over civic values, and a lack of organized political power, go a long way toward . . . making political activity unattractive and unproductive for the bulk of the citizenry."

—Robert W. McChesney, *Monthly Review* (November 2012): 19

The auto transplants, the drug war, and the Patriot Act illustrate how projects set in motion by and for the elite classes can dominate public awareness about economic, social, and political issues and confine policy debates to a narrow range of options endorsed by organizations controlled by the elite classes. As we have seen, policies implemented by the elite classes in these areas help deflect public attention from class inequalities, promote public acceptance of an unequal class system, and utilize various forms of social control to produce conformity among nonelites, including the use of force and imprisonment when necessary. It is our view that the process of pacification is further reinforced by many features of the "culture industry," which produces and disseminates a wide range of "cultural products" that typically distract public attention from class inequalities and related issues rather than call attention to them.

We mentioned the culture industry in chapter 10 during our discussion of one of its major subdivisions, the information industry. But as we noted then, the culture industry encompasses far more than the dissemination of information. It is a complex enterprise consisting of large multimedia firms that are increasingly interlocked with even larger corporate conglomerates, public relations-marketing companies, and nominally nonprofit groups (e.g., PBS—the Public Broadcasting Service). The huge corporations that form the core of the culture industry include the five firms cited in chapter 10 that dominate the information industry plus electronic-digital media giants such as Viacom (movies, cable TV), Google (Internet, advertising),

Clear Channel (radio), Sony/Columbia (movies), Yahoo! (Internet, advertising), and Sirius XM (radio), plus another group of large media firms that produce newspapers, magazines, and books in print and electronic formats (e.g., Advance Publications, Gannett, Hearst, New York Times, Inc., Tribune Co., Bertelsmann, Pearson).[1]

Culture industry firms produce and disseminate what we call "cultural products." We use this term to call attention to how these products both reflect *and* influence the content of American culture—meaning our shared vocabularies, experiences, interests, ideas, values, norms, attitudes, ways of thinking, behavioral standards, ethics, and religious orientations. Examples of cultural products include movies, television, the Internet, radio, music, DVDs, video games, newspapers, magazines, and books. Is useful to note that the term *cultural products* refers to both the *content* of such products and the *media* used to disseminate them. For example, the product called "television" typically refers to the communications medium (electronic technology) and to the programming (content) TV communicates or delivers to an audience. The content of cultural products is very diverse and includes all forms of entertainment, information, education, public relations, and advertising-marketing disseminated through all forms of electronic and print media. The diversity of content found in the products produced by the culture industry is partly a reflection of the enormous size of that industry and the resources it controls. In fact, the industry is too large and too complex to be fully explored in a single chapter, but that is not our purpose. Rather, our goal here is to present a brief overview of a limited segment of the electronic media component of the culture industry consisting of films, television, and the Internet to illustrate how these features contribute to the pacification of everyday life.

The massive scope and everyday reach of the electronic media are evident in the huge, multifaceted distribution networks that disseminate industry-produced cultural products such as movies, TV and radio programming, the Internet, DVDs, music, and video games to thousands of communities and millions of homes and consumers. In 2011, the culture industry infrastructure provided numerous links between media firms and over 5,000 hometown movie theaters (with 39,641 screens), 96 percent of households with TVs (2.4 sets per household), 87 percent of TV households with DVD players, and 83 percent of TV households with cable or satellite TV service.[2] Regarding Internet access, 71 percent of all U.S. households had Internet access in 2010 via personal computers, smartphones, or other types of mobile devices (e.g., laptops, notebooks, iPads). Another 9 percent had Internet access outside the home; only 20 percent of households did not have Internet access.[3] Regarding cell phone use, U.S. consumers owned 302 million cell phones in 2010 and about 30 percent of those were smartphones.[4] Total annual U.S. consumer media spending per household was estimated at $1,900 in 2010 compared to $790 in 2000.[5]

The extensive penetration of communities, homes, and peoples' lives by media networks has facilitated the consumption of culture industry–produced electronic media-disseminated cultural products by Americans who are spending more and more time consuming such products. Time spent by individuals on activities that do not involve electronic media products (e.g., informal socializing, nature hikes, daydreaming) produces no benefits for culture industry firms. Only time devoted to consuming electronic media products (e.g., movies, TV programs, Internet search engines, commercial websites) juices culture industry firms' market shares, sales, and profits.

The industry has an interest in channeling more and more consumer time into its commercial products. And it is succeeding. In 1988, American adults (eighteen and over) spent an average of 1,751 hours per person consuming electronic media products. TV was first at 1,490 hours followed by recorded music. In total, each U.S. adult averaged 3,310 hours consuming all forms of media in 1988 (including newspapers, magazines, and books).[6] In 2012, total media consumption by U.S. adults increased to an estimated average of 3,500 hours per person, with 3,032 of those hours devoted to electronic media (excluding cell phones). TV was first (1,596 hours) followed by broadcast and satellite radio (729 hours), Internet (197 hours), recorded music (150 hours), home video games (142 hours), out-of-home media (122 hours), home videos (59 hours), and other (37).[7] Some media are consumed simultaneously (e.g., TV viewing and Internet use), but the trend is clear: Americans are devoting more and more time to electronic media consumption.

The Colonization of Consciousness

To the extent that the waking hours of nonelites are dominated by ideas, programs, activities, and events created by the superclass-owned and credentialed-class-managed culture industry, it means that their consciousness is, in a sense, captured, or colonized, by an outside force. This elite class–directed "media force" is driven by class interests that are quite different from those of working-class consumers. For us, then, the colonization of consciousness refers to the ongoing invasion by the culture industry, especially through electronic media-delivered entertainment and advertising content, of ever larger shares of peoples' time, interests, imagination, and lives. This process is driven by many techniques, including the electronic media firms' constant tracking, creating, and linking of popular cultural trends with media content.[8] It also involves the media's use of compelling imagery (in movies, TV programming, advertising, search engine graphics, websites and video games) and its constant barrage of cleverly produced ads emphasizing the prestige and novelty features of mass, niche, and upscale-downscale consumer products.[9] While this process results in a number of consequences, including increases in culture-industry profits, from our perspective the reduction in time available to individuals for all other activities outside of media consumption is among the most important. Of particular importance in this regard is how the colonization of consciousness contributes to the marginalization of class-related issues and interests in individuals' everyday thoughts and discussions as more time and "thought space" are devoted to media products.

Although we may live in a "24-7" world (twenty-four hours a day, seven days a week), each of us can claim only about sixteen waking hours a day—or about 5,800 hours per year. If we subtract the time devoted to work (about two thousand hours per year), family and personal obligations, and the 3,032 hours spent on electronic media consumption, we find very little time remains each year for nonprivileged-class members to read, think, or talk about public issues—including class inequalities. Moreover, given the lack of corporate media attention to class issues such as class inequalities, conflicting class interests, and superclass power, we would not expect to find such issues included in most movies, TV programs, or website content "inserted" in consumers' minds as the colonization of consciousness process unfolds.

Movies: Class-Free Content?

Class-related issues or themes are rarely presented in movies. One indicator is the small number of films that include such topics. For example, consider Tom Zaniello's well-known book, *Working Stiffs, Union Maids, Reds, and Riffraff*. It is described as a "comprehensive guide to films about labor," but it identifies only 350 movies despite including films from around the world.[10] By way of comparison, the International Movie Database (IMDb) website includes 281,000 feature movie titles.[11] Another indicator of the scarcity of class issues in movies is found in the content of new, top-grossing U.S. movies released by major studios. Among the top twenty-five films by box office earnings in 2011, only one, *The Help* (Disney), dealt explicitly with inequality issues (race, gender, class discrimination) and portrayed workers' grievances sympathetically.[12]

More systematic empirical evidence supporting the claim that few movies depict working-class interests positively or critique elite-class power is provided by the findings from two content analysis studies we conducted in 1996 and 2006. In each study we selected large, random samples of movies in three general categories (dramas, science fiction, documentaries) from all movie titles listed in those categories by popular movie guides published in 1995 and 2006.[13] The release dates of all movies included in both guides spanned a wide range of years dating from early classics (1920s) to current films released in the year prior to the copyright date for each guide. In both studies we sampled 10 percent of the movies in each category and analyzed the content of the sampled films for the presence of "class inequality issues."

In the first study our sample consisted of 699 dramas, 750 science fiction films, and 263 documentaries. In this study we found about 5 percent of the films in each category (thirty-five dramas, forty science fiction films, fifteen documentaries) included story lines or themes that included "class inequality issues." This means the films either critiqued elite class power or provided sympathetic portrayals of working-class individuals or organizations (e.g., labor unions).[14] Our second study, using the same procedures as the first, included 518 dramas, 130 science fiction films, and 223 documentaries. The results essentially replicated the findings of our first study, with one slight difference. In 2006, 8.5 percent of the documentaries sampled (19 out of 223) matched our criteria, compared with 5 percent in 1996.[15] The reasons for this increase were unclear, but one interesting finding was that seven of the nineteen films were released after 2001. This means these movies could not have been part of the sample used in our first study and it suggests there was a slight increase in the number of class-inequality documentaries released after 2001 compared with earlier years.

While there may have been a slight increase in the number of class-inequality-themed documentaries released in the U.S. since 1996, such films constitute a minuscule fraction of the larger movie tide filled with pacification-inducing themes and story lines. Moreover, of the fifteen thousand new documentaries released in the United States each year, only a handful are viewed by relatively large audiences.[16] Since few documentaries, like movies generally, include class-inequality issues or themes, very few moviegoers will see films in this genre critical of class inequalities. The odds of viewing such films may increase if you attend well-known U.S. "social justice"–friendly film festivals such as Sundance, South by Southwest, or the DC Labor Film Festival, but compared to Hollywood film-promotion standards, the crowds at these events are small.

The post–financial crisis period witnessed the release of a few relatively high-profile documentaries critical of the U.S. class structure and related inequalities, but compared to big-budget Hollywood movies, few Americans saw these films. For example, how many readers saw, or even heard of, some of the *best-known* recent documentaries critical of class inequalities such as Michael Moore's *Capitalism: A Love Story* (2009, fourteenth top-grossing documentary of all time), Charles Ferguson's *Inside Job* (2010, Academy Award for best documentary), Amie Williams's *We Are Wisconsin* (2012), or Robert Greenwald's *Koch Brothers Exposed* (2012)? Perhaps in the near future these films and newer class-critical documentaries will be viewed by wider audiences as more documentary filmmakers promote and distribute their products via Web-based platforms such as Facebook, Twitter, Hulu, Netflix, YouTube, and Amazon.com.[17]

The critiques of class inequalities and concentrated superclass-corporate power included in the documentaries noted above were not evident in big-budget Hollywood movies featuring well-known stars in the post-2008 period. For the most part, the evidence we surveyed, including the findings from both of our studies, parallel what movie historian Steven J. Ross concludes in his study of class themes in the movies. In the contemporary period, he notes that class-critical films with "labor-capital" themes have virtually disappeared from the American cinema—reinforcing what we found in our studies.[18] The relative absence of class-related themes in U.S. movies was also noted by the late film critic Roger Ebert. In an interview, Ebert observed, "Class is often invisible in America in the movies and usually not the subject of the film. . . . We don't have a lot of class-conscious filmmaking."[19] And speaking to the effects of movie content on culture and class consciousness, Ross maintains that "American filmmakers have helped create a culture whose citizens either no longer view class as an important part of their lives or define the middle class so broadly that class no longer seems to matter."[20] In short, it appears most movies today reinforce rather than challenge the pacification process.

TV and ABC

So what's on TV? For openers, try advertising. A typical prime-time thirty-minute TV-network program now includes about eleven minutes of marketing content.[21] Local programs have even more. Advertisers have increased their spending on all forms of television advertising from $55 billion in 2001 to $70 billion in 2011.[22] The result is an ever increasing tidal wave of TV commercials in all programming time periods, but especially in late-night programs. "The combined load of brand appearances and network ad messages in . . . late night shows is 29:34 [minutes] per hour, or 49% of total content time."[23] This increase in TV ad expenditures reflects not only the rise in broadcast time devoted to advertising but also advertisers' faith in the power of TV to sell more stuff—despite ad-skipping DVRs.

What kinds of programming do the ads support? The really short answer is ABC: Anything But Class. If we set aside TV news as being part of the information industry (chapter 10), we find TV advertising supports entertainment programming that virtually ignores class issues and trends heavily toward distraction. Of course, this is not a surprise. Since U.S. television programming is almost totally supported by ad revenues paid by corporations interested in increasing sales and profits, we would not expect corporate sponsors to fund programs focused on class inequalities or class power issues. Advertisers favor entertaining programs that attract large, young, affluent audiences likely to buy the products or services they are selling. A tour of *TV Guide*'s program listings for network TV confirms this observation. Mornings are devoted mainly to "popular culture-newsmagazines" (e.g., *Today* [NBC], *Good Morning America* [ABC]) and talk shows. Afternoons bring game shows, soap operas, more talk shows, and "other people's problems" programs such as *Judge Judy* and *Dr. Phil*, where voyeuristic viewers are titillated by the charm, weirdness, or defiance of hapless participants. Prime-time network programming (8–10:30 p.m.) includes comedy series (e.g., *30 Rock*, NBC), "reality" programs (e.g., *Survivor*, CBS), sporting events, crime shows (e.g., all *NCSI* versions, CBS), celebrity and talent competitions (e.g., *Dancing With the Stars* [ABC], *American Idol* [FOX], the *Voice* [NBC]), dramas (e.g., *Grey's Anatomy*, ABC), paranormal or supernatural-themed series (e.g., *Grimm* [NBC], the *Mentalist* [CBS]), and more newsmagazines (e.g., *Dateline* [NBC], *20/20* [ABC]).

In addition to network TV programming, a variety of "syndicated" programs are broadcast by many local stations, often in pre-prime-time periods. (Syndicated programs are produced by various firms for distribution to local stations for a fee.) Syndicated programming frequently features game shows (e.g., *Wheel of Fortune*, *Jeopardy*) and tabloid-style TV "magazines." Programs in the latter category almost totally avoid issues of real concern to the lives of the working class (unless we count their stories on how to mimic celebrity fashions on a budget). The mission of these programs (e.g., *Access Hollywood*, *E!*, *Entertainment Tonight*, *Extra!*, *Inside Edition*) is to promote celebrities' media products (e.g., movies, TV programs, books) and to traffic in high-energy celebrity profiles and gossip about the stars—especially via reports on sex, drugs, deviance, and opulent lifestyles. Their often-titillating stories appear deliberately designed to appeal to ordinary viewers via vicarious thrills and voyeuristic gratification.[24] They seem to say, "Maybe you can't afford it or do it or would never do it, but you can watch glamorous stars own it and do it—Right here! Right now!"

Programs broadcast to paid subscribers of cable and satellite channels add more diversity to TV content, as do PBS offerings. A small number of satellite TV channels like RT (Russian Television) and Free Speech TV broadcast programs that sometimes explore class issues such as concentrated superclass power and class inequalities, but these channels attract very small audiences. Studies of widely watched, prime-time network TV content reveal a striking absence of programs that depict the lives or concerns of working-class Americans or that deal with class-based inequalities in ways that might promote critical reflection among viewers.

One study spanning four decades of TV entertainment found that of 262 domestic situation comedies, only 11 percent featured blue-collar, clerical, or service workers as heads of households. By contrast, the vast majority of the series, 70.4 percent, portrayed "middle-class" families with incomes and lifestyles that were more affluent than those of most middle-income American families. In 44.5 percent of the comedy series studied, the head of the household was a professional.[25] Another study of thirteen TV situation comedies found that the issue of social mobility across class lines is sometimes used as a source of comic tension and moral instruction. On the rare occasions when characters in the series studied aspired to or encountered upward mobility, the outcomes reminded viewers that "achieving inter-class mobility is rare, and the rewards of any substantial social movement will likely be bittersweet." This study concluded that TV situation comedies send mixed and paradoxical messages regarding social mobility. On one hand, these programs typically reinforce the myth of America as a land of opportunity where hard work and persistence pay off. On the other hand, on rare occasions when characters actually encounter social mobility, their experiences tend to be portrayed as disruptive and often undesirable.[26] The net result is the subtle reinforcement of existing class divisions, structures, and locations as normal, natural, and preferred—to the disruptive effects of social mobility.

ABC and the Oprahfication of the Mind

In situation comedies, talk shows, newsmagazines, and most other programming formats, ABC—Anything But Class—is what's on TV. ABC is an important factor contributing to the colonization of consciousness. And the ABC focus and content of most TV programming, especially talk shows, "other people's problems" programs, and tabloid magazines, contribute to another phenomena involved in the pacification process: the Oprahfication of the mind. This term refers to how the electronic media, especially television (and Internet) "infotainment" content (information presented in a "newslike" format for the purpose of entertainment), contributes to the demise of critical thinking about cultural, social, economic, and political events and issues. While the concept incorporates the first name of former

TV talk show host and current entrepreneur-billionaire Oprah Winfrey, its origins, content, and analytical utility transcend any single TV personality or media star.[27]

Oprahfication originates with the preferences of media firms' executives for light, fast-paced, engaging styles, especially as centerpieces of daytime TV talk shows and evening tabloid-style magazines. Its substance revolves around and emerges out of the relentless focus on "GSPN" (glamour, shock, perverse, novelty) topics by these popular culture–oriented programs (and their related websites). And it embraces and exudes an attractive, seemingly humane, life-affirming personal creed grounded in naive altruism, self-help, individualism, and irony. At the same time, peoples' receptivity to Oprahfication is reinforced by the increasingly common "socialization to novelty" experiences of TV viewers, website visitors, and popular culture consumers generally.

Electronic media advertising often encourages consumers to devalue stability and continuity in products, packaging, entertainment, and lifestyle trends.[28] At the same time, much electronic media content reinforces the idea that routine is boring and changes, especially fast-paced novel changes, are good. TV viewers and website visitors are encouraged to think that "been there, done that" experiences equal boring repetition and are to be avoided. Consumers are encouraged to prefer novel products, experiences, and activities because novelty is presented as a source of fulfillment and fun.[29] Preferences for novel products and activities are driven in part by the recognition, among corporate overlords of the electronic media, that novelty-infused content energized by speed, action, color, and change juice consumer interest and increase media profits.

To illustrate our view that the styles and substance that drive Oprahfication are especially evident in daytime TV talk shows and evening tabloid TV magazines, consider the high-profile anchors/hosts of such shows (e.g., talk shows: Barbara Walters, Kelly Ripa, Ellen DeGeneres; magazines: Nancy O'Dell, Terrence Jenkins, Deborah Norville). They affect confident, engaging styles and traffic in GSPN content chosen for its "infotainment" value. Projected through powerful TV (and Internet) platforms, the hosts' seemingly innocent styles and superficial content subtly encourage viewers (and website visitors) to embrace the shallow, stylish, pop-culture-centered but good-hearted conceptual framework that forms the core of Oprahfication. This framework (or variations of it) is used as a lens though which people's problems, high-profile events (GSPN), and current social issues (showcased by the corporate media) are processed by media-star anchors/hosts into short, glib entertainment segments. TV viewers (and website visitors) of all classes (especially those in the "middle" and working classes) are encouraged, by consuming these segments, to embrace this framework as a basis for understanding both the wider and personal worlds they inhabit.

Elements of this framework are used by TV talk shows and tabloid magazines (and related websites such as TMZ) as the basis for reporting on and interpreting both routine and tragic events. In one respect, these programs' coverage of even tragic events is similar to content typical of nearly all TV programs: It deflects critical attention from any consideration of class power issues or class inequalities. But programming devoted to tragic events by TV talk shows and tabloid magazines is short-lived. As soon as such events are depleted of novel and compelling story lines, shock value, and ratings utility, these programs turn their attention elsewhere. Waiting in the wings are always new angles on familiar infotainment GSPN subjects: breathless reports on pop-culture icons (e.g., movie stars, business tycoons, the Obamas, the Clintons, the Kennedys, Marilyn Monroe, Lady Gaga, and Lady Di—forever), breaking stories on British royalty, new serial killers, the latest movie trailers, hot new fashions, high-tech toys, and, from the Internet, viral video clips. Through such programming, media consumers are coached to conceptualize and think about most topics covered by TV talk shows and tabloid magazines (as well as many topics covered by TV network news programs and websites) at the most immediate, superficial, and individualized level. Any sense of how social class inequalities or wider historical or cultural contexts may be linked to current events and issues is lost to Oprahfication.

At its core, Oprahfication is a kind of truncated and compartmentalized cognitive style that not only erodes people's capacity for critical thinking but also diminishes even the legitimacy of critical thought. Oprahfication reduces (1) the likelihood that people will think of social issues or current events in terms of class analysis (too boring!); (2) people's ability to think in such terms (they have little practice or experience); and (3) people's ability to understand or appreciate a class-based analysis of problematic social conditions if it is presented to them (too confusing!). Colonization and Oprahfication are major elements in how the process of pacification of everyday life operates through the culture industry.

The Internet: Digital Pacification

Like film or television production and display equipment, the Internet is a form of electronic technology. However, unlike movies and television, the Internet is a unique digital-electronic tool that can be used for many purposes such as sending-receiving email messages and accessing websites. When used to access websites, the Internet is somewhat like telephone technology (wire, wireless, cell) that connects callers to the numbers we reach when we call (or text). But because the Internet links users with a seemingly endless variety of websites, typically with interactive qualities, this feature makes it a unique medium. The website accessing feature of the Internet is of special interest here. From our perspective, the Internet's relevance to the culture industry and pacification is inextricably tied to the *content of the websites* that can be accessed by using it, especially the most popular websites where large numbers of users spend lots of time.

It's important to distinguish between what's available via the Internet and how it is used by most people. We know that the Internet can link users to a huge range of entertainment and informational content. But to get a sense of how the Internet is most often actually used we need to look at the most popular websites (by unique audience visitors and time spent per visit). The top ten websites in the United States in 2012 were (in order) Google, Facebook, YouTube, Yahoo!, Amazon.com, eBay, Wikipedia, MSN/WindowsLive/Bing, Craiglist.org, and Twitter.[30] The search engine sites are popular because they are widely used to find other websites—like the popular entertainment and shopping destinations that make up most of the top ten, or top fifty, or top one hundred websites. And the most popular websites dominate the flow of Web traffic. "The top 10 websites accounted for 31 percent of US page views in 2001, 40 percent in 2006, and 75 percent in 2010."[31] Whether it's social networking, shopping, or consuming other media (e.g., TV, movies, porn), the Internet is largely used in the everyday lives of most Americans as a superhighway to pacification-related website destinations: shopping, socializing, entertainment.

This is not to say that the Internet fails to provide access to websites maintained by groups and organizations committed to social change. Such groups and organizations obviously exist, but their websites are visited far less frequently than the most popular commercial websites, which attract millions of visitors each day.[32] The Internet can be used to attract, inform, and mobilize people interested in all sorts of social causes, political issues, and social movements, ranging from fascist groups on the right to communists on the left, but relatively speaking, *most* Internet users go online for Facebook socializing, Amazon shopping, or Twitter-tweeting rather than radical ranting or movement planning. In short, given the huge volume of website traffic that flows through the Internet to commercial websites, we conclude that this medium facilitates the pacification of everyday life far more often than any other outcome.

PACIFICATION AND PROVOCATION: TWO SIDES OF EVERYDAY LIFE

"Those that are concerned about the growing inequality in this country . . . [are] the silenced majority, silenced by the corporate media. . . . [The] force more powerful than that . . . is people's movements calling for real democracy."

—Amy Goodman, *In These Times* (December 2012): 35

As the preceding sections illustrate, the pacification of everyday life is a pervasive, complex, and powerful process. The examples in this chapter suggest pacification promotes elite class interests through a variety of institutionalized routines and practices that for the most part legitimate and reproduce existing class inequalities and at the same time distract nonelites from these issues. However, it is also important to recognize that pacification does not proceed as an unopposed process, nor is it a seamless, one-dimensional force without internal contradictions.

The alternative class-power networks described in chapter 6 often call attention to, challenge, and contest the pacification process. The provocation efforts of these networks often operate outside the organizations and structures that dominate the pacification process—but not always. Some branches or substructures of mainstream organizations that drive the pacification process sometimes include people and ideas from the alternative power networks. For example, public and commercial TV and radio producers sometimes include individuals from alternative power networks on some programs. Perhaps such guests are occasionally included to help legitimate a program's *image* as an "open forum" for discussions of public issues. But whatever the motives of the gatekeepers for elite class–dominated media may be, whenever representatives from the alternative power networks appear on corporate-controlled TV or radio programs, their messages challenging the pacification process reach large audiences. Examples of individuals associated with alternative power networks who sometimes appear as guests on programs disseminated via corporate-controlled electronic media include AFL-CIO president Richard Trumpka, consumer advocate Ralph Nader, filmmaker Michael Moore, and elite-power critic Noam Chomsky.

Perhaps more important than token electronic media appearances by pacification critics such as those cited above are the effects of internal contradictions that are part of the routine operation of the pacification process. This means that while many features of elite class–produced pacifying "products" like the policies, programs, and cultural content described in this chapter largely facilitate the pacification process, some features of those products may generate paradoxical effects. That is, some features of products that drive the pacification process may highlight or even challenge class inequalities or concentrated superclass-corporate power rather than legitimate them. When this occurs, such products lead to contradictory outcomes—such as heightened class consciousness among workers and increased class tensions.

One illustration of how pacification and provocation can occur as a result of the routine operation of conventional institutional practices can be found in the political arena. As we have seen, the campaigns of candidates for public office are largely financed by the elite classes. But to win elections, candidates must appeal to middle- and even lower-income voters. This reality can sometimes lead elite class–funded candidates to take public positions on some issues that appear to reinforce working-class interests rather than those of the elite classes. For example, mainstream media pundits typically encourage Democratic candidates to run as "centrist unifiers" and to avoid populist or progressive stands on issues—advice offered repeatedly in the 2012 elections.[33] But Democratic candidates in high-profile campaigns who *ignored* this advice and took progressive positions on economic and social issues (e.g., stronger regulations on Wall Street, higher taxes on the rich, opposition to free trade, support for gay rights) won more often than they lost in 2012. Notable examples were progressive U.S. Senate candidates Sherrod Brown (OH), Tammy Baldwin (WI), and Elizabeth Warren (MA); all three campaigned on progressive platforms and won.[34] Even President Obama invoked populist rhetoric in portions of his reelection campaign.[35] The inclusion of progressive-populist messages in national political campaigns illustrates that the routine operation of our largely elite class–funded election process, which usually reinforces the pacification process, has the *potential* to generate *some* provocative, "class war"–like campaign messages—at least episodically.

The corporate-controlled electronic media also illustrate how institutional imperatives can produce contradictions in pacification products. While most commercially produced electronic media products help distract public attention from class issues and legitimate class inequalities, some do not. Because bottom-line-driven, profit-making media firms must deliver a constant, massive stream of novel media products to attract viewers in order to increase sales and profits, some space exists in this torrent for the development of nonpacifying products by creative, socially conscious writers, producers, actors, and related artists. Thus, in the absence of explicit censorship and in the routine course of producing creative and marketable products, some movies and TV programs are produced that include content critical of various forms of class inequalities, such as concentrated superclass-corporate power, worker oppression, and poverty.

On rare occasions Hollywood movies are made that illustrate how culture industry products that typically promote pacification can sometimes promote its opposite—class consciousness. Some movies, like *The Grapes of Wrath* (1940, starring Henry Fonda) and *Norma Rae* (1979, starring Sally Field), portray working-class characters and interests in sympathetic terms. Films such as these expose viewers to harsh class inequalities that drive working-class grievances, legitimate workers' struggles to resolve those grievances, and encourage viewers to identify with class underdogs. Thus, movie studios that typically traffic in pacification products sometimes produce provocative films critical of class inequalities. Such films can resonate powerfully with audiences, generate critical acclaim, *and* produce large box-office revenues. Of course, movie studios are *not* in business to make films that stimulate class consciousness. Even so, if movies that have that effect generate big profits, then they will be produced—at least from time to time.

Like the movies, television is also most closely associated with pacifying effects. However, even routine television products can be provocative. For example, since the 2008 financial crisis, network TV news shows and newsmagazines have broadcast some reports on topics that help call attention to class inequalities and concentrated superclass-corporate power. Examples include reports on metastasizing corporate scandals, large bonuses paid to executives of banks bailed out by U.S. taxpayers, soaring CEO pay, declining "middle-class" incomes, the Federal Reserve's ongoing rescue of Wall Street via "quantitative easing," loopholes that allow the rich and large corporations to avoid taxes (and even get refunds), plant closings engineered by private equity firms like Bain Capital (Mitt Romney's corporate home), the corrupting effects of *Citizens United* on U.S. elections, corporations looting workers' pension funds, governments breaking unions via "right-to-work" laws, predatory payday loan shops, and many others.[36] At the same time, some regularly scheduled TV entertainment programs (especially those on cable channels) have, since 2008, occasionally included content critical of Wall Street firms' excesses, super PACs, and related forms of class inequalities. *The Daily Show*, hosted by Jon Stewart, and *The Colbert Report*, hosted by Stephen Colbert, are prominent examples of cable-TV entertainment programs blending news and class inequality issues with humor and satire.[37]

As we noted earlier, the Internet, like most movies and television programs, is far more closely associated with pacification than provocation outcomes. Even so, as we also noted earlier, it does provide access to websites hosted by groups and organizations committed to social change. To the extent that Web surfers visit such websites and become involved with such groups, especially those working to reduce class inequalities, the Internet can act as a kind of double-edged sword facilitating both pacification and provocation at the same time.

Recently we caught a glimpse of the *potential* utility the Internet has for promoting social movements seeking greater economic, political, and social justice. First came the emergence, in early 2011, of what has been called the Arab Spring movements in Egypt and other nearby nations.[38] Then September 2011 witnessed the unfolding drama of the Occupy Wall Street encampment in New York City's Zuccotti Park, soon followed by similar actions in several cities across the United States.[39] In both cases the Internet, via social media websites as well as websites maintained by social justice groups and independent media (plus cell phone communications), played a significant role in attracting participants, supporters, and news coverage by the corporate electronic and print media. The new technologies were also useful in facilitating internal communications among movement participants and in coordinating movement activities. While the Internet *seemed* useful in these two cases, both movements failed to achieve substantive changes in inequality-producing institutional structures in the United States, Egypt, or elsewhere. The Arab Spring movements produced some government leadership changes (e.g., in Egypt), but institutional structures that permit or reinforce political repression and economic inequalities were largely untouched.[40] In the United States, the Occupy encampments were attacked by police actions and the movement found itself increasingly ignored by the corporate media and fragmented a year after it began.[41] Even so, these movements in different parts of the world demonstrated that the new digital technologies can do more than promote the pacification of everyday life.

The parade of examples illustrating the flip side of the pacification process could go on and on, but the point is that there is another side. The everyday, routine functioning of conventional social institutions (local communities, the criminal justice system, Congress) and the electronic media (movies, TV, Internet) mostly serves, as we have seen, to distract nonelites from class issues, defuse class tensions, and legitimate class inequalities. But at the same time, the routine functioning of those institutions and media can, and occasionally does, subvert the pacification process. On those infrequent occasions, chunks from the dark mass of conflicting class interests from beneath the waterline of the class iceberg churn to the surface and contribute to transient episodes of inconvenience, embarrassment, and even anger for members of the elite classes. Fortunately for them, such provocations are usually isolated and quickly smoothed over by the powerful and predictable elite class–controlled institutional routines and electronic media that on a daily basis largely serve to reinforce the pacification of everyday life.

14

Class in the Twenty-First Century

> "Uninformed and misinformed; pauperized or over-worked; misled or betrayed by their leaders—financial, industrial, political and ecclesiastical, the people are suspicious, weary, and very, very busy, but they are, nonetheless, the first, last, and best appeal in all great human cases. . . . And, though each individual in the great crowd lacks some virtues, they all together have what no individual has, a combination of all the virtues."
>
> —Lincoln Steffens, *Upbuilders* (1909)

In the preface to the first edition of this book we called attention to the relative absence of scholarly and popular inquiries into America's class structure and inequalities. We expressed our hope that the book's 1999 publication would help change that situation. In the third edition we noted in the preface how times had changed and observed that the period preceding its 2008 publication had witnessed the emergence of a "cottage industry" in class inequality studies. Since then, a veritable tsunami of articles, reports, books, websites, blogs, and tweets dealing with economic or class inequalities has been produced by scholars, journalists, think tanks, social justice groups, bloggers, geeks, and tweeters. It seems to us that everyone, except maybe the pizza delivery guy, has researched, written, blogged, or tweeted about inequality.

The spark for this sudden "discovery" of inequality and the huge outpouring of reports about it were obviously linked to the 2008 financial crisis and the Great Recession it produced that still hasn't seemed to end for many Americans. Since 2008, we have all read, heard, or seen numerous media reports on the trillions of taxpayer Federal Reserve dollars that were used, and are still being used, to bail out Wall Street banks and juice the salaries and bonuses of top executives in those firms. Meanwhile, the economic and social sufferings of foreclosed homeowners, indebted students, the unemployed, and the poor have been largely ignored by the same federal officials who rushed trillions in taxpayer-provided cash to aid and comfort "banksters" and billionaires.[1] Public protests over such inequities crystallized into the Tea Party and Occupy movements, with the latter group spotlighting the gaping economic divide between the 1 percent and the 99 percent.

In our view, the increase in attention given to inequality is important, but focusing on inequality is not the central issue. In fact, such a focus can distract people from learning more about how the U.S. *class structure* operates. Americans know a lot about economic inequality. Most know first-hand that it's harder and harder to stretch their stagnant wages to cover rising rent, food, and health care costs, not to mention trying to keep their used car running. And most Americans know about some of the "big-money guys" like multibillionaires Bill Gates and Warren Buffett, and they know what some big-name movie stars and athletes are paid. But what most Americans don't know much about is the *structure* of the U.S. class system and how it works—mostly against them. Without this knowledge, public concern about economic inequality will probably not rise much higher than expressions of contempt for Wall Street "banksters." It may be that the lack of a full understanding of the U.S. class system helps explain why so few Americans are moved to rage against it in public protests or join social movements to change it. Perhaps, as we noted near the end of chapter 5, many Americans really do see themselves as members of the "pre-rich class" and expect to join the actually wealthy elite one day soon: "As John Steinbeck is said to have noted, 'Socialism never took root in America because the poor see themselves not as an exploited proletariat, but as temporarily embarrassed millionaires.'"[2]

If Steinbeck's opinion was right, and if the illusion he described is widely and unshakably held by most Americans today, this book will not be useful for most readers. On the other hand, if Steinbeck was wrong, and if many Americans today are not only concerned about inequality but also interested in better understanding and reducing it, we believe this book will be a useful resource. If you've come this far, you know that the preceding chapters explored many key features of what we termed in our introduction the "iceberg" of the new class system. And you know we did so by focusing primarily on features of that system, or structure, that we believe are largely submerged below the waterline of widespread public awareness. Our purpose was to provide a readable, well-documented, and more complete picture of the U.S. class structure than one is likely to find in other sources.

In this final chapter we consider the prospects for continuity and change in the U.S. class system through a set of present, past, and future themes. The section titled "Reality Check of the Present" revisits the power of the U.S. class structure and calls attention to how the structures of racism, sexism, and classism reinforce it. In the "Past as Prologue?" section we revisit the class-based foundations of the American underdog tradition by recalling the emergence of populist movements that contested the power of elite classes in the past. And we consider the extent to which the Tea Party and Occupy movements represent contemporary expressions of our earlier populist traditions. In the final section, "The Future of Class Inequalities," we consider two general paths toward remaking the new class system. We contrast what we call the "Scrooge scenario," favored by elite-class-based "reform" leaders, with what we view as a populist-like "structural democracy scenario." The latter scenario is favored by those who envision America as a more equal, inclusive society that operates on the basis of participatory, transparent, authentic democratic practices in the political, economic, and cultural arenas. It is a vision shared by many working-class-based activists and some privileged-class members who have allied themselves with the working class in the alternative power networks described in chapter 6.

REALITY CHECK OF THE PRESENT

> "[Class] is a kind of ghost issue, there, but not there. . . . The truth is, class does count. It shapes our lives and intersects with race, ethnicity, gender, and geography in profound ways. . . . When you look at differences within the working class as a whole, you see a pattern on the part of the owners to pit one ethnic or racial group or gender against another. . . . It is a strategy of divide and conquer."
>
> —Janet Zandy, "Decloaking Class: Why
> Class Identity & Consciousness Count" (2005)

The phrase "reality check of the present" is intended to remind us not only that the highly unequal U.S. class structure is the most powerful, organizationally based social force in our lives today (as if we could forget) but also that its power is reinforced by three potent institutionalized structures associated with the "inequality scripts" described in chapter 2. As we have seen, because of its iceberg-like nature, the class structure is largely an unseen, taken-for-granted part of the social landscape. While we believe our book's exploration of the class iceberg provides readers with unique insights into many of its hidden features, it is important to note that even a richly textured description of the class structure does not diminish its power over or its reach into our lives. As you may recall from earlier chapters, for members of the elite classes and those beneath them in the larger privileged class, this structure securely anchors their possession of large shares of the four forms of capital described in chapter 2 and it ensures that their wealth, power, and privileges will remain intact far into the future. You may also recall that for most working-class members this same structure generates ever-greater levels of insecurity and uncertainty. It is a corrosive force that wears away and shrinks the life chances, choices, and opportunities for workers and their children. But because the class *structure* is largely invisible, it is unlikely that most members of the privileged or working classes ascribe their very different life chances or experiences to the force of its hidden features concealed beneath the waterline.

In addition to what we learned in earlier chapters regarding the structure and operation of our class system, reality checking the present calls attention to how the "institutionalized" structures of racism, sexism, and classism help reinforce this system. Many activities of large organizations that support and perpetuate the U.S. class structure are organized around and guided by policies and practices that are "institutionalized." This simply means that the typically unquestioned and taken-for-granted assumptions, policies, and practices elite class owners and privileged class managers use to achieve what they believe are optimal organizational outcomes (which serve their class interests) are built into the routine activities and operations of the large organizations that stand astride and dominate the new class society. These organizations include, as we have seen, the largest corporations at the core of the new economy, especially financial firms, key offices and agencies within the executive, legislative, and judicial branches of the federal government, media conglomerates, major foundations, think tanks, and the elite universities.

We view the institutionalized policies and practices that guide how executives, stockholders, employees, elected officials, job-seekers, clients, customers, students, and citizens are routinely treated by large organizations as reflecting both traditional cultural norms and the economic, political, and cultural interests of the elite classes. From our perspective, institutionalized policies and practices that involve race, sex, and class distinctions reinforce the class system for two reasons. First, they facilitate preferential treatment by resource-rich organizations for members of the elite classes and those in the larger privileged class. Second, they reinforce organizationally based forms of discrimination (often subtle) against and contribute to the marginalization of groups not typically found in the elite classes (i.e., people of color, women, and members of the working class). We refer to the organizationally based practices that generate such outcomes as institutional racism, sexism, and classism. These institutionalized forces include, but extend beyond, the inequality scripts noted in chapter 2.

Institutional Racism, Sexism, and Elite Class Dominance

Embedded in the history and culture of the United States are sets of beliefs, policies, and practices that form the bases of ideological and institutional racism and sexism. As ideas, racism and sexism are based on belief systems that link physical characteristics thought to be associated with "minority" groups (i.e., groups with less power than a distinct dominant group) to a set of psychological and behavioral characteristics assumed to be true of such groups (e.g., African Americans, women). These assumed features of minority groups are judged by members of a dominant group to be inferior.[3] This is the essence of ideological racism and sexism.[4] Ideological racism may give even the poorest working-class whites psychological gains that may come from feeling superior to others, and ideological sexism may give working-class men validation of their masculinity when they exclude women from their activities or exert control over them at home.

When the idea systems regarding race and gender become intertwined with the policies and practices of businesses, schools, the criminal justice system, the corporate media, and many other organizations, the results are institutional racism and sexism. These forms of treatment embody a principle of social domination whereby groups viewed as inferior are exploited economically and oppressed politically, so-cially, and physically. This principle of domination is carried out by schools that fail to provide students of color and women with equal preparation to assume leader-ship roles in their communities and workplaces; it is revealed in the organizational structures of corporations and governmental bodies that do not equally provide all employees with opportunities and job ladders to learn, grow, and advance; it is revealed, as we have seen, by how the drug war is waged and by the unequal incar-ceration rates the criminal justice system imposes on minorities; and it is reflected in the corporate media by TV programming that sometimes excludes minorities and women or depicts them in unrealistic or demeaning ways and by the hiring practices of media firms that limit their employment prospects.[5]

One arena where we find obvious examples of the connections between institu-tional racism and sexism and the economic and political power and interests of the elite classes is the workplace. While federal laws make discriminatory hiring, pay, and promotion practices in the workplace based on race or gender illegal, such practices nonetheless persist.[6] Their existence is evident in continued forms of occupational segregation by race and gender and by disparities in the wage and benefit levels of black, Hispanic, and female workers compared to those of white males.[7] Despite be-ing illegal, institutional racism and sexism in the workplace reinforce the interests of elite class owners and privileged class managers in various ways.

One direct benefit of institutional racism and sexism in the workplace that relates to class interests is that such practices provide business owners and managers with hidden or seemingly "neutral" ways to discriminate against blacks and women in em-ployment and wages and thereby increase profits.[8] Elite-class employers can reduce labor costs by using workers who, compared to their "core," full-time employees, are paid lower wages, denied insurance and pension benefits, and work only part-time. Such low-wage, part-time workers are often women and minorities. Of course, most employers are not likely to view their use of low-wage, part-time workers as tied to racism or sexism. Most would probably deny holding any prejudicial beliefs about blacks or women. And most would almost certainly deny discriminating against blacks or women in their businesses. Rather, their staffing practices would probably be explained on the basis of "merit," or the relative lack thereof among low-paid workers. This means employers would say that their low-paid black or women em-ployees are paid less because they have lower educational levels and are less skilled than higher-paid employees who have higher levels of education and more complex, refined job skills. Since employers seek to maximize profits and minimize costs, when they use low-wage black or female workers, they are likely to see themselves as simply taking advantage of how the "labor market" sorts workers into different skill and wage categories. They are not likely to view themselves as responsible if this "market" produces a segregated workforce.

Another benefit of institutional racism and sexism for elite-class employers is that these practices help managers maintain greater control over workers and over the entire working class as well. In U.S. labor history we find many examples where racial, ethnic, and sexual differences have been used to divide workers to enhance managerial control over the labor force.[9] In a recent book focusing on the 1830–1930 period, David R. Roediger and Elizabeth D. Esch demonstrate that elite white U.S. business owners and managers consciously developed and used management practices that took advantage of racial and ethnic divisions as well as racist beliefs held by different working-class groups as techniques to enhance their control over employees.[10] As one reviewer of their book put it, the authors explore how corporate employers have "long used racial and ethnic differences among workers to divide and conquer them . . . to maximize profits."[11] The work of these authors illustrates how at least some forms of institutional racism can be viewed as emerging out of consciously developed "racialized" management practices used by elite white business owners and managers. These authors also suggest that racialized management techniques continue to be used in the United States in a variety of occupations and in the global economy, as, for example, in situations where low-paid workers in poor nations are placed in competition with higher-paid, often white workers in the United States and other advanced industrialized nations.

Outside of the workplace, we find many other arenas where the structures of institutional racism and sexism reinforce elite and privileged class interests. Examples include both major political parties, the political process (including election campaigns), various federal and state governmental offices and agencies, the criminal justice system, the corporate media, and schools and universities. In each arena it is likely that only a small proportion of Americans endorse blatant racist or sexist views or institutionalized practices. More likely, a much larger proportion probably believe that racism and sexism as belief systems and as structured practices are "history"—part of the past but not the present. Many believe that blacks won the civil rights revolution and that women too have "come a long way, baby!"

Believing that blacks and women have made major gains in the economic, political, and social arenas, many Americans now feel that affirmative action policies in place in many organizations provide African Americans and women with unfair advantages.[12] To the extent that many white working-class Americans, especially men, believe that ideological and institutional racism and sexism are dead, although the everyday experiences of minorities and women suggest otherwise, the entire working class is rendered divided, resentful, and suspicious by its racial and gender divisions. A divided working class cannot act as a united political, economic, and cultural force. For members of the elite classes, this situation facilitates the pursuit of their class interests. Institutional racism and sexism are not structures that have resulted from a superclass conspiracy, but their existence and effects do help reinforce the economic, political, and cultural interests of the elite classes.

Institutional Classism and Elite Class Dominance

Institutional classism is another abstract label for a powerful but hidden force that also helps reinforce the class system and disguise the interests of the elite classes and of most of the rest of the privileged class. At a general level, classism refers to the unspoken but widely accepted belief in American society that the values, vocabulary, social norms, social skills, cultural knowledge, educational backgrounds, cultural tastes, and lifestyles of the privileged class, especially those in the elite segments of this class, are superior to those of the working class (and lower class).[13] While the upper and lower segments of the privileged class tend to be united in terms of sharing most of the social and cultural traits listed above, because of the extensive wealth and power held by the elite classes (the superclass and the credentialed class), these upper segments play key roles in establishing and reinforcing such traits and in rewarding their refined expression. Compared with racism and sexism (or even ageism), classism is largely a silent, hidden "ism"—partly because of the invisible nature of key features of the U.S. class structure. But classism is similar to racism and sexism in terms of its effects. It leads to prejudice toward, stereotyping of, and discrimination against members of the nonprivileged class, especially those in the lower segments of the working class. *White trash, trailer-park, low-life,* and *slacker* are only a few of the pejorative terms applied to those in lower segments of the working class.[14]

Classism is based on and justified by a widely shared belief system sometimes called the ideology of meritocracy.[15] This idea system views class location as a reflection of talent and effort. It encourages the view that privileged-class positions are occupied by people who possess widely valued and admired traits such as high intelligence, achievement motivation, and altruism. It also encourages viewing members of the new working class (especially those in the bottom segments) as being justly placed in lower ranks because they obviously lack the valued qualities necessary to "succeed" in a merit-based economic system. The ideology of meritocracy helps justify and legitimate class inequalities by making class divisions seem naturally ordained and views elites at the top of the class structure as rare and gifted visionaries. This is obviously what billionaire John D. Rockefeller Sr. had in mind when he said, "I believe the power to make money is a gift of God. . . . Having been endowed with the gift I possess, I believe it is my duty to make money and still more money, and to use the money I make for the good of my fellow man according to the dictates of my conscience."[16]

Like racism and sexism, classism is embedded, or institutionalized, in the routine policies and practices of large organizations controlled by members of the elite classes and managed by lower-ranking privileged-class members. Examples include corporations, government branches and agencies, foundations, the corporate media, public schools, the criminal justice system, and universities. As a result, the operations of nearly the entire organizational establishment of the society trend in directions that exclude, disadvantage, or otherwise marginalize people from the lower classes through everyday routine (but largely unrecognized) practices. Institutional classism refers to a form of hegemony whereby upper-tier, privileged-class-based ideas, values, norms, language styles, and social behaviors prevail in organizations dominated by this class. From schools to the workplace to government and beyond, the gatekeepers in elite-class-controlled, privileged-class-managed large organizations actively screen out or marginalize working-class-based values, norms, language styles, and behaviors.

Such gatekeeping practices were evident in a now-classic study illustrating how Harvard law students "afflicted" with the stigma of working-class origins were subtly (but powerfully) encouraged to disguise this feature of their social identity. In addition to mastering their academic endeavors, they learned the importance of distancing themselves from the working-class stigma, as well as how to do it. This was necessary to increase their chances of being selected to join elite law firms and thereby maximize their own career opportunities. The acceptance of these students by elite-class "organizational masters" in elite law firms required them to demonstrate an easy familiarity with elite cultural codes and conform to the cultural standards, social behaviors, style of dress, and manner of speech affected by those in the upper segments of the privileged class.[17]

The hidden power of elite-privileged-class communication styles illustrates yet another dimension of institutional classism. Teachers and professors in public schools and universities, especially those serving students where many already possess advanced levels of social capital, actively discourage working-class students from using the language styles of their class origins in their academic work. Students are rewarded for using elite-class language styles and their grades are penalized if they do not. The same pattern extends to job interviews, hirings, and workplace promotions, especially for "professional" positions above entry-level ranks.[18] And this pattern also applies to political candidates. Only those who demonstrate an easy familiarity with an elite-class vocabulary and style of speech will be viewed as "legitimate" candidates and be reported on as such by the corporate media. This vocabulary and style is what some sociologists refer to as the "elaborated code." In general, it involves communicating with others via a wide-ranging, nuanced vocabulary, abstract conceptual references, and complex sentences. This code (or variations of it) routinely structures communication (written and spoken) among privileged class members, especially those in the elite class segments.[19] It is a kind of "gold standard" and is the only legitimate communication style or mode of expression accepted and rewarded in most classrooms, boardrooms, and formal political and policy-making arenas.

Hidden class-linked advantages or disadvantages associated with privileged-class gatekeeping practices and with the class-based hegemony of the elaborated code as a communication style are seldom noted or explored by social scientists, journalists, or pundits. In fact, the details of these phenomena are virtually unknown to the public. The placement of workers from privileged-class backgrounds in advanced entry-level "professional" career positions as well as the pace of later career advancement are typically explained in mainstream academic research or in popular media profiles of "successful people" as functions of merit and talent and not as the result of class-biased gatekeeping practices. Similarly, the differential mastery by students of "proper" communication styles and forms (the elaborated code) is typically viewed as an indicator of merit and talent and not as the result of the advantages or disadvantages associated with privileged versus working-class origins and experiences.

Some features of privileged-class advantages are informally recognized among segments of the population, as in the commonly circulated aphorism (among the working class) concerning the basis of career success: "It's not what you know, but who you know." This statement reflects a kind of cynical realism among members of the working class, but it is obviously overly simplistic and misses the hidden institutional basis of elite-privileged-class advantages.

As tips of the class inequality iceberg, privileged-class gatekeeping practices and rewards for mastery of the elaborated code are but two examples of the myriad ways by which class-biased organizational routines, policies, and practices perpetuate elite and privileged-class interests. They are only two of the many covert threads woven into the fabric of institutional classism. Their powerful presence as sifting and sorting instruments helps make the common economic, political, and cultural successes (and rare failures) of elite and privileged-class offspring as well as the common failures and rare successes of working-class children within elite-class-controlled, privileged-class-managed organizations seem to be "fair" and "impartial" outcomes.

Our reality check of the present leads us to conclude that while the U.S. class system is indeed organizationally based and supported, the related structures of institutionalized racism, sexism, and classism powerfully reinforce that system in both obvious and subtle ways. Of the three "isms," classism is probably the least well known to most Americans as an ideology and as an institutionalized structure. The ideology of classism is particularly potent because it encourages viewing unequal class outcomes as legitimate, natural, and even inevitable or desirable by large numbers of people in all classes. At the same time, institutional classism, woven into the fabric of a variety of social and organizational practices, serves as a powerful yet largely invisible force reinforcing, on a daily basis, our highly unequal class system and the class interests of those groups at the top of that system. But seeing classism as *the* crucial force driving class inequalities is misleading because all three isms operate synergistically as institutionalized structures that together reinforce and disguise many inequalities in the U.S. class system.

THE PAST AS PROLOGUE?

"We meet in the midst of a nation brought to the verge of moral, political, and material ruin. Corruption dominates the ballot box, the legislatures, [and] the Congress. . . . The newspapers are subsidized or muzzled. . . . The fruits of the toil of millions are stolen to build up colossal fortunes. . . . From the same prolific womb of governmental injustice we breed two classes—paupers and millionaires."

—preamble to the 1892 People's Party National Platform, cited in Howard Zinn, *A People's History of the United States* (1980)

How long can the intensifying inequalities between the privileged class (especially its top segments) and the new working class continue? That's akin to asking, "How long can the stock market keep going up?" In early 2013 some optimistic market analysts predicted the Dow Jones Industrial Average (DJIA) would top 15,000 by year's end, but many others were not so sure.[20] Perhaps that's because they know that the stock market, like history, does not move in a straight line over time. This reality has been strikingly evident since the 2008 financial crisis. The DJIA fell from just over 14,000 in early October 2008 to about 6,600 in March 2009 before recovering to the low 14,000 range in early 2013.[21] Hardly a straight line!

So what are the prospects that significant social movements will develop to alter the current imbalance of power that exists between the two great opposing classes in the double diamond? To avoid utopian visions or fantasies driven by hopes or dreams more than by reality, in this section we look to America's past to help guide our understanding of the present and what might be possible in the future. We begin with those times when the forces for change converged on a single project—to change the structure of society in order to reduce economic and social inequalities. Popular movements for change have gone by many labels, but "American populism" has endured as a common frame of reference describing many movements from the past aimed at reducing material inequalities. The next section considers lessons from the American populist tradition and provides a context for understanding contemporary reform projects aimed at reshaping the new class society.

The Populist Tradition: Lessons from History

When some political candidates today criticize the concentrated power of wealthy elites and large corporations, they are following in the footsteps of earlier critics who help forge the American populist tradition. The wealthy and powerful, in the form of corporate executives, bankers, politicians, and bureaucrats, have served in the past as high-profile targets of criticism by individuals and groups attempting to mobilize discontented Americans for change. Historical movements condemning elite-class excesses and promoting working-class reforms have often juxtaposed obvious and easily understood class contrasts by using terms such as the *haves* versus the *have-nots,* the *powerful* versus the *powerless,* and the *fat cats* versus the *common man.* Such references have served as the images and language of American populism. This historical tradition of protest calling for reforms to reduce economic and social inequities has periodically emerged from the class-based grievances of the working-class majority.

Populist rhetoric has been used by numerous labor organizers, social movement leaders, and even, at times, mainstream politicians to shape and mobilize public discontent. In its classic form, populist messages seek to simultaneously elevate the masses and attack the privileged for their undeserved rewards. When the People's Party was formed in 1892, it pulled together debt-ridden small farmers, hundreds of discontented workers' groups, and several minor parties—all of whom were deeply dissatisfied with how the Democrats and Republicans had been running the country. More than a century ago, leaders of the People's Party praised the virtuous small farmers and laborers as the "producers" who created national prosperity that rightfully belonged to all Americans and heaped scorn on the "plutocrats," "parasites," and "moneyed aristocracy" who were said to wallow in idleness, extravagance, and waste. The use of sharply contrasting class-based images was a central feature of the populist message. As a noted historian of this tradition recently observed, "[Populism is] a language whose speakers conceive of ordinary people as a noble assemblage not bounded narrowly by class, view their elite opponents as self-serving, and seek to mobilize the former against the latter."[22]

The populist social movements of the nineteenth century were grounded in a rhetoric and ideology based on economic grievances and a defense of those who worked as small farmers, wage earners, and small-business people. But populist attacks on corporations, monopoly, and plutocrats were not aimed at the overthrow of capitalism. Rather, the populist reform message called for greater recognition of the importance of the common man in the economic, political, and social arenas and for a fair share of the fruits of workers' productive labor to be returned to these producers of wealth. The relatively modest scope of the populist reform agenda is underscored by author Michael Kazin's point that "through populism Americans have been able to protest social and economic inequalities without calling the entire system into question."[23] Kazin also argues that early populist critiques of American society attempted to build new bonds among people by returning to the core beliefs of the new American nation—rule by the people, reward for hard work and diligence, and faith in God.

As history illustrates, the American populist tradition has been both a powerful and ambivalent instrument for reform. Many aspiring leaders have picked up the populist instrument hoping to play a tune powerful enough to stir the sleeping masses into sweeping away corrupt elites. The power of that tradition rests with its roots in the early American experience, stressing the dignity of the common man and a rejection of the "foreign" influences of aristocracy and elitism. This thread of populism can serve as a bond unifying people to act on behalf of the common good while eschewing privilege and unfair advantage. The ambivalence associated with the populist tradition stems from its majoritarian beliefs, reflected in support for direct participatory democracy. The majoritarian emphasis does not sit well with members of religious or ethnic groups that are numerically small and therefore feel that their interests will be ignored by the usually white and Christian majority. The majoritarian emphasis also does not sit well with "privileged leftists" who support populist ideology but whose education and credentialed-class privileges make them wary of "marching with the people."

Today's Populism? The Tea Party and Occupy Movements

In recent years, two change-oriented movements with some apparent similarities to our earlier populist traditions emerged in the United States: the Tea Party (in 2009) and the Occupy movement (in 2011). The corporate media and elite-class pundits, however, have devoted far more attention to the former than the latter, and the Tea Party has received more positive media treatment than has been the case for the Occupy movement.[24] Perhaps this disparity in media coverage and treatment has occurred because, as media analysts Peter Hart and Steve Rendall have pointed out,

"The Tea Party's right-wing populism is the perfect kind for corporate news outlets at a time when the wealthy elites who own them feel threatened by more authentic populist impulses. And for that reason . . . the Tea Party movement is likely to remain a focus of media attention."[25] By contrast, corporate media coverage of the Occupy movement was slow to develop, often critical or snarky, and faded quickly in early 2012.[26] As media analyst John Knefel has noted, what the data regarding media coverage of the Occupy movement reveal is that the "corporate media and their owners have every incentive to ignore not only protest movements [in favor of reducing economic inequalities], but also the underlying causes of those movements."[27]

Despite variations in coverage, corporate media reports and elite-class pundits have often focused on three topics that relate to both movements. First, there has been a recurring focus on the movements' political effects. It has centered on the question of how or to what extent the two movements have influenced political campaigns and election outcomes. Second, there has been a focus on the movements' goals. Media reports and pundits have asked, "What do they want?" Third, there has been a focus on the movements' membership. It has involved questions about age (young or old?), race (white or nonwhite?), education (well educated or not?), work status (employed or unemployed?), and occupations (what types of jobs do members hold?). In addition to these questions, some independent media have focused on the extent to which these movements are "genuine." This means questioning whether they are authentic "grass roots" movements or artificial "astroturf" movements—the latter term referring to fake movements created by wealthy elites, most often on the right side of the political spectrum.[28]

Answers to the mainstream media–framed questions noted above have filled the corporate electronic and print media, Internet websites, blogs, Facebook posts, and tweets since these movements emerged. Some of the answers have been reasonably fact-based, such as examinations of election outcomes, the characteristics of participants, and the movements' authenticity. On the latter issue, most independent observers agree that although many Tea Party protestors appear to be genuinely angry about the economic and political status quo, many features of the Tea Party *movement* appear to be more astroturf than grassroots in nature.[29] In contrast, corporate as well as independent media reports on the Occupy movement have generally described it as having characteristics that are consistent with authentic, grassroots social movements.[30]

Compared to the fact-based answers to some of the questions noted above, many answers to questions associated with the first and second topics have often been little more than speculation based on superficial observations of movement events or interviews with small numbers of individuals associated with either of the two movements. What is missing from most corporate media reports on these two movements are serious efforts by reporters and pundits to consider their similarities and the potential that exists for both groups to merge into a single, unified movement for change. Viewing these missing topics through a class-based lens is, we believe, useful to better understand the Occupy movement and some Tea Party features as contemporary, class-based social phenomena that have much in common with our populist traditions.

One quality that most core members and sympathizers of both movements have in common is that they are part of what we call the new working class. While some movement members are drawn from the lower ranks of the privileged class, most are workers who share a number of grievances related to their position in the class structure. Out of these shared class grievances emerge shared feelings of *anger*. Such feelings shared by movement members and sympathizers are related to their common life circumstances and to how government organizations seem to side with wealthy elites against the interests of average persons.

They are angry if they are among the ranks of the unemployed and underemployed. They are angry about the demise of middle-class jobs, wages, benefits, and opportunities and tax policies that favor the wealthy and giant corporations. They are angry about growing economic inequalities, especially the widening gap in wealth and income between the haves and the have nots. Even if they currently have decent jobs, health insurance, and retirement benefits, they are angry about taxpayer-funded bailouts of the Wall Street firms responsible for the financial crisis and the multimillion-dollar bonuses and salaries received by executives in the firms responsible for the crisis. They are angry about large firms like General Electric shipping American jobs overseas while their CEOs are lionized in the corporate media for their business acumen and appointed to panels shaping government policies on jobs. One glaring example, which we noted in chapter 3, was Obama's appointment of GE's CEO to head the President's Council on Jobs and Competitiveness.[31] The palpable anger apparent in both groups echoes the sentiments that energized and unified workers, farmers, and small business owners in the past.

While the Tea Party and Occupy movements appear to differ in important ways, be focused on somewhat different inequalities, and be aimed at times at different targets, the members and sympathizers of both groups are clearly angry. In both cases, their anger is based in large part on a number of shared, *class-based* grievances. These shared qualities could serve as a unifying force. If current conditions persist, the anger, grievances, and frustrations both movements share could be qualities that, given the right "spark" of specific events or new developments, might bring them together into a unified and enlarged populist movement for change.

At this point it is difficult to know if the two movements might someday merge. We do know that the public is increasingly aware of how big business and big government often work together against the interests of average Americans. Such awareness is evident by the *lack* of confidence Americans have in major social institutions such as large corporations, banks, the presidency, Congress, and the U.S. Supreme Court.[32] The view of America as a plutocracy is difficult for many to square with traditional American ideals regarding how a fair, egalitarian, democratic government and society should work. The dissonance that results from the contrast between the reality of a corrupt economic and political system and the ideal of a democratic political system governed "of, by, and for the people" helps generate the subjective feelings of anger that help energize participants of both the Tea Party and the Occupy movements.

In some ways, the Tea Party and Occupy movements are similar to the populist movements of the past. Both then and now widespread interest among nonelites in changing unequal, unfair, and corrupt economic and political systems into forms more consistent with traditional American democratic ideals has led many citizens to create and join populist movements for change. However, just as past populist movements rose and then subsided, it may be that the Tea Party and Occupy movements will shift into a dormant mode, becoming part of what some sociologists have termed "abeyance structures."[33] But even if today's movements subside rather than merge, they are unlikely to totally disappear from public awareness because the grievances that gave rise to them have not been resolved. And if new grievances arise or if existing ones intensify anew in the future, we are likely to see new versions of these movements emerge again, perhaps in a unified form that is difficult now to envision or predict.

THE FUTURE OF CLASS INEQUALITIES

"Once I saw the mountains angry, And ranged in battle-front. Against them stood a little man; I laughed and spoke to one near me, 'Will he prevail?' 'Surely,' replied this other; 'His grandfathers beat them many times.'"

—Stephen Crane, *The Red Badge of Courage and Other Writings* (1960)

Having considered the present and recounted the past, what is the future of the new class society? We believe there is no single future. Rather, there are many possible futures. The future of class inequalities depends upon the extent to which the many organizations, trends, and structures that support and reinforce the new class system (the dominant power networks) prevail over the organizations, trends, and structures that oppose and challenge that system (the alternative power networks). As much of the information and analysis presented in the preceding chapters and in this one suggest, it is likely that elite-class-led efforts to further consolidate and harden our unequal class structure will be powerful and difficult to resist or reverse. We expect elite-class leaders to pursue policies that will produce, compared to today, even greater concentrations of investment, consumption, social, and skill capital in the hands of the elite classes and those of their allies in the larger privileged class. But a bleak future of growing class dominance by the few over the many is not inevitable. We know that reversing the antidemocratic, anti-egalitarian, plutocratic trends evident in early twenty-first-century America is possible. Our forebears united in populist movements more than a century ago beat the mountains many times.

The Scrooge Scenario versus the Structural Scenario

"Wars and revolutions have destroyed oligarchies by forcibly dispersing their wealth, but a democracy never has. Democracy . . . can, however, tame oligarchs. . . . Americans are once again asking fundamental questions about how the oligarchic power of wealth distorts and outflanks the democractic power of participation."

—Jeffrey A. Winters, *In These Times* (March 2012): 20

In the world according to Dickens, reform is a function of conscience. In *A Christmas Carol*, the ghosts of Christmas past, present, and future visit Ebenezer Scrooge. This gets results. Shown the consequences of his selfishness, Scrooge is appropriately appalled and transformed. He reforms his miserly ways, and the community becomes a better place. It is a powerful and comforting morality tale grounded in an unspoken assumption that the selfish pursuit by the rich of their narrow economic interests can be blunted and redirected by consciousness-raising experiences that awaken a latent social conscience. It seems too simplistic to be taken seriously as a way to reform the wider social world, but it is a reform message that deeply resonates within a working class intensely socialized to the individualistic credo of American culture.

The "Scrooge scenario" represents one kind of reform template favored and promoted by leaders in the elite classes and many in the larger privileged class. It is a personal-level approach that views individuals as both the sources of and solutions to our most vexing economic, political, and cultural problems and inequalities. This approach includes a willingness to view individuals in the elite classes whose activities cause societal-wide harm as redeemable. Elite-class leaders who embrace the Scrooge-based reform scenario allow that even if some "greedheads" in their class trash the economy, for example, it is possible for them, like Scrooge, to experience an epiphany of spiritual renewal that sets in motion a chain of redemption. In this chain, the spiritual renewal of flawed elites awakens within them what had been a latent social conscience, which now becomes a powerful force driving them to renounce their "sinful" greed, repent, and commit themselves to behave with virtue and henceforth work for the common good.

In the event that elite-class transgressors fail to embrace or conform to the Scrooge scenario, reformers may invoke what might be called a "due process replacement scenario." This alternative, applied in some situations today, uses conventional organizational policies and legal practices to remove flawed or unfit elite-class individuals from their positions of authority. The unfit are then replaced with more virtuous individuals with elite-class credentials who can be trusted to avoid the shame and transgressions of their disgraced predecessors. An example would be the jailing of Bernie Madoff, the Ponzi scheme shark whose illegal investment dealings were sorted out by court-appointed, elite-class professionals.

Variations of the Scrooge and replacement scenarios are evident in how the corporate media report on what seems to be an endless array of negative events and developments plaguing our society and widening inequalities. Sordid, greed-driven events, developments, and the collateral damage they cause are often attributed by corporate media reports to a few "bad apples" who, unfortunately, misused their upper-level positions of authority within corporations or major government offices (or both). When the corporate media report on topics such as financial firms crashing the economy, billionaires funding elections, corporate lobbyists crafting inside deals with Congress and federal agencies, private equity firms looting workers' pensions, and iconic American firms exploiting U.S. workers at home and child laborers abroad, all of these and other dastardly deeds are often framed as being caused by the greed or bad judgment (or both) of elite-class individuals in positions of authority in large organizations. Or, in some cases, they may be framed as caused by the extraordinary complexity of contemporary organizations and societies, in which case no one may be personally responsible or accountable for the harm such practices inflict on other individuals or the public at large.

The point is, the system is sound, or so we are told. We simply need the bad apples to repent by publicly admitting their wrongdoing, demonstrate a deep spiritual awakening, embrace their newly energized conscience, ask the public for forgiveness, and promise to go forth and sin no more. Failing that scenario, what is viewed by elites as efficacious individual-level reform may be enacted via the due process replacement scenario. In cases involving unrepentant or beyond-the-pale elite-class wrongdoers, justice may be served and public outrage assuaged by TV images of a few handcuffed, elite-class villains being led to prison by grim-faced marshals. But only a few Bernie Madoff–like elites go to jail. Most repent or pay a fine, and then go back to work.

The "structural democracy scenario" places little faith in the Scrooge or the due process replacement approaches. Reformers who oppose the new class system see undemocratic political, economic, and cultural structures embedded in large organizations controlled by the elite classes and unaccountable to the public as the problem. Supporters of and advocates for the populist-inspired "structural democracy scenario" are located in many different groups and organizations found in the alternative power networks. Examples include reformers and activists in the labor movement, social justice groups, grassroots educational and media reform groups, the alternative media, corporate accountability groups, environmental groups, LGBT groups, and many others.[34] The primary objectives of individuals and groups that embrace or endorse variations of what we call the structural democracy scenario generally include (1) revitalizing authentic democratic participation in politics and government, (2) extending the principles of democratic governance to the corporate structures that currently dominate the economic and cultural arenas of our society, (3) expanding opportunities for all citizens to participate in democratic processes essential to realize the first two objectives, and (4) increasing Americans' class consciousness—expanding awareness of not just how and why class membership is the central, defining feature of our social identities and life chances but, more importantly, understanding how the *class structure* operates and how it is organized, reinforced, and perpetuated.

The prospects for dramatically reducing structurally based class inequalities, achieving a more egalitarian society, and providing opportunities for everyone to achieve perhaps some new version of the American dream via projects inspired by the structural democracy scenario must be judged as uncertain at best. Even so, we believe this scenario and projects inspired by it can serve as useful points of departure for a national dialogue on the nature of the class structure and the many inequalities associated with it. An increasingly class-conscious public can provide the economic, political, and human resources necessary to support existing and yet-to-be-established institutions committed to the interests of the new working class and to reforming the new class society. We saw some evidence of a growing willingness by America to become involved in new social change initiatives earlier in this chapter in our brief exploration of the Tea Party and Occupy movements as possible modern-day versions of the American populist tradition.

As we have seen throughout this book, there is a pressing need for *structural changes* in our highly unequal new class system. Changes that would attempt to reform the class structure by replacing corrupt or malevolent individuals at the top of the large organizations that generate and reinforce it are clearly, in our view, inadequate. So what kinds of changes are needed? Some readers of earlier editions of this book wrote to us complaining of our failure to include a reform agenda clearly listing the structural changes necessary to transform our unequal class system. We appreciate their interest and enthusiasm. But we believe it would be presumptuous for us to provide readers with a list of changes that *we* think need to be pursued and enacted.

Only groups of Americans acting collectively can determine what needs to be done and what steps must be taken to reshape the class system and reduce class inequalities. Readers interested in participating in the reform process should explore the publications and websites of groups active in the alternative power networks. Many publications and websites of several groups in those networks are cited in various note references found in this and preceding chapters and in the bibliography. Reforms proposed or initiated by groups located in the alternative power networks provide specific examples of what structural changes aimed at reforming the present unequal class system and redressing class inequalities might look like. One small step, for example, would be the adoption of a federal "maximum wage" policy that would cap CEO compensation.[35]

As the future rushes from the present, it is necessary for concerned citizens to continue to develop new reform initiatives, strategies, and tactics that recognize, address, and build upon new conditions, circumstances, and opportunities. Developing and implementing new structural reform initiatives on an ever-increasing scale are essential if we are to make meaningful progress toward melting the iceberg of inequality before it rips open the current version of the *Titanic* known as the new class society and sends our American experiment to a permanent resting spot at the bottom of history.

Notes

INTRODUCTION

1. Robert Perrucci and Earl Wysong, *The New Class Society* (Lanham, MD: Rowman & Littlefield, 1999); Robert Perrucci and Earl Wysong, *The New Class Society*, 2nd ed. (Lanham, MD: Rowman & Littlefield, 2003); Robert Perrucci and Earl Wysong, *The New Class Society*, 3rd ed. (Lanham, MD: Rowman & Littlefield, 2008); Earl Wysong and Robert Perrucci, "Organizations, Resources, and Class Analysis: The Distributional Model and the US Class Structure," *Critical Sociology* 33 (2007): 211–46; Earl Wysong and Robert Perrucci, "Media and the Marginalization of Social Class Inequalities," *Journal of the Indiana Academy of the Social Sciences* XI (2007): 14–26; Earl Wysong and David W. Wright, "Socioeconomic Status and Gender: Recent Intergenerational Mobility Patterns in the U.S.," *Journal of the Indiana Academy of the Social Sciences* XIII (2009): 112–30; Robert Perrucci and Carolyn Perrucci, *America at Risk: The Crisis of Hope, Trust, and Caring* (Lanham, MD: Rowman & Littlefield, 2009).

2. The concept of "life chances" was developed by Max Weber as part of his exploration of class lifestyles. See Max Weber, *Economy and Society*, 2 vols., eds. G. Roth and C. Wittich (Berkeley: University of California Press, 1978). For a discussion of the meaning Weber attached to his concept of "life chances," see Ralf Daherndorf, *Life Chances* (Chicago: University of Chicago Press, 1979), 73.

3. Richard Wilkinson and Kate Pickett, *The Spirit Level: Why More Equal Societies Almost Always Do Better* (New York: Bloomsbury Press, 2009).

4. For examples of this literature, see Heather Boushey and Adam S. Hersh, *The American Middle Class, Income Inequality, and the Strength of Our Economy* (Washington, DC: Center for American Progress, May 2012); Chuck Collins, *99 to 1: How Wealth Inequality Is Wrecking the World and What We Can Do About It* (San Francisco: Berrett-Koehler Publishers, 2012); Timothy Noah, *The Great Divergence: America's Growing Inequality Crisis and What We Can Do About It* (New York: Bloomsbury Press, 2012); Sam Pizzigati, *The Rich Don't Always Win:*

The Forgotten Triumph over Plutocracy that Created the American Middle Class, 1900–1970 (Boston: Seven Stories Press, 2012).

5. James Truslow Adams, *The Epic of America* (Boston: Little, Brown, 1933). In his best-selling book, Adams wrote, "The American Dream [is] that dream of a land in which life should be better and richer and fuller for everyman, with opportunity for each according to his ability or achievement. . . . It is . . . a dream of a social order in which each man and each woman shall be able to attain to the fullest stature of which they are innately capable . . . regardless of the fortuitous circumstances of birth or position" (415).

6. Michael Ford, Dayna Dion, Casey Conway, and Jeremy Katz, "The Modern American Dream," American Family Mutual Insurance Company, August 2011, 10; MetLife, "2010 MetLife Study of the American Dream: An Uphill Climb," Metropolitan Life Insurance Company (May 2010), 13; Janny Scott and David Leonhardt, "Class in America: Shadowy Lines That Still Divide," *New York Times*, May 15, 2005, 16.

7. Robert Borosage and Katrina Vanden Heuvel, "The American Dream: Can a Movement Save It?" *Nation* (October 10, 2011): 11; Center for a New American Dream, "New American Dream Survey Report" (September 2004), 4–5, on the Internet at http://www.newdream.org (accessed August 27, 2005); Change to Win, "The American Dream Survey 2006" (August 28, 2006), on the Internet at http://www.changetowin.org (accessed October 18, 2006); MetLife, "2010 MetLife Study of the American Dream: An Uphill Climb," 8.

8. Borosage and Vanden Heuvel, "The American Dream: Can a Movement Save It?" 11.

9. See, for example, Seymour M. Lipset and Reinhard Bendix, *Social Mobility in Industrial Society* (Berkeley: University of California Press, 1959); Harry J. Crockett Jr., "The Achievement Motive and Differential Occupational Mobility in the United States," *American Sociological Review* 27 (1962): 191–204; Reinhard Bendix and Frank W. Howton, "Social Mobility and the American Business Elite—II," *British Journal of Sociology* 9 (1958): 1–14.

10. Peter Blau and Otis D. Duncan, *The American Occupational Structure* (New York: Wiley, 1967); David L. Featherman and Robert M. Hauser, *Opportunity and Change* (New York: Academic Press, 1978).

11. Joan Huber and William H. Form, *Income and Ideology: An Analysis of the American Political Formula* (New York: Free Press, 1973); James R. Kluegel and Eliot R. Smith, *Beliefs about Inequality: Americans' Views of What Is and What Ought to Be* (New York: Aldine De Gruyter, 1986); Beth A. Rubin, *Shifts in the Social Contract* (Thousand Oaks, CA: Pine Forge Press, 1996), 7–8.

12. Sarah Van Gelder, "The Legitimacy of Rule by Giant Corporations and Wall Street Banks Is Crumbling," *Yes! Magazine* (January 29, 2012): 1–3, on the Internet at http://www.yesmagazine.org (accessed July 8, 2012).

13. These examples were drawn from our review of several news media and popular culture sources over the course of the 2008–2012 period. See chapter 13, note 36 for details.

14. Peter Hart and Steve Rendall, "Journalists Love Tea Party," *Extra!* (May 2010): 7–8.

15. Peter Hart, "Surprised by Solidarity," *Extra!* (April 2011): 6–7.

16. Sam Pizzigati, "Equality Now!" *Nation* (November 14, 2011): 18–19.

17. "NBC News/*Wall Street Journal* Survey," conducted by Hart/McInturff, Study #11579 (November 2–5, 2011), Question #30, 22, on the Internet at http://www.nbcnews.com (accessed January 14, 2012).

18. "*Washington Post*-ABC News Poll," conducted by Abt-SRBI (November 3, 2011), Question #18, 11, on the Internet at http://www.washingtonpost.com (accessed January 14, 2012).

19. "Occupied Territory: A Time Poll," *Time* (October 24, 2011): 24.

20. Perrucci and Wysong, *The New Class Society*, 3rd ed., 48–49. The taboo is, of course, not complete; many alternative media outlets have often reported and continue to report on "above- and below-the-waterline" inequality issues.

21. Ronald Aronson, "The Left Needs More Socialism," *Nation* (April 17, 2006): 28–30; Robert W. Mcchesney, "This Isn't What Democracy Looks Like," *Monthly Review* (January 2013): 1–28; Robert W. McChesney and John Bellamy Foster, "The 'Left-Wing' Media?" *Monthly Review* (June 2003): 1–16; Maria Svart, "Why Not Socialism?" *In These Times* (December 2012): 27.

22. Julie Hollar, "Wealth Gaps Yawns—and So Do Media," *Extra!* (June 2010): 10–12; Janine Jackson, "13th Annual Fear & Favor Report," *Extra!* (February 2013): 9–11; Janine Jackson, "Admiring the Rich for Getting Richer," *Extra!* (June 2010): 5–6; Jim Naureckas, "Framing the Fed as Financial Philosopher Kings," *Extra!* (June 2010): 13–14.

23. G. William Domhoff, *Who Rules America?*, 6th ed. (Boston: McGraw-Hill, 2010), 55–84.

24. Thomas Dye, *Who's Running America? The Bush Restoration*, 7th ed. (Upper Saddle River, NJ: Prentice Hall, 2002), 137–39.

25. Martin N. Marger, *Social Inequality*, 5th ed. (New York: McGraw-Hill, 2011), 218–35.

CHAPTER 1: CLASS IN AMERICA: THE WAY WE WERE

1. Don Stillman, "The Devastating Impact of Plant Relocations," *Working Papers* (July–August 1978): 42–53.

2. Howard Zinn, *A People's History of the United States* (New York: Harper Colophon Books, 1980), 373–77.

3. Frederick Lewis Allen, *Since Yesterday: 1929–1939* (New York: Harper & Row, 1940), 43–52; Gilbert C. Fite and Jim E. Reese, *An Economic History of the United States*, 2nd ed. (Boston: Houghton Mifflin, 1965), 582–86.

4. Beth A. Rubin, *Shifts in the Social Contract* (Thousand Oaks, CA: Pine Forge Press, 1996), 27–33.

5. Data not shown. See Lawrence Mishel, Jared Bernstein, and Sylvia Allegretto, *The State of Working America, 2004/2005* (Ithaca, NY: IRL Press, 2005), 67.

6. See figure 5.2 in chapter 5 for the sources of these data.

7. For an orthodox Marxian view, see Charles H. Anderson, *The Political Economy of Social Class* (Englewood Cliffs, NJ: Prentice Hall, 1974). For an extensive neo-Marxian analysis of class, see Erik O. Wright, *Classes* (London: Verso, 1985), and *Interrogating Inequality* (London: Verso, 1994). Wright's early analysis emphasizes ownership and control of the means of production and control of labor as the defining conditions for determining class location; his more recent work adds control of organizational assets and ownership of skill assets.

8. Weber also posited a third order of inequality—namely, parties. Parties exist in the legal order and they are groups like political parties or trade associations that attempt to influence actions that affect a community, like property taxes or whether and where to build a new school. See Hans H. Gerth and C. Wright Mills, *From Max Weber: Essays in Sociology* (New York: Oxford University Press, 1946).

9. Thomas Abel and William C. Cockerham, "Lifestyle or *lebensführung*? Critical Remarks on the Mistranslation of Weber's 'Class, Status, Party,'" *Sociological Quarterly* 54 (1993):

551–56; Martin N. Marger, *Social Inequality: Patterns and Processes*, 5th ed. (New York: McGraw-Hill, 2011), 54.

10. For a good example of the functionalist multidimensional model of class, see Dennis Gilbert and Joseph A. Kahl, *The American Class Structure* (Chicago: Dorsey Press, 1987). For an approach that emphasizes the status or prestige of occupations, see Peter M. Blau and Otis D. Duncan, *The American Occupational Structure* (New York: Wiley, 1967).

11. Robert Perrucci and Carolyn Cummings Perrucci, eds., *The Transformation of Work in the New Economy* (New York: Oxford University Press, 2007).

CHAPTER 2: THE NEW AMERICAN CLASS STRUCTURE

1. U.S. Census Bureau, *Statistical Abstract of the United States: 1995* (Washington, DC: U.S. Government Printing Office, 1995), 814.

2. Lawrence Mishel, Jared Bernstein, and Sylvia Allegretto, *The State of Working America, 2004/2005* (Ithaca, NY: Cornell University Press, 2005), 96.

3. Barry Bluestone and Bennett Harrison, *The Deindustrialization of America: Plant Closings, Community Abandonment, and the Dismantling of Basic Industry* (New York: Basic Books, 1982); James Crotty, "The Austerians Attack," *In These Times* (February 2012): 17.

4. Thomas Byrne Edsall, *The New Politics of Inequality* (New York: W.W. Norton, 1984), 120–29, 151–78, 216–19, 228–42; Robert Perrucci, *Japanese Auto Transplants in the Heartland* (New York: Aldine de Gruyter, 1994), 23.

5. Robert Perrucci and Carolyn C. Perrucci, *America at Risk: The Crisis of Hope, Trust, and Caring* (Lanham, MD: Rowman & Littlefield, 2009), 18.

6. U.S. Census Bureau, *Statistical Abstract of the United States: 2012* (Washington, DC: U.S. Government Printing Office, 2011), 808–11.

7. Kathleen Short, "The Research Supplemental Poverty Measure: 2010," *Current Population Reports*, U.S. Census Bureau (November 2011), 6.

8. Family income data for 1969, 1979, 1989, and 2000 are from Mishel, Bernstein, and Allegretto, *The State of Working America, 2004/2005*, 88.

9. U.S. Census Bureau, *Statistical Abstract of the United States: 2012*, 619.

10. Lawrence Mishel, Josh Bivens, Elise Gould, and Heidi Shierholz, *The State of Working America*, 12th ed. (Ithaca, NY: IRL Press, 2012), 395.

11. U.S. Census Bureau, *Statistical Abstract of the United States: 2012*, 360–61.

12. Melvin Oliver, Thomas M. Shapiro, and Julie E. Press, "'Them That's Got Shall Get': Inheritance and Achievement in Wealth Accumulation," in *Research in Politics and Society*, vol. 15, ed. Richard E. Ratliffe, Melvin Oliver, and Thomas M. Shapiro (Greenwich, CT: JAI Press, 1995).

13. Lauren A. Rivera, "Ivies, Extracurriculars, and Exclusion: Elite Employers' Use of Educational Credentials," *Research in Stratification and Mobility* 29 (2011): 71–90.

14. Clifford J. Levy, "New York Attorney General Remakes Staff by Patronage," *New York Times*, November 10, 1995; Robert Granfield and Thomas Koenig, "Pathways into Elite Law Firms: Professional Stratification and Social Networks," in *Research in Politics and Society*, vol. 4, *The Political Consequences of Social Networks*, ed. Gwen Moore and J. Allen Whitt (Greenwich, CT: JAI Press, 1992).

15. Harold R. Kerbo, *Social Stratification and Inequality*, 8th ed. (New York: McGraw-Hill, 2012), 376.

16. Pew Research Center, "Inside the Middle Class: Bad Times Hit the Good Life," A Social & Demographic Trends Report (April 9, 2008), 36–53, on the Internet at http://www.pewresearch.org (accessed February 24, 2012); Pew Research Center, "The Lost Decade of the Middle Class" (August 22, 2012), 20–39, on the Internet at http://www.pewresearch.org (accessed October 15, 2012); U.S. Department of Commerce, Economics and Statistics Administration, "Middle Class in America," prepared for the Office of the Vice President of the United States Middle Class Task Force (January 2010), 25–26.

17. Gregory Acs, "Downward Mobility from the Middle Class: Waking Up from the American Dream" (Philadelphia, PA: The Pew Charitable Trusts, September 2011).

18. See Alan Neustadtl and Dan Clawson, "Corporate Political Groupings: Does Ideology Unify Business Political Behavior?" *American Sociological Review* 53 (1988): 172–90; Robert Perrucci and Marc Pilisuk, "Leaders and Ruling Elites: The Interorganizational Bases of Community Power," *American Sociological Review* 35 (December 1970): 1040–57; Robert Perrucci and Bonnie L. Lewis, "Interorganizational Relations and Community Influence Structure," *Sociological Quarterly* 30 (1989): 205–23; David Knoke, *Organized for Action: Commitment in Voluntary Associations* (New Brunswick: Rutgers University Press, 1981).

19. Sam Pizzigati, "The Hedges Get a Trim," *Too Much* (April 14, 2012): 3.

20. "Physician Compensation Report 2012," *Medscape* (February 2012), 2, 4, on the Internet at http://www.medscape.com (accessed June 4, 2012).

21. "2011–2012 Physician Salary Survey," *Profiles* (September 2011), 1–2, on the Internet at http://www.profilesdatabase.com (accessed June 4, 2012).

22. Nathan Koppel and Vanessa O'Connell, "Pay Gap Widens at Big Law Firms as Partners Chase Star Attorneys," *Wall Street Journal*, February 8, 2011, on the Internet at http://online.wsj.com (accessed October 10, 2012).

23. National Association for Law Placement, "Median Private Practice Starting Salaries for the Class of 2011 Plunge as Private Practice Jobs Continue to Erode," press release (July 12, 2012), on the Internet at http://www.nalp.org (accessed October 10, 2012).

24. John Ciaran, "The Average Median Salary for a Law Firm Lawyer," *Houston Chronicle*, August 7, 2012, on the Internet at http://www.chron.com (accessed October 10, 2012).

25. David Herzenhorn, "The Story behind the Generous Gift to Harvard Law School," *New York Times*, April 7, 1995.

26. Tamar Lewin, "23 Private College Presidents Made More Than $1 Million," *New York Times*, November 2, 2009; Graham Bowley, "At Brown, Spotlight on President's Role at a Bank," *New York Times*, March 1, 2010.

27. Mishel, Bivens, Gould, and Shierholz, *The State of Working America*, 12th ed., 280.

28. U.S. Census Bureau, *Statistical Abstract of the United States: 2012*, 367.

29. Barbara Reskin and Irene Padavic, *Women and Men at Work* (Thousand Oaks, CA: Pine Forge Press, 1994), ch. 4; Donald Tomaskovic-Devey, *Gender and Racial Inequality at Work* (Ithaca, NY: ILR Press, 1993), ch. 4.

30. Reskin and Padavic, *Women and Men at Work*, ch. 4.

31. U.S. Bureau of Labor Statistics, "Ratio of Women's to Men's Earnings by Occupation" (2010), on the Internet at http://www.bls.gov (accessed June 15, 2012).

32. U.S. Bureau of Labor Statistics, "Ratio of Women's to Men's Earnings by Occupation"; U.S. Bureau of Labor Statistics, "Employed Persons Detailed by Occupation, Sex, Race, and Hispanic or Latino Ethnicity" (2010), on the Internet at http://www.bls.gov (accessed June 15, 2012); Reskin and Padavic, *Women and Men at Work*, 140.

33. U.S. Bureau of Labor Statistics, "Employed Persons Detailed by Occupation, Sex, Race, and Hispanic or Latino Ethnicity"; U.S. Bureau of Labor Statistics, "Ratio of Women's to Men's Earnings by Occupation"; "Women CEOs in the Fortune 1000," *Catalyst* (2011), on the Internet at http://www.catalyst.org (accessed May 5, 2012).

34. Joan Williams, *Unbending Gender* (New York: Oxford University Press, 2000), 69–72.

35. Sharon M. Collins, "The Marginalization of Black Executives," *Social Problems* 36 (October 1989): 317–31.

36. Bluestone and Harrison, *The Deindustrialization of America*, 17.

CHAPTER 3: THE NEW ECONOMY
AND THE NEW CLASS STRUCTURE

1. "Americans' Economic Pessimism Reaches Record High," *New York Times*, November 26, 2007; David Leonhardt and Majorie Connelly, "81% in Poll Say Nation is Headed on Wrong Track," *New York Times*, April 4, 2008.

2. Jeffrey M. Jones, "Confidence in U.S. Public Schools at New Low, Confidence Also at New Lows for Organized Religion, Banks, and TV News," Gallup, Inc. (June 20, 2012), on the Internet at http://www.gallup.com (accessed October 4, 2012).

3. Richard Henderson, "Industry Employment and Output Projections to 2020," *Monthly Labor Review* (January 2012): 66.

4. U.S. Department of Labor, Bureau of Labor Statistics, Databases, Tables & Calculators by Subject, "Industry: Manufacturing," November 11, 2012, on the Internet at http://data.bls.gov/timeseries (accessed November 11, 2012).

5. U.S. Department of Labor, Bureau of Labor Statistics, Databases, Tables & Calculators by Subject, "Industry: Manufacturing."

6. Jane Slaughter, "Auto Companies Recover, but Jobs Are Harder," *Labor Notes* (September 2011): 10.

7. Robert Perrucci, *Japanese Auto Transplants in the Heartland: Corporatism and Community* (Hawthorne, NY: Aldine de Gruyter, 1994).

8. Lawrence Mishel, Josh Bivens, Elise Gould, and Heidi Shierholz, *The State of Working America*, 12th ed. (Ithaca, NY: IRL Press, 2012), 338.

9. Ibid., 350–51.

10. Pew Research Center, "How the Great Recession Has Changed Life in America," press release (June 30, 2010), on the Internet at http://www.pewsocialtrends.org (accessed July 1, 2012).

11. For Hayek, *liberal* was a term he applied to followers of classic free market economics. In the contemporary period, what Hayek labeled as *liberal* economic thought morphed into what is now known as *neoliberalism*. Ironically, Hayek's definition of "liberal" economics is essentially the reverse of what the term later came to mean in the United States. Since the New Deal, "liberal" economic policies have involved government intervention in the economy (often based on the ideas of English economist John Maynard Keynes). For a summary of Hayek's ideas, see Christian Parenti, "Winning the War of Ideas," *In These Times* (November 17, 2003): 18–21. See also Friedrich Hayek, *Economic Freedom* (Cambridge, MA: Blackwell, 1991); Friedrich Hayek, *The Road to Serfdom* (Chicago: University of Chicago Press, 1994).

12. William K. Tabb, "After Neoliberalism?" *Monthly Review* (June 2003): 25–33.

13. Parenti, "Winning the War of Ideas."

14. Severyn Bruyn, *The Social Economy: People Transforming Modern Business* (New York: Wiley, 1977).

15. John Bellamy Foster, "Education and the Structural Crisis of Capital," *Monthly Review* (July–August 2011): 19.

16. Ibid., 7.

17. See Peter Hart, "First, Bash the Teachers," *Extra!* (September 2010): 6–7; Pauline Lipman, "Neoliberal Education Restructuring," *Monthly Review* (July–August 2011): 114–27.

18. John Foster Bellamy, "The Financialization of Accumulation," *Monthly Review* (October 2010): 2.

19. The 1960–2009 data are from John Foster Bellamy and Hannah Holleman, "The Financial Power Elite," *Monthly Review* (May 2010): 5; John Foster Bellamy, "The Financialization of Capital and the Crisis," *Monthly Review* (April 2008): 3. The 2011 data are from U.S. Department of Commerce, Bureau of Economic Analysis, "Gross Domestic Product: Fourth Quarter and Annual 2011 (Third Estimate), Corporate Profits: Fourth Quarter and Annual 2011," table 12, press release (March 29, 2012).

20. Data sources include U.S. Census Bureau, *Statistical Abstract of the United States: 1995* (Washington, DC: U.S. Government Printing Office, 1995), 564; U.S. Census Bureau, *Statistical Abstract of the United States: 2012* (Washington, DC: U.S. Government Printing Office, 2011), 518; U.S. Department of Commerce, Bureau of Economic Analysis, "Gross Domestic Product: Fourth Quarter and Annual 2011 (Third Estimate), Corporate Profits: Fourth Quarter and Annual 2011."

21. Shannon Moriarty, ed., *Born on Third Base: What the Forbes 400 Really Says about Economic Equality and Opportunity in America* (Boston: United for a Fair Economy, 2012), 15.

22. Ken-Hou Lin and Donald Tomaskovic-Devey, "Financialization and U.S. Income Inequality, 1970–2008," *Social Science Research Network* (November 4, 2011).

23. William D. Cohan, "How We Got the Crash Wrong," *Atlantic* (June 2012), on the Internet at http://www.theatlantic.com (accessed October 15, 2012).

24. Bellamy and Holleman, "The Financial Power Elite," 13.

25. Cohan, "How We Got the Crash Wrong"; Bethany McLean, "The Meltdown Explanation that Melts Away," Reuters (March 19, 2012), on the Internet at http://blogs.reuters.com (accessed October 15, 2012).

26. Robert Scheer, *The Great American Stickup* (New York: Nation Books, 2009), 93–101, 198–99, 211–13.

27. John V. Walsh, "The Myth of U.S. Manufacturing Decline," *CounterPunch* (October 15, 2012), on the Internet at http://www.counterpunch.org (accessed October 20. 2012). This author documents the sharp increase in productivity in the U.S. manufacturing sector during 1947–2011.

28. Evan Rohar, "Longshore Workers Block Trains, Shut Ports to Protect Good Jobs," *Labor Notes* (October 2011): 1, 14–15.

29. "Foxconn Technology," *New York Times*, December 27, 2012, on the Internet at http://topics/nytimes.com (accessed January 2, 2013).

30. Roger Bybee, "NAFTA's Hung Jury," *Extra!* (May–June 2004): 14–15; Travis McArthur, "The Numbers Are In: Trade Deals Fail to Deliver," *Labor Notes* (November 2010): 11; Robert E. Scott, "NAFTA's Hidden Costs," Washington, DC: Economic Policy Institute (May 21, 2001).

31. John Sargent and Linda Matthews, "China versus Mexico in the Global EPZ Industry: Maquiladoras, FDI Quality, and Plant Mortality," *World Development* 37 (2009): 1069–82.

32. John Miller, "No Fooling—Corporations Evade Taxes," *Dollars and Sense* (May–June 2011): 11–12; Shahien Nasiripour, "Immelt, GE CEO, to Run New Jobs-Focused Panel as GE Sends Jobs Overseas, Pays Little in Taxes," *Huffington Post* (January 21, 2011), on the Internet at http://www.huffingtonpost.com (accessed October 12, 2012).

33. Robert Perrucci, "Too Big to Fail: A Network Perspective," *International Journal of Contemporary Sociology* 48 (2011): 251–78; Gretchen Morgenson and Joshua Rosner, *Reckless Endangerment* (New York: Henry Holt, 2011).

34. William Carroll and Jean Philippe Sapinski, "The Global Elite and the Transnational Policy-Planning Network," *International Sociology* 25 (2009): 501–38; David Rothkopf, *Superclass: The Global Power Elite and the World They Are Making* (New York: Farrar, Straus, and Giroux, 2008).

35. Jeffrey Kentor and Yong Suk Jang, "Yes, There Is a (Growing) Transnational Business Community: A Study of Global Interlocking Directorates 1983–1998," *International Sociology* 19 (September 2004): 355–68.

36. Leslie Sklar, *The Transnational Capitalist Class* (Oxford: Blackwell, 2001).

37. P. B. Doeringer and Michael J. Piore, *Internal Labor Markets and Manpower Analysis* (Lexington, MA: Heath, 1971); K. Hudson, "The New Labor Market Segmentation: Labor Market Dualism in the New Economy," *Social Science Research* 27 (2007): 286–312; Earl Wysong and David W. Wright, "Family Friendly Workplace Benefits: Policy Mirage, Organizational Contexts, and Worker Power," *Critical Sociology* 24 (1998): 244–76.

38. Bruce Western and Jake Rosenfeld, "Unions, Norms, and the Rise in U.S. Wage Inequality," *American Sociological Review* 76 (2011): 513–37.

39. Earl Wysong and David W. Wright, "Family Friendly Workplace Benefits: The U.S., Canada, and Europe," *Critical Sociology* 29 (2003): 337–67.

40. Audrey Williams June, "Adjuncts Build Strength in Numbers," *Chronicle of Higher Education* (November 5, 2012), on the Internet at http://www.chronicle.com (accessed December 15, 2012).

41. Western and Rosenfeld, "Unions, Norms, and the Rise in U.S. Wage Inequality," 514.

42. Thomas Byrne Edsall, *The New Politics of Inequality* (New York: W.W. Norton, 1984), 151–78; Alejandro Ruess, "What's Behind Union Decline in the United States?" *Dollars and Sense* (May–June 2011): 25–26.

43. U.S. Department of Labor, Bureau of Labor Statistics, "Union Members—2012," news release (January 23, 2013), 1; Lawrence Mishel, Jared Bernstein, and Sylvia Allegretto, *The State of Working America, 2006/2007* (Ithaca, NY: IRL Press, 2007), 180.

44. Arne L. Kalleberg, "Non-standard Employment Relations: Part-Time, Temporary, Contract Work," *Annual Review of Sociology* 26 (2000): 341–65; Arne L. Kalleberg, *Good Jobs, Bad Jobs: The Rise of Polarized and Precarious Employment* (New York: Russell Sage Press, 2011); Lawrence Mishel, Jared Bernstein, and Heidi Shierholz, *The State of Working America: 2008–2009* (Ithaca, NY: IRL Press, 2009), 252–56.

45. Randy Hodson and Teresa A. Sullivan, *The Social Organization of Work*, 4th ed. (Belmont, CA: Thomson Wadsworth, 2008), 336–39.

46. Mishel, Bernstein, and Shierholz, *The State of Working America: 2008–2009*, 253.

47. Pew Research Center, "How the Great Recession Has Changed Life in America."

48. Ann Monroe, "Getting Rid of the Grey," *Mother Jones* (July–August 1996): 29.

49. John Bellamy Foster and Fred Magdoff, *The Great Financial Crisis* (New York: Monthly Review Press, 2009); Paul Krugman, *The Return of Depression Economics and the Crisis of 2008* (New York: W.W. Norton, 2009); Henry Paulson Jr., *On the Brink: Inside the Race to Stop the Collapse of the Global Financial System* (New York: Hachette, 2010); Richard Posner, *The Failure of Capitalism: The Crisis of '08 and the Descent into Depression* (Cambridge, MA: Harvard University Press, 2009); Robert B. Reich, *Aftershock: The Next Economy and America's Future* (New York: Alfred Knopf, 2010); Nouriel Roubini and Stephen Mihm, *Crisis Economics: A Crash Course in the Future of Finance* (New York: Penguin, 2010).

50. Tyler Cowen, *The Great Stagnation* (New York: Dutton, 2011); John Bellamy Foster and Robert W. McChesney, *The Endless Crisis: How Monopoly-Finance Capital Produces Stagnation and Upheaval from the United States to China* (New York: Monthly Review Press, 2012); Thomas I. Palley, *From Financial Crisis to Stagnation* (Cambridge, MA: Cambridge University Press, 2012).

51. Quoted in Scheer, *The Great American Stickup*, 20.

52. John Bellamy Foster and Robert W. McChesney, "The Endless Crisis," *Monthly Review* (May 2012): 19.

53. Rex Nutting, "Corporate Profits' Share of Pie Most in 60 Years," *MarketWatch* (July 29, 2011), on the Internet at http://www.marketwatch.com (accessed August 14, 2011); Foster and McChesney, "The Endless Crisis," 19–20.

54. Mishel, Bivens, Gould, and Shierholz, *The State of Working America*, 12th ed., 333–34.

55. Ibid., 325.

56. Ralph Nader, "Not Made in America," *Common Dreams* (November 30, 2011), on the Internet at http://www.commondreams.org (accessed December 1, 2011).

CHAPTER 4: THE GLOBAL
ECONOMY AND CLASS INEQUALITIES

1. Carolyn C. Perrucci, Robert Perrucci, Dena B. Targ, and Harry R. Targ, *Plant Closings: International Context and Social Costs* (New York: Aldine de Gruyter, 1988).

2. Office of Technology Assessment, "Technology and Structural Unemployment" (Washington, DC: Congress of the United States, 1986); Thomas S. Moore, *The Disposable Work Force* (New York: Aldine de Gruyter, 1996).

3. Charles Koeber and David W. Wright, "W/Age Bias in Worker Displacement: How Industrial Structure Shapes the Job Loss and Earnings Decline of Older American Workers," *Journal of Socio-Economics* 30 (2001): 343–52; National Employment Law Project, "The Low Wage Recovery and Growing Inequality," data brief (August 2012), on the Internet at http://www.nelp.org (accessed October 5, 2012); John Schmitt and Janelle Jones, "Where Have All the Good Jobs Gone," Center for Economic and Policy Research (July 2012), on the Internet at http://www.cepr.net (accessed October 5, 2012).

4. Daniel Chirot, *Social Change in the Twentieth Century* (New York: Harcourt Brace Jovanovich, 1974); Immanual Wallerstein, *The Modern World System* (New York: Academic Press, 1974); Immanual Wallerstein, *The End of the World as We Know It: Social Science for the Twenty-First Century* (Minneapolis: University of Minnesota Press, 1999).

5. For an extended discussion, see Michael Stohl and Harry R. Targ, *Global Political Economy in the 1980s* (Cambridge, MA: Schenkman, 1982).

6. Lawrence Mishel, Jared Bernstein, and Sylvia Allegretto, *The State of Working America, 2004/2005* (Ithaca, NY: IRL Press, 2005), 96; see also Robert J. Samuelson, "Great Expectations," *Newsweek* (January 8, 1996): 31.

7. Thomas Byrne Edsall, *The New Politics of Inequality* (New York: W.W. Norton, 1984), 132, 151–78, 216–19, 228–42.

8. Robert B. Reich, *Next American Frontier* (New York: Times Books, 1983).

9. Quoted in Joel Bleifuss, "The Terminators," *In These Times* (March 4, 1996): 12–13.

10. Alan Downs, *Corporate Executions* (New York: AMACOM, 1995).

11. Bob Herbert, "The Worst of the Pain," *New York Times*, February 8, 2010.

12. Steve Lohr, "Offshore Jobs in Technology: Opportunity or a Threat ?" *New York Times*, December 22, 2003; Steve Lohr, "Debate Over Exporting Jobs Raises Questions on Policies," *New York Times*, February 23, 2004; Alan Reynolds, "Offshoring Which Jobs?" *Washington Times*, June 6, 2004.

13. Sheryl Wu Dunn, "When Lifetime Jobs Die Prematurely: Downsizing Comes to Japan, Fraying Old Workplace Ties," *New York Times*, June 12, 1996.

14. John Miller and Ramon Castellblanch, "Does Manufacturing Matter?" *Dollars and Sense* (October 1988).

15. Noam Chomsky, *The Common Good* (Monroe, ME: Odonian Press, 1998).

16. U.S. Census Bureau, *Statistical Abstract of the United States: 2012* (Washington, DC: U.S. Government Printing Office, 2011), 793; U.S. Department of Commerce, U.S. Census Bureau, Foreign Trade Division, Washington, DC (2005).

17. U.S. Census Bureau, *Statistical Abstract of the United States: 2012*, 808–11.

18. John Pomery, "Running Deficits with the Rest of the World—Part I," *Focus on Economic Issues*, Purdue University (Fall 1987) (emphasis added).

19. U.S. Census Bureau, *Statistical Abstract of the United States: 2012*, 808.

20. U.S. Department of Labor, Bureau of Labor Statistics, Databases, Tables & Calculators by Subject, "Industry: Manufacturing" (November 11, 2012), on the Internet at http://data.bls.gov/time series (accessed November 11, 2012).

21. U.S. Census Bureau, *Statistical Abstract of the United States: 1995* (Washington, DC: U.S. Government Printing Office, 1995), 411; U.S. Census Bureau, *Statistical Abstract of the United States: 2012*, 393.

22. Richard Henderson, "Industry Employment and Output Projections to 2020," *Monthly Labor Review* (January 2012): 66.

23. "Economic Focus," *The Economist* (September 2, 2006): 66.

24. "Largest U.S. Corporations," *Fortune* (May 21, 2012): F-1.

25. Christopher Helman, "What the Top U.S. Companies Pay in Taxes," *Forbes* (April 1, 2011), on the Internet at http://www.forbes.com (accessed October 5, 2012).

26. John Bellamy Foster, Robert W. McChesney, and R. Jamil Jonna, "The Internationalization of Monopoly Capital," *Monthly Review* (June 2011): 6.

27. Robert S. McIntyre, "Testimony on Corporate Welfare," U.S. House of Representatives Committee on the Budget (June 30, 1999), on the Internet at http://www.ctj.org (accessed June 25, 2001).

28. John Miller, "No Fooling—Corporations Evade Taxes," *Dollars and Sense* (May–June 2011): 11–12.

29. David Kocieniewski, "Biggest Public Firms Paid Little U.S. Tax, Study Says," *New York Times*, November 3, 2011, on the Internet at http://www.nytimes.com (accessed May 1, 2012).

30. Edmund L. Andrews, "Foreign-Profit Tax Break Is Outlined," *New York Times*, January 14, 2005, B2.

31. Kenneth Bradsher, "For Workers Sent Abroad, a Tax Jolt," *New York Times*, September 2, 2006, B1, B6.

CHAPTER 5: HOW THE MIDDLE CLASS DIED

1. Jon Meacham, "Keeping the Dream Alive," *Time* (July 2, 2012): 29; Pew Research Center, "Inside the Middle Class: Bad Times Hit the Good Life," A Social & Demographic Trends Report (April 9, 2008), 10, on the Internet at http://www.pewresearch.org (accessed February 24, 2012); U.S. Department of Commerce, Economics and Statistics Administration, "Middle Class in America," prepared for the Office of the Vice President of the United States Middle Class Task Force (January 2010), 1; Hope Yen, "Courting, Not Defining, Nation's Middle Class," *Indianapolis Star*, July 22, 2012, A7.

2. For examples, see Andrew G. Marshall, "Western Civilization and the Economic Crisis, the Impoverishment of the Middle Class" (March 30, 2010), on the Internet at http://www.marketoracle.co.uk/Article18282 (accessed January 6, 2012); Lawrence Mishel and Josh Bivens, "Occupy Wall Streeters Are Right About Skewed Economic Rewards in the United States," Briefing Paper #331, Economic Policy Institute, Washington, DC (October 26, 2011); Eric Michael Moberg, *Class War 2012* (London: Prescott University Press, 2011), 43–50; Jeffrey D. Sachs, "Why America Must Revive Its Middle Class," *Time* (October 21, 2011): 30–32. For a more complete review of this literature, see Earl Wysong and David W. Wright, "Shot through the Heart: Have Recent Inequality Trends Killed the Middle Class?" paper presented at the 2010 meetings of the Midwest Sociological Society, Chicago, Illinois.

3. Barack Obama, "Remarks by the President and Vice President in Announcement of Labor Executive Orders and Middle Class Working Families Task Force," White House Briefing Room (January 30, 2009), on the Internet at http://www.whitehouse.gov (accessed February 8, 2012).

4. Barack Obama, "Memorandum for the Heads of Executive Departments and Agencies." White House Press Office (January 30, 2009), on the Internet at http://www.whitehouse.gov (accessed February 8, 2012).

5. Joe Biden, *Annual Report of the White House Task Force on the Middle Class* (February 2010).

6. The U.S. Census Bureau reports that in 2010, the U.S. median household income ($49,445) was more than $3,000 below 2007 ($52,823) when the recession began (both amounts in 2010 dollars). The 2010 amount was the lowest since 1996. See Carmen DeNavas-Walt, Bernadette D. Proctor, and Jessica C. Smith, U.S. Census Bureau, Current Population Reports, P60-239, *Income, Poverty, and Health Insurance Coverage in the United States: 2010* (Washington, DC: U.S. Government Printing Office, 2011), 5, 34; Gregory Acs, "Downward Mobility from the Middle Class: Waking Up from the American Dream," Economic Mobility Project (Washington, DC: The Pew Charitable Trusts, September 2011).

7. Carl Dassbach, "The *Manifesto* and the Middle Class," *Critical Sociology* 27 (2001): 121–32; Martin N. Marger, *Social Inequality: Patterns and Processes*, 5th ed. (New York: McGraw-Hill, 2011), 119–35.

8. The term *social wage* refers to a minimum standard of material well-being guaranteed to citizens in advanced industrial societies. The U.S. social wage is based on federal and state

laws that guarantee a minimum wage, unemployment insurance, educational assistance, housing assistance, cash assistance to the poor, and old age pensions. Compared to most advanced industrial nations, the U.S. social wage is modest (low benefit levels) and incomplete (lacking universal health care). This situation is largely a reflection of the political weakness of the U.S. labor movement. U.S. industrial unions were unable to significantly expand the welfare state–social wage put in place by President Roosevelt's 1930s New Deal. In the post-WWII period, however, they were able to win for their members higher real wages and expanded workplace benefits such as job security under seniority systems, health insurance, and pension plans. As a result, unions created a kind of "private welfare state" based in major U.S. industrial firms. See Marie Gottschalk, *The Shadow Welfare State* (Ithaca, NY: IRL/Cornell University Press, 2000).

9. Bruce Western and Jake Rosenfeld, "Unions, Norms, and the Rise in U.S. Wage Inequality," *American Sociological Review* 76 (2011): 513–37.

10. As chapters 3 and 4 suggest, the new economy must be viewed as the *product* of corporate and government policy decisions and actions organized around and in support of the economic, political, and cultural interests of the superclass—the wealthiest and most powerful segment of the privileged class. It's true that various forms of advanced technology *facilitated* the emergence and continued development of the new economy, *but high-technology alone did not create it*, just as the new economy did not, on its own, create the new class system. Drawing on this perspective, we view the inequality trends identified and explored in this chapter *not as causes* of class inequalities, but rather as measurable *outcomes* or consequences of conflicting class interests and class war. In chapters 6–9 we explore how and why the conditions of *conflicting class interests* and *class war* have been central to creating and perpetuating the new economy and the new class system.

11. U.S. Department of Commerce, "Middle Class in America," 2.

12. See, for example, Brian Cashell, "Who Are the Middle Class?" Congressional Research Service Report for Congress (October 22, 2008); Pew Research Center, "Inside the Middle Class: Bad Times Hit the Good Life," 8.

13. For details on these approaches, see Wysong and Wright, "Shot through the Heart: Have Recent Inequality Trends Killed the Middle Class?" 3–11, 19–23; also see Marger, *Social Inequality*, 5th ed., 117–23.

14. We recognize that "non-workers" (i.e., people *not in the labor force* such as retirees, the disabled, the discouraged unemployed, those living on inherited wealth) may also be classified as "middle class" (or higher or lower), but such individuals are not our primary focus here.

15. U.S. Department of Commerce, "Middle Class in America," 4.

16. The income range indicative of middle-class membership for *individual workers* is based partly on information in the U.S. Commerce Report cited in note 1 and partly on findings from the Pew Research Center survey cited in note 1. In the latter source, a majority of respondents who identified themselves as members of the middle class had annual *family incomes* between $30,000–$100,000.

17. The three features that comprise the resource component of our operational definition for middle-class *workers* (secure job tenure, employer-provided health insurance benefits, defined-benefit pension plans) were included because they formed the core of the "private welfare state" (or "shadow welfare state") achieved in the post-WWII period by many unionized workers in major U.S. industrial firms. See Gottschalk, *The Shadow Welfare State*.

18. See, for example, Marger, *Social Inequality*, 5th ed., 117–19.

19. The term *real earnings* means the purchasing power of income earned in the past is expressed in current (2011), inflation-adjusted dollars. The transformation of income amounts

earned in the past allows us to see what workers' earnings in past years would be in today's dollars after adjusting those earnings for inflation over the years. To calculate inflation-adjusted incomes, we use a version of the Consumer Price Index (CPI) developed by the U.S. Bureau of Labor Statistics and multiply earnings from previous years by a CPI formula. (We also use some other statistical procedures to ensure greater accuracy.) The basic idea is simple. For example, in figure 5.1 we report the average "real" hourly wage in 1973 as $20.97 in 2011 dollars. If, for example, the CPI was 3.6 times higher in 2011 than in 1973, the 1973 average hourly wage in 1973 dollars would have been approximately $5.68. Conversely, 3.6 times $5.68 equals $20.45, which is very close to the inflation-adjusted value we report of $20.97.

20. In 2011, half of the workers in Q2 had annual earnings *above* the Q2 median ($30,000) and half of the workers in Q5 had annual earnings *below* the Q5 median ($102,400), placing both sub-groups within our middle-class definition. Since the two sub-groups each account for 10 percent of the workers in figure 5.3 and table 5.1, together, they make up 20 percent of all workers studied. Adding this 20 percent to the Q3 and Q4 groups, we find 60 percent of all full-time, full-year workers had 2011 earnings that placed them in our middle-class-by-income range. While the Q3 and Q5 subgroups each account for 10 percent of all workers included in figure 5.3 and table 5.1, they each constitute about 17 percent of the middle-class-by-income group that also includes all workers in the the Q3 and Q4 groups. (The upper half of the Q5 group, the lower half of the Q2 group, and the entire Q1 group had earnings that placed them outside the middle-class-by-income boundaries.) Table 5.1 also suggests the middle class was slightly larger in 1973 than 2011 because the 1973 median annual earnings in Q5 ($91,191) were below the $100,000 upper limit of our middle-class income range. Thus, *more* than one-half of the workers in Q5 would have been included in the middle class by our definition in 1973.

21. Sam Pizzigati, "Treadmill Time, Except at the Top," *Too Much* (January 31, 2011): 3; Sam Pizzigati, "At the Top, Pulling Away," *Too Much* (June 13, 2011): 3.

22. Lawrence Mishel, Jared Bernstein, and Heidi Shierholz, *The State of Working America: 2008–2009* (Ithaca, NY: IRL Press, 2009), 256–57.

23. U.S. Bureau of Labor Statistics, "Employee Tenure," news release (September 14, 2010), 1.

24. U.S. Bureau of Labor Statistics, "Employee Tenure," table 2.

25. Mishel, Bernstein, and Shierholz, *The State of Working America: 2008–2009*, 259.

26. U.S. Bureau of Labor Statistics, "Employee Tenure," table 2.

27. Mishel, Bernstein, and Shierholz, *The State of Working America: 2008–2009*, 259.

28. Peter Brady and Michael Bogdan, "A Look at Private-Sector Retirement Plan Income After ERISA," *Research Perspective* 16 (November 2010), 21, published by Investment Company Institute, Washington, DC.

29. U.S. Census Bureau, *Statistical Abstract of the United States: 2012* (Washington, DC: U.S. Government Printing Office, 2011), 112; Mishel, Bernstein, and Shierholz, *The State of Working America: 2008–2009*, 149.

30. Elise Gould, "A Decade of Declines in Employer-Sponsored Health Insurance Coverage," Briefing Paper #337, Economic Policy Institute, Washington, DC (January 23, 2012), 5.

31. Average monthly premiums were derived from several sources: Bridger M. Mitchell and Charles E. Phelps, "National Health Insurance: Some Costs and Effects of Mandated Employee Coverage," *Journal of Political Economy* 84 (1976): 553–71; Larry Levitt, Janet Lundy, and Catherine Hoffman, *Employer Health Benefits: 1999 Annual Survey* (Chicago: The

Kaiser Family Foundation and Health Research and Educational Trust, 1999); Gary Claxton, Matthew Rae, Nirmita Panchal, Janet Lundy, and Anthony Damico, *Employer Health Benefits: 2011 Annual Survey*, Section 6 (Chicago: The Kaiser Family Foundation and Health Research and Educational Trust, 2011); U.S. Census Bureau, *Statistical Abstract of the U.S.: 2012*, 112; Martha Remy Yohalem, "Employer Benefit Plans, 1975," *Social Security Bulletin* (November 1977): 19–28.

32. U.S. Census Bureau, *Statistical Abstract of the U.S.: 2012*, 112.

33. Drew Altman, "Rising Health Costs Are Not Just a Federal Budget Problem," *Pulling It Together*, The Kaiser Family Foundation and Health Research and Educational Trust (September 27, 2011), on the Internet at http://www.kff.org/pullingittogether/rising_health_costs (accessed March 17, 2012).

34. Claxton, et al., *Employer Health Benefits: 2011 Annual Survey*, section 6, 69.

35. John E. Buckley and Robert W. Van Giezen, "Federal Statistics on Healthcare Benefits and Cost Trends: An Overview," *Monthly Labor Review* (November 2004): 43–45; U.S. Census Bureau, *Statistical Abstract of the U.S.: 2012*, 112.

36. Mishel, Bernstein, and Shierholz, *The State of Working America: 2008–2009*, 348; U.S. Census Bureau, *Statistical Abstract of the U.S.: 2012*, 448, 456.

37. Mike Stobbe, "1 in 5 are Struggling to Pay Medical Bills, Survey Finds," *Indianapolis Star*, March 18, 2012, A13.

38. Don Trementozzi and Steve Early, "Romney, Obama Health Care Reforms Offer No Relief for Unions," *Labor Notes* (July 2011): 10.

39. Lawrence Mishel, Josh Bivens, Elise Gould, and Heidi Shierholz, *The State of Working America*, 12th ed. (Ithaca, NY: IRL Press, 2012), 201.

40. Mishel, Bernstein, and Shierholz, *The State of Working America: 2008–2009*, 150.

41. Biden, *Annual Report of the White House Task Force on the Middle Class*, 25–26.

42. Mishel, Bernstein, and Shierholz, *The State of Working America: 2008–2009*, 151.

43. Workers are also encouraged to save for retirement via "Individual Retirement Accounts" (IRAs). IRA "investment profits" are not taxed until retirement, but IRAs are funded by workers, not employers.

44. James H. Moore Jr., "Projected Pension Income: Equity or Disparity for the Baby Boom Cohort?" *Monthly Labor Review* (March 2006): 58–67.

45. "Current Labor Statistics, Tables 34 and 35," *Monthly Labor Review* (July 2005): 126–27.

46. U.S. Census Bureau, *Statistical Abstract of the U.S.: 2012*, 359.

47. U.S. Census Bureau, *Statistical Abstract of the U.S.: 2012*, 358; "Current Labor Statistics, Tables 34 and 35," *Monthly Labor Review* (January 2012): 161–65.

48. Mishel, Bernstein, and Shierholz, *The State of Working America: 2008–2009*, 151.

49. Ibid., 282.

50. Ibid., 283.

51. Ibid.

52. This trend has been exacerbated by low returns on retirement investments that are now less than half of the 7 percent researchers assumed prior to the 2008 financial crisis to estimate the percentage of workers with expected retirement income less than one-half of current income. See Mishel, Bernstein, and Shierholz, *The State of Working America: 2008–2009*, 283.

53. Brady and Bogdan, "A Look at Private-Sector Retirement Plan Income After ERISA," 29.

54. Ibid., 27.

55. James Ridgeway, "Who Shredded Our Safety Net?" *Mother Jones* (May–June 2009): 31.

56. Joan M. Weiss, "Pension Benefit Guaranty Corporation: 2011 Actuarial Report" (December 20, 2011), 22.

57. Josh Gotbaum, "2011 Pension Benefit Guaranty Corporation Annual Report" (November 14, 2011), 6, on the Internet at http://www.pbgc.gov/res/reportsar2011.html (accessed March 18, 2012).

58. Jennifer Wheary, Thomas M. Shapiro, and Tamara Draut, "By a Thread: The New Experience of America's Middle Class," Dēmos: A Network for Ideas & Action, New York, and the Institute on Assets and Social Policy, Brandeis University, Waltham, MA (November 28, 2007), 7.

59. John Schmitt and Janelle Jones, "Where Have All the Good Jobs Gone," Center for Economic and Policy Research (July 2012), 2, on the Internet at http://www.cepr.net (accessed October 5, 2012).

60. Cited in Jeanette Wicks-Lim, "Creating Decent Jobs," *Dollars and Sense* (January–February 2010): 8.

61. Mark Brenner, "The Real Deficit Problem—Good Jobs," *Labor Notes* (July 2011): 14.

62. Nir Jaimovich and Henry E. Siu, "The Trend is the Cycle: Job Polarization and Jobless Recoveries," unpublished paper, Duke University, March 31, 2012.

63. C. Brett Lockard and Michael Wolf, "Occupational Employment Projections to 2020," *Monthly Labor Review* (January 2012): 106. Also see Arne Kalleberg, *Good Jobs, Bad Jobs: The Rise of Polarized and Precarious Employment* (New York: Russell Sage Press, 2011).

64. Lockard and Wolf, "Occupational Employment Projections to 2020," 101.

65. Robert A. Rothman, *Inequality and Stratification: Race, Class, and Gender*, 5th ed. (Upper Saddle River, NJ: Pearson/Prentice-Hall, 2005), 195.

66. Biden, *Annual Report of the White House Task Force on the Middle Class*, 35.

67. Pew Research Center, "Inside the Middle Class: Bad Times Hit the Good Life," 30, 40.

68. Lockard and Wolf, "Occupational Employment Projections to 2020," 101.

69. Ibid.

70. Ibid., 106.

71. U.S. Census Bureau, *Statistical Abstract of the U.S.: 2012*, 190.

72. Ibid., 191–92.

73. Manuel Valdes, Travis Loller, Christina Silva, and Sandra Chereb, "1 in 2 New Graduates are Jobless or Underemployed," Associated Press (April 22, 2012), on the Internet at http://www.cnbc.com (accessed May 12, 2012).

74. For a review of this literature, see Earl Wysong and David W. Wright, "Is Social Mobility a Social Problem? Recent Intergenerational Mobility Trends, the American Dream, and the Media," paper presented at the 2006 meetings of the North Central Sociological Association, Indianapolis, Indiana; see also Harold R. Kerbo, *Social Stratification and Inequality*, 8th ed. (New York: McGraw-Hill, 2012), 354.

75. Marger, *Social Inequality*, 38–43.

76. Large-scale intergenerational mobility studies in the 1970s and 1980s utilized only father-son comparisons. For a review of the mobility literature on women, see Earl Wysong and David W. Wright, "Socioeconomic Status and Gender: Recent Intergenerational Mobility Patterns in the U.S.," *Journal of the Indiana Academy of the Social Sciences* XIII (2009): 112–30.

77. We used fathers in our study because their SES ranks were, on average, much higher than those of mothers; father-child comparisons allowed us to explore the widest possible range of intergenerational mobility outcomes, up or down. Fathers were higher, on average,

than mothers in SES ranks largely because in 1979 males were far more advantaged educationally, economically, and occupationally than women. Also, in 1979 far fewer married mothers were employed full-time compared to the present.

78. Mishel, Bernstein, and Shierholz, *The State of Working America: 2008–2009*, 78.

79. Alan B. Kruger, "The Rise and Consequences of Inequality in the United States," speech at the Center for American Progress (January 12, 2012).

80. DeNavas-Walt, Proctor, and Smith, U.S. Census Bureau, Current Population Reports, P60-239, *Income, Povery, and Health Insurance Coverage in the United States: 2010*, 34.

81. Emmanuel Saez, "Striking It Richer: The Evolution of Top Incomes in the United States" (updated March 2012), on the Internet at http://www.elsa.berkeley.edu/-saez/ (accessed March 17, 2012).

82. Kathleen Short, "The Research—Supplemental Poverty Measure: 2010," U.S. Census Bureau, *Current Population Reports* (November 2011): 6, 10.

83. Hope Yen, "Millions Slip Out of Middle Class," *Indianapolis Star*, December 15, 2011, A1, 17.

84. David L. Featherman and Robert M. Hauser, *Opportunity and Change* (New York: Academic Press, 1978), 535.

85. Ibid., 91.

86. Ibid., 89.

87. Sam Pizzigati, "Long Live the Statistical Middle Class!" *Labor Studies Journal* 35 (September 2010): 386–97.

CHAPTER 6: CONFLICTING CLASS INTERESTS AND CLASS WAR

1. Jeffrey M. Jones, "Confidence in U.S. Public Schools at New Low, Confidence Also at New Lows for Organized Religion, Banks, and TV News," Gallup, Inc. (June 20, 2012), on the Internet at http://www.gallup.com (accessed August 1, 2012); Pew Research Center, "Rising Share of Americans See Conflict between Rich and Poor" (January 11, 2012), on the Internet at http://www.pewsocialtrends.org (accessed July 1, 2012); Pew Research Center, "Partisan Polarization Surges in Bush, Obama Years," *Trends in American Values: 1987–2012* (June 4, 2012), on the Internet at http://www.people-press.org (accessed July 1, 2012); Lydia Saad, "Americans Decry Power of Lobbyists, Corporations, Banks, Feds," Gallup, Inc. (April 11, 2011), on the Internet at http://www.gallup.com (accessed July 1, 2012).

2. Radley Glasser and Steve Rendall, "For Media, 'Class War' Has Wealthy Victims," *Extra!* (August 2009): 9–10; Matthew Rothschild, "Class Warfare Anyone?" *Progressive* (November 2011): 7–8.

3. When violence is used, it is most often carried out by superclass surrogates—such as the police—against those who resist superclass dominance *and* who are viewed as a serious threat to superclass interests *and* who cannot be controlled, co-opted, pacified, or defeated by more peaceful means. A recent case in point: violent police attacks on Occupy Wall Street movement protestors and the violent, coordinated police-led destruction of Occupy encampments in cities across the nation in 2011–2012. See Rick Wolff, "Turning toward Solutions," *Dollars and Sense* (January–February 2012): 7–8.

4. The "6 million" figure is a near-term future projection based on information reported in the U.S. Census Bureau, *Statistical Abstract of the United States: 2012* (Washington, DC:

U.S. Government Printing Office), 491; the "over $30 trillion" amount is based on information reported by the U.S. Department of the Treasury, Internal Revenue Service, *Statistics of Income, Corporation Tax Returns* (2011).

5. Shawn Tully, "The Year of Living Profitably," *Fortune* (May 21, 2012): 237, F-25.

6. The $1.94 trillion amount represents total U.S. corporate profits in 2011 as reported by the U.S. Department of Commerce, Bureau of Economic Analysis, "Gross Domestic Product: Fourth Quarter and Annual 2011 (Third Estimate); Corporate Profits: Fourth Quarter and Annual 2011," press release (March 29, 2012): table 12.

7. "Commerical Banks, [Top] 20 Companies," *Fortune* (May 21, 2012): F-34; U.S. Census Bureau, *Statistical Abstract of the United States: 2012*, 737.

8. John Bellamy Foster and Hannah Holleman, "The Financial Power Elite," *Monthly Review* (May 2010): 9.

9. Insurance company assets were computed based on data reported in *Fortune* magazine: "Fortune 500 Largest U.S. Corporations," "Healthcare: Insurance and Managed Care, [Top] 11 Companies," "Insurance: Life, Health (Mutual), [Top] 7 Companies," "Insurance: Life, Health (Stock), [Top]10 Companies," *Fortune* (May 21, 2012): F-1–F-26, F-36, F-37; U.S. Census Bureau, *Statistical Abstract of the United States: 2012*, 731, 754.

10. U.S. Census Bureau, *Statistical Abstract of the United States: 2012*, 519–20.

11. Luisa Kroll, "Forbes World's Billionaires 2012," *Forbes* (March 7, 2012): 27, on the Internet at http://www.forbes.com (accessed May 1, 2012).

12. The authors' estimate of 5,350 director positions is based on an average of 10.7 directors per S&P firm; an analysis of a sample of S&P directors found their average wealth holdings placed them in the top 1 percent of all Americans; see also Jeffrey Marshall and Ellen M. Heffes, "Recruiter's Study Finds Change, and Progress," *Financial Executive* (November 2005), 10.

13. G. William Domhoff, *Who Rules America?*, 6th ed. (Boston: McGraw-Hill, 2010), 31–35.

14. Lawrence Mishel, Josh Bivens, Elise Gould, and Heidi Shierholz, *The State of Working America*, 12th ed. (Ithaca, NY: IRL Press, 2012), 387.

15. Citizens for Tax Justice, "Who Pays Taxes in America?" (April 4, 2012), on the Internet at http://www.ctj.org (accessed May 5, 2012).

16. Emmanuel Saez, "Striking It Richer: The Evolution of Top Incomes in the United States" (updated March 2012), on the Internet at http://www.elsa.berkeley.edu/~saez/ (accessed May 5, 2012).

17. Sam Pizzigati, "The Hedges Get a Trim," *Too Much* (April 14, 2012): 3.

18. Citizens for Tax Justice, "Who Pays Taxes in America?"

19. Ibid.

20. Lawrence Mishel, Jared Bernstein, and Heidi Shierholz, *The State of Working America: 2008–2009* (Ithaca, NY: IRL Press, 2009), 82.

21. Matt Krantz and Barbara Hansen, "CEO Pay Rises Again in 2011, While Workers Struggle to Find Work," *USA Today*, March 29, 2012, on the Internet at http://www.usatoday .com (accessed May 5, 2012).

22. Donald L. Barlett and James B. Steele, *America: What Went Wrong?* (Kansas City, MO: Andrews and McMeel, 1992), xiii.

23. Ida A. Brudnick, "Salaries of Members of Congress: Recent Actions and Historical Tables," *Congressional Research Service* (February 22, 2012): 8.

24. "CFOs Earn 40% Less Than Average CEO Salary," *BenefitsPro* (September 1, 2011), on the Internet at http://www.benefitspro.com/2011/09/01 (accessed June 2, 2012).

25. "Chief Financial Officer (CFO) Salary," *PayScale* (May 26, 2012), on the Internet at http://www.payscale.com/research (accessed June 2, 2012).

26. "Forbes 400: The Richest People in America," *Forbes* (September 19, 2012), on the Internet at http://www.forbes.com/forbes-400/list/ (accessed October 1, 2012). The six Wal-Mart heirs include Christy, Jim, Alice, and S. Robson Walton, plus Ann Walton Kroenke and Nancy Walton Laurie.

27. Sam Pizzigati, "Tip for Joe the Machinist: Watch Your Back," *Too Much* (June 25, 2011): 4.

28. Ibid.

29. Tully, "The Year of Living Profitably," 237.

30. The combined net corporate revenues reported here are derived from corporate annual reports published by each of the three auto firms in 2010 and 2011.

31. In August 2007, Daimler Chrysler sold Chrysler to Cereberus Capital Management, a privately held equity group; this ownership arrangement continued until early 2009. As a result, Chrysler CEO compensation figures are not publicly available for the 2007–2009 period. In April 2009, Chrysler filed for bankruptcy protection. A "new" Chrysler Group LLC was formed and began operation with loans and credit provided by the U.S. Treasury Department. In June 2009, Fiat, a large Italian auto firm, acquired 20 percent of Chrysler's assets. Chrysler is now effectively a subsidiary of Fiat but is also partially owned by the United Auto Workers and the U.S. government. In 2011 Fiat CEO Sergio Marchionne elected to receive no direct compensation from Chrysler LLC for his services as Chrysler CEO. Due to the complex Chrysler ownership and management structures during 2009–2011, CEO compensation levels were unclear or unavailable for this period and therefore were not included in table 6.1. The CEO incomes in table 6.1 are from executive compensation summaries in "Form 10-K" corporate reports filed by Ford and GM in 2009–2011 with the U.S. Securities and Exchange Commission.

32. Tiffany Ten Eyck, "UAW Approves Even-Deeper Concessions at Ford," *Labor Notes* (December 2007): 5.

33. Jane Slaughter, "Auto Workers Approve Ford Contract After Hard Sell," *Labor Notes* (November 2011): 13.

34. Andre Damon, "Corporations Find Cheap Labor Haven in U.S.," *World Socialist Web Site* (July 9, 2012), on the Internet at http://wsws.org (accessed July 14, 2012); Jane Slaughter, "Next Low Wage Haven: USA," *Labor Notes* (August 2011): 1, 14.

35. Michael Dolny, "Think Tank Spectrum Revisited," *Extra!* (June 2012): 14.

36. Peter Hart, "Right and Early," *Extra!* (April 2012): 10–11.

37. James Crotty, "The Austerians Attack," *In These Times* (February 2012): 17.

38. Murray L. Wiedenbaum, *Business, Government, and the Public* (Englewood Cliffs, NJ: Prentice-Hall, 1977), 5–8.

39. Vicente Navarro, "Production and the Welfare State: The Political Context of Reforms," *International Journal of Health Services* 21 (1991): 606.

40. Lawrence Mishel, Jared Bernstein, and Sylvia Allegretto, *The State of Working America, 2004/2005* (Ithaca, NY: IRL Press, 2005), 96; see also Crotty, "The Austerians Attack," 17; Robert J. Samuelson, "Great Expectations," *Newsweek* (January 8, 1996): 31.

41. Val Burris, "The Two Faces of Capital: Corporations and Individual Capitalists as Political Actors," *American Sociological Review* 66 (2001): 376.

42. Sam Pizzigati, "Remembering the Moment Our CEOs Dug In," *Too Much* (August 29, 2011): 4.

43. Crotty, "The Austerians Attack," 17.

44. Ibid., 17–18.

45. Pizzigati, "Remembering the Moment Our CEOs Dug In," 3.

46. Lewis F. Powell Jr., "Attack on American Free Enterprise System" (August 23, 1971), 25–26, on the Internet at http://www.greenpeace.org/usa (accessed June 30, 2012).

47. Powell, "Attack on American Free Enterprise System," 11.

48. Ted Nace, *Gangs of America: The Rise of Corporate Power and the Disabling of Democracy* (San Francisco: Berrett-Koehler, 2003), 168. Also see Diana B. Henriques, "Putting the Corporation in the Dock," *New York Times*, September 14, 2003, 3.

49. Business Roundtable, "About Us: Business Roundtable History," on the Internet at http://www.businessroundtable.org (accessed June 5, 2012); Lee Drutman and Charlie Cray, "The People's Business," *In These Times* (March 14, 2005): 17; John B. Judis, "The Most Powerful Lobby," *In These Times* (February 21, 1994): 22–23.

50. Navarro, "Production and the Welfare State," 606.

51. Michael Becker, "Federal Lobbying Expenditures Plateau After Years of Rapid Growth," OpenSecretsBlog (February 4, 2011): 2–3, on the Internet at http://www.opensec rets.org/news/2011/federal-lobbying-expenitures-plateau (accessed June 16, 2012).

52. Ibid.

53. FEC, *2010 Full Election Cycle Summary Data*, "2009–2010 Candidate Summary Data: 2009–2010 Financial Activity of All Senate and House Campaigns," on the Internet at http://www.fec.gov (accessed June 16, 2012); Becker, "Federal Lobbying Expenditures Plateau After Years of Rapid Growth."

54. Andy Kroll, "Follow the Dark Money," *Mother Jones* (July–August 2012): 21; Tim Murphy, "So You Want to Buy an Election?" *Mother Jones* (January–February 2012): 23; Jeffery A. Winters, "Oligarchy in the U.S.A.," *In These Times* (March 2012): 18.

55. Domhoff, *Who Rules America?*, 6th ed., 38.

56. James A. Gross, *Broken Promise: The Subversion of U.S. Labor Relations Policy* (Philadelphia: Temple University Press, 1995).

57. Domhoff, *Who Rules America?*, 6th ed., 38.

58. Sam Hananel, "Unions Lost Big on Walker Recall," *Las Vegas Review-Journal*, June 7, 2012, A1, A4; John Flesher and Jeff Karoub, "'Right to Work' Prevails in Former Labor Stronghold," *Indianapolis Star*, December 12, 2012, A2; Jane Slaughter, "Right to Work Smacks Michigan: Sneak Attack, Long Buildup," *Labor Notes* (January 2013): 1–3.

59. Hananel, "Unions Lost Big on Walker Recall," A4.

60. U.S. Department of Labor, Bureau of Labor Statistics, "Union Members—2012," news release (January 23, 2013), 1. See also Alejandro Reuss, "What's Behind Union Decline in the United States?" *Dollars and Sense* (May–June 2011): 25–26.

61. U.S. Department of Labor, Bureau of Labor Statistics, "Union Members—2012," 1.

62. Hananel, "Unions Lost Big on Walker Recall," A4.

63. Roger Bybee, "A Three-Point Plan to Save Democrats," *In These Times* (January 2011): 24–25; Roger Bybee, "NAFTA's Hung Jury," *Extra!* (May–June 2004): 14–15.

64. Roger Bybee, "Obama's Double Game on Outsourcing," *Dollars and Sense* (September–October 2012): 20–22; Dan Froomkin, "Free Trade Deals: Lobbying Fever Foreshadows Winners, Losers," *Huffington Post* (September 24, 2011), on the Internet at http://www. huffingtonpost.com (accessed December 1, 2011); Todd Tucker, "The Trade Debate That

Wasn't Reported," *Extra!* (February 2012): 9–10; Lori Wallach, "Congress Shoves through Trio of Job-Killing Trade Agreements," *Public Citizen News* (November–December 2011): 10.

65. Sam Pizzigati, "U.S. Tax Rates: The Top Drop," *Too Much* (October 10, 2011): 3.

66. Sam Pizzigati, "Our Top 400: A Little Historical Perspective," *Too Much* (June 11, 2012): 3–4; Sam Pizzigati and Chuck Collins, "The Great Regression," *Nation* (February 25, 2013): 25–26.

67. George Ritzer, *Sociological Theory*, 3rd ed. (New York: McGraw-Hill, 1988), 641–42.

68. Glasser and Rendall, "For Media, 'Class War' Has Wealthy Victims"; John Knefel, "Bored with Occupy—and Inequality," *Extra!* (May 2012): 6–7. For a discussion of class consciousness and false consciousness, see George Lukács, *History and Class Consciousness* (Cambridge, MA: MIT Press, 1968); Ritzer, *Sociological Theory*, 69–70.

69. Sam Pizzigati, "Repeating History, Reversing History," *Too Much* (February 23, 2009): 4.

70. Domhoff, *Who Rules America?*, 6th ed., 115–18; Richard L. Zweigenhaft and G. William Domhoff, *Diversity in the Power Elite: Have Women and Minorities Reached the Top?* (New Haven, CT: Yale University Press, 1998), 192–94.

71. Domhoff, *Who Rules America?*, 6th ed., 53–84.

72. Seth Ackerman, "The Most Biased Name in News," *Extra!* (July–August 2001): 10–12; Ben Bagdikian, *The Media Monopoly*, 4th ed. (Boston: Beacon Press, 1992), 216; Adolph L. Reed Jr., "The 'Public Is Bad; Private Is Better' Scam," *Labor Party News* (October 2005): 1–2.

73. For a discussion of equity and liberty, see Martin N. Marger, *Social Inequality*, 3rd ed. (Boston: McGraw-Hill, 2005), 207.

74. Charles Derber, *The Wilding of America* (New York: St. Martin's Press, 1996), 141–42.

75. Ruth Conniff, "Social Darwinism Returns," *Progressive* (July 2012): 14–16.

76. Wayne Alves and Peter Rossi, "Who Should Get What? Fairness Judgments of Distribution of Earnings," *American Journal of Sociology* 84 (1978): 541–64.

77. JoAnn Wypijewski, "Gatherer of Worlds," *CounterPunch* (September 1–30, 2012): 8.

CHAPTER 7: THE INVISIBLE CLASS EMPIRE

1. Quoted in Vicente Navarro, "Medical History as Justification Rather Than Explanation: A Critique of Starr's *The Social Transformation of American Medicine*," *International Journal of Health Services* 14 (1984): 516.

2. Gore Vidal, "The End of History," *Nation* (September 30, 1996): 11–18.

3. G. William Domhoff, *State Autonomy or Class Dominance?* (New York: Aldine de Gruyter, 1996), 25; G. William Domhoff, *Who Rules America?*, 6th ed. (Boston: McGraw-Hill, 2010), 115–18.

4. See, for example, Ben H. Bagdikian, *The New Media Monopoly* (Boston: Beacon Press, 2004), 27–54; "Ranked Within Industries: Entertainment, 7 Companies," *Fortune* (May 21, 2012): F35; Janine Jackson, "12th Annual Fear & Favor Review," *Extra!* (April 2012): 7–9; Janine Jackson, "13th Annual Fear & Favor Review," *Extra!* (February 2013): 9–11; Mark Lloyd, "Lessons for Realistic Radicals in the Information Age," in *The Future of Media: Resistance and Reform in the 21st Century*, ed. Robert McChesney, Russell Newman, and Ben Scott (New York: Seven Stories Press, 2005), 73–95; Robert W. McChesney, *Rich Media, Poor Democracy: Communication Politics in Dubious Times* (Chicago: University of Illinois Press, 1999), 48–62; Patrick Morrison, "Media Monopoly Revisited," *Extra!* (October 21, 2011): 13–15.

5. Val Burris, "The Myth of Old Money Liberalism: The Politics of the *Forbes* 400 Richest Americans," *Social Problems* 47 (2000): 360–78; Neil deMause, "Who Ate the Dessert?" *Extra!* (June 2010): 6–8; Domhoff, *Who Rules America?*, 6th ed., 55–84; Michael C. Dreiling, "The Class Embeddedness of Corporate Political Action: Leadership in Defense of the NAFTA," *Social Problems* 47 (2000): 21–48; Thomas Frank, *Pity the Billionaire* (New York: Metropolitan Books, 2012): 106–11; David Harvey, *A Brief History of Neoliberalism* (New York: Oxford University Press, 2005); Alan Neustadtl and Dan Clawson, "Corporate Political Groupings: Does Ideology Unify Business Political Behavior?" *American Sociological Review* 53 (1988): 172–90; Maynard S. Seider, "American Big Business Ideology: A Content Analysis of Executive Speeches," *American Sociological Review* 39 (1974): 802–15.

6. Not all elite-class members believe the economic and political status quo is fair and just. One organization, Responsible Wealth (RW), explicitly disavows such views. RW is a national network of over seven hundred business leaders and wealthy individuals in the top 5 percent of income and/or wealth in the United States. As beneficiaries of economic policies tilted in their favor, these individuals advocate for fair taxes and corporate accountability. Their message is simple, and surprising to some: "We can afford to pay more; we don't need any more tax breaks." United for a Fair Economy, "Projects: Responsible Wealth—About" (2011), on the Internet at http://www.faireconomy.org/responsible_wealth (accessed July 1, 2012).

7. For examples, see Eric Alterman, "Show Us the Money," *Nation* (June 25, 2012): 10; Monika Bauerlein and Clara Jeffery, "Occupied Washington," *Mother Jones* (January–February 2012): 19–21; Beau Hodai, "Zombie Lobbyists Occupy Washington," *In These Times* (November 2011): 14–18; Craig Holman, "Campaign to Clean Up Washington," *Public Citizen Urgent Campaign Memorandum* (June 20, 2012), 1–4; John Nichols and Robert W. McChesney, "Assault of the Super Pacs," *Nation* (February 6, 2012): 11–17.

8. Pew Research Center, "Super PACs Having Negative Impact, Say Voters Aware of 'Citizens United' Ruling" (January 17, 2012).

9. Lydia Saad, "Americans Decry Power of Lobbyists, Corporations, Banks, Feds," Gallup, Inc. (April 11, 2011), on the Internet at http://www.gallup.com (accessed July 1, 2012).

10. Pew Research Center, "Growing Gap in Favorable Views of Federal, State Governments" (April 26, 2012).

11. CBS News/*New York Times* poll (January 20–25, 2006), 29.

12. Michael Beckel, "Federal Lobbying Expenditures Plateau After Years of Rapid Growth," Center for Responsive Politics (February 4, 2011), on the Internet at http://www.opensecrets.org/news/2011/02 (accessed June 16, 2012); Sarah McKinnin Bryner, "From Hired Guns to Hired Hands: 'Reverse Revolvers' in the 111th and 112th Congresses," *A Center for Responsive Politics Report* (July 11, 2011); T. W. Farnam, "Revolving Door of Employment Between Congress, Lobbying Firms, Study Shows," *Washington Post*, September 13, 2011, on the Internet at http://www.washingtonpost.com (accessed July 1, 2012); Source Watch, "Lobbying," 2006, on the Internet at http://www.sourcewatch.org (accessed May 21, 2006).

13. District of Columbia Bar, "Prospective Members" (2012), on the Internet at http://www.dcbar.org (accessed July 1, 2012); District of Columbia Bar, "2004–2005 Annual Report," on the Internet at http://www.dcbar.org (accessed May 21, 2006); District of Columbia Bar, "Attorney Resources," on the Internet at http://www.dcbar.org (accessed July 8, 2001).

14. Center for Responsive Politics, "Lobbying Database" (April 30, 2012), on the Internet at http://www.opensecrets.org/lobby/index.php (accessed June 16, 2012).

15. Center for Responsive Politics, "Summary," in *Influence, Inc.* (Washington, DC: Center for Responsive Politics, 2000), 1.

16. Jeffrey H. Birnbaum, *The Lobbyists* (New York: Times Books, 1992); Alex Knott, "Industry of Influence Nets More Than $10 Billion," Center for Public Integrity (2006), 3, on the Internet at http://www.publicintegrity.org/lobby/report (accessed May 21, 2006); Kevin Phillips, "Fat City," *Time* (September 26, 1994): 51.

17. Center for Responsive Politics, "Lobbying Database."

18. LegiStorm, "Former Lobbyists Working for Congress Outnumber Elected Lawmakers" (September 13, 2011), on the Internet at http://www.legistorm.com/blog/ (accessed July 1, 2012).

19. Craig Holman, "Campaign to Clean Up Washington," *Public Citizen Urgent Campaign Memorandum* (June 20, 2012), 2.

20. Source Watch, "Lobbying."

21. LegiStorm, "Former Lobbyists Working for Congress Outnumber Elected Lawmakers."

22. Farnam, "Revolving Door of Employment Between Congress, Lobbying Firms, Study Shows," 2.

23. Kevin Bogardus and Rachel Leven, "Lobbyists Took $100K Cut in Pay to Work for Members of Congress," *The Hill* (June 28, 2011): 2, on the Internet at http://www.thehill.com (accessed July 1, 2012).

24. Lee Fang, "Analysis: When a Congressman Becomes a Lobbyist, He Gets a 1,452% Raise (on Average)," *Republic Report* (March 14, 2012): 1, on the Internet at http://www.republicreport.org (accessed July 1, 2012).

25. Birnbaum, "The Road to Riches Is Called K Street," A1; see also Domhoff, *Who Rules America?*, 6th ed., 166–68, 183–95; Phillips, "Fat City," 52.

26. Bogardus and Leven, "Lobbyists Took $100K Cut in Pay to Work for Members of Congress"; Fang, "Analysis: When a Congressman Becomes a Lobbyist, He Gets a 1,452% Raise (on Average)"; Jordi Blanes i Vidal, Mirko Draca, and Christian Fons-Rosen, "Revolving Door Lobbyists," Center for Economic Performance, United Kingdom (May 2011).

27. Fang, "Analysis: When a Congressman Becomes a Lobbyist, He Gets a 1,452% Raise (on Average)."

28. Center for Responsive Politics, *Influence, Inc.: National Trade and Professional Associations of the United States* (Washington, DC: Columbia Books, 2006); Kay L. Schlozman and John T. Tierney, *Organized Interests and American Democracy* (New York: Harper and Row, 1986), 77.

29. Burson-Marsteller, "About Us—Family of Companies" (2006), on the Internet at http://www. burson-marsteller.com (accessed November 27, 2006); see also G. William Domhoff, *Who Rules America?*, 5th ed. (Boston: McGraw-Hill, 2006), 114, 174.

30. WPP, "Lobbying Firms BKSH & Associates and Timmons & Company Announce Merger," press release (October 5, 2009), on the Internet at http://www.wpp.com (accessed July 1, 2012).

31. WPP, "WPP Company Profile" (2012), on the Internet at http://www.wpp.com (accessed July 1, 2012).

32. Dan Clawson, Alan Neustadtl, and Denise Scott, *Money Talks* (New York: Basic Books, 1992), 182; Domhoff, *Who Rules America?*, 6th ed., 28–37.

33. Harold R. Kerbo, *Social Stratification and Inequality*, 8th ed. (New York: McGraw-Hill, 2012), 162–64.

34. Domhoff, *Who Rules America?*, 5th ed., 72.

35. G. William Domhoff, *Who Rules America?*, 4th ed. (Boston: McGraw-Hill, 2002), 27, 58, 63; Lev Grossman, "2010 Person of the Year: Mark Zuckerberg," *Time* (December 27,

2010–January 3, 2011): 44–75; Richard L. Zweigenhaft, "Making Rags Out of Riches," *Extra!* (January–February 2004): 27–28.

36. Thomas Dye, *Who's Running America? The Clinton Years* (Englewood Cliffs, NJ: Prentice-Hall, 1995), 175; Domhoff, *Who Rules America?*, 6th ed., 80–83.

37. Domhoff, *State Autonomy or Class Dominance*, 25; Domhoff, *Who Rules America?*, 6th ed., 72–74; Kerbo, *Social Stratification and Inequality*, 8th ed., 371–72.

38. Domhoff, *Who Rules America?*, 6th ed., 10–11, 163–66; Robert Fitch, "How Obama Got His Start," *CounterPunch* (January 1–15, 2012): 1, 3–7.

39. Domhoff, *Who Rules America?*, 6th ed., 163–66, 170.

40. Citigroup, Inc. "Peter Orszag to Join Citi as Vice Chairman in Global Banking," press release (December 9, 2010), 1.

41. Jeffrey H. Birnbaum, "The Road to Riches Is Called K Street," *Washington Post*, June 22, 2005, A1; John Bellamy Foster and Hannah Hollemen, "The Financial Power Elite," *Monthly Review* (May 2010): 15.

42. William Greider, "Born-Again Rubinomics," *Nation* (July 31–August 7, 2006): 20–23.

43. Troy Mullaney, "Trade Deals with S. Korea, Colombia, Panama, Who Wins?" *USA Today*, October 13, 2011, on the Internet at http://www.usatoday.com (accessed July 21, 2012); Todd Tucker, "The Trade Debate That Wasn't Reported," *Extra!* (February 2012): 9–10; Lori Wallach, "Congress Shoves through Trio of Job-Killing Trade Agreements," *Public Citizen News* (November–December 2011): 10.

44. The Hamilton Project, "Advisory Council" (39 members) (2012), on the Internet at http://www.hamiltonproject.org (accessed July 14, 2012).

CHAPTER 8: POLITICAL FINANCE: IT'S MONEY THAT MATTERS

1. Supreme Court of the United States, "Citizens United *v.* Federal Election Commission," No. 08-205, decided January 21, 2010; Monika Bauerlein and Clara Jeffery, "Undoing Citizens United, the DIY Guide," *Mother Jones* (July–August 2012): 27–28.

2. Public Campaign, *Hard Facts on Hard Money* (Washington, DC: Public Campaign, 2001), 4.

3. Benjamin I. Page, Fay Lomax Cook, and Rachel Moskowitz, "Wealthy Americans, Philanthropy, and the Common Good," Institute for Policy Research, Northwestern University, *Working Paper Series* (October 16, 2011): 10–11.

4. Ibid., 9.

5. FEC, "The FEC and the Federal Campaign Finance Law" (updated February 2011), 2, on the Internet at http://www.fec.gov/pages/brochures/fecfeca.shtml (accessed July 1, 2012).

6. Ibid.

7. Ibid.

8. Andy Kroll, "Follow the Dark Money," *Mother Jones* (July–August 2012): 20.

9. FEC, "The FEC and the Federal Campaign Finance Law," 2.

10. Kroll, "Follow the Dark Money," 24.

11. FEC, "The FEC and the Federal Campaign Finance Law," 4.

12. Ibid, 3.

13. FEC, "Campaign Finance Law Quick Reference for Reporters," 1, on the Internet at http://www.fec.gov (accessed May 1, 2006).

14. Andy Kroll, "Can Harold Ickes Make It Rain?" *Mother Jones* (September–October 2012): 39–40.

15. Kroll, "Follow the Dark Money," 22.

16. U.S. Department of the Treasury, Internal Revenue Service, "Section 527 Political Organizations Revised Tax Filing Requirements," press release (November 2002); IRS, "IRS Acts to Enforce Reporting and Disclosure by Section 527 Political Groups," press release (August 19, 2004).

17. Center for Public Integrity, "527s in 2004 Shatter Previous Records for Political Fundraising" (December 16, 2004), on the Internet at http://www.publicintegrity.org (accessed May 21, 2006).

18. FEC, "Message from the Chairman," *Record* (July 2009): 1, 4; FEC, "The FEC and the Federal Campaign Finance Law," 7–8.

19. FEC, "Quick Answers to General Questions," 2, on the Internet at http://www.fec.gov/ans/answers_general.shtml (accessed July 1, 2012).

20. Stephanie Mencimer, "Mr. Precedent," *Mother Jones* (May–June 2011): 55.

21. Kroll, "Follow the Dark Money," 25.

22. Jamie Raskin, "Citizens United and the Corporate Court," *Nation* (October 8, 2012): 20.

23. Adam Lioz and Blair Bowie, "Million-Dollar Megaphones: Super PACs and Unlimited Outside Spending in the 2012 Elections" (August 2, 2012), 3, a joint project by Dēmos and USPIRG, on the Internet at http://www.demos.org (accessed August 12, 2012).

24. FEC, "Quick Answers to PAC Questions," 2, on the Internet at http://www.fec.gov/ans/answers_pac.shtml (accessed July 28, 2012).

25. FEC, "Template for Super PACs," link from "Quick Answers to PAC Questions," on the Internet at http://www.fec.gov (accessed July 28, 2012).

26. FEC, "The FEC and the Federal Campaign Finance Law," 4.

27. Tim Murphy, "So You Want to Buy an Election?" *Mother Jones* (January–February 2012): 23.

28. FEC, "Quick Answers to General Questions," 2; Adam Lioz and Blair Bowie, "Auctioning Democracy: The Rise of Super PACs and the 2012 Election" (February 8, 2012), 5–6, a joint project by Dēmos and USPIRG, on the Internet at http://www.demos.org (accessed September 8, 2012).

29. Andy Kroll, "What Citizens United Begot," *Mother Jones* (January–February 2012): 22.

30. FEC "The FEC and the Federal Campaign Finance Law," 4; Kroll, "What Citizens United Begot"; Michael Scherer, "A Rich Man's Game," *Time* (August 13, 2012): 42–45.

31. FEC, "The FEC and the Federal Campaign Finance Law," 1.

32. Center for Reponsive Politics, "2012 Presidential Race" (January 14, 2013), on the Internet at http://www.opensecrets.org (accessed January 27, 2013).

33. This amount is our estimate based on information from several sources, including data summaries from the Center for Responsive Politics, the Campaign Finance Institute, Mike Allen and Jim VanderHei, "GOP Groups Plan Record $1 Billion Blitz," *Politico* (May 30, 2012), and papers by Lioz and Bowie cited in note 23 ("Million-Dollar Megaphones: Super PACs and Unlimited Outside Spending in the 2012 Elections") and note 28 ("Auctioning Democracy: The Rise of Super PACs and the 2012 Election"). The article by Allen and VanderHei is on the Internet at http:// www.dyn.politico.com (accessed July 1, 2012).

34. Dave Gibson, "Dark Stars," *Mother Jones* (September–October 2012): 39; Kroll, "Follow the Dark Money"; Lioz and Bowie, "Million-Dollar Megaphones," 2.

35. Center for Reponsive Politics, "The Money Behind the Elections" (August 1, 2012), 2; "2012 Election Will Be Costliest Yet, With Outside Spending a Wild Card" (August 1, 2012), 2, on the Internet at http://www.opensecrets.org (accessed August 12, 2012).

36. FEC, "2008 Presidential Recipts Nearly Double 2004 Totals," *Record* (July 2009): 8–9; FEC, "Quick Answers to General Questions" (January 2012), on the Internet at http://www. fec.gov/ans/answers (accessed July 1, 2012).

37. Center for Responsive Politics, "2004 Presidential Election," 2005, on the Internet at http://www.opensecrets.org/presidential/index.asp (visited December 12, 2005); the authors used an inflation index to transform Bush's 2004 campaign receipts into 2010 dollars.

38. This amount is our estimate based on information from (1) congressional candidates' campaign contribution and spending reports to the FEC, (2) congressional PAC and super PAC contribution and spending reports to the FEC, (3) data summaries from the campaign finance-tracking organizations Center for Responsive Politics and the Campaign Finance Institute, and (4) unreported outside spending estimates developed by investigative reporters.

39. This amount reflects the authors' use of an inflation index to transform the $2.9 billion 2008 congressional total reported by the Center for Responsive Politics into 2012 dollars.

40. Center for Reponsive Politics, "The Money Behind the Elections," 2.

41. These amounts are based on the authors' use of an inflation index to transform the 2006 and 2002 congressional totals reported by the Center for Responsive Politics into 2010 dollars.

42. Center for Responsive Politics, "Total Outside Spending by Election Cycle, All Groups" (2012), 1, on the Internet at http://www.opensecrets.org/outsidespending (accessed July 2, 2012).

43. Campaign Finance Institute, "Independent Spending Roughly Equaled the Candidates' in Close House and Senate Races; Winning Candidates Raised More Than Any Previous Election" (November 9, 2012), on the Internet at http://www.cfinst.org (accessed January 13, 2013).

44. Campaign Finance Institute, "2010 Federal Elections: The Cost of Winning an Election, 1986–2010," table 3-1: House and Senate Winners (2010), on the Internet at http://www.cfinst.org (accessed June 1, 2012). The inflation-adjusted amounts reported for the 2002 winning congressional candidates (in 2012 dollars) were calculated by the authors.

45. Center for Responsive Politics, "The Big Spender Always Wins?" *Open Secrets blog* (January 11, 2012), on the Internet at http://www.opensecrets.org (accessed July 28, 2012).

46. Ibid.

47. Ibid.

48. John Nichols and Robert W. McChesney, "The Assault of the Super Pacs," *Nation* (February 6, 2012): 11.

49. Allen and VanderHei, "GOP Groups Plan Record $1 Billion Blitz"; Kroll, "Follow the Dark Money," 17–26; Andy Kroll, "The Governors' Three-PAC Monte," *Mother Jones* (January–February 2012): 24–27.

50. Robert Perrucci and Earl Wysong, *The New Class Society: Goodbye American Dream?*, 3rd ed. (Lanham, MD: Rowman and Littlefield, 2008), 154–55.

51. FEC, "2012 Presidential Campaign Finance," "Contributions to Obama, Barack, through 7/31/2012," and "Contributions to Romney, Mitt, through 7/31/2012," on the Internet at http://www.fec.gov/disclosure/pnational.do (accessed September 8, 2012).

52. FEC, "2008 Presidential Recipts Nearly Double 2004 Totals."

53. FEC, "Financial Activity of All Congressional Candidates—1992–2010," on the Internet at http://www.fec.gov (accessed July 29, 2012).

54. Ibid.

55. FEC, "2010 Full Election Cycle Summary Data," "2009–2010 Financial Activity of All Senate and House Campaigns" (January 1, 2009–December 31, 2010), on the Internet at http://www.fec.gov (accessed June 17, 2012).

56. Center for Responsive Politics, "Total Outside Spending by Election Cycle, All Groups."

57. Center for Responsive Politics, "2012 Overview, Donor Demographics" (July 9, 2012), 1, on the Internet at http://www.opensecrets.org (accessed July 28, 2012).

58. Center for Responsive Politics, "Historical Elections, Donor Demographics, Election Cycle 2010" (2010), 2, on the Internet at http://www.opensecrets.org (accessed July 28, 2012).

59. Americans for Campaign Reform, "Money in Politics: Who Gives, Fact Sheet" (December 29, 2010), on the Internet at http://www.acrreform.org (accessed July 7, 2012).

60. Ibid.

61. Lee Drutman, "The Political One Percent of the One Percent" (December 13, 2011), 1, on the Internet at http://sunlightfoundation.com/blog/201112/13 (accessed July 4, 2012).

62. Micah L. Sifry and Nancy Watzman, *Is That a Politician in Your Pocket? Washington on $2 Million a Day* (Hoboken, NJ: John Wiley & Sons, 2004), 13.

63. Spencer Overton, "The Donor Class: Campaign Finance, Democracy, and Participation," *University of Pennsylvania Law Review* 153 (2004): 76.

64. U.S. Census Bureau, *Statistical Abstract of the United States: 2006* (Washington, DC: U.S. Government Printing Office, 2005), 459, 467.

65. Center for Responsive Politics, "Historical Elections, Donor Demographics, Election Cycle 2010," 2.

66. Center for Responsive Politics, "2012 Overview, Donor Demographics," 1.

67. NextMark, "Major Republican Political Donors Mailing List" (June 28, 2012), on the Internet at http://lists.nextmark.com (accessed August 8, 2012).

68. Campaign Finance Institute, "CFI's Review of Connecticut's Campaign Donors in 2006, and 2008 Finds Strengths in Citizen Election Program but Recommends Changes," press release (March 2, 2010), 1–3, on the Internet at http://www.cfinst.org (accessed August 5, 2012).

69. FEC, "PAC Count—1974 to Present," press release (January 2012), on the Internet at http://www.fec.gov (accessed August 26, 2012).

70. The FEC classifies PACs into these six categories: (1) corporate, (2) labor, (3) nonconnected, (4) trade-membership-health, (5) cooperative, (6) and corporations without stock.

71. Despite the large sums they control today, corporate PACs as campaign-funding vehicles are relatively new. Following the Watergate-related revelations of secret corporate political donations to the Nixon campaign, it first appeared that corporate campaign contributions would be severely limited. However, in 1975 the FEC (established by federal law in 1971) ruled, by a vote of four to three, that the Sun Oil Corporation PAC could solicit funds from both stockholders and employees. After the so-called SUN-PAC decision, the number of corporate PACs increased from 89 in 1974 to 433 in 1976 and has continued to increase since that time. See Dan Clawson, Allen Neustadtl, and Denise Scott, *Money Talks* (New York: Basic Books, 1992), 32–33.

72. Val Burris, "The Two Faces of Capital: Corporations and Individual Capitalists as Political Actors," *American Sociological Review* 66 (2001): 378.

73. FEC, "2008 Presidential Campaign Finance," "Contributions to Obama, Barack, through 12/31/2008," and "Contributions to McCain, John S., through 12/31/2008," on the Internet at http://www.fec.gov (accessed August 8, 2012); "Contributions to Obama, Barack, through 7/31/2012" and "Contributions to Romney, Mitt, through 7/31/2012."

74. FEC, "Table 1, PAC Financial Activity, 2009–2010" and "PAC Contribution Summary," on the Internet at http://www.fec.gov (accessed June 16, 2012).

75. FEC, "PAC Contribution Summary."

76. FEC, "Financial Activity of All Congressional Candidates—1992–2010."

77. Ibid.

78. FEC, "PAC Count—1974 to Present."

79. Previous studies of PAC committees that manage corporate and corporate-linked PACs along with our own research on a sample of these committees support our elite-class composition conclusion. See Clawson, Neustadtl, and Scott, *Money Talks*, 161.

80. Burris, "The Two Faces of Capital," 369; G. William Domhoff, *Who Rules America?*, 5th ed. (Boston: McGraw-Hill, 2006), 148.

81. Clawson, Neustadtl, and Scott, *Money Talks*, 161.

82. Ibid., 140–41.

83. Ibid., 176, 160.

84. Lioz and Bowie, "Million-Dollar Megaphones," 8.

85. Ibid.

86. Ibid., 10.

87. Ibid., 7.

88. Ibid., 6.

89. Ibid., 1.

90. Sam Pizzigati, "The 'Dark Money' of the Ultra Rich," *Too Much* (August 20, 2012): 3.

91. Gibson, "Dark Stars."

92. Drutman, "The Political One Percent of the One Percent," 8.

93. Lioz and Bowie, "Million-Dollar Megaphones," 8–10.

94. Ibid., 8.

95. Ibid.

96. Campaign Finance Institute, "Reality Check: Obama Received about the Same Percentage from Small Donors in 2008 as Bush in 2004" (November 24, 2008), on the Internet at http://www.cfinst.org (accessed June 16, 2012).

97. Colin Delan, *Learning from Obama: Lessons for Online Communicators in 2009 and Beyond* (August 2009), 32, on the Internet at http://www.epolitics.com (accessed June 4, 2012).

98. Center for Responsive Politics, "2012 Overview: Donor Demographics"; G. William Domhoff, *Who Rules America?*, 6th ed. (Boston: McGraw-Hill, 2010), 163–68; Scherer, "A Rich Man's Game."

99. Campaign Finance Institute, "All CFI Funding Statistics Revised and Updated for the 2008 Presidential Primary and General Election Candidates" (January 8, 2010), on the Internet at http://www.cfinst.org (accessed July 28, 2012); Campaign Finance Institute, "Money vs. Money-Plus: Post-Election Reports Reveal Two Different Campaign Strategies," press release (January 11, 2013), on the Internet at http://www.cfinst.org (accessed January 27, 2013).

100. Lioz and Bowie, "Million-Dollar Megaphones," 2–3; Amitabh Pal, "Meet the 26 Billionaires Buying Our Democracy," *Progressive* (October 2012): 24–26.

101. Joe Garecht, "How To Raise Political Donations Online," *Local Victory* (August 30, 2010), on the Internet at http://www.localvictory.com (accessed July 28, 2012).

102. John Nichols, "Behind the DLC Takeover," *Progressive* (October 2000): 29.

103. Marty Jezer, "Soft Money, Hard Choices," *Dollars and Sense* (July–August 1996): 30.

104. Barack Obama, *The Audacity of Hope* (New York: Crown, 2006), 113–14.

105. James Thinda, "Time for Democrats to Pay Their Dues," *In These Times* (February 2013): 30–31.

106. Thomas Frank, *Pity the Billionaire* (New York; Metropolitan Books, 2012), 166–83.

107. The Hamilton Project, "Mission and Vision" (2012), 1–2, on the Internet at http://www.hamiltonproject.org (accessed July 17, 2012).

108. Matthew Rothschild, "The Third-Party Dilemma," *Progressive* (September 2012): 18.

109. Ibid.

110. Campaign Finance Institute, "Reality Check: Obama Received about the Same Percentage from Small Donors in 2008 as Bush in 2004"; FEC, "2008 Presidential Campaign Finance," "Contributions to Obama, Barack, through 12/31/2012," "Contributions to McCain, John S., through 12/31/2008," "Contributions to Obama, Barack, through 7/31/2012," "Contributions to Romney, Mitt, through 7/31/2012."

111. FEC, "Contributions from Individuals by Size of the Contribution," "Senate," "House," on the Internet at http://www.fec.gov (accessed July 29, 2012).

112. FEC, "2010 Full Election Cycle Summary Data," "PAC Contributions 2009–2010 Through December 31, 2010," on the Internet at http://www.fec.gov (accessed June 17, 2012).

113. Lioz and Bowie, "Million-Dollar Megaphones," 7.

114. Ibid., 10.

115. For an example, see Elizabeth DiNovella, "Sherrod Brown Beats Back Big Money," *Progressive* (October 2012): 14–18.

CHAPTER 9: POLICY PLANNING AND CLASSWIDE LOBBYING

1. Ari Berman, "The Austerity Class," *Nation* (November 7, 2011): 11–17; Kevin C. Brown, "The 'Liberal Media' and State Austerity," *Extra!* (June 2010): 9; Carolyn Cutrone and Steve Rendall, "Deficit-Obsessed Media Misinform on Causes," *Extra!* (September 2011): 4–5; Michael Dolny, "Think Tank Spectrum Revisited," *Extra!* (June 2012); G. William Domhoff, *Who Rules America?*, 6th ed. (Boston: McGraw-Hill, 2010), 97–99; Joe Klein, "These Savings Are Unreal," *Time* (April 23, 2012): 27.

2. Domhoff, *Who Rules America?*, 6th ed., 87–90.

3. Ibid., 83–84; David Harvey, *A Brief History of Neoliberalism* (New York: Oxford University Press, 2005).

4. Thomas R. Dye, "Organizing Power for Policy-Planning: The View from the Brookings Institution," in *Power Elites and Organizations*, ed. G. William Domhoff and Thomas R. Dye (Newbury Park, CA: Sage, 1987), 185–86.

5. Ibid., 188.

6. G. William Domhoff, *Who Rules America?*, 3rd ed. (Mountain View, CA: Mayfield Publishing, 1998), 128.

7. Domhoff, *Who Rules America?*, 6th ed., 97–99.

8. Thomas R. Dye, *Who's Running America? The Bush Restoration*, 7th ed. (Upper Saddle River, NJ: Prentice Hall, 2002), 174–87.

9. Val Burris, "Elite Policy-Planning Networks in the United States," in *Research in Politics and Society*, vol. 4, *The Political Consequences of Social Networks*, ed. Gwen Moore and J. Allen Whitt (Greenwich, CN: JAI Press, 1992), 115–20; Domhoff, *Who Rules America?*, 6th ed., 25–26, 48, 104, 111–12.

10. John Nichols, "ALEC Exposed," *Nation* (August 1–8, 2011): 16–17.

11. Beau Hodai, "Publicopoly Exposed," *In These Times* (August 2011): 16.

12. Nichols, "ALEC Exposed," 17.

13. Ibid.

14. American Legislative Exchange Council, "History" (2011), on the Internet at http://www.alec.org (accessed January 10, 2012).

15. Julie Underwood, "Starving Public Schools," *Nation* (August 1–8, 2011): 22–23.

16. Joel Rogers and Laura Dresser, "Business Domination, Inc.," *Nation* (August 1–8, 2011): 17–20; Mark Pocan, "Inside the ALEC Dating Service," *Progressive* (October 2011): 19–21.

17. Joel Bleifuss, "Tea Party Winter Is Coming," *In These Times* (January 2013): 5.

18. Domhoff, *Who Rules America?*, 6th ed., 98.

19. Ibid.

20. Michael Patrick Allen, "Elite Social Movement Organizations and the State: The Rise of the Conservative Policy-Planning Network," in *Research in Politics and Society*, vol. 4, *The Political Consequences of Social Networks*, ed. Gwen Moore and J. Allen Whitt (Greenwich, CT: JAI Press, 1992), 95; Domhoff, *Who Rules America?*, 6th ed., 102–3; Sam Husseini, "Checkbook Analysis," *Extra!* (May–June 2000): 23–24; Erica Payne, *The Practical Progressive: How to Build a 21st Century Political Movement* (New York: PublicAffairs, 2008), 31–40.

21. National Committee for Responsive Philanthropy, "$1 Billion for Ideas: Conservative Think Tanks in the 1990s," press release (March 12, 1999), 2.

22. This finding is based on our analysis of annual reports and Federal Form 990 Income tax returns for the twenty think tanks over the 2001–2006 period.

23. This finding is based on our analysis of annual reports and Federal Form 990 income tax returns for these two think tanks over the 2007–2011 period.

24. Thomas B. Edsall, "Rich Liberals Vow to Fund Think Tanks; Aim Is to Compete with Conservatives," *Washington Post*, August 7, 2005, A1. See also Ari Berman, "Big $$ for Progressive Politics," *Nation* (October 16, 2006): 18–24.

25. Edsall, "Rich Liberals Vow to Fund Think Tanks."

26. "Democracy Alliance Editor's Note," *Washington Free Beacon* (September 2012), on the Internet at http://www.freebeacon.com (accessed September 30, 2012).

27. "Democracy Alliance Editor's Note."

28. Domhoff, *Who Rules America?*, 6th ed., 86, 117.

29. G. William Domhoff, *State Autonomy or Class Dominance?* (New York: Aldine de Gruyter, 1996), 34, 38.

30. Ibid., 29–32.

31. Ferdinand Lundberg, *The Rich and the Super-Rich* (New York: Bantam Books, 1968), 498–505; Harold R. Kerbo, *Social Stratification and Inequality*, 5th ed. (Boston: McGraw Hill, 2003), 183.

32. The Foundation Center, "Top 100 U.S. Foundations by Asset Size," "Top 100 U.S. Foundations by Total Giving," "FC Stats, Grantmaker Set Information," on the Internet at http://www.foundationcenter.org (accessed October 1, 2012).

33. Thomas Dye, *Who's Running America? The Clinton Years*, 6th ed. (Englewood Cliffs, NJ: Prentice Hall, 1995), 11, 135, 171, 192.

34. The Rockefeller Foundation, "2010 Trustees," *Annual Report 2010*, 33.

35. This information on Brookings is derived from three sources: (1) Brookings Institution, "Brookings Annual Report 2010," (2) Brookings Institution, "The Brookings Institution Financial Statements" (June 30, 2011), and (3) Federal Form 990 income tax return 2010 for the Brookings Institution. The first two sources are on the Internet at http://www.brookings.edu (accessed August 10, 2012).

36. "Brookings Annual Report," 35–37; "The Brookings Institution Financial Statements," 3.

37. "Brookings Annual Report," 35. In 2010, Brookings received a $10 million grant from the Rockefeller Foundation. See the Rockefeller Foundation, *Annual Report 2010*, 57.

38. Dye, *Who's Running America?*, 6th ed., 225.

39. National Committee for Responsive Philanthropy, "$1 Billion for Ideas," 1–2.

40. Our analysis of annual reports issued by several conservative think tanks over the past five years supports this conclusion. See also Payne, *The Practical Progressive*, 31–40.

41. These findings are from the authors' research; source materials used include Business Roundtable, "About Us: Members" (2012), on the Internet at http://www.businessroundtable.org (accessed July 25, 2012); U.S. Department of Treasury, Internal Revenue Service, "Return of Organization Exempt from Income Tax—Form 990, The Business Roundtable," 23-7236607 (Washington, DC, 2010). See also Lee Drutman and Charlie Cray, "The People's Business," *In These Times* (March 14, 2005): 17.

42. Business Roundtable, "About Us: Executive Committee" (2012), on the Internet at http://www. businessround table.org (accessed July 25, 2012).

43. "Brookings Annual Report," 34.

44. Domhoff, *Who Rules America?*, 6th ed., 105.

45. Dye, *Who's Running America?*, 6th ed., 236–37.

46. Jared Newman, "SOPA and PIPA: Just the Facts," *PC World* (January 19, 2012): 1, on the Internet at http://www.arnnet.com (accessed March 12, 2012).

47. Ibid.

48. Ibid.

49. Art Brodsky, "PIPA and SOPA Were Stopped, but the Web Hasn't Won," *Huffington Post* (January 25, 2012), 1, on the Internet at http://www.huffingtonpost.com (accessed March 12, 2012).

50. U.S. House of Representatives, Judiciary Committee, "List of Supporters: H.R. 3261, the *Stop Online Piracy Act*" (January 2012).

51. Jill Abrams, "Understanding the Internet Piracy Bills, SOPA and PIPA," *Chicago Sun Times*, February 21, 2012, on the Internet at http://www.suntimes.com/business (accessed March 12, 2012).

52. Brodsky, "PIPA and SOPA Were Stopped."

53. Domhoff, *Who Rules America?*, 6th ed., 25–26, 104, 111–12. See also Clawson, Neustadtl, and Scott, *Money Talks*, 180.

54. This list is based on new research by the authors for this book.

55. These four contests illustrate that political support for superclass-favored policies that are backed by unified and well-funded classwide lobbying campaigns is typically bipartisan. But in one case, many Democratic House members voted *against* the 2011 free trade deals. Even when the Democratic party controls the Congress and presidency, we find important cases where classwide lobbying facilitated the enactment of legislation supporting superclass interests over those of the working class. Examples include the North American Free Trade

Agreement (NAFTA, 1993) and the welfare "reform" act of 1996; both were enacted with strong support from President Clinton and Democrats holding leadership postions in Congress.

56. Robert Scheer, *The Great American Stickup* (New York: Nation Books, 2010), 62.

57. Scheer, *The Great American Stickup*, 55.

58. Ibid., 34, 55, 102–5.

59. Ibid., 108–9; see also Kevin Connor, "Big Bank Takeover," Campaign for America's Future (2010), on the Internet at http://www.OurFuture.org; John Bellamy Foster and Robert W. McChesney, "The Endless Crisis," *Monthly Review* (May 2012): 1–28; Robert Weissman and James Donahue, "Sold Out: How Wall Street and Washington Betrayed America," *Essential Information* (March 2009), on the Internet at http://www.wall-streetwatch.org (both Web reports accessed August 10, 2012).

60. Bob Guldin, "Flawed Bankruptcy Law Rewards Finance Industry, while Families Beset by Health Costs Lose Protection," *Public Citizen News* (May–June 2005): 11.

61. Ibid.

62. Public Citizen, *Unfairness Incorporated: The Corporate Campaign Against Consumer Class Actions*, Public Citzen's Congress Watch (June 2003); Seth Stern, "Republicans Win on Class Action," *Congressional Quarterly Weekly* (February 21, 2005): 460.

63. Seth Stern, "2005 Legislative Summary: Class Action Lawsuits," *Congressional Quarterly Weekly* (January 2, 2006): 46.

64. Keith Perine, "Class Action Lawsuit Measure Advances amid Heavy Lobbying, Concern Over State Law," *Congressional Quarterly Weekly* (April 12, 2003): 882.

65. Dan Froomkin, "Free Trade Deals: Lobbying Fever Foreshadows Winners, Losers," *Huffington Post* (September 24, 2011), on the Internet at http://www.huffingtonpost.com (accessed December 1, 2011).

66. Ibid., 1.

67. Ibid., 1; see also Joshua Meltzer, "Congress Should Pass Free Trade Agreements with South Korea, Colombia and Panama," Brookings Institution, press release (July 28, 2011), on the Internet at http://www.brookings.edu (accessed June 7, 2012).

68. Todd Tucker, "The Trade Debate That Wasn't Reported," *Extra!* (February 2012): 9–10; Hillary Rodham Clinton, Secretary of State, U.S. Department of State, Remarks: "South Korea, Colombia, Panama Free Trade Agreements," press release (October 12, 2011), on the Internet at http://www.state.gov/secretary/rm (accessed June 10, 2012).

69. Froomkin, "Free Trade Deals," 2.

70. Ibid.

71. Lori Wallach, "Congress Shoves Through Trio of Job-Killing Trade Agreements," *Public Citizen News* (November–December 2011): 10.

72. Ibid.

73. Ibid.

74. Angela Bradbery, "2011 'Free Trade' Deals Haven't Lived Up to Obama's Promises," *Public Citizen News* (November–December 2012): 13.

75. Roger Bybee, "Obama's Double Game on Outsourcing," *Dollars and Sense* (September–October 2012): 21.

76. Ibid.

77. Doug Orr, "Social Security Q&A," *Dollars and Sense* (May–June 2005): 15–20.

78. Jim Hightower and Phillip Frazer, "Naming the Names Behind the Grab for Social Security," *The Lowdown* (April 2005): 1–8.

79. Other examples illustrating how labor-based coalitions have defeated superclass policy initiatives are discussed in the second edition of this book, chapter 4, 143–44.

80. Dave Lindorff, "The First Cuts Won't Be the Deepest," *CounterPunch* (October 1–15, 2012): 1–3.

81. Berman, "The Austerity Class," 14.

82. *The Moment of Truth: Report of the National Commission on Fiscal Responsibility and Reform* (December 2010), 48–55.

83. Jay Newton-Small and Michael Scherer, "Conspiracy of Two," *Time* (July 25, 2011): 40–41.

84. Domhoff, *Who Rules America?*, 3rd ed., 266–81; G. William Domhoff, *Who Rules America?*, 4th ed. (Boston: McGraw-Hill, 2002), 175.

85. Dye, *Who's Running America?*, 6th ed., 61–62.

86. Kevin Phillips, *American Dynasty* (New York: Penguin Books, 2004), 53.

87. Joseph White and Aaron Wildavsky, *The Deficit and the Public Interest: The Search for Responsible Budgeting in the 1980s* (Berkeley: University of California Press, 1989), 165–66; Donald L. Barlett and James B. Steele, *America: Who Really Pays the Taxes?* (New York: Simon and Schuster, 1994), 218.

88. The Tax Foundation, "Federal Individual Income Tax Rates History, 1913–2011," on the Internet at http://www.taxfoundation.org (accessed September 30, 2012); Barlett and Steele, *America: Who Really Pays The Taxes?*, 134–35.

89. Barlett and Steele, *America: Who Really Pays The Taxes?*, 232–33.

90. U.S. Congress, House of Representatives, *Comprehensive Tax Reform*, Committee on Ways and Means, 99th Congress, 1st sess., serial 99–41 (Washington, DC: U.S. Government Printing Office, 1985).

91. The Tax Foundation, "Federal Individual Income Tax Rates History, 1913–2011."

92. "Alternative Minimum Tax Reform Act: Chamber of Commerce of the United States of America" and "Alternative Minimum Tax Reform Act: Statement of National Association of Manufacturers," *Congressional Record* (May 8, 1997): S4236–38; "The Small Business Capital Gains Enhancement Act of 1997," *Congressional Record* (May 15, 1997): S4588–91; "Amendment No. 519," *Congressional Record* (June 26, 1997): S6449–51.

93. Details regarding the superclass-sponsored, classwide coalitions supporting BRA are presented in the third edition of this book, chapter 4, 175–76.

94. John Miller, "Tax Cuts: Clinton and Congress Feed the Wealthy," *Dollars and Sense* (November–December 1997): 43; John Miller, "More Wealth for the Wealthy: The Estate Tax Giveaway and What to Do about It," *Dollars and Sense* (November–December 1997): 26–27.

95. "The Rich Get a Good Return on Their Campaign Investments," *Sanders Scoop* (Winter 1998): 1.

96. Miller, "Tax Cuts," 43.

97. Lori Nitschke, "Tax Plan Destined for Revision," *Congressional Quarterly Weekly* (February 10, 2001): 318–21.

98. Daniel J. Parks, "Under Tight Spending Ceilings, Democrats Lower Their Sights," *Congressional Quarterly Weekly* (June 9, 2001): 1364.

99. Adria Scharf, "Tax Cut Time Bomb," *Dollars and Sense* (March–April 2004): 39.

100. Citizens for Tax Justice, "Final Version of Bush Tax Plan Keeps High-End Tax Cuts, Adds to Long-Term Cost," on the Internet at http://www.inequality.org (accessed August 8, 2001). See also John Miller, "Getting Back More Than They Give," *Dollars and Sense* (September–October 2001): 60–62.

101. Sam Pizzigati, "Stat of the Week: Estate Tax Odds," *Too Much* (June 5, 2006): 4.

102. Jane Bryant Quinn, "Tax Cuts: Who Will Get What," *Newsweek* (June 11, 2001): 30.

103. Citizens for Tax Justice, "CBO Projects $8.5 Trillion in Borrowing Over Next Decade Under Bush Policies," subtopic "Effects of the Bush Tax Cuts Enacted Through 2004 (with Sunsets) by Income Group (Calendar Years)," press release (January 26, 2006), 1–3.

104. Robert Pollin, *Contours of Descent* (New York: Verso, 2005), 97.

105. The most pernicious effect of the 2001 tax law was that it accelerated the revenue "starvation" of federal programs benefiting working-class Americans. As one progressive journalist noted, "Make no mistake. We are being set up for the repeal of the last of the hard-earned New Deal antipoverty and health care programs for the elderly and poor Americans." Ruth Conniff, "The Budget Surrender," *Progressive* (June 2001): 13.

106. Lori Nitschke, "Coalitions Make a Comeback," *Congressional Quarterly Weekly* (March 3, 2001): 474.

107. Ibid., 470, 474.

108. Ibid., 321.

109. Ibid., 474.

110. Michael Scherer, "Make Your Taxes Disappear!" *Mother Jones* (March–April 2005): 74; Public Citizen, *Unfairness Incorporated.*

111. The White House, "Fact Sheet—Extending the President's Tax Relief: A Victory for American Taxpayers," press release (May 17, 2006).

112. Scharf, "Tax Cut Time Bomb," 39.

113. Ibid.

114. Citizens for Tax Justice, "Tax Cuts on Capital Gains and Dividends Doubled Bush Income Tax Cuts for the Wealthiest in 2003," press release (April 5, 2006), 1.

115. Edmund L. Andrews, "House Passes a $2.7 Trillion Spending Plan," *New York Times,* May 18, 2006, A1.

116. Pollin, *Contours of Descent,* 97–99.

117. U.S. House of Representatives, Committee on Ways and Means, "428 Major Companies and Organizations Support the American Jobs Creation Act," press release (July 8, 2004).

118. Scherer, "Make Your Taxes Disappear!" 72.

119. Ibid., 74.

120. Kimberly Amadeo, "What Was the Stimulus Package?" About.com (September 4, 2012), on the Internet at http://www.useconomy.about.com (accessed October 1, 2012); Stephen Ohlemacher, "You Can Say Goodbye to Payroll Tax Cut," *Indianapolis Star,* October 22, 2012, A5.

121. Business Roundtable, "Statement on Bipartisan Tax Agreement," press release (December 7, 2010); National Association of Manufacturers, "Manufacturers: Tax Relief in Senate Passed Bill Is Critical," press release (December 15, 2010); U.S. Chamber of Commerce, "Letter Regarding Legislation Expected to Be Considered in the Senate to Extend Certain Expiring 2001 and 2003 Tax Cuts While Failing to Avert a Massive Tax Increase on American Small Businesses," press release (December 3, 2010).

122. Barry Grey, "Leaked 'Grand Bargain' Document Details Obama's Plan for Cuts in Entitlement Programs," *World Socialist Web Site* (November 15, 2012): 1–3, on the Internet at http://www.wsw.org (accessed November 20, 2012).

123. John Miller, "Second Coming of the Estate Tax Not So Rapturous," *Dollars and Sense* (January–February 2013): 9–10.

124. Michael Grunwald, "Cliff Dweller," *Time* (January 14, 2013): 28; Jill Stein, "Austerity's Agent: The Real Obama Emerges (Again)," *CounterPunch* (January 18–20, 2013), on the Internet at http://www.counterpunch.org (accessed January 27, 2013); Sam Pizzigati, "The Tax Legacy of George W. Bush: It Lives!" *Too Much* (January 7, 2013): 4–5; Sam Pizzigati, "Swell Times for America's Swollen Fortunes," *Too Much* (January 14, 2013): 4–5.

125. Joel Bleifuss, "Watch Out, Grandma!" *In These Times* (February 2013): 5.

126. "An Alternative to Austerity," *Nation* (January 28, 2013): 3.

127. Domhoff, *Who Rules America?*, 6th ed., 166.

128. Sam Pizzigati, "Why the Top Rate Matters," *Too Much* (March 9, 2009): 3; Gerald Freeman, "The Great Tax-Cut Experiment," *Dollars and Sense* (January–February 2013): 29–30; Sam Pizzigati and Chuck Collins, "The Great Regression," *Nation* (February 25, 2013): 25–26.

129. This information is from Mitt and Ann Romney's 1040 U.S. individual income tax return (2010), on the Internet at http://www.mittromney.com (accessed October 1, 2012).

130. In 2010, $12.6 million of Romney's total income ($21.6 million) was from capital gains.

131. G. William Domhoff, "Wealth, Income, and Power," figure 1 (January 2012), on the Internet at http://www2.ucsc.edu/whorulesamerica/power/wealth.html (accessed October 10, 2012); Edward N. Wolff, *The Asset Price Meltdown and the Wealth of the Middle Class* (New York: New York University Press, 2012).

132. Office of Management and Budget, "Historical Tables, Table 2.1—Receipts by Source: 1934–2017," in *Budget of the U.S. Government: Fiscal Year 2013* (Washington, DC: U.S. Government Printing Office, 2013), 30–31.

133. David Cay Johnston, *Perfectly Legal: The Covert Campaign to Rig Our Tax System to Benefit the Super Rich—and Cheat Everybody Else* (New York: Portfolio, 2003).

134. Kevin Drum, "Plutocracy Now," *Mother Jones* (March–April 2011): 27; Center for Responsive Politics, "Average Wealth of Members of Congress: 2004–2011," on the Internet at http://www.opensecrets.org (accessed December 27, 2012).

135. John Miller, "No Fooling—Corporations Evade Taxes," *Dollars and Sense* (May–June 2011): 11–12.

136. Damian Paletta and John D. McKinnon, "The Data Behind Romney's 47% Comments," *Wall Street Journal*, September 18, 2012, on the Internet at http://blogs.wsj.com/washwire (accessed October 1, 2012); Peter Schroeder, "Tax Policy Center Analysis Details the '47 Percent,'" *The Hill* (September 18, 2012), on the Internet at http://thehill.com/blogs (accessed October 1, 2012).

137. L. Randall Wray and Pavlina R. Tcherneva, "Romney: The Little People Don't Pay Taxes," *New Economic Perspectives* (September 19, 2012), on the Internet at http://www.new economicperspectives.org (accessed October 1, 2012).

138. Joel Bleifuss, "Warfare or Welfare," *In These Times* (December 9, 1996): 12–14; "Explosive Job Growth," *Mother Jones* (May–June 2006): 17; Heidi Garrett-Peltier, "Is Military Keynesianism the Solution?" *Dollars and Sense* (March–April 2010): 7; Huck Gutman, "Soldiers for Hire," *Monthly Review* (June 2004): 11–18.

139. Office of Management and Budget, "Department of Defense," in *Budget of the U.S. Government: Fiscal Year 2013* (Washington, DC: U.S. Government Printing Office, 2013), 84.

140. War Resisters League, "Where Your Income Tax Money Really Goes—U.S. Federal Budget 2013 Fiscal Year," on the Internet at www.warresisters.org (accessed October 1, 2012);

Office of Management and Budget, "Summary Tables," in *Fiscal Year 2013, Budget of the U.S. Government* (Washington, DC: U.S. Government Printing Office, 2013), table S-1, p. 205.

141. Mickey Huff and Adam Bessie, "Case Study of News Abuse: Framing, Propaganda, and Censorship," in *Censored 2012*, ed. Mickey Huff and Project Censored (New York: Seven Stories Press, 2011), 202; Lawrence Kudlow, "Is Obama Buying the Election With His Welfare Explosion?" *The Kudlow Report* (October 19, 2012), on the Internet at http://www.cnbc.com (accessed October 21, 2012); Louis Nayman, "Splintering the 99%," *In These Times* (October 2012): 24–25; Wray and Tcherneva, "Romney: The Little People Don't Pay Taxes."

142. Randy Albelda, "Welfare Reform, Ten Years Later," *Dollars and Sense* (January–February 2006): 6–7, 27; Randy Albelda, "Different Anti-Poverty Programs, Same Single-Mother Poverty," *Dollars and Sense* (January–February 2012): 11–17; Neil deMause, "The Smell of Success," *Extra!* (November–December 2006): 6–7; Hank Hoffman, "Time Is Tight," *In These Times* (November 12, 2001): 7–8.

143. Office of Management and Budget, "Appendix: Department of Health and Human Services, 'Administration for Children and Families, TANF,'" in *Budget of the U.S. Government: Fiscal Year 2013* (Washington, DC: U.S. Government Printing Office, 2013), 511; Office of Management and Budget, "Summary Tables," table S-1, p. 205.

CHAPTER 10: THE INFORMATION INDUSTRY

1. Peter Phillips, "The Top 25 Censored Stories of 2000," in *Censored 2001*, ed. Peter Phillips and Project Censored (New York: Seven Stories Press, 2001), 38.

2. Peter Phillips, "Preface," in *Censored 2006*, ed. Peter Phillips and Project Censored (New York: Seven Stories Press, 2005), 15.

3. Mickey Huff, "Introduction: Project Censored News Clusters and the Top Censored Stories of 2010–2011," in *Censored 2012*, ed. Mickey Huff and Project Censored (New York: Seven Stories Press, 2011), 36.

4. Ibid.

5. Robert Abele, "Drawing Back the Veil on the US Propaganda Machine," in *Censored 2012*, ed. Mickey Huff and Project Censored (New York: Seven Stories Press, 2011), 325–36; Peter Hart, "Right and Early," *Extra!* (April 2012): 10–11; Janine Jackson, "12th Annual Fear and Favor Review," *Extra!* (April 2012): 7–9; Janine Jackson, "13th Annual Fear & Favor Review," *Extra!* (February 2013): 9–11; John Knefel, "Bored with Occupy—and Inequality," *Extra!* (May 2012): 6–7.

6. These statements concerning the sources of Project Censored's top stories are based on our review of citations in the project's annual publications from 2000 through 2012.

7. Robert W. McChesney, *Rich Media, Poor Democracy* (Chicago: University of Illinois Press, 1999), 16–29. See also Ben Bagdikian, *The New Media Monopoly* (Boston: Beacon Press, 2004), 27–54; Patrick Morrison, "Media Monopoly Revisited," *Extra!* (October 2011): 13–15; Bridget Thornton, Britt Walters, and Lori Rouse, "Corporate Media Is Corporate America," in *Censored 2006*, ed. Peter Phillips and Project Censored (New York: Seven Stories Press, 2005), 245–62.

8. Pat Aufderheide, "Too Much Media," *In These Times* (May 9, 2005): 28; Mark C. Miller, "Free the Media," *Nation* (June 3, 1996): 9–15; "The National Entertainment State, Special Issue," *Nation* (July 3, 2006): 13–30.

9. Michael Dolny, "Think Tank Spectrum Revisited," *Extra!* (June 2012): 14–15.

10. David Croteau, "Challenging the 'Liberal Media' Claim," *Extra!* (July–August 1998): 9.

11. Bagdikian, *The New Media Monopoly*, 236.

12. Jeffrey M. Jones, "Confidence in U.S. Public Schools at New Low, Confidence also at New Lows for Organized Religion, Banks, and TV News," Gallup, Inc. (June 20, 2012), on the Internet at http://www.gallup.com (accessed August 1, 2012); Pew Research Center for the People and the Press, "Press Accuracy Rating Hits Two Decade Low" (September 13, 2009), on the Internet at http://people-press.org (accessed August 1, 2012).

13. Pew Research Center for the People and the Press, "Internet Gains on Television as Public's Main News Source" (January 4, 2011), on the Internet at http://people-press.org (accessed August 1, 2012).

14. News Corporation, "Australian Federal Court Approves News Corporation Reincorporation to United States," press release (November 3, 2004), 1.

15. Since our focus in this chapter is on the information industry, we limit our attention to the five companies listed because their media holdings include national television network *news* operations. Our list does not include other large firms with major U.S. media holdings such as Viacom, Google, Advance Publications, and others. See Morrison, "Media Monopoly Revisited."

16. The profiles of the five media firms, including the revenue figures, are based on information included in various corporate publications produced by each firm. These include 2012 annual reports, 2012 U.S. Securities and Exchange Commission Form 10-K reports, and additional documents found on the five corporate websites available on the Internet. See the bibliography for complete citations for each company website.

17. Pew Research Center's Project for Excellence in Journalism, "Newspapers: By the Numbers," *The State of the News Media 2012*, 17, on the Internet at http://stateof the media. org (accessed August 1, 2012).

18. Pew Research Center's Project for Excellence in Journalism, "Who Owns the News Media: Top Newspaper Companies," *The State of the News Media 2012*, 1–4, on the Internet at http://stateofthemedia.org/media-ownership/ (accessed August 1, 2012).

19. Ibid., 2.

20. "Who's on Top by Sector: Ranked within Industries," *Fortune* (May 21, 2012): F-38.

21. News Corporation, *Annual Report 2012*, 10, 23.

22. McChesney, *Rich Media, Poor Democracy*, 29.

23. Ibid.

24. Thornton, Walters, and Rouse, "Corporate Media Is Corporate America."

25. Peter Phillips, "Self Censorship and the Homogeneity of the Media Elite," in *Censored 1998*, ed. Peter Phillips (New York: Seven Stories Press, 1998), 152.

26. Matt Carlson, "Boardroom Brothers," *Extra!* (September–October 2001): 18–19. See also Stephanie Dyer, "Lifestyles of the Media Rich and Oligopolistic," in *Censored 2005*, ed. Peter Phillips and Project Censored (New York: Seven Stories Press, 2004), 189–97.

27. Bagdikian, *The New Media Monopoly*, 6–9, 15–17.

28. These percentages are based on the the authors' calculations using information from "Forbes 400: The Richest People in America," *Forbes* (September 19, 2012), on the Internet at http://www.forbes.com/forbes-400/list/ (accessed October 1, 2012).

29. Robert Parry, "The Right-Wing Media Machine," *Extra!* (March–April 1995): 7.

30. Jim Naureckas, "From the Top: What Are the Politics of the Network Bosses?" *Extra!* (July–August 1998): 21–22. See also Bagdikian, *The New Media Monopoly*, 50–54; Jim Naureckas, "Where's the Power: Newsroom or Boardroom?" *Extra!* (July–August 1998): 23.

31. Ben H. Bagdikian, *The Media Monopoly*, 5th ed. (Boston: Beacon Press, 1997), 26.

32. Ibid., 15, 51, 122; Janine Jackson, "Let Them Eat Baguettes," *Extra!* (March–April 1996): 14–15.

33. William K. Tabb, "After Neoliberalism?" *Monthly Review* (June 2003): 27. As we noted in chapter 3, note 11, Austrian economist Friedrich August von Hayek, the intellectual godfather of "free market supply side economics," used the term *liberal* to describe free-market economic thought. His meaning of this term was nearly the opposite of what "liberal" means in U.S. political-economy thought today. As we also noted earlier, what Hayek labeled as "liberal" economic thought came to be known as "neoliberal." See Christian Parenti, "Winning the War of Ideas," *In These Times* (November 17, 2003): 18–21. The importance of neoliberalism to U.S. ruling-class elites as a political-economy ideology is suggested by author David Harvey. He "argues that ruling elites in the United States [have] promoted neoliberalism—or free market fundamentalism—as 'a project to achieve the restoration of class power' which was threatened economically and politically in the late '60s and early '70s." Quoted in David Moberg, "Throw Books at Them," *In These Times* (December 19, 2005): 37.

34. G. William Domhoff, *Who Rules America?*, 5th ed. (New York: McGraw-Hill, 2006), 78–79, 106.

35. Ibid., 112, 157.

36. Bagdikian, *The Media Monopoly*, 5th ed., 6.

37. Parry, "The Right-Wing Media Machine," 7.

38. Naureckas, "From the Top," 21–22.

39. Bagdikian, *The New Media Monopoly*, 106; Robert McChesney and John Bellamy Foster, "'Left Wing' Media?" *Monthly Review* (June 2003): 10, 14–15.

40. Average CEO pay is based on the authors' analysis of total compensation for each of the five CEOs as reported in Securities and Exchange Commission filings by each of the five firms.

41. Average pay for CEOs at the three largest *publicly held* U.S. newspaper companies (Gannett, McClatchy, the New York Times Company) is based on the authors' analysis of data reported in SEC filings by these three firms. The News Corporation owns two large newspapers, which makes it the third-largest U.S. newspaper firm; however, pay for the NC CEO (Rupert Murdoch) was not included in our calculations because Murdoch oversees operations not just for the newspapers but also for the entire NC media enterprise. The second-largest U.S. newspaper company is a privately held firm (MediaNews Group); financial information for this firm, including CEO pay, is not publicly available. Newspaper revenue and profit declines cited in Pew Research Center's Project for Excellence in Journalism, "Newspapers: By the Numbers," 1, 9.

42. Suzanne M. Kirchoff, "Advertising in the Digital Age," *Congressional Research Service* (February 1, 2011): 5, 15; Kantar Media, "Kantar Media Reports U.S. Advertising Expenditures Increased 0.8 Percent in 2011," press release (March 12, 2012), on the Internet at http://www.KantarMediaNA.com (accessed May 10, 2012); U.S. Census Bureau, *Statistical Abstract of the United States: 2012* (Washington, DC: U.S. Government Printing Office, 2011), 785.

43. Robert W. McChesney, John Bellamy Foster, Inger L. Stole, and Hannah Holleman, "The Sales Effort and Monopoly Capitalism," *Monthly Review* (April 2009): 16.

44. Peter Hart and Janine Jackson, "Media Lick the Hand That Feeds Them," *Extra!* (November–December 2005): 21–23; Janine Jackson, "12th Annual Fear and Favor Review: In Advertisers We Trust," *Extra!* (April 2012): 7–8.

45. Jim Naureckas, "Corporate Censorship Matters: The Case of NBC," *Extra!* (November–December 1995): 13.

46. Lisa Myers's quotes were cited in "NBC's Dodgy Coverage of GE's $0 Tax Bill," *Extra!* (May 2011): 3.

47. Ibid.

48. Sheldon Rampton and John Stauber, "This Report Brought to You by Monsanto," *Progressive* (July 1998): 22–25.

49. Jane Akre, "We Report, They Decide: Fox TV Censors Series on Milk Hazards," *National News Reporter* (June 1998): 13.

50. Liane Casten, "Florida Appeals Court Orders Akre-Wilson Must Pay Trial Costs for $24.3 Billion Fox Television: Couple Warns Journalists of Danger to Free Speech, Whistle Blower Protection," in *Censored 2006*, ed. Peter Phillips and Project Censored (New York: Seven Stories Press, 2005), 165.

51. Sheldon Rampton and John Stauber, "Oprah's Free—Are We?" *Extra!* (May–June 1998): 11–12. See also Ralph Nader, "Product Libel," *Public Citizen News* (May–June 1998): 4.

52. Julie Hollar, Janine Jackson, and Hilary Goldstein, "Outside (and Inside) Influence on the News: Fear & Favor 2005," *Extra!* (March–April 2006): 15–20.

53. Peter Hart, "Fear and Favor 2008," *Extra!* (April 2009): 10.

54. Bagdikian, *The Media Monopoly*, 5th ed., 218. See also Andrew Jay Schwartzman, Cheryl A. Leanza, and Harold Feld, "The Legal Case for Diversity in Broadcast Ownership," in *The Future of Media: Resistance and Reform in the 21st Century*, ed. Robert McChesney, Russell Newman, and Ben Scott (New York: Seven Stories Press, 2005), 159.

55. Alex Weprin, "'Nightly Business Report' Sold Yet Again," *TVNEWSER* (November 16, 2011): 1–3, on the Internet at http://www.mediabistro/tvnewser (accessed August 1, 2012); Peter Hart, "Charlie Rose's Elite Meet-and-Greet," *Extra!* (November 2010): 13–14.

56. In radio, three examples of popular progressive radio talk-show hosts who lost their shows and jobs were Jim Hightower (ABC), Mike Malloy (WLS, Chicago), and Pat Thurston (KSRO, Santa Rosa, California). In all three cases media managers denied that their progressive views had anything to do with the decisions to fire them. See Kimberly Pohlman, "Solid Ratings Don't Protect Progressive Radio Voices," *Extra!* (July–August 2000): 22; Edward S. Herman, "The Media Mega-Mergers," *Dollars and Sense* (May–June 1996): 8–13; "Action Alert," *Extra!* (December 1995): 4.

57. Peter Hart, "Olbermann's Countdown Reaches Zero," *Extra!* (March 2011): 5; Michael Corcoran, "Uygur Out at MSNBC," *Extra!* (November 2011): 11–12.

58. Neil deMause, "Economy Is the Issue That Isn't," *Extra!* (October 2012): 10–11; Hart, "Right and Early"; Peter Hart and Julie Hollar, "Guide to Election Coverage 2012," *Extra!* (October 2012): 6–9; Janine Jackson, "New Media—but Familiar Lack of Diversity," *Extra!* (June 2012): 12–13.

59. Robert W. McChesney, *The Problem of the Media* (New York: Monthly Review Press, 2004), 98–117; McChesney and Foster, "'Left-Wing' Media?"; Parry, "The Right-Wing Media Machine," 6–19.

60. Domhoff, *Who Rules America?*, 5th ed., 201–4.

61. Joel Bleifuss, "The War on Teachers: Pick a Side," *In These Times* (November 2012): 16–17; Diana Kendall, *Framing Class: Media Representations of Wealth and Poverty in America*, 2nd ed. (Lanham, MD: Rowman and Littlefield, 2011), 125–37; Christopher Martin, *Framed!: Labor and the Corporate Media* (Ithaca, NY: Cornell University Press, 2003).

62. Robert Bruno, "Evidence of Bias in the Chicago Tribune Coverage of Organized Labor," *Labor Studies Journal* (September 2009): 385–407; Joshua Carreiro, "Newspaper Coverage of the U.S. Labor Movement: The Case of Anti-Union Firings," *Labor Studies Journal* (September 2005): 1–20; Peter Hart, "Surprised by Solidarity in Wisconsin," *Extra!* (April 2011): 6–7; Diane E. Schmidt, "Public Opinion and Media Coverage of Labor Unions," *Journal of Labor Research* (Spring 1993): 151–64; Amy Traub, "War on Public Workers," *Nation* (July 8, 2010): 4–6.

63. Salary figures were compiled from Stephen Battaglio and Michael Schneider, "Who Earn$ What," *TV Guide* (August 13–26, 2012): 16–21; and from "Celebrity Net Worth" (2012), on the Internet at http://www.celebritynetworth.com (accessed October 1, 2012).

64. "'Shared Sacrifice' at the Country Club," *Extra!* (May 2012): 3.

65. Salary figures are from the sources listed in note 63 and from Eric Boehlert, "Struggling Clear Channel and Rush Limbaugh's $400 Million Payday," Media Matters for America (March 16, 2012), on the Internet at http://mediamatters.org (accessed October 1, 2012); Oprah Winfrey's net worth is from "The Forbes 400: The Richest People in America," *Forbes* (September 19, 2012), on the Internet at http://www.forbes.com (accessed October 10, 2012).

66. Peter Hart, "This Week in Beltway Think," *Extra!* (November 2010): 15; Hart, "Right and Early."

67. Media Matters for America, "If It's Sunday, It's Conservative" (February 14, 2006), 1, on the Internet at http://www.essentialaction.org (accessed November 26, 2006).

68. Hart, "Right and Early," 10.

69. Hart, "This Week in Beltway Think."

70. Hart, "Right and Early," 11.

71. "From the Left: More Than a Figure of Speech?" *Extra!Update* (February 1996): 1.

72. Ina Howard, "Power Sources," *Extra!* (May–June 2002): 14.

73. Janine Jackson, "ABC's 'Made in America' a Shoddy Product," *Extra!* (April 2011): 5.

74. Bagdikian, *The Media Monopoly*, 5th ed., 52.

75. For examples, see Peter Hart, "Fear & Favor 10th Annual Review," *Extra!* (May 2010): 11–13; Janine Jackson, "11th Annual Fear & Favor Report," *Extra!* (March 2011): 13–15; Jackson, "12th Annual Fear & Favor Review"; Jackson, "13th Annual Fear & Favor Review."

76. For examples, see the sources cited in notes 61 and 62; see also Richard Whitmire and Andrew J. Rotherham, "How Teachers Unions Lost the Media," *Wall Street Journal*, October 2, 2009, on the Internet at http://www.wsj.com (accessed May 1, 2012).

77. Peter Hart, "Not for Teacher," *Extra!* (November 2012): 7.

78. Theresa Moran, "Chicago Teachers Raise the Bar," *Labor Notes* (October 2012): 1.

79. Hart, "Not for Teacher," 8.

80. Sady Doyle, "Learning from Karen Lewis," *In These Times* (November 2012): 19; Micah Uetricht and Jason Perez, "Democratic to the CORE," *In These Times* (December 2012): 32.

81. Peter Hart, "First, Bash the Teachers," *Extra!* (September 2010): 6–7; Hart, "Surprised by Solidarity in Wisconsin," 6–7; Whitmire and Rotherham, "How Teachers Unions Lost the Media."

82. Hart, "Surprised by Solidarity in Wisconsin," 6; Doyle, "Learning from Karen Lewis."

83. Bagdikian, *The Media Monopoly*, 5th ed., 44.

84. Dolny, "Think Tank Spectrum Revisited."

85. The 2010 total operating revenue ($81.7 million) and total operating contributions ($71.3 million) are from the Heritage Foundation *2010 Annual Report*, Washington, DC,

31; the 2010 total operating revenue listed in the *2010 Annual Report* is *slightly more* than the $78.2 million "Total Revenue" listed by the organization on page 1, line 12, of its 2010 federal tax return (see note 87); but it is *somewhat less* than the $89.9 million "Total Unrestricted Revenue and Support" figure listed in the Heritage Foundation's "Financial Report" (December 31, 2010), 3.

86. Heritage financial supporters are listed in its *2010 Annual Report*, 32–33.

87. U.S. Department of the Treasury, Internal Revenue Service, "Return of Organization Exempt from Income Tax—Form 990, The Heritage Foundation," 23-7327730 (Washington, DC, 2010), schedule J, part II.

88. Domhoff, *Who Rules America?*, 6th ed., 124.

89. Eyal Press, "Spin Cities," *Nation* (November 18, 1996): 30.

90. Robert W. McChesney, "Journalism, Democracy, and Class Struggle," *Monthly Review* (November 2000): 7.

91. Carolyn Cutrone and Steve Rendall, "Deficit-Obsessed Media Misinform on Causes," *Extra!* (September 2011): 4–5.

92. Shamus Cooke, "Democrats and the Fiscal Cliff," *CounterPunch* (November 12, 2012), on the Internet at http://www.counterpunch.org (accessed November 17, 2012); Barry Grey, "Leaked 'Grand Bargain' Document Details Obama's Plan for Cuts in Entitlement Programs," *World Socialist Web Site* (November 15, 2012), on the Internet at http://www.wsws.org (accessed November 17, 2012).

93. Kevin C. Brown, "The 'Liberal Media' and State Austerity," *Extra!* (June 2010): 9.

94. Cutrone and Rendall, "Deficit-Obsessed Media Misinform on Causes."

95. Jim Naureckas, "The Great British Mistake," *Extra!* (June 2012): 11.

96. "An Alternative to Austerity," *Nation* (January 28, 2013): 3; Michael Grunwald, "Cliff Dweller," *Time* (January 14, 2013): 25–31; Bhaskar Sunkara, "The Austerity Cliff," *In These Times* (December 2012): 5; Joel Bleifuss, "Watch Out, Grandma!" *In These Times* (February 2013): 5.

97. Jill Stein, "Austerity's Agent: The Real Obama Emerges (Again)," *CounterPunch* (January 18–20, 2013), on the Internet at http://www.counterpunch.org (accessed January 27, 2013).

98. "An Alternative to Austerity."

99. Bleifuss, "Watch Out, Grandma!"; Sarah Anderson and Scott Klinger, "A Pension Deficit Disorder," Institute for Policy Studies (November 27, 2012): 1, on the Internet at http://www.IPS-dc.org (accessed December 15, 2012).

100. Pew Research Center for the People and the Press, "Deep Divisions over Debt Reduction Proposals" (October 12, 2012), on the Internet at http://www.people-press.org (accessed November 11, 2012).

101. Randal Martin, "A Brief History of Propaganda," in *Censored 2012*, ed. Mickey Huff and Project Censored (New York: Seven Stories Press, 2011), 310.

102. These estimates of total employment in U.S. PR and news occupations are based on the authors' analyses of and extrapolations from data reported in the *Current Population Survey* (March 2012), for occupational codes that correspond to PR managers (60), PR specialists (2,825), and news analysts, reporters, and correspondents (2,810).

103. McChesney, "Journalism, Democracy, and Class Struggle," 7.

104. Bagdikian, *The New Media Monopoly*, 167; Robert W. McChesney, "This Isn't What Democracy Looks Like," *Monthly Review* (November 2012): 9–11, 25; McChesney, Foster, Stole, and Holleman, "The Sales Effort and Monopoly Capitalism," 14–16.

105. Jeff Cohen and Norman Solomon, *Adventures in MediaLand* (Monroe, ME: Common Courage Press, 1993), 45. See also McChesney, *Rich Media, Poor Democracy*, 252.

106. Bagdikian, *The Media Monopoly*, 5th ed., 58.

107. Maria Petrova, "Inequality and Media Capture," Working Paper Series, Social Science Research Network, Harvard University (February 6, 2006), 1, on the Internet at http://www.papers.ssrn.com (accessed December 28, 2006).

108. Sam Pizzigati, "Most Original Research on the Consequences of Inequality," *Too Much* (December 18, 2006): 4. Quote from Pizzigati, summarizing Petrova's findings.

109. Pew Research Center for the People and the Press, "Partisan Polarization Surges in Bush, Obama Years," *Trends in American Values: 1987–2012* (June 4, 2012), 61, 64, on the Internet at http://www.people-press.org (accessed November 11, 2012).

110. Pew Research Center for the People and the Press, "Public Support for Increased Trade, Except with South Korea and China" (November 9, 2010), 1–5, on the Internet at http://www.people-press.org (accessed November 3, 2012).

111. Lydia Saad, "Americans Decry Power of Lobbyists, Corporations, Banks, Feds," Gallup, Inc. (April 11, 2011), on the Internet at http://www.gallup.com (accessed June 3, 2012).

112. Pew Research Center for the People and the Press, "Auto Bailout Now Backed, Stimulus Divisive" (February, 23, 2012), 6, on the Internet at http://www.people-press.org (accessed November 3, 2012).

113. Pew Research Center for the People and the Press, "Little Change in Public's Response to 'Capitalism,' 'Socialism'" (December, 28, 2011), 1–5, on the Internet at http://www.people-press.org (accessed November 3, 2012).

114. Bagdikian, *The Media Monopoly*, 5th ed., 206.

115. McChesney, "This Isn't What Democracy Looks Like," 19–26.

116. McChesney, *Rich Media, Poor Democracy*, 63–77; McChesney, "Journalism, Democracy, and Class Struggle"; Mark Lloyd, "Lessons for Realistic Radicals in the Information Age," in *The Future of Media: Resistance and Reform in the 21st Century*, ed. Robert McChesney, Russell Newman, and Ben Scott (New York: Seven Stories Press, 2005), 73–95; Parry, "Right-Wing Media Machine," 6–10.

117. McChesney, "Journalism, Democracy, and Class Struggle," 1–15. See also Norman Solomon, "The Media Oligarchy: Undermining Journalism, Obstructing Democracy," in *Censored 2001*, ed. Peter Phillips and Project Censored (New York: Seven Stories Press, 2001), 277–90; and G. William Domhoff, *Who Rules America?*, 4th ed. (Boston: McGraw-Hill, 2002), 1–13.

118. Martin N. Marger, *Social Inequality: Patterns and Processes*, 5th ed. (New York: McGraw-Hill, 2011), 238–46, 375–77. See also Gail Dines, "Capitalism's Pitchmen," *Dollars and Sense* (May 1992): 18–20; and Kevin Phillips, "Fat City," *Time* (September 26, 1994): 49–56.

CHAPTER 11: EDUCATING FOR PRIVILEGE: DREAMING, STREAMING, AND CREAMING

1. Roslyn Arlin Mickelson, "The Attitude-Achievement Paradox among Black Adolescents," *Sociology of Education* 63 (1990): 44–61; Patricia A. Adler, Steven J. Kless, and Peter Adler, "Socialization to Gender Roles: Popularity among Elementary School Boys and Girls," *Sociology of Education* 65 (1992): 169–87; Karl S. Alexander, Doris R. Entwisle, and Carrie

S. Horsey, "From First Grade Forward: Early Foundations of High School Dropout," *Sociology of Education* 70 (1997): 87–107; Vincent J. Roscigno and James W. Ainsworth-Darnell, "Race, Cultural Capital, and Educational Resources: Persistent Inequalities and Achievement Returns," *Sociology of Education* 72 (1999): 158–78; Samuel R. Lucas and Aaron D. Good, "Race, Class, and Tournament Track Mobility," *Sociology of Education* 74 (2001): 139–56; Dennis J. Condron, "Social Class, School and Non-School Environments, and Black/White Inequalities in Children's Learning," *American Sociological Review* 74 (2009): 683–708.

2. Martin N. Marger, *Social Inequality: Patterns and Processes*, 5th ed. (New York: McGraw Hill, 2011), 218–35.

3. Michael B. Katz, *The Irony of Early School Reform* (Cambridge, MA: Harvard University Press, 1968).

4. Maureen T. Hallinan, "Tracking: From Theory to Practice," *Sociology of Education* 67 (April 1994): 79.

5. Robert Granfield and Thomas Koenig, "Pathways into Elite Law Firms: Professional Stratification and Social Networks," in *Research in Politics and Society*, vol. 4, *The Political Consequences of Social Networks*, ed. Gwen Moore and J. Allen Whitt (Greenwich, CT: JAI Press, 1992), 325–51.

6. Brian Doherty, "Those Who Can't, Test," *Mother Jones* (November–December 1998): 71.

7. Tiffani Chin and Meredith Phillips, "Social Reproduction and Child-Rearing Practices: Social Class, Children's Agency, and the Summer Camp Activity Gap," *Sociology of Education* 77 (July 2004): 185–210.

8. Christopher Hayes, "Why Elites Fail," *Nation* (June 25, 2012): 11–18.

9. Eric Pace, "B. Gerald Cantor, Philanthropist and Owner of Rodin Collection, Is Dead at 79," *New York Times*, July 6, 1996.

10. The *Chicago Tribune* published a much-abbreviated eight-paragraph story about Cantor obtained from the *New York Times* news service. The *Tribune* story started with the same lead sentence used in the fifty-five-paragraph *Times* story, revealing the extraordinary appeal of the rags-to-riches story, even when it may not be true in its substance.

11. Carla O'Connor, "Race, Class, and Gender in America: Narratives of Opportunity among Low-Income African American Youths," *Sociology of Education* 72 (1999): 137–57.

12. Richard Wohl, "The 'Rags to Riches Story': An Episode of Secular Idealism," in *Class, Status, and Power*, ed. Reinhard Bendix and Seymour M. Lipset (New York: Free Press, 1966), 501–26.

13. U.S. Department of Education, National Center for Educational Statistics, *Digest of Educational Statistics*, ed. Thomas D. Snyder, Charlene M. Hoffman, and Clair M. Geddes, NCES 2001–034 (Washington, DC: Government Printing Office, 2000); America's Promise Alliance, "Building a Grad Nation Report" (March 19, 2012), on the Internet at http://www.americaspromise.org (accessed July 15, 2012).

14. U.S. Census Bureau, *Statistical Abstract of the United States: 2012* (Washington, DC: U.S. Government Printing Office, 2011), 151.

15. U.S. Census Bureau, *Statistical Abstract of the United States: 2012*, 189.

16. For a discussion of these two different views of why educational requirements for many jobs have increased, see Randall Collins, *The Credential Society* (New York: Academic Press, 1979); and Randall Collins, "Functional and Conflict Theories of Educational Stratification," *American Sociological Review* 36 (1971): 1002–19.

17. Edgar Litt, "Civic Education, Community Norms, and Political Indoctrination," *American Sociological Review* 28 (February 1963): 69–75.

18. John Bellamy Foster, "Education and the Structural Crisis of Capital: The U.S. Case," *Monthly Review* (July–August 2011): 7–8; Jonathan Kozol, "'A Deeper Truth Than Newspapers and Networks Are Likely to Provide,'" *Extra!* (September 2010): 10.

19. Litt, "Civic Education, Community Norms, and Political Indoctrination," 72, 73.

20. Dean Jaros, *Socialization to Politics* (New York: Praeger, 1973); Edward S. Greenberg, *Political Socialization* (New York: Atherton, 1970).

21. Alan Wolfe, *The Seamy Side of Democracy* (New York: David McKay, 1973); Ira Katznelson and Mark Kesselman, *The Politics of Power* (New York: Harcourt Brace Jovanovich, 1975).

22. Scott Cummings and Del Taebel, "The Economic Socialization of Children: A Neo-Marxist Analysis," *Social Problems* 26 (December 1978): 198–210.

23. "School Finance," *Education Week* (June 20, 2011): 1, on the Internet at http://www.edweek.org (accessed November 10, 2012).

24. Robert S. Michael, Terry E. Spradlin, and Fatima R. Carson, "Changes in Indiana School Funding," Center for Evaluation and Educational Policy, *Education Policy Brief* 7 (Summer 2009): 1–16.

25. Ibid., 2.

26. Harold Wenglinsky, "How Money Matters: The Effect of School District Spending on Academic Achievement," *Sociology of Education* 70 (July 1997): 221–37.

27. Dennis J. Condron and Vincent J. Roscigno, "Disparities Within: Unequal Spending and Achievement in an Urban School District," *Sociology of Education* 76 (January 2003): 18–36.

28. Ibid., 20.

29. Christopher Jencks, Marshall Smith, Henry Acland, Mary Jo Bane, David Cohen, Herbert Gintis, Barbara Heyns, and Stephan Michelson, *Inequality: Reassessment of the Effect of Family and Schooling in America* (New York: Harper and Row, 1972).

30. *Education Week* (May 3, 1995), on the Internet at http://www.edweek.org.

31. Maureen T. Hallinan, "Ability Grouping and Student Learning," in *Brookings Papers on Educational Policy*, ed. Diane Ravitch (Washington, DC: Brookings Institute Press, 2003); Myra Pollack Sadker and David Miller Sadker, *Teachers, Schools, and Society*, 6th ed. (New York: McGraw-Hill, 2003).

32. Robert Rosenthal and Lenore Jacobson, *Pygmalion in the Classroom* (New York: Holt, Rinehart and Winston, 1968).

33. Karl S. Alexander, Martha Cook, and Edward McDill, "Curriculum Tracking and Educational Stratification," *American Sociological Review* 43 (1982): 47–66; Sally Kilgore, "The Organizational Context of Tracking in Schools," *American Sociological Review* 56 (1991): 189–203.

34. U.S. Census Bureau, *Statistical Abstract of the United States: 2012*, 170.

35. U.S. Department of Education, National Center for Education Statistics, *The Condition of Education 2012* (Washington, DC: U.S. Government Printing Office, 2012).

36. Ron Renchler, *Financial Equity in Schools*, ERIC Digest no. 76 (Eugene, OR: ERIC Clearinghouse in Educational Management, 1994); U.S. Department of Education, *Digest of Educational Statistics, 2000* (Washington, DC: U.S. Government Printing Office, 2001).

37. Jonathan Kozol, *Savage Inequalities* (New York: Harper, 1991).

38. Noreen Connell, "Underfunded Schools: Why Money Matters," *Dollars and Sense* (March–April 1998): 14–17, 39.

39. Ibid.

40. William A. Sewell, A. O. Haller, and G. W. Ohlandorf, "The Educational and Early Occupational Status Attainment Process," *American Sociological Review* 35 (1970): 1014–27.

41. Martha J. Bailey and Susan M. Dynarski, "Gains and Gaps: Changing Inequality in U.S. College Entry and Completion," in *Whither Opportunity? Rising Inequality, Schools, and Children's Life Chances*, ed. Greg J. Duncan and Richard J. Murnane (New York: Russell Sage, September 2011); Anthony P. Carnevale and Stephen J. Rose, "Socioeconomic Status, Race/Ethnicity, and Selective College Admissions" (New York: The Century Foundation, March 2003); William A. Sewell and Vimal Shah, "Parents' Education and Children's Educational Aspirations and Achievements" *American Sociological Review* 33 (1968): 191–209.

42. Derek Thompson, "What's the Best Investment: Stocks, Bonds, Homes . . . or College?" *Atlantic* (June 27, 2011); U.S. Bureau of Labor Statistics, "Household Economic Studies," Current Population Survey (Washington, DC: U.S. Government Printing Office, 2010).

43. John Miller, "Putting the Screws to Generation Screwed," *Dollars and Sense* (September–October 2012): 10.

44. U.S. Census Bureau, *Statistical Abstract of the United States: 2012*, 187.

45. Ibid., 186.

46. Dan Schneider, "Occupying Student Debt," *Dollars and Sense* (January–February 2012): 6.

47. Thomas Mortenson, National Council of Educational Opportunity Associations, Washington, DC, reported in Karen W. Arenson, "Cuts in Tuition Assistance Put College beyond Reach of Poorest Students," *New York Times*, January 27, 1997; Richard Kahlenberg, ed., *America's Untapped Resource: Low-Income Students in Higher Education* (New York: The Century Foundation, 2003).

48. Miller, "Putting the Screws to Generation Screwed," 10–11.

49. U.S. Department of Education, National Center for Educational Statistics, *The Condition of Education 2012*.

50. U.S. Census Bureau, *Statistical Abstract of the United States: 2012*, 189.

51. Jerry A. Jacobs, "Gender and Academic Specialties: Trends among Recipients of College Degrees in the 1980s," *Sociology of Education* 68 (1995): 81–98.

52. U.S. Census Bureau, *Statistical Abstract of the United States: 2012*, 178.

53. "Rich College, Poor College," *Business Week* (December 20, 2004): 88–90.

54. Adrian Wooldridge, "Ever Higher Society, Ever Harder to Ascend," *Economist* (December 29, 2004); Michael Schwalbe, *Rigging the Game: How Inequality Is Reproduced in Everyday Life* (New York: Oxford University Press, 2008), 75–79.

55. "Salary Offers to College Class of 2009 Are Flat," International Association of Employment (2010), on the Internet at http://www.iae.com (accessed June 10, 2011).

56. U.S. Department of Education, National Center for Education Statistics, *The Condition of Education 1996*, ed. Thomas Smith, NCES 96–304 (Washington, DC: U.S. Government Printing Office, 1996); Deshundra Jefferson, "Most Lucative College Degrees," *Money Magazine* (September 21, 2004).

57. Lauren A. Rivera, "Ivies, Extracurriculars, and Exclusion: Elite Employers' Use of Educational Credentials," *Research in Stratification and Mobility* 29 (2011): 71–90.

58. U.S. Department of Education, National Center for Education Statistics, "Projections of Education Statistics to 2016," table 24, Institute of Education Statistics (December 18, 2006), on the Internet at http://www.nces.gov (accessed January 15, 2013).

59. G. William Domhoff, *Who Rules America?*, 6th ed. (New York: McGraw Hill, 2010), 57–61.

60. James Hearn, "Academic and Nonacademic Influences on the College Destinations of 1980 High School Graduates," *Sociology of Education* 64 (July 1991): 158–71.

61. David Karen, "Toward a Political-Organizational Model of Gatekeeping: The Case of Elite Colleges," *Sociology of Education* 63 (1990): 227–40.

62. Ernest Haveman and Patricia Salter West, *They Went to College* (New York: Harcourt, Brace, 1952), 180.

63. Scott Davies and Neil Guppy, "Fields of Study, College Selectivity, and Student Inequalities in Higher Education," *Social Forces* 75 (1997): 1417–38; David Karen, "Changes in Access to Higher Education in the United States: 1980–1992," *Sociology of Education* 75 (July 2002): 191–210; Daniel Golden, *The Price of Admission: How America's Ruling Class Buys Its Way into Elite Colleges and Who Gets Left Outside the Gates* (New York: Crown, 2006); Danette Gerald and Kati Haycock, "Engines of Inequality: Diminishing Equity in the Nation's Premier Public Universities" (Washington, DC: The Education Trust, 2006).

64. Ann L. Mullen, Kimberly A. Goyette, and Joseph A. Soares, "Who Goes to Graduate School? Social and Educational Correlates of Educational Continuation after College," *Sociology of Education* 76 (April 2003): 143–69.

65. Lawrence Mishel, Josh Bivens, Elise Gould, and Heidi Shierholz, *The State of Working America*, 12th ed. (Ithaca, NY: IRL Press, 2012), 65.

66. Pew Research Center, "The Lost Decade of the Middle Class" (August 22, 2012): 84, on the Internet at http://www.pewsocialtrends.org (accessed November 14, 2012).

67. Robert Perrucci et al., "The Two Faces of Racialized Space in a Predominantly White University," *International Journal of Contemporary Sociology* 37 (2000): 230–44.

68. Bruce D. Baker, David G. Sciarra, and Danielle Farrie, "Is School Funding Fair? A National Report Card" (Newark, NJ: Education Law Center, September 2010).

69. Foster, "Education and the Structural Crisis of Capital: The U.S. Case," 6–37.

CHAPTER 12: THE PACIFICATION OF EVERYDAY LIFE

1. Martin N. Marger, *Social Inequality: Patterns and Processes*, 5th ed. (New York: McGraw-Hill, 2011), 214.

2. Robert Goodman, *The Last Entrepreneurs: America's Regional Wars for Jobs and Dollars* (New York: Simon and Schuster, 1979).

3. For details on incentive packages, see Peter Eisenger, *The Rise of the Entrepreneurial State* (Madison: University of Wisconsin Press, 1988); Milward H. Brinton and Heide H. Newman, "State Incentive Packages and the Industrial Location Decision," *Economic Development Quarterly* 3 (1989): 203–22; Robert Perrucci, *Japanese Auto Transplants in the Heartland* (New York: Aldine de Gruyter, 1994).

4. Greg LeRoy, *The Great American Jobs Scam* (San Francisco: Berrett-Koehler, 2005), 2.

5. Kenneth P. Thomas, *Investment Incentives and the Global Competition for Capital* (Basingstoke, UK: Palgrave Macmillan, 2011), 7.

6. "The New Transplants," *UAW Research Bulletin* (January–February 1995): 10–11.

7. The term *catch-22* has come to refer to any "no-win situation." It is the title of Joseph Heller's 1961 classic satirical novel and refers to a fictional military rule that prevented U.S. military personnel from avoiding combat duty. The book critiques the organization, rules, and logic of the military bureaucracy via the experiences of the members of a fictional Air Force bomber squadron in World War II, but the Cold War and McCarthyism are its real targets.

8. Naomi Klein, *The Shock Doctrine* (New York: Holt, 2008).

9. Katherine Beckett, "Setting the Public Agenda: 'Street Crime' and Drug Use in American Politics," *Social Problems* 3 (1994): 425–47; Earl Wysong, Richard Aniskiewicz, and David Wright, "Truth and DARE: Tracking Drug Education to Graduation and as Symbolic Politics," *Social Problems* 41 (1994): 448–72.

10. Josmar Trujillo, "Media Laugh Off Criticism of Drug War," *Extra!* (December 2012): 6–7.

11. For example, see Office of National Drug Control Policy (ONDCP), *The National Drug Control Strategy* (Washington, DC: National Criminal Justice Reference Service, 1992), 9. See also Office of National Drug Control Policy, *National Drug Control Strategy: 2001 Annual Report* (Washington, DC: U.S. Government Printing Office, 2001), 1–7; Office of National Drug Control Policy, *National Drug Control Strategy: 2012* (Washington, DC: U.S. Government Printing Office, 2012), v.

12. Office of National Drug Control Policy (ONDCP), *National Drug Control Budget: FY 2013 Budget Funding Highlights* (Washington, DC: The White House, February 2013), 13.

13. Jimmy Carter, "Call Off the Global Drug War," *New York Times*, June 16, 2011.

14. U.S. Department of Justice, Bureau of Justice Statistics, "Key Facts at a Glance: Correctional Populations, 1980–2009," on the Internet at http://bjs.ojp.usdoj.gov (accessed October 10, 2012); Lauren E. Glaze and Erika Parks, "Correctional Populations in the United States, 2011," *Bureau of Justice Statistics Bulletin* (November 2012): 8.

15. The Sentencing Project, *Trends in U.S. Corrections*, "Federal & State Prison Population, by Offense, 2010," and "Number of People in Prisons and Jails for Drug Offenses, 1980 and 2010," on the Internet at http://www.sentencingproject.org (accessed October 10, 2012).

16. Bruce Western and Becky Pettit, "Incarceration & Social Inequality," *Daedalus* 139 (Summer 2010): 8–19.

17. The Sentencing Project, "People in State and Federal Prisons, By Race and Ethnicity, 2010," *Trends in U.S. Corrections*, on the Internet at http://www.sentencingproject.org (accessed October 10, 2012).

18. U.S. Census Bureau, "Selected Social Characteristics in the United States, 2010," on the Internet at http://factfinder.census.gov (accessed October 10, 2012).

19. Kellie E. M. Barr, Michael P. Farrell, Grace M. Barnes, and John W. Welte, "Race, Class, and Gender Differences in Substance Abuse: Evidence of Middle Class/Underclass Polarization among Black Males," *Social Problems* 40 (1993): 314–27; William S. Harder and Howard D. Chilcoat, "Cocaine Use and Educational Achievement: Understanding a Changing Association Over the Past 2 Decades," *American Journal of Public Health* 97 (October 2007): 1790–95.

20. D.A.R.E. America, "The New D.A.R.E. Junior High/Middle School Curriculum," on the Internet at http://www.dare.com (accessed July 9, 2011); Earl Wysong and David Wright, "A Decade of DARE: Efficacy, Politics, and Drug Education," *Sociological Focus* 28 (1995): 283–311.

21. Erich Goode, *Drugs in American Society*, 8th ed. (Boston: McGraw-Hill, 2011), 325; Office of National Drug Control Policy, *National Drug Control Strategy: 2012*, 6.

22. Jeffrey Reiman, *The Rich Get Richer and the Poor Get Prison*, 5th ed. (Boston: Allyn and Bacon, 1998), 154.

23. Hannah Holleman, Robert W. McChesney, John Bellamy Foster, and R. Jamil Jonna, "The Penal State in an Age of Crisis," *Monthly Review* (June 2009): 1–17.

24. "A 40-Year Wish List," *Wall Street Journal*, January 28, 2009, on the Internet at http://online.wsj.com (accessed August 25, 2011).

25. Rachel Coen, "Are You a Terrorist?" *Extra!* (November–December 2001): 21–22.

26. Coen, "Are You a Terrorist?" 21; Ira Katznelson, Mark Kesselman, and Alan Draper, *The Politics of Power*, 5th ed. (Belmont, CA: Thomson Wadsworth, 2006), 263.

27. Charles Derber, *The Wilding of America*, 5th ed. (New York: Worth, 2011), 109–112.

28. Tom Cohen, "Obama Approves Extension of Expiring Patriot Act Provisions," *CNN Politics* (May 27, 2011), on the Internet at http://articles.cnn.com (accessed May 30, 2012).

29. Beverly Goldberg, "Patriot Act Renewal Renews Reformers' Determination," *American Libraries Magazine* (May 31, 2011), on the Internet at http://americanlibrariesmagazine.org/news (accessed May 30, 2012); American Civil Liberties Union, "Congress Reauthorizes Overbroad Patriot Act Provisions," press release (May 26, 2011).

30. American Civil Liberties Union, "ACLU Says Justice Dept.'s PATRIOT Act Website Creates New Myths about Controversial Law," press release (August 26, 2003).

31. Cohen, "Obama Approves Extension of Expiring Patriot Act Provisions."

CHAPTER 13: THE CULTURE INDUSTRY AND PACIFICATION

1. Patrick Morrison, "Media Monopoly Revisited," *Extra!* (October 2011): 13–15.

2. Motion Picture Association of America, "Theatrical Market Statistics, 2011," 18, on the Internet at http://www.mpaa.com (accessed May 10, 2012); Nielsen Company, "State of the Media: Consumer Usage Report, 2011," 1, on the Internet at http://www.nielsen.com (accessed May 10, 2012).

3. U.S. Census Bureau, *Statistical Abstract of the United States: 2012* (Washington, DC: U.S. Government Printing Office, 2011), 723.

4. U.S. Census Bureau, *Statistical Abstract of the United States: 2012*, 720; Nielsen Company, "State of the Media: Consumer Usage Report, 2011."

5. John Suhler, "VSS Communications Industry Forecast 2010," *Communications Industry Spending & Consumption Trends*, Veronis, Suhler, Stevenson (2011), on the Internet at http://www.vssforecast.com (accessed May 10, 2012).

6. U.S. Department of Commerce, *Statistical Abstract of the United States: 1996* (Washington, DC: U.S. Government Printing Office, 1995), 572.

7. "Average Time Spent with Consumer Media per User per Year," *VSS Communications Industry Forecast, 2011–2015*, Veronis, Suhler, Stevenson (2011), on the Internet at http://www.vssforecast.com (accessed May 10, 2012).

8. John Bellamy Foster and Robert W. McChesney, "The Internet's Unholy Marriage to Capitalism," *Monthly Review* (March 2011): 1–30; Suzanne M. Kirchhoff, "Advertising in the Digital Age," *Congressional Research Service* (February 1, 2011): 5–16.

9. Jerry Mander, "The Privatization of Consciousness," *Monthly Review* (October 2012): 18–41; Robert W. McChesney, John Bellamy Foster, Inger L. Stole, and Hannah Holleman, "The Sales Effort and Monopoly Capital," *Monthly Review* (April 2009): 1–23.

10. Tom Zaniello, *Working Stiffs, Union Maids, Reds, and Riffraff: An Expanded Guide to Films about Labor* (Ithaca, NY: IRL Press, 2003). A larger list of "more than 1500 films and videos that focus on working people" can be found on the "Labor Film Database" website (laborfilms.com). But compared to the total of 2,371,463 movies, videos, and TV programs listed on the Internet Movie Database website, 1,500 is an incredibly small number. See "Resources," *Labor Notes* (March 2013): 13.

11. Internet Movie Database, Inc., "IMDb Database Statistics: Feature Titles," 1880–2012 (2012), on the Internet at http://www.imdb.com/stats (accessed November 11, 2012).

12. Motion Picture Association of America, "Theatrical Market Statistics, 2011," 17.

13. Mick Martin and Marsha Porter, *1995 Video Movie Guide* (New York: Ballantine Books, 1994); Jim Craddock, ed., *VideoHound's Golden Movie Retriever: 2006* (Detroit: Thomson-Gale, 2006). We were unable to use the 2006 edition of the *DVD & Video Guide* by Martin and Porter as a source for our 2006 study because this publication no longer classifies films by genre categories. The *VideoHound* guide we used did classify films into genre categories, but these were more specific than the general categories used in our first study. To replicate the categories used in our 1996 study, we combined film titles from several specific categories used by the *VideoHound* source into the three general categories. For example, the drama category (5,180 films) from which we sampled 518 dramas for our 2006 study was created by combining films from 12 specific drama categories used to classify drama film titles in the *VideoHound* source (e.g., adventure drama, comedy drama, historical drama, etc.).

14. Earl Wysong, "Class in the Movies" (1996), unpublished paper.

15. Earl Wysong and Robert Perrucci, "Media and the Marginalization of Social Class Inequalities," *Journal of the Indiana Academy of the Social Sciences* XI (2007): 14–26. See this source for a complete description of the content analysis methodology used in both studies.

16. Internet Movie Database, Inc., "U.S. Documentary Releases, by Year," on the Internet at http://www.imdb.com/stats (accessed November 11, 2012); Michael Cieply, "A Strong Crop of Documentaries, but Barely Seen," *New York Times*, January 2, 2011, on the Internet at http://www.nytimes.com (accessed June 1, 2012).

17. Michael Atkinson, "Greenwald vs. Goliath," *Progressive* (September 2012): 33–34.

18. Steven J. Ross, *Working-Class Hollywood: Silent Film and the Shaping of Class in America* (Princeton, NJ: Princeton University Press, 1998).

19. Matthew Rothschild, "The Progressive Interview: Roger Ebert," *Progressive* (August 2003): 34.

20. Ross, *Working-Class Hollywood*, 255.

21. Marketing Charts Staff, "Average Hour-Long TV Show Is 36% Commercials," MC Marketing Charts (May 7, 2009), on the Internet at http://www.marketingcharts.com (accessed November 10, 2012).

22. U.S. Census Bureau, *Statistical Abstract of the United States: 2007* (Washington, DC: U.S. Government Printing Office, 2006), 785; Kantar Media, "Kantar Media Reports U.S. Advertising Expenditures Increased 0.8 Percent in 2011," press release (March 12, 2012), 6, on the Internet at http://www.KantarMediaNA.com (accessed May 10, 2012).

23. Marketing Charts Staff, "Average Hour-Long TV Show Is 36% Commercials."

24. Diana Kendall, *Framing Class: Media Representations of Wealth and Poverty in America*, 2nd ed. (Lanham, MD: Rowman and Littlefield, 2011), 49, 68; Karen Sternheimer, *Celebrity Culture and the American Dream* (New York: Routledge, 2011), 10–15.

25. Richard Butsch, "Class and Gender in Four Decades of Television Situation Comedy: Plus ça Change . . . ," *Critical Studies in Mass Communications* 9 (1992): 387–99.

26. Lewis Freeman, "Social Mobility in Television Comedies," *Critical Studies in Mass Communications* 9 (1992): 400–406, quote from 405.

27. The "Oprahfication of the Mind" concept was not developed as a personal criticism of or as a personal attack on Oprah Winfrey. Although Oprah ended her syndicated program, *The Oprah Winfrey Show*, in 2011 (after twenty-five years), she continues to appear on her OWN network, launched January 1, 2011, with Discovery Communications. (See Ileane Rudolph, "Oprah's Grand Finale," *TV Guide* [May 23–29, 2011]: 18–21.) Oprah's original show remains, in our view, the model that many current, popular TV-talk-show-infotainment-format programs have sought to emulate. Organized around a chatty, informal, newslike style, Oprah's show, which sometimes dealt with serious topics, typically followed this formula: "Keep it light, keep it bright, keep it moving!" Her legacy lives on in similar programs like *The View*, *Live with Kelly*, and many others.

Since TV is largely an entertainment business, the purpose of Oprah-like shows is to attract and entertain large TV audiences with the "right demographics" so as to maximize profits for the firms that produce the programs and those that advertise on them. There is nothing wrong with entertainment (we're for it!), but when shows like Oprah's focus on "serious" topics (like class or race) the treatment is necessarily superficial and often includes a touch of glamor. The end result is that viewers are often entertained, but they are also encouraged to feel as if they've been informed—which we believe is rarely the case in any meaningful sense of the term. Oprah's show and those that now imitate her style reflect institutional imperatives of the commerical media, which, among others, are to generate large profits and produce content that does not in any serious way question, challenge, or threaten the economic, political, and cultural status quo. Oprahfication is an insidious media-induced process whereby viewers are encouraged to believe that by viewing Oprah-like shows they are being informed, when in fact they are simply being entertained, bedazzled, beguiled, and, ultimately, pacified. For a sympathetic view of Oprah as a consoling cultural presence, see Bhaskar Sunkara, "Oprah-iate of the People," *In These Times* (August 2012): 40–41.

28. Vito Rispo, "How to Stop Ad Blindness: Novelty in Advertising Is Key," *Ad Savy* (2012), on the Internet at http://www.adsavy.org (accessed November 10, 2012).

29. Ronald Dahl, "Burned Out and Bored," *Newsweek* (December 15, 1997): 18; Thomas Frank, *The Conquest of Cool: Business Culture, Counterculture, and the Rise of Hip Consumerism* (Chicago: University of Chicago Press, 1997); Thomas Frank, *One Market Under God* (New York: Doubleday, 2000); McChesney, Foster, Stole, Holleman, "The Sales Effort and Monopoly Capital," 10.

30. Alexa, "Top Sites in United States" (2012), on the Internet at http://www.alexa.com (accessed December 1, 2012); Nielsenwire, "May 2012—Top U.S. Web Brands and News Websites" (June 22, 2012), on the Internet at http://blog.nielsen.com (accessed July 14, 2012).

31. Michael Wolff, "The Web Is Dead?, A Debate; Who's to Blame: Them," *Wired* 18 (September 2010): 122–27.

32. Nielsenwire, "May 2012—Top U.S. Web Brands and News Websites."

33. Peter Hart and Julie Hollar, "Guide to Election Coverage 2012," *Extra!* (October 2012): 6–9. Elite-class pundits' advice continued *after* the 2012 elections. They encouraged Obama to support "centrist" policies like cuts in Social Security and Medicare benefits. They wanted him to govern from what they viewed as the "center" and to act as if he had *lost* the election. See Jim Naureckas, "The Hall of Fame of Bad Ideas," *Extra!* (January 2013): 5.

34. The Editors, "A Progressive Surge," *Nation* (November 26, 2012): 3–6.

35. Ruth Conniff and Matthew Rothschild, "A Victory for the 99 Percent," *Progressive* (December 2012–January 2013): 10–11.

36. These examples were identified by scanning transcripts of the news content of nationally broadcast network TV news shows and newsmagazines. Transcripts were scanned for three national network evening TV news shows (ABC, CBS, NBC) and for three TV newsmagazines (*Dateline*: NBC, *20/20*: ABC, *60 Minutes*: CBS) covering the 2008–2012 period. The transcripts were accessed using the Nexis U.S. TV transcripts database.

37. Both programs are broadcast on *Comedy Central*, a Viacom-owned cable channel.

38. Samir Amin, "An Arab Springtime?" *Monthly Review* (October 2011): 8–28; Jonathan Schell, "The Revolutionary Moment," *Nation* (February 21, 2011): 3–6; Rami G. Khouri, "The Arab Awakening," *Nation* (September 12, 2011): 13–15.

39. Jeremy Gantz, "Voices from the Occupations," *In These Times* (December 2011): 16–18; Arun Gupta, "An Occupy Road Trip," *In These Times* (December 2011): 18–20; Nathan Schneider, "From Occupy Wall Street to Occupy Everywhere," *Nation* (October 31, 2011): 13–17.

40. Fadhel Kaboub, "On the Jasmine Revolution," *Dollars and Sense* (March–April 2011): 7–8; Karl Vick, "Big Brothers," *Time* (December 24, 2012): 26–30; "Newswatch: President Mohammed Morsi's Power Grab Inside Egypt's Union Federation," *Labor Notes* (January 2013): 5.

41. Rick Wolff, "Turning toward Solutions," *Dollars and Sense* (January–February 2012): 7–8; John Knefel, "Bored with Occupy—and Inequality," *Extra!* (May 2012): 6–7; Rachel Lears, "The Death and Life of Occupy," *In These Times* (September 2012): 27–28; Nathan Schneider, "Occupy, After Occupy," *Nation* (September 24, 2012): 13–17.

CHAPTER 14: CLASS IN THE TWENTY-FIRST CENTURY

1. Mariana Gates and Steve Rendall, "Media Not Concerned about the Very Poor," *Extra!* (September 2012): 5; David Graeber, "Can Debt Spark Revolution?" *Nation* (September 24, 2012): 22–24; Astra Taylor, "Occupy 2.0: Strike Debt," *Nation* (September 24, 2012): 17–20.

2. Quoted in Monika Bauerlein and Clara Jeffery, "Occupied Washington," *Mother Jones* (January–February 2012): 20.

3. Joe R. Feagin, *Racial and Ethnic Relations* (Englewood Cliffs, NJ: Prentice Hall, 1989).

4. Roberta Fiske-Rusciano and Virginia Cyrus, "Experiencing Race, Class, and Gender in the United States," in *Experiencing Race, Class, and Gender in the United States*, ed. Roberta Fiske-Rusciano and Virginia Cyrus, 4th ed. (New York: McGraw-Hill, 2005), xvii.

5. Juan Gonzalez and Joseph Torres, "The Colonial Roots of Media's Racial Narratives," *Extra!* (February 2012): 14–15; Julie Hollar, "Missing Latino Voices," *Extra!* (September 2012): 7–8; Janine Jackson, "New Media—but Familiar Lack of Diversity," *Extra!* (June 2012): 12–13.

6. Rudi Volti, *An Introduction to the Sociology of Work and Occupations*, 2nd ed. (Los Angeles: Sage, 2012), 233–37.

7. Lawrence Mishel, Josh Bivens, Elise Gould, and Heidi Shierholz, *The State of Working America*, 12th ed. (Ithaca, NY: IRL Press, 2012), 232–35.

8. Robert Cherry, "Institutionalized Discrimination," in *Experiencing Race, Class, and Gender in the United States*, ed. Roberta Fiske-Rusciano and Virginia Cyrus, 4th ed. (Boston:

McGraw-Hill, 2005), 380–86; Barbara Reskin and Irene Padavic, *Women and Men at Work* (Thousand Oaks, CA: Pine Forge Press, 1994); Chris Tilly and Charles Tilly, *Work Under Capitalism* (Boulder, CO: Westview Press, 1998).

9. For examples, see Eric Arnesen, ed., *Encyclopedia of U.S. Labor and Working Class History* (New York: Routledge, 2007); Randy Hodson and Teresa A. Sullivan, *The Social Organization of Work*, 4th ed. (Belmont, CA: Thomson Wadsworth, 2008), 84–97, 307–9.

10. David R. Roediger and Elizabeth D. Esch, *The Production of Difference: Race and the Management of Labor in U.S. History* (New York: Oxford University Press, 2012).

11. Joe R. Feagin, "Whiteness as a Managerial System," *Monthly Review* (January 2013): 53–58.

12. M. Junaid Alam, "The Unexplored Questions of Affirmative Action," *Extra!* (January 2013): 4.

13. Class Action, "What Is Classism?" and "What Do We Mean by 'Class'?" on the Internet at http://www.classism.org (accessed June 12, 2005); Fiske-Rusciano and Cyrus, "Experiencing Race, Class, and Gender in the United States," xvii; Gregory Mantsios, "Class in America: Myths and Realities," in *Race, Class, and Gender in the United States*, ed. Paula S. Rothenberg (New York: St. Martin's Press, 1995), 131–43.

14. Diana Kendall, *Framing Class: Media Representations of Wealth and Poverty in America*, 2nd ed. (Lanham, MD: Rowman and Littlefield, 2011), 152–55; Matt Wray and Annalee Newitz, eds., *White Trash: Race and Class in America* (New York: Routledge, 1997).

15. Robert Granfield, "Making It by Faking It," *Journal of Contemporary Ethnography* 20 (1991): 331–51; Christopher Hayes, "Why Elites Fail," *Nation* (June 25, 2012): 12–13.

16. Quoted in Matthew Josephson, *The Robber Barons* (New York: Harcourt, Brace and World, 1934), 325.

17. Robert Granfield and Thomas Koenig, "Pathways into Elite Law Firms: Professional Stratification and Social Networks," in *Research in Politics and Society*, vol. 4, *The Political Consequences of Social Networks*, ed. Gwen Moore and J. Allen Whitt (Greenwich, CT: JAI Press, 1992).

18. Today the term *professional* is applied to many occupations and is not limited to those traditionally identified as professions by sociologists such as law, medicine, and the clergy. See Hodson and Sullivan, *The Social Organization of Work*, 258–80.

19. Basil Bernstein, *Class, Codes, and Control*, 3 vols. (London: Routledge and Kegan Paul, 1971–1973).

20. ForecastChart, "Dow Jones Industrial Average Stock Market Index Forecast," "12 Month Forecast" (November 2012), on the Internet at http://www.forecastchart.com (accessed January 5, 2013).

21. FedPrimeRate, "A Sampled History of the Dow Jones Industrial Average From 1900 to the Present" (January 2, 2013), on the Internet at http://www.fedprimerate.com (accessed January 5, 2013); "Business," *Indianapolis Star*, February 20, 2013, A7.

22. Michael Kazin, *The Populist Persuasion* (New York: Basic Books, 1995), 1.

23. Ibid., 2.

24. Peter Hart and Steve Rendall, "Journalists Love Tea Party," *Extra!* (May 2010): 7–8; Julie Hollar, "Tea Party vs. U.S. Social Forum," *Extra!* (September 2010): 5; Jim Naureckas, "They Are the 1 Percent," *Extra!* (November 2011): 7–8.

25. Hart and Rendall, "Journalists Love Tea Party," 8.

26. Naureckas, "They Are the 1 Percent," 7–8; John Knefel, "Bored with Occupy—and Inequality," *Extra!* (May 2012): 6–7.

27. Knefel, "Bored with Occupy—and Inequality," 7.

28. Robert Perrucci and Earl Wysong, *The New Class Society*, 3rd ed. (Lanham, MD: Rowman and Littlefield, 2008), 235–37.

29. Thomas Frank, *Pity the Billionaire* (New York: Metropolitan Books, 2012), 44–59, 92–94, 122–28; Anthony DiMaggio, "A Tea Party Among Us: Media Censorship, Manufactured Dissent, and the Right-Wing Rebellion," in *Censored 2012*, ed. Mickey Huff and Project Censored (New York: Seven Stories Press, 2011), 351–66.

30. Michael Scherer, "Taking It to the Streets," *Time* (October 24, 2011): 20–24; Arun Gupta, "An Occupy Road Trip," *In These Times* (December 2011): 18–20; Allison Kilkenny, "No Longer Laughing, But Still Clueless," *In These Times* (December 2011): 20–21.

31. Shahien Nasiripour, "Immelt, GE CEO, to Run New Jobs-Focused Panel as GE Sends Jobs Overseas, Pays Little in Taxes," *Huffington Post* (January 21, 2011), on the Internet at http://www.huffingtonpost.com (accessed October 12, 2012).

32. Jeffrey M. Jones, "Confidence in U.S. Public Schools at New Low, Confidence Also at New Lows for Organized Religion, Banks, and TV News," Gallup, Inc. (June 20, 2012), on the Internet at http://www.gallup.com (accessed August 1, 2012).

33. Verta Taylor, "Social Movements Continuity: The Women's Movement in Abeyance," *American Sociological Review* 54 (1989): 761–75.

34. For examples of specific groups, see Kenn Burrows, "Signs of Health and Emerging Culture—Stories of Hope and Creative Change from 2010 and 2011," in *Censored 2012*, ed. Mickey Huff and Project Censored (New York: Seven Stories Press, 2011), 229–60; Nolan Higdon and Ryan Shehee, "Media Democracy in Action," in *Censored 2012*, ed. Mickey Huff and Project Censored (New York: Seven Stories Press, 2011), 280–92; Debra Minkoff, Silke Aisenbrey, and Jon Agnone, "Organizational Diversity in the U.S. Advocacy Sector," *Social Problems* 55 (2008): 525–48.

35. Sam Pizzigati, "The Scruffy and Stuffy Agree: Cap CEO Pay," *Too Much* (February 11, 2013): 4.

Bibliography

Abel, Thomas, and William C. Cockerham. "Lifestyle or *lebensführung*? Critical Remarks on the Mistranslantion of Weber's 'class, status, party.'" *Sociological Quarterly* 54 (1993): 551–56.

Abele, Robert. "Drawing Back the Veil on the US Propaganda Machine." In *Censored 2012*, edited by Mickey Huff and Project Censored. New York: Seven Stories Press, 2011.

Abrams, Jill. "The Most Biased Name in News." *Extra!* (July–August 2001): 10–12, 14–18.

———. "Understanding the Internet Piracy Bills, SOPA and PIPA." *Chicago Sun Times*, February 21, 2012. Available at http://www.suntimes.com/business.

Acs, Gregory. "Downward Mobility from the Middle Class: Waking Up from the American Dream." Philadephia, PA: The Pew Charitable Trusts, September 2011.

Adams, James Truslow. *The Epic of America*. Boston: Little, Brown, 1933.

Adler, Patricia, Steven J. Kless, and Peter Adler. "Socialization to Gender Roles: Popularity among Elementary Boys and Girls." *Sociology of Education* 65 (1992): 169–87.

"A 40–Year Wish List." *Wall Street Journal*, January 28, 2009. Available at http://online.wsj.com.

Aguirre, Adalberto, Jr., and David V. Baker. *Structured Inequality in the United States*. Upper Saddle River, NJ: Prentice Hall, 2000.

Akre, Jane. "We Report, They Decide: Fox TV Censors Series on Milk Hazards." *National News Reporter* (June 1998): 12–13.

Alam, M. Junaid. "The Unexplored Questions of Affirmative Action." *Extra!* (January 2013): 4.

Albelda, Randy. "Farewell to Welfare but Not to Poverty." *Dollars and Sense* (November–December 1996): 16–19.

———. "Welfare Reform, Ten Years Later." *Dollars and Sense* (January–February 2006): 6–7.

———. "Different Anti-Poverty Programs, Same Single-Mother Poverty." *Dollars and Sense* (January–February 2012): 11–17.

Alexa. "Top Sites in United States." 2012. Available at http://www.alexa.com.

Alexander, Karl S., Martha Cook, and Edward McDill. "Curriculum Tracking and Educational Stratification." *American Sociological Review* 43 (1982): 47–66.

Alexander, Karl S., Doris R. Entwisle, and Carrie S. Horsey. "From First Grade Forward: Early Foundations of High School Dropout." *Sociology of Education* 70 (1997): 87–107.

Allen, Frederick Lewis. *Since Yesterday: 1929–1939*. New York: Harper & Row, 1940.

Allen, Michael Patrick. "Elite Social Movement Organizations and the State: The Rise of the Conservative Policy-Planning Network." In *Research in Politics and Society*, vol. 4, *The Political Consequences of Social Networks*, edited by Gwen Moore and J. Allen Whitt. Greenwich, CT: JAI Press, 1992.

Allen, Mike, and Jim VanderHei. "GOP Groups Plan Record $1 Billion Blitz." *Politico* (May 30, 2012). Available at http:// www.dyn.politico.com.

Alterman, Eric. "Show Us the Money." *Nation* (June 25, 2012): 10.

"An Alternative to Austerity." *Nation* (January 28, 2013): 3.

Altman, Drew. "Rising Health Costs Are Not Just a Federal Budget Problem." *Pulling It Together*. The Kaiser Family Foundation and Health Research and Educational Trust (September 27, 2011). Available at http://www.kff.org/pullingittogether.

Alves, Wayne, and Peter Rossi. "Who Should Get What? Fairness Judgments of Distribution of Earnings." *American Journal of Sociology* 84 (1978): 541–64.

Amadeo, Kimberly. "What Was the Stimulus Package?" About.com (September 4, 2012). Available at http://www.useconomy.about.com.

American Civil Liberties Union. "ACLU Says Justice Dept.'s PATRIOT Act Website Creates New Myths about Controversial Law." Press release, August 26, 2003.

———. "Congress Reauthorizes Overbroad Patriot Act Provisions." Press release, May 26, 2011.

American Legislative Exchange Council. "History." 2011. Available at http:// www.alec.org.

"Americans' Economic Pessimism Reaches Record High." *New York Times*, November 26, 2007.

Americans For Campaign Reform. "Money in Politics: Who Gives, Fact Sheet." December 29, 2010. Available at http://www.acrreform.org.

America's Promise Alliance. "Building a Grad Nation Report." March 19, 2012. Available at http://www.americas promise.org.

Amin, Samir. "An Arab Springtime?" *Monthly Review* (October 2011): 8–28.

Anderson, Charles H. *The Political Economy of Social Class*. Englewood Cliffs, NJ: Prentice-Hall, 1974.

———. *Toward a New Sociology*. Homewood, IL: Dorsey Press, 1974.

Anderson, Sarah, and Scott Klinger. "A Pension Defect Disorder." Institute for Policy Studies (November 27, 2012). Available at http://www.IPS-dc.org.

Andrews, Edmund L. "Foreign-Profit Tax Break Is Outlined." *New York Times*, January 14, 2005, B2.

———. "House Passes a $2.7 Trillion Spending Plan." *New York Times*, May 18, 2006.

Arenson, Karen W. "Cuts in Tuition Assistance Put College beyond Reach of Poorest Students." *New York Times*, January 27, 1997.

Arnesen, Eric, ed. *Encyclopedia of U.S. Labor and Working Class History*. New York: Routledge, 2007.

Aronson, Ronald. "The Left Needs More Socialism." *Nation* (April 17, 2006): 28–30.

Atkinson, Michael. "Greenwald vs. Goliath." *Progressive* (September 2012): 33–34.

Aufderheide, Pat. "Too Much Media." *In These Times* (May 9, 2005): 28.

"Average Time Spent with Consumer Media per User per Year." *VSS Communications Industry Forecast, 2011–2015*, Veronis, Suhler, Stevenson (2011). Available at http://www.vssfore cast.com.

Bagdikian, Ben. *The Media Monopoly*. 4th ed. Boston: Beacon Press, 1992.

———. *The Media Monopoly*. 5th ed. Boston: Beacon Press, 1997.

———. *The New Media Monopoly*. Boston: Beacon Press, 2004.

Bailey, Martha J., and Susan M. Dynarski. "Gains and Gaps: Changing Inequality in U.S. College Entry and Completion." In *Whither Opportunity? Rising Inequality, Schools, and Children's Life Chances*, edited by Greg J. Duncan and Richard J. Murnane. New York: Russell Sage, September 2011.

Baker, Bruce D., David G. Sciarra, and Danielle Farrie. "Is School Funding Fair? A National Report Card." Newark, NJ: Education Law Center, September 2010.

Barlett, Donald L., and James B. Steele. *America: Who Really Pays the Taxes?* New York: Touchstone, 1994.

Barr, Kellie E. M., Michael P. Farrell, Grace M. Barnes, and John W. Welte. "Race, Class, and Gender Differences in Substance Abuse: Evidence of Middle Class/Underclass Polarization among Black Males." *Social Problems* 40 (1993): 314–27.

Battaglio, Stephen, and Michael Schneider. "Who Earn$ What." *TV Guide* (August 13–26, 2012): 16–21.

Bauerlein, Monika, and Clara Jeffery. "Occupied Washington." *Mother Jones* (January–February 2012): 19–21.

———. "Undoing Citizens United, the DIY Guide." *Mother Jones* (July–August 2012): 27–28.

Beckel, Michael. "Federal Lobbying Expenditures Plateau After Years of Rapid Growth." Center for Responsive Politics (February 4, 2011). Available at http://www.opensecrets.org.

Beckett, Katherine. "Setting the Public Agenda: 'Street Crime' and Drug Use in American Politics." *Social Problems* 41 (1994): 425–47.

Bendix, Reinhard, and Frank W. Howton. "Social Mobility and the American Business Elite—II." *British Journal of Sociology* 9 (1958): 1–14.

Berman, Ari. "Big $$ for Progressive Politics." *Nation* (October 16, 2006): 18–24.

———. "The Austerity Class." *Nation* (November 7, 2011): 11–17.

Bernstein, Basil. *Class, Codes, and Control*. 3 vols. London: Routledge and Kegan Paul, 1971–1973.

Biden, Joe. *Annual Report of the White House Task Force on the Middle Class*. February 2010.

Birnbaum, Jeffrey H. *The Lobbyists*. New York: Times Books, 1992.

———. "The Road to Riches Is Called K Street." *Washington Post*, June 22, 2005.

Blanes i Vidal, Jordi, Mirko Draca, and Christian Fons-Rosen. "Revolving Door Lobbyists." Center for Economic Performance, United Kingdom. May 2011.

Blau, Peter M., and Otis D. Duncan. *The American Occupational Structure*. New York: Wiley, 1967.

Bleifuss, Joel. "The Terminators." *In These Times* (March 4, 1996): 12–13.

———. "Warfare or Welfare." *In These Times* (December 9, 1996): 12–14.

———. "The War on Teachers: Pick a Side." *In These Times* (November 2012): 16–17.

———. "Tea Party Winter Is Coming." *In These Times* (January 2013): 5.

———. "Watch Out, Grandma!" *In These Times* (February 2013): 5.

Bluestone, Barry, and Bennett Harrison. *The Deindustrialization of America: Plant Closings, Community Abandonment, and the Dismantling of Basic Industry*. New York: Basic Books, 1982.

Boehlert, Eric. "Struggling Clear Channel and Rush Limbaugh's $400 Million Payday." Media Matters for America (March 16, 2012). Available at http://mediamatters.org.

Bogardus, Kevin, and Rachel Leven. "Lobbyists Took $100K Cut in Pay to Work for Members of Congress." *The Hill* (June 28, 2011). Available at http://www.thehill.com.

Borosage, Robert, and Katrina vanden Heuvel. "The American Dream: Can a Movement Save It?" *Nation* (October 10, 2011): 11.

Boushey, Heather, and Adam S. Hersh. *The American Middle Class, Income Inequality, and the Strength of Our Economy*. Washington, DC: Center for American Progress, May 2012.

Bowles, Samuel, and Herbert Gintis. *Schooling in Capitalist America: Educational Reform and the Contradictions of Economic Life*. New York: Basic Books, 1976.

Bowley, Graham. "At Brown, Spotlight on President's Role at a Bank." *New York Times*, March 1, 2010.

Bradbery, Angela. "2011 'Free Trade' Deals Haven't Lived Up to Obama's Promises." *Public Citizen News* (November–December 2012): 13.

Bradsher, Keith. "For Workers Sent Abroad, a Tax Jolt." *New York Times*, September 2, 2006, B1, B6.

Brady, Peter, and Michael Bogdan. "A Look at Private-Sector Retirement Plan Income After ERISA." *Research Perspective* 16. Washington, DC: Investment Company Institute, November 2010.

Brenner, Mark. "The Real Deficit Problem—Good Jobs." *Labor Notes* (July 2011): 14.

Brinton, Milward H., and Heide H. Newman. "State Incentive Packages and the Industrial Location Decision." *Economic Development Quarterly* 3 (1989): 203–22.

Brodsky, Art. "PIPA and SOPA Were Stopped, but the Web Hasn't Won." *Huffington Post* (January 25, 2012). Available at http://www.huffingtonpost.com.

Brookings Institution. "Brookings Annual Report 2010." Available at http://www.brookings.edu.

———. "The Brookings Institution Financial Statements." June 30, 2011. Available at http://www.brookings.edu.

Brown, Kevin C. "The 'Liberal Media'and State Austerity." *Extra!* (June 2010): 9.

Brudnick, Ida A. "Salaries of Members of Congress: Recent Actions and Historical Tables." *Congressional Research Service* (February 22, 2012).

Bruno, Robert. "Evidence of Bias in the Chicago Tribune Coverage of Organized Labor." *Labor Studies Journal* (September 2009): 385–407.

Bruyn, Severyn. *The Social Economy: People Transforming Modern Business*. New York: Wiley, 1977.

Bryner, Sarah McKinnin."From Hired Guns to Hired Hands: 'Reverse Revolvers' in the 111th and 112th Congresses." *A Centers for Responsive Politics Report* (July 11, 2011).

Buckley, John E., and Robert W. Van Giezen. "Federal Statistics on Healthcare Benefits and Cost Trends: An Overview." *Monthly Labor Review* (November 2004): 43–45.

Burris, Val. "Elite Policy-Planning Networks in the United States." In *Research in Politics and Society*, vol. 4, *The Political Consequences of Social Networks*, edited by Gwen Moore and J. Allen Whitt. Greenwich, CT: JAI Press, 1992.

———. "The Myth of Old Money Liberalism: The Politics of the *Forbes* 400 Richest Americans." *Social Problems* 47 (2000): 360–78.

———. "The Two Faces of Capital: Corporations and Individual Capitalists as Political Actors." *American Sociological Review* 66 (2001): 361–81.

Burrows, Kenn. "Signs of Health and Emerging Culture—Stories of Hope and Creative Change from 2010 and 2011." In *Censored 2012*, edited by Mickey Huff and Project Censored. New York: Seven Stories Press, 2011.

"Business." *Indianapolis Star*, February 20, 2013, A7.

Business Roundtable. "Statement on Bipartisan Tax Agreement." Press release, December 7, 2010. Available at http://www.businessroundtable.org.

———. "About Us: Members." 2012. Available at http://www.businessroundtable.org.

———. "About Us: Executive Committee." 2012. Available at http://www.businessround table.org

Butsch, Richard. "Class and Gender in Four Decades of Television Situation Comedy: Plus ça Change. . . ." *Critical Studies in Mass Communications* 9 (1992): 387–99.

Bybee, Roger. "NAFTA's Hung Jury." *Extra!* (May–June 2004): 14–15.

———. "A Three-Point Plan to Save Democrats." *In These Times* (January 2011): 24–25.

———. "Obama's Double Game on Outsourcing." *Dollars and Sense* (September–October 2012): 20–22.

Campaign Finance Institute. "Reality Check: Obama Received About the Same Percentage from Small Donors in 2008 as Bush in 2004." November 24, 2008. Available at http://www.cfinst.org.

———. "All CFI Funding Statistics Revised and Updated for the 2008 Presidential Primary and General Election Candidates." January 8, 2010. Available at http://www.cfinst.org.

———. "CFI's Review of Connecticut's Campaign Donors in 2006, and 2008 Finds Strengths in Citizen Election Program but Recommends Changes." Press release, March 2, 2010. Available at http://www.cfinst.org.

———. "2010 Federal Elections: The Cost of Winning an Election, 1986–2010." Table 3–1: House and Senate Winners. 2010. Available at http://www.cfinst.org.

———. "Independent Spending Roughly Equaled the Candidates' in Close House and Senate Races; Winning Candidates Raised More Than Any Previous Election." November 9, 2012. Available at http://www.cfinst.org.

———. "Money vs. Money-Plus: Post-Election Reports Reveal Two Different Campaign Strategies." Press release, January 11, 2013. Available at http://www.cfinst.org.

Carlson, Matt. "Boardroom Brothers." *Extra!* (September–October 2001): 18.

Carnevale, Anthony P., and Stephen J. Rose. "Socioeconomic Status, Race/Ethnicity, and Selective College Admissions." New York: The Century Foundation, March 2003.

Carreiro, Joshua L. "Newspaper Coverage of the U.S. Labor Movement: The Case of Anti-Union Firings." *Labor Studies Journal* 30, no. 3 (2005): 1–20.

Carroll, William, and Jean Philippe Sapinski. "The Global Elite and the Transnational Policy-Planning Network." *International Sociology* 25 (2009): 501–38.

Carter, Jimmy. "Call Off the Global Drug War." *New York Times*, June 16, 2011.

Cashell, Brian. "Who Are the Middle Class?" Congressional Research Service Report for Congress (October 22, 2008).

Casten, Liane. "Florida Appeals Court Orders Akre-Wilson Must Pay Trial Costs for $24.3 Billion Fox Television: Couple Warns of Danger to Free Speech, Whistle Blower Protection." In *Censored 2006*, edited by Peter Phillips. New York: Seven Stories Press, 2005.

CBS Corporation. "Form 10–K." For 2011. Filed with the U.S. Securities and Exchange Commission (February 23, 2012). Available at http://www.sec.gov.

CBS News/*New York Times* poll. "Foreign Trade and the U.S. Economy." January 31, 2006.

"Celebrity Net Worth." 2012. Available at http://www.celebritynetworth.com.

Center for a New American Dream. "New American Dream Survey Report." 2004. Available at http://www.newdream.org

Center for Public Integrity. "527s in 2004 Shatter Previous Records for Political Fundraising." December 16, 2004. Available at http://www.publicintegrity.org.

Center for Responsive Politics. "Summary." In *Influence, Inc.* Washington, DC: Center for Responsive Politics, 2000.

——. *Influence, Inc.: National Trade and Professional Associations of the United States.* Washington DC: Columbia Books, 2006.

——. "Historical Elections, Donor Demographics, Election Cycle 2010." Available at http://www.opensecrets.org.

——. "Average Wealth of Members of Congress: 2004–2011." Available at http://www.opensecrets.org.

——. "The Big Spender Always Wins?" January 11, 2012. Available at http://www.opensecrets.org.

——. "Lobbying Database." April 30, 2012. Available at http://www.opensecrets.org.

——. "2012 Overview, Donor Demographics." July 9, 2012. Available at http://www.opensecrets.org.

——. "The Money Behind the Elections." August 1, 2012. Available at http://www.opensecrets.org.

——. "2012 Election Will Be Costliest Yet, with Outside Spending a Wild Card." August 1, 2012. Available at http://www.opensecrets.org.

——. "Total Outside Spending by Election Cycle, All Groups." 2012. Available at http://www.opensecrets.org.

——. "2012 Presidential Race." January 14, 2013. Available at http://www.opensecrets.org.

"CFOs Earn 40% Less Than Average CEO Salary." *BenefitsPro* (September 1, 2011). Available at http://www.benefitspro.com.

Change to Win. "The American Dream Survey 2006." August 28, 2006. Available at http://www.changetowin.org.

Cherry, Robert. "Institutionalized Discrimination." In *Experiencing Race, Class, and Gender in the United States,* edited by Roberta Fiske-Rusciano and Virginia Cyrus. 4th ed. Boston: McGraw-Hill, 2005.

"Chief Financial Officer (CFO) Salary." *PayScale* (May 26, 2012). Available at http://www.payscale.com/research.

Chin, Tiffany, and Meredith Phillips. "Social Reproduction and Child-Rearing Practices: Social Class, Children's Agency, and the Summer Camp Activity Gap." *Sociology of Education* 77 (July 2004): 185–210.

Chirot, Daniel. *Social Change in the Twentieth Century.* New York: Harcourt Brace Jovanovich, 1974.

Chomsky, Noam. *The Common Good.* Monroe, ME: Odonian Press, 1998.

Ciaran, John. "The Average Median Salary for a Law Firm Lawyer." *Houston Chronicle,* August 7, 2012. Available at http://www.chron.com.

Cieply, Michael. "A Strong Crop of Documentaries, but Barely Seen." *New York Times,* January 2, 2011. Available at http://www.nytimes.com.

Citigroup, Inc. "Peter Orszag to Join Citi as Vice Chairman in Global Banking." Press release, December 9, 2010.

Citizens for Tax Justice. "Final Version of Bush Tax Plan Keeps High-End Tax Cuts, Adds to Long-Term Cost." 2001. Available at http://www.inequality.org.

———. "CBO Projects $8.5 Trillion in Borrowing Over Next Decade Under Bush Policies, Effects of the Bush Tax Cuts Enacted through 2004 (with Sunsets) by Income Group (Calendar Years)." Press release, January 26, 2006. Available at http://www.ctj.org.

———. "Tax Cuts on Capital Gains and Dividends Doubled Bush Income Tax Cuts for the Wealthiest in 2003." Press release, April 5, 2006. Available at http://www.ctj.org.

———. "Who Pays Taxes in America?"April 4, 2012. Available at http://www.ctj.org.

Class Action. "What Do We Mean by 'Class'?" Available at http://www.classism.org.

———. "What Is Classism?" 2005. Available at http://www.classism.org.

Clawson, Dan, Alan Neustadtl, and Denise Scott. *Money Talks*. New York: Basic Books, 1992.

Claxton, Gary, Matthew Rae, Nirmita Panchal, Janet Lundy, and Anthony Damico. *Employer Health Benefits: 2011 Annual Survey*. Chicago: The Kaiser Family Foundation and Health Research and Educational Trust, 2011.

Clinton, Hillary Rodham. "South Korea, Colombia, Panama Free Trade Agreements." Press release, October 12, 2011. Available at http://www.state.gov/secretary/rm.

Coen, Rachel. "Are You a Terrorist?" *Extra!* (November–December 2001): 21–22.

Cohan, William D. "How We Got the Crash Wrong." *Atlantic* (June 2012). Available at http://www.theatlantic.com.

Cohen, Tom. "Obama Approves Extension of Expiring Patriot Act Provisions." *CNN Politics* (May 27, 2011). Available at http://articles.cnn.com.

Collins, Chuck. "Horatio Alger, Where Are You?" *Dollars and Sense* (January–February 1997): 9.

———. *99 to 1: How Wealth Inequality Is Wrecking the World and What We Can Do About It*. San Francisco: Berrett-Koehler, 2012.

Collins, Randall. "Functional and Conflict Theories of Educational Stratification." *American Sociological Review* 36 (1971): 1002–19.

———. *The Credential Society*. New York: Academic Press, 1979.

Collins, Sharon M. "The Marginalization of Black Executives." *Social Problems* 36 (1989): 317–31.

"Commercial Banks, [Top] 20 Companies." *Fortune* (May 21, 2012): F-34.

Comcast Corporation. "Form 10–K." For 2011. Filed with the U.S. Securities and Exchange Commission (February 2012). Available at http://www.sec.gov.

Condron, Dennis J. "Social Class, School and Non-School Environments, and Black/White Inequalities in Children's Learning." *American Sociological Review* 74 (2009): 683–708.

Condron, Dennis J., and Vincent J. Roscigno. "Disparities Within: Unequal Spending and Achievement in an Urban School District." *Sociology of Education* 76 (January 2003): 18–36.

Congressional Record. May 8, 1997: S4236–38.

———. May 15, 1997: S4588–91.

———. June 26, 1997: S6449–51.

Connell, Noreen. "Underfunded Schools: Why Money Matters." *Dollars and Sense* (March–April 1998): 14–17, 39.

Conniff, Ruth. "The Budget Surrender." *Progressive* (June 2001): 12–13.

———. "Social Darwinism Returns." *Progressive* (July 2012): 14–16.

Conniff, Ruth, and Matthew Rothschild. "A Victory for the 99 Percent." *Progressive* (December 2012–January 2013): 10–11.

Connor, Kevin. "Big Bank Takeover." Campaign for America's Future (2010). Available at http://www.ourfuture.org.

Conrad, Joseph. "Conrad's Manifesto." In *Great Writers on the Art of Fiction*, edited by James Daley. Mineola, NY: Dover Publications, 2007.

Cooke, Shamus. "Democrats and the Fiscal Cliff." *CounterPunch* (November 12, 2012). Available at http://www.counterpunch.org.

Corcoran, Michael. "Uygur Out at MSNBC." *Extra!* (November 2011): 11–12.

Costo, Stephanie L. "Trends in Retirement Plan Coverage Over the Last Decade." *Monthly Labor Review* (February 2006): 58–64.

Cowen, Tyler. *The Great Stagnation.* New York: Dutton, 2011.

Craddock, Jim, ed. *VideoHound's Golden Movie Retriever: 2006.* Detroit, MI: Thomson-Gale, 2005.

Crane, Stephen. *The Red Badge of Courage and Other Writings.* Edited by Richard Chase. Cambridge, MA: Riverside Press, 1960.

Crockett, Harry J., Jr. "The Achievement Motive and Differential Occupational Mobility in the United States." *American Sociological Review* 27 (1962): 191–204.

Croteau, David. "Challenging the 'Liberal Media' Claim." *Extra!* (July–August 1998): 4–9.

Crotty, James. "The Austerians Attack." *In These Times* (February 2012): 16–23.

Cummings, Scott, and Del Taebel. "The Economic Socialization of Children: A Neo-Marxist Analysis." *Social Problems* 26 (1978): 198–210.

"Current Labor Statistics: Tables 34 and 35." *Monthly Labor Review* (July 2005): 126–27.

"Current Labor Statistics: Tables 34 and 35." *Monthly Labor Review* (January 2012): 161–65.

Cutrone, Carolyn, and Steve Rendall. "Deficit-Obsessed Media Misinform on Causes." *Extra!* (September 2011): 4–5.

Daherndorf, Ralf. *Life Chances.* Chicago: University of Chicago Press, 1979.

Dahl, Ronald. "Burned Out and Bored." *Newsweek* (December 15, 1997): 18.

Damon, Andre. "Corporations Find Cheap Labor Haven in U.S." *World Socialist Web Site* (July 9, 2012). Available at http://wsws.org.

DARE America. "The New D.A.R.E. Junior High/Middle School Curriculum." Available at http://www.dare.com.

Dassbach, Carl. "The *Manifesto* and the Middle Class." *Critical Sociology* 27 (2001): 121–32.

Davies, Scott, and Neil Guppy. "Fields of Study, College Selectivity, and Student Inequalities in Higher Education." *Social Forces* 75 (1997): 1417–38.

Davis, James A., and Tom W. Smith. *General Social Surveys, 1972–1998.* Storrs, CT: The Roper Center for Public Opinion Research, 1989.

Delan, Colin. *Learning from Obama: Lessons for Online Communicators in 2009 and Beyond.* August 2009. Available at http://www.epolitics.com.

deMause, Neil. "The Smell of Success." *Extra!* (November–December 2006): 6–7.

———. "Who Ate the Dessert? *Extra!* (June 2010): 6–8.

———. "Economy Is the Issue That Isn't." *Extra!* (October 2012): 10–11.

"Democracy Alliance Editor's Note." *Washington Free Beacon* (September 2012). Available at http://www.freebeacon.com.

DeNavas-Walt, Carmen, Bernadette D. Proctor, and Jessica C. Smith. U.S. Census Bureau, Current Population Reports, P60–239. *Income, Poverty, and Health Insurance Coverage in the United States: 2010.* Washington, DC: U.S. Government Printing Office, 2011.

Derber, Charles. *The Wilding of America*. New York: St. Martin's Press, 1996.

———. *The Wilding of America*. 5th ed. New York: Worth, 2011.

DiMaggio, Anthony. "A Tea Party among Us: Media Censorship, Manufactured Dissent, and the Right-Wing Rebellion." In *Censored 2012*, edited by Mickey Huff and Project Censored. New York: Seven Stories Press, 2011.

Dines, Gail. "Capitalism's Pitchmen." *Dollars and Sense* (May 1992): 18–20.

DiNovella, Elizabeth. "Sherrod Brown Beats Back Big Money." *Progressive* (October 2012): 14–18.

District of Columbia Bar. "Attorney Resources." 2001. Available at http://www.dcbar.org.

———. "2004–2005 Annual Report." Available at http://www.dcbar.org.

———. "Prospective Members." 2012. Available at http://www.dcbar.org.

Doeringer, P. B., and Michael J. Piore. *Internal Labor Markets and Manpower Analysis*. Lexington, MA: Heath, 1971.

Doherty, Brian. "Those Who Can't, Test." *Mother Jones* (November–December 1998): 68–71.

Dolny, Michael. "Think Tank Spectrum Revisited." *Extra!* (June 2012): 14.

Domhoff, G. William. *The Powers That Be*. New York: Vintage Books, 1979.

———. *State Autonomy or Class Dominance?* New York: Aldine De Gruyter, 1996.

———. *Who Rules America?* 3rd ed. Mountain View, CA: Mayfield Publishing, 1998.

———. *Who Rules America?* 4th ed. Boston: McGraw-Hill, 2002.

———. *Who Rules America?* 5th ed. Boston: McGraw-Hill, 2006.

———. *Who Rules America?* 6th ed. Boston: McGraw-Hill, 2010.

———. "Wealth, Income, and Power." January 2012. Available at http://www2.ucsc.edu/whorulesamerica/power/wealth.html.

Douglas, Susan J. "Class Consciousness Is Back." *In These Times* (January 2012): 15.

Downs, Alan. *Corporate Executions*. New York: AMACOM, 1995.

Doyle, Sady. "Learning from Karen Lewis." *In These Times* (November 2012): 19.

Dreifus, Claudia. "Interview: Gore Vidal, the Writer as Citizen." *Progressive* (September 1986): 36–39.

Dreiling, Michael C. "The Class Embeddedness of Corporate Political Action: Leadership in Defense of the NAFTA." *Social Problems* 47 (2000): 21–48.

Drum, Kevin. "Plutocracy Now." *Mother Jones* (March–April 2011): 27.

Drutman, Lee. "The Political One Percent of the One Percent." The Sunlight Foundation (December 13, 2011). Available at http://sunlightfoundation.com.

Drutman, Lee, and Charlie Cray. "The People's Business." *In These Times* (March 14, 2005): 16–19, 28.

Dye, Thomas R. "Organizing Power for Policy-Planning: The View from the Brookings Institution." In *Power Elites and Organizations*, edited by G. William Domhoff and Thomas R. Dye. Newbury Park, CA: Sage, 1987.

———. *Who's Running America? The Clinton Years*. 6th ed. Englewood Cliffs, NJ: Prentice-Hall, 1995.

———. *Who's Running America? The Bush Restoration*. 7th ed. Upper Saddle River, NJ: Prentice-Hall, 2002.

Dyer, Stephanie. "Lifestyles of the Media Rich and Oligopolistic." In *Censored 2005*, edited by Peter Phillips. New York: Seven Stories Press, 2004.

"Economic Focus." *The Economist* (September 2, 2006): 66.

Economic Report of the President. Transmitted to the Congress. Washington, DC: U.S. Government Printing Office, February 2012.

The Editors. "A Progressive Surge." *Nation* (November 26, 2012): 3–6.

Edsall, Thomas Byrne. *The New Politics of Inequality.* New York: W.W. Norton, 1984.

——. "Rich Liberals Vow to Fund Think Tanks; Aim is to Compete with Conservatives." *Washington Post,* August 7, 2005, A1.

Education Week. May 3, 1995. Available at http://www.edweek.org.

Eisenger, Peter. *The Rise of the Entrepreneurial State.* Madison: University of Wisconsin Press, 1988.

Fang, Fang. "Analysis: When a Congressman Becomes a Lobbyist, He Gets a 1,452% Raise (on Average)." *Republic Report* (March 14, 2012). Available at http://www.republicreport.org.

Farnam, T. W. "Revolving Door of Employment Between Congress, Lobbying Firms, Study Shows." *Washington Post,* September 13, 2011. Available at http://www.washingtonpost.com.

Feagin, Joe R. *Racial and Ethnic Relations.* Englewood Cliffs, NJ: Prentice Hall, 1989.

——. "Whiteness as a Managerial System." *Monthly Review* (January 2013): 53–58.

Featherman, David L., and Robert M. Hauser. *Opportunity and Change.* New York: Academic Press, 1978.

Federal Election Commission (FEC). All FEC documents cited in all chapters available at http://www.fec.gov.

FedPrimeRate. "A Sampled History of the Dow Jones Industrial Average from 1900 to the Present." January 2, 2013. Available at http://www.fedprimerate.com.

Ferris, Kerry, and Jill Stein. *The Real World: An Introduction to Sociology.* 3rd ed. New York: W.W. Norton & Company, 2012.

Fiske-Rusciano, Roberta, and Virginia Cyrus. "Experiencing Race, Class, and Gender in the United States." In *Experiencing Race, Class, and Gender in the United States,* edited by Roberta Fiske-Rusciano and Virginia Cyrus. 4th ed. Boston: McGraw-Hill, 2005.

Fitch, Robert. "How Obama Got His Start." *CounterPunch* (January 1–15, 2012): 1, 3–7.

Fite, Gilbert C., and Jim E. Reese. *An Economic History of the United States.* 2nd ed. Boston: Houghton Mifflin, 1965.

Flesher, John, and Jeff Karoub. "'Right to Work' Prevails in Former Labor Stronghold." *Indianapolis Star,* December 12, 2012, A2.

"Forbes 400: The Richest People in America." *Forbes* (September 19, 2012). Available at http://www.forbes.com.

Ford, Michael, Dayna Dion, Casey Conway, and Jeremy Katz. "The Modern American Dream." American Family Mutual Insurance Company (August 2011).

ForecastChart. "Dow Jones Industrial Average Stock Market Index Forecast." "12 Month Forecast." November 2012. Available at http://www.forecastchart.com

Foster, John Bellamy. "The Financialization of Capital and the Crisis." *Monthly Review* (April 2008): 1–19.

——. "The Financialization of Accumulation." *Monthly Review* (October 2010): 1–17.

——. "Education and the Structural Crisis of Capital." *Monthly Review* (July–August 2011): 6–37.

Foster, John Bellamy, and Hannah Holleman. "The Financial Power Elite." *Monthly Review* (May 2010): 1–19.

Foster, John Bellamy, and Fred Magdoff. *The Great Financial Crisis.* New York: Monthly Review Press, 2009.

Foster, John Bellamy, and Robert W. McChesney. "The Internet's Unholy Marriage to Capitalism." *Monthly Review* (March 2011): 1–30.

———. "The Endless Crisis." *Monthly Review* (May 2012): 1–28.

———. *The Endless Crisis: How Monopoly-Finance Capital Produces Stagnation and Upheaval from the United States to China.* New York: Monthly Review Press, 2012.

Foster, John Bellamy, Robert W. McChesney, and R. Jamil Jonna. "The Internationalization of Monopoly Capital." *Monthly Review* (June 2011): 1–23.

Foundation Center. "FC Stats, Grantmaker Set Information." Available at http://www.foundationcenter.org.

———. "Top 100 U.S. Foundations by Asset Size." Available at http://www.foundationcenter.org.

———. "Top 100 U.S. Foundations by Total Giving." Available at http://www.foundationcenter.org.

"Foxconn Technology." *New York Times*, December 27, 2012. Available at http://topics/nytimes.com.

Frank, Thomas. *The Conquest of Cool: Business Culture, Counterculture, and the Rise of Hip Consumerism.* Chicago: University of Chicago Press, 1997.

———. *One Market Under God.* New York: Doubleday, 2000.

———. *Pity the Billionaire.* New York: Metropolitan Books, 2012.

Freeman, Gerald. "The Great Tax-Cut Experiment." *Dollars and Sense* (January–February 2013): 29–30.

Freeman, Lewis. "Social Mobility in Television Comedies." *Critical Studies in Mass Communications* 9 (1992): 400–406.

"From the Left: More Than a Figure of Speech?" *Extra!Update* (February 1996): 1.

Froomkin, Dan. "Free Trade Deals: Lobbying Fever Foreshadows Winners, Losers." *Huffington Post* (September 24, 2011). Available at http://www.huffingtonpost.com.

Gantz, Jeremy. "Voices from the Occupations." *In These Times* (December 2011): 16–18.

Garecht, Joe. "How to Raise Political Donations Online." *Local Victory* (August 30, 2010). Available at http://www.localvictory.com.

Garrett-Peltier, Heidi. "Is Military Keynesianism the Solution?" *Dollars and Sense* (March–April 2010): 7.

Gates, Mariana, and Steve Rendall. "Media Not Concerned about the Very Poor." *Extra!* (September 2012): 5–6.

Gerald, Danette, and Kati Haycock. "Engines of Inequality: Diminishing Equity in the Nation's Premier Public Universities." Washington, DC: The Education Trust, 2006.

Gerth, Hans H., and C. Wright Mills. *From Max Weber: Essays in Sociology.* New York: Oxford University Press, 1946.

Gibson, Dave. "Dark Stars." *Mother Jones* (September–October 2012): 39.

Gilbert, Dennis, and Joseph A. Kahl. *The American Class Structure.* Chicago: Dorsey Press, 1987.

Glasser, Radley, and Steve Rendall. "For Media, 'Class War' Has Wealthy Victims." *Extra!* (August 2009): 9–10.

Glaze, Lauren E., and Erika Parks. "Correctional Populations in the United States, 2011." *Bureau of Justice Statistics Bulletin* (November 2012): 8.

Goldberg, Alison, Chuck Collins, Scott Klinger, and Sam Pizzigati. *Unnecessary Austerity, Unnecessary Shutdown.* Washington, DC: Institute for Policy Studies and the Program on Inequality and the Common Good, April 2011. Available at http://www.ips-dc.org.

Goldberg, Beverly. "Patriot Act Renewal Renews Reformers' Determination." *American Libraries Magazine* (May 31, 2011). Available at http://americanlibrariesmagazine.org/news.

Golden, Daniel. *The Price of Admission: How America's Ruling Class Buys Its Way into Elite Colleges—and Who Gets Left Outside the Gates.* New York: Crown, 2006.

Gonzalez, Juan, and Joseph Torres. "The Colonial Roots of Media's Racial Narratives." *Extra!* (February 2012): 14–15.

Goode, Erich. *Drugs in American Society.* 8th ed. Boston: McGraw-Hill, 2011.

Goodman, Robert. *The Last Entrepreneurs: America's Regional Wars for Jobs and Dollars.* New York: Simon and Schuster, 1979.

Gotbaum, Josh. "2011 Pension Benefit Guaranty Corporation Annual Report." November 14, 2011. Available at http://www.pbgc.gov/res/reportsar2011.html.

Gottschalk, Marie. *The Shadow Welfare State.* Ithaca, NY: IRL/Cornell University Press, 2000.

Gould, Elise. "A Decade of Declines in Employer-Sponsored Health Insurance Coverage." Briefing Paper #337. Washington, DC: Economic Policy Institute, January 23, 2012.

Graeber, David. "Can Debt Spark Revolution?" *Nation* (September 24, 2012): 22–24.

Granfield, Robert. "Making It by Faking It." *Journal of Contemporary Ethnography* 20 (1991): 331–51.

Granfield, Robert, and Thomas Koenig. "Pathways into Elite Law Firms: Professional Stratification and Social Networks." In *Research in Politics and Society,* vol. 4, *The Political Consequences of Social Networks,* edited by Gwen Moore and J. Allen Whitt. Greenwich, CT: JAI Press, 1992.

Granovetter, Mark. *Getting a Job: A Study of Contacts and Careers.* Cambridge, MA: Harvard University Press, 1974.

Greenberg, Edward S. *Political Socialization.* New York: Atherton, 1970.

Greider, William. "Born-Again Rubinomics." *Nation* (July 31–August 7, 2006): 20–23.

Grey, Barry. "Leaked 'Grand Bargain' Document Details Obama's Plan for Cuts in Entitlement Programs." *World Socialist Web Site* (November 15, 2012): 1–3. Available at http://www.wsw.org.

Gross, James A. *Broken Promise: The Subversion of U.S. Labor Relations Policy.* Philadelphia: Temple University Press, 1995.

Grossman, Lev. "2010 Person of the Year: Mark Zuckerberg." *Time* (December 27, 2010–January 3, 2011): 44–75.

Grunwald, Michael. "Cliff Dweller." *Time* (January 14, 2013): 28.

Guldin, Bob. "Flawed Bankruptcy Law Rewards Finance Industry, While Families Beset by Health Costs Lose Protection." *Public Citizen News* (May–June 2005): 11.

Gupta, Arun. "An Occupy Road Trip." *In These Times* (December 2011): 18–20.

Hacker, Jacob B. *The Great Risk Shift: The Assault on American Jobs, Families, Health Care, and Retirement and How You Can Fight Back.* New York: Oxford University Press, 2006.

Hallinan, Maureen T. "Tracking: From Theory to Practice." *Sociology of Education* 67 (1994): 79–85.

———. "Ability Grouping and Student Learning." In *Brookings Papers on Educational Policy,* edited by Diane Ravitch. Washington, DC: Brookings Institute Press, 2003.

Hamilton Project. "Advisory Council." 2012. Available at http://www.hamiltonproject.org.

———. "Mission and Vision." 2012. Available at http://www.hamiltonproject.org.

Hananel, Sam. "Unions Lost Big on Walker Recall." *Las Vegas Review-Journal* (June 7, 2012): A1, A4.

Harder, William S., and Howard D. Chilcoat. "Cocaine Use and Educational Achievement: Understanding a Changing Association Over the Past 2 Decades." *American Journal of Public Health* 97 (October 2007): 1790–95.

Hardt, Michael, and Antonio Negri. *Empire*. Cambridge, MA: Harvard University Press, 2000.

Hart, Peter. "Fear and Favor 2008." *Extra!* (April 2009): 10–12.

———. "Fear & Favor 10th Annual Review." *Extra!* (May 2010): 11–13.

———. "First, Bash the Teachers." *Extra!* (September 2010): 6–7.

———. "Charlie Rose's Elite Meet-and-Greet." *Extra!* (November 2010): 13–14.

———. "This Week in Beltway Think." *Extra!* (November 2010): 15.

———. "Olbermann's Countdown Reaches Zero." *Extra!* (March 2011): 5.

———. "Surprised by Solidarity." *Extra!* (April 2011): 6–7.

———. "Right and Early." *Extra!* (April 2012): 10–11.

———. "Not for Teacher." *Extra!* (November 2012): 7–8.

Hart, Peter, and Julie Hollar. "Guide to Election Coverage 2012." *Extra!* (October 2012): 6–9.

Hart, Peter, and Janine Jackson. "Media Lick the Hand That Feeds Them." *Extra!* (November–December 2005): 21–23.

Hart, Peter, and Steve Rendall. "Journalists Love Tea Party." *Extra!* (May 2010): 7–8.

Hartman, Thom. *Screwed: The Undeclared War Against the Middle Class—and What We Can Do about It*. San Francisco: Berrett-Koehler, 2006.

Harvey, David. *A Brief History of Neoliberalism*. New York: Oxford University Press, 2005.

Haveman, Ernest, and Patricia Salter West. *They Went to College*. New York: Harcourt, Brace, 1952.

Hayek, Friedrich. *Economic Freedom*. Cambridge, MA: Blackwell, 1991.

———. *The Road to Serfdom*. Chicago: University of Chicago Press, 1994.

Hayes, Christopher. "Why Elites Fail." *Nation* (June 25, 2012): 11–18.

"Healthcare: Insurance and Managed Care, [Top] 11 Companies." *Fortune* (May 21, 2012): F-36.

Hearn, James. "Academic and Nonacademic Influences on the College Destinations of 1980 High School Graduates." *Sociology of Education* 64 (1991): 158–71.

Helman, Christopher. "What the Top U.S. Companies Pay in Taxes." *Forbes* (April 1, 2011). Available at http://www.forbes.com.

Henderson, Richard. "Industry Employment and Output Projections to 2020." *Monthly Labor Review* (January 2012): 65–83.

Henriques, Diana B. "Putting Corporations in the Dock." *New York Times*, September 14, 2003.

Herbert, Bob. "The Worst of the Pain." *New York Times*, February 8, 2010.

Heritage Foundation. *2010 Annual Report*. Available at http://www.heritage.org.

———. "Financial Report." December 31, 2010.

Herman, Edward S. "The Media Mega-Mergers." *Dollars and Sense* (May–June 1996): 8–13.

Herzenhorn, David. "The Story behind the Generous Gift to Harvard Law School." *New York Times*, April 7, 1995.

Higdon, Nolan, and Ryan Shehee. "Media Democracy in Action." In *Censored 2012*, edited by Mickey Huff and Project Censored. New York: Seven Stories Press, 2011.

Hightower, Jim, and Phillip Frazer. "Naming the Names Behind the Grab for Social Security." *The Lowdown* (April 2005): 1–8.

Hodai, Beau. "Publicopoly Exposed." *In These Times* (August 2011): 14–19.

———. "Zombie Lobbyists Occupy Washington." *In These Times* (November 2011): 14–18.

Hodge, Robert W., and Donald J. Treiman. "Class Identification in the United States." *American Journal of Sociology* 73 (1968): 535–47.

Hodge, Robert W., Paul M. Siegel, and Peter H. Rossi. "A Comparative Study of Occupational Prestige." In *Class, Status, and Power*, edited by Reinhard Bendix and Seymour M. Lipset. New York: Free Press, 1966.

———. "Occupational Prestige in the United States: 1925–1962." In *Class, Status, and Power*, edited by Reinhard Bendix and Seymour M. Lipset. New York: Free Press, 1966.

Hodson, Randy, and Teresa A. Sullivan. *The Social Organization of Work*. 4th ed. Belmont, CA: Thomson Wadsworth, 2008.

Hoffman, Hank. "Time Is Tight." *In These Times* (November 12, 2001): 7–8.

Hollar, Julie. "Wealth Gaps Yawns—and So Do Media." *Extra!* (June 2010): 10–12.

———. "Tea Party vs. U.S. Social Forum." *Extra!* (September 2010): 5.

———. "Missing Latino Voices." *Extra!* (September 2012): 7–8.

Holleman, Hannah, Robert W. McChesney, John Bellamy Foster, and R. Jamil Jonna. "The Penal State in an Age of Crisis." *Monthly Review* (June 2009): 1–17.

Holman, Craig. "Campaign to Clean Up Washington." *Public Citizen Urgent Campaign Memorandum* (June 20, 2012): 1–4.

Howard, Ina. "Power Sources." *Extra!* (May–June 2002): 14.

Huber, Joan, and William H. Form. *Income and Ideology: An Analysis of the American Political Formula*. New York: Free Press, 1973.

Hudson, K. "The New Labor Market Segmentation: Labor Market Dualism in the New Economy." *Social Science Research* 27 (2007): 286–312.

Huff, Mickey. "Introduction: Project Censored News Clusters and the Top Censored Stories of 2010–2011." In *Censored 2012*, edited by Mickey Huff and Project Censored. New York: Seven Stories Press, 2011.

Huff, Mickey, and Adam Bessie. "Case Study of News Abuse: Framing, Propaganda, and Censorship." In *Censored 2012*, edited by Mickey Huff and Project Censored. New York: Seven Stories Press, 2011.

Husseini, Sam. "Checkbook Analysis." *Extra!* (May–June 2000): 23–24.

"Insurance: Life, Health (Mutual), [Top] 7 Companies." *Fortune* (May 21, 2012): F-36–37.

"Insurance: Life, Health (Stock), [Top] 10 Companies." *Fortune* (May 21, 2012): F-37.

Internet Movie Database, Inc. "IMDb Database Statistics: Feature Titles" (1880–2012). 2012. Available at http://www.imdb.com/stats.

———. "U.S. Documentary Releases, by Year." 2012. Available at http://www.imdb.com/stats.

Jackman, Mary R., and Robert W. Jackman. *Class Awareness in the United States*. Berkeley: University of California Press, 1982.

Jackson, Janine. "Let Them Eat Baguettes." *Extra!* (March–April 1996): 14–15.

———. "Admiring the Rich for Getting Richer." *Extra!* (June 2010): 5–6.

———. "11th Annual Fear & Favor Report." *Extra!* (March 2011): 13–15.

———. "ABC's 'Made in America' a Shoddy Product." *Extra!* (April 2011): 5.

———. "12th Annual Fear & Favor Review." *Extra!* (April 2012): 7–9.

———. "New Media—but Familiar Lack of Diversity." *Extra!* (June 2012): 12–13.

———. "13th Annual Fear & Favor Review." *Extra!* (February 2013): 9–11.

Jacobs, Jerry A. "Gender and Academic Specialties: Trends among Recipients of College Degrees in the 1980s." *Sociology of Education* 68 (1995): 81–98.

Jaimovich, Nir, and Henry E. Siu. "The Trend is the Cycle: Job Polarization and Jobless Recoveries." March 31, 2012. Unpublished Paper. Duke University.

Jaros, Dean. *Socialization to Politics*. New York: Praeger, 1973.

Jencks, Christopher, et al. *Inequality: Reassessment of the Effect of Family and Schooling in America*. New York: Harper and Row, 1972.

Jezer, Marty. "Soft Money, Hard Choices." *Dollars and Sense* (July–August 1996): 30–34, 42.

Johnston, David Cay. *Perfectly Legal: The Covert Campaign to Rig Our Tax System to Benefit the Super Rich—and Cheat Everybody Else*. New York: Portfolio, 2003.

Jones, Jeffrey M. "Confidence in U.S. Public Schools at New Low, Confidence Also at New Lows for Organized Religion, Banks, and TV News." Gallup, Inc. (June 20, 2012). Available at http://www.gallup.com.

Josephson, Matthew. *The Robber Barons*. New York: Harcourt, Brace and World, 1934.

Judis, John B. "The Most Powerful Lobby." *In These Times* (February 21, 1994): 22–23.

June, Audrey Williams. "Adjuncts Build Strength in Numbers." *Chronicle of Higher Education* (November 5, 2012). Available at http://www.chronicle.com.

Kaboub, Fadhel. "On the Jasmine Revolution." *Dollars and Sense* (March–April 2011): 7–8.

Kahlenberg, Richard, ed. *America's Untapped Resource: Low-Income Students in Higher Education*. New York: The Century Foundation, 2003.

Kalleberg, Arne L. "Non-standard Employment Relations: Part-Time, Temporary, Contract Work." *Annual Review of Sociology* 26 (2000): 341–65.

———. *Good Jobs, Bad Jobs: The Rise of Polarized and Precarious Employment*. New York: Russell Sage Press, 2011.

Kantar Media. "Kantar Media Reports U.S. Advertising Expenditures Increased 0.8 Percent in 2011." Press release, March 12, 2012. Available at http://www.KantarMediaNA.com.

Karen, David. "Toward a Political-Organizational Model of Gatekeeping: The Case of Elite Colleges." *Sociology of Education* 63 (1990): 227–40.

———. "Changes in Access to Higher Education in the United States: 1980–1992." *Sociology of Education* 75 (July 2002): 191–210.

Katz, Michael B. *The Irony of Early School Reform*. Cambridge, MA: Harvard University Press, 1968.

Katznelson, Ira, and Mark Kesselman. *The Politics of Power*. 5th ed. Belmont, CA: Thomson Wadsworth, 2006.

Kazin, Michael. *The Populist Persuasion*. New York: Basic Books, 1995.

Kendall, Diana. *Framing Class: Media Representations of Wealth and Poverty in America*. 2nd ed. Lanham, MD: Rowman and Littlefield, 2011.

Kentor, Jeffrey, and Yong Suk Jang. "Yes, There Is a (Growing) Transnational Business Community: A Study of Global Interlocking Directorates 1983–1998." *International Sociology* 19 (September 2004): 355–68.

Kerbo, Harold R. *Social Stratification and Inequality*. 5th ed. Boston: McGraw-Hill, 2003.

———. *Social Stratification and Inequality*. 8th ed. New York: McGraw-Hill, 2012.

Khouri, Rami G. "The Arab Awakening." *Nation* (September 12, 2011): 13–15.

Kilgore, Sally. "The Organizational Context of Tracking in Schools." *American Sociological Review* 56 (1991): 189–203.

Kilkenny, Allison. "No Longer Laughing, But Still Clueless." *In These Times* (December 2011): 20–21.

Kirchoff, Suzanne M. "Advertising in the Digital Age." *Congressional Research Service* (February 1, 2011).

Klein, Joe. "These Savings Are Unreal." *Time* (April 23, 2012): 27.

Klein, Naomi. *The Shock Doctrine*. New York: Holt, 2008.

Kluegel, James K., and Eliot R. Smith. *Beliefs about Inequality: Americans' Views of What Is and What Ought to Be*. New York: Aldine DeGruyter, 1986.

Knefel, John. "Bored with Occupy—and Inequality." *Extra!* (May 2012): 6–7.

Knoke, David. *Organized for Action: Commitment in Voluntary Associations*. New Brunswick, NJ: Rutgers University Press, 1981.

Knott, Alex. "Industry of Influence Nets More Than $10 Billion." Center for Public Integrity. 2006. Available at http://www.publicintegrity.org.

Kocieniewski, David "Biggest Public Firms Paid Little U.S. Tax, Study Says." *New York Times*, November 3, 2011. Available at http://www.nytimes.com.

Koeber, Charles, and David W. Wright. "W/Age Bias in Worker Displacement: How Industrial Structure Shapes the Job Loss and Earnings Decline of Older American Workers." *Journal of Socio-Economics* 30 (2001): 343–52.

Koppel, Nathan, and Vanessa O'Connell. "Pay Gap Widens at Big Law Firms as Partners Chase Star Attorneys." *Wall Street Journal*, February 8, 2011. Available at http://online.wsj.com.

Korpi, Walter. *The Democratic Class Struggle*. London: Routledge, 1983.

Kozol, Jonathan. *Savage Inequalities: Children in America's Schools*. New York: Harper, 1991.

———. "'A Deeper Truth Than Newspapers and Networks Are Likely to Provide.'" *Extra!* (September 2010): 9–10.

Krantz, Matt, and Barbara Hansen. "CEO Pay Rises Again in 2011, While Workers Struggle to Find Work." *USA Today*, March 29, 2012. Available at http://www.usatoday.com.

Kroll, Andy. "The Governors' Three-PAC Monte." *Mother Jones* (January–February 2012): 24–27.

———. "What Citizens United Begot." *Mother Jones* (January–February 2012): 22.

———. "Follow the Dark Money." *Mother Jones* (July–August 2012): 17–26.

———. "Can Harold Ickes Make It Rain?" *Mother Jones* (September–October 2012): 39–40.

Kroll, Luisa. "Forbes World's Billionaires 2012." *Forbes* (March 7, 2012). Available at http://www.forbes.com.

Kruger, Alan B. "The Rise and Consequences of Inequality in the United States." Speech at the Center for American Progress (January 12, 2012).

Krugman, Paul. "The Spiral of Inequality." *Mother Jones* (November–December 1996).

———. *The Return of Depression Economics and the Crisis of 2008*. New York: W.W. Norton, 2009.

Kudlow, Lawrence. "Is Obama Buying the Election with His Welfare Explosion?" *The Kudlow Report* (October 19, 2012). Available at http://www.cnbc.com.

"Largest U.S. Corporations." *Fortune* (May 21, 2012): F-1.

Lears, Rachel. "The Death and Life of Occupy." *In These Times* (September 2012): 27–28.

LegiStorm. "Former Lobbyists Working for Congress Outnumber Elected Lawmakers." September 13, 2011. Available at http://www.legistorm.com.

Leonhardt, David, and Majorie Connelly. "81% in Poll Say Nation is Headed on Wrong Track." *New York Times*, April 4, 2008.

LeRoy, Greg. *The Great American Jobs Scam*. San Francisco: Berrett-Koehler, 2005.

Levitt, Larry, Janet Lundy, and Catherine Hoffman. *Employer Health Benefits: 1999 Annual Survey*. Chicago: The Kaiser Family Foundation and Health Research and Educational Trust, 1999.

Levy, Clifford J. "New York Attorney General Remakes Staff by Patronage." *New York Times*, November 10, 1995.

Lewin, Tamar. "23 Private College Presidents Made More Than $1 Million." *New York Times*, November 2, 2009.

Lin, Ken-Hou, and Donald Tomaskovic-Devey. "Financialization and U.S. Income Inequality, 1970–2008." *Social Science Research Network* (November 4, 2011).

Lindorff, Dave. "The First Cuts Won't Be the Deepest." *CounterPunch* (October 1–15, 2012): 1–3.

Lioz, Adam, and Blair Bowie. "Auctioning Democracy: The Rise of Super PACs and the 2012 Election." February 8, 2012. A Joint Project by Dēmos and USPIRG. Available at http://www.demos.org.

———. "Million-Dollar Megaphones: Super PACs and Unlimited Outside Spending in the 2012 Elections." August 2, 2012. A Joint Project by Dēmos and USPIRG. Available at http://www.demos.org.

Lipman, Pauline. "Neoliberal Education Restructuring." *Monthly Review* (July–August 2011): 114–27.

Lipset, Seymour M., and Reinhard Bendix. *Social Mobility in Industrial Society*. Berkeley: University of California Press, 1959.

Litt, Edgar. "Civic Education, Community Norms, and Political Indoctrination." *American Sociological Review* 28 (February 1963): 69–75.

Lloyd, Mark. "Lessons for Realistic Radicals in the Information Age." In *The Future of Media: Resistance and Reform in the 21st Century*, edited by Robert McChesney, Russell Newman, and Ben Scott. New York: Seven Stories Press, 2005.

Lockard, C. Brett, and Michael Wolf. "Occupational Employment Projections to 2020." *Monthly Labor Review* (January 2012): 84–108.

Lohr, Steve. "Offshore Jobs in Technology: Opportunity or a Threat?" *New York Times*, December 22, 2003.

———. "Debate Over Exporting Jobs Raises Questions on Policies." *New York Times*, February 23, 2004.

Lucas, Samuel R., and Aaron D. Good. "Race, Class, and Tournament Track Mobility." *Sociology of Education* 74 (2001): 139–56.

Lukács, George. *History and Class Consciousness*. Cambridge, MA: MIT Press, 1968.

Lundberg, Ferdinand. *The Rich and the Super-Rich*. New York: Bantam Books, 1968.

Magdoff, Fred. "The Jobs Disaster in the United States." *Monthly Review* (June 2011): 24–37.

Mander, Jerry. "The Privatization of Consciousness." *Monthly Review* (October 2012): 18–41.

Mantsios, Gregory. "Class in America: Myths and Realities." In *Race, Class, and Gender in the United States*, edited by Paula S. Rothenberg. New York: St. Martin's Press, 1995.

Marger, Martin N. *Social Inequality: Patterns and Processes*. 3rd ed. Boston: McGraw-Hill, 2005.

———. *Social Inequality: Patterns and Processes*. 5th ed. Boston: McGraw-Hill, 2011.

Marketing Charts Staff. "Average Hour-Long TV Show is 36% Commercials." MC Marketing Charts (May 7, 2009). Available at http://www.marketingcharts.com.

Marshall, Andrew G. "Western Civilization and the Economic Crisis, the Impoverishment of the Middle Class." March 30, 2010. Available at http://www.marketoracle.co.uk/Article18282.

Martin, Christopher R. *Framed: Labor and the Corporate Media*. Ithaca, NY: Cornell University Press, 2004.

Martin, Mick, and Marsha Porter. *1995 Video Movie Guide*. New York: Ballantine, 1994.

Martin, Randal. "A Brief History of Propaganda." In *Censored 2012*, edited by Mickey Huff and Project Censored. New York: Seven Stories Press, 2011.

McArthur, Travis. "The Numbers Are In: Trade Deals Fail to Deliver." *Labor Notes* (November 2010): 11.

McChesney, Robert W. *Rich Media, Poor Democracy: Communication Politics in Dubious Times*. Chicago: University of Illinois Press, 1999.

———. "Journalism, Democracy, and Class Struggle." *Monthly Review* (November 2000): 1–15.

———. *The Problem of the Media*. New York: Monthly Review Press, 2004.

———. "This Isn't What Democracy Looks Like." *Monthly Review* (November 2012): 1–28.

McChesney, Robert W., and John Bellamy Foster. "The 'Left-Wing' Media?" *Monthly Review* (June 2003): 1–16.

McChesney, Robert W., John Bellamy Foster, Inger L. Stole, and Hannah Holleman. "The Sales Effort and Monopoly Capitalism." *Monthly Review* (April 2009): 1–23.

McChesney, Robert W., and John Nichols. "Political Advertising: A Bull Market." *Monthly Review* (April 2012): 1–26.

McChesney, Robert W., Russell Newman, and Ben Scott, eds. *The Future of Media: Resistance and Reform in the 21st Century*. New York: Seven Stories Press, 2005.

McIntyre, Robert S. "Testimony on Corporate Welfare." U.S. House of Representatives Committee on the Budget (June 30, 1999). Available at http://www.ctj.org.

McLean, Bethany. "The Meltdown Explanation That Melts Away." *Reuters* (March 19, 2012). Available at http://blogs.reuters.com.

Meacham, Jon. "Keeping the Dream Alive." *Time* (July 2, 2012): 29.

Meltzer, Joshua. "Congress Should Pass Free Trade Agreements with South Korea, Colombia and Panama." Brookings Institution. Press release, July 28, 2011. Available at http://www.brookings.edu.

Mencimer, Stephanie. "Mr. Precedent." *Mother Jones* (May–June 2011): 55–57, 66–67.

MetLife. "2010 MetLife Study of the American Dream: An Uphill Climb." New York: Metropolitan Life Insurance Company, May 2010.

Michael, Robert S., Terry E. Spradlin, and Fatima R. Carson. "Changes in Indiana School Funding." Center for Evaluation and Educational Policy. *Education Policy Brief* 7 (Summer 2009): 1–16.

Mickelson, Roslyn Arlin. "The Attitude-Achievement Paradox among Black Adolescents." *Sociology of Education* 63 (1990): 44–61.

Miller, John. "More Wealth for the Wealthy: The Estate Tax Giveaway and What to Do about It." *Dollars and Sense* (November–December 1997): 26–28, 33.

———. "Tax Cuts: Clinton and Congress Feed the Wealthy." *Dollars and Sense* (November–December 1997): 43.

———. "Getting Back More Than They Give." *Dollars and Sense* (September–October 2001): 60–62.

———. "No Fooling—Corporations Evade Taxes." *Dollars and Sense* (May–June 2011): 11–12.

———. "Putting the Screws to Generation Screwed." *Dollars and Sense* (September–October 2012): 10–11.

———. "Second Coming of the Estate Tax Not So Rapturous." *Dollars and Sense* (January–February 2013): 9–10.

Miller, Mark C. "Free the Media." *Nation* (June 3, 1996): 9–15.

Minkoff, Debra, Silke Aisenbrey, and Jon Agnone. "Organizational Diversity in the U.S. Advocacy Sector." *Social Problems* 55 (2008): 525–48.

Mishel, Lawrence, Jared Bernstein, and Sylvia Allegretto. *The State of Working America, 2004/2005.* Ithaca, NY: IRL Press, 2005.

———. *The State of Working America, 2006/2007.* Ithaca, NY: IRL Press, 2007.

Mishel, Lawrence, Jared Bernstein, and Heidi Shierholz. *The State of Working America: 2008–2009.* Ithaca, NY: IRL Press, 2009.

Mishel, Lawrence, and Josh Bivens. "Occupy Wall Streeters Are Right about Skewed Economic Rewards in the United States." Briefing Paper #331. Washington, DC: Economic Policy Institute, October 26, 2011.

Mishel, Lawrence, Josh Bivens, Elise Gould, and Heidi Shierholz. *The State of Working America.* 12th ed. Ithaca, NY: IRL Press, 2012.

Mitchell, Bridger M., and Charles E. Phelps. "National Health Insurance: Some Costs and Effects of Mandated Employee Coverage." *Journal of Political Economy* 84 (1976): 553–71.

Moberg, David. "Throw Books at Them." *In These Times* (December 19, 2005): 26–27, 37.

Moberg, Eric Michael. *Class War 2012.* London: Prescott University Press, 2011.

Moment of Truth: Report of The National Commission On Fiscal Responsibility and Reform. December 2010.

Monroe, Ann. "Getting Rid of the Grey." *Mother Jones* (July–August 1996): 29.

Moore, James H., Jr. "Projected Pension Income: Equity or Disparity for the Baby Boom Cohort?" *Monthly Labor Review* (March 2006): 58–67.

Moore, Thomas S. *The Disposable Work Force.* New York: Aldine de Gruyter, 1996.

Moran, Theresa. "Chicago Teachers Raise the Bar." *Labor Notes* (October 2012): 1.

Morgenson, Gretchen, and Joshua Rosner. *Reckless Endangerment.* New York: Henry Holt, 2011.

Moriarity, Shannon, ed. *Born on Third Base: What the Forbes 400 Really Says about Economic Equality and Opportunity in America.* Boston: United for a Fair Economy, 2012.

Morrison, Patrick. "Media Monopoly Revisited." *Extra!* (October 21, 2011): 13–15.

Motion Picture Association of America. "Theatrical Market Statistics, 2011." Available at http://www.mpaa.org.

Mullaney, Troy. "Trade Deals with S. Korea, Colombia, Panama, Who Wins?" *USA Today,* October 13, 2011. Available at http://www.usatoday.com.

Mullen Ann L., Kimberly A. Goyette, and Joseph A. Soares. "Who Goes to Graduate School? Social and Educational Correlates of Educational Continuation After College." *Sociology of Education* 76 (April 2003): 143–69.

Mumford, Lou. "Granholm's Hope on Jobs Plan." *South Bend Tribune,* April 16, 2006. Available at http://www.southbendtribune.com.

Murphy, Tim. "So You Want to Buy an Election?" *Mother Jones* (January–February 2012): 23.

Nace, Ted. *Gangs of America: The Rise of Corporate Power and the Disabling of Democracy.* San Francisco: Berrett-Koehler, 2003.

Nader, Ralph. "Product Libel." *Public Citizen News* (May–June 1998): 4.

———. "Not Made in America." *Common Dreams* (November 30, 2011). Available at http://www.commondreams.org.

Nasiripour, Shahien. "Immelt, GE CEO, to Run New Jobs-Focused Panel as GE Sends Jobs Overseas, Pays Little in Taxes." *Huffington Post* (January 21, 2011). Available at http://www.huffingtonpost.com.

National Association for Law Placement. "Median Private Practice Starting Salaries for the Class of 2011 Plunge as Private Practice Jobs Continue to Erode." Press release, July 12, 2012. Available at http://www.nalp.org.

National Association of Manufacturers. "Manufacturers: Tax Relief in Senate Passed Bill is Critical." Press release, December 15, 2010.

National Committee for Responsive Philanthropy. "$1 Billion for Ideas: Conservative Think Tanks in the 1990s." Press release, March 12, 1999.

National Employment Law Project. "The Low Wage Recovery and Growing Inequality." August 2012. Available at http://www.nelp.org.

"The National Entertainment State, Special Issue." *Nation* (July 3, 2006): 13–30.

Naureckas, Jim. "Corporate Censorship Matters: The Case of NBC." *Extra!* (November–December 1995): 13.

———. "From the Top: What Are the Politics of Network Bosses?" *Extra!* (July–August 1998): 21–22.

———. "Where's the Power: Newsroom or Boardroom?" *Extra!* (July–August 1998): 23.

———. "Framing the Fed as Financial Philosopher Kings." *Extra!* (June 2010): 13–14.

———. "They Are the 1 Percent." *Extra!* (November 2011): 7–8.

———. "The Great British Mistake." *Extra!* (June 2012): 11.

———. "The Hall of Fame of Bad Ideas." *Extra!* (January 2013): 5.

Navarro, Vicente. "Medical History as Justification Rather Than Explanation: A Critique of Starr's *The Social Transformation of American Medicine.*" *International Journal of Health Services* 14 (1984): 511–28.

———. "Production and the Welfare State: The Political Context of Reforms." *International Journal of Health Services* 21 (1991): 585–614.

Nayman, Louis. "Splintering the 99%." *In These Times* (October 2012): 24–25.

"NBC News/*Wall Street Journal* Survey." Conducted by Hart/McInturff, study #11579 (November 2–5, 2011), Question #30, 22. Available at http://www.nbcnews.com.

"NBC's Dodgy Coverage of GE's $0 Tax Bill." *Extra!* (May 2011): 3.

Neustadtl, Alan, and Dan Clawson. "Corporate Political Groupings: Does Ideology Unify Business Political Behavior?" *American Sociological Review* 53 (1988): 172–90.

Newman, Jared. "SOPA and PIPA: Just the Facts." *PC World* (January 19, 2012). Available at http://www.arrnet.com.

Newman, Russell, and Ben Scott. "Introduction." In *The Future of Media: Resistance and Reform in the 21st Century*, edited by Robert McChesney, Russell Newman, and Ben Scott. New York: Seven Stories Press, 2005.

The News Corporation. "Australian Federal Court Approves News Corporation Reincorporation to United States." Press release, November 3, 2004. Available at http://www.newscorp.com.

———. *News Corporation Annual Report 2012*. Available at http://www.newscorp.com.

"Newswatch: President Mohammed Morsi's Power Grab Inside Egypt's Union Federation." *Labor Notes* (January 2013): 5.

Newton-Small, Jay, and Michael Scherer. "Conspiracy of Two." *Time* (July 25, 2011): 40–41.

"The New Transplants." *UAW Research Bulletin* (January–February 1995): 10–11.

New York Times. *Class Matters*. New York: Times Books, 2005.

New York Times/CBS News Poll. January 20–25, 2006.

NextMark. "Major Republican Political Donors Mailing List." June 28, 2012. Available at http://lists.nextmark.com.

Nichols, John. "Behind the DLC Takeover." *Progressive* (October 2000): 28–30.

———. "ALEC Exposed." *Nation* (August 1–8, 2011): 16–17.

Nichols, John, and Robert W. McChesney. "Assault of the Super Pacs." *Nation* (February 6, 2012): 11–17.

Nielsen Company. "State of the Media: Consumer Usage Report, 2011." Available at http://www.nielsen.com.

Nielsenwire. "May 2012—Top U.S. Web Brands and News Websites." June 22, 2012. Available at http://blog.nielsen.com.

Nitschke, Lori. "Tax Plan Destined for Revision." *Congressional Quarterly Weekly* (February 10, 2001): 318–21.

———. "Coalitions Make a Comeback." *Congressional Quarterly Weekly* (March 3, 2001): 470–74.

Noah, Timothy. *The Great Divergence: America's Growing Inequality Crisis and What We Can Do about It.* New York: Bloomsbury Press, 2012.

Nutting, Rex. "Corporate Profits' Share of Pie Most in 60 Years." *MarketWatch* (July 29, 2011). Available at http://www.marketwatch.com.

Obama, Barack. *The Audacity of Hope.* New York: Crown, 2006.

———. "Memorandum for the Heads of Executive Departments and Agencies." White House Press Office (January 30, 2009). Available at http://www.whitehouse.gov.

———. "Remarks by the President and Vice President in Announcement of Labor Executive Orders and Middle Class Working Families Task Force." White House Briefing Room (January 30, 2009). Available at http://www.whitehouse.gov.

"Occupied Territory. A Time Poll." *Time* (October 24, 2011): 24.

O'Connor, Carla. "Race, Class, and Gender in America: Narratives of Opportunity among Low-Income African American Youths." *Sociology of Education* 72 (1999): 137–57.

Office of Management and Budget. "Appendix: Department of Health and Human Services, 'Administration for Children and Families, TANF.'" *Budget of the United States Government: Fiscal Year 2013.* Washington, DC: U.S. Government Printing Office, 2013.

———. *Budget of the United States Government: Fiscal Year 2013.* Washington, DC: U.S. Government Printing Office, 2013.

———. "Department of Defense." *Budget of the United States Government: Fiscal Year 2013.* Washington, DC: U.S. Government Printing Office, 2013.

———. "Historical Tables." *Budget of the United States Government: Fiscal Year 2013.* Washington, DC: U.S. Government Printing Office, 2013.

———. "Summary Tables." *Budget of the United States Government: Fiscal Year 2013.* Washington, DC: U.S. Government Printing Office, 2013.

Office of National Drug Control Policy. *The National Drug Control Strategy.* Washington, DC: National Criminal Justice Reference Service, 1992.

———. *National Drug Control Strategy: 2001 Annual Report.* Washington, DC: U.S. Government Printing Office, 2001.

———. *National Drug Control Strategy: 2012.* Washington, DC: U.S. Government Printing Office, 2012.

———. *National Drug Control Budget: FY 2013 Budget Funding Highlights.* Washington, DC: The White House, February 2013.

Office of Technology Assessment. *Technology and Structural Unemployment.* Washington, DC: Congress of the United States, 1986.

Ohlemacher, Stephen. "You Can Say Goodbye to Payroll Tax Cut." *Indianapolis Star*, October 22, 2012, A5.

Oliver, Melvin, Thomas M. Shapiro, and Julie E. Press. "'Them That's Got Shall Get': Inheritance and Achievement in Wealth Accumulation." In *Research in Politics and Society*, edited by Richard E. Ratliffe, Melvin Oliver, and Thomas M. Shapiro. Vol. 15. Greenwich, CT: JAI Press, 1995.

Orr, Doug. "Social Security Q&A." *Dollars and Sense* (May–June 2005): 15–20.

Orum, Anthony M., and Roberta S. Cohen. "The Development of Political Orientations among Black and White Children." *American Sociological Review* 38 (1973): 62–74.

Overton, Spencer. "The Donor Class: Campaign Finance, Democracy, and Participation." *University of Pennsylvania Law Review* 153 (2004): 73–118.

Pace, Eric. "B. Gerald Cantor, Philanthropist and Owner of Rodin Collection, Is Dead at 79." *New York Times*, July 6, 1996.

Page, Benjamin I., Fay Lomax Cook, and Rachel Moskowitz. "Wealthy Americans, Philanthropy, and the Common Good." Institute for Policy Research, Northwestern University, *Working Paper Series* (October 16, 2011): 10–11.

Pal, Amitabh. "Meet the 26 Billionaires Buying Our Democracy." *Progressive* (October 2012): 24–26.

Paletta, Damian, and John D. McKinnon. "The Data Behind Romney's 47% Comments." *Wall Street Journal*, September 18, 2012. Available at http://blogs.wsj.com/washwire.

Palley, Thomas I. *From Financial Crisis to Stagnation*. Cambridge: Cambridge University Press, 2012.

Parenti, Christian. "Winning the War of Ideas." *In These Times* (November 17, 2003): 18–21.

Parks, Daniel J. "Under Tight Spending Ceilings, Democrats Lower Their Sights." *Congressional Quarterly Weekly* (June 9, 2001): 1362–64.

Parry, Robert. "The Right-Wing Media Machine." *Extra!* (March–April 1995): 6–10.

Paulson, Henry, Jr. *On the Brink: Inside the Race to Stop the Collapse of the Global Financial System*. New York: Hachette, 2010.

Payne, Erica. *The Practical Progressive: How to Build a 21st Century Political Movement*. New York: PublicAffairs, 2008.

Perine, Keith. "Class Action Lawsuit Measure Advances amid Heavy Lobbying, Concern over State Law." *Congressional Quarterly Weekly* (April 12, 2003): 882.

Perrucci, Carolyn C., and Robert Perrucci. "Social Origins, Educational Contexts, and Career Mobility." *American Sociological Review* 35 (1970): 451–63.

Perrucci, Carolyn C., Robert Perrucci, Dena B. Targ, and Harry Targ. *Plant Closings: International Context and Social Costs*. Hawthorne, NY: Aldine de Gruyter, 1988.

Perrucci, Robert. "The Significance of Intra-Occupational Mobility." *American Sociological Review* 26 (1961): 874–83.

———. *Japanese Auto Transplants in the Heartland*. New York: Aldine De Gruyter, 1994.

———. "Too Big to Fail: A Network Perspective." *International Journal of Contemporary Sociology* 48 (2011): 251–78.

Perrucci, Robert, et al. "The Two Faces of Racialized Space in a Predominantly White University." *International Journal of Sociology* 37 (2000): 230–44.

Perrucci, Robert, and Bonnie L. Lewis. "Interorganizational Relations and Community Influence Structure." *Sociological Quarterly* 30 (1989): 205–23.

Perrucci, Robert, and Carolyn Perrucci, eds. *The Transformation of Work in the New Economy*. New York: Oxford University Press, 2007.

———. *America at Risk: The Crisis of Hope, Trust, and Caring.* Lanham, MD: Rowman and Littlefield, 2009.

Perrucci, Robert, and Marc Pilisuk. "Leaders and Ruling Elites: The Interorganizational Basis of Community Power." *American Sociological Review* 35 (1970): 1040–57.

Perrucci, Robert, and Earl Wysong. *The New Class Society.* Lanham, MD: Rowman and Littlefield, 1999.

———. "Organizational Power, Generative Capital, and Class Closure." Paper presented at the Pacific Sociological Association annual meeting, San Francisco, California (March 31, 2001).

———. *The New Class Society: Goodbye American Dream?* 2nd ed. Lanham, MD: Rowman and Littlefield, 2003.

———. *The New Class Society: Goodbye American Dream?* 3rd ed. Lanham, MD: Rowman and Littlefield, 2008.

Petrova, Maria. "Inequality and Media Capture." Working Paper Series, Social Science Research Network, Harvard University (February 6, 2006). Available at http://www.papers.ssrn.com.

Pew Research Center for the People and the Press. "Inside the Middle Class: Bad Times Hit the Good Life." A Social & Demographic Trends Report (April 9, 2008). Available at http://www.pewresearch.org.

———. "Press Accuracy Rating Hits Two Decade Low." September 13, 2009. Available at http://people-press.org.

———. "How the Great Recession Has Changed Life in America." Press release, June 30, 2010. Available at http://www.pewsocialtrends.org.

———. "Public Support for Increased Trade, Except with South Korea and China." November 9, 2010. Available at http://www.people-press.org.

———. "Internet Gains on Television as Public's Main News Source." January 4, 2011. Available at http://people-press.org.

———. "Little Change in Public's Response to 'Capitalism,' 'Socialism.'" December, 28, 2011. Available at http://www.people-press.org.

———. "Rising Share of Americans See Conflict Between Rich and Poor." January 11, 2012. Available at http://www.pewsocialtrends.org.

———. "Super PACs Having Negative Impact, Say Voters Aware of 'Citizens United' Ruling." January 17, 2012. Available at http://www.pew research.org.

———. "Auto Bailout Now Backed, Stimulus Divisive." February, 23, 2012. Available at http://www.people-press.org.

———. "Growing Gap in Favorable Views of Federal, State Governments." April 26, 2012. Available at http://www.pewresearch.org.

———. "Partisan Polarization Surges in Bush, Obama Years." *Trends in American Values: 1987–2012* (June 4, 2012). Available at http://www.people-press.org.

———. "The Lost Decade of the Middle Class." August 22, 2012. Available at http://www.pewresearch.org.

———. "Deep Divisions over Debt Reduction Proposals." October 12, 2012. Available at http://www.people-press.org.

Pew Research Center's Project for Excellence in Journalism. "Newspapers: By the Numbers." *The State of the News Media 2012.* Available at http://stateofthemedia.org.

———. "Who Owns the News Media: Top Newspaper Companies." *The State of the News Media 2012.* Available at http://stateofthemedia.org.

Phillips, Jim. "What Happens After Seattle?" *Dollars and Sense* (January–February 2000): 15–16, 31–32.

Phillips, Kevin. "Fat City." *Time* (September 26, 1994): 49–56.

———. *American Dynasty*. New York: Penguin Books, 2004.

Phillips, Peter. "Self Censorship and the Homogeneity of the Media Elite." In *Censored 1998*, edited by Peter Phillips. New York: Seven Stories Press, 1998.

———. "The Top 25 Censored Stories of 2000." In *Censored 2001*, edited by Peter Phillips and Project Censored. New York: Seven Stories Press, 2001.

———. "Preface." In *Censored 2006*, edited by Peter Phillips and Project Censored. New York: Seven Stories Press, 2005.

"Physician Compensation Report 2012." *Medscape* (February 2012). Available at http://www.medscape.com.

Pizzigati, Sam, ed. "Stat of the Week: Estate Tax Odds." *Too Much* (June 5, 2006): 4.

———. "Most Original Research on the Consequences of Inequality." *Too Much* (December 18, 2006): 4.

———. "Repeating History, Reversing History." *Too Much* (February 23, 2009): 4.

———. "Why the Top Rate Matters." *Too Much* (March 9, 2009): 3.

———. "Long Live the Statistical Middle Class!" *Labor Studies Journal* 35 (September 2010): 386–97.

———. "Treadmill Time, Except at the Top." *Too Much* (January 31, 2011): 3.

———. "At the Top, Pulling Away." *Too Much* (June 13, 2011): 3.

———. "Tip for Joe the Machinist: Watch Your Back." *Too Much* (June 25, 2011): 4.

———. "Remembering the Moment Our CEOs Dug In." *Too Much* (August 29, 2011): 4.

———. "U.S. Tax Rates: The Top Drop." *Too Much* (October 10, 2011): 3.

———. "Equality Now!" *Nation* (November 14, 2011): 18–19.

———. "The Hedges Get a Trim." *Too Much* (April 14, 2012): 3.

———. "Our Top 400: A Little Historical Perspective." *Too Much* (June 11, 2012): 3–4.

———. "This Week." *Too Much* (June 18, 2012): 1.

———. "This Week." *Too Much* (August 6, 2012): 1.

———. "The 'Dark Money' of the Ultra Rich." *Too Much* (August 20, 2012): 3.

———. *The Rich Don't Always Win: The Forgotten Triumph over Plutocracy that Created the American Middle Class, 1900–1970*. Boston: Seven Stories Press, 2012.

———. "The Tax Legacy of George W. Bush: It Lives!" *Too Much* (January 7, 2013): 4–5.

———. "Swell Times for America's Swollen Fortunes." *Too Much* (January 14, 2013): 4–5.

———. "The Scruffy and Stuffy Agree: Cap CEO Pay." *Too Much* (February 11, 2013): 4.

Pizzigati, Sam, and Chuck Collins. "The Great Regression." *Nation* (February 25, 2013): 25–26.

Pocan, Mark. "Inside the ALEC Dating Service." *Progressive* (October 2011): 19–21.

Pohlman, Kimberly. "Solid Ratings Don't Protect Progressive Radio Voices." *Extra!* (July–August 2000): 22.

Pollin, Robert. *Contours of Descent: U.S. Economic Fractures and the Landscape of Global Austerity*. New York: Verso, 2005.

Pomery, John. "Running Deficits with the Rest of the World—Part I." *Focus on Economic Issues*. West Lafayette, IN: Purdue Center for Economic Education, Fall 1987.

Posner, Richard. *The Failure of Capitalism: The Crisis of '08 and the Descent into Depression*. Cambridge, MA: Harvard University Press, 2009.

Postman, Neil. "Virtual Students, Digital Classroom." *Nation* (October 9, 1995): 377–82.
Powell, Lewis F. "Attack on American Free Enterprise System." August 23, 1971. Available at http://www.greenpeace.org/usa.
Press, Eyal. "Spin Cities." *Nation* (November 18, 1996): 30–33.
Public Citizen. *Unfairness Incorporated: The Corporate Campaign against Consumer Class Actions.* Public Citizen's Congress Watch (June 2003).
Quinn, Jane Bryant. "The Economic Perception Gap." *Newsweek* (November 20, 2006): 59.
Rampton, Sheldon, and John Stauber. "Oprah's Free—Are We?" *Extra!* (May–June 1998): 11–12.
———. "This Report Brought to You by Monsanto." *Progressive* (July 1998): 22–25.
Randall, Adrian. *Before the Luddites.* New York: Cambridge University Press, 1991.
"Ranked within Industries: Entertainment, 7 Companies." *Fortune* (May 21, 2012): F35.
Raskin, Jamie. "Citizens United and the Corporate Court." *Nation* (October 8, 2012): 17–20.
Reed, Adolf L., Jr. "The 'Public Is Bad; Private Is Better' Scam." *Labor Party News* (October 2005): 1–2.
Reich, Robert B. *Next American Frontier.* New York: Times Books, 1983.
———. *Aftershock: The Next Economy and America's Future.* New York: Alfred Knopf, 2010.
Reiman, Jeffrey. *The Rich Get Richer and the Poor Get Prison.* 5th ed. Boston: Allyn and Bacon, 1998.
Renchler, Ron. *Financial Equity in Schools.* ERIC Digest no. 76. Eugene, OR: ERIC Clearinghouse in Educational Management, 1994.
Reskin, Barbara, and Irene Padavic. *Women and Men at Work.* Thousand Oaks, CA: Pine Forge Press, 1994.
"Resources." *Labor Notes* (March 2013): 13.
Reuss, Alejandro. "What's Behind Union Decline in the United States?" *Dollars and Sense* (May–June 2011): 25–26.
Reynolds, Alan. "Offshoring Which Jobs?" *Washington Times*, June 6, 2004.
"Rich College, Poor College." *Business Week* (December 20, 2004): 88–90.
"The Rich Get a Good Return on Their Campaign Investments." *Sanders Scoop* (Winter 1998): 1.
Ridgeway, James. "Who Shredded Our Safety Net?" *Mother Jones* (May–June 2009): 28–33, 81–82.
Rispo, Vito. "How to Stop Ad Blindness: Novelty in Advertising Is Key." *Ad Savy* (2012). Available at http://www.adsavy.org.
Ritzer, George. *Sociological Theory.* 3rd ed. New York: McGraw-Hill, 1988.
Rivera, Lauren A. "Ivies, Extracurriculars, and Exclusion: Elite Employers' Use of Educational Credentials." *Research in Stratification and Mobility* 29 (2011): 71–90.
Roberts, Alison. "George Carlin: Standup's Grump-pa." *Sacramento Bee*, December 2, 2005.
Roberts, Paul Craig. "The New Face of Class Warfare." *CounterPunch* (July 2006): 1–6.
Rockefeller Foundation. "2010 Trustees." *Annual Report 2010.*
Roediger, David R., and Elizabeth D. Esch. *The Production of Difference: Race and the Management of Labor in U.S. History.* New York: Oxford University Press, 2012.
Rogers, Joel, and Laura Dresser. "Business Domination, Inc." *Nation* (August 1–8, 2011): 17–20.
Rohar, Evan. "Longshore Workers Block Trains, Shut Ports to Protect Good Jobs." *Labor Notes* (October 2011): 1, 14–15.

Romney, Mitt, and Ann Romney. 1040 U.S. Individual Income Tax Return (2010). Available at http://www.mittromney.com.

Roscigno, Vincent J., and James W. Ainsworth-Darnell. "Race, Cultural Capital, and Educational Resources: Persistent Inequalities and Achievement Returns." *Sociology of Education* 72 (1999): 158–78.

Rosenthal, Robert, and Lenore Jacobson. *Pygmalion in the Classroom*. New York: Holt, Rinehart and Winston, 1968.

Ross, Steven J. *Working-Class Hollywood: Silent Film and the Shaping of Class in America.* Princeton, NJ: Princeton University Press, 1998.

Rothkopf, David. *Superclass: The Global Power Elite and the World They Are Making.* New York: Farrar, Straus, and Giroux, 2008.

Rothman, Robert A. *Inequality and Stratification: Race, Class, and Gender.* 5th ed. Upper Saddle River, NJ: Pearson-Prentice Hall, 2005.

Rothschild, Matthew. "The Progressive Interview: Roger Ebert." *Progressive* (August 2003): 33–37.

———. "Class Warfare, Anyone?" *Progressive* (November 2011): 7–8.

———. "The Third-Party Dilemma." *Progressive* (September 2012): 18.

Roubini, Nouriel, and Stephen Mihm. *Crisis Economics: A Crash Course in the Future of Finance.* New York: Penguin, 2010.

Rousseau, Jean-Jacques. *The Social Contract.* Trans. Charles Frankel. New York: Hafner, 1947.

Rubin, Beth A. *Shifts in the Social Contract.* Thousand Oaks, CA: Pine Forge Press, 1996.

Rudolph, Ileane. "Oprah's Grand Finale." *TV Guide* (May 23–29, 2011): 18–21.

Saad, Lydia. "Americans Decry Power of Lobbyists, Corporations, Banks, Feds." Gallup, Inc. (April 11, 2011). Available at http://www.gallup.com.

Sachs, Jeffrey D. "Why America Must Revive Its Middle Class." *Time* (October 21, 2011): 30–32.

Sadker, Myra Pollack, and David Miller Sadker. *Teachers, Schools, and Society.* 6th ed. New York: McGraw-Hill, 2003.

Saez, Emmanuel. "Striking It Richer: The Evolution of Top Incomes in the United States." Updated March 2012. Available at http://www.elsa.berkeley.edu/-saez/.

"Salary Offers to College Class of 2009 Are Flat." International Association of Employment (2010). Available at http://www.iae.com.

Samuelson, Robert J. "Great Expectations." *Newsweek* (January 8, 1996): 24–33.

Sargent, John, and Linda Matthews. "China *versus* Mexico in the Global EPZ Industry: Maquiladoras, FDI Quality, and Plant Mortality." *World Development* 37 (2009): 1069–82.

Scharf, Adria. "Tax Cut Time Bomb." *Dollars and Sense* (March–April 2004): 39.

Scheer, Robert. *The Great American Stickup.* New York: Nation Books, 2009.

Schell, Jonathan. "The Revolutionary Moment." *Nation* (February 21, 2011): 3–6.

Scher, Abby. "Not the Same Old 'New Economy.'" *Dollars and Sense* (July–August 2012): 12.

Scherer, Michael. "Make Your Taxes Disappear!" *Mother Jones* (March–April 2005): 72–77.

———. "Taking It to the Streets." *Time* (October 24, 2011): 20–24.

———. "A Rich Man's Game." *Time* (August 13, 2012): 42–45.

Schlozman, Kay L., and John T. Tierney. *Organized Interests and American Democracy.* New York: Harper and Row, 1986.

Schmidt, Diane E. "Public Opinion and Media Coverage of Labor Unions." *Journal of Labor Research* (Spring 1993): 151–64.

Schmitt, John, and Janelle Jones. "Where Have All the Good Jobs Gone." Center for Economic and Policy Research (July 2012). Available at http://www.cepr.net.

Schneider, Dan. "Occupying Student Debt." *Dollars and Sense* (January–February 2012): 6.

Schneider, Nathan. "From Occupy Wall Street to Occupy Everywhere." *Nation* (October 31, 2011): 13–17.

———. "Occupy, After Occupy." *Nation* (September 24, 2012): 13–17.

"School Finance." *Education Week* (June 20, 2011). Available at http://www.edweek.org.

Schroeder, Peter. "Tax Policy Center Analysis Details the '47 Percent.'" *The Hill* (September 18, 2012). Available at http://thehill.com/blogs.

Schwalbe, Michael. *Rigging the Game: How Inequality Is Reproduced in Everyday Life.* New York: Oxford University Press, 2008.

Schwartzman, Andrew Jay, Cheryl A. Leanza, and Harold Feld. "The Legal Case for Diversity in Broadcast Ownership." In *The Future of Media: Resistance and Reform in the 21st Century*, edited by Robert McChesney, Russell Newman, and Ben Scott. New York: Seven Stories Press, 2005.

Scott, Janny, and David Leonhardt. "Class in America: Shadowy Lines That Still Divide." *New York Times*, May 15, 2005, 1, 16–18.

Scott, Robert E. "NAFTA's Hidden Costs." Washington, DC: Economic Policy Institute (May 21, 2001).

Seider, Maynard S. "American Big Business Ideology: A Content Analysis of Executive Speeches." *American Sociological Review* 39 (1974): 802–15.

The Sentencing Project. *Trends in U.S. Corrections.* "Federal and State Prison Population, by Offense, 2010." Available at http://www.sentencingproject.org.

———. "Number of People in Prisons and Jails for Drug Offenses, 1980 and 2010." Available at http://www.sentencingproject.org.

———. "People in State and Federal Prisons, by Race and Ethnicity, 2010." Available at http://www.sentencingproject.org.

Sewell, William A., A. O. Haller, and G. W. Ohlandorf. "The Educational and Early Occupational Status Attainment Process." *American Sociological Review* 35 (1970): 1014–27.

Sewell, William A., and Vimal Shah. "Parents' Education and Children's Educational Aspirations and Achievements." *American Sociological Review* 33 (1968): 191–209.

"'Shared Sacrifice' at the Country Club." *Extra!* (May 2012): 3.

Short, Kathleen. "The Research Supplemental Poverty Measure: 2010." *Current Population Reports.* U.S. Census Bureau (November 2011).

Shuldiner, Allan, and Tony Raymond. *Who's in the Lobby? A Profile of Washington's Influence Industry.* Washington, DC: Center for Responsive Politics, 1998.

Sifry, Micah L. *Spoiling for a Fight: Third Party Politics in America.* New York: Routledge, 2002.

Sifry, Micah L., and Nancy Watzman. *Is That a Politician in Your Pocket? Washington on $2 Million a Day.* Hoboken, NJ: John Wiley & Sons, 2004.

Silverstein, Ken, and Alexander Cockburn. "Why the Drug War Works: It's a Money/Class Thing, of Course." *CounterPunch* (June 15–30, 1998): 4–5.

Simmons, Robert G., and Morris Rosenberg. "Functions of Children's Perceptions of the Stratification System." *American Sociological Review* 36 (1971): 235–49.

Sklar, Leslie. *The Transnational Capitalist Class.* Oxford: Blackwell, 2001.

Slaughter, Jane. "Next Low Wage Haven: USA." *Labor Notes* (August 2011): 1, 14.

———. "Auto Companies Recover, but Jobs Are Harder." *Labor Notes* (September 2011): 10.

———. "Auto Workers Approve Ford Contract After Hard Sell." *Labor Notes* (November 2011): 13.

———. "Right to Work Smacks Michigan: Sneak Attack, Long Buildup." *Labor Notes* (January 2013): 1–3.

Solomon, Norman. "Media Moguls on Board." *Extra!* (January–February 1998): 19–22.

———. "The Media Oligarchy: Undermining Journalism, Obstructing Democracy." In *Censored 2001*, edited by Peter Phillips. New York: Seven Stories Press, 2001.

Source Watch. "Lobbying." 2006. Available at http://www.sourcewatchorg.

Stauber, John, and Sheldon Rampton. *Toxic Sludge Is Good for You: Lies, Damn Lies, and the Public Relations Industry*. Monroe, ME: Common Courage Press, 1996.

Steffens, Lincoln. *Upbuilders*. Seattle: University of Washington Press, 1968 (1909).

Stein, Jill. "Austerity's Agent: The Real Obama Emerges (Again)." *CounterPunch* (January 18–20, 2013). Available at http://www.counterpunch.org.

Stern, Seth. "Republicans Win on Class Action." *Congressional Quarterly Weekly* (February 21, 2005): 460.

Sternheimer, Karen. *Celebrity Culture and the American Dream*. New York: Routledge, 2011.

Stevenson, Richard W. "U.S. to Report to Congress NAFTA Benefits Are Modest." *New York Times*, July 11, 1997.

Stillman, Don. "The Devastating Impact of Plant Relocations." *Working Papers* (July–August 1978): 42–53.

Stites, Jessica. "Independent Media Now!" *In These Times* (December 2012): 34–35.

Stobbe, Mike. "1 in 5 are Struggling to Pay Medical Bills, Survey Finds." *Indianapolis Star*, March 18, 2012, A13.

Stohl, Michael, and Harry R. Targ. *Global Political Economy in the 1980s*. Cambridge, MA: Schenkman, 1982.

Strobel, Frederick R., and Wallace C. Peterson. *The Coming Class War and How to Avoid It*. Armonk, NY: M. E. Sharpe, 1999.

Suhler, John. "VSS Communications Industry Forecast 2010." *Communications Industry Spending & Consumption Trends*. Veronis, Suhler, Stevenson. Available at http://www.vssforecast.com.

Sunkara, Bhaskar. "Oprah-iate of the People." *In These Times* (August 2012): 40–41.

———. "The Austerity Cliff." *In These Times* (December 2012): 5.

Supreme Court of the United States. "Citizens United *v.* Federal Election Commission." No. 08–205. Decided January 21, 2010.

Svart, Maria. "Why Not Socialism?" *In These Times* (December 2012): 27.

Tabb, William K. "After Neoliberalism?" *Monthly Review* (June 2003): 25–33.

Tax Foundation. "Federal Individual Income Tax Rates History, 1913–2011." 2012. Available at http://www.taxfoundation.org.

Taylor, Astra. "Occupy 2.0: Strike Debt." *Nation* (September 24, 2012): 17–20.

Taylor, Verta. "Social Movements Continuity: The Women's Movement in Abeyance." *American Sociological Review* 54 (1989): 761–75.

Ten Eyck, Tiffany. "UAW Approves Even-Deeper Concessions at Ford." *Labor Notes* (December 2007): 5

Thinda, James. "Time for Democrats to Pay Their Dues." *In These Times* (February 2013): 30–31.

Thomas, Kenneth P. *Investment Incentives and the Global Competition for Capital.* Basingstroke, UK: Palgrave Macmillan, 2011.

Thompson, Derek. "What's the Best Investment: Stocks, Bonds, Homes . . . or College?" *Atlantic* (June 27, 2011).

Thompson, Hunter S. *Generation of Swine.* New York: Vintage Books, 1988.

Thornton, Bridget, Britt Walters, and Lori Rouse. "Corporate Media is Corporate America." In *Censored 2006,* edited by Peter Phillips and Project Censored. New York: Seven Stories Press, 2005.

Tilly, Chris, and Charles Tilly. *Work Under Capitalism.* Boulder, CO: Westview Press, 1998.

Time Warner. *Time Warner Annual Report 2011.* Available at http://www.timewarner.com.

Tomaskovic-Devey, Donald. *Gender and Racial Inequality at Work.* Ithaca, NY: IRL Press, 1993.

Traub, Amy. "War on Public Workers." *Nation* (July 8, 2010): 4–6.

Trementozzi, Don, and Steve Early. "Romney, Obama Health Care Reforms Offer No Relief for Unions." *Labor Notes* (July 2011): 10.

Trujillo, Josmar. "Media Laugh Off Criticism of Drug War." *Extra!* (December 2012): 6–7.

Tucker, Todd. "The Trade Debate That Wasn't Reported." *Extra!* (February 2012): 9–10.

Tudor, Jeannette F. "The Development of Class Awareness in Children." *Social Forces* 49 (1971): 470–76.

Tully, Shawn. "The Year of Living Profitably." *Fortune* (May 21, 2012): 237, F-25.

"2011–2012 Physician Salary Survey." *Profiles* (September 2011). Available at http://www.profilesdatabase.com.

Uetricht, Micah, and Jason Perez. "Democratic to the CORE." *In These Times* (December 2012): 32.

Underwood, Julie. "Starving Public Schools." *Nation* (August 1–8, 2011): 22–23.

United for a Fair Economy. "Projects: Responsible Wealth—About." 2011. Available at http://www.faireconomy.org.

U.S. Census Bureau. *Statistical Abstract of the United States: 1995.* Washington, DC: U.S. Government Printing Office, 1995.

——. *Statistical Abstract of the United States: 2006.* Washington, DC: U.S. Government Printing Office, 2005.

——. *Statistical Abstract of the United States: 2007.* Washington, DC: U.S. Government Printing Office, 2006.

——. Current Population Surveys. "1973 and 2010 Annual Social and Economic Supplement."

——. "Selected Social Characteristics in the United States, 2010." Available at http://factfinder.census.gov.

——. *Statistical Abstract of the United States: 2012.* Washington, DC: U.S. Government Printing Office, 2011.

——. Current Population Surveys. "1960 to 2012 Annual Social and Economic Supplement."

——. Current Population Surveys. "1974 and 2012 Annual Social and Economic Supplement."

——. Current Population Survey. "2012 Annual Social and Economic Supplement."

U.S. Chamber of Commerce. "Letter Regarding Legislation Expected to Be Considered in the Senate to Extend Certain Expiring 2001 and 2003 Tax Cuts While Failing to Avert a Massive Tax Increase on American Small Businesses." Press release, December 3, 2010.

U.S. Citizenship and Immigration Services. "H-1B Frequently Asked Questions." Available at http://www.uscis.gov/graphics/howdoi/h1b.htm.

U.S. Congress, House Committee on the Budget. *Unnecessary Business Subsidies.* 106th Congress, 1st sess. Serial 106–5. Washington, DC: U.S. Government Printing Office, 1999.

U.S. Congress, House Committee on Ways and Means. *Comprehensive Tax Reform.* 99th Cong., 1st sess. Serial 99–41. Washington, DC: U.S. Government Printing Office, 1985.

———. *Impact, Effectiveness, and Fairness of the Tax Reform Act of 1986.* 101st Congress, 2nd sess. Serial 101–92. Washington, DC: U.S. Government Printing Office, 1990.

———. "428 Major Companies and Organizations Support the American Jobs Creation Act." Press release, July 8, 2004.

U.S. Congress, Senate Committee on Finance. "Federal Tax Treatment of Individuals." Prepared by the Staff of the Joint Committee on Taxation. JCX-43–11. Washington, DC: U.S. Government Printing Office, September 12, 2011.

U.S. Department of Commerce, Bureau of Economic Analysis. "Gross Domestic Product: Fourth Quarter and Annual 2011 (Third Estimate), Corporate Profits: Fourth Quarter and Annual 2011." Press release, March 29, 2012.

U.S. Department of Commerce, Economics and Statistics Administration. "Middle Class in America." Prepared for the Office of the Vice President of the United States Middle Class Task Force (January 2010).

U.S. Department of Commerce, U.S. Census Bureau, Foreign Trade Division. Washington, DC: U.S. Government Printing Office, 2005.

U.S. Department of Education, National Center for Educational Statistics. *The Condition of Education, 1996.* Edited by Thomas Smith. NCES 96–304. Washington, DC: U.S. Government Printing Office, 1996.

———. *Digest of Educational Statistics, 2000.* Washington, DC: U.S. Government Printing Office, 2001.

———. *Digest of Educational Statistics.* Edited by Thomas D. Snyder, Charlene M. Hoffman, and Clair M. Geddes. NCES 2001–034. Washington, DC: U.S. Government Printing Office, 2001.

———. "Projections of Education Statistics to 2016." Institute of Education Statistics (December 18, 2006). Available at http://www.nces.gov.

———. *The Condition of Education 2012.* Washington, DC: U.S. Government Printing Office, 2012.

U.S. Department of Justice, Bureau of Justice Statistics. "Key Facts at a Glance: Correctional Populations, 1980–2009." Available at http://bjs.ojp.usdoj.gov.

U.S. Department of Labor, Bureau of Labor Statistics. "National Longitudinal Surveys of Youth, 1979–2006."

———. "Employee Tenure." News release, September 14, 2010. Available at http://www.bls.gov.

———. "Employed Persons Detailed by Occupation, Sex, Race, and Hispanic or Latino Ethnicity." 2010. Available at http://www.bls.gov.

———. "Household Economic Studies." Washington, DC: U.S. Government Printing Office, 2010.

———. "Ratio of Women's to Men's Earnings by Occupation." 2010. Available at http://www.bls.gov.

———. *Databases, Tables & Calculators by Subject.* "Industry: Manufacturing." November 11, 2012. Available at http://data.bls.gov/timeseries.

———. Current Employment Statistics (CES), 2012.

———. "Union Members—2012." News release, January 23, 2013. Available at http://www .bls.gov.

U.S. Department of the Treasury, Internal Revenue Service. "Section 527 Political Organizations Revised Tax Filing Requirements." Press release, November 2002.

———. "IRS Acts to Enforce Reporting and Disclosure by Section 527 Political Groups." Press release, August 19, 2004.

———. "Return of Organization Exempt from Income Tax: Form 990: Brookings Institution." 2010. 53–0196577. Washington, DC.

———. "Return of Organization Exempt from Income Tax: Form 990: The Business Roundtable." 2010. 23–7236607. Washington, DC.

———. "Return of Organization Exempt from Income Tax: Form 990: The Heritage Foundation." 2010. 23–7327730. Washington, DC.

———. *Statistics of Income, Corporation Tax Returns.* 2011. Available at http://www.irs.gov.

U.S. House of Representatives, Judiciary Committee. "List of Supporters: H.R. 3261, the *Stop Online Piracy Act.*" January 2012.

U.S. Securities and Exchange Commission. "Form 10–K, Ford Motor Company: For Fiscal Year Ended December 31, 2009." Washington, DC.

———. "Form 10–K, General Motors Company: For Fiscal Year Ended December 31, 2009." Washington, DC.

———. "Form 10–K, Ford Motor Company: For Fiscal Year Ended December 31, 2010." Washington, DC.

———. "Form 10–K, General Motors Company: For Fiscal Year Ended December 31, 2010." Washington, DC.

———. "Form 10–K, CBS Corporation: For Fiscal Year Ended December 31, 2011." Washington, DC.

———. "Form 10–K, Comcast Corporation: For Fiscal Year Ended December 31, 2011." Washington, DC.

———. "Form 10–K, Ford Motor Company: For Fiscal Year Ended December 31, 2011." Washington, DC.

———. "Form 10–K, General Motors Company: For Fiscal Year Ended December 31, 2011." Washington, DC.

———. "Form 10–K, Walt Disney Company: For Fiscal Year Ended December 31, 2011." Washington, DC.

Useem, Michael. *The Inner Circle.* New York: Oxford University Press, 1984.

Valdes, Manuel, Travis Loller, Christina Silva, and Sandra Chereb. "1 in 2 New Graduates are Jobless or Underemployed." Associated Press (April 22, 2012). Available at http://www. cnbc.com.

Van Gelder, Sarah. "The Legitimacy of Rule by Giant Corporations and Wall Street Banks Is Crumbling." *Yes! Magazine* (January 29, 2012): 1–3. Available at http://www.yesmagazine. org.

Vanneman, Reeve, and Lynn Weber Cannon. *The American Perception of Class.* Philadelphia: Temple University Press, 1987.

Vick, Karl. "Big Brothers." *Time* (December 24, 2012): 26–30.

Vidal, Gore. "The End of History." *Nation* (September 30, 1996): 11–18.

Volti, Rudi. *An Introduction to the Sociology of Work and Occupations.* 2nd ed. Los Angeles: Sage, 2012.

Wallach, Lori. "Congress Shoves through Trio of Job-Killing Trade Agreements." *Public Citizen News* (November–December 2011): 10.

Wallerstein, Immanual. *The Modern World System.* New York: Academic Press, 1974.

———. *The End of the World as We Know It: Social Science for the Twenty-First Century.* Minneapolis: University of Minnesota Press, 1999.

Walsh, John V. "The Myth of U.S. Manufacturing Decline." *CounterPunch* (October 15, 2012). Available at http://www.counterpunch.org.

War Resisters League. "Where Your Income Tax Money Really Goes—U.S. Federal Budget 2013 Fiscal Year." Available at www.warresisters.org.

"*Washington Post*-ABC News Poll." Conducted by Abt-SRBI (November 3, 2011), Question #18, 11. Available at http://www.washingtonpost.com.

Weber, Max. *Economy and Society.* 2 vols. Eds. G. Roth and C. Wittich. Berkeley: University of California Press, 1978.

Weiss, Joan M. "Pension Benefit Guaranty Corporation: 2011 Actuarial Report." December 20, 2011.

Weissman, Robert. "Democracy Campaign to Overturn *Citizens United.*" Washington, DC: Public Citizen, July 25, 2012.

Weissman, Robert, and James Donahue. "Sold Out: How Wall Street and Washington Betrayed America." *Essential Information* (March 2009). Available at http://www.wallstreetwatch.org.

Wenglinsky, Harold. "How Money Matters: The Effect of School District Spending on Academic Achievement." *Sociology of Education* 70 (July 1997): 221–37.

Weprin, Alex. "'Nightly Business Report' Sold Yet Again." *TVNEWSER* (November 16, 2011): 1–3. Available at http://www.mediabistro/tvnewser.

Western, Bruce, and Becky Pettit. "Incarceration & Social Inequality." *Daedalus* 139 (Summer 2010): 8–19.

Western, Bruce, and Jake Rosenfeld. "Unions, Norms, and the Rise in U.S. Wage Inequality." *American Sociological Review* 76 (2011): 513–37.

Wheary, Jennifer, Thomas M. Shapiro, and Tamara Draut. "By a Thread: The New Experience of America's Middle Class." New York: Dēmos: A Network for Ideas & Action; and Waltham, MA: The Institute on Assets and Social Policy, Brandeis University, November 28, 2007.

White, Joseph, and Aaron Wildavsky. *The Deficit and the Public Interest: The Search for Responsible Budgeting in the 1980s.* Berkeley: University of California Press, 1989.

Whitmire, Richard, and Andrew J. Rotherham. "How Teachers Unions Lost the Media." *Wall Street Journal*, October 2, 2009. Available at http://www.wsj.com.

"Who's on Top by Sector: Ranked within Industries." *Fortune* (May 21, 2012): F-38.

Wicks-Lim, Jeanette. "Creating Decent Jobs." *Dollars and Sense* (January–February 2010): 8.

Wiedenbaum, Murray L. *Business, Government, and the Public.* Englewood Cliffs, NJ: Prentice-Hall, 1977.

Wilder, Thornton. *Our Town: A Play in Three Acts.* New York: Coward-McCann, 1938.

Wilkinson, Richard, and Kate Pickett. *The Spirit Level: Why More Equal Societies Almost Always Do Better.* New York: Bloomsbury Press, 2009.

Williams, Joan. *Unbending Gender.* New York: Oxford University Press, 2000.

Winters, Jeffery A. "Oligarchy in the U.S.A." *In These Times* (March 2012): 16–20.

Wohl, R. Richard. "The 'Rags to Riches Story': An Episode of Secular Idealism." In *Class, Status, and Power*, edited by Reinhard Bendix and Seymour M. Lipset. New York: Free Press, 1966.

Wolfe, Alan. *The Seamy Side of Democracy.* New York: David McKay, 1973.

Wolfe, Charles, and Kip Lornell. *The Life and Legend of Leadbelly.* New York: HarperCollins, 1992.

Wolff, Edward N. "Changes in Household Wealth in the 1980s and 1990s in the U.S." Working Paper No. 407, Levy Economics Institute and New York University (May 2004).

———. *The Asset Price Meltdown and the Wealth of the Middle Class.* New York: New York University Press, 2012.

Wolff, Michael. "The Web Is Dead?, A Debate; Who's to Blame: Them." *Wired* 18 (September 2010): 122–27.

Wolff, Rick. "Turning toward Solutions." *Dollars and Sense* (January–February 2012): 7–8.

"Women CEOs in the Fortune 1000." *Catalyst* (2011). Available at http://www.catalyst.org.

Wooldridge, Adrian. "Ever Higher Society, Ever Harder to Ascend." *Economist* (December 29, 2004).

WPP. "Lobbying Firms BKSH & Associates and Timmons & Company Announce Merger." Press release, October 5, 2009. Available at http://www.wpp.com.

———. "WPP Company Profile." 2012. Available at http://www.wpp.com.

Wray, L. Randall, and Pavlina R. Tcherneva. "Romney: The Little People Don't Pay Taxes." *New Economic Perspectives* (September 19, 2012). Available at http://www.neweconom-icperspectives.org.

Wray, Matt, and Annalee Newitz, eds. *White Trash: Race and Class in America.* New York: Routledge, 1997.

Wright, Erik O. *Classes.* London: Verso, 1985.

———. *Interrogating Inequality.* London: Verso, 1994.

Wu Dunn, Sheryl. "When Lifetime Jobs Die Prematurely." *New York Times,* June 12, 1996.

Wypijewski, JoAnn. "Gatherer of Worlds." *CounterPunch* (September 1–30, 2012): 8–10.

Wysong, Earl. *High Risk and High Stakes: Health Professionals, Politics, and Policy.* Westport, CT: Greenwood Press, 1992.

———. "Class in the Movies." Unpublished paper, 1996.

Wysong, Earl, Richard Aniskiewicz, and David Wright. "Truth *and* DARE: Tracking Drug Education to Graduation and as Symbolic Politics." *Social Problems* 41 (1994): 448–72.

Wysong, Earl, and Robert Perrucci. "Media and the Marginalization of Social Class Inequalities." *Journal of the Indiana Academy of the Social Sciences* XI (2007): 14–26.

———. "Organizations, Resources, and Class Analysis: The Distributional Model and the US Class Structure." *Critical Sociology* 33 (2007): 211–46.

Wysong, Earl, Robert Perrucci, and David Wright. "A New Approach to Class Analysis: The Distributional Model, Social Closure, and Class Polarization." Paper presented at the 2002 meetings of the American Sociological Association, Chicago, Illinois.

Wysong, Earl, and David W. Wright. "A Decade of DARE: Efficacy, Politics, and Drug Education." *Sociological Focus* 28 (1995): 283–311.

———. "Family Friendly Workplace Benefits: Policy Mirage, Organizational Contexts, and Worker Power." *Critical Sociology* 24 (1998): 244–76.

———. "Family Friendly Workplace Benefits: The U.S., Canada, and Europe." *Critical Sociology* 29 (2003): 337–67.

———. "Is Social Mobility a Social Problem? Recent Intergenerational Mobility Trends, the American Dream, and the Media." Paper presented at the 2006 meetings of the North Central Sociological Association, Indianapolis, Indiana.

———. "What's Happening to the American Dream? Sons, Daughters, and Intergenerational Mobility Today." Paper presented at the 2007 meetings of the Midwest Sociological Society, Chicago, Illinois (April 4–7, 2007).

———. "Socioeconomic Status and Gender: Recent Intergenerational Mobility Patterns in the U.S." *Journal of the Indiana Academy of the Social Sciences* XIII (2009): 112–30.

———. "Shot through the Heart: Have Recent Inequality Trends Killed the Middle Class?" Paper presented at the 2010 meetings of the Midwest Sociological Society, Chicago, Illinois.

Yen, Hope. "Millions Slip Out of Middle Class." *Indianapolis Star*, December 15, 2011, A1, 17.

———. "Courting, Not Defining, Nation's Middle Class." *Indianapolis Star*, July 22, 2012, A7.

Yohalem, Martha Remy. "Employer Benefit Plans, 1975." *Social Security Bulletin* (November 1977): 19–28.

Zandy, Janet. "Decloaking Class: Why Class Identity and Consciouness Count." In *Experiencing Race, Class, and Gender in the United States*, edited by Roberta Fiske-Rusciano and Virginia Cyrus. 4th ed. Boston: McGraw-Hill, 2005.

Zaniello, Tom. *Working Stiffs, Union Maids, Reds, and Riffraff: An Expanded Guide to Films about Labor*. Ithaca, NY: IRL Press, 2003.

Zinn, Howard. *A People's History of the United States*. New York: Harper Colophon Books, 1980.

Zweigenhaft, Richard L. "Making Rags Out of Riches." *Extra!* (January–February 2004): 27–28.

Zweigenhaft, Richard L., and G. William Domhoff. *Diversity in the Power Elite: Have Women and Minorities Reached the Top?* New Haven, CT: Yale University Press, 1998.

Index

About the Authors

Earl Wysong is professor of sociology at Indiana University, Kokomo. Profiled in several *Who's Who* publications, he is a past president of the Indiana Academy of the Social Sciences and author of *High Risk and High Stakes*.

Robert Perrucci is professor of sociology at Purdue University, past president of the Society for the Study of Social Problems, and former editor of the *American Sociologist*, *Social Problems*, and *Contemporary Sociology*.

David Wright is professor of sociology at Wichita State University, where he is also associate provost for academic data systems and strategic planning.